The Roman World

The Roman World 44 BC–AD 180 deals with the transformation of the Mediterranean region, northern Europe and the Near East by the military autocrats who ruled Rome during this period. The book traces the impact of imperial politics on life in the city of Rome itself and in the rest of the empire, arguing that, despite long periods of apparent peace, this was a society controlled as much by fear of state violence as by consent.

Martin Goodman examines the reliance of Roman emperors on a huge military establishment and the threat of force. He analyses the extent to which the empire functioned as a single political, economic and cultural unit and discusses, region by region, how much the various indigenous cultures and societies were affected by Roman rule. There is a long section devoted to the momentous religious changes in this period, which witnessed the popularity and spread of a series of elective cults and the emergence of Rabbinic Judaism and Christianity from the complex world of first-century Judaea. This book provides a critical assessment of the significance of Roman rule for inhabitants of the empire, and introduces readers to many of the main issues currently faced by historians of the early empire.

This new edition, incorporating the finds of recent scholarship, includes a fuller narrative history, expanded sections on the history of women and slaves and on cultural life in the city of Rome, many new illustrations, an updated section of bibliographical notes, and other improvements designed to make the volume as useful as possible to students as well as the general reader.

Martin Goodman is Professor of Jewish Studies at Oxford. He is a Fellow of Wolfson College, Oxford, and a Fellow of the British Academy. He has written numerous books, including *The Ruling Class of Judaea* (1987) and *Rome and Jerusalem: the clash of ancient civilizations* (2007).

ROUTLEDGE HISTORY OF THE ANCIENT WORLD

Series Editor: Fergus Millar

Forthcoming:

THE ROMAN WORLD

44 BC–AD 180

Second Edition

Martin Goodman

LONDON AND NEW YORK

First published 1997.
This second edition published 2012
by Routledge
2 Park Square, Milton Park, Abingdon, Oxon OX14 4RN

Simultaneously published in the USA and Canada
by Routledge
711 Third Avenue, New York, NY 10017

Routledge is an imprint of the Taylor & Francis Group, an informa business

© 1997, 2012 Martin Goodman.

The right of Martin Goodman to be identified as author of this work has been
asserted by him/her in accordance with sections 77 and 78 of the Copyright,
Designs and Patents Act 1988.

British Library Cataloguing in Publication Data
A catalogue record for this book is available from the British Library

Library of Congress Cataloging in Publication Data
Goodman, Martin, 1953-
The Roman world, 44 BC-AD 180 / Martin Goodman. -- 2nd ed.
   p. cm. -- (Routledge history of the ancient world)
Includes bibliographical references and index.
   1. Rome--Civilization. 2. Rome--History--Republic, 265-30 B.C. 3. Rome--
History--Empire, 30 B.C.-284 A.D. I. Title.
   DG254.G66 2011
      937'.07--dc23
                              2011025444

ISBN: 978-0-415-55978-2 (hbk)
ISBN: 978-0-415-55979-9 (pbk)
ISBN: 978-0-203-14688-0 (ebk)

Typeset in Garamond
by Saxon Graphics Ltd, Derby DE21 4SZ

Printed and bound in Great Britain by the MPG Books Group

CONTENTS

LIST OF FIGURES

LIST OF MAPS

LIST OF DATES

LIST OF ABBREVIATIONS

AE	*L'année épigraphique* (Paris, 1888–)
AJA	*American Journal of Archaeology*
AJPh	*American Journal of Philology*
ANRW	H. Temporini and W. Haase (eds.) *Aufstieg und Niedergang der römischen Welt; Geschichte und Kultur Roms im Spiegel der neueren Forschung* (Berlin and New York, 1972–)
BGU	*Ägyptische Urkunden aus den Staatlichen Museen zu Berlin, Griechische Urkunden* (Berlin, 1895)
BNP	M. Beard, J. North and S. Price (eds.) *Religions of Rome 2: A Sourcebook* (Cambridge, 1998)
Braund	D.C. Braund (ed.) *Augustus to Nero: A Sourcebook on Roman History 31 BC–AD 68* (London and Sydney, 1985)
CAH	*The Cambridge Ancient History*, 2nd edn (Cambridge, 1961–)
CIL	T. Mommsen *et al.* (eds.) *Corpus Inscriptionum Latinarum*, 16 vols. (Berlin, 1863–)
CPJ	V.A. Tcherikover *et al.*, *Corpus Papyrorum Judaicarum* (Jerusalem, 1957–64)
Dio, *Hist. Rom.*	Cassius Dio, *History of Rome*
EJ²	V. Ehrenberg and A.H.M. Jones (eds.) *Documents Illustrating the Reigns of Augustus and Tiberius*, 2nd edn (Oxford, 1975)
FIRA	S. Riccobono *et al.* (eds.) *Fontes Iuris Romani Antejustiniani*, 2nd edn, 3 vols. (Florence, 1940–43)
IGRR	R. Cagnat *et al.*, *Inscriptiones Graecae ad res Romanas pertinentes* (Paris, 1901–27)
ILS	H. Dessau (ed.) *Inscriptiones Latinae Selectae*, 3 vols. (Berlin, 1892–1916)
JHS	*Journal of Hellenic Studies*
Joseph., *AJ*	Josephus, *Antiquities of the Jews*
Joseph., *JW*	Josephus, *The Jewish War*
JRA	*Journal of Roman Archaeology*
JRS	*Journal of Roman Studies*

Levick	B. Levick (ed.) *The Government of the Roman Empire: A Sourcebook* (London, 1985)
LR 1 & 2	N. Lewis and M. Reinhold (eds.) *Roman Civilization: Selected Readings*, 3rd edn, 2 vols. (New York and Oxford, 1990)
OGIS	W. Dittenberger (ed.) *Orientis Graeci Inscriptiones Selectae*, 4 vols. (Leipzig, 1903–05)
PBSR	*Papers of the British School at Rome*
Pliny, *Nat. Hist.*	Pliny, *Natural History*
POxy	*The Oxyrhynchus Papyri* (London, 1898–)
PRIA	*Proceedings of the Royal Irish Academy*, Section C, Dublin
PYadin	Y. Yadin, *The Documents from the Bar Kokhba Period in the Cave of Letters: Greek Papyri*, ed. N. Lewis (Jerusalem, 1989)
Reynolds	J. Reynolds, *Aphrodisias and Rome* (London, 1982)
RIB	R.G. Collingwood and R.P. Wright, *Roman Inscriptions of Britain* (Oxford, 1965–)
Select Papyri	*Select Papyri with an English Translation* by A.S. Hunt and C.C. Edgar, 2 vols. (London and Cambridge, Mass., 1932–34)d
SHA	*Scriptores Historiae Augustae*
SIG³	W. Dittenberger (ed.) *Sylloge Inscriptionum Graecarum*, 3rd edn, 4 vols. (Leipzig, 1915–24)
Smallwood, *Gaius-Nero*	E.M. Smallwood (ed.) *Documents Illustrating the Principates of Gaius, Claudius and Nero* (Cambridge, 1967)
Smallwood, *Nerva-Hadrian*	E.M Smallwood (ed.) *Documents Illustrating the Principates of Nerva, Trajan and Hadrian* (Cambridge, 1966)
Suet., *Aug.*	Suetonius, *Augustus*
Suet., *Claud.*	Suetonius, *Claudius*
Suet., *Dom.*	Suetonius, *Domitian*
Suet., *Gai.*	Suetonius, *Gaius*
Suet., *Tib.*	Suetonius, *Tiberius*
Suet., *Tit.*	Suetonius, *Titus*
Suet., *Vesp.*	Suetonius, *Vespasian*
Tab. Vindol II	A.K. Bowman and J.D. Thomas (eds.) *The Vindolanda Writing–Tablets (tabulae Vindolandenses II)* (London, 1994)
Tac., *Agric.*	Tacitus, *Agricola*
Tac., *Ann.*	Tacitus, *Annals*
Tac., *Hist.*	Tacitus, *Histories*
YCS	*Yale Classical Studies*
ZPE	*Zeitschrift für Papyrologie und Epigraphik*

PREFACE

I am very grateful to Matt Gibbons at Routledge for his enthusiastic encouragement for a second edition of this history.

It is good to have been able to take advantage in this new edition of comments and suggestions from many colleagues. I am particularly grateful to Alan Bowman for his comments on the penultimate draft of the new text. The book has been expanded in the light of these suggestions, as well as being brought up-to-date to reflect both new discoveries and new approaches, but the structure and tone of the original have been retained as far as possible.

It is appropriate to recall here the immense contribution to the first edition made by Jane Sherwood as my research assistant in 1995-1996. Once again I have benefited, through a grant from the Oxford Centre for Hebrew and Jewish Studies, from expert research assistance, this time provided with great efficiency and good humour by Caillan Davenport. I am immensely grateful to Neelum Ali for her continuing forbearance in deciphering my handwriting in the preparation of the text for publication.

Martin Goodman
June 2011

For Sarah

Part I

INTRODUCTION

1

SOURCES AND PROBLEMS

The Roman world from the middle of the first century BC to the end of the second century AD witnessed, after traumatic upheavals, the establishment of a stable society over one of the widest geographical areas to know political unity at any time in human history. From the achievements, ethos and writings of the Roman Empire at its height stemmed the values – moral, religious, artistic, legal, political – which have shaped European culture down to the twenty-first century. In some respects, such influence has been continuous over the last 2,000 years. Christianity, which sprang from Judaism in the early first century, and Rabbinic Judaism, which emerged from the traumas of the end of that century, evolved in an unbroken tradition through the Middle Ages. So too did the medical achievements of the High Empire, to the extent that the speculations of Galen (AD 129–c. 199) about the workings of the body remained standard theory until the eighteenth century. So also did the astronomy and astrology of Claudius Ptolemaeus (AD c. 100–c. 178) and the work of the Classical Roman jurists, whose textbooks, written in the mid- to late second century AD, provided the foundation of Late Roman and then medieval law codes. German law is based on their categories to this day.

Other achievements were forgotten until the Renaissance, when the rediscovery of Plutarch (AD c. 46–c. 120), and the philosophical discussions of the elder Seneca (c. 55 BC–c. AD 40) and others, set standards and tone for civilized morality, while a burgeoning awareness of the architecture of the grand buildings erected in the High Empire stimulated the neo-classicism of Renaissance architecture. The industriousness of Greek scholars of the second century AD ensured that the works through which the Early Modern world came to know about and love Classical Greece were themselves products of the Roman world (Plutarch, Appian, Arrian above all).[1]

To understand the evolution of the Early Roman Empire is thus to comprehend the foundations of our own society. It is not, as will be seen, an entirely easy task to achieve. For Edward Gibbon in the late eighteenth century, the consolidation of the Roman Empire saw the establishment, after violent conflict, of a balanced constitution, which under enlightened emperors led inevitably to the peace and security of the second century AD:

> If a man were called to fix the period in the history of the world during which the condition of the human race was most happy and prosperous, he would, without hesitation, name that which elapsed from the death of Domitian to the accession of Commodus.[2]

This judgement directly reflects the views of the narrative sources of political history on which Gibbon based his account. For the Roman senator Pliny (AD 61–c. 112), writing in the early second century AD, the despotic tendencies of early emperors had given way to the just and beneficent rule of Trajan. A similarly kindly filter has coloured posterity's view of subsequent emperors down to, but not including, the monster Commodus (sole ruler AD 180–92). But a history of the Roman world must be more than an account of the finer feelings of its governing élite and literati. The mass of humanity of all classes, ethnic backgrounds and cultural affiliations, and of both sexes, cannot be assumed to have concurred with the view of a Roman senator. Was the second century AD for them, too, an age in which it was good to be alive? And if not, why not?

THE EVIDENCE[3]

The problem in answering such a question lies, as always in the study of ancient history, in the selective nature of the evidence. The narrative histories of the political events of the period were composed by Roman senators – Velleius Paterculus (c. 20 BC–after AD 30), Tacitus (AD c. 56–c. 120), Cassius Dio (AD c. 163/4–c. 230) – whose stance close to, but not quite in, the centre of state power engendered an idiosyncratic, often jaundiced view – which was compounded by the requirement of the historiographical genre to concentrate on the military efforts of the state, and overt political action by the ruling class, rather than on economic or social developments or the hidden, unspoken wielding of power by emperors.

The genre of emperors' biographies effectively invented by Suetonius (AD c. 69–after 122), who had the advantage of working in the imperial household, provides something of a corrective in the latter field. But Suetonius' reliance on unchecked anecdotes, and his concern for the personal characteristics of emperors more than for their relations with their subjects, somewhat limit the usefulness of his work.

The *Augustan History* (*Scriptores Historiae Augustae*), a collection of the biographies of emperors stretching from Hadrian to the late third century AD, is even less reliable. Similar in style and organization to Suetonius' lives, these biographies descend into obvious fantasy and forgery in some of the third-century lives. The most likely explanation of the origins of the work is that, despite the pretence of multiple authorship, it was produced in the late fourth century by a single individual with a strong (if peculiar) sense of humour, which developed as he proceeded chronologically with the composition of the biographies. In that case, the biographies of Hadrian and of the Antonines can be considered among the most reliable in the collection, since the author could rely on plentiful data, and had not yet developed the tendencies which make the later lives unusable; but no uncorroborated statement found in any of the biographies can be used without caution.

For the most part, information must be culled from less direct sources than historical or biographical narratives. From the governing class in Rome there survives a mass of evidence which was preserved for its literary merit. For the beginning of the period, the last letters of Cicero (106–43 BC) and his passionate speeches against Antonius (the *Philippics*) provide an unparalleled insight into the attitudes and assumptions of one, rather idiosyncratic, politician. The other collections of letters which survive, the *Moral Letters* of Seneca, the letters of the younger Pliny, and the pedantic correspondence with his imperial pupils of the rhetorician Fronto (AD *c.* 100–166/7), offer many insights into the social and ethical assumptions of élite Roman society but, since they were mostly composed for publication, they lack the immediacy of Cicero. A cultural efflorescence under Augustus produced much poetry in Latin, the so-called 'Golden Age', while the steady stream of poets in the first century AD welled up into a second flood at the end of the first century and early second century AD, the 'Silver Age'. The origins of most Latin poetry in imitation and adaptation of Greek genres preclude use of such writings as if they described their own society directly, but frequent hints can nonetheless be culled about contemporary affairs; in this respect, the Latin genre of satire, in which contemporary morals are mocked, is particularly illuminating (thus Horace (65–8 BC) and especially Juvenal (AD *c.* 60–after 127)). Much, too, can be learnt from the compendious scholarship of gentlemen academics, which had become fashionable in the Late Republic: the antiquarian musings of Terentius Varro (116–27 BC) and the massive compilation of the elder Pliny (AD 23/4–79), his *Natural History*, contain numerous nuggets of information among the verbose speculations of the learned.

It would then be possible to compose a history simply of the upper class in the city of Rome. But it would be quite wrong to view developments among this privileged group as normal for the rest of the emperors' subjects. Little literary evidence survives from the western (Latin-speaking) part of the empire outside Rome in this period. Latin writers gravitated to the capital in search of patronage. An honourable exception was Apuleius (AD *c.* 125–after 160s), a citizen of Madaura in North Africa, whose novel, *The Golden Ass*, gives an instructive insight into provincial life as viewed by a man on the fringes of the urban élite. But from the Greek-speaking East survives a mass of literary evidence which rivals the Latin compositions in Rome in quantity, if not always in quality. Some of these authors also wrote in Rome, from the composers of Greek epigrams for Augustus, to Plutarch (in *c.* AD 92–93) and the rather greater numbers attracted by the philhellenic policy of Hadrian in the 120s AD (see Chapters 7 and 23). But many, like Pausanias (AD *c.* 115–*c.*

180), were content to stay in Greece itself, or Asia Minor, reflecting the cultural self-absorption of those areas. Only one such author composed a history of his own region in his own time: the Jewish writer Josephus (AD *c.* 37/8–after AD 93), whose accounts of the Jewish war of AD 66–70 and the history of the Jews to AD 66, in his *Antiquities of the Jews*, provide a unique insight into the nature of Roman rule as viewed from below. Much of the rest of the Greek literature of the imperial period was concerned with the remote Classical past before Alexander the Great. This fact is, in itself, an important cultural phenomenon, but it restricts the usefulness of these writings in reconstructing the history of their own times. The exceptions are few: Dio Chrysostom, rhetorician and philosopher (AD *c.* 40–after 112), whose moral discourses sometimes referred to contemporary events, or the rather more rigorous Stoic-Cynic Epictetus (AD *c.* 55–*c.* 135).

These disparate and disjointed literary sources for life outside Rome are amplified and corrected by an extraordinary mass of physical evidence, from the strictly archaeological to inscriptions on stone, metals and wood and the written records of papyri, and coins. The accumulated effect of such evidence may give the impression of a society which can be known in detail, particularly in contrast to the preceding and following periods, but the peculiar nature of this evidence and the biases inherent in it also need to be acknowledged.[4]

The frequency with which evidence for the early imperial period is reported from archaeological sites is, to a large extent, a function of the ease with which it can be recognized. That, in turn, means that only certain kinds of evidence will usually be spotted. Thus Roman villas, town plans, public buildings and roads of this period may be recovered with comparative ease because of the regularity of their construction over much of the empire and the durability of buildings constructed in stone rather than wood or other perishable materials. The wide circulation of the artefact least subject to decay, that is, pottery, enables archaeologists to correlate different areas with comparative ease; but again, only fine wares travelled far, so that the relations of poorer people are less easy to fathom. The reconstruction of settlement patterns and lifestyles of peasants can indeed be recovered from archaeological evidence, but only with great and painstaking care.

A similar bias towards the better-off prejudices use of the million or so inscriptions on stone which are currently known to survive from the Roman period.[5] Most of these can be dated to Roman imperial times, and together they provide multifarious details of the careers and family relations of individuals, the deployment of military units, and the relations between cities and between subject and emperor. The 'epigraphic habit' is a rather strange one. Cutting letters on stone requires a mason skilled in the traditional craft. The custom did not catch on in all areas of the empire and, for reasons of expense, never became common among those whose wealth fell below that of the better-off artisans (although many ex-slaves were prepared to pay to commemorate their freedom). It was thus an urban phenomenon. In the countryside, peasants could rarely afford the luxury, and only soldiers who were eager to perpetuate their memory, and were quite well paid, erected permanent monuments. In our society, the fashion survives primarily in the commissioning of grave markers.[6]

Writing on more perishable materials has survived in the last 2,000 years only through exceptional climatic conditions or by unusual chance. Papyri survive in great numbers from Roman Egypt, and reveal much about small town life and the state's bureaucracy. The peculiar society and administration of Egypt (see Chapter 27) enable this evidence to be applied to the rest of the empire only with caution. Similar care is needed in assessing the significance of evidence of social strains. Many of the papyri survived because the land in which they were buried has not been inundated since antiquity. By definition, then, they derive from caches outside or on the fringes of the land cultivable from irrigation from the River Nile. The communities who lived on such marginal land may have been more susceptible to fluctuation in climate, or in state demands, than others in the empire. Some, but fewer, papyri survive from the Near East, especially from the Judaean desert, throwing some light on the history of Judaea and Arabia. Inscriptions on wooden slats have been discovered in the excavations of the Roman fort of Vindolanda on Hadrian's Wall; it can confidently be assumed that more will appear in excavations elsewhere in the western provinces, now that archaeologists know what they are looking for.[7]

Evidence of coins can be used in a variety of ways to reconstruct history.[8] On the one hand, the inscriptions and types can be presumed to reflect a propaganda message intended by the state to influence its subjects. Whether such propaganda was very successful is unclear, but that is another matter. On the other hand, economic historians can learn much about the circulation of coinage by analysing the distribution of the places where coins of a particular issue are found; such information is especially useful when the coins are discovered as spot finds, since such individual coins will have survived in the archaeological record only because they were dropped by accident, and that in turn reveals that such coins must have been generally carried for purposes of exchange. In contrast, the discovery of deliberate hoards may be evidence of political turmoil; at the least it can be assumed that some factor prevented the hoarder from recovering his or her treasure.

In all this mass of evidence a crucial question, and a source of continuing conflicting interpretations, is how much to take at face value. What is involved must be not just the collection and collation of evidence, but an attempt, with sympathy but without uncritical acceptance of ancient evaluations, to interpret that evidence in a framework of a plausible model of how the Roman Empire might have worked.

It cannot be stressed too emphatically that the only certain fact about the ancient world is that most information about it has been lost. What survives does so mostly through the preferences and prejudices of those – mostly Christian monks – who in Late Antiquity, and through the Middle Ages, copied the manuscripts on which our texts are based. Imagination and empathy are essential to achieve even a glimpse of the lives of people long dead. Thus, all historians accept that attempted reconstructions of the past can never be allowed to ignore or contradict the surviving evidence without at least plausible justification for such a procedure, but it is equally misleading to allow credence only to those statements about the past for which direct evidence happens to survive.

THE WRITING OF HISTORY

Roman history has, for centuries, suffered from an antiquarian approach in which footnotes and citation have come to seem ends in themselves. Such historiography may reflect more the vagaries of literary survival and archaeological discoveries than the world of the Romans themselves. It is preferable to attempt to imagine a rounded picture of Roman society into which all the evidence can be fitted coherently. The choice of the framework for that picture will, of course, inevitably reflect the taste and prejudices of the historian, and sometimes imagination will lead one astray. At any time, new evidence may shift perceptions. This is a matter not for regret but for rejoicing. The historian's task is never finished.

Thus it is possible, with the benefit of hindsight, to see that the picture of the Roman empire favoured in nineteenth-century British scholarship reflected the concerns of imperial Britain, and that more recent interest in the effects of empire on subject peoples reflects a rise in post-colonial consciousness. It is not accidental that so much has been written in recent years on problems of identity in the ancient world, the place of women in Roman society, and the manipulation of memory within this society for contemporary purposes.

The use of social-scientific models for population growth or the operation of pre-capitalist economies can provide a control on the use of ancient data under a veneer of objectivity, but, valuable and suggestive although such studies often are, they too rest upon unprovable assumptions about similarities between the Roman world and other societies. Recourse to sociological, anthropological and other general theories to provide a structure for comprehending the Roman world is common – and often helpful – but such theories can be taken only as a guide to interpretation of the surviving evidence, and not as evidence in themselves.

One of the most important recent developments in theoretical approaches to ancient history has been a focus on representation – the process by which Romans individually or collectively constructed their world in literature, monuments, inscriptions and art. A major advantage of this approach is that, even when the evidence is too scattered and fragmentary for a reasonably secure comprehension of what 'really' happened, a great deal can still be learned about Roman society from the way that this society and its travails were portrayed by Romans themselves.

FROM CITY TO EMPIRE

With the assassination of Julius Caesar in 44 BC, the Roman aristocracy was thrown into a chaos from which it only emerged in 31 BC with the victory of Octavian who, under the name Augustus, set the pattern for future government of the Roman world by a sole ruler. The struggle in which Augustus had been involved had nominally been over the right to honours and magistracies in the city of Rome, but the arena for the contest was the whole area that had been conquered by Rome over the preceding three centuries. Armies marched through Italy, and fought in most of the countries bordering the Mediterranean from Spain to Egypt. In an age of slow communications, the cause of their tribulations must have been quite obscure to many of the provincials whose taxes and forced labour enabled great Roman aristocrats to fight out the Roman revolution. Hence the approach by the people of Aphrodisias in Turkey to Octavian in *c.* 38 BC, even though their territory did not lie in the region controlled by him. According to an inscription preserved at Aphrodisias, Octavian wrote to the neighbouring city of Ephesus:

> Solon son of Demetrius, envoy of Plarasa-Aphrodisias, has reported to me … how much property both public and private was looted, concerning all of which I have given a mandate to my colleague [Marcus] Antonius that, as far as possible, he should restore to them whatever he finds.

(Reynolds, no. 12; LR 1, p. 327)

For such desperate provincials, Rome was a distant, ruthless power, and the machinations of her leaders belonged to a different world. Any help from any powerful individual was to be seized on.

By AD 180 much of this had changed. The Roman world was for the most part at peace, and it was many years since aspirants to power had upset the *status quo* (although civil war was to erupt again in AD 193 on the murder of Commodus). But in any case, for many provincials of the urban aristocracy, Rome had ceased to appear alien and hostile. Partly this was as a result of the grant of Roman citizenship to increasing numbers: in AD 212 it was to become quasi-universal. Partly it was encouraged by the openness of the Roman upper class to rich provincials who wished to devote their lives to participation in the state's bureaucracy. But above all it was a product of the main change which gives the period its name. What united the 50 to 60 million or so inhabitants of the empire, whether they were scions of old Roman noble families or the humblest Syrian peasant, was simply this: that all were ruled by one man, the supreme autocrat, the emperor.

2

THE ROMAN WORLD
IN 50 BC

THE SPHERE OF ROMAN INFLUENCE

From Britain to Egypt, from Portugal to Iran, throughout the north coast of Africa and along the Rhine and the Danube, the influence and power of Rome were known by 50 BC (see Map 1), and the Roman aristocrats who busied themselves in Rome over the internal wranglings of their own small coterie knew about the places included within this vast region, and might have visited a good number of them. It was a region characterized by great diversity of geography, climate, peoples and cultures. If by AD 180 many of them had achieved a semblance of unity, it was the effect not of internal development but of their relationship with Rome. In 50 BC a tour through such countries produced wide-eyed fascination at the differences between peoples, reflected in the voluminous ethnographies of the Greek experts Posidonius (*c.* 135–*c.* 51/50 BC) and Strabo (*c.* 64/3 BC–*c.* AD 24/5).[1]

For the Romans themselves, the centre of their world was the Mediterranean, whose waters provided both transport links, which encouraged trade and cultural interchange as well as the passage of armies, and the genial climate which promoted similar lifestyles around its edges. The coastal plains of the Mediterranean in antiquity, as now, flourished under a mixed agricultural regime of grain, olive and grape crops irrigated by gentle precipitation in mild winters and warm summers and by light ploughing, but, away from the coast, there was much variety of economies, cultures and societies.

Rome itself, the hub of empire, was a strange mess of a city. A heterogeneous population, attracted by wealth culled by conquests or descended from slaves brought to Rome after such conquests, inhabited a rather drab and unplanned urban sprawl next to the River Tiber. Public buildings were still rather scarce and unimpressive by the standard of contemporary cities in the Greek world. Overpopulation led to recurrent food crises and constant reliance on imports brought by sea. The city's poor provided fertile ground for the political agitation and riots on the streets which were a feature of the late 50s BC.

Increasingly, the influential inhabitants of the city were drawn from the wider society of Italy. The whole Italian peninsula had been brought under

Roman influence long ago, by 272 BC, and the use of the Latin language and Roman coinage had become widespread by the end of the second century. But it was only as result of the Social War of 90–88 BC that all Italians had gained Roman citizenship and its attendant privileges. The merging of Italian consciousness into Roman was a feature of the first century BC already well under way in the time of Julius Caesar, but many local divergences persisted. The latest extant inscription in the Etruscan language dates from the time of Augustus, for example. Local cults persisted even when native languages such as Oscan had been given up for Latin. In two areas, in particular, a simple merging into Roman society was not easy. In the southern Apennines, where anti-Roman forces had fought not for citizenship but for Italian independence in the Social War, Samnite tribes did not take easily to Roman-style urban life; in any case, large areas of the mountainous countryside were still devastated from the war. In the southern coastal cities, which had been colonized from Greece between the eighth and fourth centuries BC, Hellenic culture and the Greek language retained their pre-eminence.[2]

Spain had been a focus of Roman interest since the Hannibalic wars of the late third century BC. Of particular interest were the fertile coastal regions, and considerable mineral resources, such as the large mines of Río Tinto in the south, which the Romans exploited principally for silver. Yet no consistent strategy governed Rome's intense but relatively brief campaigns in the province, the extensive mountainous interior made campaigning difficult, and the Celtic and Celtiberian tribes fought hard to preserve their autonomy. As Livy noted in the late first century BC (*History of Rome* 28.12.2), 'Spain, although it was the first mainland province to be entered by the Romans, was the last to be completely subdued, and held out until our own times.'

Many of Spain's inhabitants belonged to the more general category known to Romans and Greeks as Celts; the same name was used to describe the numerous tribes who lived in Gaul and Britain.[3] The scarcity of contemporary written evidence from within these societies makes it impossible to tell whether the impression of ethnic and cultural similarities between the Celtic peoples was indeed correctly observed. When they enter the detailed political narrative of Caesar's campaigns in France in the 50s BC, the Celtic tribes are more often found at war with one another than combined into any ethnic community. It was only in response to Caesar's aggression that they joined forces under Vercingetorix in 52 BC. Greek writers observed that Celts had achieved much in some areas. According to Posidonius (quoted by Strabo, *Geography* 4.4.4), their scientific and philosophical knowledge was well developed. But Caesar (*Gallic War* 6.13) confirms an essential split of authority in Celtic society between a ruling élite of warrior chieftains, whose power depended on their military competence, and a learned class of druids whose function was the oversight of legal processes and religious ceremonies. Roman fear of Celts, engendered by the tradition of the sack of Rome by Gauls in 390 BC, rendered their reports of native customs highly suspect, not

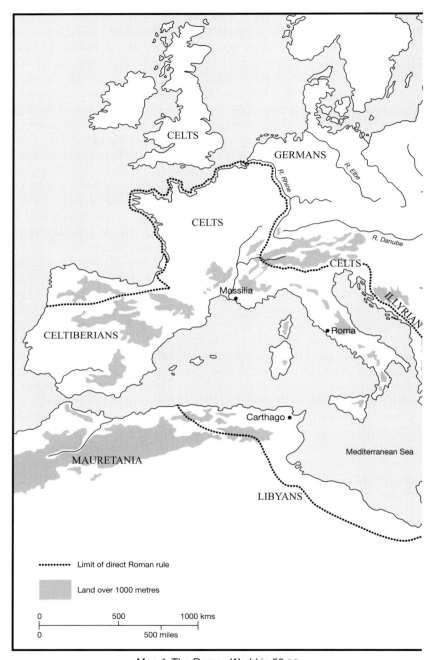

Map 1 The Roman World in 50 BC

least in the rumours that Celts in Gaul still practised human sacrifice in 50 BC (Caesar, *Gallic War* 6.16). Archaeological evidence of fortified hilltops in the mid-first century BC, as well as the co-ordinated resistance to Caesar in Gaul and Britain, suggests a well-organized society. The warrior chieftains seem to have been able to amass great wealth.

According to Caesar (*Gallic War* 6.11), the Germans who lived east of the Rhine were to be clearly distinguished from the Celts who lived west of it.[4] Such clarity may be somewhat deceptive. Caesar's claim to have conquered Gallia (Gaul) was much enhanced by the assertion that only the area west of the river should be included in the definition of the province. The archaeological remains of settlements on both sides of the Rhine in the first century BC reveal similar economies based on settled village agriculture and stock rearing in forest clearings. The Germani too seem to have been organized under war leaders, but their religious practices may have differed somewhat to those of the Celts, since in his rather idealized account, *On the Origin and Country of the Germans* (9.3), Tacitus records that they worshipped gods without images. Further east, little is known of the state of the Balkans in this period; only the tribes closest to Greece and the Adriatic are mentioned in the literary sources, where they emerge as fierce fighters under hereditary rulers zealously preserving their independence in mountainous country.

Matters were very different in Greece and in western Turkey, where the evolution of classical urban culture by which Greeks had adapted to the emergence of regional superpowers after Alexander the Great continued, little affected by the imposition of Roman rule during the second century BC.[5] The cities of Greece maintained exceptional prosperity, reflected in magnificent architecture. Greek intellectuals felt themselves to be self-consciously the centre of a higher culture, from which Romans, despite their political superiority, had much to learn. Roman aristocrats in turn came to Athens to broaden their cultural horizons. The extent of cultural Hellenization was much less in central and eastern Turkey, where the inhospitable terrain of the Anatolian plateau and Caucasus mountains encouraged separate communities to retain distinct identities: the kingdoms of Pontus and Bithynia by the Black Sea; the Galatian Celts on the plateau; the Phrygians, Lydians and Lycians of south-west Turkey; the Cilicians, whose pirate activities were curtailed by Pompeius Magnus in 67 BC, but whose mountain hideouts remained unconquered; and the independent kingdom of Commagene, whose king Antiochus I (69–34 BC) built himself a truly monumental tomb on the mountainside at Nemrud Dagh in this period.

The petty kings of Commagene were only one of the numerous successor kingdoms of the superstate of the Seleucid empire.[6] Seleucus, one of the generals of Alexander the Great, had established a kingdom which stretched at its greatest from the frontier of India to the Aegean, and from the Black Sea in the north to Egypt in the south. The break-up of this state was a gradual business from the early second century BC to the end of the Seleucid monarchy at the hands of Pompeius in 64 BC; in the last century and a half of the process, Roman pressure from the west was a major factor. Of the independent petty states which benefited from the break-up of Seleucid power, a number had in turn fallen into Roman hands, including the old kingdom of Pergamum in Asia Minor, bequeathed to Rome by its king Attalus already in 133 BC and, as the province of Asia, famous for its wealth, and Judaea in southern Syria, but many others remained independent or semi-independent, notably the Nabataeans in the northern Arabian desert, Armenia (which under Tigranes I had recently been a major regional power), and the Parthian rulers of Mesopotamia and Iran. In all these areas of the Near East, indigenous cultures survived, sometimes with a heavy overlay of Greek civilization encouraged by the Seleucid state as part of a policy of ruling through Greek-style urban aristocracies.

Incorporation into the Roman sphere of influence of these regions on the eastern frontier involved a series of major wars in the first half of the first century BC. Particularly effective in resistance to Rome was Mithradates VI Eupator (120–63 BC) of Pontus, whose own territorial ambitions spurred him to expand his territory in the first decade of the century, until he controlled, either directly or through puppet rulers, most of the Black Sea region (including Bithynia and part of Armenia) as well as Cappadocia and Paphlagonia to the south. In the early 80s BC, Mithradates conquered the Roman province of Asia, killing thousands of Romans and Italians, and won the support of most of Greece. Defeated by Sulla Felix in 87 BC, he withdrew to his ancestral base in the Crimea but came again into conflict with Romans when he invaded Bithynia in the following decade after Nicomedes of Bithnyia had bequeathed his kingdom to Rome. He was opposed first by Licinius Lucullus, who drove him out of Bithynia, and finally, in 66 BC, by Pompeius Magnus, who destroyed his power altogether, establishing Rome as saviour and protector of the Greek cities of Asia from such despotic rule.[7]

Still independent of Rome was Egypt, ruled in 50 BC by the penultimate king in the line of Macedonian monarchs descended from another of Alexander the Great's generals, Ptolemy Soter.[8] The Ptolemaic dynasty ruled Egypt through a complex Greek bureaucracy which brought in massive revenues and permitted conspicuous expenditure in the great capital of Alexandria in the Delta. The wealth generated by the Nile and long-established agriculture in Egypt was in stark contrast to the poverty of the Hamitic Kingdom to the south in Sudan. Trade in luxuries brought riches to the Aden peninsula across the Red Sea.

The rest of North Africa enjoyed less independence, although a native dynasty still ruled in Morocco under Juba I of Mauretania.[8] Both the area of Africa opposite Italy, and the interposed island of Sicily, had long been directly controlled by Rome. The cause lay back in the conflict with the Phoenicians of Carthage in the third and second centuries BC. In Tunisia, the great grain-growing rolling hills by the coast were largely owned by Roman colonists and entrepreneurs, but much of the population was native to the region and spoke the local languages, predominantly Punic in the area around Carthage and the coastal regions, and Berber in the interior.

For the Roman government in the city of Rome, there was no particular cause to object to this diversity of cultures. Nor was there need to impose uniformity in the formal relations of such areas with Rome. Some regions were controlled directly by Roman senators commanding troops, as in Gaul. In Greece, where almost no troops were stationed, the local aristocracy kept order and collected revenues for Rome, reporting back in cases of difficulty to a Roman governor. But elsewhere things were managed even less formally. Friendly kings in the Near East ruled by agreement with Rome, proud of their independence but in practice subservient to Roman whims, particularly in foreign policy. And some such kings, despite their friendship, could even afford to go their own ways, as did the kings of Parthia. But in such cases the Roman state was apt to respond by military intervention, like the 40,000 soldiers who had marched against Parthia in 53 BC under Marcus Crassus, only to be crushingly defeated at Carrhae, with the loss of the legionary standards.

The political struggles of the rulers of the Roman state in the 40s and 30s BC, and the political solution imposed by the victor Octavian, were of no great concern to most of the inhabitants of this variegated world. But the progress and results of these struggles were to have an effect on all of them which would last for centuries.

THE CITY OF ROME IN 50 BC[10]

Perhaps the greatest effect of all was in the city of Rome itself, even though the essentially rural, peasant structure of earlier Roman life had already undergone much change by the Late Republic. For two centuries the city had been enriched by booty – Pompeius is said to have amassed 36,000 talents after the defect of Mithradates alone – and increasing wealth had encouraged a rapidly growing urban proletariat.

At the end of the Republic a good proportion of Roman citizens still inhabited the city itself, despite the extension of citizenship to the rest of Italy by 83 BC. From the census he carried out in 28 BC, Augustus claimed that there were 4,063,000 Roman citizens altogether (*Res Gestae* 8.2). The accuracy of Augustus' figures may be dubious, since the census relied on self-reporting; views differ over whether the increase in the population which Augustus' figures seem to indicate was due to a previously untried attempt to include women and children in the figure. Whatever the case, it may be estimated that over one million people lived in the city.[11]

The structure of Roman life had developed in quite idiosyncratic forms during the long centuries since the city's foundation (traditionally dated to 753 BC). The social and legal structures which had evolved by the end of the

Republic were to function as the basis of the Roman culture adopted over great areas of the Mediterranean world during the Early Empire.

The city of Rome had originated as part of a group of Latin peoples, whose loose confederation was in the sixth century BC based on the plain of Latium, to the south of the Tiber. Early urbanization was heavily influenced by Etruscan and Greek models, but the intense militarism which led Rome to establish dominion first over the other Latins, and then over the rest of Italy and beyond, had no parallel in the ancient world. By the mid-first century BC, the Latin elements of Roman society had already been much influenced by Greek culture and deeply affected by the strains of an enlarged population and the wealth generated by successful warfare. None the less, a distinctively Roman way of life persisted, to be in part preserved and extended in the imperial period, in part only mentioned by conservatives in times of change.

On the public level, Roman society was highly stratified on the basis of birth and wealth. The social and political status of each adult male citizen was fixed at irregular censuses. Wealth was a prime, but not the only, criterion in the assignation of individuals to the *ordines* (status groups) in Rome. Of these the most prominent were the senators, from whose ranks most magistrates were drawn, and, below them on the social scale, the equites (literally, 'cavalry'), who generally lacked direct political involvement. In essence, select rich individuals controlled the state as a warrior élite into whose hands were placed political, religious and judicial authority. Their position was preserved by the institutionalized support of the wealthy in public assemblies.[12]

On the domestic scale, Roman society was also in principle quite rigid. In Late Republican Rome the primary social unit was still in law, as in very early times, the extended family (*familia*), even though in practice social relations centred for most Romans, as in modern Western society, on the nuclear family of parents and children in a single household.[13] In theory, the only fully legally recognized person (*sui iuris*) in each family unit was its male head, the *paterfamilias*. Anyone of any age who was directly descended from the *paterfamilias* through the male line by legitimate marriage was included within his *familia*. So too were those brought in by formal adoption, which was a custom common at least among aristocrats. Over all these people the *paterfamilias* had absolute power of life and death, although the state's magistrates could intervene in cases of gross abuse. Such power was still found in regular use in the first century BC in the decision of the *paterfamilias* about the fate of newborn babies, who would be exposed to die if unwanted. The theoretical powers of the *paterfamilias* were enshrined in the earliest code of Roman law, the Twelve Tables, which tradition held had been drawn up back in *c.* 450 BC but which were still much quoted in the Late Republic.[14]

Expectations derived from early Roman society thus still in part conditioned the lives of Romans in the Late Republic. As children, both boys and girls were educated primarily within the *familia*. In aristocratic circles it became common in the first century BC to employ professional grammarians to teach children literary skills, which were always more highly prized by Romans than numeracy. Institutionalized schools, of the type common in the contemporary Greek world, were still almost unknown in Late-Republican Rome.

Boys received full public rights as citizens from the age of about 17. Roman hopes for the future career of such young men were clear. The ideal was the soldier farmer, devoted to the state, loyal to friends. For the urban poor the ideal was hard to achieve, but there is no good reason to doubt that they shared the longing for such a way of life which is explicit in much Roman literature and rhetoric.

Expectations about the careers of girls were very different.[15] Where men were expected to be martial, the virtues praised in women were essentially domestic. In political terms women were totally excluded from power in Roman society except through their influence on their male relatives.

Domestic slaves were as common in Roman families in the Late Republic as cars are in modern European society.[16] Their presence in the city had far-reaching social effects, not least because on receiving their freedom (*manumissio*), they became part of the undifferentiated plebs.

The city in 50 BC was thus a cosmopolitan place where Greek and other languages were widely spoken in addition to Latin, and the customs and dress of non-Italians were frequently visible on the streets. On the other hand, many particularly Roman customs survived, such as the use of gladiatorial games for entertainment or the funerary processions of the rich, in which professional mourners and actors paraded in wax masks of distinguished ancestors of the deceased. And despite the introduction of new cults into the city over many centuries from the rest of Italy and from Greece and elsewhere, and a general disregard for some traditional Latin deities which had caused a few cults to fall into disuse, traditional Roman religion preserved its distinctive form:[17] thus the domestic cult, based on the hearth (*vesta*) of each home and the deities of the *familia* – the ancestors (*lares*) and the household spirits (*penates*) – was replicated on a national scale, and the magistrates and priests of the city of Rome regularly entreated the gods at national shrines, not least that of the goddess Vesta, which all lay within a clearly defined religious border, the *pomerium*.

Part II

ÉLITE POLITICS

3

THE POLITICAL LANGUAGE
OF ROME

POLITICAL POWER

Rome in 44 BC was in theory a democracy.[1] Laws (*leges*) were passed by the people as a whole – that is, the adult male citizens, who met for the purpose either in an assembly of the 35 tribes of Rome (the *comitia tributa*) or, more infrequently, in a gathering of the 193 'centuries' into which the citizen body was divided when it was drawn up on the Campus Martius in battle order (the *comitia centuriata*). It was by a system of group voting at these great mass meetings that war was declared on the state's enemies, legislation passed to regulate civil relations and criminal conduct, and magistrates appointed to lead troops into battle, conduct campaigns, convene courts, and enact the other multifarious tasks of the execution of government (see Figure 1).

Such was the theory. In practice,[2] the free exercise of democratic power had never been fully enjoyed by the Roman people, and curbs on their control of events, which had begun as simply practical restrictions, had by the Late Republic become sufficiently part of political life to appear to an outsider like Polybius in the mid-second century BC as if they must be constitutionally enshrined:

Figure 1 Silver denarius minted by order of the senator P. Nerva in 113 or 112 BC. The obverse has a bust of the goddess Roma, a personification of the city. The reverse shows the process of voting in Republican Rome: the voter on the left is being handed his ballot, while the man on the right casts his vote in the urn. Photo courtesy of CNG Coins.

> It was impossible even for a native to pronounce with certainty whether the whole system was aristocratic, democratic, or monarchical. This was indeed only natural. For if one fixed one's eyes on the power of the consuls, the constitution seemed completely monarchical and royal; if on that of the senate, it seemed again to be aristocratic; and when one looked at the power of the masses, it seemed clearly to be a democracy.
>
> (*The Histories* 6.11.11–12)

Polybius' picture was idealized under the influence of Greek political philosophy, but he had lived in Rome for many years and showed real political insight. On the one hand, the power of the leading magistrates had been much enhanced by the widened scope of their responsibilities, which could involve commands of huge armies for long periods away from Rome. Cicero in the mid-first century BC confirmed in his treatise on the *Laws* that the highest magistrates acted like kings:

> There shall be two magistrates with royal powers. Since they precede, judge, and consult, from these functions they shall be called praetors, judges and consuls. In the field they shall hold the supreme military power and shall be subject to no one. The safety of the people shall be their highest law.
>
> (*Laws* 3.3.8)

In practice, the consuls in the Late Republic often achieved this quasi-monarchical power as much after as during the period of their magistracy, since the great army commands were by law reserved for ex-consuls at least five years after their consulships; such ex-consuls technically acted in place of the consuls and hence were termed *proconsules*. Despite legal restrictions on the power of both consuls and proconsuls, ordinary citizens had little hope of opposing their power, except with the threat of prosecution when the magistracy came to an end.

On the other hand, the principle that magistracies were collegial (that is, held with a number of colleagues) engendered a certain necessary unity within the governing class. In 50 BC there were two consuls a year at the head of the state; eight praetors looked after legal jurisdiction in Rome. The four aediles (two curule, two plebeian) were responsible for urban administration in Rome, the corn supply, and the provision of public games and shows. The 20 quaestors had a variety of tasks, from the accompaniment of proconsular armies as chief of tax collection to more mundane jurisdiction in Rome. Below them ranked a variety of junior magistrates. At the bottom were the *vigintisexviri*, the 26 men whose tasks included the supervision of the sewers of Rome. The very fact that they had all stood for election to a series of these posts encouraged a sort of fellow feeling for others within their political culture. Anyone whose wealth was sufficient was in theory able to stand, but in the nature of things only those whose temperament inclined them to public life, or who were pushed forward by family or friends, chose to devote themselves to the strenuous and sometimes dangerous life of politics. But, more importantly, advancement to the next rung in this clearly stratified hierarchy was usually possible only with the active support and friendship (*amicitia*) of other politicians, so that the development of reliable political supporters (*amici*), through marriage links or assiduous attendance, was a major concern of all politicians who had any ambition.

The operation of bonds of *amicitia* were clearest on the election hustings, but they not infrequently emerged also in the senate, the public body to which all ex-magistrates of a certain rank – since 80 BC all those who had held the quaestorship – automatically belonged. The senate was in theory no more than a forum for the leading men of the state to offer their advice to the current magistrates, but in practice the influence within the senate of senior politicians whose friendship might be necessary for those magistrates to proceed further in their career rendered it dangerous to ignore the senate's advice. Such respect for the senate could even be elevated into a political principle, as by Cicero, who characterized those politicians who followed the senate's wishes as *optimates* (the best men). Those who ignored the senate, on the grounds that the people's support mattered more than that of their fellow politicians, were liable to obloquy as *populares* (panderers to the people); since all politicians needed popular support whatever the attitude of the senate, the same title of abuse could be worn with pride when addressing the wider assemblies.

It can be seen that a major factor in ensuring stability in the political influence of senate and senior ex-magistrates was the rigid hierarchy of the *cursus honorum*, the steps by which a man advanced to the peak of a political career, the consulship, or, for a select few, appointment as one of the two censors elected at irregular intervals to fix the roll of Roman citizens, weed out the unworthy from the senate and set the state back on the path of virtue.[3] Precisely the rigidity which was normal enhanced the status of those few who by charisma, luck or force circumvented the system, as did Pompeius Magnus when he was elected to the consulship in 70 BC at the age of 36, after holding no previous posts in the city of Rome. For most Romans, it seemed necessary and right that such figures should remain exceptional. Prestige was assumed to grow naturally with age and experience. It was dangerous for young men to have too much power. Men in positions of influence should have sufficient means to act as gentlemen, and the ability to point to ancestors of high achievement was a major advantage: the constant appeals to ancestral virtue in Roman political rhetoric contrast oddly with the great extension of citizenship to foreigners. Technically only those whose male ancestors were consuls or patricians (a select group of families who had held power in the Early Republic) could call themselves *nobiles*, but politicians were accustomed to appeal to their female ancestors also when it suited. Those who could not do so made a virtue of necessity by claiming that as new men (*novi homines*), their own talents compensated for poor birth, but sneers about humble origins always remained a potent weapon in the hands of opponents. The principles of canvassing are well laid out in a long letter attributed to Quintus Cicero, and purportedly addressed by him to his brother Marcus when he sought election to the consulship in 65 or 64 BC:

> Consider these three things: what state this is, what you are seeking and who you are. Then every day, as you descend to the forum, you must say to yourself, 'I am a new man; I am standing for the consulship; this is Rome.' The political newness of your name you will overcome to a large extent by your reputation as a speaker. ... Next, let the number and quality of your friends be apparent.
>
> (*On Canvassing for the Consulship* 1)

The impression is of a club devoted to the self-advancement of its members despite frequent rifts over the composition of the committee and officers.

For young men in a hurry there was an alternative, if risky, route to rapid prestige – or, depending on your point of view, notoriety – by seeking election as a tribune of the plebs. The principle that the Roman people as a whole had the power to protect their own fortunes was expressed constitutionally in a somewhat incongruous body, the plebeian assembly (*concilium plebis*). This self-constituted and self-governing body was a relic of a struggle back in the fifth and fourth centuries BC, when magistracies had been confined to a small group of families distinguished as patricians and the rest of the populace (the plebeians) had resorted to joint action to prevent arbitrary abuse of magisterial power. They extorted from the patricians greater opportunities for rich plebeians to embark on political careers. Such battles had long been won, and the majority of the state's magistrates by 50 BC were plebeians; only the name *patricius* lingered on as an honorific zealously guarded by the declining number of families entitled to boast it. But the plebeian assembly still met regularly and elected its own leaders, plebeian tribunes and aediles, whose brief now was in essence to act as ombudsmen for individual Romans against the state. Such tribunes could be of any age. Since they enjoyed two further privileges – first, that of presenting motions to the plebeian assembly which, if passed, had the force of law, and, second, that of vetoing on the people's behalf laws proposed in the main state assemblies – the position might seem to offer great opportunities for advancement and self-publicity for a young man. Such indeed had proved to be the case not infrequently during the 50s BC and, indeed, ever since the tribunate of Tiberius Gracchus in 133 BC.

POLITICAL METHODS

Analysis of the Roman constitution in the somewhat cynical fashion presented above was more characteristic of Roman politicians in their evaluation of the careers of political enemies than in their discussions of their own careers. In advocating policies and supporting individuals, the Romans shared a distinctive vocabulary.[4] All could appeal to an instinctive conservatism. Any action that accorded with ancestral custom (*mos maiorum*) was praiseworthy.

Alongside this notion went an idealization of an imaginary heroic past, when Roman peasant soldiers had embodied simple, sterling qualities. All could appeal to freedom (*libertas*), a term as slippery in antiquity as now; for politicians it sometimes meant little more than the right to advocate any policy they wished without fear.[5] All advocated promotion of the *gloria* of the Roman state, which meant more than just preserving the *status quo*. The Roman state had been geared to war throughout its history, and the extension of Roman power by military conquest was accepted by everyone. All accepted the authority of the laws, which were regarded with great reverence, as if the wording of a law alone could cure social and political ills: hence the stream of legislation passed in the 50s BC in an attempt to curb violence, bribery and murder on the streets of Rome by the simple expedient of defining them as illegal.

In their judgement of the qualities desirable in a political leader, Romans showed an essential unanimity. Skill in generalship, or at any rate success in war, was universally admired. Hence the extraordinary praise by Cicero of the conquests in Gaul by Julius Caesar, a man he cordially disliked but whose right to continue campaigning he vigorously upheld:

> Gaius Caesar's strategy I see to be far different; for he believed not only that it was necessary to wage war against those who he saw were already in arms against the Roman people, but also that all Gaul must be subjected to our sway. And so he has fought with the fiercest peoples, in gigantic battles against the Germans and Helvetians, with the greatest success. He has terrified, confined, and subdued the rest, and accustomed them to obey the empire of the Roman people. ... Previously, we possessed merely a path through Gaul, members of the senate; the other parts were held by peoples either unfriendly to this empire, or untrustworthy, or unknown, or certainly savage, uncivilized and warlike – peoples which everyone always desired to be smashed and subdued.
>
> (*On the Consular Provinces* 13.32)

Romans conceived of their empire in the Republican period not as a fixed territory but as a sphere of influence, defined by the limits of Roman power. There has been much debate as to why the Romans expanded their dominion across the Mediterranean. The defensive model, according to which Rome acquired territories haphazardly in the course of protecting its own interests, has largely given way to an explanation based on the aggression of a state driven by the ambitions of leading senators for whom success in war brought economic, social and personal rewards. Both models may be partially correct, since the circumstances leading to foreign wars over the long period of Roman expansion undoubtedly differed from one occasion to another.[6]

In any case, the acme of political success was envisaged as the triumph, a ceremonial procession through the streets of Rome to the temple of Jupiter on the Capitol. The details of the ceremony, as depicted over the centuries in a variety of literary and artistic media, varied greatly, but the underlying notion was that the victorious general should be dressed in regal fashion and accompanied not only by his army and a parade of captives and spoils but by the senate, magistrates, and people.[7] Acceptance of the imperialist ethos which justified Roman rule over other people seems to have been more or less universal among the free population of the city of Rome itself.

The prestige of the powerful was advertised not least through visual imagery. Late-Republican silver coins often bear images with historical allusions and political themes. It was common for the magistrates responsible for production of a coin issue to depict the past glories of their own ancestors, such as their military victories or the monuments they had built. The public space of Rome was filled with monuments, from basilicas to temples and triumphal arches, erected by senators for self-glorification.

Such visual reminders of Rome's leading generals exposed the tension between the empire of the people as a whole and the ambitions of individuals. The speaker's platform located in the *comitium* at Rome was the place where politicians made their case to the people, but it was also home to memorials to great generals of the past, such as a gilded equestrian monument dedicated to the dictator Sulla. Sculptural reliefs like those from the Piazza della Consolazione in Rome, depicted an array of military paraphernalia. Rome's first permanent stone theatre, erected by Pompeius Magnus in 55 BC, contained fourteen female personifications of the nations he had conquered, creating the impression that he had brought the entire Mediterranean world under his sway. Competition between Roman politicians to excel on the battlefield was thus enshrined in their monuments in Rome.[8]

Besides such militaristic virtues, skill in oratory was also highly prized: in a society without mass printing, political ideas were mostly disseminated by public speeches and passed on afterwards by word of mouth. Oratorical ability was crucial in the pursuit of political power.[9] In his *Dialogue on Oratory* 36, Tacitus looked back to the rewards available for effective orators in the Late Republic:

> The more influence a man could wield by his powers of speech, the more readily did he attain to high office, the farther did he, when in office, outstrip his colleagues, the more did he gain favour with the great, authority with the senate, name and fame with the common people.

Wealth in itself did not bring prestige, and over-indulgence was described by some as positively bad, but the leisure (*otium*) provided by a sufficient income was reckoned part of the necessary equipment for intellectual endeavour and therefore political power. Roman society had never witnessed the promotion of a leader from the impoverished, or even the artisanal class of free citizens, and when Spartacus led a slave rebellion in Italy in 72–71 BC, the free peasants sided with the state in its suppression. It was generally expected that possession of wealth would be advertised by conspicuous expenditure on fellow citizens. The aim of such 'evergetism' was not so much charity as insurance in the winning of political support. Those who were politically threatened might accordingly be particularly lavish, as was M. Vipsanius Agrippa in 33 BC, according to Cassius Dio:

> Agrippa agreed to be made aedile and without taking anything from the public treasury repaired all the public buildings and all the streets, cleaned out the sewers, and sailed through them underground into the Tiber. ... Furthermore, he distributed olive oil and salt to all, and furnished the baths free of charge throughout the year for the use of both men and women; and in connection with the many festivals of all kinds which he gave ... he hired barbers, so that no one should be at any expense for their services.
>
> (*History of Rome* 49.43.1–3)

It was taken for granted that the very poor would not benefit from any handouts. Those individuals who were specially singled out to receive particular gifts might consider themselves to be designated thereby as friends (*amici*) of the donor, although outsiders, and doubtless in private the donor, viewed such an unequal friendship rather as that of a patron to his client, mirroring the close formal ties which bound an ex-slave to his former master.[10]

Perhaps not surprisingly, the rhetoric of Republican politics thus tended to be bland and imprecise. Men praised *virtus*, which could mean anything from courage to probity. They encouraged energy (*strenuitas*), but abhorred its excess (*ambitio*). Loath to admit the selfish causes that bound them, they might describe themselves and their friends simply as 'the good' (*boni*) or 'the best men' (*optimates*). Even pure self-regard could be honoured with the title *dignitas* (dignity), without self-consciousness. At times, Roman politicians in the Late Republic, with their great estates and hordes of retainers of slaves and freedmen, could behave much like medieval barons in the wilful self-interest of their policies.

And yet the public speeches of politicians in the 50s BC reveal a continuing respect for the constitutional theory with which this survey began, namely, the right of the Roman people to control their own destiny. It was to the interest of the state, not of the individual, or of classes or pressure groups, that politicians appealed in seeking support or election. In doing so they put forward policies on specific issues of foreign and domestic policy on which the people might be expected to have a view, not least, in the former case, because in the Republican period they would be likely to serve in the armies which would put such policies into operation. It could prove worthwhile wooing the people in this way. In the tribal assembly, the rich could best afford to leave their farms regularly to vote, and their influence could predominate, especially in the decisions of the rural tribes, since there were 31 rural tribes to four urban ones. In the centuriate assembly, the better-off constituted the centuries which voted first, and if their votes were unanimous, the poor would not be called upon to vote. But when the vote of the richer centuries was split, particularly in elections for office, then the vote of even the poorest centuries could be vital for political success.[11] Voting aside, political rhetoric addressed a non-constitutional but no less real factor in Roman political life: the power of the urban mob to intimidate or cheer and to create the whole atmosphere surrounding a politician in a political system whose physical arena was the astonishingly small area of Rome around the forum and the senate house (the *curia*).[12]

4

CAESAR TO AUGUSTUS, 50 BC–AD 14

LAST YEARS OF JULIUS CAESAR

When Julius Caesar crossed the Rubicon in January 49 BC, he inaugurated the autocracy of the Caesars.[1] With great candour, the opening chapters of his account of the civil war between his forces and those of Pompeius Magnus reveal stark personal motives alongside a more respectable concern for the Roman Republic. Typically writing of himself in the third person, he gives his motives for fighting in a speech made to his troops:

> 'As for myself,' he said, 'I have always reckoned the dignity of the Republic of first importance and preferable to life. I was indignant that a benefit conferred on me by the Roman people was being insolently wrested from me by my enemies.'
> (*Civil War* 1.9)

Caesar plunged the Roman world into war to protect his own affronted *dignitas* (*Civil War* 1.7), but the outcome of three years of bloody fighting was far more than the appeasement of a hurt. It was nothing less than the establishment of the road to monarchy. It was no accident that Suetonius' series of imperial biographies began with Julius Caesar – not the first member of the Caesar family to hold office, nor yet the first to rule as later emperors did, but the first Caesar to rule alone.

Caesar's rhetoric in the seizure of power was, naturally enough, entirely in accordance with the Republican traditions within which he had made his mark. A scion of a patrician family, whose father had reached the praetorship, he had experienced no difficulty in enjoying a successful if unspectacular career until 63 BC. Then his election as *pontifex maximus*, the leading priest of the Roman state cults, propelled him to prominence, not least because of the unashamed use of bribery on his behalf by his powerful friend, M. Licinius Crassus, who had been consul in 70 BC. Still, his achievement of a consulship in 59 BC would have aroused no surprise if he had not traded on the opportunities provided by his occupation of high office for the year to do favours to the most influential ex-magistrates of the time: his benefactor, Crassus, and his future rival, Pompeius. This political accommodation, known to modern scholars as the First Triumvirate, was of brief duration in the early months of 59 BC, but it was sufficient to gain Caesar a great command in the province of Gaul, which he interpreted as a remit to conquer the whole area of what is now France north of the Alps, as far as the Channel. Exceptional generalship in the field between 58 and 51 BC, and a good deal of luck which compensated for some rash strategic decisions, won for Rome unprecedented conquests and for Caesar both immense popularity in the city and the support of a great body of soldiers. These men were tied to him both by the affection of shared military experience and by an expectation that his political power would win them rewards, suitable pensions for the soldiers in the form of land grants, and political preferment for the officers. When Pompeius' friends attempted to prevent Caesar reaping the political harvest that he expected from his campaigns by demanding that he demit his general's post in Gaul and thus lay himself open to prosecution for alleged misdeeds in office before being allowed to stand for election to a second consulship, Caesar responded by marching on Rome.

Such use of legionaries to seize power was hardly new in Roman life. Sulla Felix had marched on Rome in 82 BC, defeated his enemies and killed many of them, and won thereby election to the post of *dictator*, in which guise he had reorganized the state. Both Pompeius and Crassus had threatened the city in 70 BC in order to achieve their consulships, although in their case no fighting had been necessary. But in the previous 20 years, in which violence of a different kind had been rampant in gang warfare on the streets of Rome, no army commander had used his troops to impose his political will in such a way. And Caesar went much further than Sulla. Stopping only briefly in Rome to raid the treasury, he waged a rapid campaign against Pompeius and his supporters in Spain and Greece, where in Thessaly he won a decisive victory over Pompeius in 46 BC. Pompeius fled to Egypt, only to be murdered on his arrival by his erstwhile supporters there. Campaigns in Egypt and Syria established Caesar's control over those areas, and a final campaign in Africa subdued a further group of his political opponents. In 46 BC he could return to Rome to claim, implausibly, a great triumph for the Roman people.

Original, limited, ends soon gave ways to grander designs with the reality of unchallenged power. As Cicero put it, bitterly, immediately after Caesar's death (*On Duties* 3.21.83): 'Behold, here you have a man who was ambitious to be king of the Roman people and master of the whole world; and he achieved it!' After the death of Pompeius in Egypt, Caesar was sufficiently at ease to grant, and advertise, pardon (*clementia*) for his political opponents. Such contravention of the rules of *inimicitia* (enmity) was bound to irritate the beneficiaries little less than betrayal of *amicitia* (friendship) would do. In 48 BC Caesar was elected by the people as *dictator*, thereby following the lead of Sulla in declaring normal competitive politics in abeyance while he sorted out the ills of the state. Unlike Sulla, who resigned into private life once the legislation that he thought essential had been passed, Caesar accepted in 44

BC the title of *dictator perpetuo* (dictator for life). A great programme had been enacted in 46 and 45 BC, from the settlement of his veteran soldiers on confiscated land in Italy, to reform of the debt laws and the calendar. According to later reports, not all of them reliable, much more was intended for 44 BC, but his adoption of quasi-monarchical powers and the rumour that he might accept a royal crown, as he had already welcomed the establishment of a priesthood for his worship, proved too much for some fellow senators, who saw the dashing of all hopes for their own rise to the top in Roman politics. On the Ides of March (15 March) a large group of senators led by Marcus Brutus and Gaius Cassius Longinus, two of the supporters of Pompeius who had been granted *clementia* by Caesar, stabbed him to death at the foot of Pompeius' statue in the senate's meeting place in the theatre of Pompeius.

In proclaiming the restoration of *libertas*, as they did on their coins (see Figure 2, the murderers of Caesar were not at the time naïve. Only one man had died; the rest of Caesar's friends remained untouched. In constitutional terms there was no particular problem in the continued running of the government. One consul for the year survived, Caesar's general Marcus Antonius. Magistrates for the law courts and command of armies had been duly elected by the people, albeit at Caesar's behest. Far from a plunge into chaos, the liberators might argue that their action could bring a return to normality. And, indeed, in the days after the Ides of March, they remained peacefully in Rome, until the threat of allegedly spontaneous violence by the urban mob drove them out, first from Rome and then from Italy. Not even that flight was necessarily seen as a prelude to civil war. After all, most of those still active in politics in 44 BC remained involved because in some sense they were part of Caesar's faction – including his murderers, who had received magistracies themselves with Caesar's electoral support. Of Caesar's enemies, only Sextus Pompeius, son of Pompeius Magnus, who had held on to the independent command of six legions in Spain after his father's defeat and

Figure 2 Silver denarius minted for Cassius in 43–42 BC. The message of the depiction of the goddess Freedom is reinforced by the caption Leibertas. The rest of the caption stresses Cassius' prestige as a general (imperator); Cassius was just as eager as the followers of Caesar to seek prestige for himself. Photo courtesy of CNG Coins.

death, had a natural inclination to take advantage of Caesar's demise. For the rest of Caesar's friends there was no reason – and given Caesar's fate, little incentive – to seek promotion to the same pre-eminence that Caesar had achieved. Enough for them to accept the steady prestigious rise through the *cursus honorum* guaranteed by the presence of so many friends to canvass for them. There is no reason to suppose any greater ambition for Marcus Lepidus, who, as Caesar's lieutenant (*magister equitum*) in the latter's role as *dictator*, alone lost his job as a result of his friend's decease. As for Marcus Antonius, who was the surviving consul, Cicero, who hated him, accused him of aiming at dictatorship, but it is now impossible to know how justified the accusation was.

That all this was so can be traced in some detail through the contemporary letters of Cicero, who at the age of 62, and 19 years after his glorious consulship, stood pre-eminent in front of the senate, at least in his own estimation. Cicero applauded Caesar's murderers as liberators, praised their act to the people and hoped to counter any excessive ambitions by passionate speeches (the so-called *Philippics*) in denunciation of Marcus Antonius.[2] But speeches were of no account against the one figure for whose single-minded and ruthless determination no-one could possibly have allowed in March 44 BC. That figure was the young Octavius, the future emperor Augustus, who was to be the founder of the Roman Empire.

AUGUSTUS

On the death of Augustus in AD 14, 58 years after his eruption into Roman politics, a catalogue of his achievements, the *Res Gestae*, was inscribed in front of his vast mausoleum on the Campus Martius in Rome and in some of the many temples erected to honour him as a god all over the Roman realm.[3] In that account, the first 13 years to 31 BC were sketched with deliberate brevity and ambiguity:

> At the age of nineteen, on my own initiative and at my own expense, I raised an army by means of which I liberated the Republic, which was oppressed by the tyranny of a faction. For which reason the senate, with honorific decrees, made me a member of its order in the consulship of Gaius Pansa and Aulus Hirtius [43 BC], giving me at the same time consular rank in voting, and granted me the *imperium*. It ordered me as propraetor, together with the consuls, to see to it that the state suffered no harm. Moreover, in the same year, when both consuls had fallen in the war, the people elected me consul and a triumvir for the settlement of the commonwealth. Those who assassinated my father I drove into exile, avenging their crime by due process of law; and afterwards when they waged war against the state, I conquered them twice on the battlefield. I waged many wars throughout the whole world by land and by sea, both civil and foreign.
>
> (*Res Gestae* 1–3.1)

The anodyne words masked a sustained, ruthless assault between 44 and 31 BC on the bastions of power, in which, from the beginning, no danger and no morality were allowed to hinder Octavius' path to a power as absolute as Caesar had known.

Marcus Octavius had been born in September 63 BC of a not particularly distinguished line of Italian municipal aristocracy. His father, the first in the family to enter Roman politics and become a senator, reached only the praetorship. But it so happened that his maternal grandfather had married the sister of Julius Caesar, and the relationship had brought him, while still a boy, to his great-uncle's attention. Signs of favour were already in evidence. The childless Caesar allowed Octavius, aged 16, to join him in the triumph in Rome in 46 BC. But the news that he had been posthumously adopted by Caesar in his will, and named as chief heir to Caesar's enormous and ill-gotten fortune, must have come as a shock to all, including Octavius.

Octavius was 18 on the Ides of March 44 BC and training as a junior officer for Caesar's proposed renewal of the desultory campaigns against the Illyrian hill people on the eastern Adriatic coast, which had persisted for some time. On hearing of the murder of Caesar he returned at speed to Italy to take up his inheritance, spurred on not least by rumours that Marcus Antonius, as the man on the spot, might deprive him of a share of the money. The prospects were good. With great wealth and the name of Caesar, Octavius could now expect to move high in Roman politics – to achieve an early consulship perhaps, and be courted by an aristocratic bride. Cicero viewed him with patronizing affection as a young man of talent and promise, who should be 'praised, honoured and removed' (*Letters to Friends* 11.20.1).

But Cicero was wrong, for the signs of greater ambition were there from the start. Even before his arrival in Rome, Octavius used the promise of the vast wealth which was to come from his inheritance to lure some of Caesar's veterans from their secure but dull lives as farmers to seek adventure and greater gain under his leadership. The precise function of the two legions thus privately raised was not at first clear, but no-one objected openly. Cicero praised the young man's initiative and urged his fellow senators to invite Octavius and his mercenaries to help in the struggle to suppress the ambitions of Antonius.

Events moved rapidly in 44 BC. In May, the murderers of Caesar were forced to flee Rome by the hostility of the people, probably encouraged by Antonius. When Antonius departed to north Italy to confront one of their number, Decimus Brutus, in Mutina, Cicero pressed for the senate to declare Antonius a public enemy, but the senate preferred to issue an ultimatum for Antonius' withdrawal. It was unsuccessful. The consuls for 43 BC, Aulus Hirtius and Gaius Pansa, marched north in February and March of that year to lift the siege at Mutina. They were aided by the two legions of Octavius, who had been granted praetorian status to legalize his command of forces for the state.

In a speech made to the senate in early January 43 BC (*Fifth Philippic* 17.46), Cicero urged that Octavius be given honours by a formal decree of the senate (*senatus consultum*):

> Whereas Gaius Caesar son of Gaius, *pontifex*, propraetor, at a serious crisis of the state has exhorted the veteran soldiers to defend the liberty of the Roman people, and has enrolled them; and whereas the Martian and Fourth Legions, with the utmost zeal and the most admirable unanimity in serving the state, under the instigation and leadership of Gaius Caesar, are defending and have defended the state and the liberty of the Roman people; and whereas Gaius Caesar, propraetor, has with an army set out for the relief of the province of Gaul, has brought under his own obedience and that of the Roman people cavalry, archers, and elephants, and has at a most difficult crisis of the state come to the assistance of the safety and dignity of the Roman people; therefore for these reasons it is the pleasure of the senate that Gaius Caesar son of Gaius, *pontifex*, propraetor, shall be a senator and shall express his opinion on the praetorian benches.

Octavius' premature use of the name Caesar – he was not formally permitted to use it until his adoption by Julius had been ratified along with the rest of the will by the Roman people, which did not occur until later in 43 BC – caused Cicero some qualms, but no serious concern. A bid for popularity was standard practice in political life, even if in this case the methods lacked good taste.

Antonius was defeated, at least sufficiently to be required to take refuge in Gaul with his old comrade Lepidus, but the two consuls were both killed – not, according to rumour, without the intervention of Octavius (Suetonius, *Augustus* 11). Octavius, still not quite 20, marched to Rome with his own legions and now those of the state as well, and demanded the consulship. There was no resistance. A law was promptly passed which made Octavius legally Caesar's son, with the impressive new name of Gaius Julius Caesar Octavianus. (It should be explained that while to his contemporaries he was simply Caesar, modern historians tend to call him Octavian to prevent confusion with Julius Caesar.)

Now at last it was clear that this was no ordinary young politician. Pompeius Magnus too had raised a private army at the start of his career in 83 BC, but it had been 13 years before he threatened Rome with another army to secure his election as consul. Octavian had telescoped the process into a few months. But such single-mindedness was dwarfed by the ruthlessness of the following year. Octavian had achieved the consulship through his support of the liberators against Antonius. Within weeks he swapped sides and agreed to co-operate with Antonius and Lepidus.

In November 43 BC, Antonius, Lepidus and Octavian came to an essentially private agreement which was to have immense public consequences. The scene was described 200 years later by the historian Appian:

Octavian and Antonius composed their differences on a small, depressed islet in the Lavinius River, near the city of Mutina. Each had five legions of soldiers whom they stationed opposite each other, after which each proceeded with three hundred men to the bridges over the river. Lepidus by himself went before them, searched the island, and waved his military cloak as a signal to them to come. Then each left his three hundred men in charge of friends on the bridges and advanced to the middle of the island in plain sight, and there the three sat together in council, Octavian in the centre because he was consul. They were in conference from morning till night for two days.

(*Civil Wars* 4.1.2)

The three generals persuaded the plebeian tribune Publius Titius that the state needed a strong hand and the imposition of order. On the instigation of Titius, on 27 November the *lex Titia* was passed granting the three men a five-year task 'to set up the state' (*rei publicae constituendae*). The normal system of election and law-making was returned to the abeyance in which it had been under Caesar.

Many senators, including Cicero, and many more equites, were proscribed as enemies of the state and put to death. The process was described by Appian:

It was ordered that the heads of all the victims should be brought to the triumvirs for a fixed reward, which to a free person was payable in money and to a slave in both money and freedom. All persons were required to afford opportunity for searching their houses. Those who received fugitives, or concealed them, or refused to allow search to be made, were liable to the same penalties as the proscribed, and those who informed against such were allowed the same rewards. The proscription edict was in the following words: 'Marcus Lepidus, Marcus Antonius, and Octavius Caesar, chosen by the people to set in order and regulate the Republic, declare as follows: "Had not perfidious traitors begged for mercy and when they obtained it become the enemies of their benefactors and conspired against them, neither would Gaius Caesar have been slain by those whom he saved by his clemency after capturing them in war, whom he admitted to his friendship, and upon whom he heaped offices, honours, and gifts; nor should we have been compelled to use this widespread severity against those who have insulted us and declared us public enemies. Now, seeing that the malice of those who have conspired against us, and by whose hands Gaius Caesar perished, cannot be mollified by kindness, we prefer to anticipate our enemies rather than suffer at their hands." '

(*Civil Wars* 4.2.7–8)

The three men (*tresviri* in Latin, but commonly known in English as 'triumvirs') appointed all magistrates for years ahead. Their powers were ill-defined, because they were overwhelming. When they came to an end in December 38 BC there was no change in the triumvirs' behaviour. Their right to act as absolute rulers was simply retrospectively reconfirmed in the spring of 37 BC, by a prolongation of the *lex Titia* of 43 BC.[4]

The triumvirs divided up responsibility for the Roman world between them, but their first task was to deal with the murderers of Caesar. Brutus and Cassius controlled massive forces in the East, supported by cash ruthlessly extorted from the provincials. Antonius and Octavian carried out the campaign, while Lepidus stayed in Italy. The victory, at Philippi in Macedonia in October 42 BC, was mainly won by Antonius, even though Octavian claimed the credit as avenger of his adoptive father.

Immediately after Philippi began what in retrospect appears to have been a struggle for supremacy between the triumvirs. But at first it might not have looked quite like that to all the participants. For Antonius and Lepidus the role they had already achieved as great proconsuls might well suffice to satisfy ambition: after all, the command in the East and in Gaul handed over to Antonius after Philippi was over an area even greater than that which Pompeius had ruled in the 60s BC, and the powers of patronage enjoyed by the two men were quite sufficient to enable them to look forward to preeminence in the state on the relinquishing of their commands. Thus Antonius strikingly failed to help his brother L. Antonius (consul in 41 BC) when the latter tried to unseat Octavian in Italy, and with M. Antonius' wife Fulvia was besieged by Octavian in Perugia, finally being defeated in early 40 BC. At a dramatic meeting in October of that year in Brundisium, commemorated at the time by coin issues significantly inscribed with the word *CONCORDIA* (harmony), Antonius marked his willingness to co-operate with Octavian by marrying the latter's sister Octavia. So long as each triumvir stuck to his own agreed area of responsibility – in technical Roman terms, his own *provincia* – there was no cause for conflict, and, indeed, none is recorded between Antonius and Lepidus. Antonius preferred to concentrate on a campaign against Parthia in the hope, in the event disappointed, of glory.

In theory, the division of power was loose enough to allow interference by one triumvir in the sphere of influence of another without resentment, provided that no military activity was involved. Hence inscriptions set up in the late 40s and 30s BC record privileges granted by Octavian both to an individual, Seleucus of Rhosus, and to the city of Aphrodisias in Caria (today Turkey), despite the fact the two places lay within Antonius' *provincia*.[5]

It was thus perfectly possible for the triumvirs to rule together in amity, but Octavian had other ideas. He had already discovered what could be achieved by the judicious use of money and energy, and he could not but notice how he had leapfrogged in power over great generals like Pollio and Plancus. Left in 42 BC with the unglamorous area of Sardinia and Spain to rule, where no prestigious campaigns could easily be trumped up, he undertook the necessary but unpopular task of confiscating land in Italy in order to settle veteran soldiers in sufficient comfort to ensure their loyalty. With remarkable skill Octavian seems to have managed to dissociate himself from responsibility for the confiscations. In the contemporary poetry of Vergil (for instance, *Eclogue* 1.42), Octavian was praised for his ability to respond compassionately to appeals against the harsh consequences of the policy.

Octavian was already presenting himself as more than human on the coins which emphasized the name of Caesar and the divinity of his father, formally acknowledged by the senate and people in January 42 BC. His ambition is hardly in doubt, but more precise delineation of the development of his plans for power is difficult, for no detailed political history of the next ten years survives in any contemporary source. The fullest account is that of Cassius Dio, composed in the early third century and reliant, like the other more fragmentary accounts written in the late first or early second centuries, on sources which had been heavily infected by hindsight and Octavian's propaganda, despite the availability of a more cynical version of events by Antonius' general, the historian Asinius Pollio. None the less, the outline of Octavian's extraordinary designs is clear.[6]

A brief narrative will indicate the audacity of his actions. When by chance Calenus, Antonius' legate in Gaul, died in post in 40 BC, Octavian simply took over both *provincia* and troops, ignoring the inconvenience that the region lay under Antonius' command. Then in 38 BC Octavian attacked Sextus Pompeius, the son of Pompeius Magnus. Sextus had been outlawed in 43 BC under a law passed against Caesar's murderers, but his possession of a large force of ships based in Sicily had won him considerable political support. In 39 BC Octavian had even wooed his support and legitimated his command in Sicily, so that he could only justify his renewed hostility in 38 BC by characterizing Sextus as a pirate intent on cutting the corn supply to the city of Rome. He eventually defeated him in Sicily in 36 BC, and when Lepidus, who had helped half-heartedly in the defeat, claimed that Sicily rightfully should be under his control, Octavian won over his troops, so that Lepidus also retired suddenly to life under guard and in obscurity.[7]

After 36 BC Octavian's single-minded pursuit of sole power was now evident to all. With Lepidus out of the way, he concentrated on the defeat of Antonius. The latter, apparently unaware of the seriousness of the threat, was preoccupied with the awful failure of his attack on Parthia in 36 BC, in the course of which he lost a quarter of his army. He formed a strong attachment to Cleopatra in Egypt, perhaps not unreasonably, given the description of her by Plutarch:

> Her beauty, as is recorded, was not in and of itself incomparable, not such as to strike those who saw her. But conversation with her attracted attention, and her appearance combined with the persuasiveness of her talk, and her demeanour which somehow was diffused to others, produced something stimulating.
> (*Life of Antonius* 27.1–2)

After the Parthian disaster of 36 BC, Antonius was at least able in 34 BC to establish (by trickery), and to advertise on his coins, firm control over Armenia.

Despite such efforts, when Octavian in 32 BC began to portray Antonius as essentially un-Roman, a slave to his oriental mistress, and an incompetent drunkard, Antonius had little propaganda reply except to insist that he was one of the duly elected board of three triumvirs, who ruled the Roman state with the consent of the Roman people. Most of his coins, for instance, retained

Figure 3 Silver denarius minted for Marcus Antonius in 31 BC, just before the battle of Actium. The obverse shows the head of Antonius with his full Roman titles, advertising his role as priest (*augur*), general (*imperator*), senator (his consulships) and triumvir. The reverse depicts Victory in a laurel wreath. The portrayal of Roman magistrates on their own coins was an innovation by Julius Caesar. Photo courtesy of the Ashmolean Museum, Oxford.

a resolutely Roman façade (see Figure 3), apart from some rash issues, like those which portrayed his head on one side, that of Cleopatra on the other.[8]

Octavian, ignoring the two consuls who fled to Italy to join Antonius, sought moral support by garnering an oath of loyalty from all Italy (*tota Italia*) against the eastern queen. Only those veteran colonies in Italy which comprised Antonius' soldiers were exempted from the oath which would have bound them against their former general, although many of them in any case chose (wisely) to swear allegiance to Octavian. With such psychological backing, and many troops, Octavian set sail for the East and defeated Antonius resoundingly at Actium in Greece in September 31 BC. Rapid action by Agrippa, Octavian's general, trapped Antonius' huge forces in the harbour of Actium and reduced them by attrition. Antonius and Cleopatra were hard put even to escape with a few ships. They took refuge in Alexandria, which was in turn besieged and captured in 30 BC. Both committed suicide.

From that date Octavian was the undisputed ruler of the Roman world. All further constitutional changes did no more than dress up this fact. Success had been achieved in part through the mistakes of Antonius, who allowed Octavian to become sole master of the western Mediterranean by defeating Sextus Pompeius in 36 BC, while he himself sought for too long an elusive victory in Parthia. Antonius also failed to recognize the serious propaganda effects of his relationship with Cleopatra, giving the impression at the so-called 'Donations' of Alexandria in 34 BC that control of much of Rome's empire in the eastern Mediterranean and the Middle East would be handed over to the three children who had been born to him and the queen (see Chapter 27).

But more important than Antonius' failings were Octavian's efforts. Octavian took full advantage of every stroke of fortune, advancing his cause by skilful playing on the name and memory of Caesar in 44–43 BC; by using the gullibility of Cicero and the liberators; by capitalizing on the death of the consuls of 43 BC at Mutina and of Calenus in Gaul in 40 BC; and by exploiting the loyalty of his soldiers and the excellence of his generals, particularly M. Vipsanius Agrippa (see below), whose triumphs in Illyricum in 35–34 BC gave the impression to the Roman people that Octavian's party could achieve military glory, and whose military genius won an unexpectedly decisive victory in the Actium campaign.

But Octavian's success was owed above all to the single-minded ruthlessness which enabled him to change sides with ease and to murder erstwhile friends. Suetonius' portrayal of his behaviour during the proscriptions is chilling:

> For ten years Augustus remained a member of the triumvirate commissioned to reorganize the government, and though at first opposing his colleagues' plan for a proscription, yet, once this had been decided upon, carried it out more ruthlessly than either of them. They often relented under the pressure of personal influence, or when the intended victims appealed for pity; Augustus alone demanded that no one was to be spared, and even added to the list of proscribed persons the name of his guardian Gaius Toranius, who had been an aedile at the same time as his father Octavius.
>
> (*Augustus* 27)

In 25 BC Augustus published an autobiographical defence of his actions in seizing power, but it does not survive. His enigmatic brief account in the extant *Res Gestae Divi Augusti*, not published until after his death in AD 14, was more in keeping with the dignity of the old established politician who preferred to draw a veil over his youthful excesses.

Returning to Italy, in 30 BC Octavian disbanded about half of the huge legionary forces left in his hands, paying for their resettlement with wealth taken from Egypt. Consul every year since Actium, in 28 BC he also, with Agrippa, performed the task of a censor (but without the title), expelling from the senate the members he deemed 'unworthy' of the body – an act rendered necessary in part by the inclusion in the senate of partisans of the triumvirs who were believed to have secured their position by bribery. During 28 and 27 BC he was so secure that he could ostentatiously resign all his offices and return the state to normality. As Octavian later described it:

> In my sixth and seventh consulships, after I had put an end to the civil wars, having attained supreme power by universal consent, I transferred the state from my own power to the control of the Roman senate and the people. For this service of mine I received the name of Augustus by decree of the senate, and the doorposts of my house were publicly decked with laurels, the civic crown was affixed over my doorway, and a golden shield was set up in the Julian senate house, which, as the inscription on this shield testifies, the Roman senate and people gave me in recognition of my valour, clemency, justice, and devotion. After that time I excelled all in authority, but I possessed no more power than the others who were my colleagues in each magistracy.
>
> (*Res Gestae* 34)

In effect, regardless of the formal date when the triumvirate was thought to have ended – (a debated issue, see above, Note 4) – the job of the triumvirs, that of setting back the state to rights, was thereby announced as complete (see Figure 4).[9] A grateful senate and people voted Octavian a new name, Augustus. The new Augustus did not take on the title of *dictator*, as Julius Caesar had done, and indeed he was to refuse it when the plebs tried to press it upon him in 22 BC. He chose instead to be known by the informal title of *princeps*, a term used in the Republic to indicate the foremost statesman. But as well as his new name, and other honours (see below, Chapter 12, on his careful crafting of his image), the senate and people also voted Augustus command for ten years over the provinces of Spain, Gaul, Syria and Egypt. The real significance was that it gave him control of the vast majority of the legions still under arms.

Possession of so many legions gave Augustus an opportunity for political prestige by foreign victories as well as a means to suppress internal dissent. With some of the legions he departed in 27 BC to Spain, winning a victory over the mountainous tribes the Cantabri and Astures, which he celebrated in 25 BC by closing the gates of the temple of Janus in Rome (for the second time since 29 BC), the traditional way of symbolizing the achievement of peace throughout the Roman world. Since Augustus published his autobiography at this date, he may have felt that this victory crowned his career as a great Roman general.[10]

It is unlikely that Augustus was ever again under any threat from any of his fellow politicians in his impressively long rule, but it is impossible to be certain. The only full-scale chronological narrative about this period to survive is that of Cassius Dio, who wrote in the early third century and used sources now hard to identify.[11] The brief narrative in the short history of Rome composed by Augustus' much younger contemporary Velleius Paterculus, and the biography of Augustus composed in the early second century by Suetonius, do not adequately fill the gap.

Figure 4 Golden aureus minted for Octavian, 28 BC. The portrait of Octavian describes him as 'son of the divine (Caesar)' and as consul for the sixth time. On the reverse, on which Octavian is shown seated on a magistrate's chair holding out a scroll, the legend states: 'He has restored their laws and rights to the Roman people'.
Photo © The Trustees of the British Museum.

Thus little can be stated for certain about the significance of an incident narrated by Cassius Dio under the year 22 BC. According to one possible reconstruction of the confused evidence, Marcus Primus, the governor of Macedonia, was arraigned for illegally making war on a Thracian tribe, thereby committing *maiestas* (treason against the Roman people); the response of Primus, and his defence counsel, a certain Murena, that he had been given permission for his campaign by Marcellus, Augustus' nephew – and therefore, by implication, by Augustus himself – was severely embarrassing to Augustus, but the connection between this affair and a plot apparently to murder Augustus by the same Murena, and his close associate, one Caepio (about whom nothing else is known) is unclear, and in any case no amount of embarrassment could seriously loosen Augustus' grip on power.[12]

In 19 BC a certain Egnatius Rufus put himself forward as a candidate for the consulship, with popular support but without the correct qualifications. He was put on trial and convicted for *maiestas*, but Augustus was apparently not involved, and the entire affair was managed by the senate under a *senatus consultum ultimum* (whereby the senate increased the power of the magistrates of the state to act against public enemies by declaring a state of emergency).

The view that Augustus lurched from one crisis to another, forced at frequent intervals to readjust his image to circumvent attacks upon his position by fellow senators, is a modern hypothesis intended to explain his periodic alterations to his formal constitutional position in the state. Thus in 23 BC the people voted to Augustus *imperium proconsulare maius*, the legal right to intervene on behalf of the state even in those parts of the empire not formally under his authority, and *tribunicia potestas* for life, which permitted him to exercise a tribune's veto over all legislation, and some have interpreted these new powers as a response to the 'crisis' provoked by Murena. Such a view is possible, but its significance should not be exaggerated. Augustus' new powers may have helped in the shaping of his public image (see Chapter 12), but there is no evidence that his grip on power was itself ever threatened by his fellow senators. For the most part, Augustus' political worries derived from his continual ill-health and the rivalries of those closest to him, not least his own immediate family.[13] Far from suppressing other noble families, Augustus was concerned to strengthen the position in Roman society of the aristocracy, including not least those families brought to political prominence as his supporters during the civil wars, through a series of laws encouraging marriage, penalizing celibacy, and regulating social status. This move, as in other areas of his regime, was buttressed by traditionalist sentiment: he is said to have justified his policies by reading out a speech originally delivered by Q. Caecilius Mettelus in the second century BC, 'On Increasing the Family' (Suet. *Aug.* 89.2). For similar reasons, Augustus encouraged senators to maintain the military skills traditional in the Republic; he originally intended senators' sons to serve as cavalry commanders as well as legionary tribunes in order to increase their experience of army life.[14]

41

Augustus' victories in the 40s and 30s BC, both in the civil war and in the campaigns in Illyricum in 35–34 BC from which he gained prestige for having enlarged the boundaries of Roman power, had in fact been won entirely through the military genius of his subordinates, in particular M. Vipsanius Agrippa. Agrippa came from an obscure Italian family not previously involved in Roman politics. In his late teens on the death of Caesar, he attached his fortunes to Octavian and by loyal service achieved the heights of the consulship in 37, 28 and 27 BC and shared censorial tasks with Augustus in 28 BC. For a man lacking in inherited support and ancestral glory, and reportedly low on charm and oratorical techniques, such advance by his mid-30s was spectacular. But Agrippa had earned such favour by his military expertise, for Augustus was a notorious incompetent in warfare, rumoured to have been ill in his tent at Philippi, and conveniently absent at most of the other victories he claimed as his own.

For twenty years Octavian could rely entirely on Agrippa's loyalty precisely because of the latter's lack of outside support, but by the mid-20s BC Agrippa might reasonably have demanded an increasing share of the power earned by his efforts. In formal terms, he had held the consulate three times, and might have expected to be treated among the most senior statesmen of the senate; informally, troops might have hesitated whether to follow the charismatic Augustus and the name of Caesar or the competent Agrippa, who was more likely to deliver victory. Not that warfare ever ensued, for Augustus gradually bowed to Agrippa's pressure and, after a temporary crisis in 23 BC, when Augustus' extreme illness and the apparent prospect of his imminent death brought matters of succession into focus, Agrippa was promoted to higher and higher prominence. The process was expedited by Augustus' absence from Rome on three occasions between 27 and 12 BC, each time for three years. Agrippa was left in control, and Augustus was not compelled to define his relationship with his friend too precisely. When Agrippa died unexpectedly in 12 BC, Augustus described him as having been in effect his equal; in formal constitutional terms, this had indeed been precisely true from 13 BC, when both Augustus and Agrippa held *imperium proconsulare maius* (the formal right to intervene in provinces not assigned to them, when to the advantage of the Roman people). The words of Augustus' oration at his friend's funeral are partially preserved on a papyrus found in Egypt, in a Greek translation:

It was confirmed by a law that into whatever province the affairs of the Roman people might take you, no one in those provinces should have greater power than you. But you rose to the summit by my favour, by your own virtues, and by the consensus of all men.[15]
(ZPE 52 (1982), pp. 60–62; LR 1, p. 633)

The co-operation of the two men was symbolized in 21 BC by Agrippa's marriage to Augustus' daughter Julia, a union which produced three sons, Gaius and Lucius Caesar and, born after Agrippa's death, Agrippa Postumus. Political rivalries thus became a domestic affair, and marital affections and dislikes came to have a major effect on the distribution of power. Roman political history became the domain, not of the parliamentary correspondent, but the court gossip. That this was so is directly due to Augustus himself, who seems to have strongly believed, despite the lack of constitutional precedent or justification, that political power could in some way be bequeathed from one member of the family to another, simply by the stipulation of a private will and testament; the transmission of control of the house of Caesar. The idea was not totally foreign to Roman political life, in which the sons of *nobiles* had always expected election to magistracies as a corollary of their origins, but Augustus' interest in the subject, with an odd preference for genetic continuity, was presumably formed from his own success in using the charisma of his adoptive father's reputation in winning power. The gradual acceptance of such a notion – not necessarily complete in Augustus' lifetime – is one of the main features that marked the acceptance of autocratic rule by the Roman people.

At any rate Augustus put huge effort into the selection of a son and heir. Despite his obvious wish, two wives and a prodigious sex life which jarred uncomfortably with his encouragement of a series of legislative attempts to curb the excesses of private indulgence which had become standard in certain circles within the senatorial elite in the Late Republic (see below, Chapter 17), he himself produced only one child, his daughter, Julia. His second wife, Livia, had been transferred to Augustus by her compliant first husband, Tiberius Claudius Nero, in 39 BC, with the addition of two of his sons, Tiberius, born in 42 BC, and Drusus, born after Livia's marriage to her new spouse. The succession policy was described clearly by Tacitus:

> To consolidate his control Augustus raised his sister's son Claudius Marcellus, who was still a mere stripling, to the pontificate and curule aedileship, and Marcus Agrippa, not a noble by birth but a good soldier and his partner in victory, to two consecutive consulships. On Marcellus' death soon afterwards, he took Agrippa as his son-in-law. His stepsons, Tiberius Nero and Claudius Drusus, he honoured with imperial titles, even though his own family was still intact – for he had admitted Agrippa's children, Gaius and Lucius, into the house of the Caesars ... and he had a consuming desire, beneath a pretence of reluctance, to have them named leaders of the youth and consuls designate. After Agrippa departed his life, and premature death (or their stepmother Livia's treachery) cut off Lucius and Gaius Caesar – the former while on his way to our armies in Spain, the latter while returning, weakened by a wound, from Armenia – since Drusus had long since perished, Nero [i.e. Tiberius] alone remained of the stepsons, and everything centred on him.
>
> (*Annals* 1.3)

Thus Augustus showed favour to his stepsons Tiberius and Drusus, but preferred in the 20s BC to promote the cause of Marcellus, son of his sister Octavia and marked out as heir at least to Augustus' private property, until his career was cut short by premature death in 23 BC. Thereafter Augustus began a curious process which accurately reflected general Roman attitudes to adoption. In 17 BC Gaius and Lucius, Agrippa's two older sons and Augustus' grandsons, were formally adopted by Augustus as his sons. It was generally assumed that Gaius and Lucius would also be the main beneficiaries of his will, bypassing Augustus' stepsons Tiberius and Drusus, who up until that time had themselves been favoured with exceptional prominence in the imperial entourage. Drusus died in 9 BC, but Tiberius continued campaigning in the Balkans and received massive powers in 6 BC, only to balk at the arduous military lifestyle imposed on him by Augustus and retire to Rhodes to seek *otium* (leisure), unwilling to continue fighting for someone else's glory. After the deaths of Lucius in AD 2 and Gaius in AD 4 (after a stubborn refusal, like Tiberius, to go on working for Augustus), Augustus rather reluctantly adopted his stepson Tiberius (who, in turn, had to adopt his nephew Germanicus), as well as the youngest of his grandsons, Agrippa Postumus. By insisting on a series of astute marriages and adoptions, Augustus thus reintegrated the family so ravaged by unlucky deaths.

Concentration of power within the family had its disadvantages. Augustus compelled his daughter Julia to marry Tiberius in 12 BC on the death of her husband Agrippa. Their marital antipathy was one cause of Tiberius' decision to seek *otium* in Rhodes in 6 BC despite the high magistracies that he still held. Julia's method of comforting herself by taking lovers aroused fierce hostility from her father, either because she thereby so blatantly flouted the moral stance his propaganda proclaimed or because some of her friends were too potentially powerful to allow her amours to continue unchecked; they included the young Iullus Antonius, son of the triumvir Antonius and consul in 10 BC, and condemned to death in 2 BC for his adultery with Julia. In any case, Julia's influence was checked by exile in AD 2, and her other lovers banished. Her daughter, the younger Julia (sister of Gaius and Lucius), followed her into exile in AD 8; again, the charge was adultery, and in her case, at least, any further suspicion of treason is not very plausible. The fact that power rested in the family bred distrust. The list of those whose death was attributed by rumour to the machinations and poison of Livia is a long one.[16]

At the same time, the benefits of keeping power in the family were considerable. Augustus experimented during his long rule with the devolution of power to his sons and stepsons, who could share with him the burden of government while not threatening his ultimate control. Above all, Augustus required good generals because he continued to need foreign victories for prestige. It was essentially for glory rather than in pursuit of any overall military strategy (beyond a desire to safeguard communications between Roman possessions on either side of the Alps and the Balkans) that he embarked on an unprecedented policy of imperial expansion, with campaigns in Ethiopia (29 and 25 BC), Spain (27–25 BC, finally conquered 19 BC), against the Garamantes in Africa in 19 BC, in the Alps (16–15 BC), in the Balkans and in Germany across the Rhine in 12–9 BC, and on the Anatolian plateau against the Homanadenses in Galatia at some time between 12 BC and AD 1 (see Map 2).[17] And when, particularly after AD 6, these new conquests and other parts of the empire were racked with disturbances and revolt (in the Balkans, Asia Minor, Africa, Sardinia and Judaea), Augustus needed loyal generals for their suppression. It was not safe to allow too many ambitious, competent generals to win glory in foreign campaigns, lest they seek power for their own benefit. But members of the family might be trusted more to remain loyal to Augustus, from whose overwhelming prestige their own positions ultimately derived, and to devote their energies not to challenging but to impressing him. It was one of the main features of Augustus' rule that he extended so widely and successfully the patronage of his *familia* by judicious marriages, not least to the scions of old families of the Republic. Hence many of the consuls after 16 BC were young nobles but also, by marriage, Augustus' relatives.[18]

FRISII
GERMANIA INFERIOR
R. Elbe
R. Rhine
BELGICA
LUGDUNENSIS
GERMANIA SUPERIOR
NORICUM
RAETIA
AQUITANIA
PANNONIA
NARBONENSIS
DALMATIA
HISPANIA CITERIOR
(TARRACONENSIS)
ALPES
ITALIA
LUSITANIA
CORSICA
BAETICA
SARDINIA
MAURETANIA
SICILIA
AFRICA

- - - - Approximate provincial boundaries

0   500   1000 kms
0   500 miles

Map 2 The Roman provinces in AD 14

46

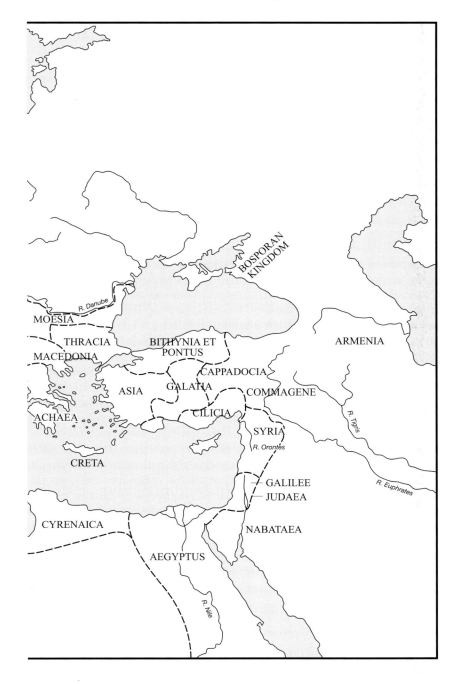

5

JULIO-CLAUDIANS, AD 14–68

TIBERIUS

When Augustus died on 19 August AD 14, aged 75, there could be no doubt what would happen in the transfer of power within the Roman state. Augustus had enjoyed exceptional formal powers granted by the state to the day of his death, with overall control of all the provinces in which more than one legion was based. But the formal powers of his stepson Tiberius, whom he had adopted ten years previously, were hardly less. Tiberius, too, had the right to overrule other provincial commanders in the interests of the state. The procession which slowly bore Augustus' body the 147 Roman miles from Nola to Rome, on foot, in the hot August of AD 14, could afford to take its time. Tiberius was already in command, and had issued orders to the soldiers throughout the empire as their new commander-in-chief (Tacitus, *Annals* 1.7).[1]

Whence came this great authority? Partly from Tiberius' formal position just outlined, but partly also from his great prestige as a soldier and a politician over many years. The scion of a proud family – the first Tiberius Claudius Nero to have been consul was believed to have held the post more than 500 years previously – Tiberius was now aged 55 and at the end of an outstandingly successful senatorial career which could put all his contemporaries into the shade. His first important public role in 20 BC, at the age of 22, had been to receive back from the Parthians the legionary standards lost to them by Crassus in 53 BC. Augustus' propaganda had trumpeted the success on coins and statues. Some eight years later, after the death of Agrippa, he took his place in command of the legions engaged in the ambitious campaigns on the Danube, 12–9 BC. After major successes there and on the Rhine in 9–7 BC, he had retired into seclusion, despite the expectation that he would campaign further. When he did so on his return to active politics in AD 4, it was with conspicuous success, though the operation largely involved the suppression of rebellions in areas previously conquered. Velleius Paterculus took part in these campaigns:

> Immediately after the adoption of Tiberius [AD 4], I was sent out with him to Germany as prefect of cavalry, succeeding my father in that position, and for nine continuous years as prefect of cavalry or as a commander of a legion I was a spectator of his

superhuman achievements, and further assisted in them to the extent of my modest ability.
(*History of Rome* 2.104.3)

Of Augustus' other great generals who might have rivalled such a record, all – Agrippa, Lollius, Varus, Tiberius' brother Drusus – were dead. According to Tacitus (*Annals* 1.13), Augustus had marked out others still in the senate in AD 14 as being capable of ruling, but there is no evidence that he wished to see any of them approach the power of Tiberius while the latter was available to rule. In the senate, too, Tiberius was in more formal terms preeminent, as the senior ex-consul. He had first held the highest office in the land twenty-seven years previously, in 13 BC.

It was an added bonus, but not necessarily the deciding factor in Tiberius' accession to power, that Augustus, the respected if hardly loved patron of everyone left active in Roman political life in AD 14, had singled out Tiberius as his son and as heir to his private fortune, and as the new head of the extensive *familia Caesaris*. Augustus' other extant (adopted) son, Agrippa Postumus, was put to death on the island to which he had been relegated by his adoptive father in AD 7. That death had been brought about at the behest of Tiberius, according to Tacitus' surmise (*Annals* 1.6.1–2), but it is more probable that it took place on Augustus' instructions, since, although he had presumably been a serious candidate for a political career in AD 4 when he was adopted, aged 16, by Augustus, he had been almost completely invisible since his exile three years later. Although entitled to expect to be an heir, he had been left out of Augustus' will, and it is hard to see why Tiberius should feel the need for his murder, and easy to gauge the hostility that it might evoke. On the other hand, the attempt by one of Agrippa's freedmen to impersonate Agrippa in AD 16 may suggest a residual level of support.

When the senate met for the first time after Augustus' death, on 17 September, it was decreed that Augustus should be elevated to the ranks of the gods, as *Divus Augustus*. But problems were aroused by Tiberius' own preeminence. It was hard for some politicians to know what to say to greet an accession to power which was already accomplished. The uneasy remarks of Tiberius' fellow aristocrats when the senate met were well described in Tacitus' ironic and hostile account (*Annals* 1.12–13), as also in the more favourable but equally misleading report put about by Tiberius' supporters at the time, and recorded by Velleius Paterculus (*History of Rome* 2.124.2) 'He is the only man to whose lot it has fallen to refuse the principate for a longer time, almost, than others had fought to secure it.'

Of the generals capable of winning the support of troops against him, Tiberius was believed to have only one serious rival, his nephew Germanicus, whom Tiberius had adopted in AD 4 at Augustus' insistence. Germanicus' charismatic personality and perhaps his youth evidently endeared him to those who found Tiberius rebarbative. None the less, Tiberius gave him every opportunity for military glory, including a triumph in AD 17 for singularly ineffective operations against the Cherusci and Chatti in Germany, and the emperor paid him the honour of sharing in his second consulship in AD 18. After his triumph, Germanicus was sent out to the eastern provinces as proconsul. What happened there is recorded in a contemporary inscription on a bronze tablet in Spain, the *Tabula Siarensis*:

> There, while engaged in those provinces and the client kingdoms of that region in accordance with the instructions of Tiberius Caesar Augustus, including installing a king in Armenia, and not sparing his efforts, until by decree of the senate an ovation was bestowed on him, he met his death giving his all to the Roman state.
> (*AE* 1984, no. 508; LR 2, pp. 524–26)

Following Germanicus' sudden death on 10 October AD 19, the senate decreed a flood of commemorative honours for him, detailed in an inscription at Rome and surviving in a number of Spanish copies like the one quoted above. Tiberius was believed, probably unreasonably, to have been involved in Germanicus' sudden death, but responsibility for the tragedy was formally laid at the door of Germanicus' adviser in the East, Gnaeus Piso, governor of Syria, with whom Germanicus had all too publicly quarrelled; Piso – protesting his innocence – committed suicide.[2]

The official version of the events surrounding Piso's fate has recently been revealed through the discovery in southern Spain of several copies of another bronze inscription, which records the senatorial decree passed in AD 20 regarding Piso's trial, condemnation and the punishment of his followers. In the text, Piso is charged with attempting to rouse the soldiers in Syria to civil war, 'when all the evils of civil war had long since been buried through the *numen* of the divine Augustus and the virtues of Ti. Caesar Augustus' (lines 46-47, trans. M. Griffin). In response, the senate decreed that Piso should not be mourned, that his statues and portraits should be removed, and that his name should be erased from a monument erected in honour of Germanicus. Piso's property was formally confiscated, but then returned to his descendants, on condition that his son relinquished the *praenomen* Gnaeus which he had shared with his father.[3]

No-one made any such accusations against the emperor on the death of his own natural son, Drusus, in AD 23, after which Tiberius seems to have lost all his zest for political life. The emperor, born in 42 BC, was in any case now at an age where retirement might seem normal, and he had already kept away from Rome in Campania for nearly two years in AD 21–22. In AD 26 he went to Capri, where he stayed in luxurious seclusion until his death in AD 37, never returning to Rome.

But for Tiberius, retirement did not include the deposition of his powers as it had for Sulla a century earlier. The hollowness of any pretence that political power was still shared by politicians as in the Republic, and still derived from the popular assemblies of Rome as Augustus had declared in his propaganda about the restoration of the Republic, was revealed all too starkly by Tiberius' self-imposed exile to Capri. That exile can in some ways be seen as the point at which overt autocracy became the accepted form of government in the Roman state. Much of the government simply ground to a halt. Senators did not dare to promote legislation which might ruin their careers if it was not to the emperor's taste, so they did nothing. Embassies from the provinces and from foreign powers joined the senators on the shore of the bay of Naples and waited endlessly for word to come from the silent autocrat.

The judgement of Suetonius, writing about Tiberius a century later, was damning:

> On his return to Capri he let all affairs of state slide: neither filling vacancies that occurred in the equestrian order, nor making new appointments to senior military posts, or the governorships of any province. Spain and Syria were left without their governors of consular rank for several years. He allowed the Parthians to overrun Armenia; the Dacians and Sarmatians to ravage Moesia; and the Germans to invade Gaul – a negligence as dangerous to the empire as it was dishonourable. But having found seclusion at last, and no longer feeling himself under public scrutiny, he rapidly succumbed to all the vicious passions which he had for a long time tried, not very successfully, to disguise.
> (*Tiberius* 41–42)

The significance of Suetonius' observations goes far beyond the issue of the effect of indecision at the heart of the state. It is clear from Suetonius' comments, and from those of numerous other contemporary observers, that in an autocracy the personality of the emperor could affect millions of his subjects. His whims could change the fate of whole nations. Thus the court gossip retailed in emperor biographies had far more importance than tittle-tattle about high society. Even though most emperors usually made decisions only in response to pressure from below,[4] the vagaries of their characters dictated their often highly personal responses. The varied and often bizarre characters of the emperors described in the rest of this book were crucial agents of political change in the principate, not least when these emperors' private excesses provoked their enemies to attempt their overthrow, often for quite personal reasons. Political history under autocrats is often just the history, or even the biography, of those autocrats themselves. The main problem for the modern historian is to account for falsifications of the record under later emperors and to distinguish between the carefully cultivated public persona of each princeps (see Chapter 12), and the real individual in each case.

In Rome Tiberius' absence on Capri encouraged the vindictive, the greedy and the ambitious among the senators to attack their enemies in court, all too frequently hoping to crush the defendant by including a charge of *maiestas*: treason against the emperor. Even from Tacitus' hostile account it is evident that this development was not encouraged by Tiberius, who had nothing to gain by advertising in such a way the existence of discontent and opposition which, from his point of view, was better suppressed in secrecy.[5]

The one man to whom Tiberius entrusted his thoughts, Lucius Aelius Sejanus, the commander (*praefectus*) of his headquarters' guard (*cohortes praetoriae*), became correspondingly powerful.[6] Sejanus, a competent soldier who had probably fought with Tiberius in his German campaigns between AD 6 and 9, might reasonably have sought a straightforward political career as senator and general, but, appointed with his father to the less prestigious but far more influential post of praetorian commander by Tiberius in AD 14, and becoming sole commander in AD 15, he achieved high status by the overt patronage of the emperor. At Tiberius' recommendation he was elected consul in AD 31 without having passed through the standard *cursus* of lower magistracies. Such an elevation was calculated to pique those senators who, for their own self-esteem, took senatorial traditions seriously. However, neither the ambition to be consul nor Sejanus' thwarted wish to marry Livilla, Germanicus' sister and widow of Tiberius' son Drusus, explains Tiberius' sudden decision to cast down his favourite in October AD 31, after the sudden end of his consulship in May. The bloody and public elimination of an enemy was the first in Tiberius' rule after seventeen years of *laissez faire* government. According to Suetonius (*Tiberius* 61.1), Tiberius himself claimed to have acted because of a rumour that Sejanus had been responsible for the death of Drusus and that of several other members of Germanicus' family, but it is hard to see that as a reason for an action clearly considered by Tiberius to be exceptionally dangerous. From Capri, the emperor had to contrive Sejanus' death at a distance in Rome in order to avoid the simply physical danger that he – old and unarmed – would be assassinated by his own bodyguard commander. The remaining members of Germanicus' family fared no better after Sejanus' fall than before: they remained for the most part in exile or in custody.

It is possible, then, that Sejanus plotted Tiberius' own death. Assassination of Tiberius would be easy. Sejanus could rely on the support of his own soldiers in the praetorian cohorts. Provincial commanders would have no incentive to urge their troops to march on Rome once the assassination had been carried out, since no alternative emperor could be presented as a rallying point. The conspiracy of Sejanus pointed out the awful truth that power really did lie in the hands of one man.

The witch-hunt for Sejanus' supporters did not extend beyond his immediate family, despite the many *amici* on whose support, at least in a tacit form, he had relied. For Tiberius there was no point in unnecessarily stirring up trouble. So long as he preserved his personal safety by the simultaneous appointment of two praetorian commanders, each of less ambition than Sejanus, there was no likelihood of a *coup* outside Capri. He neither encouraged nor prevented those senators who now added association with Sejanus to the armoury of charges to be brought against their enemies in a further series of trials. The danger to Tiberius, if any, lay rather with the motley crew of relatives who provided the emperor with company in his island retreat. Germanicus' daughters were married off to Tiberius' friends, and Tiberius' own granddaughter (by Drusus) was married to an inoffensive senator of exceptional insignificance, but Tiberius kept with him on Capri his two remaining grandsons, whom he adopted as his sons and heirs: Gaius (nicknamed 'Caligula' or 'little boot', from when he travelled with the army as a child), who was the remaining son of Germanicus, and Tiberius Gemellus, offspring of Tiberius' son Drusus. Time was to reveal how little Gaius at least was to be trusted. Thus it was rumoured that as Tiberius eventually lay dying in AD 37 and the news had already gone about that he was dead, it was his adopted grandson and heir Gaius who completed the process by smothering him with a pillow (Suetonius, *Gaius* 12).

GAIUS

Gaius' elevation to supreme power was uncomplicated in comparison to the accession of Tiberius.[7] Nothing stood in Gaius' favour except his birth (as the last of the sons of Germanicus) and Tiberius' support. Since Tiberius' death was greeted with joy in Rome, and the old man had hardly gone out of his way to court popularity, it is surprising that the latter factor proved important. At the age of almost 25, and after seven years in the stifling atmosphere of the court at Capri, Gaius was catapulated unopposed to the head of the state. The hereditary principle invented by Augustus had been accepted to an astonishing degree, although Tiberius' will, in which Tiberius Gemellus was named as Gaius' fellow-heir, was conveniently set aside on the grounds of Tiberius' insanity. Within a year, Gemellus was compelled to commit suicide.

Gaius was popular enough with the soldiers, but largely as a result of their ignorance, and optimism about his youthfulness. He had never commanded troops, and the reputation for military prowess which he inherited from his father Germanicus in fact stemmed from campaigns of 20 years before, in which Gaius himself had figured only as a toddler. He had been elected as *pontifex* in AD 31, and was quaestor in AD 33, but he had held no other public offices. The hope that youth would presage a golden age for Rome proved transitory. Gaius spent liberally in Rome on buildings, gifts to the army and people, and on games and circuses, as his predecessor had singularly failed to do. He emphasized his blood-relationship to Julius Caesar, portraying many prominent members of Caesar's family on his coins (see Figure 5). But the popularity thus gained was checked by the evidence of his unwillingness to listen to others, including the mass voice of the people in the circus. When they annoyed him, it was said, he exclaimed angrily, 'I wish they had only one neck!' (Suetonius, *Gaius* 30).

After two years true madness, or something very similar, set in. Convinced he was divine, Gaius demanded worship from all his subjects, no matter what the consequences might be. In imitation of the gods he was thought to have committed incest with his sister Drusilla, then killed her in the hope that she would bear him a divine child. It is instructive to realize how little anyone

Figure 5 Golden aureus minted for Gaius, AD 40. The obverse shows the head of Gaius wearing a laurel wreath. The reverse has an idealized portrait of Augustus, with the caption 'Divus Augustus, Father of the Country'. The legitimation of the new emperor depended on his relationship to Augustus, his great-grandfather by adoption. Photo courtesy of CNG Coins.

could do so long as the legions – mostly unaffected by such insanity, since they were in the distant provinces – remained loyal, as they had every reason to do so long as salaries continued to be paid regularly. Gaius won a certain amount of prestige by a moderately successful expedition across the Rhine in AD 39, although a plan to invade Britain was aborted, the troops getting no further than the coast of northern France:

> He drew up his army in battle array facing the Channel and moved the arrow-casting machines and other artillery into position as though he intended to bring the campaign to a close. No one had the least notion what was in his mind when, suddenly, he gave the order: 'Gather seashells!'
> (Suetonius, *Gaius* 46)

A further problem was lack of money after Gaius' extravagances, and the annexation of Mauretania, which involved the execution of its king, Ptolemy, in AD 40, was apparently motivated by the need for cash.

In AD 39, a conspiracy by Lentulus Gaetulicus, commander of the legions of Upper Germany, to replace Gaius by Marcus Lepidus, husband of Gaius' sister Drusilla, was unmasked, and the conspirators executed. In the event, Gaius' death came about in AD 41 through the purely personal grudge of a certain Cassius Chaerea, a junior officer in the praetorian guard, who resented an insult by Gaius to his masculinity. It was achieved not by armies but by a small group of assassins who stabbed the emperor to death as he was leaving the games.[8]

CLAUDIUS

What should happen next? Chaerea had no plans. Gaius was too young to have sons, adopted or natural. Senators awoke from the nightmare of the last four years to realize that they had no need after all for an emperor. Someone would need to take over the wealth of the house of Caesar, but the issue was not urgent, and the senate declined to make any immediate decision. In constitutional terms the consuls ruled the state on behalf of the people. If there was no overall magistrate to whom all must pay obedience, what reason was there to complain? The senators discussed elatedly in the senate house this unexpected restoration of their *libertas* (freedom).[9]

Among those likely to lose by the demise of autocracy were two specific groups in Rome. One was the non-Romans who relied on the emperor's patronage for their living in Rome or their power in their homeland. The other was the praetorian guard, whose only function was the protection of the emperor. Hence the full description of events after the death of Gaius given by the Jewish historian Josephus. The palace was in uproar after Gaius' death, and the praetorian guard was debating its next move:

> Claudius was disturbed by all this and alarmed for his own safety. ... There he stood in an alcove to which a few steps led, tucked away in the dark. Gratus, one of the praetorian guard, caught sight of him, but was unable to make out his features well enough to recognize him in the dim light ... He approached nearer, and when Claudius asked him to withdraw, he pounced upon him and caught him. On recognizing him, he cried to his followers, 'Here is a Germanicus: let us set him up as emperor and move fast.'
>
> (*Antiquities of the Jews* 19.216–17)

Josephus may have somewhat exaggerated the part taken in Claudius' accession by the hero of his history, Agrippa I, grandson of Herod the Great.[10] Agrippa had been raised from penury by his friendship with Gaius on Capri, and after AD 37 was rewarded for his comradeship with a territory to rule in the region of south Syria. Eager to find a new patron on Gaius' death in AD 41, he persuaded an indecisive Claudius to use the backing of the praetorian guard and allow himself to be proclaimed Caesar (*Antiquities of the Jews* 19.236–38). The news, announced by Agrippa to the dumbfounded senators as a *fait accompli*, was necessarily accepted without demur, for the senate house was surrounded by armed troops. The following year the governor of Dalmatia, a certain Scribonianus, was rumoured to be contemplating a march on Rome, but he was forestalled by the desertion of his troops and murdered by one of his soldiers. For the rest, silence and acquiescence sufficed, at least on the surface. But uneasiness remained: in a rule of 14 years, Claudius executed at least 335 members of the ruling class. As one of his first acts, Cassius Chaerea was executed, to discourage imitators of such tyrannicide. All those who came into the emperor's presence were searched to discourage imitation still further (Suetonius, *Claudius* 35).[11]

Claudius had at least the advantage of age over Gaius; he had been born in 10 BC. He also had the advantage of intelligence, although he too, a bookish scholar and physically handicapped, had had neither the opportunity nor temperament for the political and military career conventionally expected of a great Roman noble. None the less, he did his best to appear as such a noble, with repeated consulships, massive building programmes (including the eleven-year task of draining the Fucine Lake), lavish spectacles, and the wooing of new supporters by awarding the ranks of senator and of patrician to many individuals when he acted as censor in AD 47/8. He took a personal part in the invasion of Britain in AD 43, and during his reign received a record number of imperatorial acclamations (all, apart from the campaign against Britain, for victories achieved by his legates). Even the British expedition was mostly conducted by Claudius' general, Aulus Plautius, with the emperor himself spending a mere 16 days on campaign. Plautius received an *ovatio*, a minor triumph, with the true glory accumulating to the emperor himself, who assumed the triumphal *cognomen* Britannicus. A relief from the Sebasteion at Aphrodisias in Asia Minor depicts Claudius subduing the province of Britannia, represented by a female figure (see Figure 6).[12]

In addition to Britain, Claudius' reign saw the integration of several other provinces into the Roman empire. He consolidated Gaius' gains in Mauretania (now divided into Mauretania Tingitana and Caesariensis) and oversaw the creation of Thrace in AD 45 following the death of the client king, Rhoemetalces. The Alpine region of Noricum likewise formally became part of the empire in AD 46. One of the most stunning successes was the pacification of Lycia (which had been suffering from internal revolts) during AD 43-47 by the senatorial general, Quintus Veranius. The people of Lycia celebrated their incorporation into the empire through the construction of a massive monument which praised the emperor Claudius for freeing them 'from faction, lawlessness and brigandage through his divine foresight' (*SEG* 51, 1832, trans. C. P. Jones)'; according to Suetonius (*Div. Claud.* 25) and Dio Cassius (60.17.3-4), there were serious problems in the province which required Roman intervention.[13]

Claudius' sole real qualification for power was his birth as the son of Tiberius' brother Drusus, which gave him a tenuous relationship to Augustus and to Julius Caesar. But once in power he proved energetic and idiosyncratic, inaugurating change in a fashion similar to Augustus. Suetonius summed up such activity quite neatly (*Claudius* 22): 'In matters of religious ritual, civil and military customs, and the social status of all classes at home and abroad, Claudius not only revived obsolescent traditions but invented new ones.' Claudius' antiquarian leanings are clearly visible in the convoluted and verbose Latin with which he addressed his subjects in an inscription which survives from Lugdunum (Lyons) (*CIL* XIII, no. 1,668; LR 2, pp. 54–55). During his rule many elements of the eventual bureaucratic structure of the imperial state were consolidated – most notably, public recognition of the role of non-senators as public officials (procurators) in the provinces and an equestrian career structure in the army – but it is probable that such a quasi-civil service would in any case have evolved in this fashion in the principate,

Figure 6 Relief from the Sebasteion at Aphrodisias, in Asia Minor, depicting Claudius subduing the province of Britannia. The province is represented as a female figure. The emperor is shown in idealised, youthful, semi-naked, heroic pose. Such violent depictions of the emperor contrast to more common representations of the clemency of the ruler. Photo © New York University Excavations at Aphrodisias

and there is little evidence that Claudius was responsible for any major structural changes in the state. His most lasting innovation seems to have been the introduction of privileges to auxiliary soldiers on their retirement (see Chapter 11).[14]

Not surprisingly, Claudius' greatest problems came from family intrigues, described in detail both by Tacitus and by Suetonius. His divorce and execution of his wife Messalina on the grounds of her flagrant adultery in AD 48 led in AD 49 to his marriage to his niece Agrippina. Claudius himself apparently thought that this change strengthened his position, since he indulged in fewer executions, but in AD 54 his new wife contrived his murder in favour of her son by a former marriage, the young Nero, aged 16, whom the emperor had adopted as a brother to his own son, Britannicus.

NERO

There was no more talk now of the restoration of free political competition. Nero's right to rule depended on his relationship to Claudius, who was recognized by the senate as a god, but the new emperor could hardly emphasize the link, not least because it was shared with Britannicus. Nero avoided reference to his predecessor and did not stress his status as *divi filius* (son of a god), and by early AD 55 Britannicus was dead (reportedly poisoned).

Later sources referred to a happy start of Nero's rule, the *quinquennium Neronis* (Nero's first five years), a time of enlightened despotism when the young autocrat accepted the advice of his tutor, the philosopher Seneca, and moderated his appetites – or at least their display. Agrippina who had successfully engineered Nero's adoption by Claudius and his subsequent acclamation as emperor, initially exercised significant influence over the administration. Tacitus recounts how the senate voted that Agrippina should become a priestess of the newly-deified Claudius and be accompanied by two lectors. Her powerful position is strikingly illustrated by her depiction on a relief from the Sebasteion at Aphrodisias (see Figure 7). However, her power began to wane as Nero sought the company of other women, including the ex-slave Acte, and removed her leading supporters from office, notably the freedman, Pallas. But the picture may well in part be a myth conjured up by those who wanted to excuse their co-operation with Nero in his early years, when all agreed after Nero's death that in the end he had become monstrous. At any rate, all restraint had gone by AD 59, stripped away in emotional turmoil as Nero rejected excessive interference in his affairs by his mother and committed matricide.

In the following nine years it was to such vile personal practices, even though in fact they only affected a small group of close family, that much wider political opposition arose. In AD 62 he divorced, and then had murdered, his wife Octavia, despite her descent from Julius Caesar, preferring the charms of a consul's granddaughter, Poppaea, after whom he lusted. Various other female members of the Julio-Claudian dynasty were married off to members of the *gens* (clan) of the Silani, only for those Silani in AD 66 to be accused, somewhat implausibly, of conspiracy and executed.

Nero's reputation for profligacy, which permeates the ancient sources, is not entirely undeserved. In AD 64, the emperor was forced to debase the coinage, probably as a result of the great fire which ravaged much of Rome in

Figure 7 Relief from the Sebasteion at Aphrodisias, showing Agrippina crowning Nero with a laurel wreath. The image illustrates his mother's influence before Nero had her murdered. Photo © New York University Excavations at Aphrodisias

that year. The gold (*aureus*) and silver (*denarius*) coinage was reduced in weight, while the silver content of *denarii* decreased by approximately seven per cent. He is also said to have confiscated large tracts of Africa, executing the landowners. In some areas, it is possible to defend Nero's domestic policies: he showed great concern for maintaining a proper grain supply, and even planned a canal which was to run from Lake Avernus (near Naples) to

59

Ostia in order to ensure that ships could reach the port safely. The most infamous building project was Nero's *domus aurea* or 'Golden House' which was constructed in the aftermath of the great fire. Suetonius paints a vivid picture of the new palace:

> Its size and splendour will be sufficiently indicated by the following details. Its vestibule was large enough to contain a colossal statue of the emperor a hundred and twenty feet high; and it was so extensive that it had a triple colonnade a mile long. There was a pond too, like a sea, surrounded with buildings to represent cities, besides tracts of country, varied by tilled fields, vineyards, pastures and woods, with great numbers of wild and domestic animals. In the rest of the house all parts were overlaid with gold and adorned with gems and mother-of-pearl. There were dining-rooms with fretted ceilings of ivory, whose panels could turn and shower down flowers and were fitted with pipes for sprinkling the guests with perfumes.
> (Suetonius, *Nero* 31, trans. Loeb)

The majority of scholars have assumed that the Golden House consumed much of central Rome, restricting public access for the emperor's private pleasure. However, recent reassessment has shown that the palace was restricted to the area between the Palatine and the Esquiline, and its central feature, the lake, was intended as a new type of spectacle, to be shared with Nero's admirers, the populace of Rome itself. This new reading of Nero's action fits in with the other information regarding his carefully cultivated public persona, which emphasized his qualities as a performer. Nero entered musical and singing contests, performed in plays, raced chariots in the Circus Maximus, and embarked on a tour of competitions in Greece, including the Olympic Games. It was during this visit that he granted the Greeks their freedom, exempting them from taxation by Rome. Although the elite sources register their stern disapproval of Nero's actions, the fact remains that many senators and equestrians willingly participated in the emperor's public entertainment.[15]

Like his adoptive father Claudius, Nero lacked military experience and had to rely on the support of his senatorial legates. The most illustrious of these was Cn. Domitius Corbulo, governor of Cappadocia and Galatia from c. AD 54, who successfully expelled the Parthians from Armenia and installed a client king friendly to Rome on the throne. For his success, Corbulo earned promotion to the governorship of Syria, which was reserved for the most senior senators, according to Tacitus (*Agr.* 40). However, his successor in Cappadocia, Caesennius Paetus, was roundly defeated by the Parthians, and in AD 63 Corbulo was awarded a special command to deal with the situation. Nero granted Corbulo *imperium maius*, which meant that he possessed power greater than that of the other provincial governors in the region. Before full-scale hostilities could break out, the Parthians agreed to compromise: Tiridates, a member of the Parthian ruling family, was to be installed as king of Armenia, but he would be subservient to Rome. In AD 66, Tiridates travelled to Rome to receive the diadem from Nero himself in a celebration in keeping with the emperor's love of showmanship. The victory had really been Corbulo's, but Nero greeted Tiridates on the rostra in full triumphal dress, and was hailed as *imperator*. [16]

In AD 65 a conspiracy formed around a certain Piso, of ancient lineage and vague relationship to the Caesars, but indolent in character. The number and eminence of his co-conspirators who suffered in the aftermath of the conspiracy's failure, including Seneca, are evidence of the depth of disaffection with Nero.

Another conspiracy in AD 66, by a certain Annius Vinicianus, was similarly unmasked, and Corbulo, who as his father-in-law was too close to the main instigator, was ordered to kill himself. In early spring AD 68 an obscure Gallic senator, Julius Vindex, the praetorian governor of Gallia Lugdunensis, decided that enough was enough and raised the banner of revolt.

Vindex's motives were once again based on the personality of the princeps, at least according to his public pronouncements as recorded by Cassius Dio:

> And ascending a tribunal he [Vindex] delivered a long and detailed speech against Nero, saying that they ought to revolt from the emperor and join the speaker in an attack upon him, 'because', as he said, 'he has despoiled the whole Roman world, because he has destroyed all the flower of their senate, because he debauched and then killed his mother, and does not preserve even the semblance of sovereignty. Many murders, robberies and outrages, it is true, have often been committed by others; but as for the deeds committed by Nero, how could one find words fittingly to describe him?'
>
> (*History of Rome* 63.22.2–4)

Vindex had few forces, and was rapidly suppressed by the legions of Upper Germany, but Galba, governor of Hispania Tarraconensis (Spain), had time to indicate his support. When the news reached Rome and the praetorians under their commander, Nymphidius Sabinus, decided to desert, Nero panicked and stabbed himself to death with the help of his freedman Epaphroditus. Thus ingloriously ended the family of the Julio-Claudians.

6

CIVIL WAR AND FLAVIANS, AD 68–96

Vindex's coins proclaimed *PAX ET LIBERTAS* (peace and freedom) and *SPQR* (the senate and people of Rome), but it is doubtful if any senator really believed that a return to rule by the consuls, the other magistrates and the people was still possible. At any rate, after the fiasco on the death of Gaius, no-one was prepared to urge such a course openly. Yet with Nero's death, the system of recent accessions, by which proximity of relationship to the previous emperor had been the deciding factor, was clearly impossible. No descendants, even by adoption, of Julius Caesar or Augustus or of their immediate family, still survived. In any case the Pisonian conspiracy of AD 65 had thrown open the possibility that a noble with little connection to the Caesars might seize as much power if his aristocratic lineage or other qualifications could win him sufficient support.

GALBA

Apart from his greater age, Servius Sulpicius Galba was a man much in the same mould as Piso. Of a family long illustrious in Roman politics, he had enjoyed a respectable but unexceptional political career, and had ended up, since AD 60, in the undemanding job of governor of Hispania Tarraconensis. What propelled him to the forefront of political life was his favourable response to a letter from Vindex urging action against Nero. Vindex had written to all the legionary commanders urging action against the tyrant. If they had all accepted the call to revolt, Nero would have fallen bloodlessly, but most were naturally too timid, knowing their likely fate if they alone proved disloyal to the emperor. Thus it was that only Galba in Spain threw in his lot with Vindex.[1]

The precise sequence of events and the motives of the chief actors in the subsequent months are hard to reconstruct, because Tacitus' detailed account of the ensuing civil wars, preserved in his *Histories*, begins only in January AD 69, thereby omitting Vindex's uprising and Galba's accession.[2] The cause of Tacitus' silence was only partly the convention that annalistic history should deal with the events from one January to the next. Of equal significance in his decision may have been the part played in the suppression of Vindex by the governor of Upper Germany, Verginius Rufus.[3] In later years, Verginius was to claim that he had served the state well by his assault on Vindex, hence his epitaph (Pliny, *Letters* 9.19): 'Here lies Rufus, who once when Vindex had been defeated stood up for empire, not for himself but for his country.' But according to Cassius Dio (*History of Rome* 53.24), Verginius Rufus had in fact wished to enter into negotiation with Vindex and to join in the revolt against Nero, and he was pressed into battle against the uprising only by the loyalty of his troops to the emperor. Since Verginius had been a powerful friend in Tacitus' own political circle, as in Pliny's, and Tacitus had himself delivered the panegyric on his death in AD 97, these events were best passed over in silence. So there is nothing detailed in Tacitus' narrative about the events of AD 68, and it is impossible to be sure whether Galba from the start intended to seek to replace or simply to remove Nero.

At any rate, once revolt was under way, it immediately became clear that Galba would seek power for himself. Galba was acclaimed as Caesar by his troops, and supported in this by local Roman nobles. He marched with just one newly formed legion to Rome, encountering no opposition. An attempt by Clodius Macer, commander of a legion stationed in Africa, to seize power for himself, is known primarily from the coins he issued; it seems to have been suppressed by Galba. A new secret of imperial power was revealed, wrote Tacitus 40 years later (*Histories* 1.4): 'an emperor could be created elsewhere than at Rome'. The praetorian guard, which had once unseated Gaius, was, on the death of Nero, simply taken over by Galba. Their commander, Nymphidius Sabinus, who had enjoyed a brief period as ruler of Rome after Nero's death, may have hoped for more, but he was put to death, with many others.

OTHO

Galba was installed in splendour and luxury in the city of Rome, but he did not enjoy the fruits of his fortune for long. Aware of the need to clarify the succession to prevent scheming, but lacking a son, he sought popularity by stressing on his coins his relationship to Augustus' wife Livia, which was actually remote. But within weeks he took the fatal step of adopting an heir, presumably in the hope of forestalling conspiracy, since he himself was already in his early 70s. The young man chosen, another Piso, was a nonentity, with no political career behind him and no particular qualities to commend him, and this to his discredit, that he had taken no part in Galba's seizure of power. Galba's chief lieutenant in his campaign, the 36-year-old Marcus Salvius Otho, had been, in his earlier career, an energetic companion of Nero. He objected to the choice of Piso as Galba's heir, and bribed the praetorians to desert Galba and promote himself as the new emperor. Since Galba had ignored their desires, not even paying a promised bounty on his accession, the praetorians were not slow to agree. On 15 January AD 69, Galba was hunted down and assassinated in the Roman forum. Piso died close by in the temple of Vesta. The senate and people accepted Otho, if without much enthusiasm. He was the first emperor thus to seize power after open bloodshed on the streets of Rome. He attempted, according to Cassius Dio, to present himself as the people's choice, forced unwillingly to assume authority, but the attempt was hardly convincing:

> He claimed, it is true, that he had acted under compulsion, that he had been taken into the camp against his will, and had there actually risked his life by opposing the soldiers. Furthermore he was kindly in his speech and affected modesty in his deportment, and he kept throwing kisses on his fingers to everybody and making many promises. But men did not fail to realize that his rule was sure to be even more licentious and harsh than Nero's. Indeed, he immediately added Nero's name to his own.
> (*History of Rome* 64.8.1–2)

Otho evidently tried to garner support by emphasizing his (genuine) closeness to Nero and by distancing himself from the unpopular Galba.[4] Tacitus offers a similar picture:

> It was believed that he also brought up the question of celebrating Nero's memory with the hope of winning over the Roman people; and in fact some set up statues of Nero; moreover, on certain days the people and soldiers, as if adding thereby to Otho's nobility and distinction, acclaimed him as Nero Otho; he himself remained undecided, from fear to forbid or shame to acknowledge the title.
> (*Histories* 1.78)

The truth began to dawn on other legionary commanders around the empire. If Galba could seize power so easily, why not they? If the undistinguished Otho could be emperor, they could be so too. Titus, the son and emissary of Titus Flavius Vespasianus, commander of the Roman forces engaged in suppressing rebellion in Judaea, had been on his way to Rome to greet the new emperor Galba, but when at Corinth, in January AD 69, he heard of the latter's replacement by Otho, he turned back. New vistas opened, for him as for others.

VITELLIUS

In the Rhineland, the junior officers looked with envy on the power so easily won by Galba simply as an ambitious governor of Spain. Before Otho's coup, they had already persuaded their own commander, the idle Aulus Vitellius, that he too could make a bid for power, and the changed leadership at Rome made no difference. The troops followed him in the hope of reward. Otho came north to meet the German legions after they had crossed the Alps, but although the praetorians stayed loyal to him, at the battle of Cremona they proved no match for the superior number and greater experience of the battle-

Figure 8 Silver denarius minted for Vitellius in Gaul in AD 69. The obverse, with the head of Vitellius, describes him as victorious in German wars. The reverse, showing clasped hands, claims 'The Trust (*fides*) of the Armies'; such claims are characteristic of a period of civil war when in fact Roman legions fought each other. Photo courtesy of CNG Coins.

hardened troops of Vitellius. On 16 April AD 69, Otho committed suicide to prevent further shedding of Roman blood. Vitellius reached Rome in late June and took up a dissolute residence, showing surprising clemency to his surviving opponents, and emphasizing on his coins both the unity of the armies (see Figure 8) and the fact that he had a suitable son to be his heir.[5]

According to Tacitus, Vitellius' rule would have lasted far longer if he had not been tempted by the extraordinary opportunities presented by the huge private fortune which accrued to each emperor:

> In fact, if Vitellius had only moderated his luxurious mode of life, there would have been no occasion to fear his avarice. But his passion for elaborate banquets was shameful and insatiate. Dainties to tempt his palate were constantly brought from Rome and all Italy, while the roads from both the Adriatic and Tyrrhenian seas hummed with hurrying vehicles. The preparation of banquets for him ruined the leading citizens of the communities through which he passed; the communities themselves were devastated; and his soldiers lost their energy and their valour as they became accustomed to pleasure and learned to despise their leader.
> (*Histories* 2.62)

But the picture of Vitellius inherited by Tacitus had been devised under the rule of Vespasian and his sons, for whom it was essential that Vitellius' principate be portrayed as illegitimate.

VESPASIAN

It is probable that in Judaea Vespasian's plans were already well advanced some time before Vitellius seized power.[6] A man of undistinguished family – his father had not even been of senatorial rank – Vespasian's appointment by Nero to the command of three legions for the suppression of the Jewish revolt, which had begun in AD 66, may have been partly motivated by precisely this insignificance. Unlike the great general Corbulo, whose death Nero had just procured, Vespasian could never challenge the emperor for popular affection. Competent but not brilliant in warfare, Vespasian had come to prominence as a legionary legate during Claudius' invasion of Britain in AD 43, when he directed the campaign in the southern parts of the country and in the Isle of Wight. As a candidate for the principate, his only advantage in seeking power was that he had two sons, Titus and Domitian, and the elder, Titus, had already proved his worth. This was the crucial factor in the decision by the childless governor of Syria, Mucianus, to back Vespasian's bid for the purple. The conspiracy also included Tiberius Julius Alexander, prefect of Egypt, and the generals commanding the Balkan legions. On 1 July AD 69 Vespasian was acclaimed emperor in Alexandria, where Tiberius Alexander had his troops swear an oath of allegiance. The troops in Judaea followed suit two days later. Within weeks Vespasian's supporter Antonius Primus, legate of Upper Pannonia, was advancing on Italy. He was much aided by the desertion of some of Vitellius' officers to his side at a battle near Cremona, and by 21 December, the day after Vitellius' murder, he was in control of Rome on Vespasian's behalf.

In later years Primus received minimal reward for his services. His actions were alleged by Vespasian to have been against instructions, and he might be accused of irresponsibility since he had allowed Dacian tribes to cross the Danube into Roman territory. Primus had been one of the earliest supporters of Galba, when a legionary legate in Spain, and he may have seen himself as fighting for Galba rather than Vespasian. But it is more likely that Vespasian's coolness towards him was motivated by a desire to disassociate the new regime from the terrible bloodshed at Cremona. By thus disowning Primus, Vespasian could claim that he had won the empire without spilling Roman blood.

Encouraged by Civilis, a local noble, the Rhine legions were slow to accept the new regime, and in the winter of AD 69–70 an independent Gaul (*imperium Galliarum*) was mooted, but Vespasian's troops, led by Cerialis, forced their capitulation. The seriousness of such opposition is obscure, in part because Tacitus' *Histories* tail off at this point.

Vespasian himself had meanwhile taken ship, not to Italy, but to Alexandria at the mouth of the Nile Delta, in order, apparently, to halt the grain supply to Rome if the city held out against his forces. For six months, first Primus (briefly), then Mucianus ruled Rome on his behalf. The people voted Vespasian all the honours and powers of an emperor *en bloc* (for the law which detailed these powers, see Chapter 12). His younger son, Domitian, who had escaped capture by Vitellius' forces in Rome by dressing as a woman, now enjoyed unbridled licence. The new emperor himself only entered his capital in the autumn of AD 70, over a year after he had been acclaimed by his troops and after all the bloodshed had ended. He was soon able to enjoy a triumph over foreign enemies, since Titus had completed the subjugation of Judaea with the capture of Jerusalem in August AD 70. A recently published bronze coin from AD 71, which depicts Vespasian in the guise of a victorious general, shows the emperor's determination to take the credit for the victory.[7] The Flavian dynasty had begun.

Vespasian before his bid for power lacked not just prestige but also many *amici* among his fellow senators, not a few of whom, in any case, had died during the civil war.[8] Among his closest colleagues, Titus and Mucianus were naturally pre-eminent, but Vespasian also created perforce a new ruling élite of senators beholden to him, elevating some non-senatorial supporters of advanced age to the immediate rank of ex-praetor. The paraphernalia of a dynasty was soon built up. Titus was promoted rapidly to prominence as the designated heir, holding seven consulships with his father between AD 69 and 79, tribunician power from AD 71, and acting as his father's colleague in the censorship in AD 73/4. Titus was also appointed to the post of praetorian prefect, a security role usually filled by a man of equestrian rank but of exceptional sensitivity for the new regime. None the less, not all Vespasian's colleagues accepted his success unwaveringly. Vitellians such as the turncoat Caecina Alienus, who had joined the Flavian cause only at the last moment, remained the object of suspicion – hence his execution for alleged involvement with Eprius Marcellus, whose conspiracy is known only from his suicide, in AD 79.[9]

Vespasian actively pursued a policy of strengthening the border regions. The subjugation of Britain was as yet incomplete, and a series of campaigns, designed to pacify Wales and the north, was conducted by successive governors, including Tacitus' father-in-law, Julius Agricola. The eastern frontier was completely reorganized: in the aftermath of the Jewish War, Judaea received a senatorial governor (in place of an equestrian), as did the crucial frontier region of Cappadocia, now part of a larger province as it had been under Nero's general Corbulo. The nearby kingdoms of Armenia Minor and Commagene were annexed and incorporated into the province of Syria. To the north, Vespasian secured the *Agri Decumates*, a region lying between the Rhine and Danube rivers which was to be held by Rome until the mid-third century AD.

By all accounts, Vespasian lacked charm. Suetonius put it politely:

He missed no opportunity of tightening discipline: when a young man, reeking of perfume, came to thank him for a commission he had asked for and obtained, Vespasian turned his head away in disgust and cancelled the order, saying crushingly: 'I should not have minded so much if it had been garlic.' When the marine fire brigade, detachments of which had to be constantly on the move between Ostia or Puteoli and Rome, applied for a special shoe allowance, Vespasian not only turned down the application, but instructed them in future to march barefoot; which has been their practice ever since.

(*Vespasian* 8)

The new emperor seems to have revelled in his reputation for meanness and for bluntness. His thrift was at least justified, since he found the treasury in a dilapidated state as the result of Nero's extravagant spending. He instituted new tariffs, including a tax on all Jews and an infamous charge on the use of public toilets. He also rescinded Nero's order granting freedom to Greece, ensuring that tax revenues flowed from the province once again. But the emperor also embarked on an ambitious building programme, which included the *Templum Pacis* ('Temple of Peace'), a magnificent outdoor complex which displayed precious works of art, and the Colosseum, Rome's first permanent amphitheatre in stone. A recently deciphered inscription reveals that the Collosseum was built 'from the spoils' (*ex manubiis*) captured during the Jewish War (*CIL* VI 40454).[10] Vespasian was sufficiently popular, and the dynastic principle sufficiently re-established, for Titus to inherit power without difficulty after the death of his father, aged 70, in AD 79, the first peaceful demise from old age to be granted to any emperor since Augustus, if the rumours about the death of Tiberius are to be believed. Respected at least for his evident military competence, Titus wooed support among his fellow aristocrats to the extent of dismissing his paramour, the Jewish queen Berenice, daughter of Agrippa I.

TITUS

Unlike his father and brother, Titus had been brought up at the centre of the imperial court, for Claudius had chosen him when a boy as a suitable companion for his son, the young prince Britannicus, and the two had been educated together.[11] Suetonius remarks that Titus was deeply disliked on his accession due to his arrogance and flamboyant tastes, but his careful behaviour once emperor turned public opinion in his favour (*Titus* 7). According to Suetonius (*Titus* 8), he adopted an exceptionally benevolent view of the task of the princeps:

> Titus was naturally kind-hearted. … He also had a rule never to dismiss any petitioner without leaving him some hope that his request would be favourably considered. Even when warned by his staff how impossible it would be to make good such promises, Titus maintained that no one ought to go away disappointed from an audience with the emperor. One evening at dinner, realizing that he had done nobody any favour throughout the entire day, he spoke these memorable words: 'My friends, I have wasted a day.'

His short reign saw the construction of new baths on the Esquiline and the addition of new tiers to the Colosseum, which was formally dedicated in AD 80 with one hundred days of games, including naval battles, horse races and the exhibition of wild animals. The distraction of natural disasters in Italy for which he could hardly be blamed (most strikingly, the eruption of Vesuvius, which in AD 79 buried Pompeii and Herculaneum with huge loss of life), and his early death at the age of 40, left him a reputation as the 'darling of humanity' (Suetonius, *Titus* 1).

DOMITIAN

Titus' sudden, but probably natural, death in AD 81 came as a shock, not least because his successor, his younger brother Domitian, had enjoyed little limelight. Vespasian is reported to have been irritated at the young man's excesses in AD 69 and to have deliberately restrained his ambitions so as to avoid any conflict with Titus, who was considerably older.[12]

Thus, although he had been consul in AD 73 and again in AD 80, Domitian had never commanded troops, in marked contrast to Titus, victor of the Jewish war. Once emperor, the series of campaigns he led personally – against the Chatti on the Rhine, and against the Dacian king Decebalus – went only some way to build up the image of a successful soldier, not least because he ran up against exceptionally tough opponents who prevented too much glory. There were no less than three wars in Pannonia, waged against the Marcomanni, Quadi and Sarmatians on the Danube. Domitian was acclaimed as *imperator* 23 times, more than any other emperor, including his own father. After the war against the Chatti, he assumed the name Germanicus and staged a triumph in Rome. Tacitus was scornful of the emperor's achievements, writing that 'they have in recent years gratified us with more triumphs over them than victories' (*Germania* 37.6, trans. Loeb). Nevertheless, Domitian won popularity among the soldiers by raising army pay by one third, the first increase since the days of Julius Caesar. Successful campaigns in Britain were headed by the able general Agricola, originally appointed by Vespasian. Agricola conquered north Wales and advanced as far as the Scottish highlands, but he was recalled by Domitian, and many of his conquests were abandoned, including the legionary fortress which had been constructed at Inchuthill on the River Tay.

Suspicious, irascible and egocentric, Domitian had no interest in wooing the good opinion of his fellow senators by adopting the delicate polite relationship canonized by Augustus; on the contrary, he preferred to be addressed as *dominus et deus*, 'Lord and God' (Suetonius, *Domitian* 13.2 and Cassius Dio, *History of Rome* 67.4.7). Domitian actively promoted the continuity of the Flavian dynasty as a way of legitimizing his regime. Vespasian had been deified by Titus, and Domitian ensured that his brother received the same treatment, with the priests of both emperors known as the *sodales Flaviales Titiales*. Other family members soon joined them, as Domitian's baby son, who had died in Vespasian's reign, and Titus' daughter Julia, were both deified (see Figure 9). A new temple was required to house these *divi*, and the 'Temple of the Flavian *Gens*' was erected on the site of Vespasian's old house on the Quirinal. No expense was spared in the promotion of the dynasty: the poet Martial (*Ep.* 9.20, trans. Loeb) described the area 'being covered with marble and gold'.

Figure 9 Silver denarius minted for Domitian, AD 82 or 83. The obverse shows his wife, and the reverse shows his infant son, described as divus and surrounded by seven stars. The child had died some years earlier, before AD 79. Domitian strongly promoted public recognition of the continuity of the Flavian dynasty, erecting the Templ of the Flavian Gens for worship of his father and brother as well as his niece Julia and his own baby son. Photo courtesy of CNG Coins.

When in September AD 87 the Arval Brethren, a priesthood in Rome, gave thanks to the gods for the discovery of the plots of evil men (*CIL* VI, no. 2,065), they provided testimony that conspiracies against the emperor were already in motion. In AD 89 a conspiracy by L. Antonius Saturninus, legate of Upper Germany, was suppressed by the neighbouring governor of Lower Germany and its perpetrators were executed. Although immediate reper- cussions were confined to Germany, an increasingly suspicious emperor declared that no-one would believe him when he claimed that plots were being laid against him – until, that is, he was dead (Suetonius, *Domitian* 21).

The result was a reign of terror, in which the senators were compelled to convict of treason those of their colleagues who spoke out for senatorial dignity. The names of the victims were later recalled as martyrs, not least because of the ambivalent feelings about these events displayed by the main historians to record them, the senators Pliny and Tacitus. Writing from the security of Trajan's reign, they looked back with disgust at their own cowardly complicity in the judicial murder of their friends (see for example Pliny, *Letters* 8.14.2–3 and 7–10, and Tacitus, *Agricola* 44.5–45.3). Tacitus, writing of the premature death of his father-in-law Agricola, produced an image of the senate under Domitian as living in a state of constant fear (*Agricola* 45.1): 'It was not Agricola's fate to see the senate house surrounded by armed men, and in the same reign of terror so many consulars butchered, the flight and exile of so many honourable women.' It is thus difficult to know how seriously to take the later depiction of Domitian as a monster who enjoyed the sadistic manipulation of power, as in this story recounted by Suetonius:

Domitian was not merely cruel, but cunning and sudden into the bargain. He summoned a Palace steward to his bedroom, invited him to join him on the couch,

made him feel perfectly secure and happy, condescended to share a dinner with
him – yet had him crucified on the following day!
(*Domitian* 11)

Denigration of Domitian by the regime which replaced him tends to disguise
his genuine achievements, which included impressive building projects in
the city of Rome and the successful (if temporary) suppression of hostility by
the Dacian king Decebalus on the Danube. Nor were later writers inclined to
recall the extent to which the successful senators of Trajan's reign, including
Trajan himself, Pliny and Tacitus, had begun their careers through the shrewd
patronage of the same Domitian whom they now despised.

Domitian's unashamedly autocratic nature was demonstrated by his
assumption of the post of censor for life (*censor perpetuus*), which previous
emperors had only held for a fixed period. The post gave him the ability to
oversee public morals and to control membership of the senatorial and
equestrian orders. After Domitian, no emperor assumed the office, although
each received its powers as a matter of course, a transition which demonstrates
how an act originally seen as exceptional quickly became an accepted part of
imperial government. The paranoia of the emperor, whether or not it was
justified, was revealed in AD 95 by the execution of the consul, Flavius
Clemens, and his wife, Domitian's niece Flavia Domitilla: until that point,
their two sons had been intended by Domitian as his heirs. On 18 September
AD 96, an attendant stabbed Domitian to death in his bedroom. The plot was
clearly co-ordinated within Domitian's household, with the assistance of his
wife, Domitia Longina. A new emperor, Marcus Cocceius Nerva, was
proclaimed with suspicious adroitness and speed by the senate. Nerva was an
old man, coming from one of the few surviving noble families which could
trace their lineage back to the Republic. It seems clear that he was behind the
plot to kill Domitian, to the relief of all his fellow senators, but once again the
immediate perpetrator of the deed was put to death for murder, lest others
note the ease with which autocrats could be disposed of, and be tempted to
emulate his action.

7

NERVA TO MARCUS AURELIUS, AD 96–180

NERVA

Nerva was determined to set himself apart from his predecessor through a series of government measures. Many of these were fiscal reforms: he either suspended the collection of the Jewish tax or altered the mode of its collection, he instituted further exemptions from the five per cent inheritance tax, and he set up a new economic commission staffed by five senators. Many measures were commemorated on Nerva's coinage, such as the move to eliminate contributions to the imperial post in Italy. In reality, the administration of Nerva was probably little different from that of Domitian. But unlike the last of the Flavians, Nerva recognized the importance of crafting a public persona that drew a veil over imperial autocracy. The imperial palace on the Palatine was renamed the 'Public House' (*aedes publicae*), despite the fact that the imperial residence had always been open for administrative purposes, while coins proclaimed 'Public Freedom' (*libertas publica*).

This publicity campaign could not disguise Nerva's main problem, the question of who would be his heir. It is all the more striking that a formal history of the succession of power from Nerva to Commodus, who died in AD 192, should record that, apart from Commodus himself (who inherited power in AD 180 as the natural son of Marcus Aurelius), the accession of each emperor in the span of 97 years was legitimized by his adoption as son and heir by his predecessor. The impression of peaceful stability and rational choice produced by this fact is slightly illusory, as will be seen. But it was true enough that there ceased to be an expectation of assassination or civil war at periodic intervals, and life, at least for emperors, fell into a less stressful pattern.[1]

The illusion was in part a result of the effectiveness of claiming legitimacy, however reluctantly it may have been bestowed. Nerva's lack of a son was an obvious handicap to the establishment of settled power in AD 96, as the fate of Galba in AD 69 had shown. Cassius Dio described the emperor's crude but effective solution:

Nerva, therefore, finding himself held in such contempt by reason of his old age, ascended the Capitol and said in a loud voice: 'May good success attend the Roman senate and people and myself. I hereby adopt Marcus Ulpius Nerva Trajan.'
(*History of Rome* 68.3.4)

TRAJAN

Thus Nerva linked to his new dynasty a competent and respected general, Marcus Ulpius Traianus, the governor of Upper Germany, who had been consul in AD 91. Trajan was a product of the new Flavian nobility, whose father of the same name, deriving from a colony in Spain, had been a highly successful general in Syria in the mid-70s AD on behalf of Vespasian: Trajan's adoption forestalled any possible attempt to seize the purple for himself. Within a year and a half, Nerva had died of old age, and Trajan could accept the proffered power with good grace, although his dismissal of some of the praetorian guard, his rapid preparation for a foreign war, and his reluctance to return to Rome immediately on Nerva's death, may suggest that the succession was not entirely without tension.[2]

Authors like Pliny or Tacitus, who wrote in the time of Trajan and his successors, naturally portrayed his reign as a golden age, particularly in comparison to the terror of Domitian's last years. Suetonius' series of emperors' biographies came to an end with Domitian, but the lack of such biographies for Nerva and Trajan is partially compensated for by the narrative of Cassius Dio (*History of Rome* 68), which survives in epitome for Trajan's reign, and by the literary products of contemporaries, of whom Pliny and Tacitus were the most important.

Trajan seems to have enjoyed a taste for conquest over and above his need for the propaganda advantages of victory. Trajan was a natural soldier, as the younger Pliny, himself strictly civilian both in tastes and in expertise, stated in AD 100 in the traditionally overblown flattery customary in a speech made in the presence of the princeps by an incoming consul:

Indeed as tribune in the army and still of tender age, you had served and proved your manhood at the far-flung boundaries of empire, for even then Fortune set you to study closely, without haste, the lessons which later you would have to teach. A distant look at a camp, a stroll through a short term of service was not enough for you; your time as tribune must qualify you for immediate command, with nothing left to learn when the moment came for passing on your knowledge. Ten years of service taught you customs of peoples, locality of countries, lie of the land, and accustomed you to enduring every kind of river and weather as if these were the springs and climate of your native land ... . meanwhile, any soldier who is not too young can gain glory from having served with you. How many do you suppose there are who did not know you as comrade in arms before you were their emperor? Thus you can call nearly all your soldiers by name, and relate the deeds of bravery of each one, while they need not recount the wounds they received in their country's service, since you were there to witness and applaud.
(*Panegyric* 15)

The new emperor embarked on two major campaigns against the Dacians, whose relationship with Rome was still uneasy even though they had signed a peace treaty with Domitian. The first expedition, waged in AD 101-102, required the combined forces of no less than ten legions, plus auxiliaries and detachments of the praetorian guard. Though both sides suffered losses, Trajan was able to recapture the standards which had been lost by one of Domitian's generals. The Dacian king, Decebalus, eventually sued for peace when Roman forces started to bear down on his capital of Sarmizegethusa. The treaty required Decebalus to dismantle his fortifications and hand over his arms, siege engines and engineers to the Romans. In recognition of his achievement, Trajan was honoured with a new title, *Dacicus*.

As Decebalus began to regroup and rebuild his forces, it became clear that a second conflict was inevitable. Accusing the Dacian king of breaking the terms of the peace treaty, Trajan launched a second campaign in AD 105-106, in which he succeeded in capturing Sarmizegethusa itself. Decebalus committed suicide as he was about to be seized by a Roman soldier, Claudius Maximus. Trajan subsequently promoted Maximus to the rank of *decurio* 'because he captured Decebalus and brought his head to him at Ranisstorum', as the soldier recorded proudly on his tomb (*AE* 1969/70, 583). A senatorial governor was appointed to oversee the new province, which extended Rome's reach beyond the Danube and brought the Dacian gold mines under imperial control.

As Trajan was bringing the Dacian war to a conclusion, his governor of Syria successfully oversaw the incorporation of the Nabataean kingdom into the Roman province of Arabia with minimal conflict (see Figure 10). The *legio III Cyrenaica* was moved from its base in Egypt to garrison the new province, which guaranteed Roman domination over lucrative trade routes. An impressive highway, the *via Nova Traiana*, was constructed from Syria to the Red Sea.

Figure 10 Silver tridrachm or tetradrachm minted probably in Rome in AD 111. This large coin, produced for use in Arabia, has a laureate bust of Trajan and his full titles on the obverse. On the reverse is a depiction of the province of Arabia with a camel. Photo courtesy of the Ashmolean Museum, Oxford.

In contrast to the relatively peaceful acquisition of Arabia, a more dangerous conflict was brewing with the mighty Parthian empire on Rome's eastern frontier. The trouble was caused by the Parthian king installing a new monarch on the throne of Armenia without consulting Rome, as had been previously agreed. However, the historian Dio Cassius claims that this was merely a pretext for invasion, and that Trajan was actively seeking to launch a campaign against Parthia. The Roman orator Fronto, writing half a century later, had no doubt that Trajan was motivated by personal glory:

> With Trajan, as many judge from the rest of his ambitions, his own glory was likely to have been dearer than the blood of his soldiers, for he often sent back disappointed the ambassadors of the Parthian king when they prayed for peace.
> (*Princ. Hist.* 14, trans. Loeb)

Trajan arrived at Antioch in AD 114 to launch his campaign, accompanied by his senatorial generals, including the future emperor Hadrian. The Roman armies successfully annexed Armenia before turning their attention to the Parthian heartland of Mesopotamia and capturing the capital, Ctesiphon. When the news reached Rome in early AD 116, the senate acclaimed him *Parthicus*. Beneath this veneer of triumph, there were clear problems: an extensive Jewish revolt had broken out in Egypt, Cyprus and Cyrenaica, there was further trouble in Dacia, and the emperor's gains in the east were threatened by renewed Parthian strength. In response, Trajan was forced to rely on client kings in Armenia and Parthia rather than annexe the regions to Roman provinces, as he had in Dacia and Arabia.

Trajan was the first emperor since Titus to enjoy military talent, but he stretched the empire's resources to their limits to no great strategic advantage, and died in Cilicia in early August, AD 117, while returning to Rome.

According to extant contemporary accounts of Trajan's reign, he came close to the Augustan ideal of a conscientious, competent ruler. Coinage was minted acclaiming him as *Optimus Princeps*, and the title '*optimus*', ('best') was formally bestowed upon him by the senate in AD 114. He followed Nerva's example in showing respect to the senate, providing distinguished old senators like Frontinus with appropriate posts, and encouraging *alimenta* schemes which provided money to support poor children in Italy. His building efforts were prodigious, including his forum, column, and impressive baths. He claimed to have paid with his own money for the Via Traiana, the road which ran from Beneventum to Brundisium.[3] His wife, Plotina, who modestly refused to be entitled Augusta until AD 105, was much honoured.

HADRIAN

The events surrounding Trajan's death are a little uncertain. No contemporary source records what happened, and the accounts by Cassius Dio a hundred years later and by the author of the *Historia Augusta* in the biography of Hadrian are not very full.[4] In any case the evidence of the *Historia Augusta* must, as always, be used with great caution (see Chapter 1).

At any rate, Cassius Dio and the *Historia Augusta* agree that on his death bed in Cilicia, Trajan was said to have proclaimed as his successor Publius Aelius Hadrianus, a young man who had been his ward since AD 85. Hadrian came from a Spanish background similar to Trajan's, and had been put into Trajan's care while he was a boy. After military service in the Dacian wars, he was governor of Lower Pannonia in AD 107, consul in AD 108 at the age of 32, governor of Syria in AD 114, and had been designated for a second consulship in AD 118, but, despite such clear signs of imperial preferment, it was not obvious that he was to be the next emperor.

Thus, although Trajan died on 8 August, the news was kept secret until 11 August, by which time Hadrian had gained control of Antioch in Syria. It seems that other contenders for power needed some convincing of Hadrian's claim. The new emperor immediately abandoned the campaign in the East and the new Roman province of Mesopotamia, to return to Rome. Within a few months the four most senior ex-consuls in the state had been executed on a charge of treason. The rest of the governing class, which formally approved the executions, was coerced into silence.

Hadrian marked the cessation of the Parthian campaign with a triumph in Rome in AD 118, in effect taking credit for Trajan's victories. In the same year the new emperor was compelled to suppress the Sarmatians and Roxolani in Moesia. In the course of these campaigns Hadrian abandoned trans-Danubian regions which had been won by Trajan, and it is evident that, in marked contrast to his predecessor, Hadrian had no interest in expansionary campaigns, a fact interestingly not held against him in any ancient source. If, as has been suggested, Hadrian was responsible for the creation of the frieze on Trajan's column depicting the Dacian wars, it would seem that he took decisive steps to honour Trajan and his military achievements while quietly repudiating his conquests and executing his generals.[5]

Rather than campaigning, Hadrian spent many years out of Rome on tours of inspection of the settled provinces of the empire, overhauling the military establishment, particularly on the Rhine and Danube frontiers, in Africa, and in Britain (where Hadrian's Wall was built in AD 122–26). In Africa, an inscription from the base of a commemorative column records a speech made by Hadrian after his review of the legion III Augusta in AD 128. It reveals him as a strict disciplinarian, but on the parade ground in peacetime, not in war:

> You did everything in orderly fashion. You filled the field with manoeuvres. Your javelin hurling was not without grace, although you used javelins which are short and stiff. Several of you hurled your lances equally well. And your mounting was smart just now and lively yesterday. If there was anything lacking I should notice it; if there were anything conspicuously bad, I should point it out. But you pleased me uniformly throughout the whole exercise.

(*CIL* VIII, nos 2,532 and 18,042; LR 2, p. 462)

Hadrian's one major campaign, his suppression of the Jewish revolt of AD 132–35, for which he transferred his best generals to Judaea from other provinces, was not glorious, and was largely omitted from the propaganda about his regime.[6]

Like Augustus, Hadrian seems to have attempted to impose a structure on the empire from above, unlike the purely reactive policies of most other emperors. This was evident not only in his provincial policy but in his codification of important elements of the legal system, most importantly the Praetor's Edict, which was revised into a permanent form in *c.* AD 130 and laid out the framework for the administration of private law.[7] The same tidy mind may have been responsible for the increased use of equites as imperial administrators during his rule, and the introduction of a board of consular magistrates to administer law in Italy. This latter plan proved highly unpopular with senators, who saw the measure as an attack on one of the few remaining areas of direct influence by the senate as a body. In the last few years of Hadrian's rule, as at the beginning, a number of senators were convicted of treason.

Hadrian's most striking effect on his subjects derived from his cultural preferences. According to his biographer (*Historia Augusta, Hadrian* 1.3), Hadrian between the ages of 10 and 13 'grew rather deeply devoted to Greek studies, to which his natural tastes inclined him so much that some called him "Greekling"'. Despite the general problems associated with the use of this source, which often appears intended to amuse rather than inform, there is much evidence to confirm Hadrian's love of Greek culture. For some areas of the empire, this had concrete practical consequences:

> After this Hadrian travelled by way of Asia and the islands to Greece, and, following the example of Hercules and Philip, had himself initiated into the Eleusinian mysteries. He bestowed many favours on the Athenians and sat as president of the public games.
>
> (*Historia Augusta, Hadrian* 13.1–2)

Away from Greece, the emperor's example in preferring Greek culture to Latin was widely followed (see Chapter 15). During his provincial tour, Hadrian was accompanied by a young man from Bithynia, known as Antinous. The two men were lovers, but little is known about their relationship from the literary sources: it was Antinous' death and subsequent commemoration which captured their attention. Hadrian himself claimed that Antinous fell into the River Nile, but there was a rumour that he had been sacrificed as part of a ritual to prolong the emperor's life. Whatever the circumstances, Hadrian was determined to honour his memory, founding a city in Egypt in his name (Antinoopolis) and erecting statues of the young man throughout the empire (see Figure 11). In regions as far apart as Italy, Dalmatia and Asia Minor, Antinous was honoured as a god.[8]

Figure 11 Statue of Antinous (the Antinous Farnese). Idealised images of
Hadrian's young lover were erected throughout the empire. Museo Archeologico
Nazionale di Napoli. Photo © Jan Kunst.

Good health and his comparative youth made the selection of an heir less
pressing for Hadrian until the mid-130s AD, when he selected an unremarkable
senator, Lucius Aelius, for adoption, only for the selection to be rendered
useless by Aelius' premature death in January AD 138. In characteristically
orderly fashion, Hadrian, undeterred, contrived at great speed to sew up the
inheritance of his fortune and his power for generations to come. On 25
February AD 138 he adopted as his son a respected and unambitious senator of
Gallic origin named Antoninus Pius, on condition that Pius, who was

childless, should adopt an impressive young man called Marcus Annius Verus (later to become Marcus Aurelius) and also the son of the recently deceased Aelius, called Lucius Ceionius Commodus and now renamed Lucius Aelius Aurelius Commodus (and eventually to become the emperor Lucius Verus).

ANTONINUS PIUS

In accordance with these wishes, Antoninus Pius ruled from AD 138 to 161 to universal acclaim.[9] Born in Italy in AD 86, his father and grandfather, both of them consuls, had come from Nîmes. In AD 138 he had already reached the pinnacle of a senatorial career, having been proconsul of Asia between AD 133 and 136, then a member of Hadrian's *consilium* (an informal inner council). On Hadrian's death, Antoninus became emperor on 10 July AD 138, and despite senatorial hostility to his predecessor, he persuaded the senate to ratify his acts and to recognize him as a god, making the mild concession of abolishing the unpopular board of consulars to which Hadrian had handed control of Italy. In return, the senate voted to him the title *Pius* and, in AD 139, *pater patriae* (father of his country).

Antoninus' reign was not without its dramatic events, with trouble on the Rhine frontier, open revolt in Africa in *c.* AD 145–50, unrest in Dacia, and the erection of the Antonine wall, beyond Hadrian's wall, in northern Britain in AD 142, following victories in the province which earned Antoninus his second acclamation as *imperator*. But he embarked on no major campaigns, preferring to bask in the affection of his senatorial peers. His continued residence in Italy earned him the scorn of an early-fourth century orator, who criticized emperors of an earlier age who, 'while spending their days at Rome, had triumphs and cognomina of nations conquered by their general accrue to them' (*Pan. Lat,* 8.14.1; trans. Nixon and Rodgers). Nevertheless, due deference was paid to his status as the commander-in-chief of Rome's armies: the orator Fronto is said to have delivered a speech in praise of the emperor for the conquest in Britain, and coins proclaimed his achievements in foreign affairs, such as the installation of new kings over the Quadi and the Armenians. He prided himself on continuing to live in many respects like other senators, attending the regular sessions of the senate, retiring to the country in the summer, dining with his friends. The image thus cultivated was highly praised after his death by his adopted son, Marcus Aurelius:

> He was not one who bathed at odd hours, nor fond of building, no connoisseur of the table, of the stuff and colour of his dress, of the beauty of his slaves. His costume was brought to Rome from his country home at Lorium; his manner of life at Lanuvium; the way he treated the tax-collector who apologized at Tusculum, and all his behaviour of that sort. Nowhere harsh, merciless, or blustering, nor so that you might ever say 'to fever heat', but everything nicely calculated and divided into its times as by a leisured man; no bustle, complete order, strength, consistency.
> (*Meditations* 1.16)

In marked contrast to Hadrian, Antoninus apparently saw no reason to travel around the empire, thus releasing the provincials from the burden, as well as the glory, of acting as host to the imperial court. Here was a princeps who genuinely operated in the fashion advocated but hardly followed by Augustus, if the testimony of his adopted son – hardly an unbiased witness – is to be believed:

> [One should behave in] all things like a pupil of Antoninus; his energy on behalf of what was done in accord with reason, his equability everywhere, his serene expression, his sweetness, his disdain of glory, his ambition to grasp affairs. Also how he let nothing at all pass without first looking well into it and understanding it clearly; how he would suffer those who blamed him unjustly, not blaming them in return, how he was in no hurry about anything; how he refused to entertain slander; how exactly he scrutinized men's characters and actions, was not given to reproach, not alarmed by rumour, not suspicious, not affecting to be wise; how he was content with little. ... Moreover, his constancy and uniformity to his friends, his tolerance of plain-spoken opposition to his opinions and delight when anyone indicated a better course; and how he revered the gods without superstition.
>
> (Marcus Aurelius, *Meditations* 6.30)

Domestic affairs under Antoninus have to be reconstructed from the biography in the *Historia Augusta*, which, though idealized, seems to be more accurate than later lives in the collection. The biography reveals little evidence of senatorial unhappiness, although record does survive of two possible unsuccessful plots, of which the details are obscure. One of the major events of Antoninus' reign was the celebration of Rome's nine-hundredth anniversary in AD 147. This event was presaged with coin issues commemorating Rome's founding fathers, notably Aeneas, Romulus, Numa Pompilius and Augustus. Coinage was also minted to honour the emperor's wife, Faustina, who died in AD 140. Antoninus appears to have been profoundly affected by Faustina's death. She was formally deified by the senate and honoured with a temple in the Roman forum, and the emperor established a fund for orphaned children in her name, the *puellae Faustinianae*.

MARCUS AURELIUS AND LUCIUS VERUS

The wishes expressed by Hadrian in AD 138 for the succession were to be carried out meticulously. On Antoninus Pius' death on 7 March AD 161, the newly renamed Marcus Aurelius became co-emperor with his adoptive brother Lucius, now known as Lucius Aurelius Verus. Their joint rule lasted until Lucius' premature death in AD 169, after which Marcus ruled alone.

That this was so was entirely the work of Marcus Aurelius, perhaps the most unlikely of all emperors.[10] Marcus had been born in AD 121 and brought up by his grandfather, who had been given patrician status by Vespasian and held consulships in AD 97, 121 and 126. He was 17 when Hadrian, impressed by his character, required Antoninus Pius to adopt him in February AD 138, 19 when he held a consulship, and 25 when granted tribunician power and proconsular *imperium* in AD 146. His education as a young man was thus that of a future monarch. He was taught Greek by the great sophist Herodes Atticus, and Latin by the orator Fronto, with whom in later life he kept up a correspondence which is still extant. This education was shared with Lucius Verus, who had been adopted by Antoninus Pius at the same time as Marcus Aurelius, but was ten years his junior. On Antoninus' death, in AD 161, Marcus could undoubtedly have ruled alone: instead, he insisted that his adoptive brother be accorded the same powers as himself and that they should rule as colleagues. The only difference between the two emperors was that Marcus Aurelius alone held the office of *pontifex maximus*.

The continuity and stability provided by Marcus Aurelius and Lucius Verus as the heirs of the Antonine dynasty were enshrined in monuments and portraiture throughout the Roman world. An inscription from Arabia proclaimed the emperors as the 'sons of the deified Antoninus Pius Augustus, grandsons of the deified Hadrian Augustus and descendants of the deified Nerva Augustus' (*AE* 1903, 358). A relief from Ephesus dated to the same period depicts the rulers as part of a unified family group. The message was clear: the empire was in safe hands (see Figure 12).

Figure 12 Relief from Ephesus, dated to the reign of Marcus Aurelius. Hadrian stands in the centre, flanked by his heirs, Antoninus Pius and Marcus Aurelius, with the boy Lucius Verus nestled beside him. Emphasis on imperial adoptions ensured that the stability of the empire was widely advertised. Photo © Kunsthistorisches Museum, Vienna.

The two emperors were faced almost immediately by military crisis. In AD 162 the Parthians seized Armenia. If the satirical account by Lucian is to be believed, the governor of the nearby province of Cappadocia, a certain M. Sedatius Severianus, was encouraged by a local oracle to see the invasion as an opportunity for self-aggrandisement, only for him and his legion to be destroyed by the Parthians, who soon turned their attention to Syria. It was evident that imperial intervention was needed, and Lucius Verus took command of the campaign, as Cassius Dio recorded:

> Lucius, accordingly, went to Antioch and collected a large body of troops: then, keeping the best of the leaders under his personal command, he took up his own headquarters in the city, where he made all the dispositions and assembled the supplies for the war, while he entrusted the armies to Cassius. The latter made a noble stand against the attack of Vologaeses, and finally he pushed him as far as Seleucia and Ctesiphon, destroying Seleucia by fire and razing to the ground the palace of Vologaeses at Ctesiphon. ... Lucius gloried in these exploits and took great pride in them.
>
> (*History of Rome* 71.2.2–4)

Thus the campaign ended with Roman prestige sufficiently restored by AD 166.[11] But in that year, Marcus Aurelius, in turn, was prevented from enjoying his cultivated tastes in Italy to the full by the call of duty to the Danube, where Roman security was menaced by German tribes. Those tribes for the first time threatened not just to preserve their liberty from Roman interference but to invade Roman territory. In AD 167 they reached northern Italy and two new legions had to be raised to oppose them, and in AD 169 Marcus dramatically auctioned imperial property in Rome to raise funds for the campaign.

In the same year, AD 169, Lucius Verus died, on his way back to the northern frontier. By reputation he was frivolous, with a love of sports and a penchant for attending gladiatorial shows, but perhaps such triviality was only noticed in contrast to the deep moral seriousness of Marcus.

Verus' death was believed by some to have been brought about by poison, but others attributed it to the plague which had been spreading throughout the empire during this year. The Roman empire was beset by plagues throughout its history, but it is difficult always to assess their seriousness, because of the tendency of the ancient sources to describe each plague as the worst on record. Nevertheless, the so-called 'Antonine plague' which ravaged the empire in the reign of Marcus Aurelius appears to have been especially severe. The epidemic originated in the eastern provinces, where Lucius Verus was campaigning against the Parthians, and had spread to Rome by 166. The physician Galen witnessed the ravages of the plague first hand in the winter of 168/169, when he was based at Marcus Aurelius' expeditionary camp at Aquileia in North Italy. A significant proportion of Verus' army perished, and the plague spread throughout the Roman world. The sophist Aelius Aristides, a notorious hypochondriac, describes the events in Smyrna:

A plague infected nearly all my neighbours. First two or three of my servants grew sick, then one after the another. Then all were in bed, both the younger and the older. I was last to be attacked. Doctors came from the city and we used their attendants as servants. Even certain of the doctors who cared for me acted as servants. The livestock too became sick. And if anyone tried to move, he immediately lay dead before the front door. ... Everything was filled with despair, and wailing, and groans, and every kind of difficulty.

(*Or.* 48.38, trans. C.A. Behr, *P. Aelius Aristides*: *The Complete Works* Leiden, 1981).

This graphic picture seems to be supported by the archaeological and documentary evidence. There is a dramatic decrease in the number of surviving military diplomas issued from AD 165 onwards, which may indicate a reluctance to discharge soldiers, or alternatively, a break in regular bureaucratic operations. The papyrological evidence from Egypt suggests that the province may have suffered a severe population decrease which affected land prices and wages. This conclusion is controversial, but it is clear from the legal evidence that there was a significant human toll, leading the emperor to make pronouncements regarding burial plots and transport of the dead.[12]

The surviving emperor spent the next eleven years in almost continual warfare on the Danube frontiers, in AD 170–74 against the Marcomanni and Quadi, in AD 175 against the Sarmatian Iazyges, and in AD 177 in Pannonia. Some of Marcus' leading commanders perished during the conflicts, including the praetorian prefect Macrinius Vindex and the senator Claudius Fronto (not to be confused with the emperor's former tutor). These and other generals were honoured with statues in the forum of Trajan and in the temple of Antoninus Pius, which recorded their official careers and service in the wars. Claudius Fronto's statue proclaimed that he died 'bravely fighting to the very end for the state' (*ILS* 1098). Apart from a brief revolt in AD 175 by Avidius Cassius, governor of Syria, whose ambitions, having fought with conspicuous success alongside Verus in the Parthian war a decade earlier (see above), had probably been sparked by false rumours of Marcus' death and the lack of a designated heir, Marcus appears to have faced no internal political opposition. In AD 176 he briefly visited Egypt before returning to Rome for a triumph and setting off almost immediately to the embattled region of Pannonia.

As the frontiers came for the first time under nearly continuous threat, and the empire was hit by widespread plague, the role of emperor might not seem so attractive to ambitious politicians. Lonely in his tent, Marcus Aurelius composed the extraordinary *Meditations* on the nature of kingship and duty which compelled him to undertake unwillingly the role of general, which still, as with the first of the Caesars, remained central to the functions of an emperor.[13] These personal diaries expose an intense moral sensibility and a deep dislike of many of the duties incumbent on a conscientious princeps. Marcus depicted the exercise of power as a burden:

Map3 The Roman provinces in the second century AD

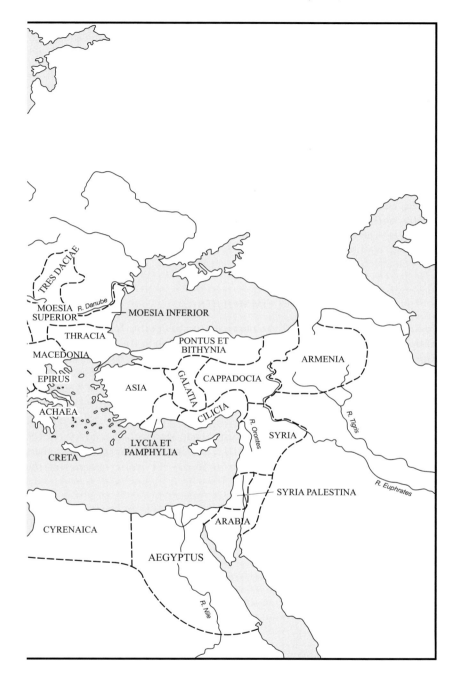

Each hour be minded, valiantly as becomes a Roman and a man, to do what is to your hand, with precise ... and unaffected dignity, natural love, freedom and justice; and to give yourself repose from every other imagination. And so you will, if only you do each act as though it were your last, freed from every random aim, from wilful turning away from the directing Reason, from pretence, self-love and displeasure with what is allotted to you. You see how few things a man need master in order to live a smooth and god-fearing life; for the gods themselves will require nothing more of him who keeps these precepts.

(*Meditations* 2.5)

It is ironic that Marcus' column and equestrian statue (still to be seen on the Capitol in Rome) both portray him as military conqueror and hero. The attitudes revealed by the emperor selected in his youth for intelligence and character, trained in the arts of civilized discourse and philosophy, contrast markedly with the lascivious delight in luxury displayed by some of his predecessors, the desire for military glory of others, and the naked political ambition of Augustus, the military autocrat with whom the principate had begun.

COMMODUS

It would be misleading to end the narrative at this point, for in AD 180 the Antonine age was close to its end. Perhaps as a reaction to the revolt of Avidius Cassius, in AD 177 Marcus ended any uncertainty about the succession by designating his son Commodus as joint ruler. The sole surviving son out of 12 or 13 children born to Marcus and his wife Faustina, the daughter of Antoninus Pius, Commodus was only 16 in AD 177, and 19 when he inherited power on his father's death in Vienna on 17 March AD 180. He had not undergone the thorough training in princely responsibility that Marcus had enjoyed. In the 12 years before his assassination in AD 192, and in particular in the last years of his rule, Commodus was to recreate in Rome the worst excesses of the reigns of Gaius and Nero.

Part III

THE STATE

8

MILITARY AUTOCRACY

The Roman emperors exercised an extraordinarily effective form of military autocracy through which their subjects were held in subjection to their rule for centuries. This is not to assert that the sources reveal a society in which the agents of the state were all-pervasive, or the movement and thoughts of individuals closely controlled. On the contrary, emperors had little interest in imposing ideology – social, political or religious – and had no means to impose surveillance on the whereabouts of all the inhabitants of the empire. But in their concern to ensure their own safety, comfort, power and prestige, emperors employed a huge military force whose main but unstated purpose was the suppression of dissent.[1]

POWER OF THE ARMY

The creation of a large standing army by Augustus was the secret weapon of the empire. It was a novel notion in the Roman state. Throughout the expansion of Roman power during the Republic, armies had been raised each year for warfare and disbanded at the end of the campaigning season. As late as the 90s BC the Roman state had in most years raised only six legions for all purposes; in one year in that decade, three legions had sufficed. In the following years, extended wars in distant places led to many legions being left *in situ* for more than the usual one year, even in some cases up to eight years, as in Gaul under the command of Julius Caesar in the 50s BC. Where wars were endemic because of fractious provincials, a military force of some kind came to be more or less permanently stationed, particularly in Spain and in Syria, but the assumption still remained that on the completion of their military task soldiers would return to farm peasant plots; since the settlement of Marius' veterans in 100 BC, if a soldier did not possess such a plot it would generally be provided by the state.[2]

Thus when in 30 BC Octavian celebrated his victory over Egypt, it would normally have been expected that he would disband all of the 60 legions under his command. These legions represented an extraordinary accumulation of troops acquired haphazardly from those who had signed on over the preceding 14 years with one or the other leader in the civil wars. That troops were no longer needed was emphasized in 29 BC by the symbolic closing of the doors of the temple of Janus by which Octavian indicated that Rome was entirely at peace. And Octavian did indeed dismiss over half of the legions at tremendous expense, as he proudly recorded in his *Res Gestae* 3.3. But in 25 BC there were still 28 legions and a huge number of auxiliary troops under arms. What were they for?

To some extent an answer may be found in Octavian's need for military victories to bolster his prestige with the Roman people.[3] It is indeed striking that the next 40 years witnessed a flurry of campaigns in Spain, the Balkans and on the Rhine. But none of these wars required more than 10 legions at any one time, and even then such a large force was unusual, as Velleius Paterculus noted in AD 7 of the campaign to put down the revolt of Pannonia and Dalmatia:

> There were now gathered together in one camp ten legions, more than seventy cohorts, fourteen troops of cavalry and more than ten thousand veterans, and in addition a large number of volunteers and the numerous cavalry of the [Thracian] king – in a word, a greater army than had ever been assembled in one place since the civil wars.
>
> (*History of Rome* 2.113.1–2)

For most of Augustus' rule, two-thirds of the legions were idle, and it was never necessary for more than half to take action at any one time. Thus up to 100,000 legionaries, fully equipped and well paid, were kept in permanent readiness for combat without ever fighting. Added to them was a number of auxiliary units, supplying perhaps 150,000 fighting men (as estimated by Tacitus of AD 23, *Annals* 4.5). The auxiliaries acted as cavalry and light infantry, and their equipment in this period was slightly less expensive and more varied than that of the legionaries. Like the legions, auxiliary units became permanent fixtures under Augustus. Altogether, before the changes made in the Flavian period, about 250,000 men were employed as troops of one kind or another by the imperial state. Most of them had nothing to do. In any case, emperors could quite easily announce victories to the Roman public without necessarily having to fight; hence, for example, Augustus' 'victories' over Parthia and Armenia in 20 BC, and the claim of *Res Gestae* 26.2 that Germany had been pacified along with France and Spain.

The decision to keep these troops on, rather than disband them, cannot have been taken lightly. To some extent frenetic campaigning can be seen as a *product* of the retention of troops. Augustus needed to prevent his huge command looking otiose, lest people ask too many questions. At the same time, the expense of the military machine was horrendous. A vast income was needed, perhaps half of the total spending of the state, constituting by far the largest single item in the state's budget, and culled by taxation of the provincials. The first ever provincial census was held in Gaul in 27 BC, and it is not accidental that during Augustus' rule the rigour of the census and tax collection sparked off revolts in Gaul, Pannonia and Judaea (see Chapter 16). Thus, ironically, the collection of taxes to pay them gave the soldiers something to do, in suppressing rebellion caused by that very taxation.

It is improbable that the reason for retaining such a force was primarily the protection of the empire from outside attack. Not only had a much smaller force proved adequate, albeit admittedly for a smaller empire, in the 90s BC, but since Roman defensive techniques relied essentially on eventual aggressive retaliation rather than sealing of a frontier to prevent incursions by outsiders or even rapid response, the permanent possession of troops was unnecessary. So long as enemies of Rome could expect eventual retaliation, they would be effectively deterred from attack. In practice the state's use of the military machine in the Early Empire seems to have reflected *ad hoc* decisions rather than any overall strategy, partly for this very reason, that there was not in general any need to worry about attacks on the borders by enemies.

The obvious reason for such massive expenditure on soldiers was to keep Octavian and his successors in power; that is, the troops under arms were intended to suppress internal dissent more than external threats. Needless to say, neither the emperors nor their subjects could often admit this fact openly. One exception will suffice. Like many deep truths it was expressed at the time as a joke, which is itself preserved within the bizarre imperial biographies known as the *Historia Augusta*:

> Favorinus [the orator from France] once had an expression he used criticized by Hadrian and conceded the point. When his friends found fault with him for wrongly conceding the point to Hadrian about a word in common use with reputable writers, he raised a hearty laugh by saying, 'You are giving me bad advice, my friends, when you don't allow me to regard a man with thirty legions as more learned than anyone else.'
>
> (*Hadrian* 15.12–13)

Usually, it did no good to the rulers or to the ruled for either of them to admit that the empire was controlled by terror. None the less, the effect of a massive army loyal to the emperor, to whom they swore an oath, and whose image was placed with their standards, was clear enough.

But why so *many* troops? The answer may lie in Octavian's awareness of his own career. His own path to power had begun with the enlisting of a private army of two legions. What he could do, others might attempt. But there was a limit to the size of an army any private individual could expect to bribe. So long, therefore, as the emperor always had more troops available and uncommitted to campaigns against external enemies than any possible opponent, he could relax. Octavian made sure that that should be the case. He ensured, also, that his own soldiers remained loyal to him, granting them honoured status, to the extent of instituting special seats for soldiers in the theatre. In fact all emperors gave frequent donations to their soldiers, who were also rewarded by the development of a complicated system of military decorations (*dona militaria*), always given in the name of the emperor.[4] Julius Caesar and Augustus both enhanced their military grip on the state by the settlement of veterans in Italy, often at important road junctions, but the unpopularity with civilians of land confiscations in Italy led to the abandoning of this procedure by later emperors, who preferred to give the soldiers cash.

Apart from the cessation of veteran colonies in Italy, no later emperor saw fit to change the method by which they retained their power. The soldiers did not in normal circumstances need to do anything. The number of soldiers changed only slightly during the first two centuries of the Empire.[5] When three legions were lost under Varus in AD 9, no attempt was made to replace them, and the 25 legions left on Augustus' death in AD 14 became a standard number. At that point they were stationed as follows: one in Africa, three in Spain, four in Lower Germany, four in Upper Germany, three in Pannonia, two in Dalmatia, two in Moesia, four in Syria and two in Egypt. However, during the first century the equipment and training of the auxiliary units came more and more to resemble those of legionaries and their units were regularized by Claudius with grants of *diplomata* (records of the privileges allowed on discharge), so that the number of heavily armed infantry in the field gradually rose.[6]

The army was complemented by a permanent navy, manned, like the auxiliaries, by non-citizen provincials. Naval forces had proved decisive in the civil wars to 31 BC, but they faced no obvious external enemy in the imperial period apart from the threat of piracy, since the Roman state controlled the whole Mediterranean coastline. By AD 23, according to Tacitus' survey of the troops available to Tiberius (*Annals* 4.5.4), there were roughly as many auxiliary troops (including the navy) as legionaries.

The pretence that the soldiers were aimed at external enemies led to the deployment of most of them at a distance from Rome, but this did not indicate constant trouble in the places where the armies were stationed. On the contrary, three legions stayed in Spain until AD 43, some seventy years after pacification, and the two Egyptian legions had almost nothing to do from 25–24 BC (the campaigns against Arabia) until a revolt broke out in the province in AD 172–73.[7]

THE PRAETORIAN GUARD

In the city of Rome itself the stationing of regular troops was a major innovation by Augustus.[8] The nine praetorian cohorts (of 500 men each) in theory acted as the emperor's headquarters' guard, assigned to him by virtue of his role as an army commander. But the use of such a guard was not standard in the Late Republic – although it became a common practice for generals in the triumviral period – and when they had held their army commands, neither Pompeius nor Julius Caesar had stationed troops permanently near the capital while living in Rome. The praetorians were chosen after Actium from among the most experienced veterans and favoured with extra pay; three cohorts were billeted in small groups around Rome, the rest in neighbouring towns. At first, Augustus kept the guard under his personal command, but in 2 BC two praetorian prefects (to hold the command jointly) were appointed for the first time, and in AD 23 Sejanus, unusually sole commander from AD 15 to 31, moved them into a strongly fortified camp on the Viminal, to the north-east of the city. By this time the praetorians were directly recruited as an élite force. Epigraphic evidence reveals that their numbers were increased to 12 cohorts in Tiberius' reign, shortly after AD 23.[9] From Domitian's reign onwards, 10 became the standard number.

Not that the praetorians were alone in enforcing the imperial will in the city. The urban prefects, appointed by the princeps, could rely on three urban cohorts to preserve the peace (unlike all magistrates in the Republic, who had available to them only their dependants). And, until the rule of Galba, each emperor had a private bodyguard of non-citizen Germans (Batavians), to protect him as he went about the city.

STATE TERROR

So long as the soldiers remained secure and loyal in their barracks, potential enemies within the political élite would remain quiescent. That, indeed, was usually the case, for the exception proves the rule. In AD 68 senators did not dare join in the revolt of Vindex against Nero because any one provincial governor always knew he would be powerless against all the rest of the legions under arms if he attempted to strike out alone. If Nero had not committed suicide it is unlikely that Galba, with his one legion from Spain, would have got far against the seven German legions under Verginius Rufus and Aulus Vitellius, who could easily have blocked his path to Rome.

Similar methods controlled the inhabitants of the empire of lower social status. State terror is only really effective if it is ruthless. In this respect the emperors simply continued a well-established trait of Roman policy.[10] Rome's expansion over the eastern Mediterranean had been partly achieved by the Romans' refusal to accept gentlemanly Greek notions of diplomacy. Those cities which opposed Rome ran the risk of annihilation. Such tactics had worked exceptionally well: for instance, the destruction of Corinth in 146 BC became legendary. It was helpful that the emperor's subjects realized that he too could act similarly. When the Pannonians and Dalmatians rebelled in 13–12 BC, many of the defeated were sold into slavery. There was no need for a constant police force to prevent anti-Roman behaviour if people knew that such action was genuinely likely.

The success of autocracy is greatest when it rarely needs to show its hand in order to produce terror. It did not need to be an everyday occurrence for the emperor's subjects to know that he could sometimes murder his enemies or arbitrarily confiscate property in Italy or the provinces. All his subjects were only too well aware that the army might at any time requisition supplies and conscripts, and that no appeal would succeed.[11] Everyone knew that banishment and exile could take place without trial; that those of the political élite who ran foul of the emperor could be compelled to commit suicide; that the emperor could ban the publication of books of which he disapproved; that imperial estates could increase through confiscation of the lands of those who opposed the autocrat; that for adult males conscription into the army, followed by long and indefinite service far from home, was a constant threat.[12] The fact that all such behaviour is attested in the extant sources at least once (and in most cases much more often) is enough to show that the arbitrary power of the autocrat was known, and could be feared. If only a few complained openly, that should hardly surprise. In practice, most subjects of the empire elected to co-operate in the functioning of the state. Since they had no choice, furthermore, they might as well make the best of their position and dignify their loyalty as an expression of honour.

Thus senators who co-operated naturally insisted, for their self-esteem, that their co-operation was voluntary, and that the emperor through whose patronage they held their status was no more than a rather powerful and much-loved *amicus* (friend); it was in the interest of emperors to encourage such self-esteem among the political élite, for emperors needed energetic and motivated men around them, not least to command on their behalf the legions on which their power was based. In the same way, provincial aristocrats co-operated in the collection of taxes for the Roman state, not least because the alternative was terror. At the same time, since Rome offered the opportunity for such provincials to hold some office within the state, they too could portray their actions as respectable careers in a Roman context. Similarly auxiliary troops, soldiers from Gaul, Spain, the Rhine, the Alps and many other regions of the empire, could justify to themselves their support for the repressive regime, which they bolstered often by serving in their own home regions, by asserting to themselves the truth that Roman rule brought benefits of peace and prosperity. The history of empires is not lacking in other examples of such native co-operation with oppression.[13]

It has to be said that most of the surviving evidence (but not all) was produced by those who co-operated with imperial rule.[14] But this should not disguise the basis of that rule in military autocracy. Modern understanding of the Roman world depends on appreciation not just of what was said but of what was left unstated from fear or from calculation.

9

THE OPERATION OF THE STATE IN ROME

IMPERIAL BUREAUCRACY

In the final analysis, power in the Roman Empire always rested with the emperor, and influence was wielded primarily through proximity to or friendship with him, as the case of Sejanus illustrated in the reign of Tiberius. The operation of the imperial household thus in time came to resemble that of a state bureaucracy, with offices, secretaries and memoranda, and bribery, patronage and corruption.[1]

This imperial bureaucracy was slow to take on a public image. The emperors at first preferred to portray themselves as, in some sense, simple senators pre-eminent in the state only by virtue of their *auctoritas* (influence). As such, it did not do to emphasize in public the power of their wives, children, slaves and freedmen. At the same time, there was nothing unconstitutional or unusual in the influence of such people over a senator's affairs, so that it did not need to be hidden, just not advertised. The clues to the operation of such influence under Augustus and Tiberius therefore survive, if only fragmentarily reported. For the reigns of Claudius and Nero in particular, there are clear accounts of the wielding of such informal power.

The Roman Republic had conquered huge territories without ever evolving a state bureaucracy.[2] Magistrates relied on their own private resources to run state business. Their own slaves acted as secretaries when they dictated letters, and totted up the accounts when public monies were involved. If extra staff were needed, friends could be asked – it was a good opportunity for young men to gain experience of public life. If a major problem arose, a family conference could be called to discuss it. Wives, mothers, neighbours, political allies, patrons, anyone might be called in to advise. The final decision and action were naturally always carried out in the name of the magistrate alone, but success might well lie with the efficacy of this informal staff of helpers.

The emperor's household was no different, except that his magistracy and his wealth were of a size and importance not previously conceived, and the problems that arose were not occasional but perennial.[3] Already by the end of the Julio-Claudian period it was quite normal for the emperor's entourage to be referred to as a court (*aula*), which gradually came to take on some of the formal trappings of Hellenistic court life, although the full imposition of formality on the imperial court was not to occur until the third century. Like other aristocrats, the princeps, when in Rome, received his friends (*amici*) in his semi-public *salutatio* at home, but admission to this particular household was a privilege highly prized, since it was from the emperor that all patronage proceeded, and in the court that it was brokered. From the point of view of the emperor, the value of the court lay in his need to spot talented young men.

That most friends of the emperor thus admitted to the court came from the highest status groups of Roman society (senators and equites) was a product not of any formal requirement but of policy in the maintenance of the emperor's image. Within the court such high-ranking nobles constantly conspired with the emperor's relatives, freedmen and slaves, and assorted other residents such as the offspring of client kings, in order to win the emperor's favour and the influence, power and wealth that favour could bring. For example, after the very recent murder of Claudius' wife Messalina in AD 48, at the instigation of the influential imperial freedman Narcissus, there was fierce competition between the imperial freedmen and their candidates as to who should take her place:

> Messalina's death convulsed the imperial household. Claudius was impatient of celibacy and easily controlled by his wives, and the freedmen quarrelled about who should choose his next one. Rivalry among the women was equally fierce. Each cited her own high birth, beauty and wealth as qualifications for this exalted marriage. The chief competitors were Lollia Paulina, daughter of the former consul Marcus Lollius, and Germanicus' daughter Agrippina. Their backers were Callistus and Pallas respectively. Narcissus supported Aelia Paetina, who was of the family of the Aelii Tuberones. The emperor continually changed his mind according to whatever advice he heard last.
>
> (Tacitus, *Annals* 13.1)

In this case it was Pallas and Agrippina who won, securing her marriage to Claudius in AD 49.

The court was filled with cabals and rumour, and the constant worry that an association might prove disadvantageous or even dangerous. Suetonius, an insider, gives a vivid portrayal of the vagaries, tension and hypocrisy of court life, in which social and political lives were inextricably mixed. One small incident from Suetonius' account of Tiberius' reign illustrates the situation perfectly (*Tiberius* 42.2): 'At a banquet a very obscure candidate for the quaestorship drained a huge two-handled tankard of wine at Tiberius' challenge, whereupon he was preferred to rival candidates from the noblest families.' The emperor's whim could set a new fashion for all courtiers, the hostility of a freedman could bar even senators from the physical access to the emperor which they prized so highly, and sexual licence and dabbling in magical practices could provide material not just for gossip but for serious intrigue.

The importance of the court as the source of patronage cannot be over-estimated, but for executive decisions, of which the emperor as magistrate had to make many each day, he relied more on his inner household, the *domus Caesaris*. It was his family, his slaves and his freedmen who saw him at his most private moments and could influence policy by their advice. Thus in Augustus' important decisions it was widely rumoured that his wife Livia had a major part to play. His adopted sons were more formally associated with his decisions, as on the execution of Herod's will in 4 BC, when Gaius Caesar attended the *consilium* (a semi-formal body of advisors to the emperor) at the age of 16. When Augustus died in AD 14 he directed the Roman people that if they wished to discuss the financial state of the empire, they should ask his freedmen and slaves (Suetonius, *Augustus* 101.4).[4]

By the time of Augustus' death, the tally of his slaves and freedmen who had wielded such enormous power for over 40 years was huge. Their names crop up primarily in their inscriptions, which proudly record (when appropriate) their servitude to Caesar as well as their winning of freedom for their services. Thus, among many such documents, a tomb inscription from Rome records (EJ[2] no. 147; Braund no. 300): 'Gaius Julius Niceros Vedianus, freedman of the divine Augustus, orderly of Germanicus Caesar in his consulship and of Calvisius Sabinus in his consulship.' Another commemorates (EJ[2] no. 149; Braund no. 302): 'Gaius Octavius Auctus, freedman of Octavia, sister of Augustus, records-clerk; Viccia Gnome, freedwoman of Gaius, his wife.'

Such imperial freedmen emerged suddenly into the limelight in the reign of Claudius, probably not because of a change in their function but in the way that it was portrayed. Both Tacitus and the younger Pliny recalled from 60 years later the disgraceful prominence of Pallas, Narcissus and others who were rewarded for their labours by the emperor and publicly proclaimed as the origin of the emperor's decisions.[5] A striking example was Claudius' honouring of Pallas in AD 52:

> Next Claudius proposed to the senate that women marrying slaves should be penalized. ... The emperor revealed that this proposal was due to Pallas; to whom accordingly rewards of an honorary praetorship and fifteen million sesterces were proposed by the consul-designate Marcius Barea Soranus. Publius Cornelius Lentulus Scipio added the suggestion that Pallas should be given the nation's thanks because, though descended from Arcadian kings, he preferred the national interests to his antique lineage, and let himself be regarded as one of the emperor's servants. Claudius reported that Pallas was content with that distinction only, and preferred not to exceed his former modest means. So the senate's decree was engraved in letters of bronze; it loaded praises for old-world frugality on a man who had once been a slave and was now worth three hundred million sesterces.
> (Tacitus, *Annals* 12.53)

Public acknowledgement of the role of freedmen continued after Claudius during Nero's reign, only to come to a sudden and almost complete end thereafter, although the *actual* tasks of imperial freedmen continued throughout the imperial period. It seems that Claudius and Nero miscalculated the likely reaction of senators to the open demonstration that their power was no greater than, indeed rather inferior to, that of ex-slaves. No senator is known to have objected to the importance of Augustus' freedmen, or their wealth, because Augustus had been careful to avoid treating his freedmen as social equals, whatever their power: he deliberately did not dine with them or permit them to parade their influence in public (Suetonius, *Augustus* 74). By contrast, the careers of freedmen under Claudius and Nero created humiliating reversals in status. On one occasion, Seneca (*Letters* 47.9) saw the former master of the powerful Callistus forced to wait outside his door whilst others were allowed inside. It was his freedmen who could procure favours from the emperor, by proffering the right advice or by putting the right paper before him at a convenient moment.

Whatever the public role of freedmen, the complexity of their administrative role evolved quite rapidly.[6] Already under Nero it was a sign of dangerous imitation of the emperor for a senator to name one of his freedmen *ab epistulis* (in charge of correspondence), another *a libellis* (in charge of petitions), another *a rationibus* (in charge of accounts), and so on (Tacitus, *Annals* 15.35). The use of such titles undoubtedly reflected the formalities of Hellenistic court practice, but the jobs themselves had real and important functions. Requests for advice or favours flooded in to the emperor from all over the empire. His secretaries dictated his replies. The normal procedure was for the reply to be checked and a *subscriptio* added at the end, often but not always written by the emperor; for ordinary letters, the *subscriptio* would be simply a greeting, but in responses to petitions it might form the substantive answer to the petitioner.[7]

By the second century AD some of these duties in the imperial house had been allocated to free Romans, who took on the tasks for the power they bestowed, despite the lack of prestige which could only be gained by a more formal political career. The first men of equestrian rank to act as imperial secretaries were two Greeks in the reign of Claudius. In a gradual process, the secretarial functions of imperial freedmen were taken over by able equites.[8] In the 120s AD the scholar Suetonius was secretary to the emperor Hadrian, a post which gave him exceptional insight into the essentially domestic government of the Roman state. That Suetonius could have had a military equestrian career is evident from a letter of the younger Pliny (*Letters* 3.8), in which Pliny revealed that through patronage he could obtain a military tribunate for the young Suetonius, an offer which Suetonius, however, declined.[9]

The whole administrative operation was carried on from wherever the emperor was at any one time. Thus when he was on campaign, the household moved with him. One effect was an extraordinarily incompetent system of record-keeping. One of Trajan's replies to the younger Pliny revealed that a search for a law passed some years previously required a rather desperate hunt through the records of earlier emperors, to no avail (Pliny, *Letters* 10.66). However, the emperor's house in Rome became increasingly large and impressive, covering much of the Palatine hill which overlooked the forum on the one side and the Circus Maximus on the other, until it became the archetype of a palace. Augustus' modest private residence on the hill was physically joined in his lifetime to a series of other houses, libraries, and public temples, culminating in the incorporation in 12 BC of the shrine of Vesta within the precincts of the palace complex; the pretext was that since Augustus was now *pontifex maximus* (chief priest of the state cults in Rome), his house had to be made over to the people. The palace was designed to permit access to the princeps by those he favoured and to ensure a luxurious lifestyle for members of the court. The staff was huge, with the responsibilities of imperial slaves and freedmen minutely differentiated.

What above all turned the imperial court into something more than the household of a particularly rich Roman magistrate was not so much its size and power as its continuity from one emperor to the next. Partly this was a result of the haphazard operation of imperial finances.[10] The emperor as head of the *domus Caesaris* had a huge private fortune (*patrimonium*), which he could arrange to be disposed of after his death more or less as he wished, like any other Roman. However, in practice, this *patrimonium*, which included huge estates in the provinces, houses and land in Italy, and the palace in Rome, passed from one emperor to the next intact, partly because it was too cumbersome to divide. With the properties went the slaves and freedmen who made them function. These were not only the butlers and chambermaids. The emperor, as a magistrate in command of a *provincia*, was responsible for a *fiscus* (literally, 'basket'), into which were collected the revenues of that *provincia*. In theory, surplus from the *fiscus*, after necessary expenditure on the province, should have passed to the state treasury (the *aerarium* of Saturn), but in practice emperors tended to keep it in their *fiscus*, perhaps for convenience as much as anything. Since they administered the *fiscus* through the same freedmen as managed their private properties, the *fiscus* and *patrimonium* inevitably became interlocked, a fact which was to the advantage of the emperor, who could sometimes claim credit for giving liberally to the state out of his *patrimonium*. Thus new emperors took over the *patrimonium* and freedmen of their predecessors along with the formal grant of powers and *provincia*. Hence the extraordinary continuity from one reign to the next, well illustrated by an inscription set up by Gnaeus Octavius Capito (Smallwood, *Nerva-Hadrian* no. 270), an eques who proudly proclaimed his services as *ab epistulis* to Nerva and Trajan but left his first master unnamed. This man's career had in fact commenced under the hated Domitian, but neither the freedman nor the new emperor found it appropriate to mention this fact in public.

For some complex decisions, or in order to flatter those invited, emperors, following the normal practice of senatorial magistrates, convened a *consilium* of advisors, which might include a select number of fellow magistrates and senior senators. In principle, the composition of a *consilium* was an *ad hoc* decision by the emperor in any particular case. When the younger Pliny was invited to join Trajan for several days at the coast to hear some legal cases, they involved questions of private law on which Pliny may have been thought moderately informed.[11] He was deeply flattered:

> I was delighted to be summoned by the emperor to act as his assessor at Centum Cellae (as this place is called). Nothing could have given me more pleasure than to have first-hand experience of our ruler's justice and wisdom and also to see his lighter moods in this sort of country environment where these qualities are easily revealed.
> (Pliny, *Letters* 6.31)

Such a semi-formal *consilium* was different from the groups of day-to-day advisors used by emperors, but never publicly acknowledged, and hence the object of much court gossip. For important matters of policy it was normal for emperors to rely on a limited group of trustworthy and intelligent friends. These might be freedmen, as for Claudius, or a non-senatorial Italian aristocrat, like Augustus' advisor, Maecenas. Women might be asked to advise; like freedmen, they evoked resentment only if they paraded their private power too openly, as Livia did after the death of Augustus. Livia's public influence is demonstrated in the text of the *Senatus Consultum de Cn. Pisone Patre* (see above, Chapter 5), which, stating that Livia had intervened in person to help in the acquittal of Piso's wife, Plancina, praises her as a woman:

> who has served the commonwealth superlatively not only in giving birth to our princeps but also through her many great favours towards men of every rank, and who rightly and deservedly could have supreme influence in what she asked from the senate, but who used that influence sparingly
> (SCPP, lines 115-118, trans. M. Griffin).

Figure 13 Brass sestertius minted in AD 37–8, depicting Gaius' three sisters, Agrippina, Drusilla and Julia, as three abstract divinities. The letters S.C. (senatus consulto) indicate that the type was approved by the senate. Photo courtesy of CNG Coins.

However, Gaius' three sisters were portrayed on coins struck in his reign by the senate; on a fine bronze coin issued in AD 37–38, they appear on the reverse in the guise of the goddesses Security, Concord and Fortune (see Figure 13). By the early second century AD, in the reign of Trajan, the developed public *personae* of the imperial women were widely advertised.

All this government of the state went on behind closed doors. In the full glare of publicity the advice given to the emperor was bound to be rather more anodyne. Since the emperor was the sole fount of the patronage which could ensure a successful political career, it would not do to be seen to contradict his wishes openly or to pander too obviously to his prejudices.

URBAN CROWDS

Hence brave public statements were more likely to be made by great urban crowds, like the mob that rushed Sejanus to his death in AD 31, than by individuals.[12] Such mass opinion was only an informal part of the system, but it could be effective, as in the riots instigated by P. Plautius Rufus in AD 6, which gave a serious shock to Augustus (Cassius Dio, *History of Rome* 55.27.1–3; Suetonius, *Augustus* 19), or the *contiones* (public political gatherings) about whose mockery Tiberius complained (Tacitus, *Annals* 5.4–5). The issues involved were rarely a desire for a change of political system, more often sympathy with particular members of the imperial family (especially women and children, like Octavia and Britannicus under Nero), or special *causes célèbres*, like the proposed death in AD 61 of all the slaves of Pedanius Secundus as a mass punishment after he had been killed by one of them (Tacitus, *Annals* 14.42–45) (see below, Chapter 17).

The main *locus* for displays of public opinion was the games. The political effectiveness of such events was recognized by the emperors through occasional rulings forbidding members of the upper classes to appear on the stage. The formal *comitia* (assemblies, see Chapter 3) still met to ratify elections to high magistracies, and occasionally to pass laws (*leges*), but these events were largely stage-managed. When there was pressure from too many eager candidates at the praetorian elections in AD 11, Augustus simply increased the number of posts available that year to equal the number of men competing (Cassius Dio, *History of Rome* 56.25.4).

THE SENATE

Similar factors caused the ineffectiveness of the body through which the governing class of Rome was meant to give its advice to magistrates, that is, the senate, even though in theory the senate appeared *more* powerful under Augustus, since its resolutions came to be treated as binding law without the authority of a vote by the people as a whole.[13] The senate had swelled to more than a thousand members by 29 BC but was reduced to around 600 in a series of culls by Augustus in 28 and 18 BC. The number remained more or less stable for the rest of the principate.

Members were usually ex-quaestors, twenty of whom were elected in each year, but, particularly from the Flavian period, emperors took to 'adlecting' older favourites directly into the senate with the senior rank of ex-praetor. The rules for senatorial procedure, hallowed by custom, were codified by Augustus under the *lex Julia de senatu habendo* of 9 BC, which also fixed the level of attendance, a lower quorum which could vary according to the business in hand, and, repeating a measure of 17 BC, fines for non-attendance, although these were in practice rarely imposed (Cassius Dio, *History of Rome* 55.3–4.1).

A good proportion of the *Annals* of Tacitus and of the *Letters* of the younger Pliny revolves around events in the senate in the first century AD. It caused these writers considerable pain that the debates which they had to report were often so trivial, and that when more important issues cropped up, the members of the senate lacked the courage for open debate. None of this was particularly surprising. It was only the requirements of the genre of Roman historiography, which had involved, as in the works of Livy, a combination of external wars and overt internal politics, that constrained Tacitus to talk about senatorial debates at all. A much clearer view of the way in which the empire was actually administered may be drawn from the non-senator Suetonius, whose biographical genre better suited the circumstances of imperial autocracy.

The senate did in fact meet regularly once a fortnight, except in the holiday months, and ostentatious non-attendance was noted and held against the culprit. Much legislation was still entrusted to the senate down to the end of our period, particularly (if the surviving evidence is representative) on matters of status, inheritance and public order, although more senatorial legislation was passed under the Julio-Claudians, Hadrian and Marcus Aurelius than under other emperors in the early imperial period.[14] Non-contentious decisions with regard to roads, water supply in the city of Rome, and minor aspects of foreign affairs might be debated in the senate, foreign embassies might sometimes be received, and issues concerning the official state religious cults discussed. But on the whole, the institution's main task became the regulation of its own members in those few posts which senators might hold without the direct patronage of the emperor. The allocation of ex-consuls to the governorships of Asia and Africa, and of other senators to the many other *provinciae* in which no legions were stationed, was conducted by drawing lots (*sortitio*); the precise details of the process are now obscure. Governors selected by the senate governed Achaea (Greece) for some of the time, and Bithynia in north-west Turkey, until the area was ruled by Pliny; and they had control of Italy after Hadrian. From some time after AD 14, perhaps after the trial of Piso in AD 20, the senate also regularly acted as a criminal court when one of its members was accused of corruption in such a provincial post, as well as in other cases involving *maiestas* (treason) or adultery by important people.[15] It was in the senate that elections to magistracies were effectively decided after AD 14, even though the Roman people as a whole continued to meet in the *comitia* to ratify the decisions until Cassius Dio's time (Cassius Dio, *History of Rome* 58.20).[16]

But, although emperors such as Tiberius might ask the senate for advice, the result, as he angrily complained, was useless. They were 'born to servitude' (Tacitus, *Annals* 3.65.3) – in other words, they found freedom of speech impossible. It cannot have helped that they met in places hallowed by connection with the princeps: most frequently in the *curia Julia* (begun by Julius Caesar), and also in the temple of Apollo on the Palatine, and from 2 BC the temple of Mars Ultor. Not even the prosecution of malefactors among their number came easily to them. The number of trials on charges of maladministration is much smaller under the Roman Empire than in the Republic. It is not likely that this reflects better government. The incentive for one senator to bring a charge against another had been considerable in the Late Republic, when rhetorical brilliance could win prominence, and prosecution, successful or otherwise, could bring the friendship of the *inimici* (enemies) of the accused. However, in the Empire, political eloquence was less needed in Rome, since speeches to the populace were no longer necessary, and any governor who achieved sufficient prominence to be worth attacking would by definition have reached such heights through the *amicitia* (friendship) of the greatest patron of all, the emperor. The prosecutor needed to be absolutely sure of the evidence before starting a trial. Hardly surprisingly, most prosecutions which are known to have taken place in the Roman Empire were thus successful.[17]

In sum, senators did have an important role in the imperial state, especially in the provinces, but it was emphatically not in the senate when it met as a body. A brief episode will illustrate the point. According to Cassius Dio (*History of Rome* 53.21.45 and 56.28.2–3), Augustus set up between 27 and 18 BC a formal system of consulting with a small council of senators with a defined but changing membership to set the agenda for the senate, and in AD 13 he went so far as to propose that the decisions of this probouleutic body should be binding, thereby making the senate's role even more otiose. Tiberius apparently revised Augustus' decision soon after taking power in AD 14, but the point about the ineffectiveness of the senate will not have been missed.[18]

MAGISTRATES AND THE COURTS

The administrative role of senators as individual magistrates in the capital should not be undervalued just because of the unimportance of senators' meetings as a corporate body, although these roles too underwent many *ad hoc* adjustments in the first century of the Roman Empire. Civil law was administered by the praetors and, on some matters, the aediles, and Augustus made a conscious effort to continue the use of senators and equites as judges, which had been an important privilege in the Republic.

For cases involving private law, Augustus in (probably) 17 BC clarified the procedure for magistrates to follow, doing away with some anachronisms which went back to the Early Republic. Under the *lex Julia de iudiciis privatis*, the old system was to continue, by which the praetors laid down the *formula* for each case and appointed a judge of the facts acceptable to both parties; but the list of acceptable judges, mostly senators and equites, was revised, and it is possible that the state began to accord special status in the creation of law to the opinions of selected legal experts (*iurisprudentes*). According to the second-century lawyer Gaius (*Institutes* 1.7), 'Juristic answers are the opinions and advice of those entrusted with the task of building up the law.' Whether such evidence shows that a formal right to give law-making answers (*ius respondendi*) existed in the first century is debated, but if it did, it will have greatly strengthened the presumptive authority of the private opinions of such designated legal experts. In any case, almost all legal experts in the Early Empire were senators, many of them of high rank.[19]

This formulary system continued to dominate the practice of Roman law everywhere (except in Egypt) for the next 200 years. The system was widespread and involved the use by quite ordinary individuals of precise legal terminology, as shown by a sizeable number of first-century legal documents found at Pompeii: the records generated in some 35 years' financial dealings by the Sulpicii at Puteoli are full of complex legal jargon.[20] A wax tablet, dated 5 October AD 51, announces the sale of slaves held by Cinnamus as security for a loan to Suavis, who has failed to repay the loan and must therefore forfeit his slaves:

> In the consulship of Tiberius Claudius Caesar, for the fifth time, and Lucius Calventius Vetus, 5 October, at Puteoli in the forum, in the Sextian portico of Augustus, on the rectangular column, a notice was affixed, on which was written what follows: the man Felix, the man Carus, the man Januarius, the woman Primigenia, the younger, and the boy Ampliatus, which chattels Marcus Egnatius Suavis was said to have given to Gaius Sulpicius Cinnamus by mancipation for one sesterce on transaction of fiducia for a debt of twenty-three sesterces, will be offered for sale on 14 October next at Puteoli in the forum in front of the Caesonian porch; the pledge became forfeit from 15 September.

(*ZPE* 29 (1978), pp. 233–34; Braund no. 766)

Alongside the formulary system there gradually emerged during the first century AD a streamlined procedure of judgement by *cognitio*, in which magistrates or their delegates decided both the law and the facts of each case at the same time. Appeal to the highest magistrate of all (the emperor) became increasingly common, and consequently imperial rescripts came by the late second century AD to rank alongside the learned opinions of the experts in persuading both judges and magistrates how to decide cases.[21] One reason for this gradual erosion of the formulary system was presumably difficulty in arranging for all the parties, and the magistrate and judges, to meet, once many of those involved might no longer live near Rome, and there was also the difficulty of enforcement: a plaintiff denied the recompense awarded by a judge had no better means of restitution than to bring another action for the money already owed. In civil cases in the imperial period, courts with multiple jurors were rare, but many of the cases brought to the panels of jurors at the centumviral court, which dealt with disputed inheritance cases of high value, became celebrated public occasions. Pliny vividly describes the court in a case where he represented one Attia Viriola:

> Here was a woman of high birth, the wife of a praetorian senator, disinherited by her eighty-year-old father ten days after he had fallen in love and brought home a step-mother for his daughter, and now suing for her patrimony in the united centumviral court. One hundred and eighty judges were sitting, the total for the four panels acting together; both parties were fully represented and had a large number of seats filled with their supporters, and a close-packed ring of onlookers, several rows deep, lined the walls of the courtroom. The bench was also crowded, and even the galleries were full of men and women leaning over in their eagerness to see and also to hear, though hearing was rather more difficult.
> (*Letters* 6.33)

The centumviral court was presided over by a praetor, as were most of the permanent criminal courts (*quaestiones*), such as those which tried charges of violence and poisoning, but after AD 20 serious charges against senators were generally heard in the senate itself, with the consuls presiding.[22]

But in many trials no senator except the princeps was involved as judge or jury, for it was increasingly common for the emperor himself to decide cases by conducting a *cognitio*. In this respect, one further development reflects one of the most crucial changes of the Early Empire, and it is disconcerting to note that its legal basis is completely obscure. The princeps rapidly became not only an active judge of first instance but also the supreme judge of appeal in place of the Roman people as a whole. There was no precedent in the Republic for a magistrate to take on this role, nor was it implicit in the emperor's *imperium*, but it is clearly assumed in the account in the Acts of the Apostles of Paul's appearance before Festus, the procurator of Judaea. Arguing his innocence of the charges of which he stood accused, Paul requested trial by the emperor in Rome: 'I appeal to Caesar' (Acts 25.11). The appeal judgements of later emperors were to form an important element in the corpus of Late Roman law.[23]

The princeps also selected senators for other, non-legal, administrative posts, such as the curatorship of the banks of the River Tiber. The most powerful job regularly allotted to a senator in the city of Rome was undoubtedly the prefecture of the city, a permanent appointment from AD 13. The incumbent was selected at the whim of the princeps, but often for long tenures. The first *praefectus urbi*, the aristocratic Messala Corvinus, appointed by Augustus in *c.* 25 BC, seems to have found it difficult to define his role (Tacitus, *Annals* 6.11.4) and resigned after six days; but after the long tenure of Lucius Piso (AD 13–32), the prefecture played an important role in the administration and policing of the city. Of other important posts entrusted to senators, the prefecture of the state treasury (the *aerarium Saturni*) involved, most importantly, the administration and supervision of the contracts of some of the tax-farmers who collected indirect taxes; in the Republic this post had been carried out by two quaestors chosen by lot; but under Augustus it was undertaken by two praetors (first selected by the senate, later by lot); under Claudius it reverted to two quaestors, but of his choice, then under Nero (and for the rest of the imperial period) two former praetors were chosen by the emperor.

The posts in the city allotted by the emperors to equites did not differ in kind from those of senators. These posts included some which were essential to the secure administration of the city, such as that of the *praefectus praetorio* (praetorian prefect), firmly established from 2 BC, the prefecture of the *vigiles* (watchmen, who acted as both police and fire brigade from AD 6), and, towards the end of Augustus' reign, the control of the corn supply. At the appeal of the people, Augustus himself had taken care of the corn supply in 22 BC. At another corn crisis in AD 6, a board of consular senators was appointed, and a few years later the office of *praefectus annonae* (prefecture of the corn supply) was created, the role being assigned permanently to equites. The division of posts owed more to emperors' concerns for the self-image of senators than any principle of administrative efficiency.

STATE FINANCES

The administrative system just described was not well suited to long-term planning, and many of the most important acts of the state occurred in reaction to events rather than out of strategy. This applied not least in the two main functions of the state: military operations and finance. About both of these, more will be said in the next chapter, which will consider the operation of the state in the provinces, but a few words about central control of the state finances are appropriate here.

Most evidence concerns the collection of tax.[24] The Roman tax regime was in general conservative, with new taxes invented to meet specific cash-flow crises: hence the introduction under Augustus of an auction tax, a tax on slave sales, a levy on inheritance by Roman citizens when the sum involved was large and the immediate family not the beneficiary, and a levy on formal slave manumissions by citizens. Tax initiatives can sometimes be ascribed directly to individual emperors, such as Tiberius' decision to halve the sales tax after the annexation of Cappadocia and addition of its wealth to the empire (Tac. *Ann.* 2.42). Vespasian's reign even saw the introduction of a tax on public lavatories (see above, Chapter 6). Precisely the fact that rates were more easily changed for indirect levies than for direct tax may have given the former extra importance in the eyes of emperors, even though the sums raised by direct taxation were much greater. For the rest, state income depended on rents from public land, which was increasingly intermingled with the emperor's private *patrimonium*, which in turn was enriched by gifts, legacies and confiscation.

The system was unwieldy. Emperors certainly kept accounts and could cite figures for the amount of coin available in the treasury, but arguments that emperors or their officials (notably the freedman *a rationibus*, 'in charge of accounts'), must have drawn up budgets of some kind for the state in advance of expenditure rest more on plausibility than explicit evidence – which need not imply that they are not correct: the literary sources give the impression that all administration was *ad hoc* but this may be only because they rarely focus on technical and financial details. In contrast, evidence from the Vindolanda tablets and papyri from Egypt clearly demonstrates that there was an intense bureaucracy at provincial level in operation throughout the empire. Taxation was based on a 15-year cycle in the provinces, with the exception of Egypt, which operated on a 14-year system. In light of this provincial evidence, it seems reasonable to suppose that the central financial administration must have planned for expected outlays such military pay and discharge bonuses, especially since army costs probably constituted three-quarters of the annual budget. Imperial officials must also have had to account for large building projects, such as the Colosseum and the Circus Maximus. If Plutarch (*Publ.* 15) was able to record that Domitian spent 12,000 talents to gild the temple of Jupiter Capitolinus, then it is likely that such expenditure was officially recorded and budgeted.[25]

The structure of government itself was more ordered than under the Republic, with senatorial and equestrian officials receiving a yearly salary when employed by the state. By the late second century AD., equestrian procurators were classified according to their pay grade: junior administrators who earned 60,000 sesterces per year were known as *sexagenarii*, and they could then progress to become *centenarii* (100,000) and *ducenarii* (200,000). The most senior equestrian officials, such as the praetorian prefects, were *trecenarii* (receiving 300,000 sesterces). The salaries of the majority of senatorial governors are unknown, apart from the proconsul of Asia, who was paid one million sesterces in the early third century AD.

The Roman administration clearly tried to exert a great deal of control over its economic situation, controlling the quarrying and distribution of materials such as marble. It also controlled the minting of coins, taking some care over the choice of types, but minting only as and when needed.[26] In or by 19 BC, Augustus reformed the Roman monetary system, so that the silver *denarius* (worth four sesterces) and the gold *aureus* (worth one hundred sesterces) became the standard coins, with the copper *as* (worth a quarter of a *sestertius*) for small change. His system, with minor modifications in the weight ratio between the coins introduced by Nero, lasted until the reign of Commodus, but minting was discontinuous. Old coins stayed in circulation a long time, and so long as the treasury had sufficient for immediate needs, nothing was minted. If the result was all too frequently a cash crisis, emperors were not necessarily unhappy. Such crises gave the ruler an opportunity to aid the state out of his own financial resources. It helped the emperor that, from at least the time of Tiberius, those resources included many of the precious metal mines of the empire,[27] so that it was possible, for instance, for Nero to disguise debasement of the coinage, when he reduced the silver content of the *denarius* to 80 per cent in AD. 64, by blanching the coins.[28]

10

THE OPERATION OF THE STATE IN THE PROVINCES

The emperors' requirements in the efficient operation of the state in the empire were simple. So long as sufficient money came into Rome for disbursement to the army and for maintenance of an imperial lifestyle, nothing else much mattered. In practice the exaction of taxes on a regular basis was possible only if good order was preserved throughout most of the provinces, or at least those which provided surplus income. Thus areas too poor to be worth crushing were often left unconquered, while in the rich lands opposition to Roman rule and taxation was ruthlessly suppressed. Much government depended on *ad hoc* decisions, reflecting what was practical at the time, but stressing precedent when it was available. No-one, not even Augustus, seems ever to have produced an overall strategy for provincial administration, although he and Hadrian interfered with provincial government more than most emperors.[1]

TAXES

The income of the Roman state was derived primarily from taxes levied on agricultural produce in those regions of the empire outside Italy.[2] In the Roman Republic, citizens had once contributed to the state's coffers when required, but foreign conquests had made this unnecessary since 167 BC, and it would be courting extreme unpopularity in Rome for any emperor to try to reintroduce the practice. Since all Italians had gained Roman citizenship by the end of the Republic, they too escaped the weight of direct taxes, but other inhabitants of the empire had to pay, even if they held Roman citizenship (as was increasingly common in the early imperial period). The tax came basically in two forms: *tributum soli*, a land tax based on the size of the plot farmed, and *tributum capitis*, a poll tax based on the size of the workforce; but there was much variety, depending on the taxation system in force before the imposition of Roman rule and on the state of local economies.

Standardization increased gradually in the first century of the Roman Empire. Thus under Augustus the inhabitants of Sicily may still have been paying a tithe of their produce to tax-farmers, and in other provinces the total

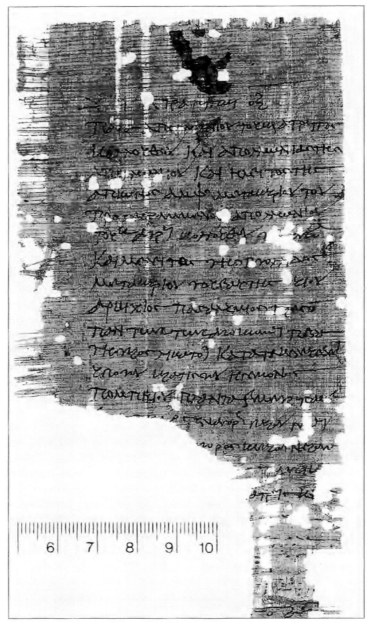

Figure 14 Oxyrhynchus papyrus POxy no. 3,910. A request to a local official in AD 99 or 100 by four Egyptians, three women and a man, for the refund of the price of requisitioned wheat which has been deposited in the public granary. The papyrus is incomplete at the foot. Photo courtesy of the Egypt Exploration Society.

payable may still have been fixed by tradition or by guesswork, but gradually the provincial census became the normal method to fix liability.[3] One should not underestimate the difficulty involved in imposing a quick new system of fiscality and monetization on the whole of north-west and central Europe, and in introducing to the eastern parts of the empire regular censuses and a poll tax, both of which were previously unknown in some areas, although long established in others, such as Egypt (see also Figure 14). Easier to impose were the indirect taxes (*portoria*) payable on goods in transit at ports, imperial frontiers and various boundaries between provinces or groups of provinces. Rates recorded were sometimes as high as 25 per cent of the value of the goods taxed but, even though the volume of long-distance trade throughout the empire was considerable, the total revenue raised was probably less than by direct taxation.[4]

PROVINCIAL GOVERNORS

Responsibility for collection of the direct taxes rested with the governors of provinces, who in turn handed over the task to more junior members of their staff. When a governor had been appointed by lot in the senate as proconsul, he used a quaestor for the purpose. When he was appointed as legatus to govern on behalf of the emperor, the latter appointed directly a non-senatorial agent called a procurator to collect the taxes. In either case the process had to begin with periodic taking of the census, which in turn generally required considerable help and advice from local leaders who knew the country and the people. Each year it was the same local leaders who were held responsible for collecting the taxes, usually in coin but sometimes partially in kind, which the quaestor or procurator would simply receive from them.[5]

The personnel employed by the state required for this operation was thus very small, but the process relied on the co-operation of the local people, in particular local aristocrats. Such aristocrats, often but not always descendants of the indigenous élite, but always defined at least partly by their wealth, were the main channel for provincials to have contact with the sources of power in the Roman Empire. Where they did not already exist, they were encouraged to emerge by state sponsorship of civilized, self-sufficient communities, sometimes (as in the north-western provinces) quite arbitrarily created out of existing tribal systems, sometimes (as in Egypt) relying on pre-existing regional units. The Roman state, itself accustomed to the rhetoric of oligarchy, preferred to rule through rich provincials, even though (as in Rome itself) lipservice could still be paid to democratic voting procedures, as is evident from municipal charters of the Flavian period recently discovered in Spain.[6] When their co-operation was denied to Rome, the governor had no means to ensure it other than violent suppression. In general, however, this was avoided because the local élite were encouraged to help the Roman state in return for the advantages offered to them: plenty of self-government, including control of magistracies, food supply, communal property, local cults, local entertainment, and so on, and the certainty of state support for their privileged status so long as they did not complain when governors chose arbitrarily to interfere, and so long as they did not subvert such rights as were guaranteed by Rome to minority populations who lived among them, such as Jews or (not surprisingly) Roman citizens.

Most of the time, then, a governor's life was peaceful. Away from the frontiers, his staff was generally small, in the hundreds even in large provinces: attendants (*lictores*), messengers (*viatores*), a few soldiers as a bodyguard, some slaves, his family, in provinces where more than one legion was stationed a few fellow-aristocrats to act as legates (commanders of individual legions within the province, under the governor's overall direction); a letter from Vindolanda in Britain (*Tab. Vindol.* III no. 645) refers also to imperial slaves and freedmen, called *Caesariani*, as assistants to the govenor. The governor's main business thus lay in the administration of justice, travelling from town to town to hold assizes.[7] In practice, the number of cases a governor could hear was severely limited by lack of time and staff, and the cases which had priority tended to be those in which the interests of the rich were involved. Only in a novel like Apuleius' *The Golden Ass* (10.28) could a poisoned woman get instant access to justice:

> The doctor's wife had an inkling straightaway of what the matter was, when the havoc wrought by the appalling potion wound its destructive way through her lungs. Soon her laboured breathing made her absolutely certain, and she rushed to the actual living quarters of the governor, shrieking loudly and calling on him for the help he was duty-bound to give. Her claim that she was going to reveal the most monstrous crimes brought a noisy crowd together, and made sure that the governor accorded her instant admission and an instant audience.

In the time of Hadrian, the practical bias towards the rich in the administration of law in provincial society was enshrined in a remarkable development of Roman law by which the legal rights of 'more honourable people' (*honestiores*) were defined as greater in a whole variety of ways than that of 'more humble people' (*humiliores*). Thus, for example, theft by a humble man was more severely punished than that by an honourable man. The dividing line was clear: it separated the provincial aristocracy from the rest of provincial society.[8]

To underline their importance, provincial aristocrats were encouraged in the West to contact the state through provincial councils (*concilia*), formed in the first instance as a focus for the cult of Rome and Augustus; *koina* in the East fulfilled the same function, but where they did not already exist before the imperial period they were not often imposed, although self-interest eventually encouraged some provincials to create such bodies, as at Ancyra (now Ankara).[9] In any case the provincial élite made great use of an attractive method of gaining direct access to the emperor through embassies, of which a large number are recorded on extant inscriptions. In a letter of 10–9 BC Augustus relates his reception of an embassy from Alexandria:

Imperator Caesar Augustus, pontifex maximus, in his fourteenth year of tribunician power, imperator twelve times, to the people of the Alexandrians, greetings. The envoys whom you sent came to me in Gaul and made your representations and in particular informed me of what seems to have troubled you in past years. ... The spokesman: 'Caesar, unconquered hero, these are the envoys of the Alexandrians. We have divided the embassy ... amongst ourselves ... according to the competence of each of us ... Theodorus on Egypt ... on the Idios Logos ... myself on the city ... not to give a defence but to request your imperial intervention.'
(*POxy* no. 3,020; Braund no. 555)

EXPANSION OF FRONTIERS

The accumulation of revenues did not require any new conquests beyond the huge area already under Roman control in 31 BC, but two factors encouraged continuing expansion. One was the simple fact that a huge army was anyway permanently in commission, and might as well be used, especially since emperors needed the prestige of victories of justify its retention. The second was the Roman method of defence by instilling terror.[10] The rumour of occasional foreign victories was publicly proclaimed on inscriptions and victory arches, such as the arch set up in Rome in honour of Titus in AD 80–81 to celebrate the defeat of the Jews:

The Roman senate and people [dedicated this] to the Emperor Titus Caesar Vespasian Augustus, son of the deified Vespasian, pontifex maximus, holding the tribunician power for the tenth year, acclaimed imperator seventeen times, consul eight times, father of his country, their princeps, because with the guidance and plans of his father, and under his auspices, he subdued the Jewish people and destroyed the city of Jerusalem, which all generals, kings, and peoples before him had either attacked without success or left entirely unassailed.
(*CIL* VI, no. 944; LR 2, p. 15)

In Pannonia in 9 BC the inhabitants were disarmed and the young men of military age sold as slaves. It was a useful way of reminding current subjects not to rebel, and free peoples not to be tempted to attack Roman possessions.

In the latter sphere the Romans were notably successful in the Early Empire. No serious attacks on the frontiers of Roman power by any outside people are recorded after 40–37 BC, when the Parthians had taken advantage of Roman civil war to retaliate for earlier Roman invasions, and this state of affairs lasted until the AD 160s, when a number of Germanic peoples attacked across the Danube, although it is now impossible to know whether the lack of attack was through fear or simply through lack of desire. At any rate there is no evidence at all of any need for a grand strategy of defence against outsiders.[11]

Nor is there any real evidence of a grand strategy of aggression, although certain patterns that make some logical sense may be glimpsed in particular areas at some times, as will become clear from a survey of the major campaigns to which reference has been made in Chapters 4-7 above. Augustus campaigned in north-west Spain in 27–25 BC; Agrippa completed the conquest in 19 BC.

Campaigns in Dalmatia in 15 BC to open up the land route from Europe to the Middle East, the military axis of the empire, were followed by a major assault across the Rhine in 12–9 BC. Revolt in the former area in 9 BC was suppressed only with difficulty and much bloodshed. Renewed efforts across the Rhine reached the Elbe in AD 5, but in AD 9, probably during an attempt to subject the region to a census and taxation, three legions under Quinctilius Varus were lost to the German tribes under Arminius. The disaster did not change Augustus' aggressive policy, but all efforts after his death were concentrated on holding the area just east of the River Rhine.

On Augustus' death, according to Tacitus (*Annals* 1.11), he had left written advice to Tiberius not to expand the empire beyond its existing boundaries. Whether or not this advice is correctly recorded, Tiberius in fact continued with the campaigns on the Rhine and Danube only for three years, and on the death of Germanicus in AD 19 all aggressive campaigns stopped for 24 years until Claudius' invasion of Britain. There was a small war to suppress rebellion in Gaul in AD 21 and a rather larger revolt by Tacfarinas in Africa between AD 17 and 24, but for the rest the legions stayed in their barracks. The main reason was perhaps simply that Tiberius had already achieved his military reputation before accession to power. Further campaigns only risked defeat and a diminution of glory.

No strategic effect of any kind from these campaigns is recorded by the sources. For instance, although Tacitus (*Annals* 2.63) records Tiberius' description of the German Maroboduus as 'more dangerous than Philip had been to Athens, or Pyrrhus and Antiochus III to Rome', there were no changes in Roman strategy as a result. Tiberius' sloth throws into relief the arbitrary nature of the campaigns of the remaining Julio-Claudians. Gaius marched to northern Gaul to threaten Britain, but gave up at the last moment and persuaded his troops to collect sea shells instead. The conquest was carried out in AD 43 by Claudius with much pomp, advertised on an arch in Rome erected in AD 51–52:

> To Tiberius Claudius Caesar, son of Drusus, Augustus Germanicus, pontifex maximus, holding the tribunician power for the eleventh year, consul five times, acclaimed imperator ... times, father of his country, the Roman senate and people [dedicated this] because he received the surrender of eleven kings of Britain conquered without any reverse and because he was the first to subject to the sovereignty of the Roman people barbarian tribes across the ocean.
> (*CIL* VI, no. 920; LR 2, pp. 36–37)

Nero campaigned against Parthia for control of Armenia, wisely not accompanying the troops in person, but sending Corbulo: after mixed success and failure, Armenia became a Roman protectorate. From this time on, that is, the latter half of the first century AD, it is interesting to note that the term *imperium Romanum* came into use to describe the area ruled by Rome (an extension of the original meaning of *imperium* as a magistrate's sphere of command).[12]

In place of a foreign victory, the first two Flavians contented themselves with trumpeting the suppression of the Jewish revolt. Domitian's campaigns in northern Britain penetrated deep into Scotland, as the biography of Agricola by Tacitus reveals. But warfare against the Chatti on the Rhine was imposed upon him rather than chosen. Only with Trajan was there a return to large-scale foreign conquest, in Dacia (in AD 106) and in Mesopotamia (in AD 115–17).[13] Again the latter territory was relinquished by Hadrian in AD 117 without any obvious problems. The rest of the emperors of the second century eschewed foreign conquests, apart from Lucius Verus in Parthia.

In all this activity it is very hard to find a single clear pattern. In general, and despite a tendency to move legions around a great deal for *ad hoc* reasons, especially in the first century of the Roman Empire, the Julio-Claudians attempted to keep a balance between forces stationed on the Rhine and Danube and those stationed in the East. In contrast, after the considerable changes in the disbanding and creation of legions after the civil war of AD 68–70, an increasing proportion of legions was stationed in the eastern part of the empire.[14]

On the whole, emperors campaigned when prestige was needed and didn't when it was not. In some areas on the edge of Roman influence, visible signs of Roman power were erected, of which the most notorious is Hadrian's Wall running between Wallsend-on-Tyne and Bowness-on-Solway, which was supplemented briefly in the middle of the second century by the Antonine wall to the north.[15] This particular example of vainglory was not directly imitated elsewhere. By the Rhine a series of little forts linked by a road was built along the frontier under Domitian, but in other places, particularly the eastern and African frontiers, it is easier to talk of a frontier zone than of a line: a defended line does not seem to be a standard feature of the empire in this period.[16] Up to Trajan's Dacian campaigns, the Danube had acted as an effective barrier. His campaigns were thus strategically unhelpful, but they were productive of gold from the mines as well as prestige. Campaigns against Parthia were a traditional activity inherited from the Republican period. Strabo (*Geography* 16.1.28) wrote under Augustus of the Euphrates as the boundary between Rome and Parthia, but no such notion was accepted by Nero or Trajan. On the other hand, there is no evidence that these later emperors had any clear notion of the strategic line it was desirable to reach in Mesopotamia. In practice, both frontier and spheres of influence fluctuated throughout the principate.[17]

It is probably a mistake to think of either Hadrian's Wall or the fortified roads as intended to be impregnable barriers, for both could be breached easily enough by any enemy which attacked *en masse*. These fortifications were as symbolic as the great stone walls which, from the time of Trajan, surrounded legionary camps throughout the western provinces in the empire, replacing earlier wooden barricades. No-one would be expected to attack a legionary camp, whatever its fortifications; to do so would be suicide. It is not too cynical to view the changing physical appearance in the archaeological record of the bases which housed legionary units as evidence not of any grand strategy but of the need to give bored and under-employed soldiers something to do. It would be no good for the soldiers' self-image to admit to themselves that their main function was to terrify the provincials into paying taxes, much of which ultimately went to the soldiers' own upkeep.

ADMINISTRATION

The management of the empire did not require a great many officials, because so much was done semi-willingly by the provincials themselves, or at least by the provincial aristocracy. The magistrates in local cities, tribal centres or other administrative units reorganized by the state collected the direct taxes and kept the peace. In the East, Greek cities also generally issued their own bronze coinage, in tandem with imperial issues.[18] By contrast, the civic pride of towns in the Latin West was often more nebulous, but, although in theory the relations of such communities to Rome might vary greatly, some being 'allies' or 'friends' of Rome rather than subjects, in reflection of their varied histories before the advent of Roman power, in practice they all served the state in the same way by relieving it of the need for a bureaucracy to fulfil such functions. Nonetheless, those who governed areas on behalf of Rome needed to be moderately competent and, even more important, trustworthy in the eyes of the emperor.

In the Republic the command of legionary armies had always been entrusted to senators, and this remained in general true in the Roman Empire, apart from the legions in Egypt which were commanded by a non-senator, the prefect (*praefectus Aegypti*). Restriction of command to persons of this high rank particularly helped to deal with the potentially serious problem that military careers might cease to appear attractive to politicians once the highest prizes of success had been taken from them. After 30 BC, triumphs were rarely permitted to senators apart from the emperor (after 19 BC only to members of the imperial family), and in 28 BC the special award traditionally granted to commanders who had personally killed the enemy leader in combat (the *spolia opima*) was denied to Marcus Licinius Crassus, who had achieved this bloodthirsty feat while waging war on a tribe in Macedonia. But it is evident that, despite this, a good number of individuals were prepared to opt for a career in effect as army officers, for Augustus greatly increased the number of senators required, by the introduction of a new military rank, the *legatus legionis*. One legionary legate presided over each individual legion under the overall direction of a provincial governor. Auxiliary troops, however, were commanded by non-senators, and correspondingly were less often mentioned in literary sources, despite their military significance in particular campaigns.

Below the rank of senator, emperors employed a great variety of functionaries who served in hope of advancement and pay.[19] The social rank and precise functions of these individuals are nicely disguised by the regular description of those in civilian roles as *procurator* (agent) and those in military roles as *praefectus* ('man in charge').[20] The term *procurator* could be used of any agent appointed by another person for any purpose. The term *praefectus* indicated any soldier put in temporary command of any task or group of men, although it had also been used in the Late Republic as a more regular title of the *praefectus fabrum,* who acted as a sort of second-in-command to the general.

This ambiguity and vagueness were highly useful to emperors in describing the agents who undertook tasks for them, which might range from the collection of taxes in provinces for which the emperor was responsible – a common role – to the governorship of a province (although the term *procurator* was only used for this purpose after Claudius, when, for instance, the governor of Judaea began to be described by this title), to an entirely private task of the collection of monies owed to the emperor as private landlord. The private role of procurators could be insisted on by the scrupulous, as by Tiberius in AD 23 (cf. Tacitus, *Annals* 4.15), but it gradually faded away, as the distinction between the emperor's interests and those of the state became more and more difficult to descry. In part the disappearance of the distinction was facilitated by the gradual increase in the amount of provincial land actually owned directly by the emperor through confiscations and bequests, since such imperial estates were naturally managed by the emperor's private agents, who in practice often wielded great political authority.

The term *praefectus* to indicate a formally appointed military officer was much used by Augustus, who thus described the first governor of Judaea in AD 6, and another in the Alps, but after Claudius it continued to be used of only one governor, the *praefectus* of Egypt, whose military role was particularly striking because he commanded two legions.

The whole system of appointments, both of senators and of *praefecti* and *procuratores,* was effectively designed to prevent any one individual accruing too much patronage to his own person through his position. Thus the procurator in a provincial province owed his post not to the governor (the *legatus*), but directly to the emperor, and it was to the latter that he reported back, sometimes in conflict or competition with the *legatus*. The system was not formally one of checks and balances, nor is it possible outside Egypt to show that each procurator had in general a precise sphere of operation different from that of the governor. The impression is rather of an overall bureaucracy in which everything, at least in theory, was referred back to the centre where power lay. The system was also highly flexible. Provinces moved freely from control by the *legatus* of the emperor to control by a proconsul, and special envoys of the emperor might take command of whole groups of provinces for specific campaigns; thus did Agrippa, Gaius Caesar and Corbulo in their time. The emperor stood at the head no matter what the official status of the governor. Thus he could (and did) issue *mandata* (instructions) to proconsuls as well as to his legates, in both cases often in response to requests for advice.

A good picture of the whole system can be found in Book 10 of the *Letters* of the younger Pliny, which were addressed to the emperor Trajan.[21] Pliny's status in Pontus and Bithynia was exceptional, according to an inscription set up at his birthplace Comum (Lake Como) in Italy which records him as 'legate of Augustus ... sent by the senate ... with proconsular power', and it is possible that this reflected his special tasks in a troubled province, but it is more likely that high status was intended to compensate him for his comparatively unimportant posting, which might otherwise have seemed an affront to a senator of his seniority. If the latter explanation of his title is correct, his actions as governor in his province may be taken as fairly typical of a provincial governor's work.

Pliny was probably exceptional in the triviality of the questions he asked of Trajan. On one occasion he wrote to inform Trajan:

> It is general practice for people at their coming-of-age or marriage, and on entering upon office or dedicating a public building, to issue invitations to all the local senators and even to quite a number of the common people in order to distribute presents of one or two *denarii*. I pray you to let me know how far you think this should be allowed, if at all.
>
> (*Letters* 10.116)

Trajan's reply acknowledges the fear which Pliny goes on to express, that excessive numbers of invitations might lead to corrupt practices, yet concludes:

> But I made you my choice so that you could use your good judgement in exercising a moderate influence on the behaviour of the people in your province, and could make your own decisions about what is necessary for their peace and security.
>
> (*Letters* 10.117)

However, it is only rarely in the extant correspondence that Trajan states that such trivial questions are inappropriate for a governor. On the other hand, Pliny's tendency to intervene in comparatively small matters does seem to reflect an increasing concern among governors from the Trajanic period to interfere in provincial life, often at the request of one or another of feuding provincial aristocrats.

In the final analysis it was never possible to prevent entirely the concentration of power in the hands of governors of exceptional energy and ambition. The province of Egypt, which was strategically placed for secession, and, after the mid-first century AD, for imposing grain restrictions on the city of Rome, was forbidden territory for senators throughout the imperial period. And where a single commander of a large number of legions was absolutely unavoidable, as in the preparations of large armies in campaigns against Parthia, emperors entrusted the command to long-standing friends or to relatives in the hope, not always justified, of their loyalty. When a governor could count on local support in his province because of his own origins there, danger most obviously threatened. Such was the case with the Syrian Avidius Cassius, governor of Syria and then given supreme control of the East, including Egypt. In AD 175 he revolted against Marcus Aurelius, and held Egypt and most of the eastern provinces for three months. After his defeat, a governor's holding office in his place of origin was forbidden.

CLIENT KINGS

But prevention of too much local support for a governor was only one half of the emperor's balancing act. All governors, whatever their rank and legal authority in Roman eyes, in practice depended on local co-operation for success in administering the empire. Where such co-operation was particularly hard to achieve, it would sometimes be enforced, not by appointing a senatorial or equestrian governor, but by choosing a ruler who already had influence in the region, and by giving him an extra incentive by appointing him as an independent ruler with a title of king or ethnarch or something else similarly impressive.

It has been customary in scholarship of the ancient world to look upon regions ruled by such friendly kings as though they were outside the Roman empire in some sense, and only in an alliance with the Roman state,[22] but it is preferable to see the use of 'client' kings (and, occasionally, queens) as part of provincial administration. Such monarchs were to be found in control of large areas of the empire during the triumviral period (when their rule in the East was particularly fostered by Antonius), and during the rule of Augustus - for example, Herod in Judaea. There were client rulers in Commagene, Emesa, Armenia and other places. When the Romans referred to such regions, they assumed they were within the Roman *imperium*. And so, indeed, they were, in the sense that the Romans could remove any client king whenever they wished to do so. They did so quite abruptly in some cases, such as the removal of Archelaus from Judaea in AD 6. They characteristically retained control of the replacement of client kings on the death of an incumbent. It was an act of kindness, not compulsion, for the will of the preceding ruler to be taken into consideration, although it usually was.

Some of these rulers were scions of the, or a, native dynasty which had ruled before Roman interference, though the Romans not infrequently ensured that the scion in question should be a less legitimate candidate (as in Armenia under Augustus and Nero), so that he might feel beholden to Rome. In a few cases, it was a queen who was put into power, like Cartimandua in the 50s and 60s AD in Britain, and on the occasions when the widow of a dead ruler was allowed to rule in her own right, such as Dynamis in the Bosporus (8 BC–AD 7/8) and Pythodoris in Pontus (8 BC–c. AD 23). In other cases, the ruler was appointed from an entirely new family, such as that of the Herods in Judaea. In such a case, loyalty to Rome was ensured. Hence descendants of Herod were appointed to kingdoms in Armenia Minor and a variety of other places with which they had no previous contact at all.

In other words, such client rulers were sometimes used as troubleshooters for difficult areas. They might be given, and use on inscriptions, Roman titles, as did Cottius, son of King Donnus, on an arch in the Alps, 9/8 BC:

> [Dedicated] to the Emperor Caesar Augustus, son of a god, pontifex maximus, holding the tribunician power for the fifteenth year, acclaimed imperator thirteen times, by Marcus Julius Cottius, son of King Donnus, prefect of the following tribes – Segovii, Segusini, Belacori, Caturiges, Medulli, Tebavii, Adanates, Savincates, Ecdinii, Veaminii, Venisami, Iemerii, Vesubianii, and Quadiates – and by the tribes which are under his command.
> (*CIL* V, no. 7,231; LR 1, p. 601)

The impression that these rulers were different from provincial governors of imperial provinces is none the less correct, since although client kings, like *legati*, were appointed by the direct patronage of the emperor and could similarly be dismissed at will, their right to present themselves as independent was zealously preserved. This was a necessary reward for a difficult job. After all, since most, perhaps all, client kings in the imperial period held Roman citizenship and were rich, it was open to any of them to seek power not just in a small fringe kingdom, but in the Roman senate. Client kings, as quasi-permanent rulers and, often, close associates on a social level with the emperor, could easily outrank ordinary senatorial Roman governors, leading to tension and enmity – like the rivalry in AD 44 between the legate of Syria, Vibius Marsus, and Agrippa I, ruler of Judaea and grandson of Herod the Great. On relinquishing their kingdoms, many client kings or their descendants did indeed become politicians on the Roman stage. Hence, the relatives of Gaius Julius Severus, recorded in a Greek inscription on a stone block found in Ancyra (Ankara), and inscribed under Trajan, AD 113–15:

> Gaius Julius Severus, descendant of King Deiotarus and of Amyntas the son of Brigatus and Amyntas the son of Dyrialus the tetrarchs and of King Attalus of Asia; cousin of the consulars Julius Quadratus, King Alexander, Julius Aquila and Claudius Severus; kinsman of a very large number of senators; brother of Julius Amyntianus; leading member of the Greek community; he held the high priesthood.
> (Smallwood, *Nerva-Hadrian* no. 215; Levick no. 215)

The advantages to the Roman state of the client king system were thus considerable. The disadvantages were few. It is probable that client kingdoms paid less to the imperial exchequer than directly governed provinces, and possible that they paid no levy to Rome at all, although voluntary gifts might come to mean much the same thing. But since client kings raised, paid and trained their own troops (often in Roman fashion and with Roman officers), and since their troops could then be called upon to serve in Roman campaigns as auxiliaries when required, it might seem that they performed all the necessary functions of the state by themselves.

A curious problem is thus the reason for the eventual elimination of client kingdoms. The process was gradual during the Julio-Claudian and Flavian periods. Cilicia became a province, with other parts of Asia Minor, in the 70s AD. Finally in AD 106 the Nabataean kingdom was reduced to a province: *ARABIA ADQUISITA*, as the coins later proclaimed. No precise reason for a partly *ad hoc* process is forthcoming. It was perhaps not inevitable: regions could revert to rule by a client king after having been directly ruled, as in the case of Judaea, which was ruled by Herod's son Archelaus from 4 BC to AD 6, by a Roman governor between AD 6 and AD 41, then by Herod's grandson Agrippa I until his death in AD 44. Gaius returned large tracts of land in Commagene, Pontus and Armenia Minor to the eastern princes who had been his companions in the imperial court before he become emperor. There was never any hint in Roman state sources that such reversion to rule by a friendly dynast implied any diminution of Roman power. Indeed, the opposite might be implied by the ostentatious homage of such dynasts to the emperor. On one side of a silver coin from Armenia, *c.* AD 14, is found a head of Augustus with the words, 'OF DIVINE CAESAR, BENEFACTOR', and on the other side a head of Artavasdes III, with the inscription 'OF GREAT KING ARTAVASDES' (EJ² no. 181; Braund no. 624).

BEYOND THE FRONTIERS

Archaeological evidence sheds light on the contacts between Rome and the peoples of Scotland and Ireland, who lay outside the territory directly controlled by the governor of Britain. The discovery of hoards of second- and third-century coins in the Scottish highlands reveals that the Roman administrators made frequent payments to tribal leaders to ensure their co-operation. Roman goods were regarded as prestige items among the native elites, even in Ireland, where the Romans never established a formal presence. The site of Drumanagh, near Dublin on the east coast of Ireland, seems to have functioned as a major trading depot through which items such as jewellery, pottery and glass were imported.

India was a major external trading partner, especially after the conquest of Egypt opened up access to the Red Sea, supplying products such as spices and perfumes. There were also diplomatic links, with both Augustus and Trajan receiving embassies from Indian kings. Despite being away from Roman territory, India featured prominently in imperialistic discourse, with the poet Propertius (*Elegies* 3.1.15-16) claiming that the region would one day be subject to Rome. This was in part the legacy of Alexander: the emperor Trajan is said to have stood at the Persian Gulf, wishing that he was young enough to cross to India in the manner of the Macedonian King (Dio 68.29.1).

Contact with Rome certainly influenced peoples beyond the frontiers, even if it was not systematically imposed in the way implied by the discourse of 'Romanization'. For example, the urbanization of the Garamantian peoples of the Sahara intensified in the first and second centuries AD, at the same time as they engaged in regular trade with Rome. These interactions between Rome and neighbouring peoples were facilitated by the fact that the frontier was not a closed border in the modern sense, with Roman troops often sent on missions beyond the limit of Roman authority. An ostracon (pottery sherd) from the military base at Bu Njem notes that one soldier had been 'sent with the Garamantes', while another records the Garamantes bringing letters to the Roman commander (*O. Bu Njem* 28, 71). Silver plate found in Mtshketa, the capital of the ancient state of Iberia in the eastern half of modern Georgia, reflects Roman diplomatic gifts to the region which began in the time of Augustus and continued throughout the early imperial period.[23]

11

THE ARMY IN SOCIETY

PROFESSIONAL SOLDIERS

In the Republic, military service had been a temporary break for soldiers from their normal life as peasants. Even when campaigns were extended over a number of years during the first century BC, most legionaries were conscripted more or less involuntarily, and assumed and hoped that they would return in time to a civilian existence. But from the time of Augustus onwards, from first enlistment many men spent their entire lives as professional soldiers, seeing in their comrades-in-arms their own social framework and the friends with whom they chose to retire when too old to fight.[1]

Augustus fixed the period of service at first at 16 years with a further four in the reserves, but in AD 5 he increased the requirement to 20 years with probably at least five in reserve. The increase seems to stem from his difficulties in raising funds to pay off those soldiers who survived to honourable retirement, until the institution in AD 6 of a special fund for the purpose (the *aerarium militare*), revenues for which were guaranteed by two new taxes. The legal fiction, probably introduced by Augustus, by which legionaries could not contract a valid marriage while under the standards, encouraged an even more extreme development of this society within a society. The male offspring of the *de facto* marriages which naturally occurred tended themselves to enlist in the legions in which they had been raised, so that military service became almost the inherited preserve of a caste. From the time of Hadrian, soldiers, their partners and children behaved just like traditional families, as can be seen from a letter of Hadrian to Rammius, the Prefect of Egypt, in AD 119, a copy of which is preserved on papyrus:

> I am aware, my dear Rammius, that those whom their parents acknowledged as their offspring during their period of military service have been debarred from succession to their paternal property, and this was not considered harsh, since the parents had acted contrary to military discipline. But for my own part I am very glad to introduce a precedent for interpreting more liberally the quite stern rule established by the emperors before me. Therefore, whereas offspring acknowledged during the period of military service are not legal heirs of their fathers, nevertheless I rule that

they, too, can claim possession of property in accordance with that part of the edict by which this right is given also to blood relatives.
(*Select Papyri* no. 213; LR 2, pp. 480–81)

It was possible to be born into military life and never leave its confines.

An insight into such domesticity in the military sphere is made possible through the writing tablets found at Vindolanda, a fort near Hadrian's Wall (see Figure 15).[2] For example, still surviving is some of the correspondence conducted by Sulpicia Lepidina, wife of Flavius Cerialis, prefect of the Ninth Cohort of the Batavians, stationed on the wall *c.* AD 97–102/3 (the laws forbidding marriage did not apply to senior officers of equestrian rank). In one letter, Sulpicia Lepidina and her husband are invited to a birthday party:

> Claudia Severa to her Lepidina greetings. On 11 September, sister, for the day of the celebration of my birthday, I give you a warm invitation to make sure that you come to us, to make the day more enjoyable for me by your arrival, if you are present (?). Give my greetings to your Cerialis. My Aelius and my little son send him (?) their greetings. I shall expect you, sister. Farewell, sister, my dearest soul, as I hope to prosper, and hail. To Sulpicia Lepidina, wife of Cerialis, from Severa.
> (*Tab. Vindol. II*, no. 291)

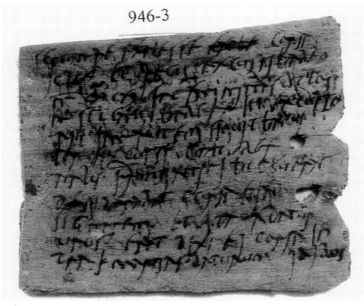

Figure 15 Wooden writing tablet from Vindolanda (*Tab. Vindol.* II no. 343), part of a letter consisting of four such tablets folded together (late first or very early second century AD). The letter, from a centurion Octavius to Candidus 'his brother', deals with the supply of goods in a military context on a large scale. Wooden tablets seem to have provided a common material for writing in the absence of papyrus. Photo courtesy of Alison Rutherford and the Vindolanda Trust.

The pride of Roman soldiers in their institutions should not be underestimated.[3] Continuity of legionary personality permitted legionaries of the High Empire to claim as their own the achievements of their regiment back in the time of Caesar and Pompeius. The legions still looked much the same, although the characteristic uniform of the Late Republic was subtly modernized: of the oval shield, throwing javelin, short sword, dagger, bronze helmet and chain mail of the Late Republic, only the shield was changed (to a rectangular shape, either flat or concave), and the chain mail mostly replaced by iron strips sewn onto leather (*lorica segmentata*), although there may have been variations between provinces. Continuity of identity of auxiliary units was achieved in some cases by the continued use of national fighting methods, like those of the oriental archer cohorts with their conical helmets, shirt mail and flowing robes, but gradually during the Early Empire much of the auxiliary infantry came to look and fight much like the legionaries. Although auxiliary cavalry remained in use, and distinctive, with their long slashing swords and spears, the specialized units of slingers and elephant riders found in the Late Republic fell out of fashion. Nonetheless, the history of many auxiliary units, as of legions, can be traced over many decades, and often over centuries. The impact on regimental pride of the only period of major upheaval in the creation and abolition of military units between Augustus and Commodus – that is, the civil war of AD 68–69 and its aftermath – was correspondingly great; the effects of other institutional changes in this period, such as the reorganization of auxiliary units stationed in the provinces of Egypt, Judaea and Syria, known through the evidence of military *diplomata*, is harder to gauge.[4]

MILITARY LIFE AND PAY

On campaign Roman soldiers prided themselves, not always with justice, on their efficiency and discipline. Evidence of these virtues in practice can be found in the stylized depiction of battles by Tacitus and other annalists, and in the detailed description of Roman techniques in setting up a camp, its daily routine, and final striking, given by Josephus (*The Jewish War* 3.76–93). This is his admiring account of daily life in camp:

> Once entrenched, the soldiers take up their quarters in the tents by companies, quietly and in good order. All their fatigue duties are performed with the same discipline, the same regard for security: the procuring of wood, food-supplies, and water, as required – each party has its allotted task. The hour for supper and breakfast is not left to individual discretion: all their meals are taken together. The hours for sleep, sentinel duty, and rising are announced by the sound of the trumpet; nothing is done without a word of command. At daybreak the rank and file report to their respective centurions, the centurions go to salute the tribunes, the tribunes with all the officers then wait on the commander-in-chief, and he gives them, according to custom, the watchword and other orders to be communicated to the lower ranks. The same precision is maintained on the battlefield.
>
> (*The Jewish War* 3.85–88)

However, some of Josephus' material was borrowed from Polybius and military handbooks, and is thus of questionable relevance for his own time. Also useful, but theoretical, is the treatise composed in the reign of Domitian by the senator Frontinus, *On Stratagems*.

Despite military rhetoric, examples of the application of extreme discipline are rare after the triumviral period, when Domitius Calvinus in 39 BC, Antonius in 36 BC, and Octavian in 34 BC all punished disobedient units with decimation, the process by which soldiers purged the guilt of mutiny by killing every tenth man of their number, the victim chosen by lot and executed by his colleagues. During the principate the harsh imposition of discipline was a rare occurrence, noted for instance at the start of Corbulo's campaign in Syria:

> Corbulo found his own men's slackness a worse trouble than enemy treachery. ... The whole army was kept under canvas through a winter so severe that ice had to be removed and the ground excavated before tents could be pitched. Frostbite caused many losses of limb. Sentries were frozen to death. ... Corbulo himself, thinly dressed and bare-headed, moved among his men at work and on the march, encouraging the sick and praising efficiency – an example to all.
> (Tacitus, *Annals* 13.35)

For most of the time, military life was not necessarily unpleasant. The obvious dangers of a soldier's career, death or injury in battle, were a distant risk for much of the Early and High Empire, particularly for legionaries. According to Tacitus (*Agricola* 35.2), his father-in-law Agricola was particularly proud to have won a great victory at Mons Graupius in the Scottish Highlands with the use of auxiliaries alone, so that no Roman blood had been shed. Most soldiers never fought in battle. When they did, the enemy was almost always chosen by the Roman commander as a reasonably easy opponent. Casualties in ancient battles were characteristically very heavy for the defeated but light for the victor, since it was in retreat that infantrymen were most vulnerable. It may be estimated that a soldier had only a one in a thousand chance of losing his life in war between 31 BC and AD 180, if the casualties of the civil war of AD 68–69 are ignored.[5]

Nor for most soldiers was life unpleasantly disjointed by arbitrary postings. Under Augustus and Tiberius, some legions were transferred for one reason or another from the Rhine frontier to the East or elsewhere, and throughout the principate it continued to be common for small units to be detailed from their legions for special purposes, which might sometimes be of quite long duration. But it gradually became normal during the first century AD for legions to stay in one place for many years. Most strikingly, legion III Augusta remained in Africa from 31 BC to AD 238, rarely undertaking anything more than police duty.

In some western provinces, such stability encouraged soldiers to turn their barracks into something resembling separate towns. This is most clearly visible in the stone-built forts which became standard under Hadrian, with especially provided baths and entertainment facilities erected at the expense of the state. In the East, the same effect was achieved by troops being stationed within existing towns. Thus at Dura-Europus on the middle Euphrates in Syria, in the late second century AD, there is good evidence for close contact between army and town, with soldiers involved in building the baths, an amphitheatre and a temple of Mithras.[6]

The illegitimate status of soldiers' marriages in Roman law did not discourage a domestic lifestyle. According to Tacitus (*Histories* 2.80.5), writing of AD 69, the soldiers of the Syrian legions enjoyed a pleasant and easy life-style:

> The provincials were accustomed to live with the soldiers, and enjoyed association with them; in fact, many civilians were bound to the soldiers by ties of friendship and marriage, and the soldiers from their long service had come to love their old familiar camps as their very hearths and homes.

It is dubious whether common-law wives stayed permanently within the camp, more probable that they set up home outside. Such a breakdown in discipline was still being deplored in the mid-second century AD, in a letter written by Fronto to Lucius Verus in AD 165:

> So by long unfamiliarity with fighting the Roman soldier was reduced to a cowardly condition. For as to all the arts of life, so especially to the business of war, is sloth fatal. It is of the greatest importance also for soldiers to experience the ups and downs of fortune, and to take strenuous exercise in the open. The most demoralized of all, however, were the Syrian soldiers, mutinous, disobedient, seldom with their units, straying in front of their prescribed posts, roving about like scouts, tipsy from one noon to the next, unused even to carrying their arms.
>
> (*Preamble to History* 11–12)

Above all, soldiers could rely on a regular income which was considerably above a standard peasant wage, and irregularly but frequently supplemented by donations handed out in celebration of imperial accessions or birthdays, or other similar occasions which gave excuse for bribery to ensure the soldiers' loyalty, as was noted cynically by Suetonius (*Claudius* 10.4): 'Claudius promised 15,000 sesterces to each man, the first of the Caesars to secure the fidelity of the soldiery by bribery.' At the beginning of the Roman Empire, the standard annual pay for legionaries was 900 sesterces (with stoppages for food and other necessities) and 1,200 from Domitian's time on. In all probability, the auxiliaries were paid on the same scale. For the legionaries, the main financial incentive apart from donatives was the lump sum of 12,000 sesterces (some 14 years' pay), or an equivalent amount of land in full or part payment, awarded on retirement to those who survived to the end of a military career.[7] For auxiliaries, the expectation on retirement was receipt of Roman citizenship and other privileges, although a proper system of a standard term of 25 years' service, with the issue of a *diploma* on retirement as evidence of citizenship, is known only from the time of Claudius.[8] A *diploma* issued in Nero's name on 2 July AD 60, and found in Vindobona, Pannonia, makes the following grants:

> to the infantry and cavalry who served in the seven cohorts ... and are in Illyricum under Lucius Salvidienus Salvianus Rufus, who have each served twenty-five years or more, their names being written below, to these men themselves, to their children and descendants he has given citizenship and *conubium* [legal marriage] with the wives they had on receipt of citizenship, or, if they were bachelors, with wives they married afterwards, provided that one man had one wife.
> (Smallwood, *Gaius-Nero* no. 296; Braund no. 532)

The majority of military *diplomata* record that auxiliaries received the right, after their service, of marriage with their wives and citizenship for their children, but a *diploma* dating to the reign of Hadrian extended citizenship to auxiliaries still in service, as well as their parents and siblings (*AE* 2003, no. 2059). Evidently there was much flexibility in the system of military awards, although after the reign of Antoninus Pius, grants of citizenship to the existing children of auxiliaries seem to have been restricted to a small number of special groups, such as sailors (*AE* 2001, no. 2156).

Stability and a sense of belonging were strengthened in this bourgeois army society by a paraphernalia of customs to emphasize corporate spirit within each legion and (to a lesser extent) each auxiliary cohort. Most obvious is the loyalty expressed to the legionary name and to the standard, before which sacrifices to the emperor and the other gods were regularly made. Military religious life was consolidated by a mass of rituals on most days, as is revealed by the religious calendar found recorded on a papyrus of *c.* AD 225–27 at Dura-Europus. It belonged to an auxiliary unit, the Twentieth Cohort of Palmyrenes, but was apparently standard for army use.[9] At the same time this was a highly ordered society in which, as in most armies, subtle gradations of rank meant a great deal. A soldier's status as *beneficiarius* (assistant to a tribune or prefect) or *cornicularius* (in charge of an officer's personal staff), and so on, are all proudly proclaimed on many thousands of inscriptions. One inscription found at Ariminum (modern Rimini), dating from AD 66, records a successful career path which culminated in the holding of equestrian posts:

> To Marcus Vettius Valens, son of Marcus, of the tribe Aniensis, soldier of praetorian cohort 8, *beneficiarius* of the praetorian prefect, awarded gifts in the British war, torcs, arm-bands, discs, ordered out by Augustus, awarded a gold crown, centurion of cohort 6 of the watch, centurion of messengers, centurion of urban cohort 16, centurion of praetorian cohort 2, driller of cavalry-scouts, headquarters first-officer of legion 13 Gemina from being scout-centurion, chief centurion of legion 6 Victrix, awarded gifts for successful achievements against the Astures, torcs, discs, arm-bands, tribune of cohort 5 of the watch, tribune of urban cohort 12, tribune of praetorian cohort 3, tribune of legion 14 Gemina Mars Victrix, procurator of Imperator Nero Caesar Augustus of the province of Lusitania, patron of the colony, scouts established this in the consulship of Lucius Luccius Telesinus and Gaius Suetonius Paulinus.
> (Smallwood, *Gaius-Nero* no. 283; Braund no. 518)

For the ambitious, army life provided an opportunity for social advancement simply by personal qualities. It was an opportunity much greater than that available to most in the outside world. The majority of centurions rose from the ranks. A proportion of the lucky few who reached the highest centurion post of *primus pilus*, the most senior of the 60 centurions in their legion, had a reasonable expectation of further promotion to *praefectus castrorum* (camp prefect). An especially talented *primus pilus* could become a *tribunus militum* (military tribune), effectively the first of the ranks of, in British terms, commissioned officers, which elevated him to the equestrian order and made a procuratorship a final possibility. But most of the tribunes of the legion would be young members of well-born and wealthy families, who accepted appointment to the post as the way to gain necessary military experience before embarking on a political career: one of the posts was usually held by a young senator, and the other five by equites who could hope to end a successful career as a procurator. Nonetheless, the army's recognition of merit, as well as wealth and status, meant that each soldier had a Field Marshal's baton in his knapsack, or could dream of it.

In the auxiliary units, the commanders under the Julio-Claudian emperors were generally the tribal nobility to whom the soldiers looked as their natural leaders, but after AD 70, and the rising led by the Batavian Julius Civilis, such links were decisively broken.[10]

The possibility of social self-advancement was one of the main lures of army service for young men outside Italy, at first as auxiliaries, since in the time of Augustus most legionaries still came from Italy, but by the mid-first century AD often as legionaries, as the Roman citizenship needed to become a legionary spread beyond Italy. The proportion of legionaries from other areas of the empire grew rapidly during the first century, and by the second century Italians were a rarity. The regions most strongly represented were Gaul, Spain and the Balkans. Few Greeks signed up, and in Asia Minor it was only the Galatian Celts and the inhabitants of Rough Cilicia who were much attracted. Syrians joined up, but few, if any, Jews. Egyptians were mostly precluded before the third century because they were excluded from Roman citizenship. Africans joined during the second century AD. Evidence for enthusiasm for military service by particular groups at certain times should not disguise the fact that some, perhaps many, soldiers in the principate were conscripts (cf. Pliny, *Letters* 10.30), although many others were volunteers. In time of crisis, conscripts could always be culled from the ranks of freed slaves, purchased by the state for this purpose as, for instance, in 37 BC for Agrippa's fleet or in AD 7 for the army in Germany.[11]

Both auxiliaries and legionaries in the Julio-Claudian period tended to be stationed within the areas from which they were recruited, but this practice was discontinued after AD 70 – hence the Syrians who were stationed on Hadrian's Wall and the Dacian auxiliary stationed at the fort of Krokodilo in Egypt with whom, according to the text on an ostracon from the site, a local prostitute fell in love[12] – only for local recruitment to creep back into practice during the second century. But it would be misleading to think of these soldiers stationed in their area of origin as a sort of citizens' militia unit. Those who joined up in the army had mostly, in a sense, left their civilian origins behind them. They did not usually represent the communities from which they sprang. The exceptions prove the rule: the Pannonian revolt in AD 6 was begun by Dalmatian auxiliaries who had been recruited by Rome to fight against Maroboduus, but preferred to fight against Rome for their own freedom.

By the second century AD the practical distinction between legionary and auxiliary services was minimal. The division into citizen and non-citizen troops was increasingly otiose with the spread of citizenship. In any case, auxiliary cohorts of Roman citizens – probably freed slaves – had been created in AD 6–9. The difference became increasingly one of physique and fighting ability, so that the legionaries became, in effect, the military élite.

For some soldiers, although not all, the comfort of mess society could be retained even after discharge. Under Augustus and the Julio-Claudians, it was quite common for veterans to be settled in special *coloniae* intended to act as bastions of the Roman state in potentially hostile territory.[13] As became clear in Boudicca's sack of Camulodunum (modern Colchester) in AD 60, such veterans could do nothing in the face of full-scale revolt, but in areas where a compliant local élite was lacking they could easily be prevailed upon to take over responsibility for tax collection as a sort of instant provincial aristocracy. The rapid foundation of many such colonies under Augustus, which included Berytus (now Beirut) and Carthage, slowed down considerably in the rest of the first century AD. As Roman citizenship became a more common attribute of provincial aristocrats, the *coloniae* tended to be no more than renamed cities and towns granted the honour by the emperor. By contrast, in veteran colonies, a military ethos and status distinctions remained paramount.

SOLDIERS AND CIVILIANS

Not surprisingly, the relationship between the soldiers and the civilians amongst whom they lived was not always easy, as in the brutal events surrounding the recent foundation of Camulodunum in AD 60, described by Tacitus:

> [The veterans] had recently been established in the colony at Camulodunum and were driving the 'prisoners and slaves' from their homes, expropriating their farms. The soldiers encouraged the lawlessness of their former comrades: they lived the same kind of life and hoped to be given the same free rein. Besides, the temple set up in honour of Claudius was seen as a citadel of a tyranny that was to have no end. (*Annals* 14.31.3–4)

Soldiers enjoyed privileged access to the provincial governor and ultimately to the emperor, neither of whom could afford to neglect their interests. The power they thus enjoyed set them apart from, and sometimes at variance with, the local people in the places where they were stationed.

Civilian hostility was usually directed to soldiers' arrogance and unaccountability. Thus Juvenal's *Satire* 16 contains a bitter attack on the violence, rapacity and greed of soldiers in Rome. Apuleius (*The Golden Ass* 9.39–10.1) narrated an evidently plausible story of the commandeering of the ass by a soldier for his own purpose. Civilians had little power to retort, since the main civilian judge in private law suits in the provinces was usually the governor, who was also the commander of the troops in the province and liable to take their side. The presence of soldiers in peace time, particularly if they passed through on campaign or manoeuvres and needed to forage, could be a disaster hardly less than war itself. Marcus Petronius Mamertinus, prefect of Egypt, admitted as much in a letter written between AD 133 and 137:

> I am informed that without having a permit many of the soldiers when travelling through the country requisition boats and animals and persons improperly, in some cases seizing them by force, in others obtaining them from the *strategi* [governors of administrative districts] through favour or obsequiousness, the result of which is that private persons are subjected to insults and abuses and the army is reproached for greed and injustice.
>
> (*Select Papyri* no. 221; LR 2, pp. 321–22)

In some provinces, soldiers behaved in effect like an occupying army for the permanent suppression of continuing disaffection (see Chapter 16).

On the other hand, some civilians became adept at harnessing the same power and influence to their own ends. The *canabae* (settlements) that sprang up around legionary camps in the West extracted great economic benefit from the regular income of the military.[14] A good description of such a settlement is given by Arrian when, as provincial governor, he inspected the auxiliary fort at Phasis on his tour of the Black Sea area in AD 132–33:

> The fort, in which four hundred select men are stationed, seems to me very strong by situation, and conveniently situated for the protection of those who sail upon the river. It was surrounded with a ditch and a double wall, each of them very broad. ... But as it is advisable that the port should be rendered safe for seafaring people, and that other places should be secured which lie without the walls of the fort, and are inhabited by people who are now exempted from military service, or by people engaged in commerce, I thought it proper to carry from the double ditch, that surrounds the wall, another ditch, as far as the river, which may include both the harbour, and the buildings, that lie beyond the walls of the fortification.
>
> (*Periplus of the Black Sea* 9)

Rich veterans, who retained the ear of the powerful in the state, became much sought-after patrons both for provincial and Italian communities, honoured for the services they could render. Hence the pride enshrined in an inscription from Matilica in Umbria:

To Gaius Arrius Clemens: private soldier in the Ninth Cohort of the Praetorian Guard; mounted trooper in the same Cohort; decorated by the Emperor Trajan with the Twisted Necklets, Armbands and Chest-pieces for service in the Dacian War; aide to the prefects of the Praetorian Guard; detailed to charge of the watchword; candidate for the centurionate; officer in charge of the pay chest; clerk to the military tribune; recalled for service as a veteran; centurion of the First Cohort of Watchmen; of the Imperial Messengers; of the Fourteenth Urban Cohort; of the Seventh Cohort of the Praetorian Guard; officer on special duties; decorated by the Emperor Hadrian with the Untipped Spear and the Golden Crown; centurion of the Third, Augustan, Legion; leading centurion; quinquennial duovir; patron of the municipality; curator of the community. The members of the city council, the Augustales members of the board of six, and the citizens of the municipality of Matilica [set this up].

(Smallwood, *Nerva-Hadrian* no. 300; Levick no. 145)

1 2

THE IMAGE OF THE EMPEROR

Most Roman emperors went to great lengths to disguise the obviousness of their reliance on naked military force for their retention of power. Among the political élite in Rome, this sometimes entailed portraying themselves as equal in status to other senatorial aristocrats, superior only by virtue of the prestige freely bestowed upon them by the people in recognition of the excellence of their qualities. But at other times in their relations with senators, and quite generally in their relations with their other subjects, especially in the provinces, it entailed the portrayal of themselves as more than mortal.[1]

AUGUSTUS: THE MODEL EMPEROR

When Octavian achieved sole control over the Roman world after Actium in 31 BC it was patent to all that his success was due to the ruthless manipulation of a huge fighting machine in the preceding ten years. To disguise such a fact was neither possible nor wholly desirable: the memory of the past would deter future challengers. For maintenance of control no constitutional change whatsoever was needed – after all, in 30 BC the whole of Italy was controlled on Octavian's behalf by Maecenas, who had no formal authority at all and was not even a senator. But it was possible to choose, more negatively, not to emphasize the crudity of the power struggle: not to mask power, but to legitimize it. In 25 BC Augustus, as he now was, issued a justification of his actions in his *Life*, now no longer extant. But in the meantime he gradually established a new image for himself in which no hint of violence, or any need for violence, could be glimpsed.

In 27 BC Octavian formally laid down his powers and returned the state (*res publica*) to the senate and people of Rome.[2] Octavian was showered with symbolic honours, which were widely advertised on the imperial coinage, from the oak-wreath, which declared that he had saved the lives of fellow-citizens, to the impressive name Augustus, which he appended to his existing name as proudly and consistently as Pompeius had used his name Magnus (see Figure 16). Since, at the same meeting of the senate in January 27 BC, Octavian was granted a command for ten years in Gaul, Spain, Syria and

Figure 16 Golden aureus minted in Spain in c. 19–18 BC. The obverse reads simply *Caesar Augustus*; the significance of Octavian's new title was so widely advertised that no more needed to be stated. The reverse depicts the oak-wreath given to Augustus in 27 BC with three words to explain the symbolism: 'On account of citizens saved'.
Photo courtesy of CNG Coins.

Egypt, and a huge number of legions to aid him in the task, the episode in no way diminished his actual power. What then was the significance of this dramatic act? In Augustus' self-portrayal in the *Res Gestae*, published on his death in AD 14, these events still loom large. But what did he reckon that he had done?

In constitutional terms, the need for a momentous occasion of some kind was probably required because of the terms of the *lex Titia*, under which in 43 BC the triumvirs, Antonius, Lepidus and Octavian, had been appointed to supreme control over the Roman state *ad rem publicam constituendam* (to set up the state). For that purpose the three men had full rights to appoint and dismiss as they saw fit all the magistrates and pro-magistrates (those who governed provinces or otherwise acted with the power of magistrates without actually holding a magistracy at the time). The granting of such powers was originally for five years, but none of the three saw it as necessary to lay down their commands when the time expired in December 38 BC, and in the spring of 37 BC their positions were prolonged for a further five years, made retrospective to January in order to legalize their decisions taken in the interim.[3] It must be presumed that in the first half of the year all the triumvirs based their authority on the undeniable fact that their task was not yet complete: the state had not yet been set back on its feet. What was true in the first half of 37 BC was presumably also true after Actium, except that now only one of the triumvirs was left to proclaim *res publica restituta* (the restoration of the state) and mark the end of the emergency period when magistrates had been appointed rather than elected, and the normal operations of the state had been in abeyance.

But if that was the issue in January 27 BC, why did Octavian not say so outright? An answer is not hard to find. In the campaign before Actium, Antonius' coins had proclaimed him vociferously as triumvir – again, incidentally, after the expiry of the five-year term voted in 37 BC. But Octavian's propaganda made no mention of the post. A triumvirate implied three people. Legitimacy earned by that title reflected equally on the other two holders of the post. It was not a legitimacy that Octavian, who had ousted the one and killed the other, was willing to confer.

January 27 BC thus marked a much-heralded return to political normality of a sort. Already in 29 BC Octavian had appeared in contemporary documents boasting the title of consul.[4] Now as Augustus he proclaimed with enthusiasm that the old political language of the Roman state would always suffice. If he was to remain pre-eminent in the state, it would not be through any formal position but because of his *auctoritas* (influence). His fellow-senators would do his bidding because they freely chose to do so, in exchange for his benevolent patronage and to boost their careers. This was the assumption that underlay the whole constitutional image of the emperor for the next two centuries. The emperor was no autocrat, he did not need to be. As first among equals – the princeps or leading man of the state – his wishes were followed because the senate and people thought them wise and him deserving. Such an image was not easy to sustain.

Actual challenges to the emperor's power were consistently met with force rather than recourse to the will of the people, and each use of force dented the picture of benevolent rule, freely accepted. A few emperors lacked patience or interest in the preservation of their image, which they perceived, in some ways rightly, as almost an irrelevant distraction from their enjoyment of despotism. Emperors like these were consistently denigrated as tyrants in the literary sources. Such was the judgement of Suetonius and Tacitus on Gaius and Domitian, who demanded that their fellow-senators treat them not as powerful friends but as divine masters. As Suetonius wrote:

> Gaius, on being reminded once that he had surpassed the heights both of princes and of kings, began from that time on to lay claim to divine majesty for himself. He made it his business to have statues of the gods which were famous for the reverence attached to them or for their artistic merit, including the Olympian Zeus, brought from Greece, so as to remove their heads and replace them with his own. … He also set up a separate temple to his own godhead, with priests and with sacrificial victims of the choicest kind. In this temple stood a golden life-size statue [of Gaius], and it was dressed each day in clothing such as he himself wore.
> (*Gaius* 22)

But such denigration of those who failed to sustain the image in many ways points up in contrast the great success of the majority of emperors in upholding the principle established, by example, by Augustus. All the authors whose disapproval is recorded did, after all, write under other different emperors who were glad to have their enlightened rule 'by universal consent' contrasted to the iniquities of their predecessors. Much of this success was due to the willing connivance in deception by the senators themselves, a self-deception quite soundly based. But it is also rash to underestimate the effort put into image-building by emperors from Augustus onwards.

The first major challenge to Augustus' image came within four or five years of the great propaganda effort of 27 BC. The restoration of free elections to the Roman people naturally left Augustus just as much in the public eye as before the Republic had been restored. He was elected consul each year to 23 BC, owing his popularity not least to his competence in ensuring the corn supply to the city. But as consul he was naturally required to share power equally with his fellow incumbent, and after 23 BC he avoided embarrassment by holding the post only rarely, and then only with a member of his family or a close personal friend.

Such a solution might have severely damaged the image which Augustus had been at such pains to create, that of a senator on equal terms with others. Over the next few years Augustus therefore gradually had himself elected to a variety of positions which between them would permit him legally to take such action as he desired without requiring his direct intervention or making him the direct and precisely equal colleague of anyone.[5]

In 22 BC Augustus refused the offer of the title of *dictator* and a perpetual consulship. The dissatisfaction of the Roman plebs in the city of Rome with this refusal was all to the emperor's advantage. Their attempts to elect him despite his reluctance in 22, 21 and 20 BC may even have been engineered. In any case, their dissatisfaction was effectively stilled by Augustus' acceptance in 22 BC, at a time of shortage, of a long-term responsibility for the corn supply (*cura annonae*), which he exercised by appointing a board of prefects (and, later, an eques) to perform the task on his behalf. In the meantime Augustus retained, under a series of grants, each for periods of five years, command of a huge *provincia* (administrative area) with the *imperium* (power) of a proconsul. Like Pompeius Magnus in 52 BC he also retained the right to hold his command while himself in Rome, ruling the provinces through legates chosen by himself. The life-long grant of *tribunicia potestas* (tribunician power) permitted him to summon the senate and to introduce legislation.

By 19 BC Augustus' accumulation of rights and positions was sufficient to ensure that a repetition of the embarrassment, even perhaps danger, of 22 BC would be always avoided. He enjoyed *imperium proconsulare maius* (for the rest of his life), which gave him the formal right to intervene in provinces not specifically assigned to him when this was to the advantage of the Roman people. In 36 BC he had been granted the sacrosanctity of a tribune, which made an assault on his person technically equivalent in Roman law to an assault on the Roman plebs as a whole. Already in 30 BC he was given some tribunician power, but from 23 BC he held the power of tribune for life, which gave him the indefinite right to veto all legislation proposed by other tribunes, thereby effectively rendering the office of tribune of the plebs so useless for other senators that it rapidly became quite hard to find candidates to fill what had once been a most desirable stepping stone for an ambitious young noble.

From about 18 BC, the years of Augustus' tribunician power began to be used throughout the empire as a useful means of marking the date, and this became a standard method for later emperors to signify regnal years. The accumulation of roles left Augustus legally unable to undertake only one desirable act that might perhaps be of use to him, namely to address the senate first, before the consuls. This problem was easily rectified: in 23 BC the people voted to him a *ius primae relationis*, the right to be the first speaker to the senate, in order to fill the gap. He was also permitted to address the senate by letter and, probably, to hold the insignia of a consul even when not occupying that office.[6]

This jumble of legal powers gathered by Augustus proved so effective that each emperor after him ensured his election to precisely the same combination. By AD 69 the process was entirely formal, and the whole parcel of rights was voted to Vespasian *en bloc* in the *lex de imperio Vespasiani*, found inscribed on a bronze tablet at Rome.[7] To take one clause at random, it was enacted:

> that he shall have the right, just as the deified Augustus and Tiberius Julius Caesar Augustus and Tiberius Claudius Caesar Augustus Germanicus had, to convene the senate, to put and refer proposals to it, and to cause decrees of the senate to be enacted by proposal and division of the house.

For Cassius Dio (*History of Rome* 53.28.2 and 54.10.5–7), writing about Augustus' rule in the early third century AD, it seemed that the emperor had in 24 BC been released from all compulsion by the law, and in 19 BC been established as the supreme authority to enact laws and supervise the morals of the Roman people. By his day it was indeed true that emperors behaved openly in this way. But the careful phrasing of Augustus' *Res Gestae* shows that this was precisely the image that the founder of the principate did not want to present.

More optional for later emperors were the titles and honours bestowed on emperors by a grateful state. The summit of Augustus' achievement as portrayed in *Res Gestae* 35 was the conferment on him, in 2 BC, of the title *pater patriae* (father of his country), which had once been enjoyed by Cicero. Most later emperors were aware of the need not to cheapen the coinage of such honorary titles, and graciously accepted both that and similar marks of respect only sparingly.

The great care spent by emperors in building up their image as Roman nobles in the Republican tradition, as upholders of Roman morals and law and heroic victors on behalf of the state against foreign enemies, was not prompted either by sentiment or by fear, for power rested ultimately not on image but on troops. It was prompted by common sense. It was possible for an emperor to preclude senatorial opposition to a limited extent simply by weeding out the disgruntled. But acquiescence in autocracy did not suffice. The emperors, who needed troops to maintain their power, needed equally trustworthy and competent army commanders to lead those troops into battle.

The gravest danger for the emperor derived from the fact that he now monopolized the glory to be won from victory. The last non-imperial triumph took place in 19 BC. The danger was that the attractions of a military career would disappear altogether for other senators, and the emperor would be left unable to exercise his military might because he had no generals. It was therefore crucial to uphold, and indeed to enhance, the prestige of an officer élite, which might as well continue with the Republican tradition of being called senators, in order to encourage energetic young men both of aristocratic and 'new' blood to devote their lives to Rome's wars. It was as much in the emperor's interests that senators should maintain their dignity as it was in theirs. Thus emperors *looked* like senators in their everyday business. The court was a standard Roman family house, writ (very) large. Behaviour at the court followed normal senatorial custom, without any special elaborate rituals.

This image of the emperor as a great Roman noble was in no way played down in his projection of himself to the plebs of Rome and to the provincials who comprised the mass of his subjects. After all, the *congiaria* (gifts of money) about which Augustus so proudly boasted in his *Res Gestae* 15.1–3 will have been of most interest to the former group:

> To the Roman plebs I paid 300 sesterces apiece in accordance with the will of my father; and in my fifth consulship I gave each 400 sesterces in my own name out of the spoils of war; and a second time in my tenth consulship I paid out of my own patrimony a largesse of 400 sesterces to every individual; in my eleventh consulship I made twelve distributions of food out of grain purchased at my own expense; and in the twelfth year of my tribunician power for the third time I gave 400 sesterces to every individual. These largesses of mine reached never less than 250,000 persons. In the eighteenth year of my tribunician power and my twelfth consulship I gave sixty denarii to each of 320,000 persons of the urban plebs.

The survival of copies of the same document in far-flung parts of the empire suggests that provincials too were expected to be in some way impressed.

The role of the emperor as a unifying figure is undoubted, but quite how the process operated has generated considerable scholarly debate. In his role as *pater patriae*, he functioned as a universal patron of the empire and its inhabitants. Inscriptions erected in provincial communities praised the emperor for his *indulgentia* (kindness) and *liberalitas* (generosity) in the remission of tax burdens or assistance in the construction of public works. The inhabitants of Forum Claudii in Etruria honoured emperor Trajan as the 'most kind emperor' (*indulgentissimus princeps*) because he provided the funds for an aqueduct (*CIL* XI 3309). What is less certain is the extent to which provincials colluded in acceptance of this image, creating a sort of consensus about the validity of imperial rule (see below, Chapter 12).

There is some evidence that the imperial image could be manipulated to appeal to different audiences. The Greek version of Augustus' *Res Gestae*, which was erected at Pisidian Antioch and Apollonia, shows subtle but perceptible differences to the Latin original, sometimes explaining unfamiliar

Roman institutions, and, on other occasions, playing down imperialist or triumphal messages which may have rankled with a provincial audience. Some scholars have proposed that different denominations of coinage could be used to target specific groups – for instance by featuring, on gold coinage, iconography and messages that would appeal to the aristocracy, but on bronzes, ideals that would resonate with the populace at large. (For example, the Colosseum is never represented on the higher denominations). There are methodological considerations to bear in mind here, however, most notably that fact that the larger bronze denominations could feature more intricate designs than the smaller *aurei*.

Statues of the emperor and his family would have been present across the Roman world – a recent estimate suggests that there were between 25,000-50,000 images of Augustus throughout the empire. But it is important to remember that these statues were not all produced in Rome by the central administration. Instead, prototype images were sent to the provinces, where they were copied by artisans and sculptors and bought by the local inhabitants. The fact that there was a market for such statues and portraits suggests that the provincials were enthusiastic consumers of this imagery, illustrating the key role they played in validating imperial rule.

Nonetheless, the emperor's senatorial image was primarily aimed at senators and those with the capacity to become such. For the Roman poor and the provincials, the political system of the Republic had led to suffering and devastation in the civil wars, and the announcement of its restoration would have evoked no great enthusiasm. For them, therefore, the image of the emperor as princeps was allied to a strikingly contrasting image of the emperor as divine.

THE EMPEROR AS A GOD

The notion that a ruler might be a god was by no means as curious to Romans as might have been expected.[9] After the death of Julius Caesar it was believed by some that a comet which had appeared in the sky was his soul ascending to heaven. In January 42 BC this fact was formally accepted by the senate and people, who thereby recognized him as a god to whom temples and altars should and could reasonably be dedicated. A temple to *Divus Julius* was built in the forum itself, and dedicated in 29 BC. Octavian, as Caesar's adopted son, exploited the relationship with enthusiasm, proclaiming himself on his coins as *divi filius* (son of a god).

There was no reason why Romans should not treat the idea with the utmost seriousness. For Greek and Roman polytheists, omnipotence was by definition not an expected attribute of divinity.[10] Gods differed from humans primarily only in their greater power (but some gods, of course, were stronger than others) and in their immortality – necessarily, as in the case of Caesar, in non-corporeal form. The notion of life after death, in the form of the continued existence of the soul, was widespread, if by no means universal, in the Roman world. It was not hard to imagine that a human of such exceptional power might retain both power and life after he or she had shed the physical body.

The nature of such ruler worship naturally varied, a fact that most emperors accepted without concern. Full-scale worship in Rome itself was confined to those who were dead, and who had been formally recognized as gods by the Roman senate; Augustus declined Agrippa's offer to include a statue of him in the Pantheon during his lifetime. For the rest, worship might be made to the other gods 'on their behalf', or their statue might be placed in the temple of *Roma* or their *genius* (undepicted) be the recipient of offerings. The religious significance of such variations is curious, but the political significance was negligible. The emperors were keen to be regarded by their subjects as more than human. Their statues, erected all over the empire, bestowed protection on the suppliant who laid hold of them. Their beneficent power preserved peace throughout the realm.

For the distant peasant in Gaul, Syria or Egypt, it was the divinity of the emperor that struck home most. For the ex-consul who discussed matters of state in the palace in Rome, it was the emperor's role as a great Roman noble. But both were also, at least potentially, aware of the other part of the emperor's image, and it was largely from the combination of two such contrasting elements that the imperial image derived its great power.

Thus the provincials' awareness of continuing Republican government was ensured in curious ways. Some documents in Roman Arabia were still dated by the consuls of the year, as well as emperors' tribunician power, well into the second century AD.[11] Decrees of the senate and people of Rome were still inscribed in far-off places, even if they were often found alongside or subordinated to the decision of individual emperors, as in an edict issued by Augustus in 4 BC, introducing a senatorial decree, which survives in a Greek translation in an inscription on a marble stele from the *agora* of the North African city of Cyrene, now known as the fifth Cyrene edict:

> The Emperor Caesar Augustus, pontifex maximus, holding the tribunician power for the nineteenth year, declares: A decree of the senate was passed in the consulship of Gaius Calvisius and Lucius Passienus, with me as one of those present at the writing. Since it affects the welfare of the allies of the Roman people, I have decided to send it into the provinces, appended to this my prefatory edict, so that it may be known to all who are under our care. From this it will be evident to all the inhabitants of the provinces how much both I and the senate are concerned that none of our subjects should suffer any improper treatment or any extortion.
> (*FIRA* I, no. 68; LR 1, pp. 590–96)

In Rome, the emperor, despite his refusal to permit temples directly in his honour, was not averse to allusions to his divinity. Horace and Vergil could describe Augustus starkly as *deus* (god) without expecting displeasure and only partly sheltering behind their poetic *personae*. Augustus positively encouraged awareness of his divinity from those around him by his penetrating stare:

> Augustus' eyes were clear and bright, and he liked to believe that they shone with a sort of divine radiance: it gave him profound pleasure if anyone at whom he glanced keenly dropped his head as though dazzled by looking into the sun.
>
> (Suetonius, *Augustus* 79)

Augustus also officially organized the *genius Augusti* cult in the city. Senators, whose main function was to govern the empire, would in any case be well aware of the ruler-cult throughout the provinces. Indeed, in some cases they were prominent in fostering the cult, as was one proconsul of Asia; his actions are recorded in a decree passed in *c.* 9 BC and inscribed in multiple copies in Asia Minor, quoted here in a text based primarily on the inscription found at Priene with additions from three other versions:

> It was decreed by the Greeks in the province of Asia, on motion of the high priest Apollonius son of Menophilus, of Azanium: Whereas the providence which divinely ordered our lives created with zeal and munificence the most perfect good for our lives by producing Augustus and filling him with virtue for the benefaction of mankind ... and whereas Paullus Fabius Maximus, proconsul of the province, sent for its preservation by that god's right hand and purpose, benefited the province with his own suggestions – the extent of which benefactions no one could succeed in telling adequately – and suggested for the honour of Augustus a thing hitherto unknown by the Greeks, namely, beginning their calendar with the god's nativity. Therefore ... it has been decreed by the Greeks in the province of Asia that the New Year shall begin in all cities on 23 September, which is the birthday of Augustus.
>
> (*OGIS* vol. 2, no. 458, lines 30–52; LR 1, pp. 624–25)

It is unreasonable to treat this action as pure cynicism. It was the senators who thronged the imperial court, part of which had from 12 BC been made over in theory to the Roman people as holy ground, while remaining the emperor's private residence. It was the senators who recognized an emperor as divine after the demise of his body and who decreed to him divine honours. On Augustus' death in AD 14, senators were proud to become *sodales Augustales*, priests of the new cult in Rome of *Divus Augustus*, with the same ritual titles as were used by the freedmen who presided over the cult in the Italian municipalities. Senators' enthusiasm for worshipping emperors was so taken for granted by the controllers of the Lyons mint that in AD 37, when the apotheosis of Tiberius was reported, they minted coins on which he was portrayed with the radiate crown of divinity, only to have to change the type when the senate (swayed by Gaius) declined to recognize the signs of divinity.[12] But when, as usually happened, senators thought that they knew that an emperor was a god immediately after his body had died – hence the practice of deification – they must surely have been aware of his divinity while he was still alive.

The emperors in practice contrived to have it both ways. Refusal of cult in Rome did not necessarily imply lack of divinity. It could merely imply that the god did not desire worship in that form. Inclusion of his *genius* and his family in the regular religious calendar helped to remind everyone that in fact he was more than human. The civility of the princeps who was willing to treat his fellow nobles as social equals was all the more acceptable to them because, as he ensured that they should remember, not least by the magnificence and inaccessibility of his palace, he could have demanded their worship. The possibility of rubbing shoulders with a god made doubly attractive the role of senator, and thus all the more effectively provided the emperor with the generals whom he so much needed.

THE CREATION OF THE IMAGE

All this of course was the ideal princeps, as embodied in Augustus for the second half of his remarkably long rule over the Roman people. Augustus bolstered his image by promotion of building styles, literature and catchwords which were absorbed by his subjects, at least in the city of Rome.[13] Already in the 30s BC, as triumvir, he had emphasized his enthusiasm for traditional Rome by putting on the Trojan games, claiming them as a revival of an ancient custom, and expelling 'alien' astrologers and magicians; this side of the image was reinforced in 27 BC by the extraordinary solemnity of the new name 'Augustus' (revered one), the significance of which cannot be overemphasized. But at the same time his buildings in Rome were remarkable for their grandiose Hellenistic triumphalism – for instance, his bizarre mausoleum, a vast building in a circular, layered shape, finished possibly by 28 BC. It was only after 23 BC that imperial buildings began to portray the sober, utilitarian, old Roman face of the regime, as in the *Ara Pacis Augustae* (the altar of Augustan peace) dedicated in 9 BC,[14] and the temple of Mars Ultor (Mars the avenger), dedicated in 2 BC in the new forum of Augustus.

Later emperors competed with their predecessors to leave their own mark on the city, hence the rapidly expanding number of buildings which consumed the area north of the *forum Romanum* in the first two centuries AD: after the *fora* of Julius Caesar and Augustus, Vespasian's 'Temple of Peace', the *forum transitorium* (completed by Nerva), and the monumental complex of Trajan's forum, complete with libraries and a basilica. Often these constructions erased the monuments of their disgraced forebears, such as Nero's 'Golden House', parts of which disappeared beneath the Baths of Titus and Trajan. Trajan's many public works, such as his Odeon, baths, forum and column, were ultimately designed to serve the specific ideological agenda of a new golden age (see Figure 17). The arch at Beneventum, inaugurated in AD 114 to celebrate the Via Traiana which ran to Brundisium, depicts the emperor in various guises as a war-leader and paternalistic figure, distributing the *alimenta* to the children of Italy. This strategy was successful, as the emperor won praise from all quarters; even the critical Fronto wrote that in 'the arts of peace scarcely anyone has excelled, if indeed anyone has equalled, Trajan in popularity with the people'. (*Princ. Hist.* 17, trans. Loeb).

Figure 17 The forum and column of Trajan. The column, with a remarkable frieze which recorded many details of Trajan's successful campaigns in Dacia, was located within a grand architectural setting designed to permit the emperor's achievements to be fully appreciated. Photo © istockphoto.com/Phillip Minnis.

The power of images lay more in cumulative associations than in direct propaganda. Thus the intensive use of coin types as propaganda in the civil wars and in 27 BC declined dramatically later in the principate, perhaps because there was less need for such issues. More effective and more subtle were such actions as the re-naming in 27 BC of the sixth month, *Sextilis*, as 'August', the gradual extension of imperial monuments into public space in the city of Rome, and the irregular but liberal donations by the princeps to the plebs and soldiers – donations that could be portrayed as pure generosity because of the institution of regular payments to which the emperor added from his own liberality. Inscriptions and literature repeated the catchwords of the regime: under Augustus, *virtus, clementia, iustitia, pietas* (valour, mercy, justice, piety), the qualities attributed to him on the golden shield presented to him by the senate in 27 BC. The city witnessed frequent pageants, to mark imperial returns, funerals and triumphs, when the princeps would be acclaimed by a grateful plebs at a series of designated places in the suburbs across the River Tiber, and coins proclaimed imperial virtues to the widest audience possible.[15]

Augustus insisted that the imperial family, as loyal supporters of the patriarch, became part of the image, as in their depiction on the *Ara Pacis*. Their devotion to the community, demonstrated not least by their own building projects in the capital city, in turn reflected glory on the princeps.

The greatest challenge to Augustus' image thus came in 6 BC, when his stepson Tiberius sullenly retreated to Rhodes, and in 2 BC, when his daughter Julia was exiled for adultery. Later emperors similarly stressed dynastic continuity and solidarity, so that imperial women often become part of the public face of the regime (see Figure 18).

All this can be demonstrated best for the age of Augustus, the first princeps so carefully to mould his image in this fashion. Other emperors portrayed themselves in a similar way, with suitable personal modifications; they were measured against Augustus' model, and did not always pass. Tiberius did not care sufficiently to demonstrate his social equality with his fellow senators. Gaius and Domitian demanded fulsome worship of themselves in Rome during their lifetime. Other emperors failed in other ways. Each earned the obloquy of historians and biographers of succeeding generations, who thereby confirmed the power of the Augustan ideal, which, though never stated by any authority or enshrined in any constitution, yet remained the model image of the princeps in the Early Roman Empire.

Figure 18 Cameo (dimensions: 12 × 15.2 cm) showing the heads of Claudius and his wife Agrippina Minor facing his brother Germanicus and Germanicus' wife Agrippina Major. (The latter pair were also parents of the younger Agrippina, since Claudius had married his niece). Claudius much valued association with the heroic military reputation of his brother. Photo © Kunsthistorisches Museum, Vienna.

13

THE EXTENT OF POLITICAL UNITY

ALLIES OR SUBJECTS?

The empire over which the princeps ruled was a huge area of variegated peoples and cultures. The core remained the inhabitants of the Mediterranean coastal strip, but Caesar's conquest of Gaul shifted the balance of empire into northern Europe. Trajan's campaigns in Dacia and against Parthia and his incorporation of Arabia as a province added much territory in the Balkans and the Near East, albeit some of it only temporary: the addition of the provinces of Armenia and Mesopotamia saw the empire reach its fullest extent. In strategic terms these accessions rendered the land-mass north of the Mediterranean the communications artery of the empire, with increasing military traffic from northern Italy across the Balkans and the Anatolian plateau. The other disparate regions of the empire were also physically linked by a network of military roads, constantly upgraded and extended, as many extant milestones proudly boast.

From the centre in Rome it was possible to view these subject populations in a variety of ways. They could be seen as foreigners conquered by Rome and controlled by force, as allies in a common culture, or as fully paid-up members of a unified society. In practice each of these attitudes is attested at one time or another in the world-view of the inhabitants of the Roman state. Provincials, too, might react to Roman rule by seeking accommodation, opposition, or integration, but the parameters within which they might adapt themselves were in essence fixed by the state. A fine visual representation of the empire as a conglomeration of varied, sometimes exotic, peoples held together by the emperor's sway is found in a series of sculptures set up in the temple of Augustus, in Aphrodisias in Turkey, in the first century AD: it is striking that the Greek city adopted an artistic motif which apparently originated in Rome and reflected so directly the Roman government's view of its empire.[1]

In the history of Livy, composed at the very start of the principate under Augustus, Roman history was the story of a city that stood alone in its struggle to win control first over Italy and then over the wider Mediterranean. Livy's account of the first century BC unfortunately does not survive, so it is impossible to state how he dealt with the enfranchisement of the Italians in the 80s BC, which resulted in the ruling élite of the Italian municipalities slowly beginning to be integrated with the political élite in Rome. But it is likely enough that the distinction between Romans and Italians still made good sense in his day: such, after all, was presupposed by Octavian's appeal to *tota Italia* before Actium. Velleius Paterculus (*History of Rome* 2.16.1–2), writing in the time of Tiberius, praised the heroes of the Italian side in the Social War, but added his own Italian ancestor to the list of heroes on the grounds of his consistently pro-Roman stance. By contrast, for Cassius Dio, whose history was composed in the early third century AD, the city of Rome no longer played any special part within the Roman system. In his day it became increasingly common for emperors to stay away from Rome for long periods when they were engrossed in campaigns, or to set up their palaces elsewhere, sometimes for the complete duration of their rule.

ROMAN CITIZENSHIP

The relationship between Rome and Italy will serve as a paradigm for the state's attitude to the population of the empire as a whole. The state was willing to grant citizenship on an ever-widening basis, culminating in the almost universal grant of citizenship by Caracalla in AD 212.[2] From the time of Julius Caesar at least, it was taken for granted that Roman citizenship could be held in conjunction with that of another state. Some emperors, notably Claudius, deliberately encouraged the spread of citizenship; none is known to have opposed it. The state encouraged urbanization, as described by Tacitus in Britain under Agricola:

> In order that a population scattered and uncivilized, and proportionately ready for war, might be habituated by comfort to peace and quiet, he [Agricola] would exhort individuals, assist communities, to erect temples, market-places, houses. ... The nation which used to reject the Latin language began to aspire to rhetoric: further, the wearing of our dress became a distinction, and the toga came into fashion, and little by little the Britons went astray into alluring vices: to the promenade, the bath, the well-appointed dinner table.
>
> (*Agricola* 21)

Emperors granted the status of *ius Latii* (Latin rights) to suitable towns, whose magistrates were thereby automatically entitled, with their families, to Roman citizenship. Another common route to citizenship was by service in the *auxilia*, which brought automatic citizenship on discharge.

Thus in the time of Augustus the empire was mostly inhabited by non-Romans, among whom Roman citizens of Italian origin were settled in scattered groups – in *conventus* (separate associations) within cities, in citizen colonies, in military camps – whereas by AD 180 many of the urban populace in all areas of the empire held Roman citizenship and could, if they so wished, think of themselves as fully Roman. It was a remarkable development, but not without a price, for the expansion of citizenship cheapened the currency, so that even those who bore their Roman names with pride might be treated by the state as little better than conquered barbarians.

ACCEPTANCE OF ROMAN RULE?

The image of the empire as the fruit of conquest is most blatant in those regions where military operations constantly recurred. Such, for instance, was the case in the highlands of Britain and in Armenia. Here, fraternization between the occupying power and the locals never removed awareness of the distinction between the rulers and the ruled, even when all were citizens. Such regions, where hostility to Rome was perceived as always latent, were quite common under Augustus but became less so with the passage of time. The Spanish legions, which had less and less to do after 19 BC, may after a while have ceased to see the inhabitants of the mountains as enemies at all.

But not all the empire had been won by conquest, and the Roman state was as keen to preserve the image of the voluntary acceptance of their rule by allies as were those allies themselves.[3] A classic expression of the vision of empire as a league of cities may be found in the panegyric *To Rome*, written and delivered at Rome by Aelius Aristides in AD 155. Born and choosing to spend most of his life in Asia Minor, Aristides saw himself as Greek by culture and social setting, although he was a Roman citizen of equestrian rank and a friend of senators. For him (*To Rome* 94), Rome was but the queen of a constellation of separate but mutually beneficent city states which respected each other's independence: 'Now all of the Greek cities flourish under you, and the offerings in them, the arts, and all their adornments bring honour to you, as an adornment in a suburb.' Such a vision had little connection with the reality of power, as shown by the correspondence of Pliny and Trajan over the city of Amisus' plans to set up a benefit society (*Letters* 10.92–93). Pliny wrote to Trajan for confirmation that he should not interfere in the affairs of Amisus, which enjoyed the privilege of administering its own laws. Trajan supplied this confirmation, but the exchange shows quite clearly that, despite the city's status as *libera et foederata* (free and confederate), Trajan could have forbidden its plans if he had so wished. Nonetheless, emperors were keen to maintain the fiction of the empire as a network of cities. The dossier of documents discovered on inscribed stone blocks erected in the theatre at Aphrodisias in Caria (Turkey) record the diplomatic niceties involved in preserving Rome's alliance with the city in the Early Empire, to the dignified satisfaction of all parties.[4] A letter from Hadrian to Aphrodisias confirms and continues the city's privileges:

Imperator Caesar Trajanus Hadrianus Augustus, son of divus Trajanus Parthicus, grandson of divus Nerva, pontifex maximus, holding the tribunician power for the third time, greets the magistrates, council and people of the Aphrodisians. Your freedom, autonomy and other (privileges) which were given you by the senate and the emperors who preceded me, I confirmed earlier. I have been petitioned through an embassy about the use of iron and the tax on nails. Although the matter is controversial, since this is not the first time that the collectors have attempted to collect from you, nevertheless, knowing that the city is in other respects worthy of honour and is removed from the *formulae provinciae*, I release it from payment and I have written to Claudius Agrippinus, my procurator, to instruct the contractor for the tax in Asia to keep away from your city.

(Reynolds no. 15)

One effect of such recognition of diverse alliances was an acceptance that a diversity of laws and legal systems should operate throughout the empire. Such tolerance of local custom extended much further than allowing the magistrates of local communities to retain their own titles and modes of election, although the latter was for good reason kept under scrutiny. Decisions on all areas of local policy, from building plans to the administration of property and family law, were left to local magistrates to carry out as they saw fit, providing they proved no danger to the Roman state. The autonomous coins produced by civic communities in many places in the eastern empire throughout this period attest strong local loyalties.[5] On the other hand, the extension of citizenship entailed a gradual spread of Roman law, which in theory, and sometimes in practice, applied to all citizens.

PROVINCIAL CO-OPERATION

The one area in which the state's intervention was seen as crucial was in the bolstering up of richer members of provincial society as local magistrates. The reason for this was only partially prejudice derived from the political language of Rome; since in Rome itself wealth was a prerequisite for political office, Romans assumed that the same should be true in the areas they ruled. The practical advantages were also considerable. Candidates for office might pay for the privilege, or a friend might pay on their behalf.[6] The rich had a greater stake in preserving peace than did the poor, and they could more easily be entrusted with the crucial task of tax collection, since in the final analysis they could be compelled to pay the sums themselves.

The structure of the state as a network of local magistrates responsible to a central authority in Rome through provincial governors was at its clearest in most provinces in the very early principate, for it was at that time that *ad hominem* grants of Roman citizenship began to be made to local nobles. Thus in Gaul in the first century AD, the peasants were controlled directly by Roman citizens usually bearing the name of Julius (see Chapter 21). Such men were normally themselves Gauls, and the descendants of the Gallic leaders who had led the opposition to the Roman invasion under Caesar in the 50s BC.[7]

Figure 19 Inscription dated to AD 53 on a limestone stele from the old forum in Lepcis Magna (J.M. Reynolds and J.B. Ward-Perkins, *The Inscriptions of Roman Tripolitania*, Rome, 1952, no. 338). The Latin text, originally in bronze letters, records at the top a dedication to the emperor Claudius by the proconsul of the province. The lower half commemorates the erection of columns and the paving of the forum at the expense of various members of the family of a certain Gaius, son of Annon. The contribution of this local magnate is recorded in similar terms in the four lines of Neo-Punic inscribed at the bottom of the stele. Photo by kind permission of Michael Vickers.

In the Early Empire, grants of citizenship of this type obscured the relationship between provincials and Rome, rather than engendering loyalty to the Roman state. The Cyrene edicts of 7–6 BC reveal Roman citizens joining forces against local Greeks, using Roman courts to get their way in disputes.[8] Some of these Roman citizens will have been Italian émigrés, who had settled in enclaves in eastern Mediterranean cities in increasing numbers from the second century BC in search of trade, but others will have been local aristocrats honoured by the state with Roman citizenship for one reason or another.

During the first century AD the franchise spread lower down the social and economic scale in all areas of the empire. But the same principle of rule by a network of rich provincials was maintained. Now that Roman citizenship had lost value as a status marker, privileges were granted to the rich simply on the grounds of their wealth. Such privileges were enshrined in law, for after Hadrian punishments considered more suitable for humble people were regularly commuted for the 'more honourable' (see Chapter 10).[9] The empire was in effect ruled by a wealth-defined élite paid by grants of privilege rather than salary, unified in their determination to keep power out of the hands of the poor. (For an illustration of some of these attitudes, see Figure 19). The characteristic institution through which their control was exercised was the city council (*ordo* in Latin, *boule* in Greek). Council membership was open only to the rich.[10] The prestige of individuals within the provincial elite was closely bound up with the prestige of the city they represented, leading to fierce competition for titles and honours bestowed on cities by the emperor.[11]

THE EMPEROR AS UNIFIER

The emperor's writ ran in all areas of the empire controlled by the state. It was true that in theory his jurisdiction in some provinces, where a proconsul had been appointed, was only marginal. His *imperium proconsulare maius* permitted intervention in such provinces only when necessary. But in practice his decisions were sought and accepted just as much in such provinces as elsewhere, as was already clear when Augustus issued the Cyrene edicts.

The emperor functioned as a universal patron of the empire and its inhabitants. Inscriptions erected in provincial communities praised the emperor for his *indulgentia* (kindness) and *liberalitas* (generosity) in the remission of tax burdens or assistance in the construction of public works. Since the position of the emperor as head of the Roman state was supported by the manufacture of coins, monuments and documents to legitimize imperial rule in the eyes of the provincials, and since the provincials themselves commemorated emperors and their families by commissioning statues and by paying gifts of 'crown gold' on significant imperial anniversaries, it might seem that such a dialogue between emperors and their subjects constituted a consensus about the validity of Roman rule, but this notion should not be pressed too hard; it is ultimately impossible to gauge the motivation of the provincials who appeared to buy in to imperial ideology, and the emperor lacked any real mass media to communicate his policies, with coin images operating as a poor substitute for the communication methods used by modern states.[12]

The pre-eminence of the emperor as the unifying force of the empire was symbolized by the importance attached to the provincial celebrations of the imperial cult.[13] The priesthoods of the imperial cult were confined to the provincial aristocracy, who were encouraged to compete for the honour. The main cultic celebrations took place at a designated provincial centre (defined according to Roman notions of a province), and were attended by gladiatorial games or other similar Roman jollifications. The high priest of the province was a man of great status and usually a Roman citizen.

Organization of the imperial cult by province reflects the continued division of the empire, in the eyes of the state, into geographical divisions based loosely on the ethnic identity of the main people with whom Rome had originally come into contact in those regions. In the Republic the term *provincia* had meant a sphere of duty, usually but not always in connection with a military campaign, but by the time of Julius Caesar a secondary use to refer to a geographically delimited area administered by Rome had developed. By the first century AD that use was standard. The Roman provincial titles (Hispania, Britannia, and so on) have in some cases passed into common currency in modern Europe, which gives an often false impression that such titles reflected existing national entities in the Roman period. The impression was not always misleading. Egypt, for instance, was clearly a recognizable political unit before the advent of Rome. But in some places the Roman view of their political order as reflected in maps of the Roman Empire demonstrates a reordering of the world, for administrative convenience, that sometimes ran counter to the interests of the native peoples or the facts on the ground. So, for instance, the tendency to view the empire as a network of cities encouraged the state to ignore the extensive autonomy of many villages in parts of Syria, where cities seem rarely to have administered village life. Thus the divisions of Part IV of this book attempt to reflect, not the geographical divisions imposed by Rome, but those that would be apparent to the subjects of Rome themselves. Even after AD 212, when all the inhabitants of the empire were citizens of Rome, their political unity was something that was imposed by the state rather than an organic expression of will.

14

THE EXTENT OF ECONOMIC
UNITY

Throughout the period covered by this history, most wealth in the Roman empire was held in the form of land, and it was traditional agriculture which brought an income to most of its inhabitants. Nonetheless, this period also witnessed, alongside such long-established modes of production, a marked increase in economic activity in many places, and this must be explained at least in part by the unification of the Mediterranean region with much of Europe as a trading area protected by the Roman peace. Quite how this was achieved has been much debated in recent years, with claims either that the redistribution of goods was mostly limited to gift exchange, with high-level trade restricted to luxuries, or that production and exchange were governed by a market economy driven by professionals in pursuit of profit. In fact, the economy of the empire seems to have had aspects in common with both models. Thus intensification of agriculture and manufacturing processes in many parts of the Roman world in the late Republic and early empire were fuelled by the market economy and its demand for new products, but these trends existed in tandem with the agricultural subsistence economy which was the way of life for the vast majority of the empire's inhabitants.[1]

It is likely that the basic need for food supply made grain the most important product of the ancient economy, and that the weight and bulk of grain made its transport over long distances by land prohibitively expensive except in times of dire shortage, and it is certain that the bulk of production in the ancient world was for local consumption. Nonetheless, there is a mass of archaeological and literary evidence that the total of goods traded over long distances in the Early Roman Empire showed a marked increase over previous periods, and it is reasonable to view the empire as, to a limited extent, an economic unity – not least because it was subjected by the state to a coherent taxation system, and exchange was facilitated by the spread of Roman currency, or at least local currencies linked to Roman currency standards, throughout the empire.

The bulk of archaeological evidence is, through the hazards of survival, in the form of ceramics.[2] Amphoras containing wine and oil were widely traded in Italy, France, Spain and Africa in the first century AD. Different centres of production flourished at different times, but the ability to transport and find markets to sell products appears to have been stable. The evidence is in any case complicated by the possibility that a shift from amphoras to non-ceramic containers such as wooden barrels might give a quite false impression of the collapse of a particular trade, such as the export of Italian wine at the end of the first century AD.[3] An even fuller picture can be derived of the spread of oil-lamps and of medium and high-class fine wares, such as the red Samian pottery made in the first century AD in Arretium (modern Arezzo) in Italy, and from the middle of that century in increasing quantities in southern Gaul.[4]

The literary evidence testifies to a flourishing trade in luxuries. A fine description may be found in the anonymous mid-first-century Greek text, the *Navigation of the Erythraean Sea* 49 (quoted here) and 56:

> Into this trading port [of Barygaza] come wine, principally Italian but also Laodicean and Arabian; copper, tin, and lead; coral and peridot; all kinds of clothing, plain and patterned; multicoloured girdles a cubit wide; storax, yellow sweet clover, raw glass; realgar, sulphide of antimony; Roman gold and silver money, which is exchanged at some profit against the local coinage; and ointment, inexpensive but not much of it. … Exported from this region are nard, costus, bdellium, ivory, onyx … agate; all kinds of cloth, Chinese [silk], molochinon, and yarn; long pepper; and the wares brought here from the trading stations in the area.

Some luxuries, such as spices and silks, were brought from China and India, and from Arabia. Amber was imported from north-western Europe. Other luxuries were exported from specialized centres within the empire, such as the balsam groves in En Gedi in Judaea. But in a way more significant for the total volume of trade is the evidence that goods of moderate rather than exceptional value were also widely traded. This, for instance, was the case with many of the products referred to by Pliny the Elder, whose curious miscellany in his *Natural History* provides the best evidence for the variety of goods traded in the Roman economy. Thus there were four types of flax from Egypt, the best medicinal salt from Spain, and so on.[5]

THE ROLE OF THE STATE IN PROMOTING TRADE

For very little of this trade is there any evidence that direct state interference was responsible.[6] There was a state monopoly of production of a few luxuries such as balsam and (probably) precious metals in places like the Río Tinto goldfields, or the mines at Vipasca (near modern Aljustrel, Portugal), where a second-century inscription shows close control of all aspects of life, such as the management of the baths:

> The lessee of the baths or his partner shall, in accordance with the terms of his lease running to June 30 next, be required to heat the baths and keep them open for use entirely at his own expense every day from daybreak to the seventh hour for

women, and from the eighth hour to the second hour in the evening for men, at the discretion of the procurator in charge of the mines. He shall be required to provide a proper supply of running water for the heated rooms, to the bath tub up to the highest level and to the basin, for women as well as for men. The lessee shall charge men one half *as* each and women one *as* each. Imperial freedmen or slaves in the service of the procurator or on his payroll are admitted free; likewise minors and soldiers.

(*CIL* II, no. 5, 181; LR 2, pp. 104–05)

The state encouraged through privileges the import of corn to the city of Rome by professional shipowners: according to the second-century lawyer Gaius:

Likewise, by an edict of Claudius, Latins acquire Roman citizenship if they build a sea-going vessel of a capacity of not less than 10,000 *modii* of grain, and if that ship, or another in its place, carries grain to Rome for six years.

(*Institutes* 1.32C)

But for the rest, the great flurry of economic activity attested particularly by the archaeological evidence must be accounted for by private initiative.

What, then, stimulated private enterprise to flourish? Some factors may usefully be ruled out. There is no evidence of *general* state inducements to merchants or craftsmen in the form of privileges or tax advantages. It is true that most of the state's income was derived from taxing agricultural land, so that owners of other forms of wealth went comparatively unscathed, but since land was much the safest investment, merchants tended in any case to plough profits back into land, and the tax system should therefore have been, if anything, a disincentive. It may be added that indirect taxation on traded goods (*portoria*) will have had the same effect. Nor is there evidence that craftsmen or traders were awarded social prestige for success. Wealth was a prerequisite for social respectability and political power, but it was not a sufficient condition, and the prejudice of the landed gentry against those who had become rich by craft or trade was strong.

It is likely, then, that the role of the state in promoting trade was less deliberate and less direct. The power of the state ensured comparative safety of transport throughout most of the empire, a fact of particular importance for the lucrative sea routes. Large investments and heavily loaded ships could produce great profits since they required little manpower, but they also ran serious risks through storms or piracy. Removal of the former factor was impossible, and there are many stories of shipwrecks. Numerous sunken ships have been excavated, and analysis of their cargoes can indicate what was being traded and where (see Figure 20). The striking increase in the number of wrecks recorded for the mid-first century AD suggests trade was prospering.[7] After Pompeius Magnus cleared the eastern Mediterranean of pirates in 67 BC, a major hazard disappeared, and the task was repeated elsewhere in later years, as an early first-century Greek inscription from Ilium (in Turkey)

Figure 20 Samian ware bowls and flagons from the second century AD recovered from a shipwreck at Pudding Pan rock, off the Kentish coast north of Whitstable. Fine pottery was produced in huge quantities and distributed over large areas of the empire. Photo courtesy of the Ashmolean Museum, Oxford.

testifies (EJ^2 no. 227; Braund no. 441): 'The council and people honoured Titus Valerius Proculus, procurator of Drusus Caesar, who destroyed the pirate vessels in the Hellespont and kept the city in every respect free of burdens.'

On land, the protection of routes from brigandage was harder to sustain, but it too was part of a governor's role. According to the lawyer Ulpian:

> It is appropriate for a good governor who takes his duties seriously to see that the province under his control is kept quiet and peaceful. He will secure this without difficulty if he takes conscientious measures to make sure that the province is free from malefactors and that he hunts them out: he ought besides hunting out temple robbers, highway robbers, kidnappers and thieves, to inflict on each of them the penalty that he deserves and to punish people harbouring them; without them a robber cannot hide for very long.
>
> (*Duty of the Proconsul*, Book 7, in *Digest* 1.18.13, Introduction)

For the most part, the actual work of controlling robbers was left to local militias of erratic competence, under local magistrates. But the paved roads built to high specification by the military for the safe movement of troops were enthusiastically adopted as trade routes, in which ease of travel on the more regular surface was only one advantage, the other being the occasional presence of troops who might deter thieves.[8]

But perhaps more significant than any of these factors was the operation of the state's payment and taxation system in encouraging the development of urban markets where coin was freely available.[9] Such fiscality and widespread monetization were entirely new in north-west Europe. On the one hand, the state paid out huge sums in coin to soldiers and officials scattered throughout the provinces. On the other hand, the state always exacted taxes, and often required that they be paid in coin. One effect of this was to discourage peasant economies from remaining entirely inward-looking and enclosed. Occasional barter with neighbours might provide sufficient to feed and clothe the family, but not to pay taxes. The peasants themselves might pay some taxes in kind to the state, as recorded in the cache of legal documents belonging to Babatha and her family, discovered in a cave close to En Gedi in Judaea. In a document of 2 and 4 December AD 127, in response to a census ordered by the provincial governor, Babatha declared her ownership of four date groves and the taxes she paid on them, in both dates and coin:[10]

> I, Babatha, daughter of Simon ... register what I possess ... a date orchard called Algiphiamma, the area of sowing one *saton* three *kaboi* of barley, paying as tax in dates, Syrian and mixed fifteen *sata*, 'splits' ten *sata*, and for crown tax one 'black' and thirty sixtieths.

Other taxes, even if assessed in coin, might be paid in kind to local collectors, who would obtain coin for the goods in local markets. In either case, urban markets were monetized, and peasants required to increase production to ensure a surplus. Once thus stimulated to produce a surplus, they would not necessarily see all of it go in tax. What was left might now have a ready market in return for coin. The cumulative spending power of large numbers of peasants was considerable, and worth the while of merchants to tap. This was a large market of small spenders rather than an élite of the very rich. But it was a consistent and reliable market, for which it was profitable to produce goods on a large scale.

The most consistent consuming centre of all was the city of Rome, whose economic interests remained dominant in state taxation policy throughout the early imperial period. Grain imports to the city, some of them distributed free, ensured a huge population in constant need of goods and services. But cumulatively no less significant was the permanent presence in frontier provinces of large bodies of troops with a regular income guaranteed by the state, and no means to expend such income except on the services provided by the locals or on goods imported by merchants. The *canabae* (settlements) which sprang up around military camps in the western and northern provinces often developed into market towns, and the collective effect of such enterprises was a general efflorescence of the economies of such frontier areas in the Early Empire.

Although the overall pattern can quite easily be discerned, and the causes of such economic change surmised with some plausibility, the sort of individuals who took advantage of the opportunities offered and benefited by the new conditions is more difficult to ascertain. Social snobbery was in part responsible for the dearth of explicit evidence about craftsmen and traders in the Early Empire. When stone inscriptions boasting about such functions are to be found, as at Lugdunum (Lyons), they generally bear the names of ex-slaves. The tombstone of one sea trader, found at Lugdunum, reveals his social status, since he was a *sevir augustalis*, one of the six freedmen priests who tended the emperor's cult in the town:[11]

> To the departed Spirits of Quintus Capitonius Probatus the elder, of the city of Rome, *sevir augustalis* in Lyons and in Puteoli, seagoing *navicularius* [maritime trader]. His freedmen Nereus and Palaemon [set this up] for their patron. He had built this tomb in his lifetime for himself and his descendants and dedicated it under the sign of the *ascia* [mason's trowel].

It is not impossible that many of the *negotiatores* (traders) who appear in Roman legal texts under this description (rather than status) were indeed of servile origin.[12]

WORKFORCE

At the beginning of the imperial period, the main focus of large-scale economic activity was Italy, where the proportion of slaves in the workforce reached an extraordinarily high level because of captives won in war.[13] The economic benefits in the use of slaves in industrial or agricultural concerns were often marginal. Slaves could be made to work hard, but they had to be fed, housed and clothed sufficiently well to make them competent to do so, and they could not be made to work well without inducements. In Roman society that inducement was customarily the promise of freedom after a limited number of years' service, the precise number being dependent on effort and conduct. There was therefore a huge number of ex-slaves in the Italian economy by the end of the first century BC. As Roman citizens, these ex-slaves were in status terms hardly distinguishable from the rest of the Roman plebs, and their economic role was constrained only by the need for capital and, crucially, the requirement not to infringe the interests of their ex-master or *patronus*, who could be the eventual heir to anything they gained.

There is little evidence that any freedmen became peasants.[14] Presumably they lacked the capital to buy land. It seems likely that many freedmen were craftsmen, perhaps because it was in the interest of craftsmen who wished to expand production by employing extra labour not to employ fellow freemen, since such individuals would be tempted to set up in competition as soon as they had served their apprenticeship. Better then to buy and train intelligent slaves and to ensure high quality in their workmanship by offering the prospect of freedom after a certain time. Such a freedman would be duty-bound not to compete with his ex-master and might therefore be happy to remain in partnership with him.

The same reasoning may well apply to long-distance trade. Rich landowners would not sully their hands with organizing such trade,[15] but they were not averse to lending money at high interest to a freedman or other person of low social status who would do so. It is striking that in Roman law the state was heavily biased towards the interest of the landowner rather than the *negotiator* in all dealings between them, such as the purchase of wine or oil from a farm.

Women and children, both free and servile, were involved in a vast array of economic activities alongside the adult male workforce. Slave children as young as five were expected to work for their masters (Ulpian, *Dig.* 7.7.6.1), and it was commonly thought that children would make good shepherds. Agriculture was a major source of employment for men and women. Varro (*De Agricultura* 1.17.2) wrote that poor men often tilled their fields with the help of their families, and women frequently participated in the collection of the harvest. Papyrological evidence from Egypt shows that when children were employed to work on large estates, they usually carried out lighter tasks, such as weeding, cutting and carrying produce, rather than tilling and digging.

Families often moved around in search of work on the land, either on their own initiative or by taking part in the foundation of Roman colonies, suggesting that the peasant population was not tied to one location. A recent estimate suggests that between two and two-and-a-half million Italians moved as a result of colonization programmes in the late Republic and early empire. For those not lucky enough to be allocated their own plot of land by the government, working on others' estates was a vital source of income, as indicated by this anecdote from Strabo (*Geography*, 3.4.17):

> Posidonius says that in Liguria his host, Charmoleon, a man of Massilia, narrated to him how he had hired men and women together for ditch-digging: and how one of the women, upon being seized with the pangs of childbirth, went aside from her work to a place near by, and, after having given birth to her child, came back to her work at once in order not to lose her pay.

The agricultural and non-agricultural sectors of the economy were bound together by a common workforce, whose jobs varied depending on the time of the year. Peasants were not required to tend to their fields all year round and often found other jobs in industries such as transport. Rural elites frequently diversified beyond agriculture, manufacturing items like clay bricks, amphorae and tiles.[16]

AGRICULTURE

Such factors helped to explain mass production of ceramics from amphoras to oil lamps, and other such crafts, but not of course agricultural products such as wine and oil. In some areas of the empire, such as Italy, Spain, southern France and northern Africa, the availability of markets and a distribution system for production stimulated, in the first century AD, a high increase in the growth of specialist crops. The phenomenon is remarkable not least because it was potentially economically wasteful of manpower costs. A farm growing primarily olives, for example, would require a large labour force at the time of harvest but almost none for the rest of the year. The early, smaller expansion of olive oil trade in Italy in the later Republic of the second century BC seems to have been achieved without the emergence of primarily cash-crop farms of this type. That cash crops such as vines were thought worthwhile in the first and second centuries AD is testimony to the stability and cumulative wealth available to producers in the fertile areas bordering the Mediterranean, and the width of their economic horizons. The calculations were made semi-successfully by Columella in the mid-first century AD:

> Those devoted to the study of agriculture must be informed of one thing first of all – that the return from vineyards is a very rich one. ... But if any who combine painstaking care with scientific knowledge receive not forty or at least thirty amphoras per *iugerum* according to my reckoning but, using a minimum estimate as Graecinus does, twenty, they will easily outdo in the increase of their ancestral estates all those who hold fast to their hay and vegetables.
> (*On Agriculture* 3.3.2, 7)

On the other hand, Columella's contemporary Pliny the Elder saw large estates as the ruin of Italy and of Africa (*Natural History* 18.35): 'If truth be told large estates have been the ruin of Italy and are now indeed the ruin of the provinces too. Six owners possessed half the province of Africa when the princeps Nero had them killed.' There was significant variety in the cost of agricultural products throughout the empire, owing to the varied costs of transport as well as ecological diversity: thus, for instance, wheat was probably four times more expensive in parts of Italy than in Egypt.[17]

INDUSTRY AND TECHNOLOGY

It has become clear in recent years that the view, long held by historians, that there was little technological development in the Roman world is simplistic, and that in fact technological changes had a considerable impact on industrial activity. The most striking evidence lies in the ice floes of the Arctic Circle, which reveal that the level of metal residues released into the world's atmosphere reached a peak in the first two centuries AD which was not to be equaled again in volume until the Industrial Revolution.[18] The evidence for technological innovations as a partial cause of this expansion lies in part in literary sources, such as the report by Suetonius of an inventor who was rewarded by Vespasian for developing a new method of moving columns (Suet. *Vesp.* 18), but the bulk of our evidence comes from the archaeological record. So, for example, the exploitation of mines in north-west Spain would not have been achievable without sophisticated hydraulic technology, and it has been suggested that the decline in the number of shipwrecks after the first century AD was the result not of economic contraction (as traditionally assumed) but of technological improvements in maritime safety.

Figure 21 Limestone lid of the sarcophagus of a certain M. Aurelius Ammianus,
rom Phrygia. Water-powered stone saws such as the one depicted here were used
to slice marble. Photo: Paul Kessener. © JRA. (Tullia Ritti, Klaus Grewe and
Paul Kessener, 'A relief of a water-powered stone saw mill on a sarcophagus at
Hierapolis and its implications', JRA 20 (200), p.138, Fig. 2.)

It is certain, at least, that, sophisticated production techniques, refined over time, allowed the Roman state to embark on vast building projects, such as the Colosseum or the Baths of Caracalla. From the Augustan period onwards, column shafts were produced in multiples of four or five Roman feet with a precise ratio in mind. The first private citizen to have marble columns throughout his whole house was a wealthy equestrian, Mamurra, who had served with Julius Caesar in Gaul (Pliny *NH* 36.7). The Romans also developed the water-powered stone saw to slice marble for their *opus sectile* floors (see Figure 21).

One of the most important innovations in Roman construction was the discovery of hydraulic concrete, made from Pozzolana, a volcanic ash found in the Bay of Naples. The process is described by Vitruvius in his work *On Architecture* (2.6.1., trans. Loeb):

> There is a species of sand which, naturally, possess extraordinary qualities. It is found about Baiae and the territory in the neighbourhood of Mount Vesuvius; if mixed with lime and rubble, it hardens as well under water as in ordinary buildings.

Hydraulic concrete facilitated the construction of impressive harbours, such as that built by Trajan at Portus, as well as the waterproofing of aqueducts. There were also important developments in manufacturing, such as the shift from a vertical to horizontal loom which allowed for a range of new designs in clothes. These improvements did not always emanate from Rome and Italy itself: Pliny the Elder (*HN* 18.48) records that two wheels were added to the plough in Raetia in order to cope with the increasing weight of the mechanism.

Technological developments therefore stimulated the Roman economy in a variety of ways, sustaining a complicated network of manufacturing and distribution across the Mediterranean. There was not, however, continuous innovation throughout this period, as many production techniques remained relatively static, such as smelting, which saw few improvements before the medieval age. Likewise, the shaduf, a device for lifting water used in Egypt and the Middle East, was originally developed in the seventeenth century BC and changed little thereafter. The advances that did occur are perhaps best regarded as refinements and improvements to existing processes rather than a complete revolution, but the economic impact of such refinements should not be underestimated.[19]

LOCAL ECONOMIES AND CONNECTIVITY

The prosperity of a particular region could depend heavily on decisions taken at a very local level. So, for instance, it used to be thought that the majority of farming which took place in the Roman world, especially in Italy, was accomplished without irrigation, but recent research has shown that, although the use of hydraulic systems to improve agricultural production was quite common, its implementation often depended on the initiative of individual landowners. A recently discovered inscription from Hispania Citerior demonstrates that local communities (*pagi*) could share an irrigation channel, taking joint responsibility for its upkeep. If individuals tasked with the cleaning or maintenance of the channel failed in their duties, they were fined 25 *denarii* per offence.[20]

On the other hand, prosperity could also be affected by access to road and sea networks. Thus the town of Beneventum in Campania grew in importance throughout the second and third centuries AD because Trajan made it the starting point for the *Via Traiana*, which crossed Italy to the port of Brundisium on the Adriatic coast – and two other communities along the route, Herdoniae and Aeclanum, benefited economically from increased traffic, and constructed upscale markets known as *macella* to take advantage of their greater integration into the trade system. At the opposite end of the spectrum, towns could be thrown into a period of decline if socio-economic networks changed trajectory. The community of Cosa on the coast of Etruria had been a major military base in the Republican period, but it lost this function as Italy ceased to be a site of frequent warfare. Emperors tried to revive the town by paying for the construction of public amenities, but their interventions reflected the absence of local landowners concerned to improve the community.

A regional economy might also be affected less directly by the implications of imperial ideology. The dramatic increase in the Flavian period in the number of villas in the province of Baetica, which had previously been home to hill forts and small farms, may be directly attributable to the investment of local elites in agriculture in order to generate the capital necessary for the holding of municipal offices and priesthoods in the imperial cult. The municipalisation of Spain was thus directly related to the intensification of agricultural production in this region.[21]

15

THE EXTENT OF CULTURAL UNITY

URBANISATION

In much of the Roman world, the most striking change produced by the imperial peace was the spread of towns. Cities and towns were the centres of administration in the eyes of the Roman state. In the eastern Mediterranean, where cities had been long established before Roman rule, civic status was granted to many village communities, which vied for the privilege. In the western and northern parts of the empire, numerous new towns were founded, often located on level sites replacing hill-top fortified settlements. The process was not universal, and in some remote regions village life remained normal even at the height of the Empire (see below, Part IV, for examples), but the main paradigms of a Roman cultured lifestyle were urban, and many provincials adopted urbanization with enthusiasm.

The casual visitor to the archaeological remains of Roman towns of the early imperial period will be struck by the uniformity of their appearance. Like modern cities with their shopping malls and office blocks, Roman towns in Britain looked much like those in Italy or Africa, and not greatly different from those in Syria or Egypt. Among the rich élite who paid for and commissioned the designs of public architecture, there developed a high degree of cultural consensus, such that a provincial aristocrat from one corner of the empire would have a great deal of cultural common ground with his counterpart in the furthermost reaches of Rome's domains. Such cultural agreement was of high value in cementing the political co-operation of the upper classes in the government of the empire. It is also reflected in, and contributed to, the extraordinary cosmopolitanism of the early Christian movement, so that St Paul, a Jew from Cilicia, could write in mutually comprehensible terms to fellow-believers from many parts of the Roman world.

This cultural unity was manifested not only in architecture and feats of engineering, such as aqueducts, but in sculpture and painting and to a rather lesser extent in literary culture. The cumulative evidence for its existence is considerable, as will be seen. What is less certain is the significance of such evidence. In many areas of the empire, 'Graeco-Roman' culture, for want of a better term, existed alongside indigenous cultural forms. It is an important but difficult task to ascertain in particular cases whether the indigenous culture was suppressed (and, if so, whether this suppression was semi-voluntary by the locals themselves, or by the state); whether the indigenous culture was confined to the lower classes, the upper classes adopting the *mores* of the imperial society from which they benefited; whether the upper class subscribed fully both to the indigenous and to Graeco-Roman culture, but for political reasons gave more public expression at least in durable materials such as stone to the latter facet of their lives. All or none of these combinations are possible. An attempt to discover something about them will be made in Part IV. But the variegated picture which will emerge there needs to be set against the quasi-uniformity of the architectural and literary remains.[1]

ARCHITECTURE AND ART

A Roman town in its fully developed form could be expected to boast a forum (an open space for markets and, at least in theory, for political meetings), temples abutting the forum (usually including a temple dedicated to Capitoline Jupiter), baths and a theatre (see Map 4).[2] Larger towns might boast an amphitheatre for gladiatorial games. Towns in the eastern half of the empire were more likely to have a less formal public open space within the city, an *agora* rather than a forum, in deference to the norms of Greek city planning. Such towns might for similar reasons also be expected to boast a gymnasium for athletic pursuits by the citizens, and perhaps an *odeion* for performance of music and poetry, and a stadium and hippodrome for athletic performances and horse racing. Small towns might only have some of these facilities, or at their first foundation even none, but it is significant that they were generally expected to acquire such facilities in time.

The architecture of the public buildings, when erected, followed quite clear norms. Forums were surrounded by pillared colonnades with decorated capitals. Temples were erected above street level on podia reached by a flight of steps and again fronted by standard columns. Theatres were built to a certain pattern, designed presumably to ease performance of the most popular form of entertainment, the mime: tiered seats were built in an extended semi-circle around a raised stage, behind which there was usually a stone screen to act as a backdrop. The external design of baths varied rather more, but the internal facilities could be expected to include hot, medium and cold baths and an open space for relaxation. Heat was provided by a system which circulated warm air beneath the floor, the *hypocaustum*.

Rich local aristocrats usually paid for such public buildings. The notion that such gifts to the city entitled the donor to greater political power ('euergetism') was deeply ingrained in both Roman and Greek society and was strongly encouraged throughout the provinces by Rome.[3] A series of

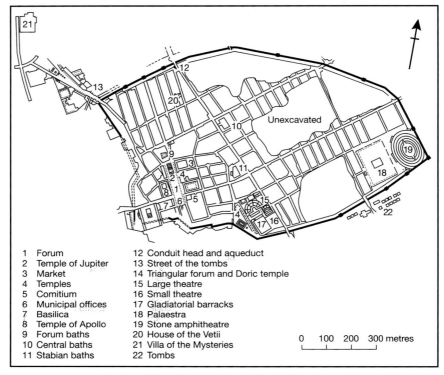

1	Forum	12	Conduit head and aqueduct
2	Temple of Jupiter	13	Street of the tombs
3	Market	14	Triangular forum and Doric temple
4	Temples	15	Large theatre
5	Comitium	16	Small theatre
6	Municipal offices	17	Gladiatorial barracks
7	Basilica	18	Palaestra
8	Temple of Apollo	19	Stone amphitheatre
9	Forum baths	20	House of the Vetii
10	Central baths	21	Villa of the Mysteries
11	Stabian baths	22	Tombs

Map 4 Plan of Pompeii in AD 79

inscriptions honour the substantial gifts given to Apamea in Syria by a prominent citizen, Lucius Iulius Agrippa, in the early second century. Originally situated on the wall of the baths complex which Agrippa had built, an inscription commemorates that:

> He performed for his city magistracies [?], liturgies and benefactions; he was a priest; he was a generous *agoranomos*, overseeing distributions of grain for six months and spending a sum of … silver; he provided oil and built a good number of miles of an aqueduct; he served as secretary to the city in an exceptional manner, taking this charge upon himself for one year and choosing his colleagues himself, and that same year he was officer of the peace and of the distribution of the grain, and he founded the baths, the *stoa* which is in front of them, and the neighbouring *basilica*, buying at his own expense all the necessary land and decorating the baths with these bronze statues.
>
> (*AE* 1976, no. 678)[4]

The extent of public construction in the Early Empire owed much indirectly to the encouragement of the state, although, so far as is known, the design was left up to locals. In some cases engineering help may have been provided by a local army unit. Hence the consistency in engineering brilliance, from the Pont du Gard erected most probably under Claudius near Nîmes to, for example, the Colosseum begun under Vespasian in Rome, even if separate provincial construction techniques continued to be used (so that, for instance, the baths constructed at Ephesus and Sardis in Asia Minor used types of brick vaulting different from those used in the baths at Rome).[5]

The same aristocrats whose Graeco-Roman taste was visible in public carried that taste into at least some of the more visible aspects of their private lives. The big town houses of the rich varied little around the empire. Impersonal high walls fronted the street, while, inside, a colonnaded courtyard (*atrium*) was surrounded by living rooms. In the countryside in some regions, the domestic villa became an increasingly attractive means of self-gratification, with more extended *atrium* and a surrounding complex of buildings, bath houses, and so on to import the civilized pleasures of the town to the country. But this partiality for comfortable country living was less common in the eastern parts of the empire than in the west.[6]

Decoration of rich men's houses followed gradual trends. For the first half of the period covered in this book, the trends can be traced clearly by examination of the great amount of evidence preserved by the volcanic ash of Vesuvius at Pompeii and Herculaneum, which were buried in AD 79.[7] By the late first century BC, Pompeian wall painting had shifted from the so-called 'first' style of coloured panels and mosaics into the 'second' style, which introduced pictures; naturalistic poses and lifelike portraits were highly favoured. Similar characteristics were much sought-after in sculpture. The Roman liking for realistic portraiture was widely adopted even in the images on Egyptian mummies (see Figure 22), and sculpture workshops such as those at Aphrodisias in Turkey enjoyed access to a huge and voracious market: the tax code of Palmyra envisaged in AD 137 the importation of statues by the camel-load.[8] A taste for such portraiture was stimulated by the wide circulation of lifelike images of emperors and their families, both on official statues and on coins in relief. On a less elevated artistic level, imperial styles in hairdressing rapidly spread to the rest of the population, and have become a useful method for dating statues.

LITERARY CULTURE

I have left literary culture until last, as it is better to speak here not of unity but of an acknowledged duality within an overall cultural consensus. The dual element was a direct product of language. West of a line drawn around the Danube area and through the southern Balkans and the Adriatic Sea the language used by the provincial élite when they consciously aligned themselves to Graeco-Roman culture was Latin. East of that line, the language was Greek.

Figure 22 Portrait from the coffin of an Egyptian mummy from el-Rabaiyat, Fayum, second to fourth century AD. The realistic conventions of Roman portraiture have been adapted for a traditional Egyptian purpose. Photo courtesy of the Ashmolean Museum, Oxford.

That this should be so was not only the product of pressure by Greek speakers from below but also of a conscious decision by the rulers of the Roman state. Thus, on an occasion when a foreigner addressed the emperor Claudius in Greek and Latin, Claudius replied, 'Since you come armed with both our languages …' (Suetonius, *Claudius* 42.1). And Roman official pronouncements in the East were almost always given in Greek except when they concerned Roman colonists (who in the Early Empire made a point of the use of Latin, as in Berytus, modern Beirut), or the army, for whom Latin was the universal language of command. The original reasons for these decisions lay well back in the Middle Republic, when Roman aristocrats enthusiastically adopted much of Greek culture and made it their own. For such people the ability to speak Greek was a mark of education for anyone who usually spoke Latin.

Both in Greek and, by the time of Augustus, in Latin, a complex literary tradition had developed. A cultured Greek speaker would be expected to know Homer well and the plays of the great tragedians, which ensured familiarity with the Greek myths. He or she could be expected to have some acquaintance with Herodotus and Thucydides, the historians of the fifth century BC, and with the greatest of the orators, such as Demosthenes and Aeschines of the fourth century BC. He or she would know something about classical Athens and Sparta, but not necessarily much about Greek history since Alexander the Great. All this engendered a great respect for the spoken as well as the written word. Professional orators who travelled the eastern empire could be assured large and enthusiastic audiences and much adulation.

The common literary culture of the western empire was more recent in origin. The cultural efflorescence under Augustus in the city of Rome (see Chapter 18) produced a mass of prose and poetry that rapidly fulfilled a role as classic texts in the education of children. The histories of Caesar and Livy, the poetry of Vergil and Horace, and the speeches of Cicero had all begun to achieve, by the first century AD, the central place in education which they continued to have in much of Europe down to the nineteenth century. An aristocrat in Africa like Apuleius could make a highly successful career as an orator and writer without straying beyond the Latin language. But Latin literature was aimed at, and consumed by, the élite alone. Evidence of more widespread knowledge of great writers is confined to tags of the *Aeneid* scribbled on the walls of Pompeii and on sherds and other materials by soldiers at forts as far apart as Masada (in Israel) and Vindolanda on Hadrian's wall. If there was any basic text which all literate people in the West would know, it was Vergil's *Aeneid*.[9]

In both Greek and Latin areas, the success of literary culture was supported by a newly competent book trade, with the result that publication of editions could lead to quite rapid dissemination of ideas. Already in the first century BC, Horace envisaged his poetry being read in Spain and by the River Rhône (*Odes* 2.20.20). One reason for such dissemination was the professionalization of education and culture. Expertise in rhetoric, which in the Roman Republic was expected of men of affairs, became the preserve of specialists who, like Aelius Aristides, might perform little or no public role. Most successful authors wrote at leisure under the patronage of others, not, like Cicero or Caesar, in the midst of other activities, although there were exceptions, such as the emperor Marcus Aurelius, whose *Meditations*, written in Greek, were incongruously composed while on campaign near the Danube. On a lower level, it had become standard in Rome in the Late Republic to entrust education to a schoolteacher, rather than for a father to attempt to instil moral values himself.[10]

Among the literary works thus disseminated was a large corpus of middlebrow philosophy. This was not a great period for philosophical innovation of any kind, and most of the writings of Seneca, Plutarch and

Marcus Aurelius are more striking for the eclecticism of their thought than for its rigour or originality. Exceptions may be Epictetus, the ex-slave whose brand of moral Stoicism was influential among some individuals of high social standing such as Arrian, and the Jewish philosopher Philo, who tried to combine the Bible with Platonism. But lack of depth was balanced by breadth of application. Philosophical notions, particularly those from the Stoic and, to a lesser extent, Cynic schools, became very widespread. Epicurean ideas spread also, but were widely regarded as more suspect. Epicureans were often accused of being atheists because of their claim that the gods were indifferent to human affairs.

The pervasiveness of such ideas had little or nothing to do with any missionary aim by philosophers to propagate their ideas. Neither Stoics nor Epicureans customarily preached on street corners, although one Epicurean, Diogenes of Oenoanda in Asia Minor, set up a huge inscription in his city in about AD 200 to educate his fellow citizens in Epicureanism.[11] Cynics, who did preach in public, were more concerned to instil doubt in their audience than to impart any systematic philosophy as a whole.

The role of the state in the emergence of the cultural norms of the Early Empire was largely but not entirely confined to passive acquiescence. Augustus as patron actively encouraged the final emergence of a distinctive Latin literary culture, strong enough to hold its head high when compared with Greek. Whether the personal tastes of other emperors percolated through the empire is less clear. Nero's love for Greek athletics sparked off no imitators outside the world in which such behaviour was in any case normal. One emperor, however, stands out as strikingly more responsible for cultural change, and that is Hadrian.

DOMINANCE OF GREEK CULTURE IN SECOND CENTURY AD

Hadrian seems to have had something of a blueprint for the empire. He was the first and, in this period, the last emperor to tour his domain systematically. As he progressed, he founded cities, erected buildings and indulged in his love for Greek art, sculpture and rhetoric:

> Hadrian travelled through one province after another, visiting the various regions and cities and inspecting all the garrisons and forts. Some of these he removed to more desirable places, some he abolished, and he also established some new ones. ... He also constructed theatres and held games as he travelled about from city to city.
> (Cassius Dio, *History of Rome* 69.9.2 and 10.1)

Of greatest significance was his preference for things Greek rather than Latin, a personal quirk rather than an inherited one, since he came from a Roman colony in Spain where Greek was very much a literary rather than an everyday language. At any rate, Hadrian's preferences (and those of his successors,

Antoninus Pius and Marcus Aurelius) elevated Greek culture to dominance throughout the empire for the rest of the second century AD, as is illustrated by the extraordinary career of a certain Favorinus of Arles who, despite coming from a Latin-speaking part of Gaul, enjoyed a most successful life as professor of Greek rhetoric in Athens and then at Rome.[12]

The ease with which Greek culture came to dominate in the second century was of course largely due to the general acceptance of Greek civilization as an (optional) part of Roman culture since the Late Republic. Its victory was illustrated by the quite widespread adoption amongst Roman aristocrats of the distinctive facial markings of an adult male Greek, that is, the beard. The same period witnessed the espousal, even beyond the élite, of two customs which might seem more obviously central to the self-identity of individuals. First, the practice of writing on stone spread very widely round the empire, as attested by thousands of epitaphs – a private habit rather than a requirement imposed by the state (see Figure 23).[13] Second, the great variety of local

Figure 23 Tombstone of Regina, from South Shields in England. This British woman had married Barathes, a soldier from Palmyra who had served on Hadrian's wall. The monument has inscriptions in both Latin and Palmyrene. Photo © Arbeia Roman Fort & Museums, Tyne & Wear Archives and Museums.

customs for disposal of the dead, including in northern Europe and Italy the widespread use of cremation, gave way during the second century to inhumation. Indeed, the vogue for carved stone coffin-shaped sarcophagi became a distinctive imperial art form. The change to burial, for which no ideological explanation has been found, seems to reflect the influence of fashion in the imperial court, first upon Rome and Italy, then upon the rest of the empire. Few other phenomena better illustrate the impulses towards cultural unity.[14]

Part IV

SOCIETY

16

REACTIONS TO IMPERIAL RULE

Approximately 50 to 60 million people lived within the confines of the Roman Empire at its height. This great mass was ruled by one man whose ability to retain power depended ultimately on brute force and terror. The emperor's subjects reacted to their powerlessness in a variety of ways: by accommodating themselves to reality in a spirit of realism or self-deception; by dissociating themselves from the state as far as was possible, and making their lives and careers within alternative value systems in which Roman politics and public affairs could be seen as irrelevant; or by committing themselves to oppose the state, by open defiance of imperial propaganda or (less commonly) by armed rebellion in the form of political conspiracies, banditry or national revolt.[1]

It is implausible that any one emperor will have elicited a uniform response across his extensive domains. In any case, some of his subjects may have reacted to him as an individual (or, at any rate, they may have reacted to the *persona* that he succeeded in conveying), whereas others may have viewed him only as a representative of the imperial system. It is reasonable therefore to expect variety in different places and periods, and the remaining chapters of this part of the book will be devoted to examining the response of different peoples in different areas of the empire.

It should be admitted at the outset that the project is not altogether straightforward, since the amount and type of evidence vary drastically from area to area, and it is rarely likely to be easy to see whether what survives represents typical attitudes or exceptional ones. In general, it can be asserted that the viewpoints of women, children and slaves are particularly hard to investigate, and the predominant trend of the evidence is to illuminate the attitude of the richer members of society who had the ability to record their ideas in durable form such as inscriptions, and who had either the education to produce the literary works preserved through the medieval manuscript traditions or the money to commission such works from others.

TYPES OF EVIDENCE

The bulk of the literary evidence, at least from the first century AD, derives from the city of Rome itself. It is tempting to see this fact as though it were significant, as if the city were somehow more Roman than more distant parts of the empire. But it has already been noted that this was not always the attitude of the state, and, as will be seen below, it was not always the attitude of the inhabitants of the empire. The survival of such literature was due almost entirely to its perceived literary merit in Late Antiquity, not because of its social or political relevance at the time of composition. Nonetheless, the preponderance of the evidence and its intrinsic interest have been allowed in this book to expand the sections below on the city of Rome to two chapters (Chapters 17 and 18).

Second only to the output of the city of Rome was a great flood of literature produced in Greece and Asia Minor between the late first and second centuries AD. Works of history, rhetoric, scholarship and philosophy were produced (and survived) in profusion, but their evidence is of a peculiar kind, since much of it emphasizes not contemporary society but that of Classical Greece before the Hellenistic period.

The third type of literary work to survive in any quantity, and again not necessarily representative of the attitudes of more than a few, is religious literature. Many Christian and Jewish writings of this period were preserved by the Early Church and to a lesser extent by later Judaism. They contain much incidental information on the life of inhabitants in the parts of the empire bordering the eastern Mediterranean, but they provide few insights into the northern or western regions of Roman rule.

For these other views, then, the reactions to imperial rule must be gauged from the ambiguous testimony of buildings, artefacts, and inscriptions. In Egypt a mass of papyri illuminates some aspects of life in villages and small towns. In Greece and in Asia Minor the strength of the epigraphic habit provides a large corpus of evidence of how local aristocrats wished themselves to be viewed. But for much of northern Europe the picture has to be built up entirely from archaeological remains, and the fragments of unreliable comments about these unfamiliar societies written by authors from the urban civilizations of the Mediterranean region.

ACCOMMODATION

The bulk of the evidence for accommodation to one-man rule by self-deception derives from the capital city and the municipalities of Italy, even though within the imperial court itself, there was no pretence: the imperial palace was a machine for the aggrandizement of its chief occupant; its other inhabitants, his huge *familia* of slaves and freedmen, existed to do his bidding. Senators and others of the higher social orders within Roman society proved highly competent in presenting themselves as willing participants in an aristocratic society of noble equals, a myth perpetuated as much by them as by the emperors themselves. A similar self-deception may be found in, for example, Aelius Aristides' image of his beloved Smyrna as one of a harmonious league of cities of which Rome too was only one city, albeit the most glorious (see Chapter 13).

In contrast the imperial cult reveals accommodation by realists who recognized that all depended on one man's whim, and that he was to be flattered and courted accordingly. A good deal of emperor worship was stimulated by pressure from below, by the worshippers, rather than imposed by the emperor. The Greek communities of Asia Minor had always competed among each other for status and power, a legacy of their days as Hellenistic city-states. This rivalry continued under the empire, except they now vied for honours bestowed by the emperor. One of the greatest privileges was the title of *neokoros* ('temple warden'), which could only be granted to communities which had a provincial temple of the imperial cult. Some cities, such as Pergamon, Smyrna and Ephesus, had acquired three provincial temples by the early third century A.D., earning the right to be known as three times *neokoros*. These privileges were advertised prominently on local coinages.

The maintenance of personal honour ensured that aristocrats played their part in the government of the empire, serving as provincial administrators and army commanders to enhance their personal status and *dignitas*, much as their predecessors had done under the Republic. In this way, the emperor functioned as the aristocrat *par excellence*, and other senators were encouraged to emulate his actions and virtues. Some senators portrayed themselves as grateful for whatever favour they received from the ruler, as in the case of L. Plotius Sabinus, who proudly recorded on his career inscription that he had earned a position in the second group of men who paid homage to Antoninus Pius at his morning *salutatio* (*CIL* VI 41111 = *ILS* 1078). Another aristocrat of the Antonine age, the jurist Salvius Iulianus, specifically noted that his salary as quaestor had been doubled by the emperor Hadrian 'on account of his distinguished learning' (*propter insignem doctrinam*) (*CIL* VIII 24094 = *ILS* 8973). These rewards enabled senators to accumulate honour and personal distinctions within the constraints of an imperial system.

In the provinces accommodation to imperial rule usually began with the local elite, for whom recognition by Rome served as a bulwark for their own authority. It sometimes took the form of adoption of aspects of Roman culture, as described by Tacitus in his biography of Agricola, who had served as governor of Britain:

> ... the nation which used to reject the Latin language began to aspire to rhetoric: further, the wearing of our dress became a distinction, and the toga came into fashion, and little by little the Britons went astray into alluring vices: to the promenade, the bath, the well-appointed dinner table. The simple natives gave the name of culture (*humanitas*) to this factor of their slavery.
> (Tac. *Agr.* 21).

The distribution of inscriptions in the Gallic provinces shows that they were usually erected in urban regions, particularly in communities on major road networks or near military zones. Epigraphic commemoration was particularly favoured by freedmen as it allowed them to display their rise through the social hierarchy and the honours that had accrued to them as the result of Roman rule, such as membership of the priesthood of the emperor (the *Augustales*).[2]

On the other hand accommodation by provincials might sometimes involve cultural choices more complex than a simple adoption of a Roman way of life, since individuals might switch between different identities depending on the circumstances, wearing a toga, for example to participate in emperor worship, but speaking their native language, rather than Latin, with members of their family. These different aspects are often now difficult to trace, since the evidence generally shows us only one aspect at a time.[3]

DISSOCIATION

Dissociation from the state was easier at a greater distance, either geographical or social, from the centre of power, although even in Rome those poets like Ovid who wrote about love, not war, in a way distanced themselves from the regime.[4] Some of the less prosperous and more inaccessible areas technically under Roman rule, such as Rough Cilicia, might witness almost none of the effects of the Roman state. With no troops stationed in the area, because there was nothing worth defending; with no urban centres, because the land produced insufficient surplus to permit their erection; with harvests too meagre to be worth the trouble to exact unpaid taxes, and routes into the territory too hilly to permit easy disciplining of the recalcitrant; in such cases, the natives' understanding of, and concern for, the Roman state may well have been negligible, although, in the nature of things, discovering much about the attitudes of such people will always be difficult. It is unusual that in the religious texts of the Jews of second-century Galilee something survives.[5]

Individual drop-outs could make their stand in any part of the empire. In some cases, they would elevate their stance to the level of a philosophy. Thus the bearded Cynics on street corners were a phenomenon frequently noted in the cities of the Mediterranean region in the Early Empire.[6] Cynics preached self-reliance and disregard for the empty trappings of public life. For many Cynics this attitude would attract no notice: only those otherwise expected to take on a public role, such as senators in mid-career, or those who proclaimed their faith in the market-place came (deliberately) to wider attention. Again, the lives of those private men and women who lived in a self-contained world of family and friends can rarely be reconstructed, and it is even more difficult to know whether that life was deliberately chosen or the unintended consequence of unknown difficulties encountered when entering on a public and political career otherwise desired. But of some, like those who sought a different explanation of life within religious groups such as Christianity, something more positive can be said; the literature produced for and by such converts reveals the creation not just of an alternative theodicy but of a society within a wider society, with its own bonds, pressures and expectations.[7]

OPPONENTS OF THE STATE

And finally, there were also explicit opponents of the state, who can conveniently be divided into those whose hostility was expressed symbolically and those who genuinely expected or hoped to change the system under which they were ruled, or at least the individual at the head of that system. In neither case is the motive of the actors always evident.

Of symbolic opponents of the imperial regime much the best known are the heroes of the 'Stoic' opposition whose exploits fill, often tragically, the pages of Tacitus' *Annals*.[8] Stoicism in itself might simply provide an antidote to the pretences and pressures of court life, but some Stoic senators and equites gained fame or notoriety by public expression of their distaste for the emperor or hatred of his immense power. By speeches in the senate or ostentatious demonstrations of defiance, they frequently brought upon their heads the displeasure of the emperor and in some cases eventual martyrdom. Such was the case with Thrasea Paetus and Barea Soranus in AD 66, as described in a lengthy narrative by Tacitus, who begins by detailing the charges against Thrasea:

> After the massacre of so many distinguished men, Nero finally coveted the destruction of Virtue herself by killing Thrasea Paetus and Marcius Barea Soranus. He had long hated them both. Against Thrasea there were additional motives. He had, as I mentioned, walked out of the senate during the debate about Agrippina. He had also been inconspicuous at the Youth Games. This gave all the more offence because during Games (the festival instituted by Antenor the Trojan) at his birthplace, Patavium, he had participated by singing in tragic costume. Besides, on the day when the praetor Antistius Sosianus was virtually condemned to death for writing offensive verses about Nero, he had proposed and carried a more lenient sentence. Again, after Poppaea's death, he had deliberately stayed away when divine honours were voted to her, and was not present at her funeral.
>
> (*Annals* 16.21)

The mode of senators' and equites' expression of opposition was tied up with their self-image as members of the Roman upper class. They never had any hope of changing the regime or threatening the autocrat. At best they won for themselves gratification, and for him embarrassment. Such opposition was as ineffective as the use of pejorative nicknames to refer to emperors or the circulation, after the death of Agrippina, of witty epigrams about Nero as a matricide (Suet. *Nero* 39.2), or the subtle cultural resistance among the provincial populations encapsulated in a reluctance to equate traditional local gods with Roman deities, or the continued use of non-Roman domestic spaces such as British roundhouses, which have been identified by archaeologists adopting post-colonial approaches to the material evidence as signs of opposition to Roman hegemony.[9]

Genuinely dangerous opposition to emperors came rather from his army commanders or from his close acquaintances, including his *familia*, or from mass uprisings by his subjects. The possibility that an imperial legate might rise up against the princeps who had selected him for command was apparent from the beginning of the Roman Empire. It had been precisely the prospect of winning power by the use of provincial legions that added fuel to the civil wars from 49 BC to Actium. Army commanders marched on Rome from all parts of the empire in AD 69. Scribonianus, legate of Dalmatia, rebelled against Claudius in AD 42, and Saturninus, governor of Upper Germany, raised a revolt against Domitian in AD 89. Other disaffected commanders were inhibited, presumably, by the fear of death as the price of failure, and the knowledge that not one of them controlled sufficient troops to expect success if faced by the concerted opposition of fellow commanders. It is worth recalling that all of Nero's legates, apart from Galba in Spain, remained loyal to him in AD 68, until in panic Nero engineered his own death. For many commanders it seemed all too likely that fellow generals would remain loyal to the man who had appointed them all. It was clearly unsafe to ask, for fear of accusation of plotting treachery.

More effectively dangerous were the emperor's close associates whose physical proximity to him gave them opportunities denied to others. The tally is long of emperors killed by trusted subordinates, praetorian guards, wives, children, freedmen and slaves. No amount of care could counteract the risks posed by the opportunity for murder. The motives for such opposition were frequently personal. Cassius Chaerea, tribune of the praetorian guard, committed murder because he had suffered a personal slight from Gaius. Nero sought power in place of his adopted father. The man who killed Domitian had probably been suborned by Nerva, who benefited so rapidly from the latter's death. None of these was trying to change the system, even though some senators in AD 41 thought the system could be changed once Gaius' murder had been effected.

MASS INSURRECTION

And finally, mass insurrection. In the nature of the Roman Empire, which favoured so strongly the rich landed class, a class struggle by the poor urban plebs might reasonably have been expected, but it is not found.[10] In the city of Rome the urban plebs had learned to play an important political role in the Late Republic, when in the 50s BC Clodius and Milo terrorized the city and controlled the political agenda, and in the triumviral period that role was maintained, though to less effect. The power of the plebs was still being demonstrated in 22 BC, when the senate was briefly barricaded inside the *curia* (senate house), and in 19 BC, when the consular candidate Egnatius Rufus garnered a dangerous amount of popular support in the city. But despite the symbolic hostility to unpopular emperors manifested at *spectacula* (shows), the urban plebs stayed strikingly quiescent through most of the early principate, bought off by 'bread and circuses'. The rural poor, both free and slave, were effectively cowed into submission; the slave revolts of the Late Republic were not repeated in the imperial period.

Revolts, when they did happen, took place at a distance from the centre of power. The tally of recorded disaffection is quite considerable in Gaul, Britain, the Balkans, Africa, Judaea and Pontus. There may also have been many other revolts which the sources do not record, since the Roman state tended to ignore such setbacks when it could and native literature rarely survives. So, for instance, the contemporary author Velleius Paterculus almost completely ignored the major insurrection by Tacfarinas in Africa in AD 17–24, and it is the chance survival of later histories that preserve an account of the episode.

What the rebels sought was not always complete independence from Roman rule. Many revolts were sparked off by the census, by the enthusiastic collection of taxes, or by conscription, and in such cases a diminution of the tax burden may have been their sole hope. But other rebellions clearly had more ambitious aims. There was a rash of revolts on the geographical fringes of Roman power, particularly in the northern provinces, in the Julio-Claudian period.[11] Led by members of the old local ruling class who had partially, but evidently not yet entirely, incorporated themselves into mainstream Roman society, these rebellions marked a last-ditch attempt to win back independence before it was too thoroughly eroded.

But it is not always easy to distinguish in the sources between local disturbances and insurrection against Rome. Where, for instance, should one place the *stasis* (civil unrest) in Alexandria under Hadrian?[12] Anti-Roman according to the accounts of such events surviving in various versions on papyrus and known to modern scholars as the *Acts of the Pagan Martyrs*, the discontent of Alexandrian Greeks was nonetheless sparked off by hostility to local Jews and to Egyptians, and the urban riots had no chance of threatening Roman power, as Trajan's and Hadrian's treatment of the city shows they were well aware. Similarly, the frequent revolts in Judaea usually expressed discontent with Rome in religious terms, but there are good grounds to suppose that the rebels hoped for far more than religious tolerance in Jerusalem. Inhabitants of Greek *poleis* (city states) always valued their freedom almost as an element of the definition of their communities, but they could, when they wanted, define freedom as local autonomy under Roman rule. Similarly, supporters of the *imperium Galliarum* (empire of the Gauls) led by Civilis and the Batavi in AD 69 may have seen themselves as an expression of Gallic nationalism, but they may also have seen themselves in the context of Roman politics, as opponents of the Vitellian regime.[13]

17

THE CITY OF ROME:
SOCIAL ORGANIZATION

In 44 BC the huge sprawling city of Rome was filled with a population of heterogeneous origin. The city had grown rapidly from *c.* 200 BC, as the presence of wealth imported by conquest attracted peasants from the countryside hopeful for a better income than the limited profits of a small farm could ever permit, and the import of slaves as domestic and skilled craft labour swelled the ranks of citizens on their release from servitude. A good proportion of the Roman plebs was probably descended from slaves, and this proportion is likely to have increased over time, although precise ratios cannot be known. The ethnic origins of such freedmen ranged from Germany to Syria, but it may be assumed that their descendants inter-married, since no record survives of definable ethnic groups within the city plebs apart from those communities, like the Jews, who maintained distinctive religious practices while encouraging endogamy.[1]

At the end of the Republic, this population was strikingly amorphous. Around the small civic centre of the forum clustered a few architecturally undistinguished buildings. On the Capitoline hill stood a huddle of ancient temples. Still to be completed was the development of a new forum by Julius Caesar, begun in 54 BC, which with its temple to Venus Genetrix and new senate house would be larger and grander than the existing Roman forum.[2] Nearby lay the great town houses of the rich, with the paraphernalia of their *familiae* increasing the size of each ménage. All round the centre stood great tenement blocks (*insulae*) for mass housing, often built leaning up against the steep sides of the hills; they were cheaply constructed from sun-dried mud brick with roofs of reeds and timber frames, liable to catch fire and dangerously overcrowded. It was here that the poor lived, the better-off owning workshops in the front of their houses, the lowest of the low taking to the streets to beg, and finding shelter at night between the buildings and under the vaults of public monuments. The streets themselves lay in random disorder, reflecting the private entrepreneurial spirit which had directed the growth of Rome to one of the greatest, but least magnificent, cities of the civilized world.

All this was to change quite substantially with the advent of Augustus. According to Suetonius (*Augustus* 28.3), Augustus claimed that he had found

Rome a city of brick and left it a city of marble. Nor did he greatly exaggerate. He could point to massive expenditure in rebuilding old temples and constructing new ones; a new forum alongside but overshadowing Julius Caesar's; great new aqueducts to increase the public water supply, impressive public baths for its consumption, and restored public drains for its disposal; paved streets; the great gardens of Messala or Maecenas become, instead of symbols of private luxury, public areas for recreation. Such care for the fabric of the city continued under later emperors, reflecting the taste of individual rulers (such as Nero's gymnasium in the Campus Martius). Claudius, Nero (with the Golden House) and Trajan (with his new forum) continued the custom, inherited from the Republic, of adding imposing new structures to the sides of Rome's hills, but other emperors preferred a less grandiose style, providing spaces for civilized public social life in colonnades and squares.[3]

Nor was change confined to external appearances. For the first time, under Augustus, care was taken for the government of Rome as urban space. The urban sprawl was divided into fourteen regions (*regiones*), each composed of a fixed number of neighbourhoods (*vici*), each with its own local magistrates for municipal services such as fighting fires and implementing the building codes laid down by Augustus. The emperor's attention to the ancient walls and the gates of the city was a symbol of the protection offered to the community by his presence. In the theatres the Roman people were assigned to seats by the *lex Julia theatricalis* according to social status: senators, equites, freedmen were all instructed to know their social position and to be proud of it.[4] It seems that Augustus and his successors wanted the inhabitants of Rome to view themselves as part of a decent, ordered, tidy society. If the evidence of many inscriptions can be trusted, some at least adopted the image thrust upon them by the state. It created civic pride at a time when it had ceased to be obvious that the term *Roma* applied only to the capital city. Within 50 years, the city became as impressive as any in the Hellenistic East. Despite imperial neglect in the third century AD, Rome was to remain down to the Middle Ages one of the wonders of the world.

As much as the physical structure of the city, the early principate witnessed substantial changes in the social relations and the social structure of the urban populace. To the extent that this was a deliberate change by the state, contemporaries explained it as a reaction to the immorality of the Late Republic. Horace opens the second book of his *Epistles* as follows (1.1–4):

> Seeing that you alone carry the weight of so many great changes, guarding our Italian state with arms, gracing her with morals, and reforming her with laws, I should sin against the public weal if with long talk, Caesar, I were to delay your busy hours.

For Augustus and his contemporaries, the strengthening of social differentiation was part of the task of tackling moral, particularly sexual, degeneracy and shameful profligacy, but for the sake of clarity I shall here examine the two issues separately.

THE IMPERIAL COURT

The social life of the city was dominated by the court of the princeps, which set fashions in dress and taste in literature, art and theatre, and provided the subject for popular gossip. Since this social prominence was directly related to the function of the court as the centre of political power, it has been discussed already in Chapter 9.

SENATORS

The prime candidates for consideration as the emperor's social equals were senators and their families, since the princeps liked to portray himself as, above all, one of their number. On senators' view of themselves, a good deal can be said, since the writings of Tacitus and the younger Pliny provide many insights into their rather curious attitudes. Senators saw themselves as the natural heirs of the full heroic political tradition of the Republic. The attainments they professed to admire were those discussed in Chapter 3: military prowess, freedom to speak one's mind (and if need be, to be obstinately determined to do so), the right to compete without hindrance for glory and honour, the preservation of the dignity of their rank. These values were, if anything, enhanced by early emperors. Augustus, who weeded out the unworthy from the senate in 28, 18 and 13–11 BC and AD 4, could claim to have achieved an optimum of quantity and quality, a genuine élite, a policy followed later by Claudius, as censor in AD 47–48, and by other emperors.

Such values seem incongruous, even ludicrous, in the mouths of men like the younger Pliny. He, like almost all his predecessors since Actium, owed his senatorial status primarily to the patronage of the emperor, whose power no ordinary senator could ever think to challenge. The subjects discussed by the senate as a body and recorded by him and by Tacitus are strikingly banal. Trials of individual senatorial governors, accused of corruption or hostility to the princeps, provide the bulk of *causes célèbres*. It is clear that all important decisions on the administration of the empire were being taken, not by the senate, but by the emperor and his advisors in the palace, many of whom might not be senators at all.[5]

What, then, did senators do to pass their time, and how could intelligent men fool themselves that a role of such little point was not only valuable but respectable and important? When not holding a magistracy, the answer seems to be that there was indeed little to do. Pliny spent much of his time in Rome either undertaking private advocacy in the centumviral courts, where disputed wills were adjudged, or attending literary salons. The echoes of Cicero's correspondence in his *Letters* indicate his desire to be seen in the same senatorial tradition. It was still possible to claim that oratory would bring a senator to prominence in the state, as Tacitus records of Vespasian's reign:

The meaner and more humble was the origin of those two men [Eprius Marcellus and Q. Vibius Crispus], and the more notorious the poverty and want that hemmed their young lives, so the more brightly do they shine as conspicuous examples of the practical advantages of oratorical power. Though they had none of the recommendations of birth or the resources of wealth, though neither of the two was of pre-eminently high moral character ... yet after being now for many years the most powerful men in Rome, and – so long as they cared for such success – leaders of the bar, they take today the leading place in the emperor's circle of friends, and get their own way in everything.

(*Dialogue on Oratory* 8.3)

But the regular meetings of the senate were only twice a month, and although deliberate prolonged abstention continued to provoke adverse comment, the lowering of the quorum for meetings in 11 BC and the introduction of a variable quorum in 9 BC demonstrate a structural problem in the organization of the institution. Quite simply, few senators really wanted to attend; the fact that they did so at all is testimony not to the interest of the proceedings but to the ambitions of members who sought imperial patronage.[6]

Senate meetings must have seemed particularly futile in the brief period from 18 BC to AD 14 when matters were effectively decided by a probouleutic council.[7] Tiberius' solicitude in bringing issues to the senate for discussion, his transfer to the senate of a major role in elections to magistracies, and the regular use from AD 20 of the senate as a court for cases involving treason or extortion and for cases of adultery in which the accused were of high rank, may have given some senators the feeling they were doing something important. If so, this self-confidence will have been somewhat dashed when in AD 26 the princeps turned his back on senatorial society by retiring to Capri.

The true glory of senatorial life, then, lay in the magistracies for which senators alone were eligible. Here the values of the Republic retained their supremacy. The proconsulship of Asia or Africa retained the highest esteem and became the acme of the senatorial *cursus*. By tradition, only the most senior ex-consuls were nominated for Africa and Asia; when in AD 36 a certain C. Galba was excluded from the ballot for the two provinces, he killed himself (Tacitus, *Annals* 6.40.2). This had nothing to do with the power of such positions, which was negligible. The governor of Africa had one legion at his disposal until the reign of Gaius, when it was transferred to the command of the imperial legate; the governor of Asia had none from the beginning of the principate. In any case, senators at a much earlier stage in their careers might wield much greater military power as legates of the princeps. But a mutual agreement among senators that it was proconsulships and priesthoods and the standard curule magistracies from quaestor to consul that really mattered kept high their self-esteem, and their hopes, since the practice, standard since 5 BC, of electing several pairs of *consules suffecti* (additional substitute consuls) each year rendered access to that high honour much easier than in the Republic. Of other honours, new but prestigious, the urban prefecture bestowed considerable glory on its holder as effective ruler of the capital city. More commonly achieved, but more transitory, was the glow derived from a taste of power at the real centre, as a member of the emperor's *consilium*.

Not many senators, even by the time of Tiberius, originated from any of the great families of the Republic.[8] By the end of the first century AD even fewer were left.[9] The causes of the disappearance of families from the record are multiple. On the one hand, senatorial status depended on a high minimum wealth census, imposed since 18 BC, which could be imperilled by division of property between more than one child — hence the tendency to rear one child only, and the dangers of childlessness and extinction of the line, avoided only by adoption, if that child should perish after the mother had passed child-bearing age. On the other hand, Augustus' grant of the right to wear the *latus clavus* (a broad purple stripe on the tunic) and other senatorial privileges to all close relatives and descendants of a senator down to the third generation rendered devotion to a senatorial career otiose for social esteem for those whose ancestors had already held office. Augustus' intention was clearly to create a separate senatorial class into which others could enter only with difficulty, but no emperor made it impossible for aspirants from outside, who simply had to wait until they had achieved the quaestorship before they could wear the broad stripe. By the 30s AD the system had effectively broken down, since in practice emperors granted the right to wear the *latus clavus* to anyone they wished to promote, regardless of family origins, and even before they had reached the quaestorship. In any case, the effect was a rapid turnover of new families of diverse regional origins, who yet retained the ethos of their predecessors.[10]

The origins of senators reflected in part the role of existing senior senators as mediators of imperial patronage. Thus in the mid-first century AD there was a rash of senators from Spain under the patronage of figures like Seneca, who came from Corduba (Córdoba). In the late first century there were many senators from southern Gaul, in the late first and second centuries from the Greek world (especially Asia), and at the end of the second century from Africa, while some regions, like Britain, produced no senators at all.

In some ways precisely the novelty of their rise encouraged 'new' senators to espouse senatorial traditions with the greater fervour in order to prove their genuineness as heirs of the past. Such an attitude was clearest in the curious behaviour of the new senators who comprised the so-called 'Stoic' opposition under Nero and the Flavian emperors.[11] For some Stoics as, for instance, the younger Seneca or the emperor Marcus Aurelius, their philosophy was essentially a private affair, but for others it encouraged a display of principles even at great personal cost. In AD 66, a certain Thrasea Paetus incurred the wrath of Nero by ostentatiously refusing to attend senatorial meetings, implying thereby that he was unable to speak freely in that body because of the autocratic stance of the emperor (see Chapter 16). Nero tried to refute the charge of tyranny by, incongruously, ordering Thrasea to commit suicide.

Thrasea's son-in-law, Helvidius Priscus, met a similar fate under Vespasian in *c.* AD 75, after continually asserting in public that he was unable to say whatever he wished because of the princeps. Helvidius' son, and various other colleagues, were martyred in a bloodbath in AD 93 by Domitian, after continuing to voice the same opinions. The attitude of Pliny and Tacitus to such behaviour was interestingly ambivalent. It was evident that these men were heroes, who had achieved in full measure a demonstration of their senatorial independence and *dignitas*. On the other hand, their public martyrdoms denounced the rest of the senators, both by the implication that they failed to stand up to the emperor only out of cowardice, and by the practical involvement of the senate as the court in which these heroes were condemned to death on the charge of *maiestas*, infringing the majesty of the Roman state.

The self-image preferred by most senators was easier to maintain without such martyrs. They saw themselves as great men, a natural aristocracy whose high status was achieved through the patronage of the noble, of whom the princeps was the most important. They persuaded themselves that they agreed with the emperor not out of fear but because they liked his views. Their self-importance depended on the preservation of this pretence (see Figure 24).

Augustus and his successors went a long way to encourage such self-importance among senators. So, for instance, they encouraged the continuation of competition at elections.[12] It may even be suggested that Augustus' law about electoral bribery (the *lex Julia de ambitu*) was, so to speak, a double bluff. Laws against bribery presupposed that senators thought it worthwhile to bribe the electorate, suggesting that there was genuine competition, even though, when there was a strong contest at the praetorian elections of AD 11, Augustus simply had all the candidates appointed to the post. Emperors, it will be recalled, needed contented, ambitious senators to hold military commands and to maintain their power. The prime danger from their point

Figure 24 Silver denarius attributed to Vindex at the start of the civil wars following revolt against Nero, AD 68–9. The obverse, depicting Victory, proclaims 'the salvation of the human race'. The reverse has simply 'the Senate and People of Rome' and an oak-wreath. The revolt of Vindex may have been the last time that any senators believed that they could govern the empire without an emperor. Photo courtesy of the Ashmolean Museum, Oxford.

of view was that young men of the requisite calibre would not be interested in a public career, when the highest honours were reserved for the imperial family. It was a genuine danger, as the shortage of recruits for the senate in some years demonstrated; the *lex Julia de senatu habendo* was to some extent aimed at the crisis of recruitment. The self-advertisement of the 'Stoic' martyrs was in part a response to the problem that such risk-taking was one of the few ways for a senator not of imperial blood to achieve the eternal fame for which Roman politicians hungered.

In recognition of, or to forestall, this problem, Augustus offered substantial salaries to provincial governors (an innovation) and invented new prestigious posts for senators, like the prefecture of the city. And above all he greatly increased the visible prestige of the senators in the city of Rome. In the Republic they had already enjoyed special seats at the circus. Now their families had special clothes, while the sweeping programme of legislation begun in 18 BC included laws like that against intermarriage by those of senatorial status with ex-slaves (the *lex Julia de maritandis ordinibus*), or that of AD 19 forbidding members of the upper classes from appearing on stage or in the arena in public, which all gave the (fraudulent) impression that senators were a caste apart.[13] At the same time, privileges granted by the same *lex Julia* to those with three children (to hold magistracies early, for example) marked an attempt to keep within the political élite the old Republican families whose continued prominence lent lustre to the new arrivals.

Emperors who encouraged senators in their self-image were fairly unanimous in disliking too much *libertas* (freedom) in senatorial debate, but they were more ambivalent about some other aspects of the aristocratic lifestyle.[14] The senators of the Late Republic seem to have evolved a hectic café society of sexual licence (both heterosexual and homosexual) and financial profligacy, not least in banquets and in the erection of private houses. Both sex and money were used to create and cement political ties between nobles. Augustus made strenuous efforts to combat this whole culture.[15] Sumptuary laws were introduced in 18 BC to control expenditure on banquets, clothes, jewellery and such like. In the *lex Julia de maritandis ordinibus* already mentioned, which was revised by the *lex Papia Poppaea* of AD 9 and (by Tiberius) in AD 20, he tried to encourage Roman citizens to settle down to the procreation of children. That Augustus' concern was to encourage *gravitas* (seriousness) in senatorial family life, rather than (as the sources implausibly allege) to create more citizen recruits for Rome's armies, is shown by his simultaneous decree that the marriages of soldiers while in service were not to be regarded as valid in Roman law. In the same broad legislative programme, Augustus promulgated a law on adultery and fornication (the *lex Julia de adulteriis coercendis*), under which, notoriously, he was himself eventually to accuse his own daughter and granddaughter. If such accusations were rare, that may have been a result of the lifestyles of the emperors themselves. Despite Augustus' laws, senatorial customs remained debauched throughout the Julio-Claudian period, and only really changed with the advent of the bourgeois values of Vespasian.

EQUITES

In some ways the new prominence of equites as a status group under Augustus marked a further attempt at the bolstering of *senatorial* privilege, as will appear below, but the process by which this occurred is a little tortuous. For the Greek historian, Polybius, in the mid-second century BC, Roman society was divided between the senators who represented the oligarchic element in society, and the rest. The equites first became prominent in Roman politics as a group only after 122 BC, when Gaius Gracchus brought it about that judges in jury trials should be chosen from their number, and their organization as a self-aware *ordo* (status group), like that of the senate, may not implausibly be assigned to Augustus himself.[16]

In the Republican period, equites had originally been those of sufficient wealth to serve as cavalry with the Roman army, a function no longer required by the end of the second century BC, when allied states provided cavalry instead. The number of equites was defined as those who belonged to the first eighteen centuries of the centuriate assembly. Their number might well have been larger than the more restricted group who served as jurors in the standing courts after the judicial reforms initiated by C. Gracchus in 122 BC. In any case, their position required property valued at 400,000 sesterces or more, so that in a loose sense any Roman citizen of that census rating could be called an eques. The same high property qualification was required of those who wished to stand as magistrates, and thus to earn entry into the senate.

Those who remained as equites were therefore those who were either too young for, or unenthusiastic about devoting themselves to, a political career. It was common for some members of a family to become senators and others to remain as equites. They shared class and economic interests, in all cases retaining most of their wealth in the form of agricultural land. On rare occasions, a group of equites might find themselves opposed to the senate as a body, as when, in the late Republic, those rich equites who took up public contracts (*publicani*) wished to change the terms of their contract, which were fixed by the senate, or when equestrian jurors tried a senator for peculation in the provinces. But equites rarely had any political voice as a group. There was no need for one, for if he was interested in politics, an adult male eques could always try to stand for office and hence become a senator. For Cicero, the equites were the epitome of disinterested, well-to-do Romans, gentlemen whose interests were also the state's, and whose political will could be asserted by placing a few of his non-senatorial friends on the senate house steps as a show of support during the Catilinarian crisis of 63 BC.

This nebulous background is worth stating, to mark the change that occurred first under Augustus and finally under Tiberius. Suddenly there is found a spread of inscriptions recording the status of individual *equites Romani* or proudly proclaiming their possession of the *equus publicus* (public horse), as can be illustrated by an inscription from Hasta, Etruria:

> To Publius Vergilius Laurea, son of Publius, grandson of Publius, of the tribe Pollia, aedile, *duumvir* for the administration of justice, prefect of engineers, judge in the four decuries, one of the equites chosen for public and private cases, prefect of Drusus Caesar, son of Germanicus, *duumvir quinquennalis*; to Publius Vergilius Paullinus, son of Publius, grandson of Publius, of the tribe Pollia, holder of the public horse, judge in the four decuries, prefect of engineers, prefect of veteran cohort 2.
> (EJ² no. 230; Braund no. 444)

A new annual parade of a select group of equites – 5,000, according to Dionysius of Halicarnassus (*Roman Antiquities* 6.13) – was organized, led by the 'flower of the youth', the young members of the imperial house who had yet to become senators. The list of jurors in the time of Augustus was somewhat smaller than this 5,000, but under Tiberius these jurors and holders of the 'public horse' came to be treated as a single *ordo*, honoured with the title *eques* and the right, exclusive to them and to senators, to wear a special gold ring and sit in the front rows of the theatre. The new corporate identity of the equestrian order is demonstrated by the *Senatus Consultum de Cn. Pisone Patre*, which refers to the *equites* as expressing opinions and delivering acclamations (probably in the theatre) as a distinct group:

> Likewise the senate particularly commends the conscientious efforts of the equestrian order in that it has loyally understood how important a matter and how relevant to the safety and devotion of all was at stake, and because it declared with repeated acclamations its sentiments and its grief for the wrongs of our Princeps and of his son and did this to the advantage of the commonwealth.
> (lines 151-154, trans. M. Griffin)

Imperial enthusiasm for this process may have been fuelled partly by the need to give the sons of senators a public role safely within the orbit of the regime, but the effect was much more widespread, as new Roman citizens throughout the empire boasted of their equestrian rank (even though, since they were not formally enrolled in the *ordo*, they were equites only in the wider sense), and procuratorships appointed directly by the princeps came to be seen almost as an equestrian *cursus* alternative to that of senators.[17]

What was the reason for such prominence for equites under Augustus? The emperor often claimed only to be restoring old customs, but that is unlikely to be true. The equites thus honoured in the city of Rome included many members of Italian municipal families. So too did the new senate. But – and this was crucial – the new prominence of equites emphasized all the more strongly the far greater honours bestowed on senators, who were for the first time distinguished from equites by the requirement that they possess one million (or perhaps 1,200,000) sesterces. This contrasted with the limit of 400,000 sesterces which was required of an eques.

POPULUS

The equites were thus clearly distinguished from the rest of the plebs of Rome by Augustus. But social engineering went further: the princeps also distinguished one group from the rest of the inhabitants as the, so-to-speak, 'official' plebs of the city.[18] The dole of free corn had been instituted by the tribune Clodius Pulcher in 58 BC, as a means to popularity when the people's vote was believed to have real power. Augustus, whose *Res Gestae* so emphatically portrayed his generosity to the plebs, redefined that body, cutting back on the number to a still large but now restricted group. For these privileged people, access to the dole was ensured by provision of a ticket by the state. Characteristically, free corn was given out not to the very poor and destitute, but to the 'respectable' plebs of moderate means, who had an interest in the preservation of the *status quo*, and whose support for the peace brought by autocracy was accordingly unwavering. In 2 BC, for example, it was this group of people who benefited from Augustus' much-vaunted largesse (*Res Gestae* 15): 'In my thirteenth consulship I gave 60 *denarii* apiece to those of the plebs who at that time were receiving public grain; the number involved was a little more than two hundred thousand.'

Within the plebs, Augustus further elevated the social self-consciousness and pride of one other group, the *liberti* (freedmen). The curious assumption in Roman law that a slave freed formally before a magistrate became a Roman citizen with (nearly) full rights has been discussed above, in terms of its economic effects.[19] In the Republic, freedmen simply merged into the general citizen population. By contrast, ex-slaves of the Early Empire often portrayed their servile origins with pride on inscriptions, as is the case in an inscription set up by the freedmen masters of the Augustales in Falerii:

> In honour of Imperator Caesar Augustus, son of a god, pontifex maximus, father of his country and the municipality, the masters of the Augustales, Gaius Egnatius Glyco, freedman of Marcus, Gaius Egnatius Musicus, freedman of Gaius, Gaius Julius Isochrysus, freedman of Caesar, Quintus Floronius Princeps, freedman of Quintus, had the Via Augusta paved with stone from the Via Annia outside the gate to the temple of Ceres at their own expense for the games.
> (EJ[2] no. 334; Braund no. 650)

Partly, such pride derived from identification with those of the emperor's freedmen whose power and influence showed what an ex-slave could do. Partly it perhaps reflected the self-esteem of the self-made man. But Augustus must again take some credit. The cult in the *vici* (Rome's 265 neighbourhoods) of the *genius Augusti* gave *liberti* their first public role as priests of the state. Petronius' picture of Trimalchio planning that he should be depicted on his funeral monument as a *sevir Augustalis* (*Satyricon* 71) shows how proud the successful freedman could be, as does the praise by Statius of the freedman father of Claudius Etruscus, who had served many emperors with distinction:

No brilliant lineage was yours, serene old man, no descent traced down from distant ancestors, but high fortune made good your birth and hid the blemish of your parentage. For your masters were not of common stock, but those to whom East and West are alike in thrall. No shame is that servitude to you; for what in heaven and earth remains unbound by the law of obedience? … a prosperous career was yours, and varied offices in due succession increased your dignity: it was your privilege ever to walk near divinities, ever to be close to Caesar's person and to share the holy secrets of the gods.

(*Silvae* 3.3.43–49, 63–66)

A rash of legislation under Augustus and Tiberius, aimed apparently at restricting the ability of owners to manumit slaves, and confining the privileges of some ex-slaves, may be seen best not as discrimination against those of slave origin but, on the contrary, as a way to emphasize the achievement of those ex-slaves regarded as respectable members of Roman society. A very high proportion of the *populus* in the city throughout the imperial period was either servile or descended from slaves. Writers such as Suetonius (*Augustus* 40.3) asserted that Augustus was keen to check the flow of servile blood into the citizen body, but in fact his legislation had the opposite effect. Those slaves informally manumitted by their owners had lived in the Late Republic in a kind of limbo, from which their ex-owners could reclaim them, their property, and their children, at whim, with little protection from the state. Under the *lex Junia* (of uncertain date, probably 17 BC or, less likely, AD 19), they were accorded the status of 'Junian Latins', which permitted them, after fulfilment of certain conditions (such as the procreation of sufficient children), to gain full citizenship. The *lex Aelia Sentia* (AD 4) clarified in full the delicate relationship between freed slaves and their former owners. Later legislation in the Roman Empire only built upon this foundation, mostly by offering further incentives for Junian Latins to become citizens by serving the state.[20]

Social distinctions between different groups within this great mass of the urban population, which in the high empire may have numbered around a million, are now difficult to discern, since they left no literary record and many will have lacked the means to commemorate their lives on monuments. Nor were the qualities that are stressed in epigraphic memorials necessarily recognized by all. What can be said is that a large but uncertain proportion of Rome's inhabitants were *peregrini* (non-citizens), about whose lives in the city remarkably little is known; that many others were slaves (see below); but that for the mass of adult male citizens not rich enough to be *equites*, status seems to have depended in their own eyes largely on occupation. Thus, although Cicero (*De Officiis* 1.150-151) famously criticized a wide variety of occupations, ranging from money-lenders and craftsmen to butchers and cooks, as unbecoming for a free man, and similar pejorative attitudes can be found in the works of Martial and Juvenal, it is clear, in light of the frequent references in epitaphs and other inscriptions to their occupations, that freed and freeborn men and women took a certain amount of pride in their work. Membership of guilds (*collegia*) provided carpenters, builders, fullers, merchants and other professionals with a sense of community as well as official recognition of the services they provided. An inscription from Rome documents personnel employed in chariot racing, including men who held the horses before the race, splashed water on them during the race, and even those who encouraged the drivers by following them round the track (*CIL* VI 10046 = *ILS* 5313). At a higher level, freeborn and freedmen alike could work for the state as *apparitores*, acting as attendants (*lictores*), heralds (*praecones*), and scribes (*scribae*) for senatorial magistrates and priests; such positions offered exceptional opportunity for building contacts within the Roman elite, opening up the possibility of social mobility for the *apparitores* and their families: thus Saturninus, scribe and later *apparitor* of Antoninus Pius, rose to the post of *praefectus vehiculorum* (head of the imperial post and transport network). Nonetheless the social status of some occupations could vary greatly. Thus Caesar bestowed citizenship on all free *medici* (physicians) at Rome, and from the late first century onwards, emperors granted exemptions to doctors from municipal burdens. Doctors serving at the imperial court, such as Xenophon, physician to Claudius, or Galen, who ministered to Marcus Aurelius and his family, were widely respected, but at the other end of the spectrum, many were regarded as charlatans. Female doctors (*medicae*) appear in the epigraphic record, though they seem to have primarily ministered to women. These *medicae* may be the same as midwives, but the fact that they used a title so similar to *medicus* may indicate that their capacities went beyond childbirth.[21]

Most of the city's population lived in high-rise apartment blocks, known as *insulae*, either in humble accommodation behind their shops (on the ground-floor) or in small apartments of one or two rooms (on the upper floors). There were also *deversoria* (inns), which housed a combination of short and long-term residents, and were notoriously crowded and noisy. It is important to note, however, that these buildings contained higher-status flats on their upper floors. The Insula Arriana Polliana at Pompeii is recorded to have had equestrian apartments (*cenacula equestria*) available for rent (*ILS* 6035). Some of these larger flats were sub-let by their owners, and were occupied by several families at once, each of whom lived in rooms off a separate corridor. A certain type of well-appointed apartment in Ostia, known as the '*medianum*' type, seem to have attracted a wealthy clientele, probably businessmen involved in shipping operations at the port.[22]

WOMEN

The analysis in this chapter of the position of different groups in Roman society in the order of their political importance reflects Roman notions of social status, but leaves in some ambiguity the social status of women of all ranks.[23] In political terms, women remained without formal rights of any kind, but this fact was less striking in the Roman Empire than under the Republic, since all men and women in Rome now lived under the domination of one man. The women of the imperial family regularly provided images of women far more prominent than ever before in Roman public life, playing an important part in official imagery because they stood for dynastic continuity and stability (see Figure 25). The younger Faustina, wife of Marcus Aurelius, was the first imperial woman to bear the title *mater castrorum* ('mother of the camps') to mark her role in accompanying her husband on campaign.

It is extremely difficult to paint a full picture of the lives of the women of the city outside the highest social ranks, but something can be said about the legal restrictions which controlled them in theory and the virtues to which in public they were expected to aspire. The public social status of a woman was defined by the status of her male relations, and early Roman law had given women little economic or practical freedom within the family; but in the Late Republic some women had begun to win increasing economic independence, and this process continued in the imperial period. Thus, although according to the law, if daughters were emancipated or found themselves without a husband on their father's death, they passed into the hands of a male guardian (*tutor*), who was usually the nearest adult male from their father's side of the family, greater financial independence might be achieved by marriage. Marriage was essentially just a private agreement between a couple to live together in a lasting union. The public ceremonies which accompanied marriage simply served to publicize the couple's intention, and did not

Figure 25 Monumental statue head of Faustina, wife of Antoninus Pius, unearthed at Sagalassos in 2008. Photo © Sagalassos Archaeological Research Project.

192

necessarily alter the property rights of the bride. In early times, the marriage had often involved the transfer of the woman from the control (*potestas*) of her male relatives into the control (*manus*) of her husband, but by the Early Empire such transfer was very rare. On the other hand, a new custom had grown up of the gift of a dowry (*dos*) by the bride's family. Since such a dowry could be demanded back from the husband on divorce, in effect it could be little more than a loan for the duration of the marriage. Divorce was easy and could be initiated by either husband or wife, and only the financial obligations of the dowry created any difficulty. It therefore became a matter for pride if a woman could declare that she had known only one husband (*univira*). If named as heirs, women could inherit property from their husbands and (more frequently) their fathers, so that widowhood might bring a fair degree of independence.

Literary sources and funerary inscriptions give a good idea of the qualities reckoned, at least publicly, to be desirable in women. Fidelity was prized; in law, adultery could in any case be punished by the wronged husband, who could also retain part of the dowry on divorce and sue his wife's lover for the outrage (*iniuria*), even though there were no corresponding legal or social bars within the *familia* to philandering by a husband. Monogamy was taken for granted or, at least, polygamy was always serial, with divorce or death separating each formal liaison.

Childbearing was considered praiseworthy, but pregnancy was dangerous, and it was a commonplace tragedy for mothers to die during or soon after childbirth. Birth control was unsophisticated and often based on magic rather than medicine. Contraceptive practices included the application of substances such as cedar gum, vinegar or olive oil to the genitals prior to intercourse, but could include folk remedies including the wearing of amulets. This type of family limitation seems to have been less popular than abortion or the exposure of infants after birth. Abortion attracted particular opprobrium from a wide spectrum of society, with opponents including the poet Ovid and the doctor Galen, who highlighted the risks to the mother. Indeed, the second-century medical writer Soranus, author of a *Gynecology*, expressly advised abortion only in event of medical need:

> The other party prescribes abortives, but with discrimination, that is, they do not prescribe them when a person wishes to destroy the embryo because of adultery or out of consideration for youthful beauty; but only to prevent subsequent danger in parturition if the uterus is small and not capable of accommodating the complete development ... or if some similar difficulty is involved. And they say the same about contraceptives as well, as we too agree with them.
> (Soranus, *Gynecology*, I 19.60, trans. O. Temkin, *Soranus' Gynecology*, Baltimore, 1956).

There were a wide range of methods thought to induce miscarriage, ranging from squatting and forced sneezing to taking draughts or undergoing surgery.

The latter was certainly an extreme option, and thus was predominantly undergone by prostitutes or adulterers. Despite widespread distaste for the practice, penalties for abortion were not introduced until the early third century AD.[24]

FAMILY

The Romans did not have a word for family in the modern sense: *familia*, although it often appears in legal texts, tended to mean the household at large (including slaves), nor does *domus* quite capture the sense. Although the Roman world was dominated by what we would call the nuclear family, high mortality rates meant that this group was constantly in flux: children would often die in infancy, male relatives might be killed at work or in warfare, while all family members were susceptible to disease. Marriages were not expected to last for decades, as indicated by the sentiments expressed in a funeral oration delivered by a husband for his wife (the so-called *Laudatio Turiae*):

> Marriages as long as ours are rare, marriages that are ended by death and not broken by divorce. For we were fortunate enough to see our marriage last without disharmony for fully 40 years. I wish that our long union had come to its final end through something that had befallen me instead of you; it would have been more just if I as the older partner had had to yield to fate through such an event.
> (*CIL* VI 41062 = *ILS* 8393, trans. E. Wistrand).

The family unit could be equally transformed by the marriage of one or both parents, resulting in blended families.[25]

Children played an important part in the ideology of Roman family life, representing stability, family continuity and hope for the future. It was thus all the more tragic that only 50 per cent of all children lived beyond the age of ten. This uncertainty translated into social customs: babies were not even given names before their eighth day (for girls) or ninth day (for boys). If they died young, they were not accorded the rites of full mourning until they had reached the age of ten. The Roman orator Quintilian wrote eloquently about the loss of his two sons, who died at the ages of five and nine, respectively:

> My youngest boy was barely five, when he was the first to leave me, robbing me as if it were one of my two eyes. I have no desire to flaunt my woes in the public gaze, nor to exaggerate the cause I have for tears; would that I had some means to make it less! But how can I forget the charm of his face, the sweetness of his speech, his first flashes of promise, and his actual possession of a calm and, incredible though it may seem, a powerful mind.
> (Quintilian 6 Pref. 6-7, trans. Loeb).

Sarcophagi and epitaphs for children featured images of their short lives, such as them learning to walk or playing with toys. This imagery first appeared at the very end of the Republic, becoming significantly more common during the empire, possibly as a direct result of the emphasis on the family in imperial ideology from Augustus onwards. Although Roman society has traditionally been seen as harsh in its treatment of children (most notably the right of the *paterfamilias* to reject the child, and expose it soon after birth), these funerary monuments demonstrate the strong bonds of love which existed between parents and their children. It was a commonplace tragedy that mothers died during or shortly after childbirth. A funerary inscription for the freedwoman Iulia Donata records that she died after her son's naming ceremony (*CIL* VI 20427).

A rhetorical education was available to children whose parents could pay for it. Children studied both Latin and Greek, primarily through reading, dictation and recitation, though the arts, such as music, were also considered important. Even the children of slaves could receive some training, but this was likely to emphasise areas which could benefit the owner, such as basic literacy and mathematics rather than rhetoric and declamation. Schooling was not always pleasant: it generally took place outside, the pupils were subjected to corporal punishment, and sometimes suffered from unwanted sexual advances, especially if they were slave children.

Adulthood arrived early: citizen boys usually assumed the *toga virilis*, a symbol of their manhood, between the ages of 13 and 18. For all children, the age of 14 marked a change in their legal status, as they were considered to have reached the age at which they were responsible for their own actions and could thus be prosecuted for crimes such as forgery and undergo torture. Girls would be married in their teenage years, but their husbands were generally older, usually in their 20s. In the intervening years, slaves and prostitutes provided the traditional sexual outlet for the Roman male citizen.

Marriages rarely came about because of romantic love, but were a social expectation. At all levels of society, Romans were expected to produce children to carry on the family, and for many upper-class citizens, political reasons may have predominated. But that does not mean that Roman marriages were soulless affairs, quite the contrary: many Romans valued the companionship and meaning they brought to their lives. The younger Pliny wrote of his affection for his wife Calpurnia:

> She is incomparably discerning, incomparably thrifty; while her love for her husband betokens a chaste nature. Her affection to me has given her a turn to books; and my compositions, which she takes a pleasure in reading, and even getting by heart, are continually in her hands. ... When at any time I recite my works, she sits close at hand, concealed behind a curtain, and greedily overhears my praises. She sings my verses and sets them to her lyre, with no other master but love, the best instructor.
> (Pliny, *Letters*, 6.19. trans. Loeb)

This unity and devotion also finds expression in art, particularly funerary monuments (see Figure 26).

Figure 26 Relief busts of a husband and his wife, the Gratidii, in close physical contact, evoking notions of a supportive and loving marriage. Photo © Vatican Museums.

For the majority of Romans, their life would not be a long one, with life expectancy at birth between 20 and 30 years. There were always exceptions, of course: according to the surviving evidence (of which the accuracy cannot of course be checked), the longest-lived known Roman, the freedman L. Sempronius Lethaeus, died aged 113 (*CIL* VI 6835). It is probable that only six to eight per cent of the empire's population were over the age of 60, which meant that grandparents were not the commonplace part of the family life that they are in the modern West. The Roman view of the elderly, as it appears in the extant literature, is somewhat contradictory. There is the exaggerated picture of toothless and wrinkled men and women (often sexually depraved), but at the other end, there were older senators, respected for their experience, and idyllic images of the loving couple supporting each other into old age.

What is clearer, however, is that there were no institutional support system for the elderly: retirement as a modern concept did not exist, though Roman senators could be excused from attending the senate, if they so wished, after the age of 60 or 65. Likewise, men over the age of 55 could be excused some, but not all, public *munera* (compulsory duties). Roman children were expected to care for their elderly parents as an act of filial duty, or *pietas*, but this was never enforced through legislation as it was in ancient Athens. Indeed, the Roman state showed an obsession with enforcing the production of children, but seemed to pay little heed to the other end of the life course. Provided that they were still in full control of their faculties, it was up to elderly people to prove they were still useful by carving out their own niche in society.[26]

SLAVES

The huge servile population of Rome was extremely visible within the city. Slavery was an integral part of Roman society, and there is little evidence to suggest that elite Romans ever questioned this fact (see above, Chapter 14, on their role in the workforce). There were three main sources of slaves: warfare, infant exposure, and reproduction among the slave community. The wars of the mid to late Republic resulted in the importation of three to four million slaves into Italy, though the total population of slaves at any one time is unlikely to have exceeded one million. Slaves continued to be captured in the imperial period, most notably in wars fought by Vespasian, Domitian and Trajan. Slaves were also acquired through the Roman tradition of infant exposure: babies would be rescued and then brought up as slaves by their new owner, a practice which caused legal problems if slaves became aware later in life that they were born free. By far the largest source of slaves in the early imperial period, however, was the birth of children to slave women, though it must be emphasized that the fathers were often citizens. The children became slaves regardless, and were known as *vernae*, a term which denoted that they had been born a slave, rather than captured.[27]

Slaves were treated as items of property, sold near the Temple of Castor in the forum, and were made to stand on a platform (*castata*) for inspection by their prospective owners, who were free to inspect the merchandise to ensure it was in top condition. The slave sellers (*mangones*) were required by law to inform buyers of any defects or problems, and Roman legal authorities debated what exactly constituted a healthy slave:

> One with warts or with tumours in the nose is diseased. Pedius writes that a man who has one eye or one jaw bigger than the other is healthy, so long as he can use both properly. ... But imbalance, or the fact that one leg is shorter than the other, can be a hindrance. ... It should also be known that left-handedness is neither a defect nor a disease, unless the slave uses his left hand by reason of the weakness of the right: such a slave is not left-handed but defected. It has been asked whether one whose breath smells is healthy. Trebatius says that it is not a disease that one's breath smells like that of a goathered or scabrous person, for this is an accident of exhalation. But if it be due to a bodily defect, such as a liver or lung complaint or something similar, the slave is diseased.
> (*Digest* 21.1.12, trans. A. Watson)

It is difficult to reconstruct the lives of slaves, since the majority of our literary testimony comes from elite Romans. But it was likely to have been a harsh existence, particularly for those slaves who laboured on rural estates. Food allowances were designed to meet minimal subsistence needs, and predominantly consisted of bread, porridge, wine, oil and a relish known as *pulmentarium* made from olives or fruit. Housing was likewise in basic rooms (*cellae*), set off from the main part of the house, and usually sparsely furnished. Since slaves were such valuable commodities, their masters were concerned to prevent the possibility of escape, and some were fitted with collars stating the name of their owner and where they should be returned if found. At the other end of the spectrum, slaves could develop relationships with their masters which could eventually lead to them being granted their freedom. These relationships are unlikely to have approached the standard of genuine friendships, whatever the pretensions of elite Romans such as the younger Pliny, who portrayed themselves as generous and attentive masters.

As in the Roman world at large, slave society possessed a distinct social hierarchy. Slaves who formed part of the domestic household (*familia urbana*) ranked more highly than rural slaves (part of the *familia rustica*) They could be promoted to higher offices within the household, such as treasurer (*arcarius*), chamberlain (*cubicularius*) or bailiff (*vilicus*). In the imperial household (*familia Caesaris*), slaves filled important bureaucratic roles, which gave them the opportunity to serve in the provinces as well as in Rome itself. After manumission, which usually occurred after the age of thirty, they continued to act as imperial freedmen, being appointed as assistants (*adiutores*) to equestrian and senatorial officials, with the opportunity for promotion to the procuratorial level, where they would administer imperial finances and properties. A slave might have slaves of his own: one slave of the emperor Tiberius, a certain Musicus Scurranus, owned 16 slaves when he died, including a doctor, cooks, attendants and secretaries, but his case was doubtless an exception (*ILS* 1514).

In law, slaves were objects, owned absolutely as chattels. Their owners were simply expected to use them. On the other hand, slaves were recognized as humans, and even a crude calculation of their utility as domestic labour required acknowledgement of this fact. Thus, for instance, quasi-marriage (*contubernium*) between slaves might be recognized and encouraged by the owner, but any children produced by such a union belonged to the master, who could in any case separate the slave couple on a whim. Such cruel behaviour may have been inhibited in some cases by the need to keep slaves willing to work well, especially since in the Late Republic they sometimes took on managerial roles. Legal recognition of such *de facto* responsibilities may be glimpsed in the development of rules about a slave's *peculium*, money assigned by the master as a reward for good work; some slaves might expect eventually to buy their freedom with their *peculium*.[28] Despite the eventual incorporation of so many slaves, after manumission, into the wider plebs, attested instances of fellow feeling between the plebs and slaves were rare. One, however, is striking. When in AD 61 the senate voted to put to death all the slaves belonging to the city prefect, Lucius Pedanius Secundus, because he had been killed by one of their number, there was an outcry among the plebs:

After the murder, ancient custom required that every slave residing under the same roof must be executed. But a crowd gathered, eager to save so many innocent lives; and rioting began. The senate house was besieged. Inside, there was feeling against excessive severity, but the majority opposed any change. ... Those favouring execution prevailed. However, great crowds ready with stones and torches prevented the order from being carried out. Nero rebuked the population by edict, and lined with troops the whole route along which those condemned were taken for execution.

(Tacitus, *Annals* 14.42–45)

* * * *

It would be wrong to suggest that this newly stratified society of the city of Rome, or the moral platitudes of the emperors, or the impressive new buildings, entirely changed the disorganized character of the great city in the Early Empire. On the one hand, numerous stories about the descendants of slaves who reached the pinnacles of society show that stratification still permitted great social mobility. On the other hand, although the emperor's *praefectus vigilum* commanded light-armed troops who acted as a sort of fire brigade and police force, much of the city still burned down in the great fire of AD 64 when Nero was emperor. And descriptions of the city in the first century suggest an urban sprawl in which only those with wealth could live comfortably, and even they would regularly evacuate the city in the heat of summer to escape the illnesses which inevitably circulated among the crowded population. It is true that there is no evidence that the state was worried by any criminal counter-culture among the plebs, but it is a moot question, as in all discussions of reactions to imperial rule, whether this lack of evidence reveals the concern of emperors to win support from the respectable, self-supporting plebs as part of their imperial self-image, or the ability of rulers to turn a blind eye to disaffection so long as it was not dangerous.

18

THE CITY OF ROME: CULTURE AND LIFE

The culture of the inhabitants of the city of Rome in the High Empire reflected their diverse origins. Greeks, Syrians, Jews and others retained Greek as their main language, and other minority groups continued to use their

Figure 27 Tombstone of the doctor Claudius Agathemerus and his wife Myrtale, from Rome, second half of the first century AD. The deceased were evidently of eastern origin, since the inscription is in Greek, but he wears a Roman toga and her curled wig is characteristic of fashionable hairstyles in the city in this period. The last line of the inscription reads 'We are with the pious in Elysium'. Photo courtesy of the Ashmolean Museum, Oxford.

national tongues, at least for the first generation or so after immigration (see Figure 27). Their religious customs, from cultic worship to the Sabbath and other practices, spread beyond the confines of such groups to the rest of the population. So too, doubtless, did tastes in food and entertainment, though these are more difficult to document, but this lively cultural interchange was only marginally reflected in the prestige culture based on the imperial court, and about which most can be said.

The long period of Augustus' sole rule witnessed a great efflorescence of the cultural life of the highest social strata in the city of Rome. Between 31 BC and AD 14, Latin poetry was enriched by the work of Vergil, Horace, Tibullus, Propertius and Ovid, and Latin historiography was transformed by the history of Livy; the great Pantheon of Agrippa and the mausoleum of Augustus were built in extravagant Hellenistic style, and the classically restrained temple of Mars Ultor erected; the relief sculptures of the Ara Pacis and the free-standing statue of the emperor at Prima Porta were carved. According to the literary artists themselves, such riches were not accidental. They attributed their output to the benefits of peace brought by the princeps. This was only part of the truth. The princeps was indeed largely responsible, but not (just) because peace gives leisure for creative arts (which can in fact also thrive in conditions of great political uncertainty). More positively, it was his patronage and that of his intimate friends which drew artists and writers to the capital city both from the provinces as well as from Italy, and within a few years changed the face of Latin culture.[1]

LITERATURE

The key to the change is the new role of intellectuals and artists within what was in effect a monarchy rather than a Republic. In the 60s and 50s BC, the great writers and thinkers in the city of Rome had on the whole been men of good social status and of assured private incomes – thus Catullus and Varro, let alone Cicero, Atticus, Sallust or Caesar. In the second century BC there had been literary figures of lesser social standing who won an audience by popular acclaim through public performance, such as Terence and Plautus, who made a living through their plays. But by the mid-first century such people were rare. Intellectuals who flocked to Rome from, for example, the dying regime in Ptolemaic Alexandria sought aristocratic patrons whose salons they might adorn – a hazardous process when the aristocrats themselves became embroiled in civil strife.

With the dominance of an emperor, all this gradually changed, but the process was not immediate. The histories of Sallust in the 30s BC, and the life of Atticus written by Cornelius Nepos for the most part before 32 BC, still concentrated on the political themes, uncertainties and ambitions of the Late Republic. The great antiquarian Varro did not die until 27 BC, and his major work *On Farming* was published in 37 BC. Even after 27 BC some aristocrats still proclaimed their intellectual independence, such as Asinius Pollio, whose history of the civil wars took a decidedly Antonian stance, or Propertius, who, like Catullus, wrote poetry primarily for his own gratification or that of his friends. But many writers in Rome in the first century of the principate came from southern Gaul or Spain (if they wrote in Latin), or from Asia Minor, Sicily or Syria (if they wrote in Greek), and most such writers came to prominence because of the patronage of the imperial court, which became as central to Roman culture as the Ptolemaic Museum and Library had been in Alexandria. Hence the emergence of patriotic literature, counterbalanced by a fashion for romantic poetry set in an unreal world, and the dominance in literary circles of close friends of the emperor such as, under Augustus, the munificent Maecenas or Cornelius Gallus, the first prefect of Egypt. Gallus' immense poetic influence over Vergil and his contemporaries is still hard to assess and explain after the chance find of some of his poetry on a fragmentary papyrus discovered at Qasr Ibrim in Egypt.[2] His complimentary epigram to Julius Caesar is the most complete piece of his poetry to survive:

> My fate will then be sweet to me, Caesar, when you are the most important part of Roman history, and when I read of many gods' temples the richer after your return for being hung with your trophies.

When the Latin writers discussed their patrons, they naturally did so in terms of Roman social conventions, which precluded the open recognition of dependence more natural in Hellenistic monarchies. Vergil and Horace portrayed themselves as close friends of Maecenas, who in turn was Augustus' friend and confidant. As friends they gave each other presents; Horace might send a birthday ode, Maecenas respond with a gift of a farm in Sabine country for Horace's amusement. Horace was capable of writing pure propaganda, as in the *Carmen Saeculare*, a lengthy ode commissioned by Augustus to celebrate the Secular Games of 17 BC, but most of his poems which begin this way veer off into private musings, and much of the poetry of the Augustan age promoted values directly opposed to the professed moral base of the court. Horace, Tibullus, Propertius and, most blatantly, Ovid, celebrated the promiscuous café lifestyle of the Late Republican aristocracy which Augustus' moral reforms publicly attacked, but only Ovid suffered for his preferences by a sentence of exile in AD 8.[3]

The delicacy of the patronage relationship is highlighted by expression in the careful metaphors of poetry. But it should not disguise the fact, obvious enough to Greek intellectuals in the city of Rome like Nicolaus of Damascus (who wrote a panegyric of the young Augustus), or the composers of epigrams now found in the *Palatine Anthology*, that Augustus was a monarch to be flattered and fêted, not least because he was prepared to pay for the privilege. Apart from flattery, which could backfire if it appeared too gross and therefore ironic, like the praise for Nero at the start of Lucan's epic *Pharsalia*, writers adapted best to writing under autocracy by avoiding dangerous themes. Those rash authors who attempted historiography either hoped to please the current emperor by blackening the reputation of his predecessors with scandalous anecdotes like those scattered through the biographies by Suetonius or, like the elder Pliny and Aufidius Bassus, took refuge in dull annals. Only a few, like Cremutius Cordus, who under Tiberius praised too much the murderers of Caesar, suffered for their art. At his trial in 25 BC, Cremutius argued for the historian's freedom of speech:

> Among us there has always been complete, uncensored liberty to speak about those whom death has placed beyond hatred or partiality. Cassius and Brutus are not in arms at Philippi now. I am not on the platform inciting the people to civil war. They died seventy years ago! They are known by their statues – even the conqueror did not remove them. And they have their place in the historian's pages. Posterity gives everyone his due honour. If I am condemned, people will remember me as well as Cassius and Brutus.
>
> (Tacitus, *Annals* 4.35)

But such candour proved fatal. Wise historians stuck safely to the distant past, like Curtius Rufus, who in the early to mid-first century AD wrote a life of Alexander the Great.

The Augustan 'Golden Age' witnessed Augustus' erection of two libraries to celebrate intellectual endeavour, and Vergil's composition of the founding epic of Rome, the *Aeneid*, reflecting Rome as a capital city whose splendour eclipsed her old rivals in Egypt, Syria and Macedon. Latin writing forged for the first time a truly independent path, neither wholly imitative of, nor parodic of, its Greek models, although the ruling constraints of genre were as strong as they had been for Cicero. Thus Quintilian at the end of the first century AD could point to a Greek origin for all the genres used in Latin literature except satire, which itself was an established Latin genre long before its adoption by Horace in his *Sermones*. But despite such constraints on originality, some of the writings of this period became great classics in the Latin-speaking world.

With hindsight it may seem that the literary life of Rome was in constant decline from this peak at the start of the Roman Empire. At any rate, such a profusion of innovation, at least in the transposition into Latin of existing Greek genres and ideas, was not to be witnessed again. Much literature of the late Julio-Claudian period simply repeated stock formulas established under Augustus. Exceptions were treated by scholarly critics like Quintilian as aberrations. Hence there was little interest at the time in Petronius' *Satyricon*, a picaresque novel composed under Nero, which mixed erotic farce with sophisticated literary parody, or Seneca's prose satire on the deification of Claudius, the *Apocolocyntosis*, let alone the charming version of Aesop's fables written in simple Latin verse by a certain Phaedrus, an imperial freedman in the age of Augustus. Latin oratory went into decline as an art with the loss of its political function in Rome, despite the rise of rhetorical schools in the capital, in which professionals taught aspiring politicians how to impose the greatest possible variation on limited material.

The Flavian age saw a continued interest in sensationalism in literature, for the most part safely located in the distant past, by Silius Italicus, Valerius Flaccus and Statius. Attempts by Persius under Nero, by Martial under the Flavians and early Trajan, and by Juvenal under Trajan and Hadrian, to bring Latin literature back to normal speech and real people foundered on the preciousness that had become inherent in literary culture. With rare exceptions, such as Frontinus' *On the Water Supply of Rome*, composed in the time of Nerva, not even didactic writings could avoid pretentiousness. Vitruvius *On Architecture*, Pomponius Mela *On Geography*, and Celsus *On Medicine*, all wrote genuinely useful works, but Columella's handbook *On Agriculture* sacrificed utility to literary artifice.

Not surprisingly, many intellectuals of the first two centuries AD do not seem to have believed that literature was in decline in their time. It is a salutary shock to find the younger Pliny, who spent much time and effort both on his own compositions (mostly rhetorical) and in the encouragement of other writers such as Martial in self-consciously literary salons, proclaiming his circle as the greatest literary flowering known in Roman history (for instance, *Letters* 5.17; 6.21). The 'silver age' of Latin literature was believed by some participants to be golden.

Certainly, productivity did not cease. Partly this was due to the continued interest of the imperial court, which sometimes retained its influence over taste. The philhellenism and decadence of Nero were reflected by the homosexual romps and Campanian setting of the main characters in the *Satyricon* of Petronius; they also elicited in reaction the moralizing Stoicism of the *Moral Letters* of the younger Seneca, although Seneca's other works, such as the bloodthirsty tragedies, never intended for performance, reflected well enough the sensationalist tastes of the imperial court. Above all, the great increase of Greek writings in the capital city owed much to Hadrian, although Vespasian had already founded a chair of Greek rhetoric in Rome as a rival to the chair in Athens. Hadrian's (adopted) grandson, Marcus Aurelius, was to compose his philosophical meditations entirely in Greek, although he was not averse to the Parthian wars led by his co-emperor Lucius Verus being celebrated in a Latin panegyric by his own teacher of Latin oratory, Cornelius Fronto.

But much of the capital's culture after the period of Augustus moved under its own momentum. Literary genres were now fixed. Lucan's *Pharsalia* followed the epic model of Vergil. Tacitus' *Annals* imitated Livy in organization and content, Sallust in literary style. Pliny's letters mimicked the classic collection of the epistles of Cicero. Juvenal continued the tradition of Lucilius and Horace in writing satire; the popularity of his work is uncertain, since in the late fourth century his poems had to be revived for a public which had forgotten them. Some of these authors were senators, as in the Republic, whose literary activity was part of their adoption of a Republican persona (thus Tacitus and Pliny). Others were intellectuals who sought patronage wherever they could get it, thus, the Spanish writers of the time of Nero, and Martial, also from Spain, who won the support of Pliny.

Of new literary endeavours in Rome after Augustus, the most important was perhaps the composition of serious philosophy in the city, both from within court circles by the younger Seneca, Nero's tutor, and on its fringes by such Stoic-Cynics as Epictetus, a freed slave and the teacher of consuls, including Arrian, consul AD 129 or 130, who collected his writings.[4]

But the most long-lasting literary works were undoubtedly the products of the jurists, whose classical period began with Augustus and culminated in the early third century AD in a new articulation of Roman law. This efflorescence of legal scholarship was only indirectly a product of imperial intervention, in the sense that Augustus and emperors after him may have chosen to strengthen the earlier system current in the Republic, by which the private thoughts of legal experts had persuasive force in private law cases. Thus, despite the fact that in practice the principate saw a gradual shift from the formulary system and reliance on private *iurisprudentes* (jurists) (see Chapter 9), the system was still sufficiently in force until the late second century AD for a mass of scholarship to be produced.[5]

Most legal scholars in the first 150 years of the principate were senators, often of high rank. Apart from one Masurius Sabinus, founder of the Sabinian school in the first half of the first century AD, and granted equestrian status, only in the second century AD did many legal experts of lower rank come to prominence, and the change coincides with the opening of public schools of law away from the city of Rome. The writings of the classical *iurisprudentes* are mostly known through excerpts in the *Digest*, compiled in the sixth century AD; only Gaius' *Institutes*, an elementary work, survives largely intact from the second century AD. In the Augustan period writers divided between the attitude to legal interpretation of M. Antistius Labeo (active from *c.* 30 BC to AD 10 or 11) and that of C. Ateius Capito (active a little later), and from Tiberius' reign they diverged into the two 'schools' of Proculians and Sabinians. The main issue to divide jurists was apparently the extent to which law should be construed from the precise wording of a document or from its probable intention.

The nature of legal schools – whether they met, how they taught, how they selected leaders – is entirely unknown, but it is worth nothing that legal expertise often ran in families. Legal writings frequently took the form of commentaries on the praetor's edict, or on specific legal problems, or on other jurists' work. They were, until the second century AD, deliberately technical and esoteric – insiders' literature. It is probably right to associate the gradual emergence of legal professionals in the second century with the innovation by Claudius in AD 47 that an advocate could receive limited payment for his work.

PAINTING, SCULPTURE AND ARCHITECTURE

Painting, sculpture and architecture underwent a revolution in the 20s BC, only to stagnate after Augustus.[6] A dramatic shift by Octavian immediately after Actium favoured a spare, idealized version of classical Attic style in all of the plastic arts, in marked contrast to the Asiatic imitations of Hellenistic royalty which had characterized the taste of later Republican nobles. Official imperial art in the following centuries revealed a constant tension between Hellenistic baroque and classical serenity.

It is a curious fact that little is known about the painters and sculptors themselves, and that few of their works were signed. They were not high status members of society, and many seem to have been slaves or freedmen, such as Famulus, responsible for some of the art in Nero's 'Golden House'. The evidence of Diocletian's Edict of Maximum Prices, from the early fourth century AD shows that painters were paid more than most other craftsmen, but still earned less on average than scribes and lawyers. This situation contrasts sharply with the great honour in which famous Greek artists, such as Apelles and Phidias, were held by the Romans. Ever since the days of the Republic, when Greece first fell into Roman hands, victorious generals had been dedicating such masterpieces to the gods. Vespasian's Temple of Peace was designed to ensure that these works of art were widely accessible to the public at large (Pliny the Elder, *NH* 34.84). It is unlikely that portraits or statues were often commissioned by the people they depict, since most are found in honorific or commemorative contexts such as tombs, although in one instance (*CIL* XIII 5708) a wealthy man's wishes for the design of his tomb are recorded on an inscription. More often depictions on sarcophagi followed a standard repertoire, illustrating an idealized life in war, peace and marriage or, from the second century AD, mythological scenes. Architects, who needed (according to Vitruvius (*On Architecture* 1.1-18)) to be qualified in geometry, history, philosophy, law, astronomy and medicine, could be more public figures, like Trajan's architect, Apollodorus, who was eventually executed by Hadrian for insulting his attempts at building design (Dio 69.4.1-5).[7]

Thus public architecture, the best-attested plastic art in Rome, evinced little development after the first emperor. The flamboyant style of the numerous public buildings, mostly temples, erected by Octavian and his supporters in the 30s BC exhibited an Egyptianizing trend, probably in imitation of the Ptolemies; it culminated in the florid architecture of the temple of Apollo on the Palatine, dedicated in 28 BC. The shift to sober neo-classicism, a mixture of Athenian and old Roman simplicity best exemplified in the temple of Mars Ultor, dedicated in 2 BC, must be attributed directly to the image of himself cultivated by Augustus, but, as often, imperial taste percolated through the rest of upper-class society, not least because in Rome the emperor and his friends had a near-monopoly on the erection of public buildings. Conventional Italian architectural forms, such as the temple on a podium at the end of a porticoed square, remained characteristic of Rome. What was new was the grandeur. In ensuing centuries there were great engineering achievements, such as the Flavian Colosseum, the huge building projects of Domitian (on which craftsmen from the eastern Mediterranean were employed), and the forum of Trajan. But styles remained fixed, in an over-blown neo-classicism.

The main architectural change after Augustus thus owed more to new construction techniques than to changed taste. Use of rubble and concrete with stone facings remained common, but the invention of kiln-fired bricks permitted more structurally sound, high-rising, free-standing *insulae* (apartment blocks) like those excavated at Ostia.[8] After the failure of Nero to create a baroque fantasy of *rus in urbe* (the countryside in the city) in his Golden House, later emperors more tactfully achieved the same in the countryside itself; Hadrian's villa - complex at Tibur (Tivoli) is the best known such residence, including around 900 rooms and originally covering 120 hectares (see Figure 28).[9] The luxurious villa in the Italian countryside, with its regular layout around a central courtyard, had become a common feature of the lifestyle of wealthy Romans in the Late Republic and, despite the strongly urban focus of court and political life, villas became increasingly widespread in the Early Empire, valued both for their privacy and for the comfort they offered for those who needed to escape the heat of a Roman summer.[10] Pliny paints an idyllic picture of his own villa in Tuscany:

Figure 28 The so-called 'Maritime Theatre' in Hadrian's villa at Tivoli from a part of the villa presumed to have housed the emperor's private apartments.. Photo © DeA/G. Nimatallah.

I can enjoy a profounder peace there, more comfort, and fewer cares; I need never wear a formal toga and there are no neighbours to disturb me; everywhere there is peace and quiet, which adds as much to the healthiness of the place as the clear sky and pure air. There I enjoy the best of health, both mental and physical, for I keep my mind in training with work and my body with hunting. My servants too are healthier here than anywhere else; up to the present I have not lost a single one of those I brought here with me – may I be forgiven for saying so, and may the gods continue to make this the pride of the place and a joy to me.

(*Letters* 5.6.45–46)

As for imperial sculpture, the statue of Augustus in Livia's villa at Prima Porta just north of Rome, and the sculpture of the Ara Pacis, set the norm for imperial portraiture for generations, so that monuments erected on behalf of the regime became so stereotyped that a set of relief statues originally intended to celebrate Domitian's embarkation on the German campaigns was remodelled after his death by the simple substitution of a new head to represent the accession to power of Nerva.[11] Only on Trajan's column, erected to celebrate his victories on the Danube in Dacia, did a new artistic approach materialize, with the meticulous depiction of scenes from the campaigns. Unfortunately, at such a height in the column, the full details were indistinguishable to all but the gods, or viewers from the top floors of Trajan's new library, erected alongside. The production of standard sculptures of these types was much aided by the residence in Italy of huge numbers of Greek craftsmen, most of them now anonymous. These craftsmen already in the Late Republic staffed workshops which shared moulds, models and techniques. Standardization was also encouraged by the imperial monopoly of many marble quarries, and the location of some workshops within imperial palaces, like that in the first imperial palace on the Palatine, built by Tiberius or possibly Nero. The same factors encouraged the adoption of the classical style of imperial sculpture by bourgeois patrons, and the popularization of aristocratic taste.

While public façades conformed to classical norms, craftsmen in some minor art forms, like silverware and wall painting, continued Hellenistic styles for private patrons. The history of Roman wall painting is primarily known at second hand, through its influence on styles in Pompeii and Herculaneum, buried by the ash of Vesuvius in AD 79, and by literary descriptions, such as those of Vitruvius in *On Architecture* and Petronius in the *Satyricon*.[12] Excavation in Rome itself also permits some knowledge of the great buildings of the Palatine in the High Empire. Thus the Pompeian third style, a severe classical technique in which paintings were placed against plain black (painted) tapestries, was already widespread in Rome by the middle of Augustus' rule, although its use in Pompeii was much later. In wall painting, as in architecture, there was a fascination with Egyptian motifs. By the time of Claudius there was a reaction against classicism, with fantastic, theatrical scenes (the Pompeian fourth style), which fit well with the baroque excesses of writers like Seneca and Lucan. For wall painting after AD 79 the surviving archaeological evidence from Rome shows that second-century wall painting favoured white, open spaces, framed by columns and porticoes. The remains of an *insula* (apartment block) of Hadrianic date preserve white backgrounds enclosed by striking red lines, which were probably designed to give the impression of outside space beyond the actual confines of the walls. Similar stylistic compositions have been found in *insulae* at Ostia, as in the case of the House of the Muses, which features painted balconies intended artificially to extend the house. The attempt at architectural realism does not create a true impression of depth, but this may have been a deliberate design to challenge the viewer. Other developments included a decline in mythological themes and a new emphasis on ceiling decoration, which was designed to draw attention to the techniques used to construct vaults and domes (see Figure 29).[13]

In funerary art, classical restraint was never pervasive, perhaps because the design of Augustus' own grandiose mausoleum had preceded his adoption of classicism. The tradition continued from the Republican period that great store was set, by those who could afford it, on the dignified disposal of the dead (see Figure 30). For the poor this was achieved by burial in communal

Figure 29 Ceiling of Room IV of the'House of the Painted Vaults' from Ostia (early third century A.D.). Eight white panels radiate outwards in the manner of an umbrella from the red central section. FU 6182, Insula delle volte dipinte, volta affrescata, circa metà del II sec. d.C., 1958. ©American academy in Rome, Photographic Archive

Figure 30 Columbarium of Pomponius Hylas, a freedman of the first century A.D., in Rome. Photo © Christie A. Ray.

sepulchral chambers (*columbaria*), with a pigeon-hole for each chest or urn. Slaves and freedmen were often buried with the rest of the *familia* to which they belonged, while the free poor clubbed together into funerary societies (*collegia*). For the very rich the Republican custom of building ostentatious mausolea flanking the roads which led out of Rome evolved into tombs of increasingly whimsical and exotic designs, often erected in close proximity to their gardens. The unexplained shift during or after the reign of Hadrian from cremation to inhumation as the normal technique for disposal of the dead was shared by the inhabitants of Rome with the rest of the empire (see Chapter 15), and some of the finest examples of extravagant stone sarcophagi come from the city. Similar baroque taste predominated in the gem cutting, fine glassware and fine pottery of the High Empire. The classical ethos encouraged by Augustus was thus taken up and internalized by the wealthy Roman élite – but only in part.

ORDINARY TASTES

How much did all or any of this cultural activity matter to those ordinary people in the city of Rome who did not belong to the wealthy élite?[14] As regards the literary culture, probably not a great deal. It is worth recalling that, for many people in Rome, Greek rather than Latin was their literary language, and that the Latin literature produced in court circles was self-consciously élitist. Books were published first by public recitation to a selected audience, then by deposition in public libraries and by copies being produced by slaves, a laborious process in which only the enthusiastic and rich would indulge; even they, unless exceptionally keen, might not choose to have a private library, and only one library was found in all the excavations at Herculaneum and Pompeii. Since there was no intellectual public entertainment, like drama in classical Athens, there was no medium for the wider dissemination of these ideas, except for those of the few select authors whose work became part of the common currency of basic education. In early imperial Rome this privilege was restricted to writers of the Late Republic and the Augustan period. Knowledge of Vergil was accordingly very widespread; acquaintance with the writings of Lucan was rare. Of all the higher arts, only sculpture and architecture were obviously addressed to, or noticed by, a wide audience in the city of Rome.

Nonetheless, we should be wary of assuming that ordinary people were unsophisticated or that Roman culture was restricted to the elite. So, for instance, after Pompey the Great brought myrrhine ware to Rome from the east, the new material was soon used to make tables and vases. The fondness for Egyptian motifs, which bloomed in Italy after Egypt was incorporated into the empire by Augustus, was embraced by the owner of the House of the Fruit Orchard in Pompeii, who does not appear to have been of high social status. The invention of glassblowing in the late first century BC ensured that glass vessels could be produced on a much wider scale than previously. Workshops were established in Italy at Rome, at Puteoli and at Aquileia, according to Pliny the Elder (*NH* 33.66), and use of glass by all levels of society is recorded by the geographer Strabo:

> At Rome, also, it is said that many discoveries are made of both for producing the colours and for facility in manufacture, as, for example, in the case of glass-ware, where one can buy a glass beaker or drinking-cup for a copper.
> (Strabo, *Geography*, 16.2.25, trans. Loeb).

Similar trends can be seen in the use of elaborate wall paintings in Roman houses. We are rarely able to link these residences to occupants from a specific social group, but the size of houses may give some indication of the wealth of the people who lived there, and popular styles of wall paintings are found in both small and large residences in Italy. As a result, it is difficult to characterize certain types of art as belonging to aristocrats, freedmen, or even a nebulous middle class. For example, the 'Flavian' female hair-style, distinguished by its tight ringlets, appears in depictions of both senatorial women and prostitutes.[15]

For all, however, it is likely that the images made popular by the imperial regime played a vital part in enabling the inhabitants of the city to internalize the fact of imperial rule.[16] Private individuals' enthusiastic embrace of literature and art which reflected the glory of the regime reveals not gullibility but acceptance of the new realities of power, which were in any case inevitable. Hence the appearance of motifs echoing imperial propaganda on private artefacts, such as tableware.

The transformation of taste to accommodate imperial rule is nowhere more obvious than in the wholesale adoption by people in Rome of the religious reforms of the principate. Augustus' pride in his restoration of cults fallen into disuse disguises the extent of innovation in public religious practice during his rule, not least in the inclusion of the princeps and his family in all kinds of worship. The performance of such rituals in the city necessarily included the populace, whose eager participation was an essential prerequisite. Presumably the provision of food by the princeps at these ceremonies helped to stimulate enthusiasm, but the thousands of extant private dedications to or on behalf of emperors, using the pious language favoured by the regime, reveal the extent to which the religious atmosphere of the principate was adopted by the urban populace – precisely because they felt that the new, peaceful society into which the emperors invited them really was theirs to enjoy.[17] One such from Rome of AD 27 reads:

> To the *genius* of Tiberius Caesar Augustus, son of the divine Augustus; Gaius Fulvius Chryses, master of the lesser Amentine district, dedicated this on 28 May, in the consulship of Lucius Calpurnius Piso and Marcus Crassus Frugi.
> (EJ² no. 133; Braund no. 163)

Apart from participation in religious ceremonies, for ordinary people public entertainment came in the form of shows, of which the most popular in the theatre were mimes, a form of comedy, usually lewd, where obscenity was often combined with spectacular violence.[18] Popular plays included a type known as Milesian tales, essentially sexual romps; Romans did not develop a sense of prudishness in discussing sex until the spread of Christian influence. For special occasions, nothing surpassed chariot racing and the amphitheatre. In Rome, imperial munificence enshrined these different forms of entertainment in public buildings of increasing size and magnificence: Caesar's rebuilding of the ancient *Circus Maximus*, the theatre of Marcellus, the *Circus Vaticanus* built by Gaius, the amphitheatres built by Nero and by Vespasian and Titus (the Colosseum), the *odeion* and the hippodrome of Domitian, Trajan's extension and restoration of the *Circus Maximus*.

Gladiatorial fights were a well-entrenched part of Roman culture long before the imperial period. Originally devised apparently as part of the celebration of funerals, with a religious significance attached to what was in effect the ritual sacrifice of the gladiators participating, by the Late Republic the shows had become an end in themselves, put on to celebrate important days and as evidence of munificence by the donor, who was usually a magistrate. Under the Roman Empire, the popularity of such shows was greatly increased (see Figure 31). Emperors could afford far greater spectacles

Figure 31 Gladiator mosaic from a villa in Zliten in North Africa, showing the aftermath of a gladiatorial combat. Musicians sit on one side; on the other, the referee holds the hand of the gladiator as they await the decision whether to kill or spare his defeated opponent.
Photo © The German Archaeological Institute, Rome.

than other benefactors, and some excelled in their ingenuity to entertain, such as Titus, who flooded the newly built Colosseum in AD 80 to stage a sea fight and other water-borne displays:[19]

> Large numbers of individuals fought in single combat, whereas others competed against each other in groups in infantry and naval battles. For Titus had suddenly filled this same theatre with water, and he had brought in horses and bulls and other domestic animals that had been taught to do in water everything that they could do on land. He also brought in people on ships; they engaged in a naval battle there representing the Corcyraeans versus the Corinthians.
> (Cassius Dio, *History of Rome* 66.25.2–3)

Despite the occasional moralizing by some writers, there is little to gainsay the immense enthusiasm with which such exciting sights were greeted. Gladiators became sex symbols when successful. The frequency of fights was restricted primarily by the expense.

Stone amphitheatres for gladiatorial bouts had been built in some Italian communities already in the second century BC, but Rome itself did not receive its first permanent amphitheatre until 29 BC. Theatres and amphitheatres were highly politicized public spaces. The Roman elites – senators, *equites* and municipal magistrates – had reserved seats at the front, marking out their status for all to see. Magistrates were required to hold public games during their tenure, the memories of which would, they hoped, secure their election to further office. Julius Caesar secured a lasting reputation for his aedilician games, which were reportedly the first time that gladiators fought with silver weapons (Pliny the Elder, *NH* 33.53)

The emphasis of the games themselves was spectacle: the bigger the better. The emperor Augustus boasted in the *Res Gestae* (22) that the *venationes* (beast hunts) he staged were responsible for the deaths of 3,500 animals. Criminals were often dressed in costumes and forced to reenact mythological events for the audience's enjoyment. Thus, a man might be chained up like Prometheus and eaten by wild beasts, or a woman proffered as a mate for a bull like the maiden Pasiphae. In the eyes of the Romans, convicted criminals deserved their fates, but moral condemnation attached to those who revelled in bloodshed for its own sake: Suetonius (*Claud.* 34) censures Claudius for enjoying the sight of defeated gladiators having their throats slashed in front of his eyes.

Emperors and elites also served as patrons of less homicidal forms of entertainment, such as the theatre. Pliny the Younger (*Ep.* 7.24) reports that Ummidia Quadratilla, a woman of senatorial rank, had her own personal troupe of pantomime actors which earned her enormous popularity:

> ...people who were nothing to Quadratilla were running to the theatre to pay their respects to her – though 'respect' is hardly the word to use for their fawning attentions – jumping up and clapping to show their admiration, and then copying every gesture of their mistress with snatches of song. (trans. Loeb)

Leading actors and actresses could earn enormous amounts of money – the sum of 4,000 sesterces a day in one instance – but their social standing could never match their wealth. From the third century BC, they can be found forming guilds to protect their own interests, and senior performers acted as mentors to up-and-coming talent.[20]

For more everyday thrills people flocked instead to the circus, where chariot racing became an embedded part of the city's life, with individuals, including emperors, devoting themselves to one faction or another. Betting was heavy, and the skill of the charioteers considerable. Many graffiti in Pompeii record the gamblers' loyalties to the blues or the greens.

* * * *

These were the changes in the imperial city which made the place pleasanter to live in for the mass of its inhabitants. There was more water, brought by efficiently administered aqueducts. Public baths abounded and could be used by all. The construction of the Baths of Trajan in Rome ushered in a stylistic change which saw public baths transformed into large-scale leisure centres. They now came complete with libraries and sporting facilities, such as *palaestrae* (exercise arenas). Trajan's complex was elegant and symmetrical, with the principal rooms – the *calidarium* (hot bath), *tepidarium* (warm bath), *frigidarium* (cold bath), and *natatio* (swimming pool) – aligned along a central axis.[21]

The growing sophistication of Roman bathing establishments in the imperial period is memorably recounted by the philosopher Seneca:

> We think ourselves poor and mean if our walls are not resplendent with large and costly mirrors; if our marbles from Alexandria are not set off by mosaics of Numidian stone, if their borders are not faced over on all sides with difficult patterns, arranged in many colours like paintings; if our vaulted ceilings are not buried in glass; if our swimming-pools are not lined with Thasian marble...
>
> (Seneca, *Ep.* 86.6; trans. Loeb)

Such changes in public bathing represented a fusion of Roman bathing customs with aspects of Greek gymnasia, so that the baths became cultural centres for the urban populations as a whole.

There were public gardens for the people to stroll in. The *vigiles* kept at least a token guard against fire and violence. No-one, apart from the agents of the state, regularly carried weapons on the streets of Rome. For those with a modicum of wealth, it had become a civilized place in which to live.

19

ITALY AND SICILY

ITALY

When in 32 BC 'all Italy' (*tota Italia*) vowed to support Octavian, this expressed a novel kind of unity for the Italian peninsula. On the only previous occasion when 'Italia' was named as a political concept, it had been in 90–89 BC, when silver coins proclaimed the state of Italia in opposition to Rome.[1] Now in contrast Italy was fully Roman, viewed by those in the capital as different from, indeed superior to, the other regions conquered by Rome.

During the Late Republic civic leaders from all over Italy had made their mark on national politics or benefited from the farming out of public contracts. Italians had fought as Roman legionaries all over the world, and had been deeply involved in the struggles of the civil wars, suffering the loss of many lives and much confiscated land in the 40s and 30s BC. Unity had been forged by this military service, and by the resettlement of soldiers often far from their original homes, since the prime loyalty of the veterans settled in disparate parts of Italy after Actium was to the emperor in Rome. Veteran colonies formed a focus for Romanization in a land already receptive to the process. Already in the Late Republic documents from all areas of Italy used the names of the consuls as the means of dating. Italy could not help being affected by change in Rome. It had all the advantages and disadvantages of lying at the centre of an empire in the midst of turbulent change.

The history of Italy in the early principate, then, is a story of the continuing disappearance of local cultural differences, and the reactions of the peninsula as a whole, first to its central role within the empire under Augustus, who specially favoured the region, then to its partial deposition – partial only, since as late as the early second century AD Trajan was still insistent that senators without land in Italy must acquire a certain amount, and Italian farms still enjoyed freedom from land tax until the end of the third century AD.

That local cultural differences did not immediately disappear with political union was partly the result of geography, partly of the ethnic composition of the population. Geography was most obviously important in the identification with Rome by cities in its close vicinity, whether in Latium or as far south as

Campania (see Map 5); cities within a roughly 50-mile radius of the capital were in effect included by emperors in the space in which they chose to demonstrate their power, *auctoritas* and beneficence. Elsewhere, there were wide differences between the indigenous cultures of the Celtic villages in the Po valley, the inhabitants of the ancient cities of Etruria, the Samnite mountain communes of the Appenines, and the Greeks of the southern

Map 5 Italy

maritime towns. Massive population transfers between 80 and 30 BC went some way to break down the contrasts but still left many others *in situ*.

With the advent of peace after Actium, much of the fertile Po Valley was parcelled out into lots for veteran colonies, and little evidence of the Celtic background of the inhabitants since the fourth century BC can any longer be traced. Tradition clung on longer in the north of Etruria, where the Etruscan language, with its marked structural differences from any Indo-European tongue, survived into the mid-first century AD; thus Varro knew a number of Etruscan words, and Etruscan inscriptions of the Early Empire have been found.[2] To some extent survival was the effect of antiquarianism, marked in the claim of Maecenas to be descended from Etruscan kings or in the case of the emperor Claudius, who was fascinated by the Etruscan past and himself composed twenty books about the Etruscans, the *Tyrrhenica*.

The continuation of some Samnite culture in the region of the southern Appenines is harder to trace. Inscriptions in the local languages of Oscan and Osco-Umbrian are hardly to be found after *c.* 100 BC. Certainly stone inscriptions are an unreliable guide to language use, but the cessation of Oscan at Pompeii is quite striking.[3] In Anagnia in the mid-second century a native had to explain a local term in a (Latin) religious formula to the emperor Marcus Aurelius (Fronto, *Letters* 4.4, ed. Naber, pp. 66–67), but this perhaps signified only antiquarianism. By Caesar's time there had already been an increase in the number of recognized *municipia* in the mountains in place of scattered villages of Roman citizens, but the settlements concerned rarely grew very large, constrained by difficulties of food supply, both locally and by road transport in the hills. Of the culture of these communities little can be said. They presented a Roman face to the world, with uniform town centres and Latin inscriptions, and magistrates with similar titles and functions. Some of the uniformity may have been created by Roman instructions, through detailed statutes like those quoted on the *lex Rubria* of 49–42 BC (from Veleia in the Po valley) and the *Tabula Heracleensis* of 44 BC (from Heraclea in southern Italy),[4] one clause of which latter document reads:

It shall not be lawful for any persons who within a municipality, colony, prefecture, forum, or *conciliabulum* are forbidden by this law to be senators or decurions or *conscripti* to stand for or to hold the office of *duovir* or *quattuovir* or any other magistracy or minor office from which they would pass into the said body, nor to sit in or be spectators in the space assigned to senators, decurions, or *conscripti* at the public games or gladiatorial contests, nor to be present at a public banquet; nor shall any person, elected or returned contrary to this law, rank as *duovir* or *quattuovir*, or hold any magistracy or minor office within such communities. Whosoever shall act in contravention of this clause shall be condemned to pay to the people the sum of 50,000 sesterces and may be sued at will by any person for that amount.

Local communities performed their own police functions, not always to the benefit of the wider Italian economy: an inscription of AD 169–72 from

Saepinum (modern Altilia) reveals the harassment by the town authorities of transhumant shepherds, who were travelling long distances.[5]

Distinctive forms of local nomenclature died out in the first century AD not only on official inscriptions but also on tombs, and the distinctive variety of funerary monuments in different areas of Italy disappeared during the same period. However, to some extent, and despite the Roman veneer which extended to the establishment of municipal courts in imitation of those in the capital, local law may have continued, although the forms of the *lex Rubria* reveal that local jurisdiction could have an upper limit, after which cases had to be tried by magistrates in Rome.

In contrast to the gradual disappearance of regional variation elsewhere in Italy, Greek culture, towards which the Roman aristocracy had long been ambivalent, retained its hold on some Greek cities, most noticeably in Campania and Tarentum (modern Taranto). Magna Graecia, as the region was still considered by Strabo in the time of Augustus, had escaped much of the convulsion of the civil wars. In Neapolis (Naples), Greek plays continued to be shown in the theatres, and Greek games were established there under Augustus. Greek remained in common use as the language of the streets down to the end of the principate.

After Augustus, in many towns local cults continued to flourish in conjunction with those of the Roman state, but the form was Roman: hence, for instance, the wide diffusion through Italy of the Julian religious calendars inscribed on stone.[6] Municipal aristocrats had opportunities to achieve greater wealth on the wider Roman stage, which was often ploughed back into their home town. Thus Comum benefited greatly from the munificence of the younger Pliny,[7] as for instance in his offer to contribute towards the running of a school:

> I was visiting my native town a short time ago when the young son of a fellow citizen came to pay his respects to me. 'Do you go to school?' I asked. 'Yes,' he replied. 'Where?' 'In Mediolanum.' 'Why not here?' To this the boy's father (who had brought him and was standing by) replied: 'Because we have no teachers here.' ... 'Now, as I have not yet any children of my own, I am prepared to contribute a third of whatever sum you decide to collect, as a present for our town such as I might give to a daughter or my mother. I would promise the whole amount were I not afraid that someday my gift might be abused by someone's selfish practices, as I see happen in many places where teachers' salaries are paid from public funds.'
> (*Letters* 4.13)

For some of this Romanization the state was still responsible. Trajan's insistence that senators should buy land in Italy has already been mentioned, as has the immunity of the land from direct taxation. Italy was a primary source for legionary recruitment throughout the Julio-Claudian period, as in the Late Republic, although by the second century AD legionaries from Italy were rare. The emperors still thought of Italy as home until the end of the Antonine dynasty. Thus Trajan set up a charitable scheme providing child assistance funds (*alimenta*) to increase the stock of free-born Italian citizens, an action widely publicized and imitated by some senators (such as Pliny, *Letters* 1.8, 7.18).[8] Yet in practice much of the benefit of the empire increasingly went elsewhere, either to the city of Rome alone, where the emperor showed off his wealth, or to the military provinces to pay for the army. A gradual decline in the economic prosperity of the peninsula as a whole from the mid-first century AD is highly probable, although it is very hard to document.

Archaeological surveys of the rural landscape present a complex picture of agrarian change. There was evidently much regional variation. Thus in some areas, such as southern Etruria and Lucania, the surveyed material suggests an increase in rural settlement. Elsewhere, the decline of rural smallholdings seems to have been largely the result of the consolidation of agricultural land into large plantations, or the abandonment of farmsteads by peasants lured into transhumant pastoralism by the generally peaceful conditions in mountainous regions which encouraged the herding of flocks across the Apennines. In the Sangro valley, settlement hierarchies which dated back to the fourth century BC, when the area was controlled by Samnites, continued into the imperial period around the administrative centre in Monte Pallano, only to crumble when Monte Pallano was abandoned in the second century AD; the collapse seems to indicate the dependence of the local satellite population on this central place.[9]

Thus the evidence for economic decline depends essentially on literary anecdote, not a source to be used with much confidence.[10] Pliny recorded difficulties in getting in rents in the early second century AD (*Letters* 3.18, 9.37, 10.8). A story in Suetonius suggests a need to protect Italian wine production:

> Domitian was such a prey to fear and anxiety that the least sign of danger unnerved him. The real reason for his reprieving the vineyards, which he had ordered to be rooted up, is said to have been the publication of this stanza:
> > You may tear up my roots, goat,
> > But what good will that do?
> > I shall still have some wine left
> > For sacrificing you.
>
> (*Domitian* 14.2)

At the same time evidence for extensive export of Italian wine comes to an end, since no amphoras of the type in which wine had previously been exported from Italy can any longer be found. But the anecdotes need mean no more than temporary local difficulties in bad years, and the absence of amphoras may signify only a change in wine containers. Nonetheless, wider considerations suggest that a change in Italy's economic role over the first century AD was indeed likely.

Nothing about the Italian climate or other resources made the peninsula an obvious region for large-scale agricultural or industrial exports. The Italian success in exporting large quantities of olives and other agricultural products in the Late Republic may have been partly due to the availability of cheap slave labour for extensive *latifundia* (large estates), in which case the decline of the trade might be attributed to the diminution of the slave supply. However, slaves were still available from traders across the *limes* (the empire's frontier), and home-born slaves required no purchase price. In any case, it is unclear whether slave labour was often cheaper than that of tenant farmers (see Chapter 14). It seems more likely that the change which came about was caused by a change in the markets available for selling goods.

Similar arguments apply to the changing role of Italian industry. Successful exports of industrial products in the Late Republic had been achieved primarily through manufacturing expertise and the presence of a stable market throughout Italy, hence the use of identical Arretine red glaze tableware in all areas in the Early Empire.[11] In time such expertise was learned and put into practice elsewhere, in Spain and Gaul (which began producing oil and pottery), in Africa (which began producing oil), and so on. Italian producers therefore needed to look to a local market for their products.

For those in central Italy, that market was, above all, the city of Rome itself. It has been plausibly argued that Italian wine in the second century AD was still made in huge quantities, but aimed at the mass consumers of the city of Rome rather than the specialist drinkers of the provinces.[12] Here was a market which would not go away or dry up. Italy was also particularly well supplied with military roads to ease the transport of goods.

One result of such shifting trade patterns was that the areas of Italy away from Rome began increasingly to resemble provincial regions. By the midfirst century AD it is hard to discern any difference in lifestyle between the inhabitants of northern Italy in the Po valley and the inhabitants of Provence in southern Gaul further to the west.

SICILY

The contrasting history of Sicily in the first century of the principate provides interesting evidence that the Italian consciousness of Romans could have a considerable effect on the lives of inhabitants of the empire. Long settled by Greeks and Carthaginians (whose urban centres dominated the local Sicels), but conquered by Rome in the third century BC, Sicily in the Late Republic was treated simply as a source of income for the imperial city. The same attitude continued well into the first century AD.[13]

Sicily was, from the Greek point of view, at the end of the Republic as much a part of Magna Graecia as south Italy, despite the settlement of many Romans on the island during the Republic and the grant by Julius Caesar of Latin rights to all Sicilians, and despite the grant by Marcus Antonius in 44 BC of full Roman citizenship. Little Latin was used by the locals, and city constitutions remained obstinately Hellenistic in the triumviral period.

This prosperous Greek society was to be changed drastically by the awful events of the ensuing years. From late 43 to 36 BC the island lay under the control of Sextus Pompeius, who milked its inhabitants to pay his forces and cut them off from the main market for their grain in Rome. But far worse was the revenge taken by Octavian, after Pompeius' defeat, against those who had harboured his enemy. Messana (modern Messina) was sacked and huge tracts of land were confiscated (to become, in time, imperial estates). It is possible that the Sicilians were stripped of their status as Roman citizens.

By 21 BC the memory of the civil wars had faded and the process of Romanization in Sicily began. The province was evidently not considered dangerous, since Augustus was happy to allow the appointment of its governor to be left to the drawing of lots (*sortitio*). At least four, possibly six, veteran colonies were founded in this year, forming a new nucleus of Italian settlers on the north and eastern coasts of the island, convenient for the Italian mainland. The state treated Sicily like an extension of Italy: senators could travel there without having to request permission.

Some of the natives responded appropriately. Latin began increasingly to be used in inscriptions. It became the standard language on coins, and was occasionally employed even on private tombstones. A spurt of urban building in coastal settlements attests an economic recovery in the Early Empire, doubtless based on the renewed availability of Rome as a market for Sicilian grain. By contrast, many cities in the interior, and especially those sited on hill tops, declined rapidly. The population of the mountain regions apparently moved to sprawling agricultural settlements in the valleys, now that protection was no longer an issue.

However, Greek culture did not disappear completely. The rural population remained stubbornly Greek for the most part, using Greek building styles and the Greek language. An inscription of AD 35 shows a Greek calendar still in use, and as late as *c.* AD 200 an honorific inscription in Greek was set up in Rome by the *colonia* of Tauromenium (modern Taormina).[14] Whether Punic also continued in the far west of the island is uncertain, but possible. The Carthaginian heritage is curiously invisible in Sicily, but Apuleius (*The Golden Ass* 11.5), in a reference in the mid-second century to the 'three languages of Sicily', must have had Punic in mind.

In overall terms it is probable that the Sicilian economy flourished in the Early Empire. Strabo asserted (*Geography* 6.2.6) that north and western Sicily were deserted in his day (the latter days of Augustus), but his claim is not confirmed by archaeological discoveries. More likely is a change in the pattern of landholding. Proximity to Italy encouraged rich Italians to invest in Sicilian land, profiting from exports not only of grain but also of wine and wool, and of timber from Mount Etna.

20

THE IBERIAN PENINSULA AND THE ISLANDS OF THE WESTERN MEDITERRANEAN

THE IBERIAN PENINSULA

Many of the inhabitants of the Iberian peninsula had been affected by Roman imperialism long before the fall of the Republic, for there had been a constant Roman presence in the south and east of the region since the late third century, when the second Punic war against Carthage had been fought and won by Rome largely on Spanish soil. For two hundred years after the conclusion of that war in 201 BC, Roman troops continued to fight in Spain, with recurrent campaigns against the mountain tribes of the interior.[1] Campaigning was particularly intense in the triumviral period: six triumphs were awarded to proconsuls between 36 and 27 BC for victories in Spain. In the propaganda of Augustus, his victory over the Cantabri in the Pyrenees in 26–25 BC, with the help of seven legions, was portrayed as the culmination of the long process of subjugation (a culmination which, embarrassingly, had to be repeated by Agrippa in 19 BC). Augustus' administrative system in the peninsula, at least as established by the end of his life, was to last. Three provinces were established: from the former province of Hispania Ulterior were created Baetica in the south and Lusitania in the west, with the huge province of Hispania Citerior (also known as Tarraconensis) incorporating all the land from the north-west of Spain to the Mediterranean seaboard in the east (see Maps 6 and 7). The continued stationing in Tarraconensis of three legions (one after AD 63) for the next 150 years may suggest something less than total pacification, let alone Romanization. Rather, this was peace through fear, at least in some parts of the peninsula.

The population of the peninsula was in fact varied both in ethnic origin and in attitude to the Roman state.[2] The Pyrenees, the last area to be conquered, were inhabited by indigenous Iberians whose retention of a non-Indo-European language (Basque) to modern times testifies to an abiding independence. Such stubborn cultural vitality survived a particularly strong onslaught by Rome at the start of the imperial period, for this was one of a number of areas of the empire where the local population was forced by the Romans to migrate to ensure stronger military control over their activities.

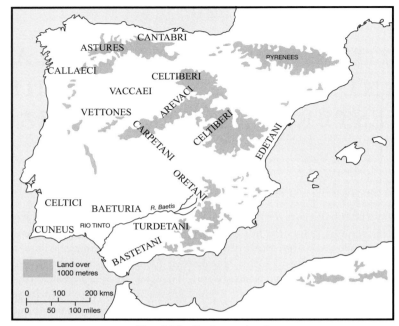

Map 6 The Iberian peninsula

Map 7 The Roman Provinces of the Iberian peninsula

Specifically, the inhabitants of the mountains were compelled by Agrippa to move to level ground, presumably of the plateau of central Spain, which was also the area where the Spanish legionary forces were quartered throughout the principate. Nevertheless, fighting against mountain bandits was still recorded under Nero. In the nature of things, the legionary camps flourished with their surrounding areas. But for the rest, towns were few and small, and none of the aristocracy of this part of Spain, the leaders of the indigenous tribes and their descendants, made any mark on the wider Roman world.

In the south and east of the peninsula, the story was rather different.[3] The population here was a mixture of Iberians and Celts, whose forebears had invaded over the Pyrenees in the fourth century BC, and Italian settlers. Part of the southern coastal area, in particular, which lay within the province of Baetica, was home to a series of colonies which were founded by Augustus as a means to divest himself of surplus veterans. Under Augustus *municipia* of Roman citizens were also founded and many native towns were granted the *ius Latii* (Latin rights). Here, peace was long-standing, until an invasion by Moors in AD 171, and integration into the wider Roman world much greater. The city laws from the Flavian period of a number of towns in Baetica (Malaca, Salpensa, and, most recently discovered, Irni) survive almost intact on a series of bronze tablets; they reveal imperial legislation for each community tailored to local needs and dealing with most aspects of civic life, from religious affairs, magistracies, the manumission of slaves and guardianship of wards, to elections, the seating of spectators at games and the exercise of jurisdiction. Chapter 62, from Tablet VIIA of the *lex Irnitana*, may give an idea of the detailed provisions in the laws[4]:

No-one in the town of the Municipium Flavium Irnitanum or where buildings are continuous with that town, is to unroof or destroy or see to the demolition of a building, except by resolution of the decuriones or conscripti, when the majority of them is present, unless he is going to replace it within the next year. Whoever acts against these rules, is to be condemned to pay to the municipes of the Municipium Flavium Irnitanum as much money as the case is worth, and the right of action, suit and claim of that money and concerning that money is to belong to any municeps of that municipium who wishes and who is entitled under this statute.

The integration of Baetica into the Roman economy was aided by a number of factors. The fertility of the coastal lands of the Mediterranean, and in particular the valley of the River Baetis which enables exceptional productivity on the huge plain it waters as it flows south-west of Corduba into the Atlantic just north of Gades, encouraged the growth of the export trade in olive oil which was to rival that of Africa and surpass that of Italy by the early second century AD. Grain, wine and *garum* (a popular fish sauce) were also exported, according to Strabo (*Geography* 3.2.6). Both private individuals and the state profited from the exploitation of the Río Tinto and other gold and silver mines and later from the patronage given to their home region by Trajan and

Hadrian, who both hailed from the colony of Italica (modern Santiponce) in the Baetis valley.[5] But the olive oil export trade was much the most significant element in the success of the Baetican economy in the Early Empire. Its success is attested by the mountainous quantity of smashed Spanish amphoras which make up Monte Testaccio by the banks of the Tiber in Rome, still today over 50 metres high.

The deep involvement of Spanish aristocrats of Italian origins in the life of the capital dated from the early first century AD, when men such as Seneca (elder and younger), Columella and Lucan formed an enclave of Spanish patronage in Rome during the late Julio-Claudian period. Such men did not lose contact with their home towns. Spain was not drastically distant from Italy, and a rather touching letter from the younger Pliny indicates that even a cynical and ambitious poet like Martial could get homesick and wish to return:

> I am distressed to hear that Valerius Martial is dead. He was a man of great gifts, with a mind both subtle and penetrating, and his writings are remarkable for their combination of sincerity with pungency and wit. I had made him a present of his travelling expenses when he retired from Rome [to his home town in Spain], in recognition of our friendship and the verses he wrote about me.
> (*Letters* 3.21)

It is hard to tell if any of the Spanish senators of the second century were of Celtic origin; it is in any case likely enough that intermarriage made such ethnic distinctions irrelevant.

Nonetheless, it was certainly the colonies and the military who dominated the landscape of Iberia in the Roman period, with the erection of complex aqueducts in the south and an impressive road system in central Spain. But the identity of those who exploited the wider market for oil and other specialist products such as salt remains a mystery. An exception is the case of those who took over mining concessions in the region from the government, whose terms and conditions are revealed on the detailed inscription from Vipasca of the Hadrianic period, quoted briefly above (Chapter 14).[6] Some individuals achieved immense wealth from precious metals, like a certain Sextus Marius, whose death in AD 33 is described by Tacitus:

> Sextus Marius, the richest man in Spain, was thrown from the Tarpeian rock. The charge was incest with his daughter. But the real cause of his ruin was his wealth. This became clear from Tiberius' personal appropriation of his gold and copper mines – though the state was ostensibly their confiscator.
> (*Annals* 6.19)

The language in use on state inscriptions was naturally Latin, and, except in the Pyrenees, that seems to have become the standard language of Roman Spain, although pre-Roman place names and personal names continued into (and even beyond) the imperial period, as did inscriptions in indigenous languages. In fine art, architecture and pottery, Romanization was pervasive but not absolute; for example, Celtic art survived in central Spain and Lusitania, and indigenous Iberian pottery continued alongside Roman *terra sigillata* (wares with decoration in relief) into the first century AD and even later.[7]

In marked contrast to the intensive urbanization of southern and eastern Spain, especially Baetica, the province of Lusitania (approximately modern Portugal) was less changed in the Early Empire.[8] One main cause presumably lay in the comparative infertility of the land. There was little settlement by Italians; the impressive Roman colony of Emerita Augusta (Merida) lay on the border between Lusitania and Baetica. The only natural resources to be fully exploited were the metal deposits, which were intensively mined, and fish sauce. By dividing Lusitania into districts (*civitates*) usually based on the boundaries of pre-Roman tribes, Rome permitted local administration to remain in the control of these tribes, insisting (with a few exceptions) only on the break-up of the larger tribal units, which had focused opposition to Rome. The army built roads and recruited native men into the *auxilia*, but no legion was stationed in this western province, and the state showed no interest in stimulating any trade on the Atlantic coast, presumably because of the dangers to shipping. The far west of Hispania Citerior (Tarraconensis) was similarly ignored by Rome, except for the extortion of gold. It was symbolic that the temple of Augustus erected by the provincials and the site of annual meetings of the provincial council lay in Tarraco (modern Tarragona), which had given its name to the province, and that Tarraco lay on the Mediterranean, rather than the Atlantic, coast.

SARDINIA AND CORSICA

In striking comparison with the Romanization of the Baetis valley and the Mediterranean coast of Spain were the histories of the islands of the western Mediterranean, whose contact with Rome in the Republic had been similar to that of Spain, but which fared very differently in the Early Empire.[9]

Sardinia, like Sicily, was an important source of grain for the city of Rome, but in Roman eyes the island had a reputation for banditry and an unhealthy climate, and both Romanization and urban prosperity were slow to come. The population of Sardinia was formed from the descendants of Carthaginian settlers, who inhabited the cities on the west coast, and native tribes in the mountainous interior. Throughout the early principate the mountain peoples caused problems for those living on the coastal plains. Roman attempts to suppress such activity were haphazard and half-hearted. A few Roman *coloniae* were established, but they did not include veteran soldiers. Latin rights were gradually extended to the inhabitants of the existing cities during the first century AD, but still in the second century a neo-Punic inscription set up in one town described local magistrates as *suffetes*, and cultic inscriptions reveal the continued worship of Punic divinities only thinly disguised behind Roman names.[10] The mountains lay effectively outside Roman control altogether, with Sardinian apparently still the standard language in use. This lack of control apparently caused no concern in Rome. Suetonius (*Tiberius* 36) and Tacitus report that Tiberius sent Jewish men of military age to Sardinia, but they imply that the emperor's aim was not the pacification of the island but the demise of the conscripts:

> Another discussion concerned the expulsion of Egyptian and Jewish rites. The senate decreed that four thousand adult ex-slaves should be transported to Sardinia to suppress banditry there. If the unhealthy climate killed them, the loss would be small.
>
> (*Annals* 2.85)

Corsica was ignored by the Roman state even more than Sardinia, despite its close proximity to Italy. Timber from the island was exported to the mainland, and Rome colonized Mariana and Aleria on the east coast, but Corsica's rugged interior remained untamed.

21

GAUL AND BRITAIN

Parts of Provence, dominated by the Greek city of Massilia (Marseilles) which had been founded *c.* 600 BC, were integrated into the Mediterranean world of trade, and shared cultural and culinary values with Italy long before the principate. Not so Gaul north of the Massif Central, let alone Britain, which was not finally to be conquered by Rome until the mid-first century AD. Here reactions to Roman rule differed greatly from region to region, and from one section of the population to another. Study of the history of Gaul and Britain is complicated, and perhaps skewed, by the comparative wealth of surviving literary evidence for the first centuries BC and AD, particularly in the writings of Caesar, Strabo, Tacitus and Cassius Dio, followed by almost a complete dearth of such evidence for the second century AD, and by a proportionate increase in epigraphic evidence for the later period.

ROMAN CONQUEST OF GAUL

In the Late Republic, Provence (called by the Romans simply *Provincia*, 'The Province') was inhabited by mountain tribes, with only pockets of urban civilization in Narbo (modern Narbonne) and around Massilia, and with Roman influence largely confined to Italian traders (see Maps 8 and 9).[1] But under Caesar, life started to change dramatically: between his arrival in the province in 58 BC and his death in 44 BC many of the native communities of the region were granted Latin status, and veteran colonies were founded at the existing colony of Narbo and elsewhere, thereby stimulating the economy. In 27 BC, Augustus created a new southern province with the name of Narbonensis to replace Provincia, and intensive Romanization began, symbolized by his gift to the town of Nemausus (Nîmes) of walls and gates, and the erection there of the Maison Carrée as a temple dedicated (after their deaths) to Gaius and Lucius Caesar, his grandsons. Urbanization was not uniform in the region, but it was impressive.

The process was aided rather than hindered by Caesar's destruction in 49 BC of the long domination of the region by Massilia. The city lost control of its lands, and during the imperial period it, and its Greek culture, faded into the background. In contrast, Augustus put many small settlements under the control of the urban centres of Nemausus and Vienna (modern Vienne), which accordingly flourished.

Celtic names for urban magistracies were slow to die out, but after Caesar Latin rapidly replaced Celtic in inscriptions and even in graffiti. From early in the first century AD the local élite also achieved success in the Roman governing class, as equestrian officials of the state, and as senators, such as Tacitus' father-in-law, Agricola. In AD 49 the Roman state began officially to treat Narbonensis as equivalent to Italy, with the ruling that Roman senators

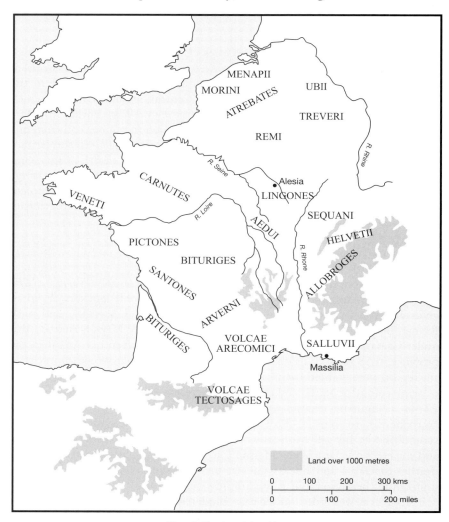

Map 8 Gaul and the Alps

needed no permission to visit the province any more than to leave Rome for Italy or Sicily.

Political incorporation into the Mediterranean world accompanied an economic boom in the first century AD, fuelled not so much by exports as by the role of the region in the redistribution of goods to northern Europe. Peace throughout Provence, now untroubled by attacks from the north, undoubtedly aided the process. As the elder Pliny noted in the 70s AD (*Natural History* 3.4.31), Provence was 'more Italy than province'.

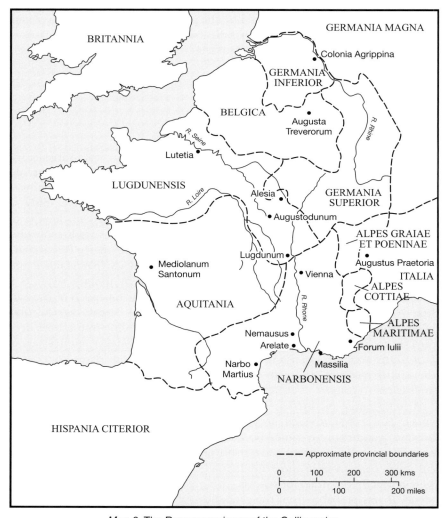

Map 9 The Roman provinces of the Gallic region

231

Central and northern Gaul came into the Roman orbit only in the 50s BC in the campaigns of Julius Caesar (when they were known as *Gallia Comata*, 'Long-haired Gaul'). They were regions quite different from all other areas of Rome's empire.[2] With a climate unlike that of the Mediterranean core of the Roman world, neither central and northern Gaul nor Britain were ever fully integrated into Roman society. Even under Augustus, Roman knowledge of the geography of northern Gaul was minimal, as can be seen from the incompetent account given by Strabo (*Geography* 4.2–4). The Roman image of Gauls throughout our period was coloured by the assumption that they were barbarous. The cliché was fed by the tradition of Gallic invasions of Rome in the fourth century BC and by the proximity of Gaul to the Germans across the Rhine, who were never fully brought under Roman control. In contrast to Provence, in northern Gaul the indigenous Celtic culture proved at first highly resistant to Rome, and the population suffered a dramatic change in their lifestyle and power structure during the first century of the principate.

CELTIC SOCIETY

The evidence for Celtic society before Julius Caesar is not very satisfactory. Writers in the Hellenistic world were strikingly incurious about the 'barbarians' to the north, and it was only in the ethnography of Posidonius, *c.* 90 BC, that any full account was given. This account survives only in fragmentary form and in the use probably, but not certainly, made of it by Caesar and by Strabo later in the first century BC, and was itself somewhat compromised by a tendency to over-schematize.[3] Caesar's fairly full account of the Gallic social system in his *Gallic War* was based on first-hand knowledge, but the extent to which his neat version was shaped by literary accounts is debated. Archaeological evidence, which confirms that for much of the Late Iron Age in Gaul and Germany the population was largely agricultural, inhabiting small settlements cleared out of the surrounding forest, does little directly to illustrate the social order.[4] Considerable evidence survives about *later* Celtic societies in Irish ballads and the like, but none dates from before the eighth century AD, and their relevance to pre-Roman Celtic life is impossible to gauge.

A compromise picture based upon Caesar's description reveals a society in which power was divided between a warrior élite, who characteristically became paramount in times of war, and wise men called druids, whose expertise in native wisdom gave them pre-eminence as advisors in religious cult and, perhaps even more influentially, in law cases. The warrior chiefs were normally rewarded for success with great wealth in the form of precious metal. It was probably from their fondness for the display of precious metals that the cliché arose among Romans that Gaul was a place of great wealth. For druids, by contrast, wealth was not an inevitable concomitant of their calling.

It seems that nothing, apart from the time taken to study sacred law, prevented a warrior achieving respect also for druidic wisdom, as was the case with Caesar's ally and Cicero's acquaintance, Divitiacus. As Cicero described him, using the voice of his brother Quintus:

> Nor is the practice of divination disregarded even among uncivilized tribes, if indeed there are druids in Gaul – and there are, for I knew one of them myself, Divitiacus, the Aeduan, your [Cicero's] guest and eulogist. He claimed to have that knowledge of nature which the Greeks call 'physiologia', and he used to make predictions, sometimes by means of augury and sometimes by means of conjecture.
> (*On Divination* 1.41.90)

But it is fair to surmise that such doubling of roles as warrior chief and druid was rare.[5]

EFFECTS OF ROMAN CONQUEST

For such a system, Roman conquest was bound to produce changes far more traumatic than in Italy or those areas of the Greek East where city magistrates not dissimilar to the Roman aristocracy held sway. The fairly loose administrative system imposed by Julius Caesar was greatly tightened over the following decades. Augustus and later emperors already viewed all 'Long-haired Gaul' as in some sense a political unity, since the altar for worship of Rome and Augustus set up at Lugdunum (modern Lyons) by Drusus in 12 BC was intended for aristocrats from the whole region. Under Augustus, Gallia Comata was divided into three provinces (Aquitania, Lugdunensis and Belgica), known collectively as *Tres Galliae*, the Three Gauls. But the three provinces were imposed regardless of ethnographic realities, and the inhabitants themselves seem to have retained only local loyalties to their *civitates* (native communities).

By the mid first-century AD, both Gaul and Britain were still ruled by native chiefs, in some, perhaps most, cases descended from the warrior chiefs of pre-Roman days. In Britain, many such warriors ruled still as client kings, such as Cogidubnus, king of a realm covering Hampshire, Sussex and part of Berkshire, who ruled from his comfortable villa at Fishbourne, close to Noviomagus (modern Chichester), from *c.* AD 43 to his peaceful death in the late 60s or 70s AD.[6] But in Gaul the status and role of the chiefs had in many places expanded greatly to fit in with that of Roman élites elsewhere. Particularly notable in Gaul were the so-called Gallic 'Julii', aristocrats who had gained Roman citizenship serving under Caesar or Octavian and had taken their family name of Julius.[7] They did not just fight on behalf of their people, although of course they did do that, primarily as commanders of auxiliary units within the Roman army. Besides that role they became the magistrates of new towns set up in imitation of the Roman towns of Italy, and acted as priests of the imperial cult. Not least as a reward from Julius Caesar for loyalty they often possessed great wealth, but they enshrined their wealth not in cattle but in land, so that their clients, with whom their ancestors had jointly grazed cattle in earlier days, became their tenants. As for the druids, under Augustus druidic practices were forbidden to Roman citizens in Gaul, and under Tiberius druidic practices were banned altogether by decree of the senate (Pliny, *Natural History* 30.4), although they clearly did not disappear as a result, since Claudius made a further attempt at suppression (Suetonius, *Claudius* 25).

In other words, the impact of Roman rule on Celtic society was dramatic, sudden and drastic. The whole social order was effectively changed.[8] Whatever of the old system continued, did so in this period underground. In the third century elements of Celtic art were to reappear. In the eighth century so did some druidic myths, but the rest was gone forever.

ROMAN CONQUEST OF BRITAIN

The inhabitants of Britain conquered by Rome came from a variety of different groups. The northern Britons were Caledonians, but those in the south were mostly descendants of Celts who had migrated from northern Gaul in the Late Iron Age (see Map 10). The quite recent arrival of most of the tribes in southern Britain explains the power struggles and the shifting formulations of tribal units before the Roman conquest, as revealed by coins. Such inter-tribal rivalries much aided the imposition of Roman domination.

The Roman attitude to Britain (*Britannia*), and native response, were similar to that in northern Gaul.[9] Julius Caesar had attempted to conquer the country in 55–54 BC but had been compelled to withdraw. Octavian is said to have planned expeditions in 34, 27 and 26 BC, but in the event he contented himself with befriending client kings in the south of the country; both he and Tiberius avoided intervention, despite appeals from their clients when the balance of power between tribes was upset by squabbles. Gaius' intention to invade in AD 40 stopped at the Channel, but Claudius, intent on propaganda, invaded in force in AD 43, conquering England up to a line between the Humber and the Severn rivers. In the following century Roman forces gradually incorporated more of Britain, without ever reaching a satisfactory boundary; attempts to conquer Wales in the 50s AD and Scotland in the 80s AD were only partially successful (see Map 11).

The revolt of Boudicca and the Iceni of East Anglia in AD 60–61, with the sack of Camulodunum (Colchester), Verulamium (St Albans) and Londinium (London), provided evidence that simple containment of existing territories would be hard for Rome to ensure. After the partial success of the campaigns of Agricola between AD 78 and 84/5, along the eastern edges of the Scottish Highlands, most of Scotland was left alone, and most Roman troops had withdrawn by the early second century, a fact which Hadrian marked symbolically in the 120s AD by the erection of a great stone wall between

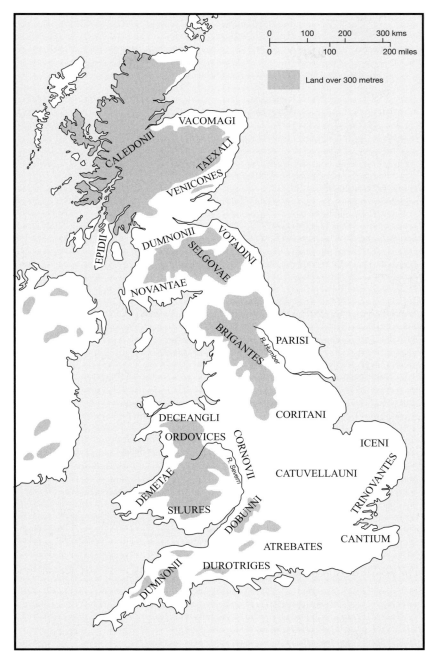

Map 10 Britain

Map 11 Roman Britain in the second century AD

Wallsend-on-Tyne and Bowness-on-Solway. The wall, which boasted regular fortlets, a ditch in front and a much larger one behind, was a novel idea in Roman military strategy, and major modifications were introduced over the period of its construction. Antoninus Pius erected another wall further north in *c.* AD 142, but it was abandoned (for the second time) by *c.* AD 163, and Hadrian's wall became the definitive frontier.

If the Romans were ambivalent about Scotland, they were even less enthusiastic about Ireland. Agricola seems to have entertained hopes of establishing some control in Ireland, according to Tacitus:

> He also manned with troops that part of the British coast which faces Ireland, in hope of future action rather than out of fear; for Ireland, I believe, which lies between Britain and Spain and also commands the Gallic Sea, would unite, to their mutual advantage, the most effective portions of our empire.
>
> (*Agricola* 24.1–2)

The discovery of a large number of Roman goods in a coastal fort in Drumanagh, in the east of Ireland, suggests substantial trade with the British mainland in the first and early second century AD.

REBELLION AGAINST ROME IN GAUL AND BRITAIN

Reactions to Roman rule were not uniformly favourable either in Gaul or in Britain. Both areas witnessed violent uprisings under the Julio-Claudians.[10] In Gaul there may have been a disturbance by the Allobroges in Vienne following the death of Caesar, and there were disturbances in 38 BC (in Aquitania), in 31–28 BC, in 12 BC, in AD 21 and in AD 68 and 69. How widespread such unrest was, and what the underlying causes were, are much more difficult to tell. In Britain the rebellion of Boudicca in AD 60–61 inflamed much of the country. Not that the cause of the resentment lay simply in the cultural and social change brought by Rome. Some of the uprisings in Gaul were sparked off by elements of the state's taxation system, from the holding of a census to assess tax, to, at its most extreme, the violent methods employed by such as the procurator Licinius in its extraction:

> This man, whose behaviour combined the greed of the barbarian with something of the dignity of the Roman, tried to pull down anyone who was ever regarded as superior to him, and to eliminate everyone who for the time being showed strength. He provided himself with ample funds for the office to which he had been appointed, and also secured large sums for himself and his friends. His unscrupulous methods went so far that in some cases where people paid their taxes by the month he represented the months in the year as totalling fourteen; thus he claimed that December was really the tenth month, and that for this reason they must reckon two more (which he called the eleventh and twelfth respectively) as the last, and pay in the money that was due for these months.
>
> (Cassius Dio, *History of Rome* 54.21.2–8)

The immediate cause of the Boudiccan revolt was the insulting treatment of the royal family of the Iceni. But the desperate viciousness of much of the fighting may be seen as a mark of the natives' awareness that the last of their culture was under threat. And it is probably no accident that it was believed that druids were in some way involved in the revolts of Boudicca and of AD 69.

URBANIZATION OF GAUL AND BRITAIN

Given such drastic changes, and the evidence for strong hostility to them, it is reasonable to wonder how deep those changes went when they were finally effected. Thus 'Roman' towns were to be found all over northern Gaul and Britain by the second century AD. But how urbanized were their inhabitants and to what extent did they identify with the Roman state?

Variety is to be expected. In northern Gaul urban life can only be traced from after the death of Augustus, except at Lyons (which was designated as the site of the imperial cult and became a major distribution centre) and at Autun (Augustodunum), a fine new town with a magnificent city wall, regular streets, theatre and amphitheatre, and a 'university', apparently built for the Aedui, Rome's old allies, to replace their old capital Bibracte. The site of Verulamium in Britain in the 50s AD may stand as a prime example of a town which was little more than a name, in marked contrast to Colchester (Camulodunum), about 30 miles away, which had a Roman *colonia* (*colonia Victricensis*) founded close by in AD 49 with a population mostly comprised of legionary veterans, and which served as a model of urbanization.

Verulamium was probably in Roman legal terminology a *municipium* from *c.* AD 49, although Tacitus' testimony on this point (*Annals* 14.33) is a little ambiguous. It lay on the site of an Iron Age centre of the Catuvellauni.[11] It is possible that there originally existed numerous timber buildings, and that these were totally destroyed during the Boudiccan revolt, but the archaeological evidence for the town before AD 60 reveals little more than a row of shops built according to a standard design, perhaps by, or under the guidance of, Roman soldiers. The Celtic settlement of Prae Wood, which lay on the hills above the new town, seems to have fallen into disuse, but there is no archaeological evidence that Verulamium had become a place for settlement. Instead, the early town seems to have been simply a notional administrative centre where some trade (by outsiders?) provided imported ceramics for a minority of the population. Local Celtic fine wares were still being much used in the town until the 80s AD. By the mid-second century the local aristocrats had built a stone theatre, baths, forum and temples on the site, but at the beginning of Verulamium, such local enthusiasm for urban life was yet to be evident.

Similarly, in northern Gaul Celtic hill-top sites, like Alesia (Alise-Ste-Reine), the centre of opposition to Julius Caesar in 52 BC, rarely stayed in occupation in the imperial period. Beginning under Augustus, the existing Celtic communities (*civitates*) were each administered through a single settled centre.[12] Life in the centres of *civitates* already situated on lowland sites seems to have continued under Augustus little changed from the Late Iron Age, with a small population in each settlement, little trade and few stone public buildings. Most new settlement was in small centres along the main routes. It was only from the time of Tiberius that new towns began to spring up along the northern Atlantic seaboard, particularly after the conquest of Britain in AD 43.

Reluctance to adopt urban culture can be found in some places in Britain and northern Gaul down to the end of the principate. Thus it is probably significant that Lutetia, the capital of the *civitas* of the Parisii, which lay on the site of Paris, preserved after antiquity its tribal rather than its urban name, even though the town had a regular street plan, forum, public buildings and other appurtenances of a standard Roman town. In many such areas, the local élite, who did so well out of Roman rule, gradually in the second century AD exhibited their enthusiasm for things Roman by adopting with a will the Italic fashion for luxurious countryside villas.[13] The siting of villas differed somewhat between regions. In early imperial Gaul, they were usually found related to villages rather than towns, whereas in contemporary Britain they were found close to urban centres, becoming more widespread only in the second century. But ostentatious expenditure on public buildings in towns, which required an assumption that at least some of one's fellows amongst the populace would appreciate such evergetism, was rare.

The exceptions to this general tendency to non-involvement were mostly settlements of Roman veterans, of which there were a large number in Britain, where the Roman state kept four legions (three after AD 86) in permanent occupation. The sheer bulk of inscriptional evidence for standard Roman-style evergetism in colonies such as Glevum (modern Gloucester) or Lindum (modern Lincoln), compared to the near dearth of evidence from major administrative centres ruled by locals such as Verulamium, despite extensive excavation at the latter, may be highly significant. In Gaul, writing increased markedly in the early imperial period, but never to the level found in Italy. Whether the failure of Britons and northern Gauls to pick up the epigraphic habit more than they did should be attributed to a reluctance to adopt Latin, or to a previous druidic monopoly of writing, or to a lack of qualified stone-cutters, is uncertain.[14]

ASSIMILATION AND INDEPENDENCE

The progress towards assimilation into wider Roman society may have been more rapid in middle and northern Gaul than in Britain because of the role of the previously mentioned Gallic Julii, the warrior leaders who were drafted into the Roman *auxilia* on the conquest of northern Gaul by Caesar. Some such warriors achieved considerable prominence as fighters in the Roman civil wars. They and their relations competed for the honour of presiding at the great altar of the imperial cult at Lyons, which rapidly became the lynch-pin of the three provinces. It was from their descendants that the emperor Claudius, in a deliberate act of inclusion, chose a select few to enter the senate in the late 40s AD. Only three are known from before AD 70, but of these, at least one, the Julius Vindex who raised the banner of revolt against Nero in AD 68–69, adopted Roman senatorial values, at least on the surface. The coins issued in his name proclaimed the senate and people of Rome (*SPQR*) and declared Rome restored to freedom (*ROMA RESTITUTA*) (Smallwood, *Gaius–Nero* no. 70). Gallic senators became less common after AD 69, for no discernible reason, but they did not disappear, and in the mid-third century AD independent Roman emperors were to rule from northern Gaul. By contrast, British senators are not to be found at all in this period, and Britons even as commanders of *auxilia* are rarely attested. The crucial difference seems to have been the later date of the conquest of Britain. By AD 43, the need for large numbers of impressive warriors was much reduced in the Roman world, and competition for prestige was sufficient among already incorporated peoples for newly conquered Britons to stand little chance of consideration.

Against this trend of greater assimilation in Gaul lie the curious events of AD 69–70, in which Julius Classicus and Julius Tutor, from the Treviri tribe of Augusta Treverorum (modern Trier) in Belgica, and Julius Sabinus of the Lingones in Upper Germany, proclaimed an independent *imperium Galliarum* (empire of the Gauls) in northern Gaul.[15] The episode, which occurred in the middle of the Roman civil war, and at the very least capitalized on this fact, was characterized by Tacitus (*Histories* 4.57 ff.) as an attempt to break away from Roman domination, a not entirely irrational aim when the Roman state was in such turmoil. If this political aim was genuinely present, 120 years after conquest by Julius Caesar, it is testimony both to a remarkable lack of assimilation despite the surface signs and to the continuing self-awareness of national Celtic bonds among tribes divided between different Roman *provinciae*. It may be, indeed, that it was precisely the continuation of Late Iron Age institutions under a Roman veneer that enabled the Gallic Julii to keep their power in Gaul throughout the Julio-Claudian period. In the Gallic *civitas* of the Santones in Aquitania, one C. Iulius Marinus was described on an inscription of the imperial period as holding office as a quaestor then as a *vergobret*, the title of a Gallic magistracy. This may be significant not just for the continued use of an archaic name, but also for the subjection of the community to an individual ruler, in Celtic style, as well as to collegial magistrates. Such bonds had produced a powerful coalition in the first place against Julius Caesar and perhaps had not been forgotten. It may be significant that a druidess, a certain Veleda, is said to have prophesied success for the revolt of AD 69–70:[16]

> This maiden of the tribe of the Bructeri enjoyed extensive authority, according to the ancient German custom, which regards many women as endowed with prophetic powers and, as the superstition grows, attributes divinity to them. At this time, Veleda's influence was at its height, since she had foretold the German success and the destruction of the legions.
>
> (Tacitus, *Histories* 4.61.2)

The appearance of a druidess at all comes as a surprise in AD 69, since such practices had been banned by the emperor Claudius under pain of death. It suggests that the archaeological and epigraphic evidence about Gallo-Roman religion and the sprouting of characteristic temples in the new 'Roman' towns, presided over by the warrior leaders or their descendants, may present only the picture of culture in Gaul and Britain that the Roman state wished to be seen. The establishment's hope to disguise the quintessentially Roman cult of the emperor in Gallic dress, with sacred groves and Gallic names, and to disguise Celtic cults by instituting formal Roman-style worship, did not necessarily suppress local desires for their ancient culture. It is impossible to know how Celts approached the 'Roman' temples, with their characteristic double square plan, built, presumably deliberately, on the site of pre-Roman shrines. But it is likely that, for instance, the popular shrine of Sulis Minerva at Aquae Sulis (Bath) retained all its local associations throughout the Roman period, regardless of the Roman accoutrements of the site. It is after all significant that druidic rites of some kind were still to be found in Gaul in the fifth century AD, however attenuated.[17]

ECONOMIC PROSPERITY UNDER THE ROMANS

In the end, the economic consequences of Roman rule were perhaps the most significant in both Gaul and Britain. On a wider scale, the northern parts of the empire exported raw materials, such as cattle, slaves and metals, and imported manufactured goods, like wine and oil. More locally, in Britain the high concentration of troops in northern Britain near Hadrian's wall and on the western frontier near Deva (modern Chester) produced a boom in production in both areas. The army provided a ready market and also distributed small-value coin, which greatly enhanced trade. The lead mines of Charterhouse and the salt-workings of Middlewich and Droitwich (both called Salinae by the Romans) flourished in parasitic relationship with the military.[18] Partly controlled by the Roman army at first, they continued production for a civilian market across wide swathes of the country.

At all times some areas of both Gaul and Britain remained effectively free of state interference, regardless of the theory that they lay within a governor's *provincia*. In the countryside most farmsteads continued unchanged, unaffected by political upheavals. In Gaul this is particularly true of north-west Brittany, where few towns were to be found and no soldiers were stationed. In the late third century the local peasants, termed the *bagaudae*, were to set up an independent state there.[19] In Britain similar non-interference in western Wales and Scotland, north of Hadrian's Wall, was more openly resented by the Roman state. It may be surmised that the success of such tribes in preserving political independence sometimes acted as an incentive to other inhabitants of the region to seek similar opportunities for themselves.

22

THE RHINELAND AND
THE BALKANS

THE RHINELAND

For the first century of the principate the Rhineland was the site of much intermittent intensive fighting by the Roman state. In the process the culture and economy of much of the region was transformed.[1]

Julius Caesar's conquest of Gaul had left the River Rhine as a frontier of Roman power (see Map 12). The choice was bound to prove unsatisfactory because it left the Roman state directly responsible for preventing the migrations from the east into north-west Europe which had been going on for centuries – and whose renewal in the late Roman period would eventually precipitate the downfall of the Roman Empire itself. The migrations continued under Augustus, with or without Roman approval.

Under Augustus immense efforts were made between 17 BC and AD 9 to extend control eastwards as far as the River Elbe. A defeat at the beginning, with the loss by Lollius of a legionary standard, was followed by great successes, including an 'immense war' of AD 1 (Velleius Paterculus, *History of Rome* 2.104.2) which confronted, but did not defeat, the great coalition of the Marcomanni. Success was brought almost to nothing by the Varian disaster of AD 9, in which three legions were destroyed in difficult country by Arminius, the chief of the Cherusci, despite which Augustus claimed in his *Res Gestae* (26.2) to have conquered Germany: 'I brought peace to the Gallic and Spanish provinces as well as to Germany, throughout the area bordering on the Ocean from Cadiz to the mouth of the Elbe.'

The campaigns of Germanicus from AD 14 to 16 against the Chatti, Cherusci and Bructeri were intended to establish Roman power indefinitely in the territory east of the Rhine (see Map 13), and he was credited with avenging Varus – it was planned his victory should be recorded on his memorial arch at Rome:

with gilded representations of the conquered peoples, and an inscription on the front of that gateway stating that the senate and the Roman people dedicated this marble monument to the memory of Germanicus Caesar, and recording that he, after conquering those Germans in war, removed them from Gaul and recovered the

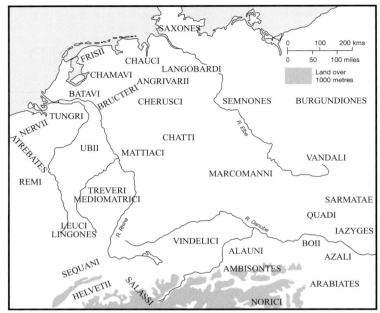

Map 12 The Rhineland region

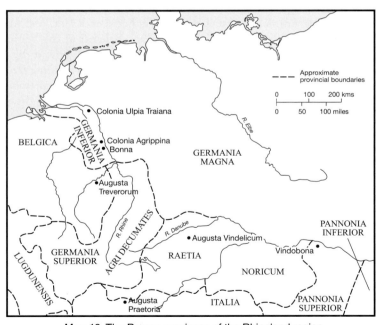

Map 13 The Roman provinces of the Rhineland region

244

military standards, and, having avenged the deceitful destruction of an army of the Roman people, and having re-established the condition of the Gauls, he was sent as proconsul to the transmarine provinces.

(*AE* 1984, no. 508; LR 2, p. 524)

But the opposition of Arminius, described by Tacitus (*Annals* 2.88) as 'without doubt, liberator of Germany', persuaded Tiberius in AD 17 to withdraw his troops back to the Rhine region. Though dignified from the late first century AD with the name of two provinces (Upper and Lower Germany), this region became in effect a military area controlled by eight legions under two legates – a small, narrow appendage to the huge province of Gallia Belgica.

The upper Rhine region was treated already under the Julio-Claudian emperors as a single settlement zone, the river being continually crossed, until, between AD 73 and 98, the Flavian emperors annexed the territory, including the Black Forest and the Neckar Basin, known as the *Agri Decumates* (perhaps a Gaulish expression meaning ten cantons), thereby shortening communications between the Rhineland and the Danube. Under Hadrian, the number of legions kept on the Rhine was reduced to four, and a palisade was erected in Upper Germany, with close-spaced forts along the lower Rhine. The palisade in Upper Germany was advanced eastwards by Antoninus Pius. The lack of reserve legions in the heart of Gaul throughout the Early Empire suggests that Rome was not seriously concerned at the possibility of major incursions in this period. Defences were against small-scale border violations at the most.[2]

Before the arrival of Rome, the inhabitants of these regions were divided into quite small tribal units. The earliest home of the Germans was south Scandinavia, Jutland and the north German coast. Separate groups had migrated south and westward since *c.* 1000 BC, coming into hostile contact first with Celts and then with Rome. According to Tacitus:

The name of 'Germany' is new and a recent application. The first tribes in fact to cross the Rhine and expel the Gauls, though now called Tungri, then bore the name Germans: so little by little the name – a tribal, not a national, name – prevailed, until the whole people were called by the artificial name of 'Germans', first only by the victorious tribe Tungri in order to intimidate the Gauls, but afterwards by themselves also.

(*Germania* 2)

The Germans themselves also believed that they had a common identity based on shared myths of origins and religious federations centred on sacred grounds, although rarely realized in political unity; the great coalition of the Marcomanni under Maroboduus in the early first century AD was an exception whose success proved the rule. Of those who defined themselves as Germans, quite a number were already to be found settled on the western bank of the Rhine even before Caesar's invasion of Gaul, but identities seem to have been fluid. Thus, the Treveri and the Nervii, according to Tacitus (*Germania* 28.4), thought of themselves as Germans, even though their names in the first and second century AD were often Celtic. Archaeological and linguistic evidence suggests that the Rhine itself was not a major cultural frontier, and differences in the Late Iron Age were more marked between the north Rhineland and the south than between the two banks of the river.[3]

The *Germania,* or *On the Origin and Country of the Germans*, composed by Tacitus in AD 98, is a description of the various tribes north of the Rhine and of the Danube. It is a rather disjointed ethnographical treatise, which draws much of its material from older works and tends to idealize the Germans as noble savages. Nonetheless, his testimony can be accepted that in his day the Germans were primarily pastoralists but also engaged in agriculture. Among some tribes there were permanent chiefs, but among others specific leaders were elected for special campaigns. On important matters decisions were taken by the warriors in assembly. The archaeological record reveals much Roman trade beyond the Roman borders into free Germany, but imported artefacts evidently did not greatly alter a long-established lifestyle. Furthermore, the shifting nomenclature of the groups who came into contact with Rome in the north-eastern Rhineland suggests that the movement of peoples, arrested within the empire by Roman might, continued unabated across the frontier, sometimes with dire consequences.

The contrast between free Germany and the Rhine region after the Roman conquest was thus striking. Here, the concentration of Roman troops and the foundation of new military colonies, among them Colonia Agrippina (modern Cologne) which was established by Claudius in AD 50 (Tacitus, *Annals* 12.27.1), proved a massive boost to commerce, and the Rhine itself rapidly became a trade route, protected by the Rhine fleet stationed upstream from Cologne. The beneficiaries of the Roman peace included some German tribes who had positively sought Roman protection. Thus of the Ubii, a German tribe originally found east of the Rhine, some had been brought across the river either in 38/37 BC or 19/18 BC by Agrippa at their own request to the land where Cologne was later to be founded. Others crossed into the empire after AD 9. Service in the auxiliaries enabled many of them to achieve Roman citizenship, and loyalty to Rome was encouraged in the first decades AD by the establishment of the altar of the Ubii (*ara Ubiorum*) for worship of the emperor, in imitation of the Gallic altar at Lyons. They intermarried with the colonists sufficiently to express dismay when cajoled into joining the great revolt of AD 69–70 by Julius Civilis.[4]

The history and the rhetoric of that revolt bear testimony to the continuation of a desire for freedom long after the decisive success of Arminius in preserving the freedom of those who remained far enough east of the Rhine.[5] The revolt of AD 69–70 was led by the Julius Civilis mentioned above, a Batavian, who was asked by Antonius Primus to create a diversion to prevent more troops of the Vitellians marching to Italy against Vespasian in the Roman civil war. The Batavi, a Germanic people, were an offshoot of the Chatti who had helped

Rome in the temporary conquest of western Germany in 12 BC and remained allied to Rome despite their own location east of the Rhine in part of what is now Holland. They provided auxiliary troops to Rome under their own chieftains until their leader Civilis, for reasons unexplained in the ancient sources, led them into insurrection. It is likely that this episode, like many others, reflects the constant conflict of pro-Roman against more traditional forces in each tribe. What is interesting is its continuation so long after Roman conquest, and the on-going ambivalence of even the most Romanized German auxiliary commanders. The Germans had before them not only the example of Arminius to emulate but also that of the Frisii on the northern tip of the Rhineland. Despite intensive campaigning by Corbulo in AD 47, the Frisii, who were determined to maintain their freedom while co-operating with Rome as they had always done, were left to their own devices on the east side of the river.

Despite such impulses to rebellion, large areas of the Rhineland flourished remarkably. Numerous inscriptions record the success of local long-distance traders with Gallo-Germanic names. Most striking is the archaeological evidence of the prosperity of second-century Augusta Treverorum (today Trier), apparently derived from intensive agriculture, presumably for the military market, which itself consisted increasingly of Gallic and Germanic soldiers.[6] Nonetheless, urbanization in the region was slow, despite its beginnings under Augustus and Claudius. In general, the state's reliance on the *civitas* system, as in Gaul, and on colonies of Italian veterans, discouraged the transformation of most native centres into *municipia* until the reigns of Trajan and Hadrian.

THE ALPS

The history of the Alpine region between Germany and Italy in this era is closely linked to Roman policy in Germany to the north.[7] The Romans in the Republican period had largely ignored the small tribes who dwelt in the Alpine valleys north of the Po basin. Although these tribes, of partly Illyrian and partly Celtic origins, were linked by linguistic and cultural bonds, they lacked any political unity, and never showed any signs of threatening Italy to the south; on the contrary, in the 40s BC they took the brunt of Germanic tribal movements which would otherwise have affected Roman territory. But they did control the Alpine passes, and could exact tolls and impede Roman troops. The Salassi had successfully fought Caesar's soldiers on the Swiss side of the Great St Bernard Pass; in 25 BC, Augustus gained control of the pass with a campaign in the Salassi's territory of the Val d'Aosta, defeating them on the Italian side of the pass:

Once these men [the Salassi] robbed even Caesar of money and threw crags upon his legions under the pretext that they were making roads or bridging rivers. Later on, however, Augustus completely overthrew them, and sold all of them as booty, after carrying them to Eporedia, a Roman colony. ... Now although the number of the other persons captured proved to be thirty-six thousand and, of the fighting men, eight thousand, Terentius Varro, the general who overthrew them, sold all of them under the spear. And Caesar sent three thousand Romans and founded the city of Augusta in the place where Varro had pitched his camp, and at the present time peace is kept by all the neighbouring country as far as the highest parts of the passes which lead over the mountain.

(Strabo, *Geography* 4.6.7)

The Roman campaigns of 15 BC seem to have had no other aim than to win glory for Tiberius and Drusus and to block off the southern route for German tribes who might wish to avoid the Roman onslaught across the Rhine. Hence the main results of that campaign were the proud claim of victory over numerous tribes, advertised on Augustus' prominent victory monument, the *Tropaeum Alpium*, set up at La Turbie above Monaco; the establishment of forts on the foothills of the northern Alps; and the incorporation of a new province, Raetia, ruled by equestrian prefects.[8]

[TX1[In later years Roman conquest seems to have produced exceptionally little resistance, partly perhaps because it required little change by the inhabitants of long-established lifestyles. The tribes paid their tribute peacefully. Augustus built many roads for easy military access. Some of the young men took service in the *auxilia* (Cassius Dio, *History of Rome* 54.22.5). But few troops were stationed permanently in the region, the *civitates* were left intact and in peace, and the few colonies of Roman citizens were confined to the northern edge of the Alps, with the exception of Augusta Praetoria (now Aosta), founded after Varro's defeat of the Salassi. Only one Roman *municipium* is attested for the whole area: *municipium Aelium Augusta Vindelicum* (now Augsburg), which was granted municipal status under Hadrian. The inhabitants were not necessarily uncivilized – inscriptions prove that some of them were literate before the Roman conquest – but land so mountainous was not worth anything to Rome, and they were left alone.

THE DANUBE AND THE BALKANS

In the region of the Danube and the Balkans, military activity was rather spasmodic, as on the Rhine.[9] The Balkan ranges were already quite well known to Greek writers before the Roman imperial period, but information was greatly expanded by Roman conquests: thus Strabo in the later years of Augustus described the course of the Danube with considerable accuracy (for instance, *Geography* 7.3.13). The river had a strong symbolic value to the Romans. Augustus boasted that in his reign Roman rule had reached its banks:

Through Tiberius Nero, who was then my stepson and legate, I conquered and subjected to the empire of the Roman people the Pannonian tribes, to which before

my principate no army of the Roman people had ever penetrated: and I extended
the frontier of Illyricum to the bank of the Danube river.

(*Res Gestae* 30.1)

However, there is no evidence for occupation of the middle and lower Danube
during the Augustan period. Augustus' much vaunted 'extension of the
frontier' in fact seems to have comprised compelling tribes south of the river
to accept client status, rather than military occupation. There was no concerted
push to the Danube before the middle of the first century AD, and direct
military control of the lower Danube does not appear to have been established
until the late Flavian, or even Trajanic, period (see Map 14).[10]

The Balkans in the mid-first century BC were inhabited by a variety of
peoples, divided primarily by the great mountain barrier which runs from
north to south through Bosnia, Montenegro and Albania, and linked in the
north by the great highway of the Danube itself. In the north-west, between
the Alps and the Danube, the population was predominantly Celtic, according
to the evidence of place names and the weapons placed in their graves. The
Celts had arrived in the region in the mid-fourth century BC and had long had
trading relations with Italy, as evidenced by the commercial settlement at the
Magdalensberg in Carinthia (in modern Austria). In the south-west (modern
Albania), a variety of Illyrian tribes inhabited fortified hill-top settlements in
mountainous and wooded terrain; they had long come under Greek influence,
particularly near the Adriatic coast. The eastern Balkans, south of the Danube,
were occupied by Getae north of the Haemus mountains, and south of these
mountains by Thracians, who were settled in hill forts and fortified villages,
with only minimal urban life as a relic of Macedonian interference in the
fourth century. Finally, north of the eastern reaches of the Danube flourished
the Dacian tribes, from *c.* 60 to 44 BC dominated by their king Burebista and,
temporarily at least, sufficiently unified to be seen as a threat to Rome.

The Illyrian tribes on the extreme west of the Balkan range had come into
sporadic conflict with Rome from the late third century BC, but the
mountainous terrain made conquest by Rome extremely difficult (see Map
15).[11] Octavian's campaigns against the Iapodes and Pannonians in 35 BC,
and against the Delmatae in 34–33 BC, were undertaken primarily for military
prestige to rival Antonius, and perhaps to counter Roman fears of the Dacians
far further to the north. They had few long-lasting effects, beyond securing
the Adriatic coast. It was only in the Pannonian war of 13–9 BC that the
region was effectively pacified, with the clear aim of securing a land route for
armies along the middle Danube from Europe to the Middle East. The
defeated Pannonians were disarmed and the young men sold as slaves.
Rebellion in AD 6 was begun by the Pannonians assembled by Rome to attack
the Marcomanni in free Germany. When they turned this force against Rome,
the uprising was only suppressed, with difficulty, in AD 9. It was probably
then that Illyricum was divided into two provinces, known at first as Upper

Map 14 The Danube region and the Balkans

Map 15 The Roman provinces of the Danube region and the Balkans
in the late second century AD

and Lower Illyricum, later as Pannonia and Dalmatia. The Dalmatian coast was rapidly urbanized, but the interior had no more than villages. Cities were founded in Pannonia under Claudius and the Flavians, as the move towards the Danube took place and the interior was handed over to civilian authority. The area was sufficiently peaceful to be left without a garrison by the end of the first century AD. The Alpine province of Noricum to the east of Raetia and south of the Danube, formed out of an organized Celtic state which had produced its own coinage as far back as the second century BC, had a similar history of conquest and pacification. Some *municipia* appeared, named after Claudius, following the same pattern of progressive urbanization which occurred in Pannonia, but this time linked to military movement east to the Danube bank. In general the area was, like Raetia, left in peace.[12]

The region of Moesia, situated on the lower Danube in present day Serbia, was almost unknown to Greeks and Romans until the Bastarnae there were defeated and subdued by Marcus Crassus in 29–28 BC (Cassius Dio, *History of Rome* 51.23.2–27.3). Almost no inscriptions from the province are found from before the Flavians, and it seems likely that the region was hardly affected by Roman rule until the Flavian emperors decided to found a series of forts along the south banks of the Danube.[13] The region always remained, from the point of view of the Roman state, little more than a site for military operations; as Ovid complained from his exile in neighbouring Tomis (modern Constanta) between AD 9 and AD 17, he was surrounded by barbarians (*Tristia* and *Letters from Pontus*). Except for the old-established Greek cities on the Black Sea, like Tomis, which was finally incorporated into Moesia under Claudius, almost all its chief towns grew out of the military camps strung along the Danube from the Flavian period and after, although there was a wave of urban foundations, probably all quite small, in the late Antonine period both in Upper Moesia and on the lower Danube.[14]

In the region south of Moesia, Rome was frequently drawn during the Julio-Claudian period into the affairs of the kingdom of Thrace, both by conflict between the Odrysians settled on the eastern plains and the Bessi in the more mountainous west, and by strife within the ruling dynasty of Rhoemetalces and his relatives. In AD 46 Claudius ended all intrigues by incorporating the region into the empire as a new province. But even after this act, and despite long contacts with the Greek world, Thracians remained little inclined to adopt an urban lifestyle.[15] In the part of Thrace north of the Haemus, cities like Nicopolis appear to be artificial creations, inhabited not by natives but by immigrants from Asia Minor (Nicomedia and Nicaea especially).

The main clue to change in the region as a whole under Roman rule lies in the gradual impact of the Roman army, a fact that is in some ways rather surprising, since the Balkans had been conquered essentially for strategic reasons not connected to the regional population. Rome made little attempt to encourage independent towns like those standard in the Mediterranean world. On the contrary, the state instituted military government and introduced Italian settlers in colonies to ensure security. For similar reasons, Augustus changed local structures in Pannonia and Dalmatia by splitting larger native groups into smaller units, sometimes by forced resettlement. Romanization away from the coast was sporadic throughout the Julio-Claudian period.

However, the recruitment of Thracians, Illyrians and Celts for service in the *auxilia* gradually spread the use of Latin and the privilege of Roman citizenship, and under Hadrian, or soon after, the camps in Moesia were constituted as colonies or *municipia*. The wheat and orchard lands in the lower Danube valley were developed for the military market. Latin became the main language in use, attested in thousands of inscriptions.

DACIA

Concentration of military expertise in the region of the Danube was greatest during the most significant expansion of the empire after Augustus, the conquest of Dacia by Trajan.[16] The Dacians were an agricultural people who inhabited primarily the plateau of Transylvania, to the north of the loop of the lower Danube. From the fourth century BC they had begun to develop the gold, silver and iron mines of the region, and export of precious metals had brought them, from *c.* 300 BC, into trading contact first with Greeks, and then, from the second century BC, with Italians. They also had strong links with the Black Sea, both through the wine trade and in construction, hence the use of Greek artisans in building fortifications at the hill fort of Costesti (close to Sarmizegetusa) in the first century. The separate Dacian tribes had enjoyed a period of extensive political power when unified between *c.* 60 and 44 BC by Burebista, in which period they expanded to the south and west, threatening Roman control of Macedonia. Thus Julius Caesar was planning a campaign against them just before his death (Suetonius, *Julius Caesar* 44.3). On the death of Burebista himself in the same year as Caesar, the Dacian coalition fragmented. But it was still of sufficient importance in the 30s BC for it to be alleged, probably by malevolent Antonian propagandists, that Octavian sought a marriage alliance by offering his daughter Julia to Cotiso, one of the rival Dacian kings (Suetonius, *Augustus* 63).

For the next century and beyond, Roman interest in Dacia seems to have been minimal despite a Dacian raid across the frozen Danube in 10 BC, which had to be suppressed, and occasional evidence that movements of new peoples in the plains beyond the lower Danube were creating turmoil in the area. According to Strabo (*Geography* 7.3.10), late in Augustus' reign 50,000 Getae were permitted to cross the river to settle in Moesia. In AD 69 Moesia was invaded by Sarmatian tribes taking advantage of the Roman civil war. In general, Rome was happy to deal with Transdanubian peoples by diplomacy. A long inscription on a marble tablet of *c.* AD 57–67 found near Tibur records the activities of a governor of Moesia under Nero, detailing his dealings with the inhabitants: an extract reads:

> Kings hitherto unknown or hostile to the Roman people he brought to the bank which he guarded, to honour the Roman standards. He restored to the kings of the Bastarnae and the Rhoxolani their sons, and to the king of the Dacians his brothers, who had been captured or rescued from the enemy. From other kings he received hostages. By these measures he both strengthened and advanced the peace of the province.
>
> (*ILS* 986; LR 2, p. 39)

Roman interest in Dacia was sharply reawakened by the reunification of the Dacian tribes by Decebalus in the 80s AD, when the Dacians were victorious over Roman armies in AD 85 and 86.[17] Despite defeat at Tapae, near Sarmizegetusa, by Domitian, Decebalus succeeded in compelling Rome to recognize him as king, inaugurating a brief period of cultural efflorescence. Many of the extant remains of the great citadel and sanctuary at Sarmizegetusa, already Burebista's capital in the first century BC, belong to the period of Decebalus' rule. Roman tolerance of Dacian power broke down in AD 101–2 with a renewal of war, whether as a result of Decebalus' ambitions or Trajan's, and hostilities began again in AD 105, with a serious Dacian incursion into Moesia, which led Trajan into full-scale invasion of Dacian territory and the capture of Sarmizegetusa and the suicide of Decebalus in AD 106 (cf. Cassius Dio, *History of Rome* 68.6–14). Almost immediately, Sarmizegetusa was replaced by a new Roman colony, sited on ground to the north of the ancient hill fort.

Roman Dacia comprised most of Transylvania. It was subdivided into Upper and Lower Dacia by Hadrian in AD 118–19, and a third province (Porolissensis) was formed, probably in AD 124, but in AD 168 the *Tres Daciae* were reunited under one governor. The effects of direct Roman rule on the region were dramatic. Many immigrants came from Illyria and elsewhere, some as miners. The attractions for immigrants were agricultural as well as mineral wealth. A number of cities developed, and the Latin language became standard with remarkable speed. Very few native names appear on inscriptions from the region, suggesting a dominant immigrant culture and little Romanization of the native inhabitants. The territory became the modern area of Romania, in which, despite the difficulty of demonstrating continuity on Dacian sites beyond AD 200, claims about the Roman heritage remain significant. The Romanian language retains close grammatical links to its Latin origins, and national ideology proudly stresses the Roman past.

23

GREECE AND THE AEGEAN COAST

The civilization of mainland Greece and the Aegean coast of Turkey had a continuous literary and political tradition from the eighth century BC. With the exception of areas such as Thessaly, and Arcadia in the Peloponnese, Greek culture was based on numerous *poleis* (city-states), most comprising a settled centre and its surrounding countryside (*chora*). Even in the Classical period of the fifth century BC, when the Athenian empire flourished, but especially since the rise to power of Alexander of Macedon in the fourth century BC, such urban communities had sometimes been combined into wider political units, either under the control of Macedonian kings, or in the form of defensive leagues. But in the beginning of the Roman imperial period, loyalties were still primarily local.

GREEK ATTITUDES TO ROMAN RULE

In the eyes of the Greeks, when political contact with Rome began in the third century BC, Rome had been treated like another Hellenistic power. The Achaean league in the Peloponnese welcomed Roman offers of 'liberation' from Macedonian rule in 197 BC. As it became clear in the ensuing decades that Roman control would be far more prone to interference in the internal politics of each community than that of Hellenistic kings, only then did resistance grow; it was to be crushed mercilessly by Rome, ending in the sack of Corinth in 146 BC. The incorporation of the Aegean cities of Turkey into the Roman sphere was partly brought about as a by-product of conflict with the Seleucid state in 192–188 BC, and partly through the voluntary bequest of their territories to Rome by the last king of Pergamum in 133 BC and by the last king of Bithynia, on the southern coast of the Black Sea, in 75/74 BC.

By the mid-first century BC all the inhabitants of the Aegean region were thus accustomed to being ruled by Rome. In the turmoil of the Late Republic, it had not been a happy experience. The topography of mainland Greece, with much of the country infertile and mountainous and coastal strips narrow, provided only a weak economic base in comparison to the Aegean coast of Turkey, which benefited from continual enrichment of the coastal plain through silt brought down by rivers from the Anatolian plateau. But both economies were badly hit by the depredations of Roman aristocrats in the civil wars. The decisive defeats of both Pompeius and Antonius had taken place after major campaigns on Greek soil. At the beginning of the imperial period the attitude of many Greeks to Roman rule was decidedly hostile.

Nonetheless, in formal political terms little was to change during the principate.[1] No Greeks are known to have made any direct bid for freedom from Roman control. The region was divided at first into the provinces of Achaea, Macedonia, Pontus and Bithynia, and Asia (see Map 16). Of these, only Macedonia had a legionary garrison (possibly two), which was primarily required in the Early Empire for operating against Thracian tribes to the north.

The Roman status of Achaea underwent periodic changes in the Early Empire, but these were a matter of terminology rather than substance. Detached from the province of Macedonia in 27 BC, Achaea was governed by a proconsul of praetorian rank until AD 67, apart from an interlude from AD 15–44 when it was again joined to Macedonia under the control of the emperor's legate in Moesia. In AD 67 Nero proclaimed freedom for Greece, a meaningless act of propaganda withdrawn by Vespasian in AD 70 or 74. Thessaly was detached from Achaea and added to Macedonia; Epirus became a separate province, at the latest under Antoninus Pius. Similar changes were imposed on the province of Pontus and Bithynia in north-west Asia Minor, which began as a public province (with a senatorial governor selected by

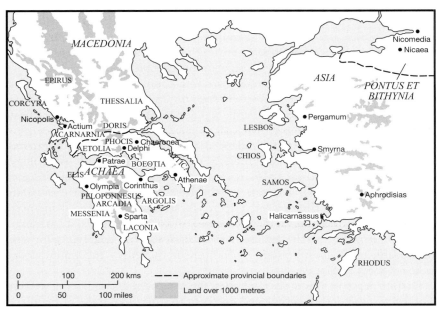

Map 16 Greece and the Aegean coast

seniority and lot), but under Marcus Aurelius was taken over by the emperor, perhaps because of the importance of the route which passed through this territory from the Balkans to the eastern frontier of the empire. The province of Asia, which comprised basically the territory of the ancient kingdom of Pergamum, remained throughout this period a rich and impressive province under the command of a senior proconsul assisted by three legates and a quaestor.[2]

In none of these provinces was any large military force stationed, except briefly under Augustus in Macedonia. Peace was taken for granted, or perhaps the troops on the Danube frontier were reckoned sufficiently close to suppress insurrection. However, a complete lack of disaffection cannot be taken for granted.

ECONOMIC MALAISE

Mainland Greece suffered from an economic malaise in the Early Empire, deepened rather than eased by the opening up of the Mediterranean to inter-regional trade and the availability in cities of imported wine and oil cheaper than anything that could be produced locally.[3] Strabo described Arcadia, Messenia and Laconia as depopulated, and many cities of Boeotia as reduced to mere villages or in ruins.[4] However, the evidence of archaeological surveys reveals that decline was not universal; whilst the countryside does indeed seem to have suffered from depopulation, the cities appear to have been growing.[5] Direct intervention by Rome in the founding of colonies (such as Corinth, begun by Julius Caesar in 44 BC, and Patrae, founded by Augustus in 14 BC) did something to stimulate the economy, as did Augustus' flourishing new city of Nicopolis, created near the site of Actium through synoecism (bringing together the surrounding people). Many emperors paid obeisance to Athens with generous gifts on account of her past glories. But according to Cassius Dio (*History of Rome*, 55.28.2), discontent was rife in many cities in AD 6. Thessaly at some unknown date lost its formal status as a free region.[6]

Greek assumptions about the independence of *poleis* were bound to interact uneasily with Roman rule, but problems ran deeper than a clash of ideology. In the later second century AD, Pausanias, in his learned description of Greece (*Guide to Greece* 7.17.1), was able to look back on the two centuries before Nero as the worst of times, when 'Greece was struck with universal and utter prostration'. But even in his day, the Greek mainland remained a backwater in economic terms, partly because it was a backwater in strategic terms and thus unable to benefit from state expenditure on the army – the nearest troops were far north in Moesia.

Despite depredations in the civil wars, the prosperity of the cities of western Turkey was too deeply entrenched for them to suffer like those of mainland Greece. Similarly, the tradition of subservience to powerful monarchs –

Lydian, Persian, Macedonian – had instilled the habit of obedience, or, at least, the avoidance of open opposition. Hence the efficiency with which the provincial council (*koinon*) of Asia took the initiative in 29 BC in asking Octavian for permission to set up temples in his honour, resulting in the temple of Augustus and Rome at Pergamum (Cassius Dio, *History of Rome* 51.20.6–8). The cities were adept at such flattery, which was just as well, since they had supported Antonius in the civil war. In such an urbanized environment there was little for the Roman governor to do, except to cream off the taxes and, all too often, to enrich himself.[7]

GREEK ÉLITES AND GREEK CULTURE

In these provinces, as elsewhere, Rome naturally relied on the support of the rich. Anti-Roman sentiment might thus express itself in the form of class warfare. In Bithynia while Pliny was governor, the emperor Trajan remained sufficiently nervous of public disorder to forbid the creation of a fire brigade for fear of organized unrest:

> You may very well have had the idea that it should be possible to form a company of firemen at Nicomedia on the model of those existing elsewhere, but we must remember that it is societies like these which have been responsible for the political disturbances in your province, particularly in its towns. If people assemble for a common purpose, whatever name we give them and for whatever reason, they soon turn into a political club.
> (Pliny, *Letters* 10.34)

All such private clubs, apart from licensed associations like those of the ephebes (youths), had been forbidden from the time of Caesar and Augustus.[8]

Most of the evidence for this region survives through the efforts of the aristocracy of the Greek cities. They reveal an interesting ambivalence towards Roman rule. Back in the second century BC, Greeks like Polybius had seen Rome as a powerful barbarian state, whose astonishing political success had to be explained through the theories of Greek political philosophy, but whose culture was assumed to be markedly inferior to that of the Greeks themselves. By the time of Augustus, Greeks like Strabo of Amaseia in Pontus and Dionysius of Halicarnassus were sufficiently integrated into Roman society to migrate to the city of Rome and write about the Roman world in Greek for a Roman audience using Roman categories. Such authors discussed Rome with sympathy but as outsiders. In contrast, Plutarch of Chaeronea in Boeotia (*c.* AD 50–120) was a Roman citizen of high rank, who held a procuratorship from Hadrian and perhaps the *ornamenta consularia*, and who could therefore have merged fully into the governing class of Rome, as did many other provincial aristocrats from other regions of the empire. It is thus significant that he elected to portray himself as a Greek, devoting himself for the last 30 years of his life to the revival of the ancient shrine of Apollo at Delphi. In his series of *Parallel Lives*, he analysed and contrasted the two cultures of Greece and Rome through the virtues exemplified in the careers of their great men. Such an attitude can usefully be compared to that of the historian Cassius Dio from Nicaea in Bithynia, who entered the senate under Commodus and eventually was twice consul. In his *History of Rome*, despite his use of the Greek language, he identified himself entirely with Roman society.[9]

Greek aristocrats were slow to throw in their lot with the élite of the empire, for a variety of reasons. First was the continuity of Greek cultural traditions, bolstered by a literature which formed part of a common Greek education. The 'classics', from Homer to the Attic tragedians, had been canonized in the Hellenistic period, and the value of *paideia* (education) enshrined in Greek consciousness by the emphasis put upon it by the political authorities of the period. Second was the recognition by Roman aristocrats of the value of Greek culture, which had been treated with respect by them from their first contacts in the third century BC. In the mid-first century BC, young Italian aristocrats still went to Athens to gain a cultural veneer. The adoption of the Greek language by Italians as a mark of high education paid obeisance to the superiority of Greek civilization. It is noticeable that at no time in the Roman Empire did Greeks feel any similar compulsion to learn Latin. In some periods imperial favour further strengthened Greek feelings of superiority, favour offered by Nero, who competed in all the great Greek games, including the Olympics, and by Hadrian with his Greek-style beard, and by his successors.

Hence the temptation for Greeks to feel that their own society was, despite lack of political power, both separate from and superior to that of Rome.[10] In some circles from the late first century AD to the end of the second, such a conscious claim to superiority was sometimes explicitly expressed. Thus according to the hagiography composed by the orator Philostratus in the early third century, the great neo-Pythagorean sage, Apollonius of Tyana, a city which actually lies upon the Anatolian plateau, once berated fellow Greeks for taking on 'barbarian' (that is, Roman) names. The orator and philosopher Dio Chrysostom in Bithynia viewed the governor and other agents of the Roman state as outsiders who could be manipulated by tactful handling by the aristocrats of the Greek cities. Such champions of Greek culture tended to hark back to the glory of Greece before Alexander's conquests. They made a fetish of oratorical display. The greatest exponents of rhetoric were dignified by their historian, Philostratus, as a 'Second Sophistic', to be compared in brilliance to the great sophists of Classical Athens.

This enthusiasm for the distant past included the recreation of lost traditions, as in the revival of the Spartan *agoge* (training regime for young men) in the late first century AD.[11] The city of Athens, as a glorious tourist centre, built consciously archaizing monuments and sold to outsiders the right to set up their statues in the city. The same attitude also created a rich literature. To those writers already mentioned could be added, among others, the mid-second-century historian Arrian from Bithynia, the orator Aelius Aristides of Smyrna, and various scientists, such as the medical writer Galen from Pergamum, Artemidorus the dream interpreter from Ephesus and the traveller Pausanias from Lydia. Many intellectuals who settled in Athens came originally from parts of the Greek world outside the Aegean centre of Greek culture, thus some of the orators celebrated by Philostratus originated in Syria. Shared Hellenic culture created a self-conscious internationalism among the urban aristocrats of the areas which had been ruled by Macedonian kings before Roman conquest. Their unity was symbolized by such institutions as the Ecumenical Synod of the Artists of Dionysus, who provided professional entertainment at the great religious festivals in many parts of the eastern empire; to this body, Claudius twice made grants, addressing them in AD 43 as 'the Dionysiac conquering victors of the empire and their company' (Smallwood, *Gaius-Nero* no. 373a; Braund no. 580a).

The impressive architectural remains of Greek cities in the Early Empire are to a large extent a testimony to the same pride in the Classical past. Some of the buildings erected were financed by the emperor, such as the new quarter of Athens built by the emperor Hadrian. But most were the product of intense competition among civic aristocrats to impress their fellow citizens by public benefactions. Such evergetism was further encouraged by rivalry between cities. In the absence of political disputes, cultural superiority and honorific titles became the main areas of competition. The title *metropolis* (chief city) was highly coveted (cf. Dio Chrysostom, *Oration* 38, for the fierce competition between Nicomedia and Nicaea), and local traditions were proudly displayed on coins and on buildings. In essence, money which in other provinces, such as Spain and Gaul, might had gone to promote the richest civic aristocrats on the wider political stage of the senate in Rome, was concentrated in Greece and western Asia Minor on the embellishment of their home cities. An inscribed letter of AD 145 from the emperor Antoninus to the people of Ephesus bears witness to the public generosity of one wealthy citizen:

> The munificence which Vedius Antoninus lavishes upon you I learned of not so much from your letter as from his own. For, desiring to obtain assistance from me for the embellishment of the public works which he offered you, he made known to me how many and what great buildings he is adding to the city, but you do not properly appreciate him. I granted him all he requested, and I welcomed the fact that he prefers, not the usual method of those participating in public affairs, who for the sake of immediate popularity expend their munificence on shows and doles and prizes for games, but means whereby he hopes to make the city more stately in the future.
>
> (*SIG*³ no. 850; LR 2, p. 261)

The intensity of such local patriotism was at its highest in the early second century. It did not long survive after the Antonine age. From the mid-first century, a few Greek aristocrats had become Roman senators. That they mostly came from Asia Minor rather than mainland Greece is presumably explained by the greater prosperity of the former area. They must have taken up residence, at least temporarily, in Italy. By the mid-second century the number of such senators was much increased, and a network of Greek senatorial patronage in Italy beckoned young aristocrats to leave the certainty of local glory in their home cities for the greater prizes but increased uncertainty of politics on the Roman stage.[12]

Arrian is a good example of someone who participated fully in both the Greek and Roman worlds at a high level. Born and educated in Nicomedia, Bithynia, he held Roman citizenship from his father or grandfather. He held a priesthood of the Greek goddesses Demeter and Kore, and from his study under Epictetus at Nicopolis in Epirus developed an interest in philosophy and meteorology. His subsequent pursuit of a public career in the Roman world was very successful; he was consul, probably in AD 129, and governor of Cappadocia from AD 132 to 137. After his spell as governor, he retired to Athens where he became a citizen and held the office of *archon* in AD 148/9. Arrian also produced a prolific literary output, writing in Greek and covering subject matter from the distant past (such as the campaigns of Alexander) to the present.[13]

CITY LIFE

The main agents and beneficiaries of this prosperous culture were the urban rich. For city communities as a whole, aristocratic competition was a mixed blessing. Building projects were often overblown and thus left uncompleted. If Pliny's letters to Trajan from Pontus and Bithynia reflect typical problems for a province in this region, as I argued above (Chapter 10), such unfulfilled promises were a constant problem (for example, Pliny, *Letters* 10.37–40). All democratic underpinnings to city life were undercut by the Roman preference for leaving the power to collect taxes and keep order in the hands of the rich members of civic councils.[14]

The urban poor could therefore do little except riot, as they did in time of food shortages, as witnessed in particular by a vivid speech of Dio Chrysostom, *Oration* 46, in which he describes an attack made at Prusa on his property and that of a neighbour's by a crowd reacting angrily to the rising price of grain. As for the inhabitants of the countryside, the medical writer Galen unwittingly revealed their almost total isolation from civic wealth in his reference to starvation among peasants who were left with very little to eat during a famine, when all the grain had been harvested for city dwellers:

> The city dwellers, as it was their practice to collect and store enough grain for all the next year immediately after the harvest, left what remained to the country people, that is, pulses of various kinds, and they took a good deal of these too to the city. The country people finished the pulses during the winter, and so had to fall back on

unhealthy foods during the spring; they ate twigs and shoots of trees and bushes, and bulbs and roots of indigestible plants; they filled themselves with wild herbs, and cooked fresh grass.

(*On Digestible and Indigestible Foods* 1.1–7)

Even in the most urbanized regions of the Aegean coast of Turkey, Aelius Aristides was willing to endure long, hurried journeys in order to reach a town by nightfall (for example, *Sacred Tales* 5.13–15). Thus the cities flourished but, in some parts, land fell into the hands of a small number of wealthy men, and regions away from the big cities, such as the island of Euboea, where the copper mines were exhausted by the Roman period, suffered serious decay and depopulation.

24

CENTRAL AND EASTERN TURKEY

The geography of Anatolia away from the Aegean coast permitted the persistence of local cultures. Most native societies had resisted full assimilation into Greek culture, despite the fact that Greeks had influenced them since the Classical period and Hellenistic states had ruled them intermittently from the mid-fourth century BC; the same resistance continued in many places under Rome.

The hills of Anatolia slope away gradually from the western coast up to an arid plateau, rising to the rugged Taurus mountains in the east and to the mountains of Lycia in the south (see Map 17). On the western side of the plateau, the mountains are broken by the large river valleys which made the western part of Turkey so fertile. Some of the inhabitants of the plateau, such as the Lydians with their capital at Sardis, were indigenous. Others, such as the Celts of Galatia, had migrated only in recent centuries. In some regions, such as Pamphylia, Greek-style civic communities (*poleis*) were the standard political form by 50 BC, and the Lycians continued to show a rare talent for political co-operation in a confederacy which had long performed all the functions of a sovereign state. But the Galatian Celts were still organized into tribes, and in general the whole area was politically and economically underdeveloped.

In formal Roman terms, this region, which had lain within Rome's orbit since the early second century BC, and was effectively controlled by Rome from the mid-first century, underwent major administrative changes only in Galatia, Lycia and Cappadocia during the Early Empire, but a general pattern can clearly be discerned. Many areas which were considered difficult to control were left at the start of the period in the hands of a variety of client rulers. Gradually during the century after Actium, and with a notable hiatus in the reign of Gaius, when he favoured his friends among the client kings, these areas were incorporated as Roman provinces, and began to take their place as an integral part of the imperial system.[1]

In the years after Caesar's death the sufferings of much of inland Asia Minor were terrible. In 43 BC Brutus extracted contributions from the cities of Lycia and forced the client kings of the region to send levies. Then in the vacuum

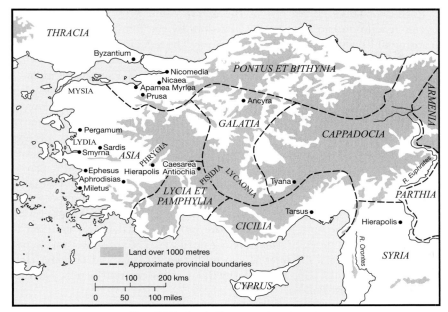

Map 17 Turkey in the second century AD

after Philippi the whole area fell into the plundering hands of the Parthians between 40 and 38 BC. Antonius brought something closer to normality; he too needed funds, but his organization of the region was statesmanlike. Apart from the plains of Cilicia, which he gave to Cleopatra, the rulers he chose for the principalities in Anatolia all came from families which had long held sway in the region, including the grandson of the great Mithridates. Hence Octavian made little change after Actium or indeed later, except sometimes to move monarchs to new territories on the death of an incumbent. Intermarriage between the dynasties gave emperors a suitable pool of princes from whom to choose.

GALATIA, CAPPADOCIA AND THE LYCIAN FEDERATION

The exception to Augustus' *laissez-faire* policy was the huge kingdom of Galatia, which lay on the important main overland route between Asia and Syria, but whose vulnerability to attack by the Homanadenses in the Pisidian mountains to the south was dramatically demonstrated when Amyntas, king of Galatia, was killed there in 25 BC. Galatia was incorporated as a province under a legate of Augustus. Pisidia itself was gradually pacified: six colonies of military veterans were established, linked by a new road, the *Via Sebaste*.[2] A successful campaign was fought *c.* 6–3 BC against the Homanadenses, whose tribe was broken up, and a rising of AD 6 was subdued.

Political change in the rest of the region came with less violence. The Lycian federation had been granted freedom by the Romans in 169 BC after its original liberation from Seleucid control. The federation retained nominal independence, continuing to produce its own coins until AD 43, when Claudius established the new province of Lycia and Pamphylia under a praetorian legate. The reason for the change may have been no more than Claudius' desire to add another province to the empire, since the confederacy continued to operate within the province, albeit with reduced autonomy. Changes in Cappadocia were more obviously connected to military strategy on the eastern frontier with Parthia. After various vicissitudes, a native dynasty descended from the Persian satrap Ariarathes, who had fought against Alexander in the fourth century BC, had been restored to power by Pompeius in the settlement of the East in the 60s BC, only for a new puppet ruler, Archelaus, to be installed by Antonius in the 30s BC. Despite efforts by his subjects to remove him, he retained the province until it was annexed to Rome in AD 17. A procuratorial province until AD 72, Cappadocia was joined with Galatia under a consular legate with two legions, and at some time between AD 107 and 113, Trajan formed out of the region the new province of Cappadocia with Pontus.

SOCIAL AND CULTURAL EFFECTS OF ROMAN RULE

Roman state interest in the Anatolian plateau lay primarily in military communications. The main military roads ran across the plateau from Byzantium through Galatia or further south to Tarsus and through the Cilician Gates, making use of existing routes apart from the *Via Sebaste*. Control was kept in most regions through cities. A number of new foundations were created in the Early Empire, but in other cases new names professing loyalty to the imperial regime were simply attached to existing settlements, hence the many places with 'Caesarea' or 'Sebaste' (from the Greek for Augustus) in their nomenclature. But elsewhere the Romans seemed quite happy to rule through the existing tribes, many of which, like the Tmolitae of Lydia, are known only from inscriptions. Since in much of the region the population was sparse and scattered over wide areas, tribal organization suited, and urbanization, when it came, was mostly through requests by local communities for the status of *polis*.

How were such areas affected by Roman rule? Apart from the Homanadenses in the mountainous region of Pisidia, there is no evidence of active opposition to Roman control during this period. However, some mountainous areas, such as Cilicia Tracheia (Rough Cilicia), remained effectively outside Roman interference. Places which proved insufficiently fertile to produce much revenue were left to their own devices. Even in those areas with rather closer Roman control there is some evidence for the unchanged continuation of local cultures. In Lycaonia the local language was still in use alongside Greek, according to the report in Acts 14.11–12. The chance survival of such information warns of the strong likelihood that other languages, such as Mysian and Celtic, continued to be spoken, despite the lack of evidence in the epigraphic record. Thus Lycian was still spoken, according to Strabo (*Geography* 14.2.3), and there is evidence for the use of Lydian and Phrygian as everyday languages to the end of the principate.[3]

What survives in greater abundance is epigraphic evidence of the continuation of local religions. The Phrygian religion, in which the male god Papas and the old Anatolian mother goddess were worshipped, is still attested in the great Phrygian religious centre of Hierapolis. So too continued the high status of women in some Anatolian societies, which may have rubbed off onto some of the minority communities living in their cities, such as the Jews. In general, the relationship between the distinctive *theos hypsistos* (highest god) cults and the Judaism of local Jewish communities is very curious.[4]

The evidence for flourishing Jewish communities in many cities on the Anatolian plateau provides an insight into the varied and international flavour of those cities after long years of rule by Hellenistic kings.[5] The intermingling of cultures between immigrants and locals was evidently considerable. There is no evidence that it created tension. Perhaps most strikingly absent from the cultural mix is a distinctively Latin strand, except in colonies of veterans, in contrast to the culture of Roman Syria to be considered in the next chapter.

ECONOMIC EFFECTS OF ROMAN RULE

Economic changes on the Anatolian plateau and in surrounding areas are harder to document. One factor was the considerable number of large imperial estates, many of them inherited from the royal dynasties which preceded Roman rule. Rainfall was always low and winters always severe, so productivity could never be really high. Apart from the production of grain and the pasturing of cattle and sheep, which gave rise to a textile industry, the main natural resources of the area lay in minerals, which were in general exploited by the imperial *fiscus*, and in fine marbles which were exported widely. On the other hand, in the eastern parts of Cilicia, on the plain, wine, olives and corn were produced in great quantities.[6]

Self-identification of the natives of Anatolia with the Roman Empire was only partially achieved by AD 180, despite the extent of Hellenization and urbanization, but the process had undoubtedly begun. Thus in Galatia the inhabitants continued to identify themselves by their tribes long after the establishment of the province in 25 BC, despite the foundation of cities like Ancyra (modern Ankara), the centre of the provincial cult of Rome and Augustus. But by the second century AD inscriptions refer only to the cities and ignore tribal names: the combination from the time of Vespasian of a large military presence in Galatia and Cappadocia as part of the emperor's strategy against Parthia with the wide spread of the imperial cult and taxation by the state infiltrated a distinctively Roman culture into nearly all parts of Anatolia. In the fourth century AD the region was to become the core of the eastern Roman empire, and in the Early Middle Ages it was to be, under the rule of Byzantium, the last bastion of Roman civilization.

25

THE NORTHERN LEVANT AND MESOPOTAMIA

THE NORTHERN LEVANT

The northern section of the fertile crescent is here treated as a separate region not because of any geographical unity, nor because it formed any distinct entity in Roman times, but because in this period the whole area bore the brunt of operations by the Roman state against the only superpower capable of aggression against Rome, namely Parthia. In many ways, the region was a frontier zone throughout the early imperial period.[1]

The geography of the area is quite complex (see Map 18). Behind the narrow coastal plain lie two parallel chains of mountains. Through a valley in one of the chains, the River Orontes flows northwards. East of the mountains are vast tracts of semi-desert, or rather, arid steppeland. In the north the Taurus and Anti-Taurus mountains mark off the region from Anatolia, and provide a strategic base for control of the Mesopotamian river valleys of the Euphrates and Tigris. The cultivable regions were very prosperous, with vines and olives on the Mediterranean coast and fruit and grain in the foothills of the mountain ranges. On the edge of the desert there flourished oases, such as Palmyra, home to Arab tribes.

The western half of this region had come into the orbit of Rome in the mid-first century BC. The central core of the remnant of the Seleucid kingdom in northern Syria around the capital Antioch had fallen, with much of the surrounding area, to Tigranes I of Armenia who had taken advantage of civil strife within the warring Seleucid dynasty. Tigranes himself was ejected by Rome, and a new province of Syria established by Pompeius Magnus in 64 BC. From then on this area became the base for hostile operations against Parthia.

The inhabitants of the northern Levant at the start of the imperial period are surprisingly difficult to characterize. The cities of the old Seleucid heartland around Antioch seem to have established a genuine urban, Hellenic culture based partly on an originally Graeco-Macedonian population. But on the steppe, in the Taurus foothills and the mountains of Lebanon, village life was normal, and numerous petty kingdoms and tetrarchies (such as Commagene, Osrhoene and Ituraea) retained independence through lack of

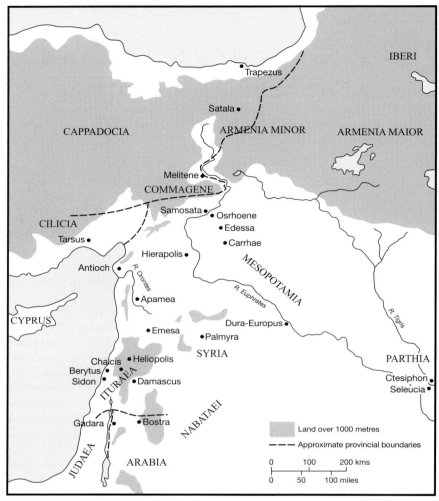

Map 18 The Northern Levant

superpower interference. In many such areas the indigenous population is likely to have spoken different dialects of Aramaic. On the coast of Lebanon, the Phoenician cities retained proud memories of a glorious past, while in the Lebanese mountains and on the desert fringe lived Arab tribes, in Ituraea and Chalcis settled as villagers, but on the desert fringe remaining nomadic. Throughout the region, in both cities and countryside, were settled communities of Jews.

PARTHIA

By 44 BC the stage was already set for this region as the arena for confrontation with Parthia. The Parthian state had arisen, like so many others, out of the ruins of the Seleucid empire.[2] The Parni had originally been a nomadic tribe in northern Iran, but by the mid-first century BC they had gained firm control of southern and central Mesopotamia. A militaristic dynasty with few cultural pretensions, they made little alteration to the societies over which they ruled. So, for instance, excavations reveal that the Greek city of Dura-Europus on the middle Euphrates, which had originally been a Macedonian military colony, retained its Greek constitution and political language during centuries of Parthian rule, despite adoption of some aspects of Parthian dress and of local religious traditions.[3] The unity of the Parthian state thus depended entirely on the small ruling class of Parthian nobles, organized as a feudal landowning military aristocracy, skilled in hunting and horseriding.

The decision of Marcus Crassus in 55 BC to march against this Parthian state seems to have been prompted simply by desire for glory, conquest, and prestige on the Roman political scene. Crassus' failure and death near Carrhae in 53 BC established the tone of Roman-Parthian relations for over two and a half centuries.[4] Crassus lost not only the campaign and his life but also the legionary standards. The need for their recovery was a political assumption shared by all Romans, until it was achieved through diplomacy by Augustus in 20 BC. In the meantime, the Parthians in 40–39 BC proved that, unlike other neighbours of Roman power, they were not content to remain passive. Taking advantage of the Roman civil war, and instigated by Quintus Labienus, who had been sent to Parthia by Caesar's murderers in 43 BC to request help against the triumvirs, they invaded North Syria and part of Asia Minor, and went down as far south as Judaea, causing extensive damage. Their ejection, achieved by 39 BC, required an intensive campaign by Marcus Antonius and his lieutenant, Ventidius. In massive campaigns in the following years, Marcus Antonius attempted to avenge the defeat of Crassus, without success. After Actium, Octavian was expected to do the same, but did not, preferring diplomatic methods. In 20 BC Tiberius, and in AD 1 Gaius, came to the Euphrates with impressive pageantry to make treaties with Parthia. But Roman armies did march from Antioch against Parthia later in the imperial period, under Nero, Trajan and Lucius Verus. Although in fact Parthia proved too fragmented a power to initiate hostilities, the danger that it might do so (a danger that was apparently quite real under Marcus Aurelius), and the effectiveness of Parthian cavalry tactics against Roman legionaries, made this region one of continuous military interest.

The most obvious effect of this was the gradual shift of the bulk of the Roman military machine to the Near East, a procedure well advanced but not yet quite complete by AD 180.[5] In the Late Republic two legions had been kept in Syria. Under the Julio-Claudians, there were four; they were based in the region of North Syria, and recruited locally. The number in northern Syria remained static over the following decades, although their bases were gradually moved to the east, but additional legions in Judaea, Arabia and eventually, in the 190s AD, Mesopotamia took over much of the role which the legions in Antioch had originally exercised, thus greatly increasing the total military pressure. The final steps were to be taken in the early third century by Septimius Severus and his successors.

The strategic role against Parthia of Armenia Maior, whose mountains overlook the north Mesopotamian plain, was recognized primarily by designating the country as a protectorate.[6] Since the Parthians tried to keep control by similar means, the dynasty in Armenia of Arsacid kings maintained a successful balance for most of the imperial period. The hill country of Armenia Minor, west of Armenia Maior, was in contrast granted by Rome to a succession of neighbouring kings up to AD 72 when it was finally incorporated by Vespasian into the province of Cappadocia. All of this required few military excursuses by Roman troops into the Armenian hills. Antonius in 36 BC attacked Parthia through Armenia, to avoid the Parthian cavalry on the open plains to the south, but most invasions in the north of the fertile crescent, whether from west to east or in the opposite direction, traversed the flat lands of the river basins rather than the mountains. That Rome could ignore Armenia was fortunate, since the terrain was notoriously inhospitable, especially during the bitter winters. There were two exceptions. In 34 BC Marcus Antonius annexed Armenia, claiming that its king, Artavasdes, had deserted him in 36 BC. Artavasdes was captured by a trick and led in Antonius' triumph in Alexandria, later to be executed by Cleopatra; coins proclaimed *ARMENIA DEVICTA*. The other exception was Trajan, who annexed the whole territory of Armenia during the campaign against the Parthians in AD 114–17. This turned out to be only a temporary affair.

MESOPOTAMIA

Trajan's Parthian campaign briefly created new provinces not just of Armenia but also of Mesopotamia and just possibly Assyria, although the existence of a province of Assyria in his day is attested only in fourth-century sources which may be mistaken.[7] There can be no doubt that these regions, which had been conquered only by brilliant and organized campaigns, were intended as permanent Roman territories. But they were discarded by Hadrian on his succession, partly because of uprisings in Mesopotamia and the Jewish revolts in Africa and Egypt, partly because of the emperor's own lack of political security. There was to be no further annexation until Lucius Verus, who, intent on the same fantasy of conquest on the model of Alexander the Great, reduced parts of upper Mesopotamia in AD 162–65; the area was eventually to be formed into the separate province of Mesopotamia by Septimius Severus. Armenia, by contrast, remained under client kings.

SYRIA

How did all this military activity affect local people? Some answer can be given in political and economic terms; judgement of the cultural effects is more difficult. Of the political effects, the most obvious was the grant of city status to long-established communities in Syria which had not previously held such rank. The city of Antioch, which had declined in the last years of Seleucid rule, gained a massive boost through its Roman military role, becoming a great city to rival Rome and Alexandria – not least through gifts to the city by Roman emperors and by client kings like Herod[8]:

> And for the Antiochenes, who inhabit the greatest city in Syria, which has a street running through it lengthwise, he [Herod] adorned this street with colonnades on either side, and paved the open part of the road with polished stone, thereby contributing greatly to the appearance of the city and to the convenience of its inhabitants.

(Josephus, *Antiquities of the Jews* 16.148)

The city also became the mint where silver provincial coinage was struck. But elsewhere, villages seem still to have retained much independence.

When Pompeius had annexed Syria he had little interest in any of the region apart from the narrow strip along the Mediterranean coast, and he left most of the region in the hands of allied rulers, in Commagene, Armenia, Emesa, Chalcis and elsewhere; his immediate successors followed a similar policy.[9] In 20 BC Augustus reorganized the client states into fewer but larger kingdoms, restoring eastern Cilicia and Emesa to their respective dynasties. But, as elsewhere, such client kings did not last. The Iranian ruling dynasty of Commagene was ejected and reinstated on a series of occasions, until it was finally removed in AD 72, only for some of its number to become Roman senators. The smaller principalities were similarly incorporated piecemeal, mostly by the Flavian period, at the latest under Trajan. Those few buffer states that were left, like Armenia, sometimes positively increased their independence because of their value in strategic terms to the Roman state.

The process may be illustrated by the history of Palmyra, which happens to be well known because of the survival of numerous inscriptions as well as buildings on the site.[10] Palmyra was an oasis lying in the desert south of the centre of the fertile crescent. A city there by the name of Tadmor is attested in the Hebrew Bible (2 Chronicles 8.4, written probably in the fourth century BC), when it was already a centre for the caravan trade. But it began to reach its greatest prosperity from the end of the first century BC, when it started to act as the main power controlling the route from the Euphrates to the west. Palmyrenes used Aramaic as their main language, in a distinctive local dialect. They were organized into tribes, whose main function seems to have been the protection of the camel caravans. Annexed by Germanicus in around AD 17, Palmyra rapidly began to take on some of the aspects of a Greek city, using

Greek titles for magistrates and Greek in official inscriptions, although almost always such language was used alongside an Aramaic version, which was usually longer, and presumably the one intended to be read by the local populace. A great new temple of Bel, dominating the city and built with magnificent classical decorations (most probably carved by imported craftsmen), had already been dedicated in AD 32. Inscriptions from the Syrian desert reveal the role of the Roman governor in fixing the boundaries of the new city.[11] But it was because it lay between Rome and Parthia that Palmyra was to win the status of *colonia* from Septimius Severus or Caracalla, and later in the third century to become an independent power in its own right.

The efflorescence of Palmyra in the Early Empire suggests that the main economic effect of Roman rule in Syria was the provision of a market and peaceful conditions for trade. There is no direct evidence that the state was involved in the caravan trade, but the first attested Palmyrene caravans are dated to AD 19, just after annexation. The Palmyrene tax law of AD 137, which records the tariff for taxes on goods coming in and out of the city and the services provided within it, shows a close interest by governors in the conduct of the Palmyrene economy.[12] It is possible that the growth in the hills behind Antioch of large villages primarily involved in olive oil production should be dated as early as the second century.[13] If so, they are testimony to the attractiveness of producing for the huge city market. In the mountains of Lebanon the timber was intensively harvested, according to inscriptions, as an imperial monopoly at least from the time of Hadrian.[14] But in much of Syria, and in the rich valleys and upland pastures of Commagene, and probably everywhere in Armenia and in the alluvial country of Mesopotamia during its brief period of Roman rule, agriculture continued, fairly much unaffected by the presence of the Roman state, with grain production on the plain of North Syria and animal-grazing on the steppes.

CULTURAL CHANGE

What of cultural change? The Greek cities retained their Greek culture, although Antioch produced surprisingly few great scholars; the writers from the region whose reputations became widespread were the historian Nicolaus of Damascus, the Epicurean philosopher Philodemus from Gadara, and, from the north, the satirist Lucian of Samosata. Outside the cities, the question of cultural change is complicated by uncertainty about the extent of Hellenization before Roman conquest. So, for instance, in Commagene the local religion was a form of Zoroastrianism, but the monumental royal tomb of Antiochus I at Nemrud Dagh, built in the mid-first century BC, consisted of a Greek-style statue of the deified king, albeit that the whole notion of such a colossal statue of royalty seated among deities was a patent imitation of Iranian practice.

Aramaic must have continued in extensive use – it is the language both of Syriac Christianity and the rabbinic Judaism which flourished in Mesopotamia from the third century AD – but precisely where and when it was employed is difficult to state, simply because it was not a language customarily put down on inscriptions. The same is true of the native language of Armenia. It is therefore true, but not very helpful, to say that there is little evidence that any of these local languages or cultural habits were much changed in the Roman period. It is hard to know how much to deduce from the fact that many pre-Roman semitic place names in the Middle East reappeared in common use after the advent of Islam.[15] Latin was found in common use in places where Roman veteran colonies were found, such as Berytus (modern Beirut), established by Augustus; it is worth noting that when Latin gradually fell into disuse in the third century, it was Greek which took its place. Aramaic was still used by some in the villages around Antioch in the late fourth century.[16]

The great temple at Heliopolis (Baalbek), built on a monumental scale and dedicated to Jupiter Optimus Maximus, was sited on the ancient religious centre of the Ituraeans, but since most of the dedications on the site are in Latin, it may be that it attracted mainly the colonists from Berytus. In any case, elsewhere local cults continued little affected, as can be seen from the detailed, if humorous, description by Lucian of worship of Atargatis at Hierapolis, with its sacred fish:

> There is also a lake, not far from the temple, in which many different holy fish are kept. Some of them are very large. These have names and come when they are called. When I was there, one of them was wearing gold. On his fin lay a golden ornament and I often saw him and he had the ornament.
> (*On The Syrian Goddess* 45)

The use of Greek names to describe local deities, such as Zeus for Baalshamin in Palmyra, made no discernible difference to the conduct of the cult. Essentially, the whole region had been subjected to Hellenistic influence for centuries before Roman rule, and the limited extent of such cultural adoption had already long been achieved.

One of the greatest changes, only partly belonging to this period, was in the enthusiastic adoption of Christianity by some in this region.[17] Antioch was an important place for the first-century Church, perhaps because it had long housed a large Jewish community, which flourished remarkably throughout this period despite tensions during the revolt in Judaea of AD 66–70 and the uprisings in other parts of the diaspora, including Mesopotamia during Trajan's campaign.

The survival of Christian material enables historians to trace not only the continuation of a local literary culture in Armenia through the Christian church, but also the appearance of such a culture from the second century onwards in Edessa, the old capital of Osrhoene.[18] Edessa, originally a Macedonian military settlement, but under heavy Parthian influence because of its position on the fringes of Roman power until the last part of the second century, was the centre of Syriac culture. Syriac (a form of Aramaic) was used for Christian writings, which were to become of immense importance in the Syrian church in later antiquity. It is reasonable to suggest that even the survival of such Syriac material owed something to Greek influence, in so far as the writing down of Syriac may be an imitation of Greek habits. The first Syriac inscriptions found in this region come from the first century AD. By the end of the second century AD, a Syriac culture was widespread throughout the region of northern Mesopotamia, and Syriac documents have been found as far away as Dura-Europus on the Euphrates. The survival in Syriac from the fifth century AD of the Syro-Roman law book, which bears testimony to the continuation of semitic practices in marriage and inheritance in Syriac-speaking areas, shows that local cultural forms continued in these regions all the way through Roman rule.[19]

But the Syro-Roman law book also shows that inhabitants of these areas could portray their culture as Roman, since the point of the compilation was probably to claim the authority of Roman emperors for local practices. One of the peculiar features of the Roman Near East is that the aristocracy of the cities, including the great city of Antioch, rarely entered the Roman senate in the High Empire, unlike their counterparts in western Asia Minor. One partial explanation may have been the slow spread of Roman citizenship which, until well into the second century, was in Syria mostly confined to the members of client dynasties, to veteran soldiers who had immigrated from Italy, and to those who received citizenship on discharge from the *auxilia*. In the Julio-Claudian period, such auxiliaries were mostly culled from the Greek cities, but, with the incorporation of client states into the province, mountain peoples like the Ituraeans, long famed as archers, were recruited into the Roman war machine. Against this background of the limited extension of citizenship, Lucius Iulius Agrippa of Apamea in Syria stands out. In several inscriptions recording his substantial benefactions to his home town, he boasts of how his ancestors' names are displayed in Rome as longstanding friends and allies, and that his great-grandfather was the first high priest of the province in the time of Augustus (see p. xxx for one of his inscriptions).[20]

Whatever the reason for the slow entry of Syrian aristocrats into the Roman governing class, it was more than compensated for in the late second century by the extraordinary success of the marriage, at some time around AD 180, of Julia Domna of Emesa to the future emperor Septimius Severus, a marriage that in the third century was to produce Emesan rulers of Rome (see below, Chapter 32).[21]

26

THE SOUTHERN LEVANT

The impact of Roman rule in this period on at least one group of inhabitants of the Levant can be traced with a degree of detail impossible in almost any other part of the empire. The history of the Jews is preserved through a continuous literary tradition which stretches back to the first half of the first millennium BC. The vicissitudes of the early imperial period were particularly well recorded, partly because the first century marked major changes within Judaism, including the birth of Christianity, and partly because it spawned the only provincial historian of the empire to describe his own society in detail, Josephus. His writings also provide insights into the history of the region as a whole and of nearby gentile peoples, but his remarks about Near-Eastern non-Jews were naturally always from a Jewish perspective, and for much of the history of the gentile inhabitants of the area recourse must be made to the remarks of geographers and antiquarians like Strabo and the elder Pliny, and to archaeology, coins and inscriptions, as elsewhere in the empire.[1]

In the early 60s BC the southern Levant was effectively controlled by two regional superpowers which had emerged from the break-up of the Seleucid empire.[2] The Jewish state was based in Judaea and especially the temple city of Jerusalem, but a policy of conquest since the 120s BC had encompassed Idumaea to the south, Galilee to the north, and the coastal plain from Gaza in the south to Ptolemais (Akko) in the north (see Map 19). The country was ruled by the Hasmonaean dynasty in Hellenistic royal style, but with a distinctively Jewish rationale, since the Hasmonaeans were High Priests as well as kings. The foundation myth of the dynasty, which justified its retention of power, was its central role in the ejection of the Seleucids from the Jerusalem Temple after its desecration in 167 BC, an event recorded in some detail in the still extant books of the Maccabees. The Nabataean kingdom is less well known, but its power seems to have extended by the first century BC from Transjordan (as far north as Damascus until 70 BC) to the Arabian peninsula alongside the Red Sea. The Nabataeans were caravan traders from north Arabia, with distinctive cults and an idiosyncratic dialect of Aramaic which was widely used on inscriptions.

Map 19 The Southern Levant

The rest of the region before the Roman conquest was controlled by a number of petty dynasts and city states. Its inhabitants were village people, famed as archers and as bandits. Other petty rulers were too insignificant to enter the history books, such as a certain Bacchius Judaeus, dynast probably in southern Lebanon, whose submission was recorded on enigmatic Roman coins of the 50s BC.[3]

The advent of Pompeius Magnus with a brief from Rome to settle the eastern provinces in the 60s BC immediately changed the political appearance of the region. The petty kingdoms were left intact, but the power of the two greatest of them, the Hasmonaean and the Nabataean, was severely curtailed. The main beneficiaries were the Greek cities, some of which were foundations of the Hellenistic period, while others were ancient centres granted *polis* status by the Seleucid state. Of these, most commemorated their liberation from Jewish or Nabataean control by starting new civic eras from around the date of Pompeius' intervention in 63 BC.

Such, more or less, was still the political scene in 44 BC. The only major change after Pompeius was the favour that had been shown by Julius Caesar to the ruling Hasmonaean, Hyrcanus II, in return for his help in the civil war against Pompeius. Change came more rapidly with the wars after Caesar's death. First was the impact made by the liberators, Brutus and Cassius, whose pressing need was for money to arm their forces against the triumvirs. Josephus (*Antiquities of the Jews* 14.271–76) attests the efficiency in raising funds in Galilee 'at the expense of others' of the young Herod, an Idumaean official of Hyrcanus II of Judaea.

Not that Herod therefore suffered on the defeat of the liberators. In 40 BC, when the whole region was invaded by the Parthians at the instigation of Labienus, Hyrcanus was carried off as captive and invalidated for the Judaean high priesthood by the mutilation of one of his ears. Marcus Antonius therefore turned to Herod. An outsider to Judaean politics and, as an Idumaean, descended from converts, Herod had no great local standing in Jewish society, but he might be thought all the more likely to show loyalty to Rome. He was designated king of Judaea by the Roman senate in 40 BC, and captured his capital Jerusalem with the help of Roman legions from Syria in 37 BC. He remained a loyal ally of the Roman state through all political vicissitudes until his death in *c.* 4 BC.[4]

In contrast to Judaea and most other states in the Roman Near East, the Nabataean kingdom contrived, just, to retain independence, throughout the civil wars, despite the predatory intentions of Cleopatra in 34 BC and frequent tensions with the Judaean state, only partly resolved by a dynastic marriage between Herod and a Nabataean princess. The political history of the region over the next 200 years is one of gradual, piecemeal incorporation of independent states into the Roman provincial system, punctuated by occasional inter-communal conflict, and by two major wars against Rome in Judaea.[5] Such gradual incorporation into the provincial system seems to have happened *ad hoc* rather than as the result of any general strategic plan by the Roman state. In contrast to the northern Levant, this region in the south had no great tactical role as a buffer region against Parthia or as a base for invasion. Greed for control of the lucrative incense route, and the sea trade between India and Egypt, led to the invasion of Arabia Felix (Sabaea) by the prefect of Egypt, Aelius Gallus, in 25–24 BC, but after the failure of that expedition Roman strategic interest in the region was minimal. Almost the only evidence of any tactical role was the great military road built by Trajan in *c.* AD 106, from the borders of Syria to the Red Sea, running along the plateau to the east of the Jordan rift valley, presumably intended for the transport of supplies needed for his Parthian campaign. It is just possible that it was this campaign that encouraged Trajan to bring to an end in AD 106 the Nabataean dynasty, which had survived as a loyal ally of Rome up to that time. No such strategic reason can be surmised for the decision by Augustus to remove Judaea from Herodian rule in AD 6, or for Claudius to restore it to Agrippa I in AD 41, or for the same emperor to return it to provincial status on Agrippa's death in AD 44.

JUDAEA

The changes in the political status of Judaea reflect less the condition of the population as a whole than the fortunes of the large family of Herod.[6] As an outsider even in Judaea, Herod's reliance on Roman support for his rule led to uncommon loyalty to Rome, and to uncommon rewards. His descendants ruled over an extraordinary bounty of principalities in the region during the first century AD, extending their power northwards into the Lebanon and eastwards into Transjordan. Thus parts of Ituraea in Lebanon were ruled by Herod's son Philip from 4 BC to AD 34 and by his grandson Agrippa I from AD 37 to 44, in the latter case as part of an extended Judaean kingdom after AD 41. Another grandson, Herod, ruled a separate kingdom of Chalcis in Lebanon from AD 41 to 48, as did Agrippa II, the son of Agrippa I, from AD 50 to 53. Agrippa II was transferred in AD 53 from Chalcis to a kingdom which encompassed the whole of the former tetrarchy of Philip, including part of Ituraea, together with some parts of Galilee, Peraea and neighbouring areas. Despite the fact that most of his subjects were gentile, he retained the right to appoint High Priests in the Jerusalem Temple. His loyalty to Rome during the Jewish revolt of AD 66–70 ensured his retention of his territory, which was only incorporated into the province of Syria on his death in *c.* AD 93 or 100.

Roman favour to Herod and his descendants as individuals caused the re-emergence of Judaea as a temporary regional superpower for two periods in the Early Empire, first under Herod himself from 37 to 4 BC, when Augustus' beneficence gradually enlarged his kingdom to the size of the Hasmonaean state at its peak, and then under Agrippa I as king from AD 41 to 44, with territories of similar extent. Both Herodians were fully aware of their regional role. They were ostentatious benefactors to surrounding cities and, despite the occasional outbreak of hostilities which occasioned strong Roman disapproval, they exercised a careful policy with the Nabataeans to the south, including diplomatic intermarriage. The undoing of Agrippa I came when he convened a conference of client kings of Rome in Tiberias in AD 44 and aroused the antagonism of Marsus, the governor of Syria, who suspected conspiracy against Rome. Agrippa's sudden death 'eaten up with worms' prevented any action being taken against him:[7]

> He had for some time been furiously angry with the people of Tyre and Sidon, who now by common agreement presented themselves at his court. ... So, on an appointed day, attired in his royal robes and seated on the rostrum, Herod harangued them; and the people shouted back, 'It is a god speaking not a man!' Instantly an angel of the Lord struck him down, because he had usurped the honour due to God; he was eaten up with worms and died.
>
> (Acts 12.20–23)

As Roman puppets, a status signified on the part of Herod by his requirement that his subjects take an oath of loyalty to Augustus, Herodian kings won little support among the Jews. Herod did not come from a priestly family, and thus could not usurp the high priesthood as the Hasmonaeans had done. Since, according to Josephus (*Antiquities of the Jews* 20.251), Jews naturally assumed that the High Priest should be the leader of their nation, this disability was a serious obstacle to secure control. Herod's selection of High Priests from insignificant families, and a rapid turnover of the holders of that position, helped to prevent the priesthood becoming a source of organized opposition to the regime, but his lack of security was in any case evident from the fortified palaces such as Masada in which he chose to dwell.

On Herod's death in 4 BC, Jewish antagonism spilled over in a series of revolts, suppressed by Varus as governor of Syria. Succession was disputed primarily because of the multiplicity of Herod's sons, itself a product of the large number of Herod's wives. The solution imposed by Augustus was a division of Herod's kingdom. There was to be no king, but Archelaus became ethnarch of Judaea, Antipas became tetrarch of Galilee, and Philip was to rule as tetrarch a region east of Galilee and in part of the Transjordan. Archelaus lasted for only 10 years. In AD 6 he was removed from power and sent into exile in Vienne in southern Gaul, at the instigation of his subjects and, probably, the governor of Syria. Judaea was placed under the rule of a praefectus of equestrian rank, who was immediately required to call in troops from Syria to suppress unrest in opposition to the provincial census.

In the next 60 years, with a brief intermission from AD 41 to 44 when Agrippa I ruled, Judaea was kept more or less under control by the Roman governor termed, by AD 44 at least, *procurator*. The exceptional detail of Josephus' narrative in his *Antiquities of the Jews* and the traditions of the Early Church about the career of Jesus reveal frequent incidents and some tension, but the military garrison of Judaea, based mostly in Caesarea, consisted of only five cohorts and one cavalry unit, and local uprisings in the late 40s AD were easily suppressed by the Syrian legions.

The causes of the great revolt of AD 66 to 70 are thus likely to be complex.[8] It is not plausible simply to see Judaism as a religion liable to provoke unrest, since it was too varied in this period for any such simplistic conclusion (see Chapter 30). Josephus, who wrote a history of the war, blamed lower-class Jews and incompetent Roman governors in his summary of the causes of the war:

> Somehow those days had become so productive of every kind of wickedness among the Jews as to leave no deed of shame uncommitted; and even if someone had used all his powers of invention, he could not have thought of any vice that remained untried: so corrupt was the public and private life of the whole nation, so determined were they to outdo each other in impiety towards God and injustice to their neighbours, those in power ill-using the masses, and the masses striving to overthrow those in power. One group was bent on domination, the other on violence and on robbing the rich. First to begin this lawlessness and this barbarity to kinsmen were the Sicarii, who left no word unspoken, no deed untried, to insult and destroy the objects of their foul plots.
>
> (*The Jewish War* 7.263–69)

By thus attributing blame to others, Josephus exculpated his own class, but his summary is balanced by his own detailed narrative, which reveals his own deep involvement and that of many other members of the Judaean ruling class. A cluster of factors may plausibly be blamed for the revolt. The strange economy of Judaea, with the influx of wealth into Jerusalem for the Temple, made the rich richer and encouraged the rural poor to settle in the city, rather as was the case in Rome itself. The excessive surplus wealth of the rich, available to invest in land or elsewhere, pushed up the price of such land and encouraged reckless borrowing by the poor. The poor were in any case under demographic pressure in the countryside since Jews did not practise contraception, abortion or infanticide, as was standard elsewhere in the ancient world. The Jewish notion of charity kept children alive to compete for scarce resources. Hence there was class antagonism directed by the poor against a rich élite, who held power through the favour of Rome but lacked influence and prestige in Jewish eyes.[9]

When the war broke out, the pressure behind it was undoubtedly primarily that of poor peasants. But it was led by members of the ruling class, since the captain of the Temple, Eleazar, son of Ananias, who caused the sacrifices in the Temple on behalf of the emperor to cease in AD 66, was one of the prime movers. This change of side from their natural alliance with Rome seems to have been undertaken by such members of the Judaean ruling class only unwillingly. It was forced on them by the incompetence of the Roman procurator, Gessius Florus, who reacted in AD 66 to the inability of the Judaean nobility to control the urban mob by punishing the nobility, as if their incompetence was in fact a product of bad faith.[10]

In any case, the independent Jewish state founded in AD 66 was to last for four years. Based on the Temple in Jerusalem, this state issued a large coinage of distinctive type, including not only fine silver shekels whose metallic purity was ensured by its use for payment to the Temple which it would be sacrilege to cheat, but also quantities of small change. Roman attempts to recapture the city were at first lacklustre. Cestius Gallus, governor of Syria, was defeated with heavy losses while withdrawing from the city in October AD 66. Vespasian, put in charge of the war by Nero in AD 67, did not hurry to attack the capital until his son Titus led the assault in the spring of AD 70, when victory was urgently needed to bring prestige and bolster Vespasian's claim to the principate after his proclamation in AD 69. The Jewish state was riven by internal faction, but the influx of many pilgrims in spring AD 70 demonstrates the assumption of a large number of Judaeans that Rome would not bother to besiege a city as strong and strategically unimportant as Jerusalem. In any case, the disputes among the Judaean leaders may have been exaggerated by later tradition, since the commander-in-chief, Simon, son of Gioras, was evidently fully in control of the defence of the city by the time of his eventual overthrow. Defeat when it came, with the destruction of the Temple, was catastrophic. Much of Jerusalem was reduced to rubble; pockets of resistance, even in remote places like Masada, were resolutely wiped out.

The effect on Judaean society was dramatic. Before AD 70, social, political and religious status had been defined primarily in relation to the Jerusalem Temple. The priests performed the sacrificial cult on behalf of the people and acted as expert interpreters of the traditional law enshrined in the Hebrew Bible (see Chapter 30). All this ended in AD 70. Despite Jewish hopes, the cult was never revived, even though priests sometimes continued to receive tithes. Most of the old ruling class simply disappeared from the pages of history. Hundreds of thousands of Jews were killed or sold into slavery. A Roman legion was quartered in Jerusalem.

In AD 132 revolt broke out again under the leadership of a certain Simeon ben Kosiba, known in some later rabbinic traditions as 'Bar Kokhba', meaning 'son of a star'.[11] The causes of this rebellion are even less certain, but like the rebels of AD 66–70 the Jews marked their temporary independence by issuing fine coins with inscriptions in Palaeo-Hebrew (a form of Hebrew lettering that had fallen out of common use many centuries earlier). Letters of Ben Kosiba found in the Judaean desert reveal his concern for proper observance of the Jewish festivals: a papyrus in Aramaic about the celebration of the feast of Tabernacles reads:[12]

Shim'on to Yehuda Bar Menashe, to Qiryat 'Arabaya. I have sent to you two donkeys that you shall send with them two men to Yehonatan Bar Ba'ayan and to Masabala in order that they shall pack and send to the camp, to you, palm branches and citrons. And you, from your place, send others who will bring you myrtles and willows. See that they are tithed and send them to the camp ... be well.

Such sentiments, and later rabbinic traditions, which partly portray him as a hero, partly as a villain, may reflect a religious motivation. In any case, his government was sufficiently organized to lease out state land. The rebels' main strategy according to Cassius Dio (*History of Rome* 69.12.3) was the use of underground hiding complexes, some of which have been excavated in recent years:

> They did not dare meet the Romans in the open field, but they occupied the advantageous positions in the country and strengthened them with mines and walls, in order that they might have places of refuge whenever they should be hard pressed, and might meet together unobserved underground; and they pierced these subterranean passages from above at intervals to let in air and light.

The revolt was based on the eastern part of the Judaean hills and down by the Dead Sea. It is uncertain whether Jerusalem was captured by the rebels at all, or (more probably) was simply one of their goals. The revolt lasted until AD 135, when it was suppressed by Hadrian only after heavy losses.[13]

After the revolt, Judaea was renamed Syria Palaestina. The Roman state took the unusual step of forbidding Jews to live in the region of Jerusalem, which became a Roman colony renamed Aelia Capitolina. Exclusion of Jews may only have involved the prohibition of Jewish customs by those living in the area, if Jewish identity was defined by Rome by this period in religious terms (see Chapter 30). The rabbinic sources suggest that some refugees at least escaped north to Galilee, which became the new centre for rabbinic academies. Other Jews escaped to Egypt, Asia Minor and elsewhere.

The two revolts involved primarily Judaea. Galilee was held by the rebels for one year, in AD 67, but was only feebly defended. The evidence for Galilean involvement in the Bar Kochba war is minimal, but a second legion was placed just south of Galilee in Caparcotna already by the 120s AD, perhaps to anticipate and prevent trouble.

SAMARIA

The Samaritans mostly remained aloof from Jewish society in this period, reflecting the separate development of Samaritan theology since the period of Persian rule which ended in 332 BC and the hostility between the Samaritans and the Hasmonaeans in the 120s BC, when the Samaritan sanctuary on Mount Gerizim was destroyed by the Judaean state.[14] Samaritans were massacred by Roman troops at the instigation of Pontius Pilate in AD 35, on allegation of rebellious tendencies. For the rest of the period they usually remained quiet, although there was unrest in AD 67 which was quelled by Vespasian with much bloodshed. They continued to treat Mount Gerizim as a holy site despite the lack of a sanctuary on the spot. The Roman colony of Sebaste, founded by Augustus and peopled with local pagans, retained firm control over the whole region of Samaria. A new formally Greek city, Flavia

Neapolis, was founded under Vespasian in AD 72/3 close to the main Samaritan centre of Shechem, but no evidence survives about its purpose or who formed its population. In the third or fourth centuries a series of fundamental Samaritan religious texts were composed, testifying, along with anti-Samaritan legislation in late Roman legal codes, to the continued existence and importance of the native population, but for the history of the Samaritans between AD 70 and AD 180 it is only possible to cull information from the unreliable medieval Samaritan chronicles, preserved by Samaritan communities to the present day.

ARABIA

In Arabia, the early imperial period witnessed an extraordinary efflorescence of Nabataean culture, with a growing economy and stable political regime.[15] The Nabataean kings retained their independence until AD 106, partly because they were long-lived, thereby giving emperors only five occasions between 58 BC and AD 106 to consider after the death of a monarch whether to uphold the succession of his son, and partly by keeping a low profile in Roman politics. Unlike most client rulers, Nabataeans did not receive Roman citizenship, and no Nabataean king is known ever to have visited Rome. Similarly, after abortive attempts at marriage alliances with the Herodian family between the last decades BC and the 30s AD, the Nabataeans avoided involvement with their fellow dynasts. Since the governor of Syria was far to the north, Nabataean contact with Rome was largely confined to the provision of troops for Roman campaigns when requested. According to inscriptions of the first century AD from Hegra (modern Mada'in Saleh, in Saudi Arabia), Nabataean power was extended deep into the Hejaz, perhaps on behalf of Rome.

The economic boom within the Nabataean kingdom in the first century AD is rather surprising. The exploitation of long-distance trade routes, which had brought the Nabataeans to prominence in the Late Hellenistic period, declined rather than increased as a result of peace brought by Rome. New alternative routes from the east through the northern Syrian desert and Palmyra, or by sea up the Arabian Gulf, presented effective competition. Nabataeans turned instead to farming. From the late first century BC the kingdom controlled tracts of the Hauran to their north, which were exploited both by sheep-grazing and by agriculture, and there survives impressive evidence of Nabataean farming in the Negev semi-desert by the careful husbandry of the very limited rainfall. The total benefit to the ruling dynasty and upper class from this economy is plain from the development of Petra in the first century AD. Money was available for numerous monumental tombs carved out of the rock, and the erection of the great Qasr el-Bint temple, on which numerous foreign artisans must have worked.[16]

Down to the end of the dynasty the structures of Nabataean society remained tribal. Transliteration into Nabataean on inscriptions of Greek titles like *strategoi* (*strg*) does not disguise the fact that royal commanders were also tribal chieftains, and Nabataean kings, unlike their counterparts elsewhere, made no effort to found cities in the Graeco-Roman style. The precise function of the capital Petra, with its monuments and tombs, surrounded by land that was cultivable with care, remains a matter of dispute. Greek literary sources, like Strabo (*Geography* 16.4.21), paint a picture of a peaceful society given to feasting, but some of this may be idealization of a barbarian lifestyle.

The cultural independence of Nabataea under its kings makes all the more remarkable the rapid change in the region after the cessation of the Nabataean kingdom in AD 106, when Trajan created from it the province of Arabia. The large series of Nabataean stone inscriptions, both honorific and funerary, rapidly declined. Both inscriptions, and city coinage produced at Petra and Bostra, were written in Greek after AD 106.

Most striking evidence of change comes from an archive of documents found in the Judaean desert belonging to a Jewish woman called Babatha, who died during the Bar Kochba war of AD 132–35.[17] The legal documents that she preserved were in Nabataean up to AD 106, in Greek and, because she was Jewish, Aramaic afterwards. Dating of the documents was by the emperors and, remarkably, by the consuls of the year. In a dispute with the guardians of her fatherless son, Babatha had commissioned documents which lay out a relevant praetor's judiciary rule in Greek translation (the Latin version of the formula is cited in Gaius, *Institutes* 4.47).[18] One cause of the rapid impact of Roman rule on local society may have been the apparently considerable participation in local administration (including the filing of census returns) of Roman troops, with small detachments scattered throughout the province in addition to the legion stationed at Bostra. Despite or because of the presence of such soldiers, the province seems to have remained peaceful down to the end of the period. One document preserved by Babatha records a large short-term loan made to her second husband Judah in AD 124 by the centurion at the camp in En Gedi:

In the consulship of Manius Acilius Glabrio and Torquatus Tebanianus one day before the nones of May, in En-gedi village of lord Caesar, Judah son of Elazar Kthousion, En-gedian, to Magonius Valens, centurion of Cohors I Miliaria Thracum, greetings. I acknowledge that I have received and owe to you in loan sixty denarii of Tyrian silver, which are fifteen staters, upon hypothec of the courtyard in En-gedi belonging to my father Elazar Kthousion ... which money I will repay to you on the kalends of January in the same year during the said consulship, and the interest of the said money I will deliver to you monthly at the rate of one denarius per hundred denarii per month. If I do not repay you on the specified terminal date as aforewritten, you will have the right to acquire, use, sell and administer the said hypothec without any opposition.

(*PYadin* no. 11)

27

EGYPT

Egypt, the site of an ancient stable civilization and from 323 BC the base of the kingdom of the Ptolemies, was much changed, almost entirely to the detriment of the majority of its inhabitants, by the advent of Roman rule. The Roman annexation of Egypt in 30 BC, some ten months after the battle of Actium, marked a decline in status, power and wealth from which the country was not to recover until well into the Byzantine period, and perhaps not even then.[1]

The history of Egypt in antiquity tended to differ from that of other countries bordering the Mediterranean, simply because of its geography. Egyptian agriculture relied not on rainfall but on the regular annual flooding of the Nile. Fields watered by irrigation produced a rich harvest, particularly of cereals. The three main areas for cultivation and habitation were the Nile valley and delta, and the Fayum, which lay about 60 miles to the southwest of the delta's apex. Land beyond the reach of the river waters was almost entirely desert, so optimum agricultural production required firm government to maintain irrigation channels and ensure rational distribution. A static population was tempted to escape into the inhospitable desert only in dire emergency. In the western desert, there were a number of oases supporting a small and scattered nomadic population, while the desert to the east contained mines and quarries. The desert protected the country from attacks from west or east, the settled populations of the oases in the western desert being particularly useful in controlling the threat of nomadic incursions. Defence of the Nile delta in the north was comparatively easy (see Map 20). In the south, garrisons were installed to prevent invasions by tribes of Nubians.

Egyptian memories of national glory since the fifth millennium BC were kept alive by the great pyramids and temples of past generations and the continuous collective tradition of the priesthood, who alone used and understood the hieroglyphic script in which Egyptian history was incised on stone records in temple precincts. In the third century BC one Egyptian high priest, Manetho, explained that history for a Greek readership and created an order of dynasties. By his time the Egyptian Pharaoh was a Graeco-Macedonian king.

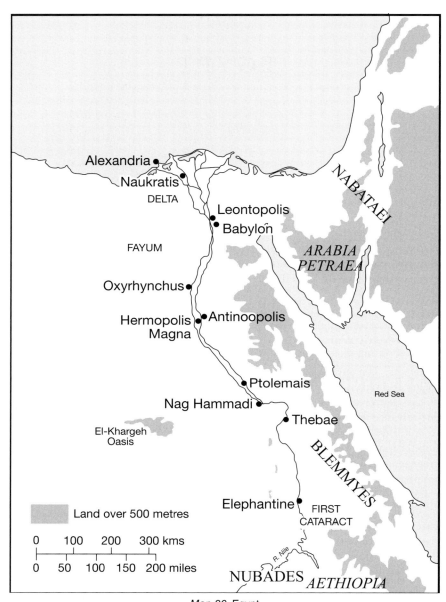

Map 20 Egypt

THE PTOLEMAIC DYNASTY

Ptolemy I was one of the generals who supported Alexander the Great in his campaigns of conquest. In 323 BC he was appointed satrap of Egypt, and after nearly 20 years of struggle following Alexander's death, in 305 BC he declared himself king. The Ptolemaic dynasty proved highly successful as rulers of Egypt. In almost continuous control until 30 BC, the Ptolemies exploited the wealth of Egypt with ruthless efficiency. A great bureaucracy was set in place, staffed mostly by Greeks at first, increasingly penetrated by Hellenized Egyptians from the late third century BC onwards. Peasants were heavily taxed; export trade was encouraged to bring in precious metals; registers were drawn up of land, animals and persons, compiled in villages and recorded in summaries in central and regional registries. This was a highly stratified society, in which Greek culture was the road to political power. Control was kept through military settlers granted land in villages in return for their role as preservers of security; into this mercenary army, by the end of the dynasty, some native Egyptian levies were also incorporated. Egyptian loyalty was also encouraged by full recognition of the native priesthood. The Ptolemies collaborated in the erection of the greatest extant Egyptian temples and received the support of the native religious institutions. The beneficiary of all this wealth was the royal family. Expenditure was lavished primarily on Alexandria, and above all the ostentatious magnificence of the Royal Palace, Museum and Library, which formed a separate quarter of the city.

On the death in August 30 BC of Cleopatra VII, the last ruler in the line of the Ptolemies, much of this came to an abrupt end. Cleopatra had enjoyed remarkable success since she became ruler of Egypt in 51 BC, sharing power jointly with her brothers Ptolemy XIII in 51–47 BC and Ptolemy XIV in 47–44 BC. She exploited the ambitions and affections of Roman politicians to preserve Egyptian independence, and indeed, during her liaisons with Julius Caesar in 48 BC and with Antonius from 41 BC, to expand Egyptian power into the ancient Ptolemaic possessions of Cyprus and Cyrenaica.

Such reliance on Roman support was a long-standing Ptolemaic policy. Diplomatic relations had existed between Rome and Egypt since c. 273 BC. In the summer of 168 BC, the status of Egypt as in effect a client of Rome was dramatically confirmed on the celebrated occasion when Rome compelled the Seleucid Antiochus IV to withdraw from Egypt after a successful invasion. Reliance on the personal support of particular Roman senators by Cleopatra marked a continuation of the policy of her father Ptolemy Auletes, who had sought the help of Pompeius, and mortgaged his kingdom to Roman creditors in 58 BC in order to win back his realm with the help of Roman legions. But Cleopatra strengthened social ties by sexual relationships, bearing a son, so she claimed, by Julius Caesar in 47 BC, and, after a formal marriage, twins (acknowledged by their father) by Antonius in 37 BC, with a third child in 36 BC.

By 34 BC the result of Cleopatra's policies was a Ptolemaic kingdom striving for a magnificence to rival that of two centuries earlier. In that year Antonius and Cleopatra held the so-called 'Donations' at Alexandria, in which all the lands once ruled by Alexander the Great, from the Hellespont to the Indus, were nominally shared out amongst Cleopatra and her children. She was, of course, the last surviving ruler descended from Alexander's successors. She and her son by Julius Caesar, nicknamed Caesarion, were hailed as 'Queen of Kings' and 'King of Kings'. Of her children by Antonius, Alexander Helios (aged three) was proclaimed king of the lands east of the Euphrates, his younger brother Ptolemy Philadelphus was to rule the area west of the Euphrates. His twin Cleopatra Selene became queen of Cyrenaica. Since much of this territory was not in fact controlled either by Rome or by Egypt, and since the kings were only infants, the donations were obviously theoretical, but that did not deprive them of considerable religious and national symbolic significance.[2]

From such magnificence, the downfall after Actium was all the more devastating. Antonius and Cleopatra fled back to Egypt after the battle, but both committed suicide; in her case death by the asp, a royal symbol in Egypt, seemed preferable to figuring in the triumph of Octavian in Rome. Caesarion was put to death. The three children by Antonius were sent to Rome to be brought up by Octavia, sister of the conqueror and once Antonius' wife. From now on the ruler of Egypt was to reside, with only the briefest of interludes, outside the country. Egypt ceased to have any central role in the wider politics of the Mediterranean for the rest of the imperial period, except briefly in AD 69, when Vespasian threatened to block the corn supply from Egypt to Rome as part of his bid for power, and in AD 175, when the pretender Avidius Cassius made Egypt his base.

ROMAN RULE IN EGYPT

In his *Res Gestae* (27.1), Octavian described the new situation briefly enough: 'I added Egypt to the empire of the Roman people.' But this was no ordinary province. Egypt was already assigned under Augustus a special function in the empire as the chief provider of grain to the city of Rome. Huge numbers of papyri testify to the vast scale of the grain supply and its complex organization at all levels. To ensure regular supplies the province was always kept as part of the *provincia* of the emperor. Revenue from the province was huge. After an abortive attempt in 25–22 BC to expand Roman control to the south, leading to a brief occupation of Qasr Ibrim, the frontier facing Meroe in the south was fixed some 50 miles south of the first cataract of the Nile. The border was stable, with few recorded clashes in later years.

It may be that the appointment in 30 BC of C. Cornelius Gallus, an eques rather than a senator, as first prefect of Egypt occurred simply because he was the man on the spot, but later policy was probably deliberate. To exclude potential leaders of disaffection from using Egypt as a power base, as Antonius had done, the governor appointed was never a senator. Prefects, who normally held the position for three years, were usually equites, although in AD 32 a freedman filled the post. No prominent Roman was permitted even to enter Egypt without express permission from the princeps.

Augustus retained much of the complex Ptolemaic bureaucracy, but he also introduced major changes which were to last for centuries, and whose originality is often masked by the continuation of terminology from the Ptolemaic period.[3] For instance, the existing division of the country into about forty administrative districts (*nomoi*) each governed by a *strategos*, was retained, but the *strategoi* were given a much greater part in the collection of taxes than they had played in the Ptolemaic period, reporting directly to the prefect. They were of immense importance in the supervision of compliance by local authorities in villages and towns. Military control was transferred first to three, then after AD 23 to two, Roman legions stationed in fortified camps at Alexandria, Thebes and Egyptian Babylon, with small detachments placed in garrisons at key places such as mines and quarries and the depots of the grain supply; under Hadrian, this legionary force was reduced still further, to one, but soldiers still performed an important administrative role in building and guarding roads, and as police in the countryside.

Other administrative changes of the Roman period included a new definition of the role of the head of the *Idios Logos* or 'Special Account', which in Ptolemaic times administered crown possessions. The *Gnomon*, or regulatory code, of the *Idios Logos* is known from a surviving copy of the Antonine period and from earlier fragments, and shows that this official, a senior Roman usually of equestrian rank, dealt with judicial problems arising out of such matters as ownerless property, land intended for sale, and admission to the priesthood. It is a long papyrus document, with 115 clauses; for example:

4. The estates of those who die intestate and who have no legal heirs fall to the fisc.
6. An Alexandrian may not bequeath to his wife, if he has no offspring by her, more than a fourth part of his estate; and if he has children by her, he may not allot to his wife a larger share than what he bequeaths to each of his sons.
92. A child who has been exposed on a dung heap may not become a priest.

(*BGU* no. 1,210; LR 2, pp. 298–302)

A new account, the *ousiakos logos* (estates account), dealt from the Flavian period with the emperor's patrimonial properties.

Further changes in the bureaucracy at the top level, such as the introduction by Hadrian of a Roman eques as *archiereus* (high priest) to oversee Egyptian religious institutions, were perhaps less significant than the greatly increased importance of the *metropoleis*, the main towns in each nome, which had a state-given role similar to that of *poleis* in other eastern provinces, as administrative centres for archives, organization and the dispensation of justice.[4] In a significant innovation, the local Graeco-Egyptian élite of these *metropoleis* were granted a major role in communal government as magistrates. Their independence differed from that of local aristocracies elsewhere in the empire principally because of their lack of councils; since there was thus no mechanism from within the *metropoleis* to check on the competence of magistrates, this duty reverted to the *strategos*. On the other hand, the social status of these local aristocrats was jealously preserved by the Roman state, which permitted such positions only to those of the 'gymnasial' class. Entry into this select class, in Ptolemaic times a private matter, was carefully controlled after AD 4/5 by *epikrisis*, a formal hearing in front of a Roman official. Entry required documentation of pedigree. The interest of the state was involved not least because such status carried tax privileges

The change in government was felt most keenly in Alexandria. A huge sprawling city under the Ptolemies, it contained a diverse population originally attracted by the wealth of the royal court. Citizens were, either in fact or fictitiously, of Greek or Macedonian stock, but many inhabitants were Egyptians settled illegally, and the Jewish population was large and influential enough to inhabit a special area with their own ethnarch and council. The presence of the kings seemed to have rendered a city council otiose by the end of the Ptolemaic period, a fact which would create much ill-feeling in the Roman period.[5]

As the capital of his avowed enemies, Alexandria was not likely to fare well under Octavian. The drastically reduced prestige of the governor, who resided in the old palace but without the same pomp and circumstance as Ptolemaic kings, robbed the city of its imperial pretensions. The privileged status of Greeks within the city continued, but the community was amorphous, with no *boule* (city council) of the type standard in the rest of the Greek East. Alexandria was not to have such a council until *c.* AD 200, and control was kept firmly in the hands of the prefect, who was supported by the permanent presence of a legion for the suppression of dissent. The Jews were allowed to retain their privileges, although for liability to the poll tax they were ranked with native Egyptians.

This political downgrading of the city led to consistent anti-Roman feelings among the Alexandrian Greeks, not least because it contrasted so blatantly with the physical splendours of the city, which reached their apogee in the early imperial period, as the contemporary Strabo remarked (*Geography* 17.1.8–10). It contrasted too with Alexandria's economic role, which became if anything more important now that it acted as entrepôt not only for grain shipments to Rome but also for the luxury trade from the East, as well as of artefacts such as glassware and mosaics manufactured in the city itself. The loss of royal patronage undoubtedly diminished the once famous intellectual life of the city, but Alexandria remained a centre for the study of philosophy and medicine, and in the second century was the home of the polymath, geographer and astronomer, Claudius Ptolemaeus.

This disappointment fuelled the already fickle nature of the Alexandrians. Their opposition to Roman rule was notorious, according to a speech made *c.* AD 71–75 by Dio Chrysostom (*Oration* 32.71–72).[6] Their demand for a city council was a real political request, illustrated by the so-called *boule* papyrus, which represents ambassadors from Alexandria asking the emperor (probably Augustus) to restore the council which the city had once had under the early Ptolemies:

> It is necessary for us to speak at some length. I submit, then, that the Council will see to it that none of those who are liable to enrolment for the poll tax diminish the revenue by being listed in the public records along with the ephebes for each year; and it will take care that the pure (?) citizen body of Alexandria is not corrupted by men who are uncultured and uneducated. And if anyone be unreasonably burdened by taxes exacted by the *Idiologos* or by any other tax-agent who may be oppressing the people, the Council, in assembly before your prefect, might lend support to the weak and prevent the income that could be preserved for you from being plundered by casual persons, simply through lack of a remedy. ... We ask, then, that it be permitted for the Council to convene annually and at the end of each year to submit a report of its transactions. ... Caesar said, 'I shall come to a decision about these matters (after I have visited?) Alexandria.'
>
> (*CPJ* vol. 2, no. 150)

The desire for a council was also symbolic of resistance to Rome, which was expressed in literary form in a series of martyr acts found in a number of papyri mostly of the second to third century AD, and known to modern scholars as the *Acts of the Pagan Martyrs*.[7] These remarkable documents portray heroic Alexandrian leaders, usually ranked as gymnasiarchs, fiercely confronting the emperor. The heroes are mostly executed for their efforts to demonstrate the justice of their call for greater Greek rights in the city. In much of the literature, violent hatred was expressed not just of Rome but of Rome's protégés, the Jews.

JEWS IN EGYPT

Of the Jewish population of Alexandria in the early Roman period, quite a lot can be said.[8] The historian Josephus included in his *Antiquities of the Jews* (18.257–309) a description of the community and accounts of its difficulties in the late 30s AD. The philosopher Philo, who was a native of Alexandria (*c.* 30 BC-*c.* AD 45), was also a politician of high standing among the Jews, and gave a detailed account of the troubles of the late 30s and early 40s AD in his *Embassy to Gaius* and *Against Flaccus*. Philo's voluminous works were preserved for their religious contents by Christian copyists, and his motivation for composing a narrative of recent events seems not to have been historiographical but more to illustrate divine retribution on the opponents of the Jews. But his writings still permit a fairly full picture of Alexandrian Jewish politics in this part of the first century.[9]

The Jews seem to have inhabited two of the five areas into which the city was divided, the 'delta' quarter, and much of 'beta'. Engaged mostly as small craftsmen, they were rich enough to erect a huge main synagogue in basilica form, and numerous enough to have a strong political effect on the life of the city. Relations with Alexandrian Greeks seem to have been prickly at most times. Greeks accused the Jews of attempting to steal into the gymnasia, thus acquiring Alexandrian citizenship. For some Jews the charge must have been true, as Philo and others acquired Roman citizenship, which was only available to those who already held Alexandrian citizenship status. But most of the resentment of the Greeks probably came from the special rights of the Jews, inherited from the Ptolemaic period, to govern themselves, with their own courts and magistrates.

Resentment boiled over in AD 38 into riots, fomented by the venal governor, Flaccus, according to Philo (*Against Flaccus* 54). The Jews sent an embassy to the emperor in Rome to complain, but it was at first physically prevented from sailing by the governor and then on arrival in Rome treated contemptuously by Gaius. The Jews retained their privileges only by the intervention at Rome of Agrippa I, friend both of Gaius and of Claudius. Even with such patronage they were treated with some disdain by Claudius in a letter written to Alexandria by the emperor in the early 40s AD.[10] In AD 66 there were further riots, instigated by the Greeks according to Josephus (*The Jewish War* 2.487–98), but suppressed with ferocity by the prefect, who used two legions and extra troops from Africa. The harsh treatment meted out to the Jews was made more piquant, perhaps, by the origins of the governor responsible: Tiberius Julius Alexander, the prefect from AD 66 to 70, was an apostate Jew from the city and a nephew of Philo.

The end of the Jewish community in Alexandria was part of a wider disaster, the diaspora Jewish revolt of AD 115–17.[11] Something has been said above (p. 270) about the simultaneous uprisings in Mesopotamia, where many Jews lived. In the Mediterranean region, Jews rebelled in Cyprus, Cyrene and all over Egypt. If the chronology suggested by Cassius Dio is correct (*History of Rome* 68.32), the revolt may have begun in Mesopotamia as a reaction to the Roman invasion of Parthian territory, but an Egyptian origin is also possible, and the rebellion, once spread, involved more than just political calculation. In Cyprus and Cyrenaica there were vicious attacks on the local gentile population as well as on representative of the state, and it seems likely that pagan temples were deliberately destroyed. Papyri from the Egyptian countryside reveal the fear of native Egyptian peasants as well as Greeks and Roman officials. Religious motivation is likely. At any rate, one casualty was the Jewish community of Alexandria, which is hardly attested by any source during the rest of the imperial period.

EGYPTIAN VILLAGES

Outside Alexandria, one impact of Roman rule on Egypt was a tightening up of tax collection, which had become lax under the last Ptolemies.[12] Augustus introduced a detailed provincial census, carried out at first every seven years, then every fourteen, with periodic updating. It was used as the basis for calculating the poll tax and tax on domestic property. Unsurprisingly, in so complex a system complaints were rife. The edict issued at the start of Galba's reign in AD 68 by the prefect Tiberius Julius Alexander, which survives in an inscription from the oasis of El-Khargeh, shows that the governor was well aware of the problems:[13]

> Since ... practically from the moment I entered the city I have been assailed by clamours of petitioners, both in small groups and in throngs, both from the most respectable people here and from the country farmers, complaining about the recent abuses, I have lost no time in righting pressing matters to the extent of my authority. ... First of all, I recognize the complete reasonableness of your petition that persons not be forced against their will, contrary to the general practice of the provinces, into tax farming or other leases of imperial estate; no little harm has been done by the compulsion of many persons inexperienced in such duties, when [the collection of] taxes was imposed upon them.
>
> (LR 2, pp. 295–98)

Villages were administered by elders (*presbyteroi*), who supervised leases, tax assessments and such like, but all under the close supervision of the village clerk (*komogrammateus*) appointed by the state. Reluctance or inability to pay was not uncommon. During the reigns of Claudius and Nero, for example, a number of people deserted their villages in the Fayum to avoid paying their taxes. Philo recounts the brutal methods espoused by one tax-collector in similar circumstances:

> Recently a certain collector of taxes was appointed in our area. When some of the men who apparently were in arrears because of poverty fled in fear of unbearable punishment, he laid violent hands on their wives, children, parents, and other relatives, beating and trampling and visiting every outrage upon them to get them either to betray their fugitive or to pay on his behalf. But they could do neither, the first because they did not know, the second because they were no less poverty-stricken than the fugitive. But the collector would not let them go before he had racked their bodies with twistings and tortures or killed them off with newly contrived modes of death. ... And when there were no relatives left, the scourge even spread to the neighbours, sometimes even to whole villages and towns, which soon became deserted and emptied of their inhabitants, who fled their homes and scattered to places where they thought they might escape detection.
>
> (*On Special Laws* 3.30)

The bureaucracy also imposed a great variety of liturgies – essentially, services in kind – on the whole population. In liturgies that started to become compulsory from the mid-first century AD, the rich supervised tax collection, while the poor provided their own labour, on work such as the building of irrigation dykes.

A partial compensation for this ruthless extraction of wealth from the country was the effect of the relaxation of the close supervision that had been exercised by the Ptolemaic state over the production of important commodities such as oil and papyrus. Such industries, and long-distance trade with the East, flourished in the early imperial period. *The Navigation of the Erythraean Sea*, written in the mid-first century AD by a Greek merchant of Egypt, describes two major lines of trade to Arabia and India which began from Egypt's Red Sea ports.[14] The trade concentrated on luxury goods, as shown for example by the items listed as exported from Egypt to the port of Muza in South Arabia (Chapter 14):

> Merchandise for which it offers a market are: purple cloth, fine and ordinary quality; Arab sleeved clothing, either with no adornment or with the common adornment or with checks or interwoven with gold thread; saffron; *cyperus* [a reed]; cloth; cloaks; blankets, in limited number, with no adornment as well as with traditional local adornment; girdles with shaded stripes; unguent, moderate amount; money, considerable amount; wine and grain, limited quantity because the region produces wheat in moderate quantity and wine in greater. To the king and governor are given (?): horses and pack mules; goldware; embossed silverware; expensive clothing; copperware.

Ideological acceptance of Roman rule was in some ways easier, and there is little evidence of resentment by Egyptian peasants. The revolt of Avidius Cassius in AD 175 was not based on any specifically Egyptian nationalism, although the uprising in AD 172 in the delta known as the revolt of the *boukoloi* ('herdsmen'), which Cassius himself had suppressed, seems to have had a local origin. Emperors were worshipped in traditional style as foreign Pharaohs, like the Persian and Ptolemaic kings before them. On the temple walls, Roman emperors appear with all the trappings of traditional Egyptian royalty, although no Roman emperor attempted to win popularity with the Egyptian populace by regular participation in Egyptian rites as the Ptolemies had done. Egyptians had little incentive to identify with Rome; they were the only free inhabitants of the empire who were excluded from Roman citizenship, although this could be circumvented by an Egyptian first becoming a citizen of Alexandria. Recruitment of Egyptians into the *auxilia* was slow, a trickle in the first century AD, more in the second century.[15] The army had detachments scattered throughout the province, so that soldiers were integrated into Egyptian life, but largely as an unwanted presence. Many papyri reveal complaints about requisitioning and billeting of troops. One example from AD 133–37 reads:

> Marcus Petronius Mamertinus, perfect of Egypt, declares: I am informed that without having a permit many of the soldiers when travelling through the country requisition boats and animals and persons improperly, in some cases seizing them by force, in others obtaining them from the *strategoi* through favour or obsequiousness, the

result of which is that private persons are subjected to insults and abuses and the army is reproached for greed and injustice. I therefore command the *strategoi* and the royal secretaries in any case not to furnish to any person whatsoever, whether travelling by river or by land, any contribution for the journey without a permit, understanding that I will vigorously punish anyone who after this edict is discovered receiving or giving any of the aforesaid things. Year ... of the lord Hadrian Caesar, Thoth 8.

(*Select Papyri* no. 221; LR 2, pp. 321–22)

About the life of Egyptian peasant families, or at least the more prosperous village landowners, a surprisingly large amount can be said, because of the survival of huge quantities of papyri in the Egyptian sands.[16] Papyri have been discovered in small quantities since the eighteenth century, but the greatest amounts were dug up deliberately in expeditions sent for that purpose in the late nineteenth and early twentieth centuries. The papyrological evidence is concentrated in a few areas of Egypt, principally the villages of the Fayum, and the nomes of Oxyrhynchus and Hermopolis. The material found encompasses public records, legal contracts, accounts, private letters and jottings, as well as a great number of literary texts, and texts used as part of the educational process in schools of the Roman period.

Thus peasant families can be found in the papyri saving up for a set of good clothes to be worn on a family occasion, most often marriages and births. Brother-sister marriages, an anathema in the rest of the Roman world, were quite common; it has been argued that this custom reflected not just an inheritance strategy to preserve property within the family but an assertion of Egyptian identity all the more powerful because of the taboo against such unions in the rest of Mediterranean society.[17] Family size varied, although village families were often larger than those in the towns. Traditionally, Egyptians, like Jews and Christians, objected to the common Greek custom of exposing unwanted infants to die, but town-dwellers began to follow the Greek practice; exposed babies were often adopted or reared as slaves.[18] Egyptian inheritance practices continued in much of the countryside, and consequently placed quite a large proportion (perhaps a third) of privately owned property in the hands of women.

A significant change in the imperial period was the substantial increase in privately owned land. Nevertheless, the majority of land belonged either to the Roman state (known as 'public' land, or 'Royal' land as in Ptolemaic times) or to the emperors as personal property. Large estates were granted to the emperor's friends and relatives, reverting to the emperor's *patrimonium* on their death. The once vast holdings of temple lands were reduced during the Roman period. Individual farmers sometimes worked a number of plots of land rented from a number of different landlords, engendering a great mass of paperwork produced to record rent agreements in cash or kind, which in turn provides an unrivalled insight into the working of the Egyptian peasant economy. The papyri also reveal that slave labour was rarely used in agricultural work, and that wage labour was common. Local trade evidently mostly involved the use of coins, which have been found extensively in excavations of Egyptian villages.

The greatest mass of papyri cover criminal and civil legal affairs, which were dealt with by the *strategos* and other officials in each administrative district. The main problems here lay in the existence of conflicts between legal systems, since upwardly mobile Egyptians seeking Greek status by entering the gymnasium might object, for instance, to being judged by Egyptian law, and all Roman citizens in theory came under Roman law.[19] In practice, it is likely that officials judged cases as they saw fit, and only those with sufficient resources appealed to the prefect or other higher authority if they believed that use of a different legal system might benefit their cause. The eventual formal solution, reached only in the second century AD, was to judge cases according to the language of the documents in which agreement had originally been reached. Documents in demotic, a form of Egyptian, are still found in the second century AD.

Egyptian religious practices continued well into the imperial period, despite the scorn of Greeks or the Latin poet Juvenal for animal worship and extreme religious enthusiasm (see Figure 32).[20] The temples lost economic power, but the priestly caste continued, and even produced one literary apologist for this tradition, a certain Chaeremon. Syncretism of Egyptian gods with Greek deities was left to Greeks and Romans, but Roman styles of painting, for instance, did influence the mummy portraits still produced by the Egyptians to honour the dead (see Figure 22, on p. xxx). Hieroglyphic and demotic writings were still produced in the Early Empire. Translations into Greek of demotic texts even in the third century AD show a continuing sense of Egyptian nationalism. One such text is the *Oracle of the Potter*, a nationalist prophecy of *c.* 130–115 BC aimed against the Ptolemies and their city of Alexandria, and forecasting that Memphis will rise again; it was still circulating in Greek versions in the second and third centuries AD:[21]

> And then the Guardian Spirit will desert the city which they founded and will go to god-bearing Memphis and it will be deserted. ... That will be the end of our evils when Egypt shall see the foreigners fall like leaves from the branch. The city by the sea will be a drying-place for the fisherman's catch because the Guardian Spirit has gone to Memphis, so that passers-by will say, 'This was the all-nurturing city in which all the races of mankind live.'
> (*POxy* no. 2,332)

The role of Greeks in the countryside was further reinforced under Hadrian, when the new Greek city of Antinoopolis was founded in memory of the emperor's deceased lover, Antinous. Antinoopolis, and the existing Greek *poleis* of Naukratis and Ptolemais, held a status outside the general administrative system of the province, in much the same way as Alexandria. The inhabitants jealously guarded their privileges and restricted their citizenship.

Figure 32 Image of the Egyptian god Horus, with bird head, dressed as a Roman soldier, second to third century AD. Such a zoomorphic deity was only worshipped by native Egyptians. The trappings of the Roman army were presumably intended to indicate the power of the god. Photo courtesy of the Ashmolean Museum, Oxford.

The Egyptian Jews, previously settled in villages throughout the Egyptian countryside, disappeared after the awful events at the end of Trajan's reign, like the Jews of Alexandria. They had already seen in AD 73 the closure of the temple of Leontopolis, a shrine modelled on Jerusalem and functioning as a centre for sacrificial worship for local Jews since its foundation by a High Priest from Jerusalem in the mid-second century BC. The shrine seems to have been ignored by the Jews of Alexandria, who preferred to look towards Jerusalem, but, despite its inoffensiveness, the Temple was closed down by Vespasian in the aftermath of the Judaean revolt.[22]

It is clear that Egypt under the Roman Empire had a special history different from that of other provinces. The impression of a closed society is reinforced by the idiosyncratic use of Ptolemaic terminology in the Egyptian bureaucracy and by the use in Egypt of a distinctive coinage. The Alexandrian mint continued after Actium to produce the silver *tetradrachma*, but since the Roman state overvalued this coin by decreeing it to be equivalent to a *denarius*, it was unacceptable outside Egypt. Nevertheless it is important to be aware of the probability that many of the apparently unique elements of life in Roman Egypt may in fact have been shared by other provincials in the empire, and that Egyptian society differed primarily only in that it left behind a detailed record in the sand.[23]

28

NORTH AFRICA

By 44 BC the whole of the North African coastline already lay within the Roman sphere of influence, and in general, from the viewpoint of the Roman state, the region remained untroublesome for the next three centuries, whether by the cooperation or the suppression of the natives. Change consisted of urbanization and increased prosperity through intensive agricultural exploitation, even of marginal land, and the production for export of olive oil, grain and pottery artefacts.[1]

AFRICA BEFORE 44 BC

The nature of African societies before Roman interference was much affected by geography. Ancient Cyrenaica (now north-east Libya) (see Map 21) was settled by Greeks from the seventh century BC, and from that time onwards the fertile coastal plain and its hinterland plateau were controlled by the four long-established Greek cities of Cyrene, Ptolemais, Arsinoe and Berenice, to which a fifth, Apollonia, was added in the Hellenistic age, when other outsiders, such as Jews, were also encouraged to settle. A large indigenous population remained, especially in the semi-desert and the desert to the south and west of the cities; these people are labelled 'Libyans' by modern writers to distinguish them and their language from the Punic peoples and language of the region, but no ancient collective name for them survives.[2] These natives developed villages and larger settlements, but much of their economy depended on transhumant pastoralism, moving from the cultivable zone in the north to the steppe in the south, and marketing their pastoral products through the cities.

Further west along the coast there was a similar picture. Only in a Mediterranean climate was there sufficient fertile ground and rainfall for some cities to flourish. In pre-Roman times all such cities west of Cyrenaica were Phoenician settlements, colonized primarily as trading posts, in some cases since the seventh century BC (even earlier in the case of Carthage), although the Phoenician imprint on the hinterland of Carthage in modern Tunisia was not as intense as the Greek imprint on Cyrenaica. The three coastal cities of Tripolitania, namely Sabratha, Oea and Lepcis Magna, grew to prosperity

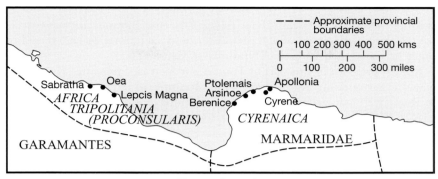

Map 21 Cyrenaica

from their part in the trade across the Sahara; they were subject first to Carthage and then to the kings of Numidia. South and west of Carthage, the Berber kingdom of Numidia (today north-west Tunisia and north-east Algeria) had maintained its nominal independence until it was annexed by Julius Caesar in 46 BC. Numidia was fertile; corn, wine and olives were grown on the plains, and horses, sheep and cattle reared on the uplands. Under Punic influence, town life developed in the second century BC in places such as Vaga and Cirta, and partial political unity was encouraged, not least as defence against predations by Carthage or Rome. In contrast, Mauretania, the land of the Moors, which spanned the western half of the Atlas Mountain range, remained distinctively Berber into the imperial period. Mauretania (now Algeria and northern Morocco) is high and rocky, supporting mostly sheep, with corn and olives only on the coast and in a few river valleys and plains. Here in pre-Roman times there were few cities to be found. The nomadic tribes of the pre-desert ranged over large distances, not infrequently coming into conflict with those in settled agricultural areas. Despite cultural links between them, there is no evidence of any wider African unity.

Rome's first interference in Africa was through conflict with Carthage. Carthage was a Punic trading city which had become the main power in the western Mediterranean by the third century BC. War with Rome originated in a struggle over control of Sicily in 264 BC, but in time conflict spilled over into a general struggle for supremacy. In the last decade of the third century BC Hannibal invaded Italy, only to suffer eventual defeat. In 146 BC Rome finally brought the contest to an end in the third Punic war by the total destruction of Carthage and the levelling of its site. One product of this continual series of wars was the first Roman province in Africa, which consisted of a relatively small area of northern Tunisia, the part of Africa closest to Italy. Roman interest in the province during the Republic was largely confined to the extraction of taxes, particularly grain for the city of Rome. There were some Italian immigrants in trading communities such as that at Cirta in Numidia, but not many, and an attempt to refound Carthage as a Roman colony in 122 BC came to nothing. A second product was an abiding rhetoric of suspicion about *Punica fides*, the notorious untrustworthiness of the Carthaginians. Such prejudice could sometimes be transferred to other Africans, such as those of Numidia or Mauretania.

Roman presence in this part of Tunisia put increased pressure on relations with the surrounding allied kings, whose attempts to retain suitable patrons in Rome were not always successful. In Numidia, Jugurtha, who ruled from 118 to 106 BC, was overthrown in a long and notorious war. Juba I was ejected by Caesar in 46 BC for his unwise support of Pompeius. His Numidian kingdom was added to the old province of Africa Vetus as Africa Nova. In Mauretania the native dynasty had supported Julius Caesar in the war against Pompeius: hence it maintained by skilful diplomacy a precarious independence until it came to an end with the (natural) death of Bocchus in 33 BC. By contrast, Cyrenaica had fallen into Roman hands quite willingly. In the Hellenistic period it had been annexed at various times by the Ptolemies in Egypt and then ruled by an independent dynasty, by whose bequest Rome received the kingdom in 96 BC. By 74 BC, it had been organized as a regular province, to which Crete was added in 67 BC.

CYRENAICA

The main lines of Roman control in Africa were thus clearly set out by 44 BC. Cyrenaica passed to control by Antonius after the battle of Philippi, then in the 'Donations of Alexandria' to Cleopatra (see Chapter 27), and after Actium to Octavian. No fighting took place in the region, but constant demands for contributions may have drained the province. In 27 BC the province was put under the command of a proconsul without troops, but soldiers had to be drafted in at some date between 5 BC and AD 3 to deal with raids on the settled area by the Libyan tribe of the Marmaridae. The problem was solved under Tiberius by the erection of a line of forts managed by auxiliaries along the edge of the desert. Other disturbances were caused by the minority groups in the cities – the Jews, who demanded special rights, and Roman citizens, who by 5 BC had twisted the administration of justice so far in their favour that the cities co-operated in winning from the emperor rules for a fairer system (EJ[2] no. 311; LR 1, pp. 594–96). In any case, from the end of the Marmaric war the province seems to have flourished. The only setbacks recorded in the first century AD are the destruction (possibly by over-grazing) of the special silphium plant, used for medicinal purposes and once a precious export (Pliny, *Natural History* 5.5.33, 19.15.38–45), and efforts, recorded on numerous *stelai*, to recover public land occupied by squatters. Most of the province was unaffected, and from the mid-first century AD, more and more rich aristocrats are attested as Roman citizens.

In the second century AD Cyrenaica was particularly badly affected by the savage revolt of the Jews in the last years of Trajan, from 115 to 117, during which, according to Cassius Dio (*History* 68.32.2), 220,000 people died. The insurrection was vigorously suppressed by Trajan, though it was his successor, Hadrian, on whom the heaviest burden of reconstruction fell. An inscription from Cyrene records that the emperor ordered the rebuilding of the baths next to the sanctuary of Apollo which had been destroyed and burned down in the Jewish uprising (*AE* 1928,2). Retired soldiers were settled in large numbers in the major cities of Cyrene and Apollonia, as well as in the emperor's own city, Hadrianopolis, founded on the site of the existing settlement.[3]

AFRICA PROCONSULARIS AND NUMIDIA

Rome was almost as successful in her control of the rest of Africa (see Map 22). In 30 BC Augustus reinstated to the throne of Numidia the son of Juba I, also called Juba, but in 25 BC the princeps united the territory with the old province of Africa.[4] One legion was stationed in the new united province of Africa Proconsularis, legion III Augusta. A series of wars is recorded against tribes on the pre-desert border of the Sahara in the south: three generals triumphed between 34 and 28 BC, and conflicts broke out in 21 BC, 19 BC, *c.* 15 BC, *c.* AD 3, and in AD 6. All these episodes probably reflect native resistance to Roman expansion into southern Tunisia towards the desert rather than a threat to Roman rule. An exception was the wide-ranging insurrection led in AD 17 by Tacfarinas, an auxiliary soldier in the Roman army who took to brigandage in protest at the imposition of tax and Roman military recruiting. He was captured and killed only in AD 24, despite three defeats in separate pitched battles.[5] One of the tactics used to crush Tacfarinas was the erection of permanent military fortifications at strategic points, to separate him from his base. Roman control of the land was further extended by the cadastration of southern Tunisia (dividing the land into large blocks for tax assessment), which was completed by AD 29/30, according to surviving inscriptions on the

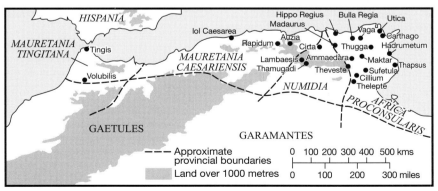

Map 22 Africa

boundary markers.[6] As well as raising taxes, the intention was to limit the customary freedom of movement of the southern tribes. The province was governed by a proconsul based in Carthage, which had been refounded by Augustus as a Roman *colonia*. During the Julio-Claudian period Carthage became a splendid city, controlling a huge territory, which incorporated both Italian settlers and native villages.

In AD 37 command of the legion was transferred by Gaius to a *legatus Augusti*; the original decision was probably *ad hoc*, but the arrangement became permanent. Since the legate's headquarters, originally in Ammaedara, moved under Vespasian further west to Theveste and under Trajan still further west to Lambaesis, he took effective control of that region as well as the sparsely inhabited desert which bordered on Tripolitania.

MAURETANIA

Juba II was compensated for the loss of Numidia in 25 BC by the grant of a huge kingdom, consisting of Mauretania with the addition of parts of Gaetulia, the region to the south. He was faced by chronic opposition from nomadic tribes, who resented his opposition to traditional, seasonal movements, and evidently felt no loyalty to a native ruler wielding power on such an untraditional scale. Patently dependent on Rome for his power, he was naturally loyal, encouraging the spread of Roman law and of Greek art, of which he was a notable patron. One of his two capital cities, Iol Caesarea (modern Cherchel), was a showplace of urban architecture. In *c.* AD 6 he required the help of Roman forces to suppress a rebellion by the Gaetuli (a blanket term used by the Romans to cover a number of southern tribes). In turn he contributed to the war against Tacfarinas in Africa Proconsularis. His diplomatic tact was rewarded on his death in AD 23 by the transfer of the kingdom to his son Ptolemy. The latter was executed in Rome in AD 40 by Gaius, resulting in disturbances in Mauretania. The region was pacified by Suetonius Paulinus (AD 41–42), and by Hosidius Geta. Suetonius Paulinus' campaign report, as recounted by the elder Pliny (*Natural History* 5.1.14–15), contains a vivid description of the area:

> Suetonius Paulinus, who was consul in our own times, was the first Roman commander who actually crossed the Atlas range and advanced a distance of many miles beyond it. His report as to its remarkable altitude agrees with that of all the other authorities, but he also states that the regions at the base of the range are filled with dense and lofty forests of trees of an unknown kind. ... The summit (the report continued) is covered with deep snow-drifts even in summer. Ten days' march brought him to this point and beyond it to the river called the Ger, across deserts covered with black dust occasionally broken by projections of rock that looked as if they had been burnt, a region rendered uninhabitable by its heat, although it was winter when he explored it. He states that the neighbouring forests swarm with every kind of elephant and snake, and are inhabited by a tribe called the Canarii, owing to the fact that they have their diet in common with the canine race and share with it the flesh of wild animals.

In AD 44 the region was turned into two provinces, Mauretania Tingitana and Mauretania Caesariensis, ruled by imperial procurators with capitals at Tingis (modern Tangiers) in the west and Caesarea in the east; only very occasionally was a senatorial governor appointed. In general the following years seem to have been marked by peace, apart from small-scale insurrection on the desert frontier.

EFFECTS OF ROMAN RULE

This was more or less the end of large-scale Roman military activity in Africa before the third century. Under Vespasian the southern parts of Numidia in the Aurès mountains were encircled by a series of forts and roads. The system was characteristically given a clearer physical expression by Hadrian, under whose rule the *fossatum Africae*, consisting of curious discontinuous stretches of ditch and wall, was built in various places, presumably to control nomadic movements in the mountains. In Mauretania Caesariensis the auxiliary forts between Auzia and Rapidum were kept quite far north. There was no attempt to build a military land route to the west; troops and supplies had to go by sea. In Tingitana in the extreme west the auxiliary units were stationed inside the province. External pressures by neighbouring tribes like the Baquatae were dealt with by diplomatic agreements.

The main effect on the northern parts of Africa of Roman control was extensive urbanization.[7] Partly this was due to the arrival in Africa Proconsularis of many immigrants from Italy under Caesar and Augustus. Some were settled in *coloniae*, but many settled privately, buying up land in the north for intensive cereal agriculture and in the mountainous southern areas for olive production (although this happened more after AD 100). In Mauretania a number of colonies were founded by Claudius, some of veteran soldiers, some local communities granted the title of *colonia*. Increased agricultural productivity was further encouraged by the control and taxation of traditional pastoral movements by natives in the southern parts of the province.

From the time of Augustus, the Roman state granted the status of *municipium*, and with it local administrative powers, to hundreds of small indigenous communities in Africa Proconsularis.[8] There was no need to create urban communities, simply to organize existing villages into manageable administrative units. Many of these native towns, such as Lepcis Magna, a mixed community of Phoenicians and native Libyans on the Mediterranean coast, developed into full-blown Roman cities. Lepcis gained from Trajan the status of a Roman *colonia*, and seems to have been lavishly appointed, although the most impressive buildings still preserved were the gift in the early third century of the emperor Septimius Severus, who was a native of the place.[9] By the end of the second century a dense urban life had been created, consisting of the network of Roman *coloniae* of Italian immigrants, of transformed

Phoenician towns like Lepcis Magna and Hadrumetum, of Numidian royal settlements such as Thugga, with its distinctive Roman architecture but with Punic titles for its magistrates, and of colonies of settled veterans such as Thamugadi (modern Timgad), founded in AD 100 on an extraordinarily regular grid plan. Carthage was the largest city in the western Mediterranean region after Rome, flourishing particularly as the entrepôt for the export to Italy of goods such as oil, grain, wine, African Red Slip ware (lamps, for example), the fish sauce *garum*, and even wild beasts.

The wealth of these communities derived mainly from local agriculture and the availability of a huge market for grain and oil in the city of Rome and elsewhere in the empire. Such goods could quickly be transferred by sea a short distance across the Mediterranean. Production was also presumably aided by investment from outside, which helped to open up the olive-growing areas in the south; olive cultivation had already been well developed by the Carthaginians, and the treatise of the Carthaginian Mago on estate management was highly regarded in Rome in the first century AD, but the availability of land after expansion by Augustus and Tiberius greatly increased production. Economic growth was heavily dependent on the careful use of Africa's scant water resources.[10] In Tripolitania, for instance, access to overseas markets stimulated large-scale olive production, which was only made possible by using effective indigenous water-management techniques.[11]

Much land in Tunisia was owned by the emperors, particularly in the fertile valleys in the north. The administration of such *saltus* (imperial estates) by procurators, who acted through *conductores* (tenants) responsible for each estate, is illuminated by a number of surviving inscriptions of the early second century AD.[12] Other estates were similarly administered on behalf of absentee landlords in Italy. The elder Pliny (*Natural History* 18.7.35) asserted that half of Africa was controlled by six great landowners until they were executed by Nero; the large imperial estates of central Tunisia were presumably the product of the confiscations. Ultimately ownership may not have been all that important for the prosperity of the region. There is no evidence of extensive use of slaves, and farms presumably went on being worked by free peasants; it might matter little to them if their landlords sported Roman names. Whether as owners or tenants, many provincials evidently prospered. Already under Vespasian two consuls from Cirta are recorded, and in the second century a good number of the African élite entered the senate in Rome. The rich left a record of their achievements in a vast number of stone inscriptions. A Latin inscription of AD 112/17 on a marble panel from Sabratha proudly records the evergetism of one affluent family:[13]

> To Gaius Flavius Pudens, son of Quintus, of the Papirian tribe, *flamen* of Liber Pater, *duumvir, flamen perpetuus*, whose father Flavius Tullus after many acts of generosity by which he embellished his native town brought in an aqueduct at his own expense and also built twelve fountains and adorned them with marble veneer and statues, and moreover promised and paid to the town 200,000 sesterces for the

upkeep of the same aqueduct; because Pudens himself, on top of the manifold munificence which he bestowed on his fellow citizens, was also the first in his town to put on a most splendid spectacle of a gladiatorial show lasting five days, the town council of Sabratha by popular request voted to put up a four-horse chariot statue to him at public expense. Flavius Pudens, content with the honour [alone], erected it with his own money.

(*AE* 1925, no. 103)

Urbanization in Mauretania was much less widespread, although this region too knew prosperity from the cultivation of olives from the second century.[14] Juba II turned his two capitals, Iol in the east (refounded by him as Caesarea) and Volubilis in the west, into fine cities. Two inscriptions commemorate Claudius' granting of the Roman citizenship to the people of Volubilis in AD 44, after receiving help to crush a revolt: dating to after AD 54, and inscribed on a stone found on the steps of a temple, the later and more detailed account reads:

To Marcus Valerius Severus, son of Bostar, of the tribe Galeria, aedile, *sufes, duumvir*, first flamen in his municipality, prefect of auxiliaries against Aedemon, who has been subdued by war; this man the ruling body of the municipality of Volubilis honoured for his services to the state and an embassy successfully accomplished, in which he sought and gained from the divine Claudius for his people Roman citizenship and *conubium* with foreign women, immunity for ten years, local settlers and the property of citizens killed in war who have no surviving heirs. Fabia Bira, daughter of Izelta, his wife, to her most indulgent husband, having held office, returned the cost and made the dedication at her own expense.

(Smallwood, *Gaius–Nero* no. 407b; Braund no. 680b)

Mauretania contained a few *coloniae*, founded in the first century and settled by Italian immigrants. But the Atlas Mountains in the south remained quite untamed.

For the cultural history of Africa Proconsularis, there is much evidence in the survival of urban architecture and the products of African literature in the second century. The best known second-century African writers are the orators Fronto and Apuleius. Fronto was born *c.* AD 100 in Cirta, Numidia, but his career took place mostly in the city of Rome. Apuleius, born of wealthy parents in *c.* AD 123 in Madaurus, was a much celebrated figure in Africa in his time, ending his career at Carthage as chief priest of the province. One of his works in particular, the *Apology* or *Pro se de Magia*, provides a fine insight into African municipal life. Apuleius had married a rich widow in the town of Oea (modern Tripoli) in *c.* AD 155, but was accused by the brother of her former fiancé of having won her love by magic. Apuleius was put on trial at Sabratha before the proconsul Claudius Maximus. He was acquitted, but his speech for his defence reveals much about the pretensions and superstitions of such small-town life.[15]

Evidence of this type applies mainly, of course, to the lives of the rich urban élite. Debate continues over the attitudes of most natives in Africa

Proconsularis to Roman rule.[16] Despite the spread of municipal status, there remained many towns and villages in northern Tunisia unrecognized by the state as independent administrative entities; in many of these, the chief magistrates were still called *sufetim*, on the Punic model, long into the imperial period. The south of Tunisia, the area conquered by Augustus and Tiberius, and placed under the rule of a prefect, was later to foster a number of Romanized towns, such as Sufetula, Thelepte and Cillium. But in the mid-first century AD, Pomponius Mela (*Geography* 1.42) still wrote about Africa as a land of nomadic wanderers and country peoples living in huts under their own leaders. Roman troops, both legionary and auxiliary, kept themselves strikingly separate from the surrounding population, in contrast to the social mingling in some other provinces. It may, however, be over-simple to take this as evidence that such troops acted as the police force of a suppressive state. Many soldiers originated from families within Africa itself, and a separate lifestyle may have owed more to the need to preserve military discipline in conditions of inactivity than the hostility of the local population.

Evidence of considerable Romanization in Africa is the widespread use of Latin on inscriptions; the epigraphic evidence from the region is exceptional, due both to the existing Punic epigraphic habit and to military bureaucracy.[17] However, Punic also continued as a spoken language even in great cities like Lepcis Magna, and it was used in the countryside in some places down to the fourth century AD at least, when St Augustine still knew of Punic-speaking villages (for instance, *Letters* 66.2). Libyan funerary inscriptions from eastern Algeria include names of some Roman citizens who, despite their evident success in the Roman world, yet preferred their final commemoration to be within a Libyan-speaking community. Family tombs erected at Ghirza in the pre-desert region of northern Libya in the fourth century AD illustrate the continuing power of local traditions, despite the impact of the Roman occupation of the coastal areas. They contain little iconography which is demonstrably Roman, although Latin is used in the accompanying inscriptions. The tombs themselves depict chieftains receiving traditional emblems of office, a remarkable demonstration of the continuing relevance of native status and power in the region. Religious continuities with pre-Roman times are also well attested. There is much evidence from Roman Carthage for the cult of the local Cereres (corn gods) and for worship of the Punic moon-goddess Tanit, revered under the name Dea Caelestis, and Baal-Hammon, worshipped as Saturnus; in the early third century the Christian Tertullian (*Apology* 9.2–3) even claimed that child sacrifice had continued as a public element in the cult of Saturnus in Roman times.[18]

Part V

HUMANS AND GODS

29

RELIGION

Much of what we would call religion was so integrated into ancient social and cultural behaviour that its separate treatment here may seem an anachronistic reflection of the role of religion as a distinct sphere in western societies since the Enlightenment. Much has indeed already been said about religious practices in Part IV of this book. Nonetheless, Romans were capable of talking about *religio* and *pietas* as important qualities and even (if rarely) of discussing the correct relationship between the human and the divine in abstract terms, and they would have recognized the value of a separate discussion of this aspect of their public and private lives, even if they themselves lacked suitable terminology for its description – thus, for instance, 'paganism' is not a word to be found, in any language, in any ancient writings of the Early Roman Empire, for it was a term used and defined only by Christians of later periods, as a way of describing the religious beliefs and practices of the rest of humanity apart from themselves and the Jews. In the first centuries AD pagans themselves had no need of a term to describe the religious beliefs they had in common. For most of them, apart from the minute fraction confronted by Judaism or Christianity or assailed by philosophical doubts, their religious life was as obvious and unchallengeable as the other most basic elements of their society.[1] Atheism was almost unknown.[2]

TRADITIONAL CULT IN THE EARLY EMPIRE

In the Early Roman Empire it was indeed possible to make religious choices, but, in contrast to European societies since the Reformation, and the Roman Empire after the conversion of the emperor Constantine to Christianity in AD 312, the Early Empire was not a time of intense religious ferment and change, and to the vast majority of ordinary people the idea of making a choice never occurred.

Lack of challenge was one factor which discouraged the production of any sizeable theological literature to explain and justify pagan beliefs; another factor was the relative unimportance of written texts in pagan liturgy, compared to their importance in Judaism and Christianity. The few literary sources which do survive have to be used with care. In the Late Republic Varro wrote extensively on 'divine matters', in his *Human and Divine Antiquities* and *On Religion*, but his main interests lay in the antiquarian origins of particular cult practices. Cicero's philosophical musings on the nature of the gods may reflect more general speculations at least among the philosophically aware, as may the moralizing of Plutarch in the late first century in his brief treatises on superstition, on oracles, and on specific cults.[3] But for a description of religious emotion and reverence parallel to those found in some abundance in contemporary Jewish or Christian literature, scholars have to rely on the fictional depiction of Lucius, the hero of Apuleius' novel *The Golden Ass*, whose devotion to Isis is described with such intensity in the last book that it probably reflects the religious experience of Apuleius himself.[4] Here is the impassioned prayer Lucius prays when Isis orders him to return home to Rome from Corinth, where he has just been initiated into her rites:

> I fell prostrate at the goddess's feet, and washed them with my tears as I prayed to her in a voice choked with sobs which convulsed my speech: 'Holy and perpetual Saviour of Mankind, you whose bountiful grace nourishes the whole world; whose heart turns towards all those in sorrow and tribulation as a mother's to her children; you who take no rest by night, no rest by day, but are always at hand to succour the distressed by land and sea, dispersing the gales that beat upon them. ... The gods above adore you, the gods below do homage to you, you set the earth spinning, you give light to the sun, you govern the universe, you trample down the powers of Hell. ... My eloquence is unequal to praising you according to your deserts; my wealth to providing you with sacrificial victims; my voice to uttering all that I think of your majesty – no, not even if I had a thousand tongues in a thousand mouths and could speak for ever. Nonetheless, poor as I am, I will do as much as I can in my devotion to you; I will keep your divine countenance always before my eyes and the secret knowledge of your divinity locked deep in my heart.'
>
> (*The Golden Ass* 11.24.6–25.6)

Such scattered items of evidence do not in themselves provide any very clear picture of the multifarious religious practices and beliefs in the Roman world. Hence most of the picture has to be built up from a mass of archaeological and epigraphic evidence, which together reveal the popularity of different cults in different places and something of their rituals.[5] The iconography of cult, sensitively interpreted, and prayers recorded on some inscriptions, may also give some clue to the beliefs and hopes of worshippers, although it is very difficult to avoid importing Judaeo-Christian presuppositions about the nature of religion into such interpretations. Informative too are the hymns in praise of particular divinities which survive in manuscript and on stone, in poetry and in prose, from almost all over the empire. But the lack of a continuous tradition for any of these cults to modern times, and the scarcity of confessional texts and theological tracts, require students of ancient religions other than Judaism and Christianity to employ much imaginative empathy if all these cults are not either to seem an empty collection of meaningless rituals, which was how Jewish and Christian authors polemically portrayed them, or to be described in Judaeo-Christian terms, and thus with the use of inappropriate categories. Much can be learned by comparison with aspects of the operation of religion in more recent and contemporary societies, such as the relationship in the eyes of Hindu worshippers between an image of a deity in a shrine and broader religious discourse about the role of the divine in the cosmos.

RELIGIOUS BELIEFS AND PRACTICES

Ancient religious practice and theology allowed for almost infinite variety in detail, but central underlying beliefs were common to all. Most people in the ancient world believed that it was obvious that they were surrounded by innumerable supernatural beings who affected their lives. Much as most modern people will take on trust the existence of germs which, though they cannot themselves be sensed, are accepted as the cause of illnesses, so ancient peoples recognized the presence of divinities by their actions. Such actions could range from care over the most fundamental aspects of human life, like ensuring the regular procession of the agricultural seasons, to the most mundane and trivial, like causing a branch to drop unexpectedly off a tree. Some divinities were immensely powerful (although it was logically impossible for any one to be omnipotent in a polytheistic world), but others were assumed to be comparatively weak.

What above all distinguished deities from man was the immortality of the former. Some divinities might not always have existed in the past (like deified humans, such as Asclepius), but none could cease to exist in the future, though they might change their nature. Thus Romans recognized that more gods existed than they could ever worship, not least because each nation was known to have its own distinctive gods. The relation between many of these divinities was unknown – perhaps, as in human society, people assumed that most gods did not come across each other. However, there were attempts to explain the relationships of those gods whose worship coincided in a particular society. Hence the elaboration of myths about a divine society in which hierarchies of heroes, nymphs and others could be postulated,[6] and gods with similar attributes could be alleged to be different aspects of a single divinity.

The wide perspective of pagans in the Roman Empire ensured that they could know that religious syncretism and genealogical myths about the Olympians varied greatly both in literary sources and in worship, but they seem to have been quite unmoved by inconsistencies in such matters. Aelius Aristides in the second century implied in his speeches in praise of Serapis, Asclepius and Zeus that each of them was all-powerful, admittedly in separate orations. Monotheistic ideas were common both in the language of worship and among philosophers, regardless of polytheistic practices.[4] The notion that the gods care greatly that humans should achieve accurate conceptions about them is a distinctively Christian idea which non-Christians did not share. For most Romans, the gods wanted to be worshipped and respected, not written about.

What did such Romans think would happen if the gods were not properly worshipped? In theological terms, this question is not easy to answer, since polytheists took it for granted that some gods existed whom humans had not yet recognized. Human misfortune, particularly when unexpected, could always be explained as the result of divine anger, but, according to Plutarch, although the gods could sometimes behave arbitrarily, only the superstitious thought that they were constantly antagonistic to men:

> Superstition, as the very name (dread of deities) indicates, is an emotional idea and an assumption productive of a fear which utterly humbles and crushes a man, for he thinks that there are gods, but that they are the cause of pain and injury. In fact, the atheist, apparently, is unmoved regarding the divinity, whereas the superstitious man is moved as he ought not to be, and his mind is thus perverted.
> (*Superstition* 2)

On the other hand, gods who demanded worship by appearing in dreams or visions or by transmitting their desires through an oracle were ignored only with great danger. In general, it was assumed that the gods, like many children, would always desire as much attention as possible, and that they would punish those who failed to continue rites previously performed, but that they would not usually attack those with whom they had enjoyed no previous relationship, unless instructions to worship had been sent and ignored.

Humans thus worshipped gods to win their favour in all their undertakings. Everyone (except Epicureans, whose preaching that the gods did not care about humans was treated by ordinary people as atheism) assumed that the gods intervened in human affairs. As a curse tablet from Rome shows, people did not hesitate to ask the gods for all sorts of help, regardless of morality:

> I conjure you up, holy beings and holy names; join in aiding this spell, and bind, break, enchant, thwart, strike, overturn, conspire against, destroy, kill, break Eucherius, the charioteer, and all his horse tomorrow in the circus at Rome. May he not leave the barriers well; may he not be quick in the contest; may he not outstrip anyone; may he not make the turns well; may he not win any prizes; ... but may he meet with an accident; may he be bound; may he be broken; may he be dragged along by your power, in the morning and afternoon races. Now! Now! Quickly! Quickly!
> (*IGRR*, vol. 1, no. 117; LR 2, p. 534)

In very general terms, it was thought that the gods might punish evil-doing. However, there was no notion of a divine sanction for any one system of morality. The gods' main care was for themselves: they wanted worship.

The salvation which the gods could bring was foremost a firmly this-world matter. Beliefs about the afterlife varied greatly, from doctrines about resurrection and the transmigration of souls (among Pythagoreans) to the defiant tombstones with the Latin abbreviation *NFFNSNC* (*non fui, fui, non sum, non curo*: 'I was not, I was, I am not, I care not'). It would be quite wrong to imagine many people in the Roman world preoccupied with the world to come or weighed down by guilt for sin. For most, these Judaeo-Christian concerns had to be imported.

Almost every part of ordinary life could be protected by appropriate attention to some divinity. The gods might answer prayer anywhere, but for most of them particular places (shrines, temples or some special locality to which they belonged) were reckoned most effective for making contact. In many respects most religions of the Roman empire operated as expressions of place. Rites, myths and legends clustered around specific localities, which might be marked by temples, built to house and honour the god, but more often by altars, or piles of stone, or simply heaps of votive offerings no longer visible in the archaeological record. Of religious spaces, the most significant in daily worship was the site of domestic cult in the home. Offerings of grain, liquids and incense to the protective deities (in Rome, especially the *lares* and *penates*) will have seemed to many the most important expression of the *pietas* which ensured prosperity for them and their families. Such local rituals naturally varied in detail from one place to another, and it was common for miniature figurines to be kept in a household niche of a god worshipped in grander style by the community as a whole in a nearby temple.[8]

Individuals could show respect in words or by libations of liquids or offerings of food.[9] The sacrifice of animals and birds was reserved for important occasions of communal worship, or for special family or individual rites of passage, or for the fulfilment of a vow; an instance of the latter is commemorated in an inscription, probably of the early imperial period, found on the road to Ostia outside Rome:

> Felix Asinianus, public slave of the *pontifices*, discharged his vow of a white heifer, gladly and sincerely to rustic Bona Dea Felicula for the restoration of his eyesight. The doctors had abandoned him after ten months, but he was cured by favour of the Mistress and her remedies. All [i.e. the commemorative monument] restored under the care of Cannia Fortunata.
> (*CIL* VI, no. 68; BNP 9.5b)

Much more common were the smaller gestures: Jewish rabbis believed that any gentile left alone with an opened jar of wine might immediately offer a libation from it, thereby rendering the wine unusable by a pious Jew:

> If an Israelite was eating with a gentile at a table, and he put flagons [of wine] on the table and flagons [of wine] on the side-table, and left the other there and went out, what is on the table is forbidden and what is on the side-table is permitted; and if he

had said to him, 'Mix your cup and drink', that which is on the side-table is forbidden also.

(*Mishnah, Avodah Zara* 5.5)

This image of the non-Jew as prone to compulsive libation is probably something of a caricature, and indicative of the ability of adherents of one ancient religion to fail to try to understand another, but numerous reliefs showing libation in practice confirm the importance of the rite in many cults.

In general, the gods were pictured in Graeco-Roman religion in anthropomorphic form; Egyptian cults were exceptional in the use of animal shapes, Syrian cults in the use of special stones which were not representational. Individuals might possess little idols to represent the divinity whose help they requested, and would place offerings in front of the statues (see Figure 33). Philosophers at least were well aware that the statues were not themselves divine, but represented divinities who existed elsewhere, but the distinction was not always remembered. Thus a temple functioned as the special house of a god, and the fact was symbolized by the installation of a cult-statue or other object in the interior, usually larger than life size. In pagan eyes one of the oddest aspects of Judaism was the lack of a cult-statue in the Jerusalem temple:

> The Jews with the mind alone conceive a single deity and think those impious who with perishable materials fashion images of the gods in the likeness of men; that supreme being is eternal, inimitable and imperishable. Therefore they allow no statues in their cities, much less in their temples.
>
> (Tacitus, *Histories* 5.5)

Figure 33 Statuette of a Lar (household god), said to be from Rome. The image stands only c. 18 cm high. Photo courtesy of the Ashmolean Museum, Oxford.

Worship at communal shrines followed a fairly standard pattern, with numerous minor local variations. Often a procession to the cult centre culminated in an animal sacrifice, perhaps with hymns and prayers, and the distribution of part of the meat to the onlookers. Sacrifice was a skilled business, not just in the slaughtering and butchery (which in the city of Rome at least was usually carried out by experts), but in the correct ordering of the ritual, which was essential to ensure divine acceptance.

As can be seen from the remarks of Pausanias about the different practices in specific cults in Greece, the preservation of local traditions was deemed vital to ensure the good will of the gods. Isis, who elsewhere was believed to accept freely worship by all, was said to treat as sacrilegious any intruder into her shrine at Tithorea in Phocis to whom she had not previously appeared in a dream (Pausanias, *Description of Greece* 10.32.13). The many-breasted Artemis of Ephesus was known throughout Greece according to Pausanias (4.31.8), but it was in Ephesus itself that the silversmiths who made figurines in her honour were said to have led the campaign against the apostles Paul and Barnabas whose preaching against idolatry would, if it succeeded, put their livelihood at risk (Acts 19.24-7; see below, Chapter 31).[10] The elder Pliny emphasized the need for the right words of supplication to accompany the sacrifice:

> To slaughter a sacrificial victim without a prayer does not seem to be of any avail or to constitute due consultation of the gods. In addition, there is one formula for obtaining favourable omens, another for averting evil, another for praising the gods. And we see that the highest magistrates employ definite formulas in their prayers, that not a single word may be omitted or said out of its proper place, that someone dictates from writing [the formula to the magistrate], and another is assigned as watcher to listen carefully, and a third is placed in charge of ordering that ceremonial silence be maintained, while a flautist plays to prevent any other words from being heard. There are memorable instances on record of the times when unlucky portents impeded and spoiled [the ceremony], and when there was a mistake in the prayer; then suddenly the head of the liver, or the heart, has disappeared from the entrails, or these have been doubled, while the victim was standing.
> (*Natural History* 28.3.10–11)

In the city of Rome the priests for the most important cults were generally elected from within a distinct group of citizens, but elsewhere in the empire (most strikingly in Egypt and Syria) the office might be hereditary and priests might form a separate caste.[11] Both the roles of religious leaders and the terminology used to refer to them might vary considerably. Some, like many Roman priests, were public figures whose task was primarily to offer prayers to the gods on behalf of the community; others, like Egyptian priests, brought the gods' teachings to the worshippers. The expertise required for the former function might be minimal – a senator elected to a priesthood was not sent off for training but relied on specialist advisers and aides. By contrast, freelance experts who specialized in divination and oracular responses relied entirely on their own skills and knowledge. The oracle established by Alexander of Abonuteichos in Paphlagonia by the Black Sea in the mid second century was mocked by the satirist Lucian (Lucian, *Alexander of Abonuteichos*, 14–15), but inscriptions attest to enthusiastic reverence for the oracle long after Lucian's attack on its integrity.[12]

When ancient writers referred to religious rites, they did so in terms of human relations to the gods, but the same rituals also fulfilled an obvious social function. Within the family everyone worshipped together in the house; religious differences between husband and wife were not impossible, but they created great strains. On the social level, public cult provided the main focus of communal identity, particularly in civic communities whose political function was now limited by the great authority of the imperial state. Citizens brought glory to themselves and their followers by erecting temples to house the gods and by funding festivals and games to please the deities; the gods brought the citizens together in a glow of proud social unity, as (people believed) they had always done. Thus religion helped to sanction the social order; only a cynical observer, able to take a stance at least somewhat outside the society, was likely to view religion as a means for an élite to maintain control. Such a man was Polybius, writing about the city of Rome in the mid-second century BC:

> I believe it is … superstition which maintains the cohesion of the Roman state. These matters are clothed in such pomp and introduced to such an extent into their public and private life that nothing could exceed it, a fact which will surprise many. My own opinion at least is that they have adopted this course for the sake of the common people. It is a course which perhaps would not have been necessary had it been possible to form a state composed of wise men, but as every multitude is fickle, full of lawless desires, unreasoned passion, and violent anger, the multitude must be held in by invisible terrors and suchlike pageantry.
>
> (*Histories* 6.56.7–11)

The younger Pliny, who expressed his delight at nomination to a priesthood in the city of Rome (*Letters* 4.8), and the immensely serious Arval Brethren who solemnly recorded the care of the gods for the emperor and the state in a detailed calendar, may have benefited from the religion of the state, but they did so as participants, not manipulators.[13] In the Early Empire, numbers of *iurisconsulti* (lawyers) and antiquarians were sufficiently involved to write learned works on religious law, codifying the performance of the state rites of Rome.

Traditional religion as thus far described had flourished in the world which was later to become the Roman Empire long before that Empire began. Undoubtedly in the two centuries and more of the early principate there were developments both of attitude and practice, and it is a fault of much scholarship that ancient cults are sometimes portrayed as a stable religious system, so that evidence from early Greek history may be mixed with that from the late Roman period. On the other hand, worshippers were indeed instinctively conservative, because ritual and myths were believed to be sanctified by antiquity.[14] In the Greek world the ancient myths reflected in the Homeric poems and Classical drama of the fifth century BC still gave structure to beliefs about the Olympian gods; in the city of Rome, people took pride in the antiquity of state cults like the worship of Vesta. The Vestal Virgins were the priestesses who presided over the cult of Vesta; in the second century AD, writers such as Plutarch (*Life of Numa*) and Aulus Gellius were interested in tracing the ancient customs surrounding their priesthoods:[15]

> As to the custom and ritual of taking a Virgin, we do not possess ancient writings, except that the first one was taken by Numa [715–673 BC] when he was king. ... The word 'taken' is used, so it seems, because the *pontifex maximus* literally takes her by the hand and leads her away from the parent in whose power she is, as though she had been captured in war. In his first book, Fabius Pictor gives the words the *pontifex maximus* must say when he takes a Virgin. They are: 'I take you, Amata, to be a Vestal priestess, who will carry out sacred rites which it is the law for a Vestal priestess to perform on behalf of the Roman people, on the same terms as her who was a Vestal on the best terms'. ... The *pontifex maximus* calls the girl 'Amata' when he takes her because that is the traditional name of the first Vestal Virgin to be taken.
>
> (Aulus Gellius, *Attic Nights* 1.12)

When Christian apologists like Justin and Tatian began in the second century to ridicule pagan beliefs, it was the pantheon of classical myths that they chose to attack.[16] To quote an extract from such an argument of Justin's:

> Secondly, we alone in the world used to worship Dionysos the son of Semele and Apollo the son of Latona (who in their affairs with males did unmentionably shameful things) and Persephone and Aphrodite (who were driven wild by Adonis, and whose mysteries you celebrate), or Asklepios or any other of those called gods; although we are threatened with death, through Jesus Christ we have come to despise these deities, and have given ourselves to the unbegotten and impassive god. We believe that he was not driven wild by Antiope or other such women nor by Ganymede; that he was not rescued by the hundred-handed giant [Briareus] through the offices of Thetis, nor did he for this reason plan that Achilles the son of Thetis would destroy many Greeks for his concubine Briseis. We pity those who believe these stories and we recognize that demons are responsible for them.
>
> (*First Apology* 25)

Thus most inhabitants of the Roman empire, for most of the period discussed in this book, continued their religious practices and beliefs undisturbed by change. When change did occur, it was often disguised; Augustus claimed to have restored numerous traditional cults, though he might better be thought to have restructured them.[17] The notion first propagated by Christians in antiquity as evidence of the readiness of the world for the advent of the new Christian faith, that traditional cults were on the wane in the high empire, is not well founded. On the contrary, ordinary people continued to show their devotion to the ancestral gods in very practical ways, not least by expenditure on shrines and offerings for their delectation.

Of the new trends to be found in the evidence for religious beliefs in the Early Empire, some may be simply a product of greater epigraphic survival. Thus the names of divinities preserved on many dedications in the provinces reveal a tendency to call local deities by Greek names in Asia Minor and Syria, by Roman names in France and Britain. Two Latin inscriptions from Britain clearly show a local deity being treated like a Roman god, following Roman religious customs:

(1) Pectillus gave to the god Nudens Mars the votive offering which he had promised.
(2) To the god Mars Alator Dum Censorinus, son of Gemellus, willingly and deservedly fulfilled his vow.

(*RIB* nos 307 and 218; BNP no. 2.9b)

Such transfer of names could of course only occur when societies had come into contact; it may well have been common long before the Roman Empire, but be less well known to us because the epigraphic habit was less widespread. So, for instance, a Jewish author in the mid-second century BC described the Jewish God as Zeus (Ps.-Aristeas, *Letter to Philocrates*, 16), but Jewish inscriptions with a similar message are exceptionally rare. More problematic is the assessment of the significance of such names. To describe this tendency as 'syncretism' is too simplistic, because the use of a name does not in itself show that any of the Greek or Roman ideas about the deity were also adopted by the worshippers who used it. Worshippers must have had a fairly clear idea of the recipient of their prayers, but (if we assume that none of these divinities did indeed exist) the precise nature of the god was a construct of the worshippers' minds alone. So, for example, those who set up a Roman-style temple to Sulis Minerva in Aquae Sulis (Bath) at the end of the first century AD may have believed, among various possibilities, that they were honouring the local Celtic goddess Sulis with the accoutrements of a 'modern' cult, or that they were worshipping the Roman goddess Minerva in the way she would expect, or that Sulis and Minerva were two aspects of a single divinity.[18] It is not likely that the buildings and inscriptions can by themselves reveal which of these alternatives is correct, although it is perhaps safe to assume that devotion to the Capitoline triad of gods (Jupiter, Juno and Minerva), evidence for which spreads rapidly through the western provinces in this period, was aimed specifically at the divinities who guarded the Capitol in Rome, since dedications are most common at first in settlements containing Italians, such as Baelo (modern Bolonia) in southern Spain in the first century AD.[19]

A second apparent change is equally difficult to evaluate. In Greece of the fifth century BC the gods (according to contemporary literature) were sometimes believed to act arbitrarily and in frightening fashion. By contrast, numerous inscriptions show that individuals in the Early Empire believed that the gods would first inform humans of their desires and would react badly only if their instruction was ignored. In general, such inscriptions presuppose that the gods act reasonably and fairly in their dealings with humans, that they will appreciate piety and approve of moral behaviour. Two prayers for a priestess from Ephesus in the first century AD, inscribed in verse, request children as a reward for the devout fulfilment of her priestly duties:[20]

(1) Hestia, oldest of the gods, you who watch over the immortal fire, to you Zeus the ruler has given the right to control the eternal flame for the city. You who were born before the other gods, grant to Tullia – since she has fulfilled her term of office without blemish in your temple – grant her children like in all respects to herself, and who think the way she does. Grant her this wish, I pray, because of her unblemished chastity and her wisdom, because she has surpassed in these respects all mortals, both in the past and those who were born in our own time.

(2) O goddess of the excellent and wise city founded by Androclos, Hestia, eternal virgin, and Artemis, you who have the greatest name among the gods, be helpers to Tullia in all respects, because she served as your *prytanis* [chief priestess] eagerly and willingly and generously provided her wealth for every purpose.

Of a third development something rather more definite can be said. During the last centuries BC in both the Hellenistic world and in Italy there began to proliferate groups whose main purpose was the worship of a particular divinity. The paradigm of this tendency in the second century BC were the groups in Italy which worshipped Bacchus, to the irritation of the Roman senate, which severely restricted their activities in 186 BC; the paradigm of such groups in the Early Empire were Christian communities. The proliferation of such groups gave religious choice to those who might find insufficient satisfaction in traditional cults. But it must be emphasized that, except for those who elected to adopt Judaism or Christianity, such new cults were adopted in addition to, rather than in place of, normal worship of family and communal deities, and that there is very little evidence that devotion to any of these new, elective cults formed the main elements in an individual's social identity. To put it crudely, an enthusiast, when challenged to state his country and citizenship, might state roundly, 'I am a Christian' (Eusebius, *Church History* 5.1.20), but no-one would identify himself or herself outside the immediate context of worship as a devotee of Mithras, Isis or Jupiter Dolichenus.[21]

These three cults, among the most popular of the new religions, were all aimed at oriental divinities little known in the western Mediterranean before the imperial period.[22] Their oriental origin had little impact on the form of cult to which they were treated, except in iconography, but it was probably not irrelevant to their popularity; as 'displaced' divinities, no longer attached to specific shrines in their place of origin, they could be treated as more universal in their interests and power. Devotees of Mithras and Jupiter Dolichenus were in large measure soldiers, devotees of Isis tended to come from higher up the social scale and included members of the urban aristocracy. Of the worship of Jupiter Dolichenus almost nothing is known (see Figure 34).[23] Mithraic groups were highly secretive, meeting in underground shrines, with a complex hierarchy of grades through which the initiates (all male) had to pass; information about the sect is derived mostly from hostile Christian authors, but is confirmed by inscriptions and iconography, which reveal sufficient similarities between different Mithraic communities to justify referring to them as members of a single religion.[24] Worship of Isis is known not just from archaeology but from the inside, from the novel of Apuleius.[25] Isiacs also had a strong sense of communal identity, such that Lucius (*The Golden Ass* 11.26–30) could be portrayed in the novel as sent by the devotees in Corinth to their brethren in Rome (where, however, he had to be reinstated into Isis worship). But not all who worshipped Isis were devotees; a temple in her honour was built in Rome by Augustus, and the less committed could pray to her there as part of the panoply of state gods.

Figure 34 Fragment of a large bronze triangular plaque depicting Jupiter Dolichenus and Juno. Jupiter Dolichenus wears military uniform and a Phrygian cap, carries a thunderbolt and stands on a bull. Juno faces him across the altar. Photo courtesy of the Ashmolean Museum, Oxford.

It is difficult to gauge the extent of the popularity of these elective cults. The evidence may be biased by the hazards of survival. Mithraic shrines are more easily identified in all areas of the empire than shrines of other cults, because of their distinctive design; and the soldiers of the northern provinces, who set up many of the extant Mithraic inscriptions, also set up a disproportionate number of the surviving inscriptions of all kinds from these areas, so that they may tell us little about the religious preferences of the civilian population. Nonetheless, there is good evidence of the wide geographic spread of such religions. Mithraism is attested in Dura-Europus on the Euphrates and on Hadrian's Wall in Britain; there is evidence that Isis was worshipped in all the countries bordering the Mediterranean.

There is little reason to suppose that these new cults were spread by missionary activity.[26] According to Apuleius (*The Golden Ass* 11.21), Isis offered 'salvation' to initiates, by which he may have meant a prolongation of life or even some (temporary?) existence after death. The benefits of initiation into Mithraism are less clear, but the close feeling of community provided by membership of the all-male group may have been particularly attractive to those who, like soldiers and merchants, far from home, might feel themselves to be without sufficient social support, and the progression through the seven grades from 'raven' to 'father' may have given a sense of purpose and fulfilment. Tertullian describes the third Mithraic grade of 'soldier' when he compares it with the soldier for Christ, in his third-century treatise about the martyrdom of a Christian soldier who refused to wear the usual laurel wreath crown when the troops received a donation from the emperor:

> You should be ashamed now, fellow soldiers [of the soldier of Christ], not of being judged by him but by some soldier of Mithras. When he is initiated in the cave, the real camp of darkness, he is offered a crown on a sword point, a sort of mockery of martyrdom, which is then fitted on his head, but he is instructed to remove it with his hand from his head and to transfer it, if possible, to his shoulders, saying that Mithras is his crown. And from then on he never wears a crown, and has that as a mark of his initiation, whenever he is put to the test at the oath-taking, and is immediately recognized as a soldier of Mithras, if he rejects the crown, if he says that in his god he has his crown. Let us recognize the devices of the devil, especially when he creates imitations of divine rites so as to shame and condemn us with the faith of his followers.
>
> (*On the Soldier's Crown* 15.3–4)

Whatever the benefits of following Mithras were, others in time would have learned of them and requested membership. The geographical spread of these religions is best explained by the travels of their members, who set up new centres in the places where they were sent by their military or commercial occupations.

THE IMPERIAL CULT

Compared to the fragmentary evidence for adoption of such new cults by an unknown proportion of the inhabitants of the empire, the evidence for observance of the imperial cult is overwhelming.[27] In almost every urban centre of the empire could be found some sort of ruler worship, even if in Italy distinctions tended to be made, at least by senators, between honours paid to the emperor as ruler and those which recognized his absolute divinity: cult paid to the emperor's *genius* (guardian spirit) were seen as more appropriate for freedmen than the upper classes, and it is notable that more formal worship of individual deceased emperors as *divi* tended to fade over time. Worship of the emperors was the only religion in the Roman Empire for which there existed province-wide organization and direct encouragement by a central administration – in this case, the emperors themselves. By definition, it did not exist before the imperial period, although many of its elements were traditional. By AD 180 it formed a major part of the religious activity of many in the Roman world.

In Roman society in previous generations, worship of living humans had always specified the precise element of the person concerned in which a divine spark was considered to adhere. Thus the *genius* or rational soul of Gaius Marius, the great general whose skill had saved Rome from the Cimbri and Teutones in the last years of the second century BC, was plied with libations by the people at the height of the invasion. Augustus encouraged similar worship to his own *genius* in Rome, Italy and the western provinces; in formal state prayers, his *genius* was included among the divinities. Characteristically, he wanted such worship to be more permanent. In Italy boards of priests (*seviri*, that is to say, of six men) were appointed, selected from the freedmen to organize his cult in each of the districts (*vici*) of Rome and the municipalities of Italy.

In some eastern provinces, by contrast, ruler cult was more haphazard because more spontaneous. Organized worship of rulers had been common in Hellenistic states since Alexander the Great demanded that he be treated as divine. Such worship took quite widely differing forms, from the worship of a king's *daimon* (close to the Roman notion of a *genius*) to the great paraphernalia of Egyptian state cult, which was inherited by the Ptolemies from the Pharoahs. Roman generals active in the East had grown accustomed to the language of divine honours and to accepting games and temples in honour of them and of *Roma* with grace. Cult was part of the language of flattery of ruler by subject, as Antonius well knew when he identified himself publicly with Dionysus. For the leading citizens of Greece, Asia Minor and Syria, such cult must rarely have seemed more obviously appropriate than after Actium, when so many had been so firmly allied to the losing side, and wished now to demonstrate allegiance to the victor, whose power completely eclipsed that of all who had preceded him (except perhaps the god Alexander, whose image

Octavian's effigy suspiciously resembled in the eastern coinage of the time). A rash of temples in honour of Augustus, or more often Augustus and *Roma*, were dedicated in the years immediately after 31 BC. If the idea was ancient, the zeal of the participants and the extent of their efforts were new. One crucial factor was the evident pleasure of the emperor in their efforts. They must have known that he was pleased with their desire to worship him – and those provincials slow to spend money and effort in the same direction would be stung into action by the need to compete for imperial favour. Cassius Dio (*History of Rome* 51.20.6–8) noted the precedent set by Augustus in encouraging worship of Rome and its emperors:

> [Octavian] granted permission that precincts sacred to Rome and to his father Caesar, whom he named the hero Julius, should be dedicated in Ephesus and in Nicaea. These had become the most important cities in the province of Asia and in Bithynia, respectively, at that time. He laid it down that the Romans who lived in those places should honour the two divinities. At the same time he allowed the aliens, under the name of Hellenes, to consecrate precincts to himself, those of the Asiatic province in Pergamum and those of the Bithynians in Nicomedia. This practice began with Octavian and it has been carried on under other emperors, not only with regard to the Hellenic peoples, but to all others in so far as they acknowledge Roman rule. In Rome itself and in Italy generally, no emperor, however greatly venerated he may have been, has so far ventured to do this. However, even there other divine honours are conferred after their death upon those emperors who have ruled virtuously, and in fact shrines are built in their honour.

The imperial policy in the East of shaping local enthusiasm was supplemented in the western part of the empire, where no such traditions existed, by a deliberate policy of installing cult. In 12 BC, Drusus, Augustus' stepson, founded an altar to *Roma* and Augustus at Lugdunum (Lyons); the fact was celebrated on coins. Later another similar altar was set up for the German tribe of the Ubii at Cologne, and other altars were established elsewhere in the northern provinces. Emperors from Augustus onwards wished to be worshipped.

It will be evident that, like 'paganism', the 'imperial cult' is a scholarly construct which does not directly reflect any term in the ancient evidence. In its most formal and public (and therefore archaeologically and historically most visible) manifestation, the cult consisted of sacrifices conducted by a special priesthood and addressed to dead emperors whose statues were housed in temples like those of other gods. The most impressive form of cult was held at the altars where the different communities of a particular province were expected to worship together, as at Lugdunum (Lyons), Oppidum Ubiorum (Cologne) and Ancyra (Ankara). The high priest of the imperial cult was a leading aristocrat of the province, expected to display his munificence by putting on an impressive display of gladiatorial contests in honour of the god. The rules governing the worship of the *numen* of the emperor Augustus by the inhabitants of Narbo (Narbonne) in Gaul are recorded on two inscriptions on the altar, one (quoted here in part) put up on its erection in AD 11, the other on its formal dedication in AD 12 or 13:

> In the consulship of Titus Statilius Taurus and Lucius Cassius Longinus, September 22. Vow taken to the divine spirit of Augustus by the population of the Narbonensians in perpetuity: 'May it be good, favourable, and auspicious to the Emperor Caesar Augustus, son of a god, father of his country, *pontifex maximus*, holding the tribunician power for the thirty-fourth year; to his wife, children, and house; to the Roman senate and people; and to the colonists and residents of the Colonia Julia Paterna of Narbo Martius, who have bound themselves to worship his divine spirit in perpetuity!'
>
> The populace of the Narbonensians has erected in the forum at Narbo an altar at which every year on September 23 – the day on which the good fortune of the age bore him to be ruler of the world – three Roman equites from the populace and three freedmen shall sacrifice one animal each and shall at their own expense on that day provide the colonists and residents with incense and wine for supplication to his divine spirit. And on September 24 they shall likewise provide incense and wine for the colonists and residents. [There follows a list of sacrifices to be made on other significant dates in the rule of Augustus.]
>
> (*CIL* XII, no. 4,333; LR 1, pp. 623–25)

It was also quite common to worship other gods to entreat their aid for the emperor. An inscription from an altar in Lugdunum records the conduct of the ritual of the *taurobolium* (bull sacrifice), normally performed in the cult of the Magna Mater, for the prosperity of the emperor Antoninus Pius and his family, and the sacrificing community:[28]

> In the *taurobolium* of the Great Idaean Mother of the Gods, which was performed on the instruction of the Mother of the Gods, for the well-being of the emperor Caesar Titus Aelius Hadrianus Antoninus Augustus Pius, father of his country, and of his children, and of the condition of the *colonia* of Lugdunum, Lucius Aemilius Carpus, *sevir Augustalis* and at the same time *dendrophorus* [officer of Magna Mater cult] received the 'powers' and transferred them from the Vaticanum, and consecrated an altar adorned with an ox-head at his own expense. The priest, Quintus Sammius Secundus, was honoured with an armlet and garland by the *quindecimviri*, and the most holy town-council of Lugdunum decreed him a lifelong priesthood. In the consulship of Appius Annius Atilius Bradua and Titus Clodius Vibius Varus [AD 160]. Ground was given for this monument by decree of the town-council.
>
> [On the right side of the monument] The midnight ceremony was performed on the fifth day before the Ides of December.
>
> (*CIL* XIII, no. 1,751; BNP no. 6.7b)

At its most informal, the cult consisted of the insertion of the names of emperors into lists of divinities whose beneficence was requested by the Salii (a priesthood at Rome), the placing of their statues in household shrines, and libations to the emperor at banquets. In between was great variety, including worship of a living emperor in conjunction with the personification of the city of Rome (*Roma et Augustus*), worship of the emperor's deceased relatives, and, from 7 BC, offerings to the images of the emperor's *genius* and *lares* (household gods) at shrines set up at the crossroads of each ward of the city of Rome. Offerings to other gods on behalf of the emperor, which were very common, cannot be said in theological terms to constitute part of the imperial cult, any more than temples at Rome erected to the emperor's favourite gods, but they did often reflect a similar view of the ruler's special relationship to the divine. Even when he was worshipped directly, the emperor might be thought of in different ways: as *deus* or *theos* (god), or more indirectly as *divus* or *theios* (divine), an ambivalence sometimes well illustrated by the offering not of black or white sacrificial animals but of speckled.

The justification for treating these varied forms of worship as a single phenomenon is that they seem all to have been encouraged by the emperors themselves (see Chapter 12). From the point of view of the worshippers, the cult fulfilled a very useful role in helping those who served under a system of military autocracy to explain their lives as part of a divine plan. If the emperor is a god, it is surely right to obey him; if he is sometimes arbitrary, that is in the nature of divine behaviour. For pagan polytheists, enthusiastic adoption of the ruler cult helped them to make sense of their lives.

30

JUDAISM

SPECIAL CHARACTERISTICS OF JUDAISM

The religion of most Jews was inherited from their ancestors, but non-Jews attracted to the cult were welcomed into Jewish communities not least in diaspora settlements such as in Rome, although the number who became full proselytes, rather than more loosely affiliated to Judaism, is unknown. Their religion differed from the other religions of the pre-Christian Roman Empire above all in one respect – the Jewish God was believed to demand the exclusive obedience of his Jewish worshippers, such that cult paid to any other divinity was treachery. This attitude was almost incomprehensible to polytheists, who responded to such deliberate snubbing of powerful forces sometimes with admiration but often with disgust at what they termed 'atheism'.[1]

Ancient sources, both Jewish and gentile, stress the peculiarities of Jewish religious practice and belief, but it is worth noting at the outset that in some ways the religious assumptions of the Jews were the same as those of others. Thus Jews like others held a variety of views about the nature of existence after death, and Jews shared the common belief that the most efficacious form of worship was by sacrifice and libations in the temple in which the divinity was housed. Indeed, the Jerusalem Temple cult is the best attested sacrificial cult in the Roman world.

For pagans, the oddity of Judaism, apart from the refusal to worship other gods, lay primarily in the lack of a cult image for worship and in the personal behaviour required of Jews, in particular the Sabbath. Pagans regarded Jews as fanatical in their devotion to Sabbath rest and their strictness in observance of sacred time, which occasionally even led them to die rather than fight on the sacred day:

> The Homeric warrior prayed to God for success in battle, but the Jews sitting unwashed on the Sabbath, when the enemy were putting up ladders to the walls and capturing them, did not get up, but remained as if bound together in a single net by superstition.
>
> (Plutarch, *On Superstition* 8)

Other aspects of Judaism most stressed by gentile writers were food taboos and the circumcision of boys, but such external views were not always well informed, and the best evidence for the special characteristics of Judaism is to be found in the Jewish sources themselves.

Such Jewish evidence is abundant, but not always easy to interpret. The abundance is accounted for in part by the high premium placed on the written word by ancient Jews, but even more significant was the preservation of Jewish writings from this period through the continuous traditions since antiquity of Rabbinic Judaism and Christianity. Both traditions placed high value on the copying of earlier writings, but each selected differently from the corpus of such writings, in accordance with the different religious preoccupations of later rabbis and Christians. The extent of such selectivity is evident from a comparison between the picture of Judaism which can be derived from the Hebrew and Aramaic works produced by the rabbis, especially the *Mishnah* (complied *c.* AD 200), the *Tosefta* (*c.* AD 250), the *Palestinian Talmud* (*c.* AD 400), the *Babylonian Talmud* (*c.* AD 500 or later) and various *midrashim* (Bible commentaries),[2] with the picture to be derived from the writings in Greek, or translations from the Greek, preserved by the Church (the *apocrypha*: additions to the Jewish Bible incorporated into the manuscripts of the Greek translation of the Bible, the Septuagint) and the *pseudepigrapha* (other Jewish writings of various types considered valuable by Christians):[3] the two pictures can be reconciled only with ingenuity, and disagreements between modern students of Judaism in this period depend primarily on differing judgements on the extent to which such reconciliation is desirable. The discovery of the Dead Sea Scrolls near Qumran in 1947 has not resolved the issue, since although these sectarian documents survive independently of both the Jewish and the Christian later traditions, and the teachings of the sect or sects who produced them do not conform precisely to anything previously known from those traditions, it remains possible (but not necessary) to interpret the evidence to make it more or less compatible with what was already known before the scrolls were discovered.[4]

This varied evidence about Judaism in the early Roman period attests above all the variety of both practice and belief which was tolerated within the religion. It is thus at first sight rather surprising to find that one of the main characteristics of Judaism singled out by Josephus in his defence of Jewish customs in *Against Apion* 2.179–81 was precisely its uniformity:

To this cause above all we owe our admirable harmony. Unity and identity of religious belief, perfect uniformity in habits and customs, produce a very beautiful concord in human character. Among us alone will be heard no contradictory statements about God, such as are common among other nations, not only on the lips of ordinary individuals under the impulse of some passing mood, but even boldly propounded by philosophers; some putting forward crushing arguments against the very existence of God, others depriving him of his providential care for mankind. Among us alone will be seen no difference in the conduct of our lives. With us all act alike, all profess the same doctrine about God, one which is in harmony with our Law and affirms that all things are under his eye. Even our womenfolk and dependants would tell you that piety must be the motive of all our occupations in life.

The unity which Josephus praised was in fact striking in contrast to the plurality of cult practices and myths espoused by Greek polytheists; Josephus explicitly emphasized the contrast in *Against Apion*. Most Jews believed that sacrifices to the Jewish God should be carried out in only one temple, that in Jerusalem; another temple, in Leontopolis in Egypt, functioned from the mid-second century BC until it was closed down by the Romans in AD 73 (Josephus, *The Jewish War* 7.421–36), but it never rivalled the central shrine in Judaea.[5] Thus Jews alone in the ancient world came on mass pilgrimages to a single shrine. The Bible enjoined all adult males to visit the shrine three times a year (Exodus 23.17; Deuteronomy 16.16) and, although most Jews who lived in the diaspora away from the homeland came far less often, the city of Jerusalem was packed at these pilgrim festivals, which frequently proved to be times of political unrest. Evidence for mass international pilgrimage is not to be found before the time of Herod in the late first century BC, and it can be assumed that the attraction of the journey to Jerusalem for women and children as well as men will have been much enhanced by the great rebuilding of the Temple, which began in 22 BC, and made the shrine one of the wonders of the world, and by the comparative ease and security of travel from diaspora communities within the Roman Empire. That the Temple was the religious focus of the Jewish insurgents in the war against Rome from AD 66–70 (see above, Chapter 26) is evident not only from Josephus' detailed narrative of the revolt, in which the Temple site was the centre of resistance to Roman forces, but from the rebel coinage, with its depiction of the sacred utensils and its proclamation, in archaic palaeo-Hebrew, of the holiness of Jerusalem (see Figure 35). Over 60 years later, the coinage of the rebels from AD 132–35 placed similar emphasis on the Temple, with idealized images of the destroyed sanctuary and slogans proclaiming 'freedom', 'redemption' and 'Jerusalem'.[6]

Figure 35 Silver shekel minted by the rebels in the third year of the Jewish revolt, AD 68/9. The obverse shows a vessel used in the Temple; the reverse has a stem with three pomegranates. The caption is written in Palaeo-Hebrew, a form of lettering archaic by the first century AD. The Jewish coins always avoid human images. Thicker and heavier than contemporary Roman issues, the coin is made from pure silver for payment of dues to the Temple. Photo courtesy of CNG Coins.

INTERPRETATIONS OF THE *TORAH*

Josephus' claim that Jews shared common ideas about the divinity was also true in contrast to polytheists, since all religious Jews accepted the importance of the covenant between God and Israel enshrined in the *Torah*, the first five books of the Jewish Bible (the Pentateuch).[7] The biblical books had all been composed by the mid-second century BC, but, although the notion that some books were more sacred than others was generally accepted, it is uncertain whether there was yet a fully recognized canon.[8] Nonetheless, the religious status of the Pentateuch was exceptional; many of the manuscripts found among the Dead Sea Scrolls were fragments of the Pentateuch or commentaries on it, and the reverence shown towards scrolls of the Pentateuch by Jews encouraged pagans to treat such scrolls as the equivalent for Jews of cult statues for pagans. In the Greek-speaking diaspora the Greek translation of the Hebrew Bible, the Septuagint, was treated by some Jews as divinely inspired like the Hebrew original, although attempts to revise the Greek text to conform more closely to the Hebrew began in the first and second centuries AD. The main function of synagogues, communal meeting places sometimes (but not always) housed in purpose-built buildings, was the reading and exposition of the Pentateuch; the name *proseuche* ('prayer') ascribed to such buildings in the Egyptian diaspora from the second century BC suggests that synagogues might also be used for communal prayer, but that was a secondary use, and synagogues were rarely treated as holy places in themselves until the late Roman period: when a synagogue was attacked in Caesarea in AD 66, the local Jews did not try to protect the site but took to safety the sacred scroll (Josephus, *The Jewish War* 2.285–91).[9]

All Jews thus accepted the importance of the *Torah*: the pluralism characteristic of Judaism in the first century AD resulted from disagreement about how the text should be interpreted. Some, like the philosopher Philo, believed that the practical injunctions of the *Torah* held also more general ethical meanings to be discovered by allegorical interpretation. Others, like the Pharisees as described by Josephus (*Antiquities of the Jews* 13.297), taught that the law should be understood in the light of customs which had grown up over the generations. The sectarians at Qumran accepted the teachings of their Teacher of Righteousness in addition to the *Torah*.[10] Some extreme allegorists believed, according to Philo (*On the Migration of Abraham* 89–93), that only the allegorical meaning of the laws mattered, so that it was not necessary to keep the laws in practice at all (but it is worth noting that such extreme allegorists were mentioned in no other Jewish literature and that Philo was at pains to insist that they were rare and lacked influence in Alexandria in his day).

The areas of greatest variety in this period in the interpretation of the *Torah* were themselves quite heterogeneous. The sacrificial cult in the Jerusalem Temple was performed by an hereditary caste of priests, but all Jews could have ideas about the details of its performance, which were laid out in somewhat confusing and incomplete fashion in the Pentateuch. The Pharisees disagreed with Sadducees over the correct way to carry out some rituals; according to Josephus (*Antiquities of the Jews* 13.298, 18.15) the views of the Pharisees usually prevailed. Copies of what appears to be a letter on this topic apparently sent from the Teacher of Righteousness to the High Priest in Jerusalem (4QMMT) were discovered among the Dead Sea Scrolls.[11] Many groups had a deep concern for the physical purity both of their own bodies and of food and drink. Pollution as a metaphor for immorality was a notion already found in the Bible but it was carried much further by Jews in this period: many ritual baths (*mikvaoth*) have been excavated in the upper city of Jerusalem near the Temple site, and the prevailing assumption that purity was desirable is nicely illustrated by widespread taboos based (so far as is known) on custom rather than any biblical text or religious authority, against the consumption of gentile milk, bread or wine, or the use of olive oil produced by gentiles for washing (like soap), eating or lighting.[12] It is hard to know what connection there was, if any, between such concern for purity and the high premium put by some Jews on asceticism, as attested by Josephus' description of his time spent with a certain Bannus in the desert:

> On hearing of one named Bannus, who dwelt in the wilderness, wearing only such clothing as trees provided, feeding on such things as grew of themselves, and using frequent ablutions of cold water, by day and night, for purity's sake, I became his devoted disciple. With him I spent three years.
> (*Life* 11)

Such asceticism was not widespread; for most Jews fasts were restricted to the Day of Atonement, a solemn annual day of repentance, to commemoration of calamities, and to times of emergency such as droughts.

HOPES AND SPECULATIONS

Other preoccupations of Jews in this period included a concern (apparently novel in Judaism from the second century BC) about the possibility of life after death. According to Josephus, some Jews affirmed that such life occurred, but Sadducees denied it (*Antiquities of the Jews* 18.14, 16), and according to Acts of the Apostles 23.6–7) the issue could lead to violent altercation:

> Now Paul was well aware that one section of them [the Council] were Sadducees and the other Pharisees, so he called out in the Council, 'My brothers, I am a Pharisee, a Pharisee born and bred; and the true issue in this trial is our hope of the resurrection of the dead.' At these words the Pharisees and Sadducees fell out among themselves, and the assembly was divided.

It is more difficult to find evidence for polemic in the popularity of apocalyptic literature which portrayed the revelation by angels to Jewish sages, usually of great antiquity, of religious truths which were not often themselves particularly unusual;[13] but the anonymity or pseudonymity of these writings may be significant: despite attestation in the works of Josephus and elsewhere of individuals described as prophets, including Josephus himself (*The Jewish War* 3.352), there was a general agreement that at some time in the distant past there had been 'a failure of the exact succession of the prophets' (*Against Apion* 1.41), so that religious authors hid behind ancient names.[14]

Jews subscribed to a linear concept of time in which the eschatological age to come would in some way vindicate Israel with a victory by a Messiah over gentile powers and (in some formulations) a general resurrection of the dead, but the effect of this idea on behaviour varied greatly.[15] The only group in antiquity derived from Judaism and known to have defined itself by its messianic beliefs was the Christians-*Christianos* means a follower of *Christos*, the Messiah – and imminent messianic expectation is little found in the writings of Philo and Josephus or the early rabbinic texts. Many Jews may have assumed that the end of the world would come in due course and that it was unnecessary or even undesirable to try to force the divine timetable, and there was much disagreement about the precise form that the messianic age would take. On the other hand, such evidence as there is for widespread eschatological expectation is not simply the effect of selection by the later Christian tradition in an attempt to bolster Christian claims, since such expectation is also a striking element of the Qumran sect, not least in the picture of the battle between the sons of light and the sons of darkness to be found in the War Scroll:

> On the day when the Kittim fall, there shall be battle and terrible carnage before the God of Israel, for that shall be the day appointed from ancient times for the battle of destruction of the sons of darkness. At that time, the assembly of gods and the hosts of men shall battle, causing great carnage; on the day of calamity, the sons of light shall battle with the company of darkness amid the shouts of a mighty multitude and the clamour of gods and men to (make manifest) the might of God. And it shall be a time of [great] tribulation for the people which God shall redeem; of all afflictions none shall be as this, from its sudden beginning until its end in eternal redemption.
> (*IQM* 1.9–12 (Sukenik))

PHARISEES, SADDUCEES AND ESSENES

It was a feature of the late Hellenistic period that within Judaism there emerged groups or philosophies which enjoyed distinct separate identities while remaining within the bounds of common Judaism. Josephus described three such types of Judaism in a set-piece passage (*The Jewish War* 2.119–61, repeated in somewhat shorter form in the *Antiquities of the Jews* 18.11–22):

> The Jews, from the most ancient times, had three philosophies pertaining to their traditions, that of the Essenes, that of the Sadducees, and, thirdly, that of the group called the Pharisees. To be sure, I have spoken about them in the second book of The Jewish War, but nevertheless I shall dwell on them for a moment.

There is no reason to believe that most Jews belonged to any one of these groups; indeed, the whole motive for Josephus' description was to assert the existence of a fourth, anarchist philosophy, on which he tried to put the blame for the outbreak of the Jewish revolt against Rome, even though adherents of the 'fourth philosophy' are unattested in any other ancient source and play no role in the events preceding the outbreak of war as described by Josephus himself.[16] On the other hand, the fact that *some* Jews could align themselves with a particular party was a distinctive development in post-biblical Judaism.

The precise nature of the three groups described by Josephus is debated. Of the Pharisees, he says:

> The Pharisees simplify their standard of living, making no concession to luxury. They follow the guidance of that which their doctrine has selected and transmitted as good, attaching the chief importance to the observance of those commandments which it has seen fit to dictate to them. They show respect and deference to their elders, nor do they rashly presume to contradict their proposals. Though they postulate that everything is brought about by fate, still they do not deprive the human will of the pursuit of what is in man's power, since it was God's good pleasure that there should be a fusion and that the will of man with his virtue and vice should be admitted to the council-chamber of fate. They believe that souls have power to survive death and that there are rewards and punishments under the earth for those who have led lives of virtue or vice: eternal imprisonment is the lot of evil souls, while the good souls receive an easy passage to a new life. Because of these views they are, as a matter of fact, extremely influential among the townsfolk; and all prayers and sacred rites of divine worship are performed according to their exposition. This is the great tribute that the inhabitants of the cities, by practising the highest ideals both in their way of living and in their discourse, have paid to the excellence of the Pharisees.

(*Antiquities of the Jews* 18.12–15)

Josephus' evidence about Pharisees can be supplemented from the New Testament and rabbinic texts, but the testimonies of the different sources do not easily cohere.[17] The Gospels have a picture of Pharisees as opponents of Jesus and as particularly zealous with regard to purity, tithing and the Sabbath (cf. Matthew 23); similar concerns are to be found ascribed by later rabbis to those named sages of the early to mid-first century AD seen by the rabbis as their forebears. However, such early sages were never described by the rabbis as Pharisees, and only one of them, Rabban Gamaliel, was described as a Pharisee in another source (Acts 5.34). When the rabbis referred specifically to Pharisees, they described their arguments against Sadducees over purity and the administration of the Temple cult. Josephus, who claimed to follow the teachings of the Pharisees with regard (at least) to public life (*Life* 12), ascribed an interest in purity and the Sabbath to Essenes, and in tithes to priests, but made no mention of such issues in his description of Pharisees. The only other writer known to have been a Pharisee at one time was St Paul (Philippians 3.5), and he also showed a striking lack of interest in purity, tithing and the Sabbath. It may be best to admit that the only certain fact about Pharisees is that they existed as a self-conscious group and that they exercised a great deal of influence beyond the confines of that group, perhaps in part because (unlike Sadducees) they treated as sacred traditional behaviour, thus in effect sanctifying and validating common custom.

Of the Sadducees, Josephus writes:

> The Sadducees hold that the soul perishes along with the body. They own no observance of any sort apart from the laws; in fact, they reckon it a virtue to dispute with the teachers of the path of wisdom that they pursue. There are but few men to whom this doctrine has been made known, but these are men of the highest standing. They accomplish practically nothing, however. For whenever they assume some office, though they submit unwillingly and perforce, yet submit they do to the formulas of the Pharisees, since otherwise the masses would not tolerate them.
>
> (*Antiquities of the Jews* 18.16–17)

The name of Sadducees (in Hebrew, *tzadukim*) was connected to the name of the priest Zadok, but despite the gloss in Acts 5.17, which refers to the followers of the High Priest as Sadducees, there is no reason to suppose that most Sadducees were priests or most priests Sadducees, and the picture of this group given in rabbinic texts accords with that in Josephus: they interpreted the law without regard to custom, and hence could be harsh in their judgements (so Josephus, *Antiquities of the Jews* 20.199, on the execution of James, the brother of Jesus).[18]

Josephus' description of the Essenes is huge in the version in *The Jewish War,* and disproportionately long even in the shorter version in the *Antiquities of the Jews*:

> The doctrine of the Essenes is wont to leave everything in the hands of God. They regard the soul as immortal and believe that they ought to strive especially to draw near to righteousness. They send votive offerings to the Temple, but perform their sacrifices employing a different ritual of purification. ... Otherwise they are of the highest character, devoting themselves solely to agricultural labour. ... Moreover, they hold their possessions in common, and the wealthy man receives no more enjoyment from his property than the man who possesses nothing. The men who practise this way of life number more than four thousand. They neither bring wives into the community nor do they own slaves, since they believe that the latter practice contributes to injustice and that the former opens the way to a source of dissension. Instead they live by themselves and perform menial tasks for one another. They elect by show of hands good men to receive their revenues and the produce of the earth and priests to prepare bread and other food.
>
> (*Antiquities of the Jews* 18.18–22)

The extraordinary attention paid to the Essene community by Josephus and Philo may be most plausibly ascribed to the desire of these authors to bring out the similarities between these ascetic regimes of this small group or groups and that of gentile philosophical sects such as Pythagoreans.[19] The Essenes were the only Jewish group known to non-Jewish observers such as Pliny. The relationship between the Essenes and the Qumran sect which produced the Dead Sea Scrolls is unknown: the similarities are striking, but there are also many small differences, and those who postulate identity have to allow for change over time or the existence of different kinds of Essenes (both quite plausible hypotheses, especially since in *The Jewish War* (2.160–61), Josephus referred to a second order of Essenes which countenanced the marriage of members). It may be thought preferable to treat the Qumran sect as a group previously totally unknown. It would in fact have been surprising if documents discovered by chance had fitted neatly into a full picture of Judaism in the early Roman period which itself is manufactured from a variety of very partial sources.[20]

PHILO

In his summary of the Jewish philosophies, Josephus made no reference to Philo, although he knew of his existence – at *Antiquities of the Jews* 18.259, Philo is described as 'not inexpert in philosophy'. A pious Jew from one of the leading families in the city in the first century AD, Philo was highly educated in Greek literature and Platonic philosophy. In his theological works he tried systematically to interpret the Bible as an esoteric allegory of Greek moral philosophy; he claimed this exercise to be a necessary corollary to, rather than substitute for, the literal interpretation of scripture. A brief quotation from the treatise *Questions and Answers on Genesis*, which survives mostly only in an Armenian translation of the Greek, may give a flavour of Philo's extensive works:

> (Gen. 16.2) Why does Sarah say to Abraham, 'Behold, the Lord has closed me up so as not to bear. Go into my maidservant that thou mayest beget children from her'?
> In the literal sense it is the same (as) not to be envious and jealous (but) to look out for the same wise man and husband and genuine kinsman. ... But as for the deeper meaning, it has somewhat the following argument. Those who are unable by virtue to beget fine and praiseworthy deeds ought to pursue intermediate education, and in a certain sense produce children from the school studies, for wide learning is a sort of whetstone of the mind and reason.

Caution is, however, necessary in extrapolating from Philo's evidence to the religion of the rest of the Jewish diaspora. Other Jewish Greek writers are known to have existed, but, of non-Christian Jewish authors, only Philo's theology was sufficiently congenial to the Early Church to be extensively preserved; by the third century AD most of the rest of this literature was known to Clement of Alexandria and later patristic authors only in very fragmentary selective quotations from earlier, often non-Jewish, compilations, particularly that by Alexander Polyhistor.[21] Unless the only special characteristic of Philo's theology was the fact that it was written down, it is therefore unlikely that Philo's theology was typical of Greek-speaking Jews.

DESTRUCTION OF THE JERUSALEM TEMPLE

The assumption which underlay these different forms of Judaism suffered a great jolt in AD 70 when the Jerusalem Temple was destroyed by Titus. The sacrificial cult had belonged to all Jews, hence the contribution by each adult male of an annual offering of half a shekel (see Figure 35) to pay for the purchase of sacrificial animals, a custom observed by diaspora Jews as well as those in Judaea (cf. Cicero, *In Defence of Flaccus* 28.66–69). The priests who performed the daily rituals preserved the relationship between God and Israel. The cessation of the cult was a blow even for those Jews who rarely or never visited the Temple themselves. The flood of Flavian propaganda which resulted in the destruction of the Temple, graphically displayed in the triumphal procession in Rome and later on the arch of Titus gave little hope for immediate restoration of the Temple.

And yet hope for such restoration must have been the first reaction of Jews to the disaster. The first Temple had been destroyed in 586 BC but was rebuilt some half a century later, and the rebuilding of destroyed shrines was not uncommon in the Roman world. As Josephus' description of Judaism in *Against Apion* makes clear, Josephus at least at the time of composition of the work (after AD 93) still assumed that sacrificial worship in Jerusalem was the main way for Jews to approach God:

> We have but one temple for the one God (for like ever loveth like), common to all as God is common to all. The priests are continually engaged in his worship, under the leadership of him who for the time is head of the line. With his colleagues he will sacrifice to God, safeguard the laws, adjudicate in cases of dispute, punish those convicted of crime. Any who disobey him will pay the penalty as for impiety towards God himself. Our sacrifices are not occasions for drunken self-indulgence – such practices are abhorrent to God – but for sobriety. At these sacrifices prayers for the welfare of the community must take precedence over those for ourselves; for we are born for fellowship, and he who sets its claims above his private interests is specially acceptable to God.
> (*Against Apion* 2.193–96)

Quite when such hopes began to fade is uncertain. The main reason for the refusal of Vespasian and Titus to permit such building must lie in their reliance on the capture of Jerusalem as justification to the Roman people for their seizure of power within the Roman state. Nerva and Trajan, who owed nothing to the Flavians and therefore had no need to continue their anti-Jewish policies, might have been expected to permit the rebuilding, and their refusal to do so must have been a severe blow, but even in the *Mishnah*, redacted in *c.* AD 200, rabbis discussed in great detail the way in which the sacrifices should be carried out, without any hint that their discussion was only theoretical.

It is also unlikely that the shock of the destruction would have brought to a sudden end the tolerance of variety within Judaism so characteristic of the period before AD 70.[22] In fact the description of the different types of Judaism given by Josephus was composed first in the AD 70s (in *The Jewish War*), but repeated in the 90s (in the *Antiquities of the Jews*), without any sign that these groups were now a thing of the past. Nothing more is heard after AD 70 of the allegorical interpretation of the Jewish texts favoured by Philo, but this silence may not be significant if it was simply a product of methods of transmission: by the end of the first century AD Jewish texts written in Greek ceased to be preserved by Christians, who now had their own literature, and since rabbis preserved only writings in Hebrew and Aramaic all further Jewish Greek literature was lost; that some such literature was composed in late antiquity is a reasonable surmise, since Greek remained the standard language of Jewish inscriptions in the western diaspora, and it is methodologically unsound to assume that any form of Judaism unmentioned in rabbinic texts cannot have existed.

RABBINIC JUDAISM

Among those who began gradually to adapt to the loss of their Temple were the rabbis. In fact this adaptation comprised a specific acceptance of changed circumstances; for instance, the rabbinic sages in the decades after AD 70 were said to have decreed that various rituals previously confined to the Temple precincts or to Jerusalem, such as the ceremonial blowing of a ram's horn on special occasions, could now be carried out elsewhere (the text in *Mishnah, Rosh haShanah* 4.1 attributes the innovation to the leading rabbi of the first generation after the destruction, Rabban Yohanan ben Zakkai), although there seems to have been no attempt to encourage sacrificial cult in places other than Jerusalem.[23] In other ways the rabbinic reaction was less direct. Rabbinic Judaism claimed descent from the revelation of the *Torah* to Moses on Mount Sinai by a continuous chain of tradition, as expressed in the programmatic introduction to the tractate *The Sayings of the Fathers* in the *Mishnah*:

> Moses received the Law from Sinai and committed it to Joshua, and Joshua to the elders, and the elders to the Prophets; and the Prophets committed it to the men of the Great Synagogue. They said three things: Be deliberate in judgement, raise up many disciples, and make a fence around the Law. Simeon the Just was of the remnants of the Great Synagogue. ... Antigonus of Soko received [the Law] from Simeon the Just. ... Jose ben Joezer of Zeredah and Jose ben Johanan of Jerusalem received [the Law] from them.
>
> (*Mishnah, Aboth* chapter 1)

This claim to legitimacy through continuous tradition makes it hard to trace precisely the features of rabbinic religion which distinguished it from earlier forms of Judaism, but one of the most striking novel elements was the religious value accorded by rabbinic sages to the study of the *Torah* for its own sake: study came to be seen as a form of worship.[24]

The early rabbinic texts are an esoteric form of literature, highly formulaic, and the records of rabbinic discussions preserved in the *Mishnah* and *Tosefta* involved only a small number of individuals in each generation of sages. It is thus debatable when rabbinic authority in the period after AD 70 spread beyond the confines of the rabbis themselves.[25] In the period before AD 132 their academies were mostly to be found in the coastal plain of Judaea and after the Bar Kochba revolt mostly in Galilee. The specific cases in which rabbis were portrayed as judges almost all concerned very limited areas of religious law – issues involving purity, the food laws, the annulment of vows, the observance of fasts in time of drought, and so on – and the rabbinic texts themselves assume that rabbinic rulings were disregarded by the many Jews termed either neutrally *ammei haaretz* (those who do not fulfil rabbinic injunctions on purity and tithing) or in more hostile terms as *minim* (heretics). If rabbis had any influence at all outside their own circles, it may be because of their expertise in fixing the calendar. The task of announcing the beginning of months had been one of the functions of the Temple authorities, and the rabbis record no opposition to their arrogation of this role, which was significant for all Jews, since observance of, for instance, the Day of Atonement on the wrong day would be a grave sin. By the late fourth century AD the Roman state was to treat the most prominent of the rabbis, the patriarch (*nasi* in Hebrew, *patriarcha* in Latin), as the religious representative of all Jews within the empire, and some scholars have suggested that this recognition may have been accorded to earlier patriarchs soon after AD 70; but good evidence for such early recognition is lacking, and it is not obvious why the Roman government in AD 70, just after the destruction of the Temple, should have felt any need to treat any one Jew as the spokesman of the religion as a whole.[26]

31

CHRISTIANITY

EARLY HISTORY OF CHRISTIANITY

Christianity began and was shaped in its first, decisive, two centuries within the confines of the Roman Empire.[1] It was recognized both by adherents and by opponents as a novel religious phenomenon, some aspects of which had no previous parallel in religious history. But many of the elements of theology and cult from which Christianity was constructed were inherited and adopted from contemporary Judaism and other religions; from the perspective of the ancient world it can be seen as a peculiarly successful oriental cult, in many ways similar to Mithraism and (most obviously) Judaism.

The peculiar success of the Church was only very partially reached by AD 180, for most inhabitants of the empire would still not by that date have had much, if any, contact with Christians. Scrutiny of the pagan and Jewish sources about Christians in the first few centuries provides a different perspective to the triumphalist and concentrated focus of the Christian documents which provide the insiders' story. Of the pagan literary sources, none composed in the first century seems to have been aware of Christians. In the early second century, the younger Pliny (*Letters* 10.96) wrote to Trajan to ask about procedure in dealing with Christians, about whose practices and legality he was uncertain. Tacitus (*Annals* 15.44) included a brief reference to the career and execution of 'Christus', and to the continued existence of his followers, in describing the fire in Rome in AD 64, for which Christians were held responsible by Nero; a similar brief reference is found in Suetonius' account of the reign of Claudius (*Claudius* 25.4). The first pagan writer known to have written a treatise against the Christians was the neo-Platonist Celsus, with his (now lost) *True Discourse* of *c.* AD 178; his arguments survive because they were quoted extensively in a refutation, *Against Celsus*, composed by the Christian Origen in the mid-third century.[2]

Jewish sources are almost equally unforthcoming. No Jewish writings composed before AD 70 reveal any awareness of the early Christian movement; attempts to find references to Christianity in the Dead Sea scrolls have not won general acceptance. According to the extant manuscripts of his history,

Josephus referred to Jesus' crucifixion in the context of the governorship of Pontius Pilate in his *Antiquities of the Jews* (18.63–64), published in the 90s AD:

> About this time there lived Jesus, a wise man, if indeed one ought to call him a man. For he was one who wrought surprising feats and was a teacher of such people as accept the truth gladly. He won over many Jews and many of the Greeks. He was the Messiah. When Pilate, upon hearing him accused by men of the highest standing amongst us, had condemned him to be crucified, those who had in the first place come to love him did not give up their affection for him. On the third day he appeared to them restored to life, for the prophets of God had prophesied these and countless other marvellous things about him. And the tribe of the Christians, so called after him, has still to this day not disappeared.

The precise wording of this description of Jesus has undoubtedly been much altered by Christian copyists, but its main contents, which, unlike the additions (such as 'He was the Messiah'), are not so favourable to Christianity as to exclude the possibility that a non-Christian could have written them, may plausibly be ascribed to Josephus himself, including the reference to the continued existence of a 'tribe' of Christians in Josephus' own day. Later Jewish writings, all preserved within the rabbinic tradition, are more or less silent about Christians until the emergence (undated, but in part reflected in the anti-Christian arguments cited by the pagan Celsus) of a scurrilous tradition about Jesus' origins and earthly career, which was to be much elaborated in the Early Middle Ages.

Pagan and Jewish testimonies thus suggest that Christianity was a movement of singularly little importance in the religious history of the Early Empire. In contrast, the internal evidence of Christianity, which survives in great quantities because the Medieval Church was responsible for the preservation and copying of most literature from this period, places the developments within Christianity at the centre of human history. The detailed internal history of the Early Church which such preservation of the evidence permits must be balanced against the more or less static view, which is necessarily all that can be achieved when considering most of the other religions of the Early Roman Empire.

Church history as salvation history is explicit in the *Church History* written by Eusebius, bishop of Caesarea in Palestine, in several editions in the late third and early fourth century AD. Eusebius' history of the Church as an institution provides the framework as well as much of the documentation for later histories of the Church in this period. The clarity of Eusebius' account, and the wealth of material, mask distinct problems in the use of his account. Eusebius wrote at what he believed to be the crowning triumph of the Church, the conversion to Christianity of the emperor Constantine in AD 312, and the establishment of the Church throughout the empire as the religion most favoured by the state.[3] He saw the Church in the preceding centuries as having followed an unerring path, directed by the divine, towards this goal. One major problem that arises from this perspective is his assumption that the Church was always a clearly identifiable body: he knew and wrote about numerous heresies, but he took it for granted that these were only minor, if irritating, deviations by a few from a generally agreed norm. This view was problematic enough in Eusebius' own day, but, as will be seen, it was even less obviously true in the first two centuries, when many different groups presented themselves as the true followers of Christ, without the advantage of Eusebius' hindsight as to which groups and theologies were eventually to become more or less standard.

Much evidence survives from within Christianity to correct and expand the narrative provided by Eusebius. Primary are the texts preserved in the New Testament, to which may be added many Christian gospels, narratives and epistles which were excluded from the canonical collection but preserved in early papyri and medieval manuscripts. For the second century also a number of apologetic tractates defended Christianity to pagans and Jews (for example, those by Aristides and Justin Martyr) and in *c.* AD 180–85 Irenaeus, bishop of Lyons, inaugurated a new and significant genre of polemic with his *Against Heresies*.[4] The problem in the use of all this evidence is that it was all composed quite openly for religious purposes, which might permit quite a loose attitude to the actual events of the historical past. Since archaeological and epigraphic evidence for Christianity in this period is almost non-existent, and (as has been seen) non-Christian evidence is not very informative, the early history of Christianity has to be puzzled out by examination and elucidation of inconsistencies within the Christian literature itself. The preservation of so much literature makes such an investigation possible on many topics – thus, for instance, the different accounts of Jesus' career and teaching in the four canonical Gospels can profitably be compared – but it is not easy, and the theological preoccupations of most modern scholars who study early Christianity so predispose them to particular interpretations of the evidence that the subject has achieved much less scholarly consensus than any other in the history of the Early Empire.

JESUS

Most contentious of all is the reconstruction of the life and teaching of Jesus himself, which need to be placed firmly within the context of first-century Judaism in the land of Israel.[5] The accounts of Jesus' career in the four canonical Gospels included in the New Testament agree on the main events of his life, and Luke and Matthew agree so closely on some of Jesus' teaching that a common (oral) source ('Q') is often posited, but the Gospels differ in detail, and in some of the teaching ascribed to Jesus; the apocryphal gospels differ even more, which is probably one reason for their exclusion from the canon by Christians of the second century. The problem arose because of the use of these biographical accounts as the main vehicles of theological ideas from the first generation of the Church, so that religious significance was from early on read into each of Jesus' recorded actions and statements. A minimalist solution for such conflicting testimony is to accept as true only those elements of the tradition which conflict with later Christian doctrine, on the grounds that such material cannot owe its inclusion to later invention, but even this procedure is hardly secure: too much of the history of the first generation of Christians after the resurrection is itself obscure to state for certain that any particular teaching was not found among them, and *some* continuity between Jesus' teaching and his followers is inherently plausible precisely because they took his name to define themselves.

Jesus was a Jew from Galilee who during the period when Pontius Pilate was governor of Judaea gathered a considerable following of Jews, first in his home region, then in Jerusalem. His disciples seem to have been peasant Galileans, but his activities aroused sufficient interest in Jerusalem to attract opposition from the ruling élite in Jerusalem, who then handed him over to Pilate for execution like a common criminal. After his death, his followers believed that he was physically resurrected for a brief period before his ascent to heaven, and that he was the Messiah, a belief that he probably encouraged while he was alive. Specific teachings are more difficult to attribute to Jesus with any certainty. Those doctrines ascribed to him in the Gospels which cannot be paralleled in contemporary Judaism (and there are few) all coincide too closely with later Christian teachings for certainty that they are not a reflection of such later communities; but his unparalleled emphasis on the Kingdom of God (either in the present or the near future) seems to reflect a distinctive intensity in his call to individuals to repent.

It is evident from the slight embarrassment of the Gospel authors about the relationship of the two that Jesus' mission and following were similar to, but later than, the career of John the Baptist. About John, Josephus included a few remarks in his *Antiquities of the Jews* (18.116–19), where he was described as a popular preacher of repentance, with a large following which had political repercussions:

> But to some of the Jews the destruction of Herod's army seemed to be divine vengeance, and certainly a just vengeance, for his treatment of John, surnamed the Baptist. For Herod had put him to death, though he was a good man and had exhorted the Jews to lead righteous lives, to practise justice towards their fellows and piety towards God, and so doing to join in baptism. ... When others too joined the crowds about him, because they were aroused to the highest degree by his sermons, Herod became alarmed. Eloquence that had so great an effect on mankind might lead to some form of sedition, for it looked as if they would be guided by John in everything that they did. Herod decided therefore that it would be much better to strike first and be rid of him before his work led to an uprising.

Josephus' account of John's demise at the hands of Herod Antipas in Galilee also agrees in essence with the Gospel account. Josephus was thus aware of

John as a remarkable Jew, but saw him firmly within the context of other first-century prophetic and similar figures; in contrast to Jesus, he left behind no movement known to Josephus.

MISSION TO THE GENTILES

The most difficult aspect of early Christianity to explain is its development from a parochial form of Judaism, aimed at Jews alone, to a distinctive separate religion with a mission to convert all humanity.[6] Jesus seems to have been uninterested in gentiles: his willingness to heal the daughter of a Syro-Phoenician woman (Mark 7.25–30) because 'even the dogs under the table eat the children's crumbs' contrasts strikingly with the missionary presuppositions of later Christians, and is therefore likely to be true. It is possible that some within the early Christian movement continued in much the same way. According to the Acts of the Apostles, the Christians in Jerusalem in the 30s and 40s AD insisted that gentiles who wished to join the Christian community must first become Jews; the fact that this was expressed as a demand for circumcision reflects the male presuppositions of Christianity, like most other religions in the Classical world.[7] The Christians in Jerusalem may have been hardly noticeable among the varied types of Judaism in the first century. The Acts of the Apostles, intending to impress the reader with the increase of the Church under the leadership of Peter, gives figures in the hundreds, and in one case the low thousands – hardly enough to have been noticeable in the teeming pilgrimage city. There is little evidence that the Jerusalem church suffered persecution from the Jewish authorities until AD 62, when (so Josephus records) James, the brother of Jesus, was put to death by the High Priest (*Antiquities of the Jews* 20.200); the martyrdom of Stephen (Acts 7.54–8.2), stoned by his accusers outside Jerusalem, is exceptional.

The mission to the gentiles was wholly different in its intention and effect. Most of the evidence for the gentile Church in the first generation is concerned with the figure of Paul, whose writings fill a large proportion of the New Testament, and whose deeds are the main single focus of interest in the Acts of the Apostles.[8] Paul was a Jew from Tarsus in south-east Turkey. Either he or his father had obtained Roman citizenship, and in Jerusalem he was evidently a person of some importance; although precisely in what office and capacity, if any, he went to Damascus as agent of the Jerusalem high priestly authorities, and indeed by what right and for what reason he attempted to interfere in the activities of a Jewish sect outside the land of Israel, is unknown. What is beyond doubt is the dramatic effect on him of his conversion on the road to Damascus: a bright, blinding light, a voice calling him to cease persecuting Jesus, and, on his arrival in Damascus, his adoption by the community he had intended to persecute (Acts 9.3–9). The precise theological significance of the message Paul heard was interpreted by him on numerous different occasions (cf. Galatians 1.11–17; 1 Timothy 1.12–17). When it actually occurred he may have thought about it in terms familiar in Jewish mysticism (that is, as a vision of the holy presence), but within a few years he had begun to interpret it as a vision of the resurrected Christ, and himself as Christ's apostle, called to his service as decisively as the disciples who had known Jesus in the flesh:

> For there is one God, and there is one mediator between God and men, the man Christ Jesus, who gave himself as a ransom for all, the testimony to which was borne at the proper time. For this was I appointed a preacher and apostle (I am telling the truth, I am not lying), a teacher of the Gentiles in faith and truth.
> (1 Timothy 2.5–7)

The direction in which Paul's new belief and enthusiasm took him at first is surprisingly difficult to reconstruct – surprising, because there is no lack of evidence in the New Testament. The problem is that, according to the Acts of the Apostles, Paul went first to the Jews of Asia Minor and Greece, and only after their rejection to the gentile godfearers who attached themselves to the synagogues, perhaps as fellow-worshippers, certainly as sympathizers; according to Acts, it was the enthusiasm of gentile godfearers that brought into the open the possibility, indeed desirability, of bringing into the Church gentiles who had not previously become Jews. The picture is clear enough, and the verisimilitude of Acts in its description of Greek city life and of Jews within it is great, but the picture conflicts directly with the picture of his mission given by Paul himself. According to Paul in his letters, which constitute the earliest extant Christian documents, he was pre-eminently the apostle to the gentiles. He gave no hint that he had previously tried to persuade Jews and failed, and the main aspect he stressed of the previous life of the gentiles he had converted was their paganism. Either the account in Acts is a later (late first-century?) theological construct intended to explain and justify the mission to the gentiles (which is quite possible) or Paul systematically ignored his earlier, less successful, career in his later epistles (which is also not at all unlikely).

Paul's teachings were based firmly on the figure of Jesus Christ, and, according to Acts (11.26), it was during his ministry in Antioch *c.* AD 40–44 that the name 'Christian', meaning essentially 'enthusiast for Christ', first came to be used. But, unlike the compilers of the Gospel story and 'Q', Paul exhibited no interest in Jesus' life apart from the crucifixion, about which the significant fact was the resurrection, and markedly little knowledge of Jesus' teaching, which he only very rarely quoted and which he failed to use even in the course of arguments where it should have provided him with clinching authority. For Paul, all life had simply changed for ever as a result of Christ's resurrection. At times this led him to talk about the present as the last times, but sometimes he looked forward to Christ's Second Coming in glory, and it is a reasonable hypothesis that some of the enthusiasm he exhibited in his mission to the gentiles was fuelled by a desire to wipe away the disappointment of the delayed end. Paul stressed the sin of men to an extent quite novel to pagans, arguing that worship of other gods in itself was a severe sin for all.

It is hard to know how many other Christians shared Paul's missionary enthusiasm. His theology evidently struck a chord with more than a few, since his epistles were imitated in the next generation and they were included by the compilers of the New Testament, but Paul's own polemic bears witness to the existence in his day of a wide variety of different Christianities. On the one hand, there was the 'circumcision party' (Galatians 2.12; Titus 1.10–15, etc.), who saw belief in Christ as no more than a desirable adjunct to the keeping of the *Torah*; on the other hand, there were the Christians such as those attacked in 1 Corinthians, who seem to have believed that those born again in Christ could jettison their previous relationships and moral codes:

> I actually hear reports of sexual immorality among you, immorality such as even pagans do not tolerate: the union of a man with his father's wife. And you can still be proud of yourselves! You ought to have gone into mourning; a man who has done such a deed should have been rooted out of your company.
> (1 Corinthians 5.1–2)

Paul was ambivalent and contradictory about whether Jews who were Christians should continue to observe distinctive Jewish practices and morality (cf. Romans 2.17–3.31), but he was very clear that for gentiles to do so would demonstrate a lack of faith (for example, Galatians 5.2–12), and this left him a considerable problem in combating the view that no moral rules applied to Christians at all. From the evidence of his epistles it appears that he used essentially his personal authority as an 'apostle of Christ' to impose a morality not unlike that of ordinary bourgeois Greek life in his day, but with the addition of a strong sexual asceticism which was later to become a hallmark of Christian supererogatory piety.[9]

ORGANIZATION OF THE EARLY CHURCH

By the end of the first century the Church had a strong sense of its own identity, and each individual community (*ecclesia*) within it was clearly organized under the leadership of an *episkopos* ('overseer', or bishop) and deacons. In Hermas' *The Shepherd*, which probably belongs to the end of the first century, the Church was envisaged as a woman, or sometimes as a castle. According to 2 Clement, travelling charismatics still had some influence as in earlier generations, but the *Didache*, an anonymous treatise dated probably to the early second century, which lays out pastoral rules for rituals such as baptism and the eucharist, seems to envisage some tension between such informal authorities and local leaders. On the other hand, distant Christians still remained in contact with each other through letters, and they continued to take for granted the notion that the nature and will of the divine were appropriate topics for argument. By the second half of the second century it became increasingly common for regional bishops to assemble in synods to achieve consensus on difficult theological issues; by the end of the century, ecclesiastical administrative boundaries followed those of secular provinces, providing episcopal authorities with a degree of control over their fellow Christians over a wide area unparalleled in the hierarchy of any other ancient religion.

Christians were to be found in the coastal cities bordering the eastern Mediterranean, particularly in Greece, Macedonia, Asia Minor and Syria. There were influential communities particularly in Antioch, Ephesus and Corinth; Jerusalem ceased to be an important centre after AD 70. Already in the first century there were smaller clusters of Christians in cities on the Anatolian plateau, and a growing community in the city of Rome. The church in Carthage must have been well established by the late second century, when Tertullian, the first Christian to compose extensive theological treatises in Latin, was converted in the city.

Identifying more precisely the geographical spread of Christianity in this period is problematic not least because of the near-total lack of identifiably Christian art and architecture before *c.* AD 180, rendering the Church virtually undetectable in the archaeological record, and because the grandiose claims of Christian writers of the time are hard to evaluate. Thus, when Paul claimed (Romans 15:19) to have 'completed the Gospel from Jerusalem and in a circle as far as Illyricum', on the grounds that he had brought to faith in Christ some people in some cities in these areas, he must be considered to have treated the churches he established as in some sense representative of these regions as a whole. It is probable that the number of those who considered themselves Christian in AD 180 was still a very small fraction of the total population of the empire.[10] The extant Christian literary tradition suggests that Christianity was essentially an urban phenomenon, but Pliny (*Letters* 10.96) in the early second century referred to the large number of Christians in the countryside in Pontus, on the southern shore of the Black Sea, and second-century Christian papyri from Egypt testify to a flourishing Christian presence there about which nothing else is known.

Converts were mostly gentiles rather than Jews, and from all levels of society: prosopography of known Christians reveals a preponderance of urban craftsmen and not a few richer members of the local aristocracies – although pride in such converts may have exaggerated their importance in the evidence, much of which is found in the greetings and valedictions at the beginning and end of epistles, such as in 2 Timothy 4.19–22:[11]

> Greetings to Prisca and Aquila, and the household of Onesiphorus. Erastus stayed behind at Corinth, and I left Trophimus ill at Miletus. Do try to get here before winter. Greetings from Eubulus, Pudens, Linus, and Claudia, and from all the brotherhood here. The Lord be with your spirit. Grace be with you all!

In a spiritual sense in Christ there was neither Jew nor Greek, neither slave nor free, neither male nor female (Galatians 3.28), but in practical terms the existing social structure was taken for granted – slaves were expected to obey their masters, and wives their husbands (cf. Titus 2.1–9). On the other hand, it is a striking feature of martyrdom stories that religious heroism could be ascribed as much to the slave girl Felicitas as to her owner, the noble Perpetua, when both were put to death in Carthage in AD 203.[12]

This strong sense of the Church as a united community with one theology, a notion already present in Paul's epistles, co-existed with great theological variety: in essence, all Christians agreed that there should be (or 'was') only one Church, but they disagreed vehemently over which doctrines, and therefore which community, constituted that Church. In practice, it would be hard to exaggerate the extent of variety within the practices and doctrines found among those calling themselves Christians in the second century. All Christians might be expected to accept the notion that there is one God, that Christ is Lord, and that the divine will has been revealed in authoritative writings preserved by their community, but there was no agreement at all about the relationship of Christ to God the Father or about the contents of authoritative scripture. It is one of the more remarkable facts about early Christianity, in contrast to other religions in the Roman world, that there was such a lack of clarity about the deity to whom Christians addressed worship. Ignatius of Antioch seems to have been the earliest writer to state explicitly that Christ was both God and man, writing in opposition to (among others) docetics who claimed that Christ was human in appearance only, and therefore had not suffered (Ignatius, *Philadelphians* 6). Basilides of Egypt asserted that God is too exalted for anything at all to be said about him, but that the ineffable divine Father revealed himself through three descending sonships (Hippolytus, *Refutation* 7.2-27). And Valentinus, in the mid second century, developed a complex myth about the rule of *Sophia* (wisdom) in relation to the Godhead and to Christ. Very difference were the forms of Christian doctrine and practice adopted by those accused by their fellow Christians of Judaising by (for instance) observing too literally the laws laid down in the Old Testament: the parting of the ways between Judaism and Christianity was a complex business in which borders were then, and are now, hard to draw.[13]

In reaction to such doctrines, mainstream Christians in the second century came increasingly to identify themselves by what they were not; writers like Irenaeus of Lyons attacked heresies with a vehemence far exceeding the routine scorn for paganism in Jewish and Christian writings.[14] The need for uniformity of doctrine was a major theme of many of the so-called Apostolic Fathers, authors in the second century of the Church like Justin Martyr (c. AD 100–165), a convert to Christianity from pagan philosophy who sought vehemently to appeal to both pagan and Jewish contemporaries. The writings of the Apostolic Fathers came to be revered by later Christians only marginally less than those canonized in the New Testament.

Two main motives for this preoccupation with orthodoxy may be identified. First, the expansion and popularity of various types of Gnosticism, for which there is evidence not only in the attacks of the Church Fathers but in the survival of numerous papyri in the sands of Nag Hammadi in Egypt.[15] 'Gnosticism' is, like 'paganism', a modern scholarly construct devised to make sense of some of the varied features of the Christian literature which were declared heretical by the orthodox of the period. Gnostic writers in this period saw themselves as Christians and, even though they undoubtedly made use of earlier Jewish and pagan motifs, there is no reason to suppose they represented a conscious pre-Christian and non-Christian tradition.

The common element in the various Gnostic systems is a belief that all that is required for salvation is knowledge (in Greek, *gnosis*). The varieties came in part from differences over the nature of the knowledge in question. In the case of Valentinian and 'Sethic' gnostics, it was enshrined in highly complex myths. Gnostics in their mundane lives could react to their knowledge of their salvation either by extreme asceticism (on the grounds that the body is disgusting, so should be denied) or by abandonment to sensual pleasures (on the grounds that what the body does is unimportant, so it might as well be enjoyable). Both attitudes are attested, but only the latter was dangerous for other Christians trying to establish themselves in an often hostile environment. Irenaeus is vehement in his denunciation of such teachings of Valentinus and the practice of his followers:

> So they assert that good works are necessary for us [ordinary Christians]; otherwise salvation would be impossible. But they hold the doctrine that they themselves will be completely saved because they are spiritual not by works but by nature. ... For this reason the most 'perfect' of them do without fear everything that is forbidden, of which scriptures assure us that 'those who do them will not inherit the kingdom of God' [Galatians 5.21]. ... Some who are intensely addicted to the pleasures of the flesh say that they render things of the flesh to the flesh, and things of the spirit to the spirit. And some of them secretly seduce women who are taught this doctrine; women who were seduced by some of them, but then returned to the church of God, have often confessed this along with the rest of their error.
>
> (*Against Heresies* 1.6.2–4)

The love feasts of which Irenaeus accused gnostic heretics were sometimes described in the same terms by pagans with reference to Christians in general.

The second main impulse to the imposition of orthodoxy was the threat of the heretic Marcion, who taught a severe dualist doctrine that the God of the Hebrew Bible, the 'Creator God', was wicked, in contrast to Christ.[16] Marcion accordingly taught that the Hebrew Bible itself was vehemently to be rejected. In reaction, mainstream Christians created a canon of the Old Testament (naturally, in its Greek version). The creation of the canon of the New Testament was similarly induced in reaction to heretics who claimed as sacred texts which were not accepted by the mainstream.[17]

By AD 180 the need for unambiguous doctrine had thus become quite clear within the Church, but there was still room for new prophecies, like those of a certain Montanus and two women associates, Priscilla and Maximilla, in

Phrygia (in Turkey); their prophetic revelation of a new covenant in the latter half of the second century was the basis of Montanism.[18] Eusebius (*Church History* 5.16–19) quotes from the polemic of Apollinarius, bishop of Hierapolis, against the heretics:

> A recent convert named Montanus, while Gratus was proconsul of Syria, in his unbridled ambition to reach the top laid himself open to the adversary, was filled with spiritual excitement and suddenly fell into a kind of trance and unnatural ecstasy. He raved and began to chatter and talk nonsense, prophesying in a way that conflicted with the practice of the Church handed down generation by generation from the beginning. ... Then he [the devil] secretly stirred up and inflamed minds close to the true Faith, raising up in this way two others – women whom he filled with the sham spirit, so that they chattered crazily, inopportunely, and wildly, like Montanus himself.

But in general by AD 180 the Church was no longer an institution in dramatic flux and growth (as a century earlier), and most Christians were now born into the faith rather than converts. Nonetheless, it would be quite wrong to imagine their religious life was comfortable and settled. Christianity was still not an easy option.

OPPOSITION TO THE CHURCH

One obvious factor which made being Christian difficult was the opposition to the Church from adherents of other religions.[19] Such opposition was a fact of life for Christians throughout the first three centuries – after all, Christ himself had been crucified. But its strength varied greatly, from disapproval to social ostracism and murderous violence, and its effects were by no means entirely negative. As Tertullian remarked in the early third century, 'the blood of martyrs is the seed of the Church' (*Dialogue with Heracleides* 454).

The opposition of Jews to Christians is one theme of the Gospel of John, which portrays 'the Jews' as an undifferentiated group responsible for the crucifixion of Jesus (unlike the other Gospels which specify the role of the High Priest and his advisors, and, of course, the governor Pilate). The Acts of the Apostles recounts specific acts of hostility by Jews to individual Christians, such as the stoning of Stephen by a Jewish crowd (Acts 7.54–8.2) and the ejection of Paul and Barnabas from the synagogue of Antioch in Pisidia (Acts 13.50). Jewish antagonism is summarized in the prophetic words of Jesus to his disciples (Mark 13.9): 'you will be beaten in synagogues'.

Hostility in this case derived from similarity, for this was a family argument. Paul claimed with pride to have been subjected five times by the synagogue authorities to the official (that is, biblical) penalty of thirty-nine lashes (2 Corinthians 11.24). Since he was a Roman citizen, and the synagogue leaders were not Roman magistrates, such punishment was illegal in Roman law, and the Jewish courts would only have dared to inflict it if the accused had agreed to put himself under their jurisdiction. It was evidently important in Paul's eyes to be seen by other Jews as a Jew, and he succeeded: punishment implies inclusion. In its first generation, Christianity was a Jewish movement, and the prime cause of persecution was the painful process of separation.

Precisely which aspect, if any, of Christian theology or behaviour led Jews to persecute Christians in the first century is debated. The varieties of belief that co-existed in first-century Judaism (see Chapter 30) preclude an easy assumption that any particular doctrine could cause other Jews to react so violently. Different Jews always had different ideas about most of the topics on which Christians took a stand, such as the identity and characteristics of the Messiah, life after death, the desirability of sexual abstinence, and so on; but such disagreements did not usually lead even to social separation, let alone to physical violence, a fact reinforced by the apparent lack of persecution of the Jerusalem Church.

If one then hunts for a social and political, rather than theological, explanation for persecution in the context of diaspora Jews, one possible answer does come to hand. Jewish communities in cities like Damascus, Philippi and Corinth were tolerated by their pagan compatriots largely because they did not interfere with the religious lives of others – if Jews had strange customs, that was their business alone. It may therefore have seemed very dangerous to the delicate standing of such communities when some Jews began proclaiming in their cities that all gentile pagans were sinners just because they continued to worship their ancestral gods. Hence the need to prevent such Christian apostles who were publicly identified as Jews from doing precisely what they were most keen to do – that is, preaching to gentiles. But it must be emphasized that this is only a hypothesis, and that causes of hostility may have varied at different times and places.

It was Christians who brought about the separation between Christianity and Judaism, since such separation was essentially one of self-definition. The picture of the Jews expelling Christians from their communities may be true in individual cases, but despite much scholarship on the history of the *Birkat haMinim* (a special blessing of God for punishing heretics, composed by or for some rabbis in the late first century AD), it cannot explain the separation as a whole, simply because Judaism had no central institution capable of imposing a ban on heretics of any kind. It is most likely that the gradual preeminence in the first century in churches of gentiles who never had any contact with Jewish communities, and the claims of such churches in any case to be the 'true Israel', carrying on God's covenant in the way he desired (unlike the Jews), led to a drifting apart rather than a sudden break.

Thus, by the second century AD much of the passion against Jews was spent – they had become irrelevant to Christians. To Justin Martyr, composing his *Dialogue with Trypho the Jew* in the 150s AD, it was simply odd that Jews had not yet seen the light (Chapter 68):

Thus, for instance, they [the Jews] have taught you that this scripture which we are discussing ['Behold, the virgin shall conceive', Isaiah 7.14] refers to Hezekiah, in which, as I promised, I shall show they are wrong. And since they are compelled, they agree that some scriptures which we mention to them, and which expressly prove that Christ was to suffer, to be worshipped, and [to be called] God, and which I have already recited to you, do indeed refer to Christ, but they venture to assert that this man is not Christ. But they admit that he will come to suffer, and to reign, and to be worshipped, and to be God; and this opinion I shall in like manner show to be silly and ridiculous.

Theophilus, bishop of Antioch, who in *c.* AD 180 wrote an apology in three books addressed to a pagan, Autolycus, put forward a Christian claim to the Jewish biblical traditions, for example describing Moses as 'our prophet' (3.9, 18, 23). By this period, Christian authors referring to Jews and persecution were usually thinking about the position of Jews in the Old or the New Testament. For them in their own day, the persecutors were pagan.

Pagan opposition to Christians had begun with the crucifixion of Jesus, and was endemic, if not always openly expressed, throughout Late Antiquity. From the point of view of the Roman governor Pilate, Jesus was probably executed simply as a trouble-maker; his theological views will have been of interest only to his fellow Jews. But pagan hostility to the early Christian movement from the 40s AD onwards was based more clearly on pagan theology. Christians, like Jews, refused to worship divinities other than their own, but, as the pagan philosopher Celsus put it in his great attack on Christianity in the second century, Christians were more objectionable than Jews because they lacked the Jews' excuse that they were at least continuing their ancestral customs (Origen, *Against Celsus* 2.1). Christianity's stance towards the standard polytheism of their day was in fact calculated to provoke deep hostility. They portrayed belief in pagan divinities as not just foolish (as Jews did) but as wicked, and, worst of all, they taught that all people – and not just existing Christians – should follow their faith, with the corollary that the normal worship of the gods on which, in the eyes of pagan polytheists, society had long relied, should be abandoned by all.[20] In the eyes of the polytheists themselves, then, Christians were not just atheists but proselytizers for atheism.

Popular pagan opposition to the Early Church generally took the form of riots, or of pressure on the authorities to take action against Christians. Thus, according to the Acts of the Apostles, the silversmiths of Ephesus whipped up feelings against St Paul in the 50s AD in the fear that the famous cult of Artemis in their city would be threatened by Paul's preaching against it:

A man named Demetrius, a silversmith, who made silver shrines of Artemis, brought no little business to the craftsmen. These he gathered together, with the workmen of like occupation, and said, 'Men, you know that from this business we have our wealth. And you see and hear that not only at Ephesus but almost throughout Asia this Paul has persuaded and turned away a considerable company of people, saying that gods made with hands are not gods. And there is danger not only that this trade of ours may come into disrepute but also that the temple of the great goddess Artemis may count for nothing, and that she may even be deposed from her magnificence, she whom all Asia and the world worship.'

(Acts 19.24–27)

In Lyons in AD 177 a number of Christians were publicly executed during the games by the governor of Gallia Lugdunensis under pressure from the local population: hostility may have been exacerbated by the foreign origin of many Christians in the city, since they were apparently Greek speakers even in this Latin-speaking part of the empire.[21]

Official state opposition to the Christians was rather more sporadic. Christians were publicly expelled from Rome by the emperor Claudius, although the reference in Suetonius (*Claudius* 25.4) to riots by the Jews 'at the instigation of Chrestus' may refer to another Jew altogether. More certain is Nero's use of the Christians as a scapegoat for the great fire in Rome in AD 64; Tacitus graphically described the crucifixions and the mockery:

Their deaths were made farcical. Dressed in wild animals' skins, they were torn to pieces by dogs, or crucified, or made into torches to be ignited after dark as substitutes for daylight. Nero provided his Gardens for the spectacle, and exhibited displays in the Circus, at which he mingled with the crowd – or stood in a chariot, dressed as a charioteer. Despite their guilt as Christians, and the ruthless punishment it deserved, the victims were pitied. For it was felt that they were being sacrificed to one man's brutality rather than to the national interest.

(*Annals* 15.44)

But the legal basis for suppression of Christians was evidently unclear to the younger Pliny in *c.* AD 110, when he wrote to Trajan to seek clarification (*Letters* 10.96). And Trajan's reply (*Letters* 10.97) – that Christians were to be punished only if recalcitrant, were to be given an opportunity to recant, and were not to be hunted down – is distinctly ambivalent. It seems evident that Christian cult was not itself a crime in the eyes of the Roman state, since there was no punishment for having been a Christian in the past, only for protestation of the name of Christian in the present.

Hence governors generally had to be pushed into action against Christians. Those pushing would in the first century sometimes be Jews, but in the second century they were generally pagans. But there were exceptions, like the Jews in Smyrna who joined the mocking pagan crowd at the martyrdom of Polycarp, Smyrna's bishop, in AD 155 or 156:

What he [the Governor] did next was to send his crier to give out three times, from the centre of the arena, 'Polycarp has admitted to being a Christian!' At the crier's words, the whole audience, the heathens and the Jewish residents of Smyrna alike, broke into loud yells of ungovernable fury: 'That teacher of Asia! That father-figure of the Christians! That destroyer of our gods, who is teaching whole multitudes to abstain from sacrificing to them or worshipping them!' Interspersed with shouts of this kind there were loud demands for the Asiarch Philip to let loose a lion at Polycarp. However, he told them that the rules would not allow him to do this, since he had already declared the beast-fighting closed; whereupon they decided to set up a unanimous outcry that he should have Polycarp burnt alive. ... It was all done in less time than it takes to tell. In a moment the crowd had collected faggots and kindling from the workshops and baths; the Jews, as usual, being well to the fore with their help.

(*The Martyrdom of Polycarp* 12–13)

The number of Christians who died for their faith in the first two centuries was probably not large, since the value of their actions in exhorting their fellow Christians was so widely recognized that the memory of their behaviour tended to be preserved, and the total of names recorded is only in the hundreds. Organized state opposition lay in the future, in the persecutions of Decius (AD 250–51) and Diocletian (AD 303–12), when many hundreds died. But such persecution as there was fed a strand within Christianity which was simply antagonistic to the Roman state.

The clearest expression of that strand may be found in the last book of the New Testament, Revelation, which was composed by an unknown author in about AD 90. Here Rome was portrayed as the scarlet whore of Babylon (Revelation 17–19.3), whose wickedness guaranteed her eventual awful destruction. But by contrast at other times Christians claimed the compatibility of Christianity with the Roman state. The contradiction was implicit in the Acts of the Apostles, which showed the unwillingness to suppress the new faith of right-thinking Roman pagans, including some of senatorial rank like Gallio. Acts 18.12–17 records how when St Paul was brought before Gallio, proconsul of Achaia, by Jews at Corinth, Gallio dismissed them, saying, 'If it is some bickering about words and names and your Jewish law, you may see to it yourselves; I have no mind to be a judge of these matters.' It was also explicit in a series of defences of Christianity written in the mid-second century AD. In the earliest surviving such apology of *c.* AD 124, Aristides of Athens asserted that, far from opposing the secular world, Christians alone preserved it by their prayers (*Apology* 16). According to Eusebius (*Church History* 4.3), Aristides explicitly addressed his apology to the emperor Hadrian; whether he ever read it is unknown.

With the establishment in the fourth century of Christianity as the religion of the Roman emperor, it became almost unimaginable that Christians had once felt themselves to be outsiders within Roman society, but in the mid-second century such a feeling was entirely possible.[22] It is likely to be significant that those Christians who decided in the mid-second century which of their books should be included in the New Testament chose to incorporate the apocalyptic vision of the book of Revelation, with its prophecy of the end of the might of Rome:

'Alas, alas, for the great city, where all who had ships at sea grew rich by her wealth! In one hour she has been laid waste. Rejoice over her, O heaven, O saints and apostles and prophets, for God has given judgement for you against her!' Then a mighty angel took up a stone like a great millstone and threw it into the sea, saying, 'So shall Babylon the great city be thrown down with violence, and shall be found no more; and the sound of harpers and minstrels, of flute players and trumpeters, shall be heard in thee no more; and a craftsman of any craft shall be found in thee no more; and the sound of the millstone shall be heard in thee no more; and the light of a lamp shall shine in thee no more; and the voice of bridegroom and bride shall be heard in thee no more; for thy merchants were the great men of the earth, and all nations were deceived by thy sorcery. And in her was found the blood of prophets and of saints, and of all who have been slain on earth.'
(Revelation 18.19–24)

The impressive prophecy of the author of Revelation survives because it became a sacred text in the continuing Christian tradition. No-one knows how many other inhabitants of the Roman Empire prayed with equal vehemence for the end of the corrupt society in which they lived, without leaving behind any record of their views. But it is certain that the author of Revelation was not alone.

PART VI

EPILOGUE

32

SEVERANS TO
CONSTANTINE

The view of Rome promulgated by Christians in the entourage of the emperor
Constantine in the fourth century could hardly have been more different from
the antagonistic stance of the author of Revelation, as we have already noted
in the case of the Church historian Eusebius (see Chapter 31). For Constantine,
his role as Christian was to be presented by the end of his life in AD 337 as
indivisible from his duties as emperor, and the special mausoleum he prepared
for himself in his new capital Constantinople presented him in death as the
Thirteenth Apostle.[1] What had changed in the Roman world to bring about
this reconciliation between Christians and the state?

IMPERIAL POLITICS

The century and a half between the accession of Commodus and the death of
Constantine witnessed political upheavals far greater than anything
experienced in the Roman world in the preceding two centuries.[2] For the first
fifty years after AD 180, the causes of chaos were essentially integral to the
political class. Commodus, who succeeded Marcus Aurelius as emperor while
still a youth, devoted his energies to performing as a gladiator in Rome and
creating an image of himself as more than human. Claiming that his reign
constituted a new golden age for the city, he renamed Rome as Colonia
Commodiana and added 'Hercules' to his own nomenclature. Too many
members of his entourage and the senate were executed in a series of purges
for the regime to survive, and the emperor was strangled on the last day of
December AD 193 in a conspiracy led by his concubine Marcia and the
praetorian prefect.

There followed a civil war similar to that in AD 68–69, but more protracted
and even more bloody. The eventual victor, Septimius Severus, backed by the
Rhine and Danubian legions, was originally of Punic origin, from Lepcis
Magna in Africa. He was married to Julia Domna, the daughter of a priest of
the Invincible Sun-god Elagabalus, the oracular deity of the city of Emesa in
Syria, but he sought legitimacy in traditional fashion, claiming fictitious
kinship to Marcus Aurelius and embarking on ambitious expansionary

campaigns against Parthia and, towards the end of his rule, in Britain. The Severan dynasty he founded was not without its own internal tensions, not least through the machinations of Julia Domna and her extended family: the appointment as emperor in AD 218 of her great nephew, known to posterity by his nickname Elagabalus, lasted for only four years before his intention to make Romans accept his ancestral Syrian cult throughout the empire at the expense of Roman religious traditions led to a palace coup and his replacement by his cousin, Severus Alexander, during whose rule (from AD 218 to 235) Cassius Dio composed his account of Roman history.

Already by the death of Severus Alexander, who had gone to the frontier to counter a threat from a loose confederation of Germanic tribes, the location of campaigns was decided less by the ambition of emperors than the hostile intentions of peoples from outside the empire. Over the ensuing decades frontier wars were to become endemic both on the Rhine and the Danube, and against the new Sassanian dynasty in Persia to the east. Emperors primarily engaged in such defensive warfare were vulnerable to the whims of the soldiers on whose service they relied, and they rarely held on to power for long: many emperors, military men themselves, were killed by their own troops when an alternative candidate, likely to be either more competent or more favourable, was identified within their ranks. From AD 260 to 274, large parts of the empire were subjected to separate regimes. Many emperors spent their entire reigns on campaign, and never enjoyed the fruits of their power in Rome itself. About some emperors no evidence survives at all, apart from their names on coins.

The restoration of unity and control at the centre of Roman politics began in a series of successful campaigns by Aurelian from AD 270 to 275, but it was not until AD 284, when the soldiers proclaimed as emperor Diocletian, another military man of humble origins, that consolidation really began. In a series of original and sweeping reforms, Diocletian established a tetrarchy, a new system of administration which sought to combine centralised control with sufficient devolved government to prevent the central organs of the state being overstretched, demonstrating his confidence in his reforms by retiring into private life in AD 305.

The new system collapsed almost immediately when Constantius, designated as Augustus in the West, died prematurely in York in AD 306. Constantius' son Constantine was proclaimed Augustus by the troops, reinstating the hereditary assumptions which Diocletian had tried to replace by a meritocracy, and leading to a series of campaigns to establish his authority. In AD 312 Constantine marched on Rome, defeating his rival Maxentius (like Constantine himself, son of a former Augustus who had failed to be awarded power by Diocletian when he abdicated in AD 305) in a battle at the Milvian Bridge just outside the city. The victory, against unequal odds, was achieved, so Constantine asserted, through the miraculous aid of the Christian God.

STATE AND SOCIETY

As a result of this tumultuous history, the role of the state in the Roman world changed considerably between Marcus Aurelius and Constantine. The military and political crises of the mid third century left the state financially stretched, and the silver coinage underwent dramatic debasement. State expenditure was concentrated on the frontier provinces to the detriment of the Mediterranean heartland of the empire, not least Italy. Concentration of power in the hands of military men often without political pedigree weakened the consensus through which the state could rely on provincial elites to support the imperial system in return for access to influence. In many provinces, the public civic display through which such elites had advertised their loyalty both to their fellow citizens and to the state simply stopped, with the wealthy preferring to reserve their wealth for more private expenditure. In many places, in the mid-third century, the practice of commissioning honorific inscriptions seems to have ceased. In some areas more distant from the troubled frontiers, and insufficiently prosperous to be subjected to intensive taxation, the lack of state attention may have been positively welcomed.

The imposition of more efficient administrative control by Diocletian and the tetrarchy was all the more shocking for those who had become accustomed to Roman rule with a light touch. The reforms affected many areas of life, including not only the tax system but a novel attempt to fix maximum prices for a huge range of goods and services.

CHRISTIANITY AND THE STATE

Among the most affected were Christians. Widespread persecutions by Decius and Valerian in the 250s were provoked by an attempt to unite the empire at a time of military crisis through ensuring that everyone in the empire could be shown to have sacrificed to the gods on behalf of the welfare of the state. The persecution initiated by Diocletian in AD 303, by contrast, was more obviously targeted at the Church, with the demolition of churches and the burning of Christian books. It is possible that an attack on Christians was attractive to the emperor precisely because they were widespread, and state action against them as 'atheists' would be widely witnessed by the rest of his subjects, but it is impossible to know how many Christians there were by the late third century: natural increase within Christian families will have ensured substantial growth in numbers, but we have no idea how many lapsed in times of persecution, nor how many returned to the faith when persecution ended.

What we do know is that the vision of Constantine at the Milvian Bridge in AD 312 was to have an immediate and dramatic effect, and not only through the Edict of Toleration in AD 313 which lifted from Christians the threat of persecution and ensured the restoration of their property.[2] Constantine was rapidly drawn into deciding between the opposing parties in the Donatist schism in Africa (in which hardliners confronted those Christians who had given in to persecution), and by AD 325 he was to be found presiding over an Ecumenical Council in Nicaea which endeavoured to end disputes about the relations of the different persons of the Trinity. Constantine affirmed abundantly, in somewhat flowery rhetoric, his own personal devotion to Christ, and directed imperial funds to Christian communities, thus rapidly turning a minority sect into a major conduit of state beneficence to the emperor's subjects.

It is a testimony to the conservative forces in ancient religion that the conversion of the empire to Christianity was not instantaneous upon the transfer of imperial largesse to the well-established institutions of the Church, for the consequences to traditional cults were as negative as those for Christians were positive. Constantine did not, in most places forbid such cults to continue, but he resolutely (and with vituperative rhetoric) declined to provide them with funding – and without funds, religious ceremonies based on expensive sacrificial offerings simply come to a natural end. It took time for the wealthy elite throughout the empire to follow the emperor's lead, but towards the end of the fourth century most did so, and in the last decade of the century the power of the state was enlisted to bring public paganism to an end. The theological arguments within the framework of tradition religion were not complicated. If those who had worshipped the ancestral gods did not find that the cessation of cult brought divine retribution, did that not show the validity of the Christian argument, as now espoused also by the emperor, that their funds and prayers were better diverted to the Christian God?

The paradox of the Roman world in these centuries is that a religion which had emerged from one obscure corner of this world in the first century, and which had begun so inauspiciously with the crucifixion of its founding figure by the Roman state, and developed an ideology which gloried in persecution by authority, would by the fourth century come to be identified with the state itself, and to provide one of the most enduring legacies of the Roman world to western societies of the present day.

NOTES

1 SOURCES AND PROBLEMS

1   See R. Lane Fox, *The Classical World: an epic history from Homer to Hadrian*, London, 2005, for a description of the classical world from the perspective of the second century AD; S. Price and P. Thonemann, *The Birth of Classical Europe: a history from Troy to Augustine*, London, 2010.

2   E. Gibbon, *The History of the Decline and Fall of the Roman Empire*, ed. J.B. Bury, vol. 1, London, 1896, p. 78.

3   For brief summaries of the careers and writings of authors, with useful bibliographies, see *The Oxford Classical Dictionary*, 4th edn, Oxford, 2010; on historiography, see A. Feldherr (ed.) *The Cambridge Companion to the Roman Historians*, Cambridge, 2009.

4   For recent discussions of the archaeology of the Roman Empire and its interpretation, see S. Johnson, *Rome and its Empire*, London, 1989.

5   On the use of inscriptions by historians, see F.G.B. Millar, Chap. 2, in M. Crawford (ed.) *Sources for Ancient History*, Cambridge, 1983. For recent inscriptions see the epigraphic surveys in the *Journal of Roman Studies*, published twice in each decade, e.g. A.E. Cooley, S. Mitchell and B. Salway, 'Roman Inscriptions 2001–2005', *JRS* 97 (2007), pp. 176–263.

6   For important arguments that epigraphic habits varied across regions as well as social classes, see H. Mouritsen, 'Freedmen and Decurions: epitaphs and social history in imperial Italy', *JRS* 95 (2005), pp. 38–63.

7   For an introduction to the Greek papyri, see E.G. Turner, *Greek Papyri: An Introduction*, 2nd edn, Oxford, 1980. On using papyri as evidence, see R.S. Bagnall, *Reading Papyri, Writing Ancient History*, London and New York, 1995. On papyri relating to the Near East, see H.M. Cotton, W.E.H. Cockle and F.G.B. Millar, 'The papyrology of the Roman Near East', *JRS* 85 (1995), pp. 214–35. On the Vindolanda documents, see A.K. Bowman and J.D. Thomas, *The Vindolanda Writing-Tablets (tabulae Vindolandenses II)*, London, 1994.

8   On the use of coins for history, see C. Howgego, *Ancient History from Coins*, London and New York, 1995; C.H.V. Sutherland, *Roman History and Coinage, 44 BC–AD 69*, Oxford and New York, 1987; M. Grant, *Roman History from Coins*, Cambridge, 1958.

2 THE ROMAN WORLD IN 50 BC

1   On Greek ethnographic writings in the Late Republic and Early Empire, see A. Momigliano, *Alien Wisdom: The Limits of Hellenization*, Cambridge, 1975, Chap. 2, 'Polybius and Posidonius'.

2 See Chapter 19.

3 On Celts, see J.J. Tierney, 'The Celtic ethnography of Posidonius', *PRIA* 60 (1960), pp. 189–275, with D. Nash, 'Reconstructing Poseidonios' Celtic ethnography: some considerations', *Britannia* 7 (1976), pp. 111–26; B.W. Cunliffe, *The Celtic World*, 2nd edn, London, 1992; M.J. Green (ed.) *The Celtic World*, London and New York, 1995.

4 On Germans, see M. Todd, *The Northern Barbarians 100 BC–AD 300*, rev. edn, Oxford, 1987.

5 On the Hellenistic world, see F.W. Walbank, *The Hellenistic World*, 3rd impression with amendments, London, 1992.

6 See ibid., and F.G.B. Millar, *The Roman Near East 31 BC–AD 337*, Cambridge, Mass., 1993.

7 On Mithridates, see A. Mayor, *The Poison King: the life and legend of Mithradates, Rome's deadliest enemy*, Princeton, N.J., 2009.

8 On Egypt, see Chapter 27.

9 On North Africa, see Chapter 28.

10 See G. Alföldy, *The Social History of Rome*, London, 1985. For the changes in the Late Republic, see M. Crawford, *The Roman Republic*, 2nd edn, London, 1992.

11 See P.A. Brunt, *Italian Manpower 225 BC–AD 14*, Oxford, 1971, Chap. 9, 'The Augustan census figures', for the view that the figures included women and children, and for the view that they did not, E. Lo Cascio, 'The size of the Roman population: Beloch and the meaning of the Augustan census figures', *JRS* 84 (1994), pp. 23–40.

12 See P.A. Brunt, *Social Conflicts in the Roman Republic*, London, 1971.

13 For guides to the copious modern literature on the Roman family, see B. Rawson (ed.) *Marriage, Divorce and Children in Ancient Rome*, Canberra and Oxford, 1991; S. Dixon, *The Roman Family*, Baltimore and London, 1992.

14 On the impact of Roman law on everyday life, see J.A. Crook, *Law and Life of Rome*, London, 1967; J.F. Gardner, *Being a Roman Citizen*, London and New York, 1993.

15 On women in Roman society, see especially the collection of sources in J.F. Gardner, *Women in Roman Law and Society*, London, 1986.

16 On slaves in the Late Republic, see K. Hopkins, *Conquerors and Slaves*, Cambridge, 1978; sources in T. Wiedemann, *Greek and Roman Slavery*, London, 1981.

17 On specifically Roman cults, see R.M. Ogilvie, *The Romans and Their Gods in the Age of Augustus*, London, 1969.

3 THE POLITICAL LANGUAGE OF ROME

1 On the theoretical constitution of the Roman Republic, see H.H. Scullard, *From the Gracchi to Nero: A History of Rome from 133 BC to AD 68*, 5th edn, London, 1982. For a useful general survey of the Republic, see M. Crawford, *The Roman Republic*, 2nd edn, London, 1992.

2 On the actual workings of government in the Late Republic, see T.P. Wiseman (ed.) *Roman Political Life, 90 BC–AD 69*, Exeter, 1985; M. Beard and M. Crawford, *Rome in the Late Republic: Problems and Interpretations*, London, 1985. On the extent of democracy, see F.G.B. Millar, 'The political character of the classical Roman Republic, 200–151 BC', *JRS* 74 (1984), pp. 1–19.

3 For a discussion of how the censors controlled the private lives of citizens, see A.E. Astin, 'Regimen morum', *JRS* 78 (1988), pp. 14–34.

4   On Roman political vocabulary, see D. Earl, *The Moral and Political Tradition of Rome*, London, 1967; C. Edwards, *The Politics of Immorality in Ancient Rome*, Cambridge, 1993.

5   See C. Wirzubski, *Libertas as a Political Idea at Rome during the Late Republic and Early Principate*, Cambridge, 1950.

6   W.V. Harris, *War and Imperialism in Republican Rome, 327–70 BC,* Oxford, 1979; J.S. Richardson, '*Imperium Romanum* between Republic and Empire', in L. de Blois et al (eds.) *The Representation and Perception of Roman Imperial Power*, Amsterdam, 2003, pp. 137–47.

7   M. Beard, *The Roman Triumph*, Cambridge, Ma., 2007.

8   P.J. Holliday, *The Origins of Roman Historical Commemoration in the Visual Arts*, Cambridge, 2002., E.E. Welch, 'Art and architecture in the Roman Republic, in N. Rosenstein and R. Morstein-Marx (eds.) *A Companion to the Roman Republic*, Oxford, 2006, pp. 496–542.

9   W.J. Dominik (ed.) *Roman Eloquence: rhetoric in society and literature*, London, 1997.

10 On 'evergetism', see P. Veyne, *Bread and Circuses*, abridged O. Murray, London, 1990; on patronage, see R.P. Saller, *Personal Patronage under the Early Empire*, Cambridge, 1982.

11 On the assemblies, see L.R. Taylor, *The Voting Districts of the Roman Republic*, Rome, 1960; C. Nicolet, *The World of the Citizen in Republican Rome*, London, 1980; A. Yakobson, '*Petitio et largitio*: popular participation in the centuriate assembly of the Late Republic', *JRS* 82 (1992), pp. 32–52. See also H. Mouritsen, *Plebs and Politics in the late Roman Republic*, Cambridge, 2001.

12 See F. Millar, *The Crowd in Rome in the Late Republic*, Ann Arbor, Mi., 2002.

4 CAESAR TO AUGUSTUS, 50 BC–AD 14

1   On the civil war and Caesar's dictatorship, see M. Gelzer, *Caesar: Politician and Statesman*, Oxford, 1968; Z. Yavetz, *Julius Caesar and his Public Image*, London, 1983.

2   For Cicero's letters, see the commentary by D.R. Shackleton Bailey, *Select Letters of Cicero*, Cambridge, 1980. On the letters from this period, see M.M. Willcock, *Cicero: The Letters of January to April 43 BC*, Warminster, 1995.

3   See P.A. Brunt and J.M. Moore (eds) *Res Gestae Divi Augusti*, Oxford, 1967, text and translation with extensive commentary.

4   On the length of the terms for which triumviral powers were voted, see F.G.B. Millar, 'Triumvirate and principate', *JRS* 63 (1973), pp. 50–67.

5   For the Seleucus inscription, see R.K. Sherk, *Roman Documents from the Greek East: senatus consulta and epistulae to the Age of Augustus*, Baltimore, 1969, no. 58, pp. 294–307; for the Aphrodisias inscriptions, see J. Reynolds, *Aphrodisias and Rome*, London, 1982.

6   On the narrative sources, see A.M. Gowing, *The Triumviral Narratives of Appian and Cassius Dio*, Ann Arbor, Michigan, 1992. On Asinius Pollio's history, see A.B. Bosworth, 'Asinius Pollio and Augustus', *Historia* 21 (1972), pp. 441–73.

7   On Lepidus, see R.D. Weigel, *Lepidus: The Tarnished Triumvir*, London, 1992.

8   On Antonius, see E.G. Huzar, *Mark Antony: A Biography*, Minneapolis, 1978; H. Bengtson, *Marcus Antonius: Triumvir und Herrscher des Orients*, Munich, 1977.

9   J.W.Rich and J.H.C. Williams, '*Leges et Iura P.R. Restitut*: A new aureus of Octavian and the settlement of 28–27 BC' *Numismatic Chronicle* 159 (1999), pp. 169–213; C.H. Lange, *Res Publica Constituta: Actium, Apollo and the Accomplishment of the Triumviral Assignment*, Brill, 2009.

10 For an assessment of Augustus' career, see A.H.M. Jones, *Augustus*, London, 1970; W. Eck, *The Age of Augustus*, transl. D.L. Schneider, Oxford, 2003.

11 On Dio's history of Augustus' rule, *Hist. Rom.* 51–56, see F.G.B. Millar, *A Study of Cassius Dio*, Oxford, 1964; B. Manuwald, *Cassius Dio und Augustus: philologische Untersuchungen zu den Büchern 45–46 des dionischen Geschichts-werkes*, Wiesbaden, 1979.

12 Dio, *Hist. Rom.* 54.3. On Primus and Murena, the more straightforward account by J.A. Crook, 'Political history, 30 BC to AD 14', *CAH* vol. X, 2nd edn, pp. 87–88, may be preferable to the ingenious reconstructions of confused evidence in D.L. Stockton, 'Primus and Murena', *Historia* 14 (1965), pp. 18–40, and L.J. Daly, 'Varro Murena, *cos.* 23 BC: [*magistratu motus*] *est*', *Historia* 27 (1978), pp. 83–94. The details of the crisis are best left obscure but the outline is clear.

13 On the political crises of Augustus' reign, see J. Crook, in *Cambridge Ancient History*, vol. X, 2nd edn, 1996, Chap. 2, 'Political history, 30 BC to AD 14'.

14 See *ILS* 911 for the career of a senator's son who had served in the cavalry as well as in the role of military tribune.

15 L. Koenen, 'Die "Laudatio funebris" des Augustus für Agrippa auf einem neuen Papyrus', *ZPE* 5 (1970), pp. 217–83, with M. Gronewald, 'Ein neues Fragment der Laudatio Funebris des Augustus auf Agrippa', *ZPE* 52 (1983), pp. 61–62; LR 1, p. 633. On the career of Agrippa, see J.-M. Roddaz, *Marcus Agrippa*, Rome, 1984.

16 On Julia, see E. Fantham, *Julia Augusta, the Emperor's Daughter*, London and New York, 2006.

17 On Augustus' campaigns, see P.A. Brunt, review of H.D. Meyer, *Die Aussenpolitik des Augustus und die Augusteische Dichtung*, in *JRS* 53 (1963), pp. 170–76.

18 See the prosopographical studies in R. Syme, *The Augustan Aristocracy*, Oxford, 1986.

5 JULIO-CLAUDIANS, AD 14–68

1 Suet., *Tib.* 23–24. On Tiberius' accession, see B. Levick, *Tiberius the Politician*, London, 1976, Chap. 5.

2 For rumours about Tiberius' hostility to Germanicus, see the snide narrative in Tac., *Ann.* Book 1. On Tiberius' rule in general, see Tac., *Ann.* 1–6; Suet., *Tib.*; Dio, *Hist. Rom.* 57–58; Levick, *Tiberius*.

3 W. Eck, A. Caballos and F. Fernández, *Das Senatus Consultum de Cn. Pisone Patre*, Munich, 1996; M. Griffin, 'The Senate's story,' *JRS* (1997), pp. 249–63.

4 This is a key argument of F.G.B. Millar, *The Emperor in the Roman World (31 BC–AD 337)*, 2nd edn, London, 1992.

5 On treason trials under Tiberius, see R.S. Rogers, *Criminal Trials and Criminal Legislation under Tiberius*, Middleton, 1935 and R.S. Rogers, 'Treason in the early empire', *JRS* 49 (1959), pp. 90–94.

6 On the conspiracy of Sejanus, see A. Boddington, 'Sejanus. Whose conspiracy?', *AJPh* 84 (1963), pp. 1–16; H.W. Bird, 'L. Aelius Seianus and his political significance', *Latomus* 28 (1969), pp. 61–98.

7 On Gaius Caligula, see Suet., *Gaius*; Dio, *Hist. Rom.* 59; J.P.V.D. Balsdon, *The Emperor Gaius (Caligula)*, Oxford, 1934.

8 The detailed narrative of the conspiracy is found in Joseph., *AJ* 19.14–118; cf. T.P. Wiseman, *Death of an Emperor: Flavius Josephus; Translation and Commentary*, Exeter, 1991.

9 Joseph., *AJ* 19.166–84.

10 Joseph., *AJ* 19.236–77. Dio's account (60.8.2–3) of Agrippa's part in creating Claudius emperor is much briefer.

11 On Claudius see Tac., *Ann.* 11–12; Suet., *Claud.*; Dio, *Hist. Rom.* 60–61.35; B. Levick, *Claudius*, London, 1990; A. Momigliano, *Claudius: The Emperor and His Achievement*, Oxford, 1934.

12 R.R.R. Smith, 'The imperial reliefs from the Sebasteion in Aphrodisias,' *JRS* 77 (1987), pp. 83–138.

13 C.P. Jones, 'The Claudian monument at Patara', *ZPE* 137 (2001), pp. 137, 161–168; A.E. Cooley, S. Mitchell and B.Salway. 'Roman inscriptions 2001–2005', *JRS* 97 (2007), pp. 181–82.

14 C. Thomas, 'Claudius and the Roman army reforms', *Historia* 53 (2004), pp. 424–52.

15 On Nero, see Tac., *Ann.* 13–14; Suet., *Nero*; Dio, *Hist. Rom.* 61.36–63.29.3; M. Griffin, *Nero: The End of a Dynasty*, London, 1984; M. Grant, *Nero*, London, 1970; V. Rudich, *Political Dissidence under Nero: The Price of Dissimulation*, London and New York, 1993. E. Champlin, *Nero*, Cambridge, Ma., 2003, stresses the extent to which Nero's image may have been sought deliberately by the emperor.

16 On the career of Corbulo under Claudius, see Tac., *Ann.* 11.18–20, and under Nero, Tac., *Ann.* 13.8–9, 13.34.2–41.3, 14.23–6, 15.1–17, 15.24–31.

6 CIVIL WAR AND FLAVIANS, AD 68–96

1 On Galba, see Suet., *Galba*; Tac., *Hist.* 1.5–49; Dio, *Hist. Rom.* 63.29.4–64.6.

2 On the civil war, see K. Wellesley, *The Long Year AD 69*, London, 1975; P.A.L. Greenhalgh, *The Year of the Four Emperors*, London, 1975.

3 On Vindex and Verginius, see especially P.A. Brunt, 'The revolt of Vindex and the fall of Nero', *Latomus* 18 (1959), pp. 531–59.

4 On Otho, see Suet., *Otho*; Tac., *Hist.* 1–2.51 *passim*; Dio, *Hist. Rom.* 64.7–15.

5 On Vitellius, see Suet., *Vitellius*; Tac., *Hist.* 1.51–3.86; Dio, *Hist. Rom.* 65.1–22.

6 On Vespasian's rise to power, see Suet., *Vesp.*; Joseph., *JW* 4.585–658; Tac., *Hist.* 2.74–5.26; Dio, *Hist. Rom.* 66.1–17; B. Levick, *Vespasian*, London, 1999.

7 P.F. Mittag, 'Ex Oriente pax: Zu einem neuen Sesterz des Vespasianus', *Jahrbuch für Numismatik und Geldgeschichte* 58 (2008), pp. 81–88.

8 On Vespasian's supporters, see J. Nicols, *Vespasian and the Partes Flavianae*, Wiesbaden, 1978.

9 On Caecina and the conspiracy of AD 79, see Suet., *Tit.* 6.2; Dio, *Hist. Rom.* 66.163.

10 G. Alföldy, 'Ein Bauinschrift aus den Colosseum', *ZPE* 109 (1995), pp. 195–226.

11 On Titus, see Suet., *Tit.*; Dio, *Hist. Rom.* 66.18–26; B.W. Jones, *The Emperor Titus*, London and New York, 1984.

12 On Domitian, see Suet., *Dom.*; Dio, *Hist. Rom.* 67.1–18; Pliny, *Letters* especially 1.5, 3.9, 3.11, 4.9, 4.11, 4.22, 8.14, 10.58, 10.60, 10.66, 10.72; Tac., *Agric.* 1–3, 39–40.2, 42, 44.5–45.3; B.W. Jones, *The Emperor Domitian*, London and New York, 1992.

7 NERVA TO MARCUS AURELIUS, AD 96–180

1 For a general political history of this period, see A. Garzetti, *From Tiberius to the Antonines: A History of the Roman Empire, AD 14–192*, London, 1974; for a detailed discussion of events immediately after the murder of Domitian, see J.D. Grainger, *Nerva and the Roman Succession Crisis of AD 96–99*, London, 2003.

2 For a narrative of Trajan's rule, see Dio, *Hist. Rom.* 68.3.4–33.3; J. Bennett, *Trajan, Optimus Princeps: a life and times*, London, 1997.

3 P.A. Roche, 'Selling Trajan's *Saeculum*. Destiny, abundance, assurance', *Athenaeum* 94 (2006), pp. 199–229.

4 On the accession of Hadrian, see Dio, *Hist. Rom.* 69.1–2.5; *SHA Hadrian* 3.10–6.5; A.R. Birley, *Hadrian: the restless emperor*, London, 1997.

5 For Hadrian's rule, see Dio, *Hist. Rom.* 69.1–23.3; *SHA Hadrian*; A. Claridge, 'Hadrian's Column of Trajan, *JRA* 6 (1993), pp. 5–22; eadem, 'Hadrian's lost Temple of Trajan, *JRA* 20 (2007), pp. 54–94.

6 W. Eck, 'The Bar Kokhba Revolt: the Roman point of view', *JRS* 89 (1999), pp. 76–89, takes a monumental arch recently discovered near Scythopolis as evidence of propaganda about the war, but for other views about the arch and the war, see P. Schäfer (ed.) *The Bar Kokhba War Reconsidered: new perspectives on the second Jewish revolt against Rome*, Tübingen, 2003.

7 A reconstruction of the edict can be found in O. Lenel, *Das Edictum Perpetuum: ein Versuch zu seiner Wiederherstellung*, 3rd edn, Leipzig, 1956.

8 On Antinous, see. C. Vout, *Power and Eroticism in Imperial Rome,* Cambridge, 2007, Chapter 2; C.P. Jones, *New Heroes in Antiquity from Achilles to Antinous*, Cambridge, Ma., 2009.

9 On Antoninus Pius, see *SHA Antoninus*.

10 On Marcus Aurelius, see especially Marcus Aurelius, *Meditations*; Fronto, *Letters; SHA Marcus*; Dio, *Hist. Rom.* 71.1–72.36; A. Birley, *Marcus Aurelius: A Biography*, rev. edn, London, 1987.

11 On Lucius Verus, see *SHA Verus*; Arrian, *Parthica* (on Parthian campaigns).

12 R. Duncan-Jones, 'The impact of the Antonine plague', *JRA* 9 (1996), pp. 108–36; W. Scheidel, 'A model of demographic and economic change in Roman Egypt after the Antonine plague', *JRA* 15 (2002), pp. 97–114.

13 See R.B. Rutherford, *The Meditations of Marcus Aurelius: A Study*, Oxford, 1989.

8 MILITARY AUTOCRACY

1 See M. Goodman, 'Opponents of Rome: Jews and others', in L. Alexander (ed.) *Images of Empire*, Sheffield, 1991, pp. 222–38.

2 On the recruitment of the army in the Republic, see P.A. Brunt, *Italian Manpower, 225 BC–AD 14*, Oxford, 1971.

3 On Augustus' campaigns, see Chapter 4.

4 See V.A. Maxfield, *The Military Decorations of the Roman Army*, London, 1981.

5 See G. Webster, *The Roman Imperial Army of the First and Second Centuries AD*, 3rd edn, London, 1985; G.R. Watson, *The Roman Soldier*, London, 1969; L.J.F. Keppie, *The Making of the Roman Army: From Republic to Empire*, London, 1984; Y. Le Bohec, *The Imperial Roman Army*, London, 1994; J.B. Campbell, *War and Society in Imperial Rome, 31 BC–AD 284*, London, 2002. For primary sources, see J.B. Campbell, *The Roman Army, 31 BC–AD 337*, London and New York, 1994. See also Chapter 11.

6 On auxiliaries, see D.B. Saddington, *The Development of the Roman Auxiliary Forces from Caesar to Vespasian (49 BC–AD 79)*, Harare, 1982; D.B. Saddington, 'The Development of the Roman Auxiliary Forces from Augustus to Trajan', *ANRW* II.3 (1975), pp. 176–201.

7 Contrast the explanations of legionary deployments in E.N. Luttwak, *The Grand Strategy of the Roman Empire from the First Century AD to the Third*, Baltimore and London, 1976, with

those in B. Isaac, *The Limits of Empire: The Roman Army in the East*, rev. edn, Oxford, 1992, and Goodman, 'Opponents of Rome'.

8   On the praetorian guard, see M. Durry, *Les cohortes prétoriennes*, Paris, 1938; D.L. Kennedy, 'Some observations on the praetorian guard', *Ancient Society* 9 (1978), pp. 275–301.

9   See *AE* 1978, no. 286.

10 See A. Ziolkowski, Chap. 3, '*Urbs direpta*, or how the Romans sacked cities', in J. Rich and G. Shipley (eds) *War and Society in the Roman World*, London, 1993.

11 See R. MacMullen, *Soldier and Civilian in the Later Roman Empire*, Cambridge, Mass., 1963.

12 Important new light is shed on the confiscations by the *senatus consultum* of Piso (see above Chapter 5, note 3).

13 On senators' self-images, see Chapter 12; on provincial aristocrats, see Chapter 10.

14 For cases of non co-operation, see Chapter 16.

9 THE OPERATION OF THE STATE IN ROME

1   On the whole subject of this chapter, see F.G.B. Millar, *The Emperor in the Roman World (31 BC–AD 337)*, 2nd edn, London, 1992.

2   On government without bureaucracy, see P. Garnsey and R. Saller, *The Roman Empire: Economy, Society and Culture*, London, 1987, Chap. 2.

3   See A.F. Wallace-Hadrill in *The Cambridge Ancient History*, vol. X, 2nd edn, 1996, Chap. 7, 'The imperial court'.

4   See J.A. Crook, *Consilium Principis: Imperial Councils and Counsellors from Augustus to Diocletian*, Cambridge, 1955.

5   Tac., *Ann.* 11.29–38; 12.25, 53, 57, 65; 13.1, 2, 14; 14.65. Pliny, *Letters* about Pallas: 7.29, senate's decree on his tombstone; 8.6, award of praetor's insignia and fifteen million sesterces.

6   On the tasks of imperial freedmen, see Millar, *Emperor*, pp. 69–83.

7   For the frequency with which the emperor wrote the subscriptions, see W. Turpin, 'Imperial subscriptions and the administration of justice', *JRS* 81 (1991), pp. 101–18.

8   On equestrian secretaries, see Millar, *Emperor*, pp. 101–10.

9   On Suetonius, see A.F. Wallace-Hadrill, *Suetonius*, 2nd edn, London, 1995.

10 On imperial finances, see Millar, *Emperor*, pp. 133–201.

11 See in general Crook, *Consilium Principis*.

12 On the image projected of imperial women, see E. Bartman, *Portraits of Livia: imaging the imperial women in Augustan Rome*, Cambridge, 1999; on the role of the crowd in Roman imperial politics, see Z. Yavetz, *Plebs and Princeps*, Oxford, 1969.

13 On the senate in the Roman Empire, see R.J.A. Talbert, *The Senate of Imperial Rome*, Princeton, New Jersey, 1984; A. Chastagnol, *Le sénat romain à l'époque impériale: recherches sur la composition de l'assemblée et le statut de ses membres*, Paris, 1992.

14 On the senate as a legislative body, see Talbert, *The Senate of Imperial Rome*, Chap. 15.

15 On the senate as a court, see ibid., Chap. 16; P. Garnsey, *Social Status and Legal Privilege in the Roman Empire*, Oxford, 1970. On other courts, see below, note 19.

16 On election under the principate, see B. Levick, 'Imperial control of the elections under the early Principate: *commendatio, suffragatio,* and "*nominatio*" ', *Historia* 16 (1967), pp. 207–30.

17 On trials for provincial maladministration, see P.A. Brunt, 'Charges of provincial maladministration under the early principate', *Historia* 10 (1961), pp. 189–227.

18 On this council, see Crook, *Consilium Principis*, pp. 9–10, 14–15.

19 See R.A. Bauman, *Lawyers and Politics in the Early Roman Empire: A Study of Relations between the Roman Jurists and the Emperors from Augustus to Hadrian*, Munich, 1989.

20 For these documents, see G. Camodeca, *L'archivio puteolaneo dei Sulpicii I*, Naples, 1992; on their significance, see J.F. Gardner, *Being a Roman Citizen*, London, 1993, pp. 33–6.

21 On the function of imperial rescripts, see Millar, *Emperor*, pp. 213–28, 'imperial correspondence' and pp. 240–52, 'answers to written petitions'.

22 On civil courts under the principate, see Pliny, *Letters*, 1.5, 2.14, 4.16, 4.24, 5.9, 6.12, 6.33, 9.23 on the centumviral courts. On criminal courts, see A.H.M. Jones, *The Criminal Courts of the Roman Republic and Principate*, Oxford, 1972.

23 On appeal to the emperor, see Millar, *Emperor*, pp. 507–16.

24 On the Roman taxation system in general, see K. Hopkins, 'Taxes and trade in the Roman empire (200 BC–AD 400)', *JRS* 70 (1980), pp. 101–25. See also Chapter 10.

25 On the proportion of the budget devoted to the army, see R. Duncan-Jones, *Money and Government in the Roman Empire,* Cambridge, 1994; on the setting of a budget, see E. Lo Cascio, 'The Early Roman Empire: State and Economy', in W. Scheidel, I. Morris, and R. Seller (eds.) *The Cambridge Economic History of the Greco-Roman World,* Cambridge, 2007, pp. 592–647; for general arguments for imperial control of the economy, see J. Paterson, 'Autocracy and political economy', *Mediterraneo Antico* 7.2 (2007), pp. 571–89.

26 On minting policy in the Early Empire, see C.H.V. Sutherland, *The Emperor and the Coinage: Julio-Claudian Studies*, London, 1976; C.H.V. Sutherland, *The Roman Imperial Coinage. I*, rev. edn, London, 1984; A. Burnett, M. Amandry and P.P. Ripollès, *Roman Provincial Coinage. I: From the Death of Caesar to the Death of Vitellius (44 BC–AD 69)*, London and Paris, 1992.

27 On imperial ownership of mines and quarries, see C. Domergue, *Les mines de la péninsule ibérique dans l'antiquité romaine*, Rome, 1990; H. Dodge and B. Ward-Perkins (eds) *Marble in Antiquity: Collected Papers of J.B. Ward-Perkins*, London, 1992, Chap. 5.

28 M. Ponting, 'Roman silver coinage: mints, metallurgy and production', in A.K. Bowman and A. Wilson (eds) *Quantifying the Roman Economy: methods and problems,* (Oxford, 2009), pp. 269–80.

10 THE OPERATION OF THE STATE IN THE PROVINCES

1 On the lack of an overall strategy, see F.G.B. Millar, 'Emperors, frontiers and foreign relations, 31 BC to AD 378', *Britannia* 13 (1982), pp. 1–23; for this chapter in general, see B. Levick, *The Government of the Roman Empire: a sourcebook*, London, 2000.

2 On the operation of the Roman taxation system, see A.W. Lintott, *Imperium Romanum: Politics and Administration*, London, 1993, Chap. 5, 'Taxation and corvées'.

3 On the provincial census, see P.A. Brunt, *Roman Imperial Themes*, Oxford, 1990, Chap. 15, 'The revenues of Rome'.

4 On indirect taxation, see ibid., Chap. 17, 'Publicans in the principate'; S.J. de Laet, *Portorium: étude sur l'organisation douanière chez les romains surtout à l'époque du Haut-Empire*, Bruges, 1949.

5 For payment in kind as well as in money, see the tax assessment of four date groves to pay specified types and amounts of dates, in Y. Yadin, *The Documents from the Bar Kokhba Period in the Cave of Letters: Greek Papyri*, ed. N. Lewis, Jerusalem, 1989, no. 16.

6　For these charters see *FIRA* I, nos 13, 16–26 (Latin texts); text, translation and commentary of the *lex Irnitana* in J. González, 'The Lex Irnitana: a new copy of the Flavian municipal law', *JRS* 76 (1986), pp. 147–243; H. Galsterer, 'Municipium Flavium Irnitanum: a Latin town in Spain', *JRS* 78 (1988), pp. 78–90. Voting procedures are described in the *lex Malacitana* (and to a small degree in the *lex Irnitana*), Chaps 51–60, cf. González, 'The Lex Irnitana', pp. 188–90. On the general decline of democracy under Roman rule, see G.E.M. de Ste Croix, *The Class Struggle in the Ancient Greek World: From the Archaic Age to the Arab Conquests*, London, 1981.

7　On the assize system, see G.P. Burton, 'Proconsuls, assizes and the administration of justice under the empire', *JRS* 65 (1975), pp. 92–106.

8　On this development, see P. Garnsey, *Social Status and Legal Privilege in the Roman Empire*, Oxford, 1970.

9　On provincial councils, see F.G.B. Millar, *The Emperor in the Roman World (31 BC–AD 337)*, 2nd edn, London, 1992, pp. 385–94.

10　On both these factors, see Chapter 8.

11　See Chapter 8, note 7.

12　See J.S. Richardson, 'Imperium Romanum: empire and the language of power', *JRS* 81 (1991), pp. 1–9.

13　See F.A. Lepper, *Trajan's Parthian War*, London, 1948.

14　For the shift eastwards, see F.G.B. Millar, *The Roman Near East (31 BC–AD 337)*, Cambridge, Mass. and London, 1993.

15　On Hadrian's wall, see R. Birley, *The Building of Hadrian's Wall*, Greenhead, 1991; D.J. Breeze and B. Dobson, *Hadrian's Wall*, 3rd edn, London, 1987; S. Johnson, *English Heritage Book of Hadrian's Wall*, London, 1989. On the Antonine wall, see A.S. Robertson, *The Antonine Wall*, Glasgow, 1990.

16　See B. Isaac, 'The meaning of the term *limes* and *limitanei*', *JRS* 78 (1988), pp. 125–47; C.R. Whittaker, *Frontiers of the Roman Empire: A Social and Economic Study*, Baltimore, 1994.

17　See B. Isaac, *The Limits of Empire: The Roman Army in the East*, rev. edn, Oxford, 1992.

18　On the coinages of Greek cities, see C. Howgego, *Greek Imperial Countermarks: Studies in the Provincial Coinage of the Roman Empire*, London, 1985; A.M. Burnett et al., *Roman Provincial Coinage*, 2 vols., London and Paris, 1992–99.

19　On Roman provincial administration in general, see Lintott, *Imperium Romanum*.

20　On the titles *procurator* and *praefectus*, see A.H.M. Jones, *Studies in Roman Government and Law*, Oxford, 1960, Chap. 7, 'Procurators and prefects in the early principate'.

21　For a detailed commentary on these letters, see A.N. Sherwin-White, *The Letters of Pliny: A Historical and Social Commentary*, Oxford, 1966. For the inscription from Como, see *CIL* V, no. 5,262; the personal inscriptions of Pliny are printed in Sherwin-White, *The Letters of Pliny*, pp. 732–3.

22　See D. Braund, *Rome and the Friendly King: The Character of the Client Kingship*, London and New York, 1984.

23　On Scotland and Ireland, see D.J. Mattingly, *An Imperial Possession: Britain in the Roman Empire*, London, 2006, pp. 428–52; on India, see G. Parker, *The Making of Roman India*, Cambridge, 2008; on the Garamantes, see D.J. Mattingly, 'Impacts beyond Empire: Rome and the Garamantes of the Sahara', in L. De Blois and J. Rich (eds.) *The Transformation of Economic Life under the Roman Empire*, Amsterdam, 2002, pp. 184–203; on Bu Njem, see R. Marichal, *Les Ostraca de Bu Njem*, Tripoli, 2002; on Georgia, see D. Braund, *Georgia in Antiquity: a history of Colchis and Transcaucasian Iberia, 550 BC–AD 562*, Oxford 1994. On

Roman attitudes in general to those beyond the imperial borders, see I.M. Ferris, *Enemies of Rome: barbarians through Roman eyes*, Sutton, 2000.

11 THE ARMY IN SOCIETY

1   On the emergence of a permanent professional army, see R.E. Smith, *Service in the Post-Marian Roman Army*, Manchester, 1958; L.J.F. Keppie, *The Making of the Roman Army: From Republic to Empire*, London, 1984.

2   A.K. Bowman and J.D. Thomas (eds) *The Vindolanda Writing-Tablets (tabulae Vindolandenses II)*, London, 1994.

3   On life for ordinary soldiers, see G.R. Watson, *The Roman Soldier*, London, 1969.

4   On the transfers of units in AD 69, see G.E.F. Chilver, 'The army in politics, AD 68–70', *JRS* 47 (1957), pp. 29–36; on the evidence of *diplomata*, see P. Holder, 'Auxiliary deployment in the reign of Hadrian', in J.J. Wilkes (ed.) *Documenting the Roman Army: essays in honour of Margaret Roxan*, London, 2003, pp. 101–45.

5   For the army on campaign, see A. Goldsworthy, *The Roman Army at War, 100 BC – AD 200*, Oxford, 1996; Y. Le Bohec, *The Imperial Roman Army*, London, 2000; on the proportion of a career spent on campaign, see R. McMullen, *Soldier and Civilian in the Later Roman Empire*, Cambridge, Mass., 1963; A. Goldsworthy and I. Haynes (eds.) *The Roman Army*, Portsmouth, R.I., 1999.

6   On Roman military architecture, see J. Lander, *Roman Stone Fortifications: Variation and Change from the First Century AD to the Fourth*, Oxford, 1984; A. Johnson, *Roman Forts of the First and Second Centuries AD in Britain and the German Provinces*, London, 1983. On the auxiliary unit at Dura-Europus, see J.F. Gilliam, 'The Roman army in Dura', in C.B. Welles *et al.*, *The Excavations at Dura-Europos, Final Report V.i: The Parchments and Papyri*, New Haven, CT, 1959, reprinted in J.F. Gilliam, *Roman Army Papers*, Amsterdam, 1986.

7   On legionary pay, see R. Alston, 'Roman military pay from Caesar to Diocletian', *JRS* 84 (1994), pp. 113–23; M.A. Speidel, 'Roman army pay scales' *JRS* 82 (1992), pp. 87–106. A number of writing tablets from Vindonissa (in Switzerland) record details of legionary pay in the Early Empire.

8   On auxiliaries' pay, see Alston, 'Roman military pay' and Speidel, 'Roman army pay scales'; D.B. Saddington, *The Development of the Roman Auxiliary Forces from Caesar to Vespasian: 49 BC–AD 79*, Harare, 1982; P.A. Holder, *Studies in the Auxilia of the Roman Army from Augustus to Trajan*, Oxford, 1980.

9   For the religious calendar from Dura, see R.O. Fink, A.S. Hoey and W.F. Snyder, *The Feriale Duranum, YCS* 7 (1940), pp. 1–222; A.D. Nock, 'The Roman army and the Roman religious year', *Harvard Theological Review* 45 (1952), pp. 186–252; LR 2, pp. 529–30 provides an English translation.

10 See Chapter 21.

11 On the extent of conscription for the imperial army, see P.A. Brunt, *Roman Imperial Themes*, Oxford, 1990, Chap. 9, 'Conscription and volunteering in the Roman imperial army'.

12 V.A. Maxfield, 'Ostraca and the Roman army in the eastern desert', in Wilkes (ed.) *Documenting the Roman Army*, pp. 152—73; see also O. Krok, 98 in H. Curigny, *Ostraca de Krokodilô: la correspondence militaire et sa circulation*, Cairo, 2005.

13 On veteran colonies, see especially B. Levick, *Roman Colonies in Southern Asia Minor*, Oxford, 1967; J.C. Mann, *Legionary Recruitment and Veteran Settlement during the Principate*, London, 1983.

14 On the economic effects of the Roman army, see Chapter 14.

12 THE IMAGE OF THE EMPEROR

1 For a general discussion of this whole issue, see A.F. Wallace-Hadrill, 'Civilis princeps: between citizen and king', JRS 72 (1982), pp. 32–48.

2 On the significance of January 27 BC, see Chapter 4 above, and W.K. Lacey, 'Octavian in the senate, January 27 BC', JRS 64 (1974), pp. 176–84, with reference to numerous earlier discussions;W.K. Lacey, Augustus and the Principate: the evolution of the system, Leeds, 1996.

3 See Chapter 4.

4 Octavian appears as consul in a recently discovered document from 29 BC. See D. Knibbe, H. Engelmann and B. Iplikçioğlu, 'Neue Inschriften aus Ephesos XII', no. 2, in Jahreshefte des Österreichischen Archäologischen Instituts in Wien 62 (1993), p. 114.

5 On the constitutional base of the principate, see G.E.F. Chilver, 'Augustus and the Roman Constitution 1939–1950', Historia 1 (1950), pp. 408–35.

6 On Augustus' precise powers, see A.H.M. Jones, 'The imperium of Augustus', in A.H.M. Jones, Studies in Roman Government and Law, Oxford, 1960, pp. 1–17; also A.H.M. Jones, 'The censorial powers of Augustus', ibid., pp. 19–26.

7 For the Lex de Imperio Vespasiani, see FIRA I, no. 15, also CIL VI, no. 930, and LR 2, pp. 11–13; cf. P.A. Brunt, 'Lex de imperio Vespasiani', JRS 67 (1977), pp. 95–116.

8 On the notion of a consensus between emperors and subjects, see C. Ando, Imperial Ideology and Provincial Loyalty in the Roman Empire, Berkeley, Ca. and London, 2000; for provincial interpretations of the Res Gestae, see A.E. Cooley, Res Gestae Divi Augusti: Text, Translation and commentary, 2009, pp. 26–30; on possible targeting of coin messages, see O. Hekster, 'Coins and messages: audience targetting on coins of different denominations', in L. de Blois, et al. (eds.) The Representation and Perception of Roman Imperial Power, Amsterdam, 2003, pp. 20–35; on the distribution of the imperial image in statues, see P. Stewart, The Social History of Roman Art, Cambridge, 2008, pp. 80–94.

9 On the imperial cult, see L.R. Taylor, The Divinity of the Roman Emperor, Middle-town, Conn., 1931; D.S. Potter, Prophets and Emperors: Human and Divine Authority from Augustus to Theodosius, Cambridge, Mass. and London, 1994; I. Gradel, Emperor Worship and Roman Religion, Oxford, 2002.

10 On the theological basis of the imperial cult, see Chapter 29.

11 Examples can be found in Babatha's archive, Y. Yadin, The Documents from the Bar Kokhba Period in the Cave of Letters: Greek Papyri, ed. N. Lewis, Jerusalem, 1989.

12 On these coins, see C.H.V. Sutherland, Roman History and Coinage 44 BC–AD 69: Fifty Points of Relation from Julius Caesar to Vespasian, Oxford, 1987, pp. 66–8.

13 On the artistic expression of this, see P. Zanker, The Power of Images in the Age of Augustus, Ann Arbor, Michigan, 1988.

14 On the Ara Pacis, see ibid., pp. 172–83, 203–6; M. Torelli, Typology and Structure of Roman Historical Reliefs, Ann Arbor, Michigan, 1982, pp. 27–61; J.M.C. Toynbee, 'The Ara Pacis reconsidered and historical art in Roman Italy', Proceedings of the British Academy 39 (1953), pp. 67–95.

15 C. Noreña, 'The communication of the emperor's virtues', JRS 91 (2001), pp. 146–68.

13 THE EXTENT OF POLITICAL UNITY

1 See R.R.R. Smith, '*Simulacra gentium*: the *ethne* from the Sebasteion at Aphrodisias', *JRS* 78 (1988), pp. 50–77.

2 On the spread of citizenship, see A.N. Sherwin-White, *The Roman Citizenship*, 2nd edn, Oxford, 1973.

3 On treaties with subject states, see A.W. Lintott, *Imperium Romanum: Politics and Administration*, London, 1993, Chap. 2, 'Elements of empire'.

4 J. Reynolds, *Aphrodisias and Rome*, London, 1982.

5 See P. Garnsey and R. Saller, *The Roman Empire: Economy, Society and Culture*, London, 1987, Chap. 2, 'Government without bureaucracy'; on the coins, see A.M. Burnett et al., *Roman Provincial Coinage*, 2 vols., London and Paris, 1992–99.

6 See G.E.M. de Ste Croix, *The Class Struggle in the Ancient World: From the Archaic Age to the Arab Conquests*, London, 1981.

7 On the Gallic Julii, see J.F. Drinkwater, *Roman Gaul: The Three Provinces, 58 BC–AD 260*, London, 1983.

8 On the Cyrene edicts, see F. de Visscher, *Les édits d'Auguste découverts à Cyrène*, Louvain, 1940.

9 P. Garnsey, *Social Status and Legal Privilege in the Roman Empire*, Oxford, 1970.

10 On local government, see Lintott, *Imperium Romanum*, Chap. 9; on council buildings, see J.C. Balty, *Curia Ordinis: recherches d'architecture et d'urbanisme antiques sur les curies provinciales du monde romain*, Brussels, 1992.

11 See B. Burrell, *Neokoroi: Greek cities and Roman emperors*, Leiden, 2004.

12 On the consensus model, see C. Ando, *Imperial Ideology and Provincial Loyalty in the Roman Empire*, Berkely, Ca. and London, 2000, with a critique in J.E. Lendon, 'The legitimation of the Roman emperor: against Weberian legitimacy and imperial 'strategies of legitimation'', in A. Kolb (ed.) *Herrschaftsstrukturen und Herrschaftspraxis: Konzepte, Prinzipien und Strategien der Administration im römischen Kaiserreich*, Berlin, 2006, pp. 53–63.

13 On the imperial cult as a unifying force, see K. Hopkins, *Conquerors and Slaves*, Cambridge, 1978, Chap. 5, 'Divine emperors or the symbolic unity of the Roman empire'.

14 THE EXTENT OF ECONOMIC UNITY

1 For a general discussion of the economy of the Roman Empire, see P. Garnsey and R. Saller, *The Roman Empire: Economy, Society and Culture*, London, 1987, Chap. 3, 'An underdeveloped economy'; R.P. Duncan-Jones, *Structure and Scale in the Roman Economy*, Cambridge, 1990; W. Scheidel, I. Morris and R. Saller (eds.) *The Cambridge Economic History of the Greco-Roman World*, Cambridge, 2007; W. Scheidel and S.J. Friesen, 'The size of the economy and the distribution of income in the Roman empire', *JRS* 99 (2009), pp. 61–91. For ancient written sources, see F. Meijer and O. van Nijf, *Trade, Transport and Society in the Ancient World: A Sourcebook*, London and New York, 1992. For archaeological evidence, see K. Greene, *The Archaeology of the Roman Economy*, London, 1986; for general theories about the ancient economy, see N. Morley, *Trade in Classical Antiquity*, Cambridge, 2007; for market and subsistence economies working together, see P. Erdkamp, 'Beyond the limits of the 'Consumer City'. A model of the urban and rural economy in the Roman world', *Historia* 50.3 (2001), pp. 332–56; on domestic weaving, see P.M. Allison, *Pompeian Households: an analysis of the material culture*, Los Angeles, Ca., 2004, pp. 146–50; on transport, G. Adams, *Land Transport in Roman Egypt: a study of economics and administration*

in a Roman province, Oxford, 2007, on extensive use of land transport even in Egypt, despite the Nile.

2   On pottery, a brief introduction is provided by K. Green, *Roman Pottery*, London, 1992; see too D.P.S. Peacock, *Pottery in the Roman World: An Ethnoarchaeological Approach*, London and New York, 1982; D.P.S. Peacock and D.F. Williams, *Amphorae and the Roman Economy: An Introductory Guide*, London and New York, 1986. On *terra sigillata*, see C. Johns, *Arretine and Samian Pottery*, rev. edn, London, 1977; M. Bulmer, *An Introduction to Roman Samian Ware*, Chester, 1980.

3   See discussion by N. Purcell, 'Wine and wealth in ancient Italy', *JRS* 75 (1985), pp. 1–19.

4   For studies of oil lamp production and trade, see W.V. Harris, 'Roman terracotta lamps: the organisation of an industry', *JRS* 70 (1980), pp. 126–43. See also W.V. Harris (ed.) *The Inscribed Economy: Production and Distribution in the Roman Empire in the Light of instrumentum domesticum*, Ann Arbor, Michigan, 1993.

5   See Pliny, *Nat. Hist.* 19.14–15 for four types of Egyptian flax, and 31.80 for medicinal Spanish salt; T. Frank (ed.) *An Economic Survey of Ancient Rome*, 6 vols, Baltimore and London, 1933–40.

6   On the part played by the state in the grain trade, see L. Casson, 'The role of the state in Rome's grain trade', in J.H. D'Arms and E.C. Kopff (eds) *The Seaborne Commerce of Ancient Rome*, Rome, 1980, pp. 21–33.

7   On shipwrecks, see A.J. Parker, *Ancient Shipwrecks of the Mediterranean and the Roman Provinces*, Oxford, 1992, with a useful index of recorded wrecks in date order, pp. 10–15.

8   On piracy, see P. de Souza, *Piracy in the Graeco-Roman World*, Cambridge, 1999; on brigandage, and the use of brigand terminology to brand enemies of the state, see T. Grünewald, *Bandits in the Roman Empire: myth and reality*, London, 2004.

9   For this argument, see K. Hopkins, 'Taxes and trade in the Roman empire (200 BC–AD 400)', *JRS* 70 (1980), pp. 101–25. On the evidence for the circulation and availability of coins, see C. Howgego, 'The supply and use of money in the Roman world 200 BC to AD 300', *JRS* 82 (1992), pp. 1–31; R.P. Duncan-Jones, *Money and Government in the Roman Empire*, Cambridge, 1994. For a partial correction, see W.V. Harris, 'A revisionist view of Roman money', *JRS* 96 (2006), pp. 1–24, on the use of paper credit within the Roman monetary economy.

10 The Babatha archive is published in Y. Yadin, *The Documents from the Bar Kokhba Period in the Cave of Letters: Greek Papyri*, ed. N. Lewis, Jerusalem, 1989. The census document is no. 16.

11 For text and translation, see *ILS* no. 7,029; Meijer and van Nijf, *Trade, Transport and Society*, no. 103.

12 On the 'invisibility' of craftsmen and traders, see P. Garnsey (ed.) *Non-Slave Labour in the Greco-Roman World*, Cambridge, 1980; for evidence of bankers, see J. Andreau, *Banking and Business in the Roman World*, Cambridge, 1999.

13 On the economic effects of slavery, see, for example, the survey by C. Wickham, 'Marx, Sherlock Holmes, and Late Roman Commerce', *JRS* 78 (1988), pp. 183–93.

14 On the economic role of freedmen, see P. Garnsey, 'Independent freedmen and the economy of Roman Italy under the principate', *Klio* 63 (1981), pp. 39–71; S. Treggiari, *Roman Freedmen during the Late Republic*, Oxford, 1967; K. Hopkins, *Conquerors and Slaves*, Cambridge, 1978; H. Mouritsen, *The Freedman in the Roman World*, Cambridge, 2010.

15 On social snobbery as a bar to trade, see M.I. Finley, *The Ancient Economy*, 2nd edn, London, 1985; J.H. D'Arms, *Commerce and Social Standing in Ancient Rome*, Cambridge, Mass. and London, 1981.

16   On women and labour, see W. Scheidel, 'The most silent women of Greece and Rome: rural labour and women's life in the ancient world', *Greece and Rome* 42 (1995), pp. 202–17; on the role of women more generally, E. D'Ambra, *Roman Women*, Cambridge, 2007. On children, see B. Rawson, *Children and childhood in Roman Italy*, Oxford, 2003; C. Laes, *Children in Roman Society*, Cambridge, 2010; for the Egyptian evidence for child workers, see M. Mirkovic, 'Child labour and taxes in the agriculture of Roman Egypt', *Scripta Classica Israelica* 24 (2005), pp. 139–49; on population movements, see W. Scheidel, 'Human mobility in Roman Italy. I.: The Free Population', *JRS* 94 (2004), pp. 1–26.

17   D. Rathbone, 'Earnings and costs: living standards and the Roman economy (First to Third Centuries AD), in A.K. Bowman and A. Wilson (eds.) *Quantifying the Roman Economy: Methods and Problems*, Oxford, 2009, pp. 299–326.

18   S. Hong, J.-P. Candelone, C.C. Patterson and C.F. Boutron, 'Greenland ice evidence of hemispheric lead pollution two millennia ago by Greek and Roman civilizations', *Science* 265 (1994), 1841–3.

19   On technology in general, see J.P. Oleson (ed.) *The Oxford Handbook of Engineering and Technology in the Classical World*, Oxford, 2008; on the Spanish mines, see A. Wilson, 'Machines, power and the ancient economy', *JRS* 92 (2002), pp. 1–32.

20   F. Beltrán Lloris, 'An irrigation decree from Roman Spain: the *Lex Rivi Hiberiensis*', *JRS* 96 (2006), pp. 147–97, with new epigraphic evidence.

21   On the theory of connectivity, with numerous examples of the impact on local economies of links with the wider Mediterranean world, see N. Purcell and P. Hordern, *The Corrupting Sea*, Oxford, 2000; on the Italian cities, see J. R. Patterson, *Landscape and Cities: Rural Settlements and Civic Transformation in Early Imperial Italy*, Oxford, 2006, pp. 92–101, 106–115, 164; on Flavian Spain, see E. Haley, 'Rural settlement in the Conventus Astigitanus (Baetica) under the Flavians', *Phoenix* 50 (1966), pp. 283–303.

15   THE EXTENT OF CULTURAL UNITY

1   On the difficulties in defining what is 'Roman' about Roman culture in this period, see E. Dench, *Romulus' Asylum: Roman identities from the age of Alexander to the age of Hadrian*, Oxford, 2005.

2   On Roman town-planning, see J. Stambaugh, *The Ancient Roman City*, Baltimore and London, 1988.

3   See P. Veyne, *Bread and Circuses: Historical Sociology and Political Pluralism*, abridged O. Murray, London, 1990.

4   See also nos 677 and 679–83, and J.-P. Rey-Coquais, 'Inscriptions grecques d'Apamée', *Annales archéologiques de Syrie* 23 (1973), pp. 39–84; Jean Ch. Balty, 'Apamea in Syria in the second and third centuries AD', *JRS* 78 (1988), pp. 91–104.

5   The Pont du Gard used to be dated to the Augustan period, but new excavations suggest the aqueduct was built AD 40–80, most probably in Claudius' reign. See G. Fabre, J.-L. Fiches and J.-L. Paillet, 'The aqueduct of Nîmes and the Pont du Gard', *Journal of Roman Archaeology* 4 (1991), pp. 63–88, especially pp. 72–3; on the baths in Asia Minor, see L. Lancaster, 'Roman engineering and construction', in J.P. Oleson (ed.) *The Oxford Handbook of Engineering and Technology in the Classical World,* Oxford, 2008, pp. 256-84.

6   On the villa, see J. Percival, *The Roman Villa: An Historical Introduction*, London, 1976.

7   Introduction to the evidence from Pompeii in A.F. Wallace-Hadrill, *Houses and Society in Pompeii and Herculaneum*, Princeton, New Jersey, 1994. See too R. Laurence, *Roman Pompeii:*

Space and Society, London and New York, 1996; M. Beard, *Pompeii: the life of a Roman town*, London, 2010.

8   On the Aphrodisias workshops, see C. Roueché and K.T. Erim (eds) *Aphrodisias Papers: Recent Work on Architecture and Sculpture*, Ann Arbor, Michigan, 1990; on the Palmyra tax law, see J. Matthews, 'The tax law of Palmyra: evidence for economic history in a city of the Roman East', *JRS* 74 (1984), pp. 157–80.

9   For literary graffiti, see H.M. Cotton and J. Geiger, *Masada II: the Yigael Yadin Excavations 1963–1965: Final Reports. The Latin and Greek Documents*, Jerusalem, 1989; A.K. Bowman and J.D. Thomas (eds) *The Vindolanda Writing-Tablets*, London, 1994.

10 On Roman education, see H.I. Marrou, *A History of Education in Antiquity*, rev. edn, Madison State and London, 1977; T. Wiedemann, *Adults and Children in the Roman Empire*, London, 1989.

11 On the inscription of Diogenes of Oenoanda, see the translation and commentary of C.W. Chilton, *Diogenes of Oenoanda: The Fragments*, London and New York, 1971; M.F. Smith, 'Diogenes of Oenoanda, new fragments 115–121', in *Prometheus* 8.3 (1982), pp. 193–212.

12 Philostratus, *Lives of the Sophists* 489–92.

13 See E.A. Meyer, 'Explaining the epigraphic habit in the Roman empire: the evidence of epitaphs', *JRS* 80 (1990), pp. 74–96.

14 See I. Morris, *Death-ritual and Social Structure in Classical Antiquity*, Cambridge, 1992.

16 REACTIONS TO IMPERIAL RULE

1   See in general the analysis in M. Goodman, 'Opponents of Rome: Jews and others', in L. Alexander (ed.) *Images of Empire*, Sheffield, 1991, pp. 222–38

2   On the role of honours as a means to achieve accommodation, see J.E. Lendon, *Empire of Honor: the art of government in the Roman World*, Oxford, 1997; on Greek cities, see B. Burrell, *Neokoroi: Greek cities and Roman Emperors*, Leiden, 2004; on the epigraphic habit in Gaul, see, G. Woolf, *Becoming Roman: the origins of provincial civilization in Gaul*, Cambridge, 1998, pp. 77-105.

3   On switching between identities, described as 'code-switching', see A.W. Wallace-Hadrill, *Rome's Cultural Revolution*, Cambridge, 2008; on post-colonial approaches to the issue of Roman imperialism, with a critique of the notion of 'Romanisation', see D.J. Mattingly, (ed.) *Dialogues in Roman Imperialism: power, discourse and discrepant experience in the Roman empire*, Portsmouth, R.I, 1997.

4   See R. Syme, *History in Ovid*, Oxford, 1978.

5   See M. Goodman, *State and Society in Roman Galilee, AD 132–212*, 2nd edn, London and Portland, Or., 2000.

6   See D.R. Dudley, *A History of Cynicism from Diogenes to the Sixth Century*, London, 1937.

7   See Chapter 31.

8   On the 'Stoic' opposition, see for example Tacitus, *Ann.* 13.49, 14.12, 14.48–50, 14.57–9, 15.23, 15.79, 16.21–35; C. Wirszubski, *'Libertas' as a Political Idea at Rome during the Late Republic and Early Principate*, Cambridge, 1950; R.A. Bauman, *Impietas in principem: A Study of Treason against the Roman Emperor with Special Reference to the First Century AD*, Munich, 1974.

9   C. Bruun, 'Roman emperors in popular jargon: searching for contemporary nicknames', in L. De Blois et al. (eds.) *The Representation and Presentation of Roman Imperial Power*,

Amsterdam, 2003, pp. 69-98; J. Webster, 'Translation and subjection: *interpretatio* and the Celtic gods', in J.D. Hill and C.G. Cumberpatch (eds.) *Different Iron Ages: studies of the Iron Age in temperate Europe*, Oxford, 1995, pp. 175-83; R. Hingley, 'Resistance and domination: social change in Roman Britain', in D.J. Mattingly (ed.) *Dialogues in Roman Imperialism*, pp. 81–100.

10 On the urban plebs, see Z. Yavetz, *Plebs and Princeps*, Oxford, 1969.

11 On these revolts, see S.L. Dyson, 'Native revolt patterns in the Roman empire', *ANRW* II.3 (1975), pp. 138–75; J. Pekary, 'Seditio, Unruhe und Revolten in Römischen Reich von Augustus bis Commodus', *Ancient Society* 18 (1987), pp. 133-50.

12 On this unrest, see D. Delia, *Alexandrian Citizenship during the Roman Principate*, Atlanta, Georgia, 1991; E.M. Smallwood, *The Jews under Roman Rule: From Pompey to Diocletian: A Study in Political Relations*, Leiden, 1976.

13 So P.A. Brunt, *Roman Imperial Themes*, Oxford, 1990, Chaps 2 and 3.

17 THE CITY OF ROME: SOCIAL ORGANIZATION

1 On the ethnic mix of the inhabitants of Rome in the Early Empire, see A.M. Duff, *Freedmen in the Early Roman Empire*, Cambridge, 1928; D. Noy, *Foreigners at Rome: citizens and strangers*, London, 2000; C. Edwards and G. Woolf (eds.) *Rome the Cosmopolis*, Cambridge, 2003.

2 For the complex process of the creation of the Forum Iulium, see Roger B. Ulrich, 'Julius Caesar and the creation of the Forum Iulium', *AJA* 97 (1993), pp. 49–80.

3 On the transformation of the city's public architecture in the Early Empire, see P. Zanker, *The Power of Images in the Age of Augustus*, Ann Arbor, Michigan, 1988.

4 See E. Rawson, '*Discrimina ordinum*: the *lex Iulia theatralis*', *PBSR* 55 (1987), pp. 83–114.

5 See Chapter 9.

6 On the senate's procedures, see R.J.A. Talbert, *The Senate of Imperial Rome*, Princeton, New Jersey, 1984.

7 See Chapter 9.

8 On the origins of senators, see K. Hopkins, *Death and Renewal*, Cambridge, 1983, Chap. 2; D. McAlindon, 'Entry to the Senate in the Early Empire', *JRS* 47 (1957), pp. 191–5.

9 One family still to survive were the Acilii Glabriones, see M. Dondin-Payre, *Exercise du pouvoir et continuité gentilice: les Acilii Glabriones du IIIe siècle av. J.-C. au Ve siècle ap. J.-C.*, Rome, 1993.

10 On senators of provincial origin, see A. Chastagnol, *Le Sénat romain à l'époque impériale: recherches sur la composition de l'Assemblée et le statut de ses membres*, Paris, 1992, Chap. 11, 'Nuances sociologiques dans le Sénat: patriciens et provinciaux'.

11 See above, Chapter 16. On Thrasea and Helvidius, see P.A. Brunt, 'Stoicism and the principate', *PBSR* 30 (1975), pp. 7–35.

12 On elections in the Roman Empire, see B. Levick, 'Imperial control of the elections under the early Principate: *commendatio, suffragatio*, and "*nominatio*" ', *Historia* 16 (1967), pp. 207–30.

13 For the law of AD 19, which is known in part from an inscription on a bronze tablet, see B. Levick, 'The *senatus consultum* from Larinum', *JRS* 78 (1988), pp. 14–34.

14 On attitudes to this lifestyle in general, see C. Edwards, *The Politics of Immorality in Ancient Rome*, Cambridge, 1993.

15 On Augustus' social legislation, see K. Galinsky, 'Augustus' legislation on morals and marriage', *Philologus* 125 (1981), pp. 126–44; B. Rawson (ed.) *The Family in Ancient Rome*, London, 1986, Chap. 1.

16 On the origins and definition of equestrian status, see T.P. Wiseman, 'The definition of "eques Romanus" in the Late Republic and Early Empire', *Historia* 19 (1970), pp. 67–83; P.A. Brunt, 'The *equites* in the Late Republic', in P.A. Brunt, *The Fall of the Roman Republic and Related Essays*, Oxford, 1988, Chap. 3; P.A. Brunt, 'Princeps and equites', *JRS* 73 (1983), pp. 42–75.

17 See Chapter 10. On equestrian acclamations, see. G. Rowe, *Princes and Political Cultures: the new Tiberian senatorial decrees*, Ann Arbor, Mi., 2002. On the public role given to sons of senators in the equestrian parades, see Z. Yavetz, 'The *Res Gestae* and Augustus' public image', in F.G.B. Millar and E. Segal, *Caesar Augustus: Seven Aspects*, Oxford, 1984, p. 16.

18 See Z. Yavetz, *Plebs and Princeps*, Oxford, 1969.

19 See Chapter 14.

20 On this legislation, see K.R. Bradley, *Slaves and Masters in the Roman Empire: A Study in Social Control*, Brussels, 1984; S. Treggiari, 'Social status and social legislation', *CAH* vol. X, 2nd edn, pp. 893–7; H. Mouritsen, *The Freedman in the Roman World*, Cambridge, 2011.

21 On inscriptions, see S.R. Joshel, *Work, Identity and Legal Status at Rome: a study of the occupational inscriptions*, Norman, 1992; N. Purcell, 'The apparitores: a study in social mobility,' *PBSR* 51 (1983), pp. 125-73; R. Jackson, *Doctors and Diseases in the Roman Empire*, London, 1988; R. Flemming, *Medicine and the Making of Roman Women*, Oxford, 2000.

22 B.W. Frier, 'The rental market in early imperial Rome', *JRS* 67 (1977), pp. 27-37; J. Delaine, 'Designing for a market: 'medianum'(?) apartments at Ostia', *JRA* 17 (2004), pp. 146-76.

23 On the lives of women in imperial Rome see B. Rawson (ed.) *Marriage, Divorce, and Children in Ancient Rome*, Oxford, 1991; S. Dixon, *The Roman Mother*, London, 1988; J. Evans Grubbs, *Women and the law in the Roman Empire: a sourcebook on marriage, divorce, and widowhood*, London, 2002.

24 K. Hopkins, 'Contraception in the Roman Empire', *Comparative Studies in Society and History* 8 (1964-65), pp. 124-51; E. Eyben, 'Family Planning in Graeco-Roman antiquity', *Ancient Society* 11/12 (1980-81), pp. 5-82; K. Kapparis, *Abortion in the Ancient World*, London, 2002.

25 E. Wistrand, *The so-called Laudatio Turiae*, Güteborg, 1976.

26 For a collection of evidence on the family, see J.F. Gardner and T. Wiedemann, *The Roman Household: A Sourcebook*, London, 1991.

27 W. Scheidel, 'Qantifying the sources of slaves in the early Roman empire', *JRS* 87 (1997), pp. 156-69; idem, 'Human mobility in Roman Italy, II: The Slave Population', *JRS* 95 (2005), pp. 64-79.

28 H. Mouritsen, *The Freedman in the Roman World*, Cambridge, 2011.

18 THE CITY OF ROME: CULTURE AND LIFE

1 On the role of patronage in literature and art, see B.K. Gold (ed.) *Literary and Artistic Patronage in Ancient Rome*, Austin, Texas, 1982.

2   See R.D. Anderson, P.J. Parsons and R.G.M. Nisbet, 'Elegiacs by Gallus from Qasr Ibrim', *JRS* 69 (1979), pp. 125–55, text and translation from p. 140.

3   On Latin literature in the Early Empire, see Parts IV and V of *The Cambridge History of Classical Literature*, vol. II, *Latin Literature*, Cambridge, 1982.

4   On Epictetus, see F.G.B. Millar, 'Epictetus and the imperial court', *JRS* 55 (1965), pp. 141–8; P.A. Brunt, 'Stoicism and the principate', *PBSR* 30 (1975), pp. 7–35. On philosophy in Rome in general, see J. Barnes and M.T. Griffin (eds.) *Philosophia Togata: Essays on Philosophy and Roman Society*, 2. vols., Oxford, 1989-1997; M. Trapp, *Philosophy in the Roman Empire: ethics, politics and society*, Aldershot, 2007.

5   For the history of legal scholarship in Rome, see F. Schulz, *History of Roman Legal Science*, Oxford, 1946.

6   See P. Zanker, *The Power of Images in the Age of Augustus*, Ann Arbor, Michigan, 1988.

7   On the status of artisans, see P. Stewart, *The Social History of Roman Art,* Cambridge, 2008, pp. 10-38, 71–6.

8   On buildings at Ostia, see R. Meiggs, *Roman Ostia*, 2nd edn, Oxford, 1973.

9   On the Tivoli villa, see T. Opper, *Hadrian: Empire and Conflict*, London, 2008, pp. 130-65.

10   On villa design and use, see J. Percival, *The Roman Villa: An Historical Introduction*, London, 1976.

11   For an illustration of the *profectio Domitiani* (Domitian setting out), see N.H. Ramage and A. Ramage (eds) *The Cambridge Illustrated History of Roman Art*, Cambridge, 1991, p. 133.

12   On wall painting, see R. Ling, *Roman Painting*, Cambridge, 1991; A. Barbet, *La peinture murale romaine: les styles décoratifs pompéiens*, Paris, 1985.

13   R. Ling, *Roman Painting*, Cambridge, 1991, pp. 175-86; on these compositions as intended to challenge the viewer, see E.W. Leach, *The Social Life of Painting in Ancient Rome and on the Bay of Naples*, Cambridge, 2004, pp. 265-86; on Roman art in general, see T. Hölscher, *The Language of Images in Roman Art*, Cambridge, 2004.

14   For an attempt to characterize non-elite culture in Rome, with numerous anecdotal insights, see N. Horsfall, *The Culture of the Roman Plebs*, London, 2003.

15   For the general argument, see A. Wallace-Hadrill, *Rome's Cultural Revolution*, Cambridge, 2008, Chapter 7; on glass, see S.J. Fleming, *Roman Glass: reflections on cultural change*, Pennsylvania, 1999.

16   This is the argument of Zanker, *The Power of Images*.

17   On religion in the city of Rome in the Early Empire, see S.R.F. Price, in *The Cambridge Ancient History*, vol. X, 2nd edn, 1996, Chap. 16, 'The place of religion: Rome in the early Empire'.

18   On forms of entertainment, see J.-C. Golvin and C. Landes, *Amphithéâtres et gladiateurs*, Paris, 1990; T. Wiedemann, *Emperors and Gladiators*, London, 1992; A. Cameron, *Circus Factions: Blues and Greens at Rome and Byzantium*, Oxford, 1976.

19   See K.M. Coleman, 'Launching into history: aquatic displays in the Early Empire', *JRS* 83 (1993), pp. 48–74.

20   See E. Köhne and C. Ewigleben (eds.) *Gladiators and Caesars: the power of spectacle in ancient Rome*, transl. R. Jackson, Berkeley, Ca., 2001; C. Holleran, 'The development of public entertainment venues in Rome and Italy', in K. Lomas and T. Cornell (eds.) *Bread and Circuses: Evergetism and Municipal Patronage in Roman Italy*, London, 2003, pp. 46-60; on performers, see D.S. Potter, 'Entertainers in the Roman Empire', in D.S. Potter and D. Mattingly (eds.) *Life, Death and Entertainment in the Roman Empire*, Ann Arbor, Mi., 1999, pp. 256-325.

21 See J. Delaine, 'New models, old modes: continuity and change in the design of public baths', in H.-J Schalles, H. von Hesberg and P. Zanker (eds.) *Die Römische Stadt in 2. Jahrhundert n. Chr.: Der Funktionswandes des öffentlichen Raumes*, Bonn, 1992, pp. 257-75; J. Delaine and D.E. Johnston, (eds.) *Roman Baths and Bathing*, Portsmouth, R.I., 1999.

19 ITALY AND SICILY

1 See in general E.T. Salmon, *The Making of Roman Italy*, London, 1982; T.W. Potter, *Roman Italy*, London, 1987; S.L. Dyson, *Community and Society in Roman Italy*, Baltimore and London, 1991; on the extent of Italian unity by 44 BC, see E. Bispham, *From Asculum to Actium: the municipalization of Italy from the Social War to Augustus*, Oxford 2008; see also W. Morley, *Metropolis and Hinterland: the city of Rome and the Italian economy, 200 BC–AD 200*, Cambridge, 1996. For primary source material, see K. Lomas (ed.) *Roman Italy, 338 BC–AD 200: A Sourcebook*, London, 1996. There is a survey of Roman Italy in E. Curti, E. Dench and J.R. Patterson, 'The archaeology of Central and Southern Roman Italy: recent trends and approaches', *JRS* 86 (1996), pp. 170–89.

2 On Etruscan relics in the imperial period, see P. Bruun *et al., Studies in the Romanisation of Etruria*, Rome, 1975.

3 On the continued use of non-Latin languages, see W.V. Harris, *Rome in Etruria and Umbria*, Oxford, 1971.

4 On the *Tabula Heracleensis*, see LR 1, pp. 440–4 and 449–53. On the *lex Rubria*, see M.W. Frederiksen, 'The *lex Rubria*: reconsiderations', *JRS* 54 (1964), pp. 129–34; F.J. Bruna, *Lex Rubria*, Leiden, 1972.

5 *CIL* IX, no. 2,438. See M. Corbier, '*Fiscus* and *patrimonium*: the Saepinum inscription and transhumance in the Abruzzi', *JRS* 73 (1983), pp. 126–31.

6 For these calendars, see R.M. Ogilvie, *The Romans and Their Gods in the Age of Augustus*, London, 1969, Chap. 5, 'The religious year'.

7 Pliny, *Letters* 1.8, 3.6, 4.13, 5.7, 7.18.

8 On the alimentary schemes, see R.P. Duncan-Jones, *The Economy of the Roman Empire: Quantitative Studies*, 2nd edn, Cambridge, 1982, Chap. 7, 'Government subsidies for population increase'; N. Criniti, *La tabula alimentaria di Veleia*, Parma, 1991.

9 On the Sangro Valley, see T. Bell, A. Wilson and A. Wickham, 'Tracking the Samnites: landscapes and communication routes in the Sangro Valley, Italy', *AJA* 106 (2002), pp. 169-86; on Monte Pallano, see A. Faustoferi and J. Lloyd, 'Monte Pallano: a Samnite fortified centre and its hinterland', *JRA* 11 (1998), pp. 1–22; more general studies in G. Barker et al., *A Mediterranean Valley: landscape archaeology and Annales history in the Biferno Valley*, London and New York, 1995; J. R. Patterson, *Landscapes and Cities: rural settlement and civic transformation in early imperial Italy*, Oxford, 2006. R. Witcher, 'Settlement and society in early imperial Etruria', *JRS* 96 (2006), pp. 88-123, shows how much different areas within quite a restricted region had different fortunes in this period.

10 For a discussion of the evidence, see N. Purcell, 'Wine and wealth in ancient Italy', *JRS* 75 (1985), pp. 1–19.

11 On the trade in Italian Samian ware, see D.P.S. Peacock, *Pottery in the Roman World: An Ethnoarchaeological Approach*, London and New York, 1982.

12 See N. Purcell, 'Wine and wealth in ancient Italy'.

13 On Sicily under Roman rule, see R.J.A. Wilson, *Sicily under the Roman Empire: The Archaeology of a Roman Province, 36 BC–AD 535*, Warminster, 1990.

14 For the calendar, see ibid., pp. 279–81; on the inscription from Taormina, see ibid., pp. 315–16.

20 THE IBERIAN PENINSULA AND THE ISLANDS OF THE WESTERN MEDITERRANEAN

1 On Roman campaigns in Spain, see J.S. Richardson, *Hispaniae: Spain and the Development of Roman Imperialism, 218–82 BC*, Cambridge, 1986.

2 On Roman Spain in general, see L.A. Curchin, *Roman Spain: Conquest and Assimilation*, London, 1991; S.J. Keay, *Roman Spain*, London, 1988; W. Trillmich *et al.*, *Hispania Antiqua: Denkmäler der Römerzeit*, Mainz, 1993; J.S. Richardson, *The Romans in Spain*, Oxford, 1996; S. Keay, 'Recent archaeological work in Roman Iberia (1990-2002)', *JRS* 93 (2003), pp. 146-211.

3 For the province of Baetica, see A.T. Fear, *Rome and Baetica: Urbanization in Southern Spain c. 50 BC–AD 150*, Oxford, 1996.

4 J. González, 'The Lex Irnitana: a new copy of the Flavian municipal law', *JRS* 76 (1986), Latin pp. 166–7, English translation p. 190.

5 On the mines, see C. Domergue, *Les mines de la Péninsule Ibérique dans l'antiquité romaine*, Rome, 1990; G.D.B. Jones, 'The Roman mines at Riotinto', *JRS* 70 (1980), pp. 146–65; P.R. Lewis and G.D.B. Jones, 'Roman gold-mining in north-west Spain', *JRS* 60 (1970), pp. 169–85; R.J.F. Jones and D.G. Bird, 'Roman gold-mining in north-west Spain, II: workings on the Rio Duerna', *JRS* 62 (1972), pp. 59–74. On imperial patronage, see R. Syme, 'Hadrian and Italica', *JRS* 54 (1964), pp. 142–9.

6 For the mining inscription, see C. Domergue, *La mine antique d'Aljustrel (Portugal) et les tables de bronze de Vipasca*, Paris, 1983, pp. 48ff.

7 See Curchin, *Roman Spain*, Chap. 9, '"Resistance" to Romanisation'.

8 On Roman Portugal, see J. de Alarcão, *Roman Portugal*, 2 vols, Warminster, 1988.

9 On Sardinia, see M.S. Balmuth and R.J. Rowland, Jr (eds) *Studies in Sardinian Archaeology*, vol. 1, Ann Arbor, Michigan, 1984; R.J.A. Wilson, 'Sardinia and Sicily during the Roman Empire: aspects of the archaeological evidence', *Kokalos* 26–7 (1980–1), pp. 219–42. On Corsica, see J. Jéhasse, 'La Corse antique d'après Ptolemée', *Archeologia Corsa: Études et Mémoires*, vol. 1, Ajaccio, 1976; J. and L. Jéhasse, 'La Corse romaine', in P. Arrighi (ed.) *Histoire de la Corse*, Toulouse, 1971, pp. 97–128.

10 On the use of neo-Punic, see M.G. Guzzo Amadasi, *Iscrizioni fenice e puniche delle colonie in Occidente*, Rome, 1967, pp. 133–6.

21 GAUL AND BRITAIN

1 For the history of Provence, see S. Piggott, G. Daniel and C. McBurney (eds) *France Before the Romans*, London, 1974; R. Chevallier, *Provincia: villes et monuments de la province romaine de Narbonnaise*, Paris, 1982; A.L.F. Rivet, *Gallia Narbonensis: Southern Gaul in Roman Times*, London, 1988. For individual sites, see J. Bromwich, *The Roman Remains of Southern France: A Guidebook*, London, 1993.

2 See in general J.F. Drinkwater, *Roman Gaul: The Three Provinces, 58 BC–AD 260*, London, 1983; T. Blagg and M. Millet (eds) *The Early Roman Empire in the West*, Oxford, 1990.

3 See D. Nash, 'Reconstructing Poseidonios' Celtic ethnography: some considerations', *Britannia* 7 (1976), pp. 111–26.

4 See M. Todd, *The Northern Barbarians 100 BC–AD 300*, rev. edn, Oxford, 1987.

5 On druids and their suppression, see N.K. Chadwick, *The Druids*, Cardiff, 1966; S. Piggott, *The Druids*, London, 1968; M. Goodman, *The Ruling Class of Judaea: The Origins of the Jewish Revolt against Rome AD 66–70*, Cambridge, 1987, pp. 239–47.

6 For the few details known of Cogidubnus, see A.A. Barrett, 'The career of Tiberius Claudius Cogidubnus', *Britannia* 9 (1979), pp. 227–42. See too D. Braund, *Ruling Roman Britain: Kings, Queens, Governors and Emperors from Julius Caesar to Agricola*, London and New York, 1996.

7 On the Gallic Julii, see J.F. Drinkwater, 'The rise and fall of the Gallic Iulii: aspects of the development of the aristocracy of the Three Gauls under the Early Empire', *Latomus* 37 (1978), pp. 817–50.

8 See G.D. Woolf, *Becoming Roman: the origins of provincial civilization in Gaul*, Cambridge, 1998.

9 See, in general, P. Salway, *Roman Britain*, Oxford, 1981; M. Millett, *The Romanization of Britain: An Essay in Archaeological Interpretation*, Cambridge, 1990, with the review by R.J.A. Wilson in *JRS* 82 (1992), pp. 290–3; T.W. Potter and C. Johns, *Roman Britain*, London, 1992; D.J. Mattingly, *An Imperial Possession: Britain in the Roman Empire, 54 BC – AD 409*, London, 2006. For primary sources, see S. Ireland (ed.) *Roman Britain: A Sourcebook*, London, 1986.

10 See the discussion of these uprisings in S.L. Dyson, 'Native revolt patterns in the Roman empire', *ANRW* II.3 (1975), pp. 138–75.

11 On the site of Verulamium, see S.S. Frere, *Verulamium Excavations*, 3 vols, London, 1972–84.

12 On the *civitates* and *civitas*-capitals, see Drinkwater, *Roman Gaul*, pp. 103–10.

13 On villas in Britain and Gaul, see J. Percival, *The Roman Villa: An Historical Introduction*, London, 1976, especially Chap. 4, 'Regional types and distributions'.

14 See the discussion by G. Woolf, Chap. 6, 'Power and the spread of writing in the West', in A.K. Bowman and G. Woolf (eds) *Literacy and Power in the Ancient World*, Cambridge, 1994.

15 On the *imperium Galliarum*, see Tac., *Hist.* 4.57f.

16 On the *vergobret*, see *CIL* XIII, no. 1,048; J.F. Drinkwater, 'A note on local careers in the Three Gauls under the Early Empire', *Britannia* 9 (1979), pp. 89–100. On Veleda, see Tac., *Hist.* 4.61.2; 4.65.3–4; 5.22.3; 5.24.1; Tac., *Germania* 8.3; Statius, *Silvae* 1.4.90.

17 On Romano-British religion, see M. Henig, *Religion in Roman Britain*, London, 1984; on Gallo-Roman religion, see T. Derks, *Gods, Temples and Religious Practices: the transformation of religious ideas and values in Roman Gaul*, Amsterdam, 1998.

18 For industrial sites, see B.C. Burnham and J. Wacher, *The 'Small Towns' of Roman Britain*, London, 1990, Chap. 10.

19 On the *bagaudae*, see E.A. Thompson, 'Peasant revolts in Late Roman Gaul and Spain', *Past and Present* 2 (1952), pp. 11–23; B. Czuth, *Die Quellen der Geschichte der Bagauden*, Szeged, 1965.

22 THE RHINELAND AND THE BALKANS

1 For a general discussion, see A. King, *Roman Gaul and Germany*, London, 1990; T. Blagg and M. Millett (eds) *The Early Roman Empire in the West*, Oxford, 1990; M. Todd, *The Early*

Germans, Oxford, 1992; and on Augustus' reign, C.M. Wells, *The German Policy of Augustus: An Examination of the Archaeological Evidence*, Oxford, 1972.

2   On the whole subject of this frontier, see H. Schönberger, 'The Roman frontier in Germany: an archaeological survey', *JRS* 59 (1969), pp. 144–97.

3   So M. Todd, *The Northern Barbarians, 100 BC–AD 300*, rev. edn, Oxford, 1987.

4   On Cologne, see P. La Baume, *Colonia Agrippinensis: A Brief Survey of Cologne in Roman Times*, Cologne, 1967; O. Doppelfeld, 'Das römische Köln, I: Ubier-Oppidum und colonia Agrippinensium', *ANRW* II.4 (1975), pp. 715–82; W. Eck, *Köln in Römischer Zeit*, Cologne, 2004.

5   On the revolt of Civilis, see Tac., *Hist.* 4.28–36, 4.54–5.26; P. Brunt, 'Tacitus on the Batavian revolt', *Latomus* 19 (1960), pp. 494–517.

6   On Trier, see E.M. Wightman, *Roman Trier and the Treveri*, London, 1970; H. Heinen, *Trier und das Trevererland in römischer Zeit*, Trier, 1985.

7   For the *Tropaeum Alpium*, see *CIL* V, no. 7,817 and J. Formigé, *La Trophée des Alpes (La Turbie)*, Paris, 1949.

8   On the Roman period in Switzerland, see W. Drack and R. Fellman (eds) *Die Römer in der Schweiz*, Stuttgart, 1988.

9   For the military frontiers of the Rhine and the Danube, see V.A. Maxfield, 'Mainland Europe', Chap. 8, in J. Wacher (ed.) *The Roman World*, vol. 1, London, 1987.

10 On use of the Danube, see J. Šašel, 'Trajan's canal at the Iron Gate', *JRS* 63 (1973), pp. 80–5; for the present state of knowledge about the Roman Danube, see J.J. Wilkes, 'The Roman Danube: an archaeological survey', *JRS* 95 (2005), pp. 124-225; R. Batty, *Rome and the Nomads: the Pontic-Danubian realm in antiquity*, Oxford, 2007.

11 On the Western Balkans, see J.J. Wilkes, *The Illyrians*, Oxford, 1992; J.J. Wilkes, *Dalmatia*, London, 1969; A. Mócsy, *Pannonia and Upper Moesia: A History of the Middle Danube Provinces of the Roman Empire*, London, 1974; P. Oliva, *Pannonia and the Onset of Crisis in the Roman Empire*, Praha, 1962.

12 On Noricum, see G. Alföldy, *Noricum*, London and Boston, 1974.

13 See A.G. Poulter, 'The Lower Moesian Limes and the Dacian wars of Trajan', in 13. Internationaler Limeskongreß, *Studien zu den Militärgrenzen Roms III*, Stuttgart, 1986, pp. 519–28.

14 On Moesia, see Mócsy, *Pannonia and Upper Moesia*.

15 On Thrace, see A.G. Poulter (ed.) *Ancient Bulgaria*, Nottingham, 1983; R.F. Hoddinott, *The Thracians*, London, 1981; A. Fol and I. Marazov, *Thrace and the Thracians*, London, 1977.

16 On Dacia, see J.J. Wilkes, 'Romans, Dacians and Sarmatians in the first and early second centuries', in B. Hartley and J. Wacher (eds) *Rome and Her Northern Provinces*, Gloucester, 1983, pp. 255–89; I.H. Crişan, *Burebista and His Time*, Bucharest, 1978; I. A. Oltean. *Dacia: landscape, colonization, Romanisation,* London, 2007.

17 On Decebalus, see K. Ziegler *et al.* (eds) *Der Kleine Pauly*, vol. 1, Stuttgart, 1964, pp. 1404–5; on Trajan's campaigns, see Wilkes, 'Romans, Dacians and Sarmatians'.

23 GREECE AND THE AEGEAN COAST

1   For a general discussion of Roman Greece, see S.E. Alcock, *Graecia Capta: The Landscapes of Roman Greece*, Cambridge, 1993.

2　On the strategic significance of the region, see B. Levick, *Roman Colonies in Southern Asia Minor*, Oxford, 1967.

3　See Alcock, *Graecia Capta*; for the most recent work, see the Archaeological Reports published by the British School at Athens and the Society for the Promotion of Hellenic Studies.

4　Strabo, *Geography* 8.8.1 (Arcadia), 8.4.11 (Messenia and Laconia), 9.2.5 (Boeotian cities become villages), 9.2.25 (in ruins).

5　This is the evidence presented by Alcock, *Graecia Capta*.

6　On individual cities, see J.H. Oliver, *The Civic Tradition and Roman Athens*, Baltimore, 1983; A.J. Spawforth, 'Roman Sparta', in P. Cartledge and A.J. Spawforth, *Hellenistic and Roman Sparta: A Tale of Two Cities*, London, 1989, pp. 93–211. On Thessaly, see G.W. Bowersock, 'Zur Geschichte des römischen Thessaliens', *Rheinisches Museum für Philologie* 108 (1965), pp. 277–89.

7　On the province of Asia, see D. Magie, *Roman Rule in Asia Minor to the End of the Third Century after Christ*, 2 vols, Princeton, New Jersey, 1950.

8　Pliny, *Letters* 10. On clubs in general, see J. Kloppenborg and S. Wilson (eds) *Voluntary Associations in the Graeco-Roman World*, London and New York, 1996.

9　On these writers, see *The Cambridge History of Classical Literature*, vol. I: *Greek Literature*, Cambridge, 1982, Chap. 20, 'The literature of the Empire'; on Plutarch, see C.P. Jones, *Plutarch and Rome*, Oxford, 1971; on Cassius Dio, see F.G.B. Millar, *A Study of Cassius Dio*, Oxford, 1964.

10　See E.L. Bowie, 'The Greeks and their past in the Second Sophistic', *Past and Present* 46 (1970), pp. 3–41; G. Woolf, 'Becoming Roman, staying Greek: culture, identity and the civilizing process in the Roman east', *Proceedings of the Cambridge Philological Society* 40 (1994), pp. 116-45; T. Whitmarsh, *Greek Literature and the Roman Empire: the politics of imitation*, Oxford, 2001; S. Goldhill (ed.) *Being Greek under Rome: cultural identity, the Second Sophistic and the development of empire*, Cambridge, 2001.

11　See Cartledge and Spawforth, *Hellenistic and Roman Sparta*; S. Swain, *Hellenism and Empire: language, classicism and power in the Greek world, AD 50–250*, Oxford, 1996.

12　On Greek senators, see R. Syme, 'Greeks invading the Roman government', in his *Roman Papers IV*, Oxford, 1988, pp. 1–20; J.H. Oliver, 'Roman senators from Greece and Macedon', in S. Panciera (ed.) *Epigrafia e ordine senatorio: Atti del Colloquio Internazionale AIEGL, Roma, 14–20 Maggio 1981*, Rome, 1982, pp. 583–602.

13　See P.A. Stadter, *Arrian of Nicomedia*, Chapel Hill, North Carolina, 1980.

14　See G.E.M. de Ste Croix, *The Class Struggle in the Ancient Greek World*, London, 1981.

24　CENTRAL AND EASTERN TURKEY

1　On the region as a whole, see especially S. Mitchell, *Anatolia: Land, Men, and Gods in Asia Minor*, 2 vols, Oxford, 1993.

2　On the colonies, see B. Levick, *Roman Colonies in Southern Asia Minor*, Oxford, 1967.

3　On local languages, see Mitchell, *Anatolia*, vol. 1, pp. 170–6.

4　On religion in Asia Minor, see ibid., vol. 2; note also the arguments in B. Dignas, *Economy of the Sacred in Hellenistic and Roman Asia Minor*, Oxford 2002, that some temple cults in the Roman state operated independently from the local cities.

5 P. Trebilco, *Jewish Communities in Asia Minor*, Cambridge, 1991; on the relations of these communities to Rome, see M. Pucci ben Zeev, *Jewish Rights in the Roman World: the Greek and Roman documents quoted by Josephus Flavius,* Tübingen, 1998.

6 On the economy of the region, see T. Frank (ed.) *An Economic Survey of Ancient Rome*, vol. IV, Baltimore, 1938.

25 THE NORTHERN LEVANT AND MESOPOTAMIA

1 Fundamental for this chapter and the next is F.G.B. Millar, *The Roman Near East 31 BC–AD 337*, Cambridge, Mass., 1993.

2 On the Parthians, see M.A.R. Colledge, *The Parthians*, London, 1967.

3 On Dura-Europus, see C. Hopkins, *The Discovery of Dura-Europos*, New Haven, Conn., 1979; Millar, *The Roman Near East*, Chap. 12, 'The Euphrates and Mesopotamia'.

4 See B. Isaac, *The Limits of Empire: The Roman Army in the East*, rev. edn, Oxford, 1992.

5 So Millar, *The Roman Near East*, Chap. 3, 'Imperialism and expansion AD 74–195'.

6 For the tortuous history of Armenia in this period, see M. Chaumont, 'L'Arménie entre Rome et l'Iran. I. De l'avènement d'Auguste à l'avènement de Dioclétien', *ANRW* II.9.1 (1976), pp. 71–194; D. Timpe, 'Zur augusteischen Partherpolitik zwischen 30 und 20 v. Chr.', *Würzburger Jahrbücher für die Altertumswissenschaft* 1 (1975), pp. 155–69.

7 On the Parthian campaign, see F. Lepper, *Trajan's Parthian War*, London, 1948. For the debate as to whether Trajan established a province of Assyria, see C.S. Lightfoot, 'Trajan's Parthian war and the fourth-century perspective', *JRS* 80 (1990), pp. 115–26.

8 See G. Downey, *A History of Antioch in Syria: From Seleucus to the Arab Conquest*, Princeton, New Jersey, 1961; on the army in Syria, see. N. Pollard, *Soldiers, Cities and Civilians in Roman Syria*, Ann Arbor, Mi., 2000.

9 On these client rulers, see R.D. Sullivan, *ANRW* II.8 (1977), 'The dynasty of Emesa', pp. 198–219 and 'The dynasty of Commagene', pp. 732–98.

10 On Palmyra, see E. Will, *Les Palmyréniens: la Venise des sables (Ier siècle avant – IIIème siècle après J.-C.)*, Paris, 1992; J. Starcky and M. Gawlikowski, *Palmyre*, Paris, 1985; J. Teixidor, *Un port romain du désert: Palmyre*, Paris, 1984; I.A. Richmond, 'Palmyra under the aegis of Rome', *JRS* 53 (1963), pp. 43–54; R. Stoneman, *Palmyra and its Empire: Zenobia's Revolt against Rome*, Ann Arbor, Michigan, 1992.

11 *AE* 1979, no. 179.

12 For Palmyra's tax law, see J.F. Matthews, 'The tax law of Palmyra: evidence for economic history in a city of the Roman East', *JRS* 74 (1984), pp. 157–80.

13 On these villages, see G. Tchalenko, *Villages antiques de la Syrie du Nord: le massif du Bélus à l'époque romaine*, 3 vols, Paris, 1953–8; on their date, see Millar, *The Roman Near East*, pp. 251–2.

14 See J.-F. Breton, *Les inscriptions forestières d'Hadrien dans le Mont Liban (Inscriptions grecques et latines de la Syrie*, VIII.3), Paris, 1980.

15 A.H.M. Jones, *The Cities of the Eastern Roman Provinces*, 2nd edn, Oxford, 1971, pp. 228–31.

16 On Berytus, see Millar, *The Roman Near East*, pp. 274–85.

17 On Christianity in Syria, see ibid., pp. 462–7.

18 On Edessa and Syriac Christianity, see J.B. Segal, *Edessa: 'the blessed city'*, Oxford, 1970; S. Brock, *Studies in Syriac Christianity*, Aldershot, 1992.

19 On the Syro-Roman law book, see A. Vööbus, *The Syro-Roman Lawbook: The Syriac Text of the Recently Discovered Manuscripts Accompanied by a Facsimile Edition and Furnished with an Introduction and Translation*, Stockholm, 1982–3.

20 See Jean C. Balty, 'Apamea in Syria in the second and third centuries AD', *JRS* 78 (1988), pp. 91–104. For the texts of the inscriptions, see J.-P. Rey-Coquais, 'Inscriptions grecques d'Apamée', *Annales archéologiques de Syrie* 23 (1973), pp. 39–104.

21 On this family, see A.R. Birley, *The African Emperor: Septimius Severus*, London, 1988, Chap. 8, 'Julia Domna'.

26 THE SOUTHERN LEVANT

1 For the sources, see E. Schürer, rev. G. Vermes *et al.*, *The History of the Jewish People in the Age of Jesus Christ*, 3 vols, Edinburgh, 1973–87, vol. 1, pp. 17–122; on Josephus, see T. Rajak, *Josephus: The Historian and His Society*, London, 1983; for general interpretations of the history of Judaea in this period, see S. Schwartz, *Imperialism and Jewish Society. 200 BCE to 640 CE.*, Princeton, N.J., 2001; M. Goodman, *Rome and Jerusalem: the clash of ancient civilizations*, London, 2007.

2 For the history of the region before the Roman conquest, see the revised Schürer, *The History of the Jewish People*, vol. 1, pp. 125–242; G.W. Bowersock, *Roman Arabia*, Cambridge, Mass. and London, 1983.

3 Details of the coins can be found in H.A. Grueber, *Coins of the Roman Republic in the British Museum*, vol. 1, London, 1910, pp. 490–1.

4 On Herod's origins and rule, see Joseph., *AJ* 16–18; P. Richardson, *Herod: King of the Jews and friend of the Romans*, Columbia, South Carolina, 1996.

5 See the revised Schürer, *The History of the Jewish People*, vol. 1, pp. 287–557; Bowersock, *Roman Arabia*; F.G.B. Millar, *The Roman Near East 31 BC–AD 337*, Cambridge, Mass., 1993.

6 On Herod's family and descendants, see A.H.M. Jones, *The Herods of Judaea*, Oxford, 1938.

7 See D.R. Schwartz, *Agrippa I: The Last King of Judaea*, Tübingen, 1990.

8 See M. Goodman, *The Ruling Class of Judaea: The Origins of the Jewish Revolt against Rome AD 66–70*, Cambridge, 1987; idem, *Rome and Jerusalem*, Chapter 11.

9 On class tensions in Judaea, see P.A. Brunt, *Roman Imperial Themes*, Oxford, 1990, pp. 267–87.

10 Joseph., *JW* 2.301–8. See Goodman, *The Ruling Class of Judaea*, Chap. 7, 'The outbreak of revolt'.

11 On Bar Kochba and the revolt, see the careful survey of evidence in P. Schäfer, *Der Bar Kokhba-Aufstand: Studien zum zweiten jüdischen Krieg gegen Rom*, Tübingen, 1981; B. Isaac and A. Oppenheimer, 'The revolt of Bar Kokhba: ideology and modern scholarship', *Journal of Jewish Studies* 36 (1985), pp. 33–60; P. Schäfer (ed.) *The Bar Kokhba War Reconsidered*, Tübingen, 2003.

12 First publication of the text and translation in Y. Yadin, 'The expedition to the Judaean desert, 1960', *Israel Exploration Journal* 11 (1961), p. 48.

13 For the Judaean desert documents, see especially the series *Discoveries in the Judaean Desert*, Oxford, 1955 onwards; other documents listed in the appendix of Millar, *Roman Near East*. For underground complexes, see A. Kloner, 'Underground hiding complexes from the Bar Kochba war in the Judaean Shephelah', *The Biblical Archaeologist* 46.4 (December 1983), pp. 210–21.

14 On Samaritan history, see A.D. Crown (ed.) *The Samaritans*, Tübingen, 1989.

15 See Bowersock, *Roman Arabia*. On the Nabataeans, see also A. Negev, 'The Nabataeans and the Provincia Arabia', *ANRW* II.8 (1977), pp. 520–686 and A. Negev, *Nabataean Archaeology Today*, New York, 1986.

16 On Petra, see J. McKenzie, *The Architecture of Petra*, Oxford, 1990.

17 For the Babatha documents, see Y. Yadin, *The Documents from the Bar Kokhba Period in the Cave of Letters: Greek Papyri*, ed. N. Lewis, Jerusalem, 1989; Y.Yadin, J.C. Greenfield, B.A. Levine and A. Yardeni (eds) *The Documents from the Bar Kokhba Period in the Cave of Letters (Hebrew, Aramaic and Nabataean Documents)*, Jerusalem, 2002.

18 See Yadin, et. al., *Documents … Greek Papyri*, nos 28–30, relating to Babatha's disputes with her son's guardians, recorded in documents 13–15 (AD 124–5).

27 EGYPT

1 See A.K. Bowman, *Egypt after the Pharaohs: 332 BC–AD 642: From Alexander to the Arab Conquest*, 2nd edn, Oxford, 1990; N. Lewis, *Life in Egypt under Roman Rule*, Oxford, 1983.

2 See D.J. Thompson, Chap. 8c, 'Egypt, 146–31 BC', in *Cambridge Ancient History* IX, 2nd edn, 1994.

3 On administrative structures in Roman Egypt, see Bowman, *Egypt after the Pharaohs*, Chap. 3, 'State and subject'; L. Capponi, *Augustan Egypt: the creation of a Roman province*, London, 2005.

4 See A.K. Bowman, *The Town Councils of Roman Egypt*, Toronto, 1971.

5 See P.M. Fraser, *Ptolemaic Alexandria*, 3 vols, Oxford, 1972, Chap. 3, 'City and sovereign'.

6 See C.P. Jones, *The Roman World of Dio Chrysostom*, Cambridge, Mass., 1978, p. 134.

7 For text, translation and commentary on the *boule* papyrus, see V.A. Tcherikover *et al.*, *Corpus Papyrorum Judaicarum*, Jerusalem, 1957–64, vol. 2, no. 150. On martyr acts, see H.A. Musurillo (ed.) *The Acts of the Pagan Martyrs: Acta Alexandrinorum*, Oxford, 1954.

8 See J.M. Modrzejewski, *The Jews of Egypt: From Rameses II to Emperor Hadrian*, Philadelphia and Jerusalem, 1995, Chap. 3, 'Alexandrian Judaism and its problems', Chap. 8, 'The "Jewish Question" in Alexandria', Chap. 9, 'The time of misfortunes', Chap. 10, 'The remembrance'; A. Kasher, *The Jews in Hellenistic and Roman Egypt: The Struggle for Equal Rights*, Tübingen, 1985.

9 On Philo, see S. Sandmel, *Philo of Alexandria: An Introduction*, Oxford, 1979.

10 For the letter of Claudius to the Alexandrians, see *CPJ* vol. 2, no. 153.

11 On this revolt, see M. Pucci, *La rivolta ebraica al tempo di Traiano*, Pisa, 1981; T.D. Barnes, 'Trajan and the Jews', *Journal of Jewish Studies* 40 (1989), pp. 145–62; M. Pucci, *Diaspora Judaism in Turmoil, 116/117 CE: ancient sources and modern insights*, Leuven, 2005. See above, Chapter 7.

12 On taxation in Egypt, see Lewis, *Life in Egypt*, Chap. 5, 'Census, taxes, and liturgies'.

13 For the text and translation of the edict of Tiberius Julius Alexander, see H.G. Evelyn-White and J.H. Oliver, *The Temple of Hibis in El Khargah Oasis*, Part II, nos 3 and 4, New York, 1938, and LR 2, pp. 295–8; for a study, see G. Chalon, *L'édit de Tiberius Julius Alexander*, Olten-Lausanne, 1964.

14 For a text, translation and commentary, see L. Casson, *The Periplus Maris Erythraei*, New Jersey, 1989.

15 For the Roman army in Egypt in general, see R. Alston, *Soldier and Society in Roman Egypt: A Social History*, London, 1995.

16 On the use by historians of papyri in general, see R.S. Bagnall, *Reading Papyri, Writing Ancient History*, London and New York, 1995; E.G. Turner, *Greek Papyri: An Introduction*, 2nd edn, Oxford, 1980.

17 J. Rowlandson and R. Takahashi, 'Brother-Sister marriage and inheritance strategies in Greco-Roman Egypt', *JRS* 99 (2009), pp. 104–39.

18 For a population study, see R.S. Bagnall and B.W. Frier, *The Demography of Roman Egypt*, Cambridge, 1994.

19 On conflicts of law, see R. Taubenschlag, *The Law of Greco-Roman Egypt in the Light of the Papyri, 332 BC–AD 640*, 2nd edn, Warszawa, 1955.

20 On Egyptian religion in this period, see H.I. Bell, *Cults and Creeds in Graeco-Roman Egypt*, Liverpool, 1953; D. Frankfurter, *Religion in Roman Egypt: assimilation and resistance*, Princeton, N.J., 1998.

21 For a translation of *POxy* no. 2,332, see Lewis, *Life in Egypt*, pp. 206–7.

22 On the closure of the Leontopolis Temple, see Joseph., *JW*, 7.420–36. On Jews in Egypt in general, see Modrzejewski, *The Jews of Egypt*; V.A. Tcherikover in *CPJ* vol. 1, especially pp. 48–93.

23 See A.K. Bowman and D. Rathbone, 'Cities and administration in Roman Egypt', *JRS* 82 (1992), pp. 107–27.

28 NORTH AFRICA

1 For a basic general introduction, see S. Raven, *Rome in Africa*, 3rd edn, London, 1993. Also, G.C. Picard, *La civilisation de l'Afrique romaine*, 2nd edn, Paris, 1990. For the archaeology, see the survey article of D.J. Mattingly and R.B. Hitchner, 'Roman Africa: an archaeological review', *JRS* 85 (1995), pp. 165–213.

2 For the term 'Libyan', see F.G.B. Millar, 'Local cultures in the Roman empire: Libyan, Punic and Latin in Roman Africa', *JRS* 58 (1968), pp. 126–34.

3 On Cyrenaica, see G. Barker, J.A. Lloyd and J. Reynolds (eds) *Cyrenaica in Antiquity*, Oxford, 1985; on the Jewish revolt, see M. Pucci, *Diaspora Judaism in Turmoil, 116/117 CE: ancient sources and modern insights*, Leuven, 2005; on rebuilding under Hadrian, see M.T.Boatwright, *Hadrian and the Cities of the Roman Empire*, Princeton, N.J. 2003, pp. 173–84.

4 On Numidia, see E.W.B. Fentress, *Numidia and the Roman Army: Social, Military and Economic Aspects of the Frontier Zone*, Oxford, 1979.

5 On the revolt of Tacfarinas, see Tac., *Ann.* 2.52; 3.20–1, 32, 73–4; 4.23–6.

6 For tax inscriptions, see *CIL* VIII, nos 22,786, 22,789; A. Merlin, *Inscriptions latines de la Tunisie*, Paris, 1944, nos 71, 73–4; P. Trousset, 'Les bornes du Bled Segui: nouveaux aperçus sur la centuriation romaine du sud Tunisien', *Antiquités africaines* 12 (1978), pp. 125–77; J.M. Reynolds and J.B. Ward-Perkins, *The Inscriptions of Roman Tripolitania*, Rome, 1952.

7 See J.-M. Lassère, *Ubique populus: peuplement et mouvements de population dans l'Afrique romaine de la chute de Carthage à la fin de la dynastie des Sévères (146 a.C.–235 p.C.)*, Paris, 1977.

8 On Africa Proconsularis, see T.R.S. Broughton, *The Romanization of Africa Proconsularis*, reprinted New York, 1968; J. Gascou, *La politique municipale de l'empire romain en Afrique proconsulaire de Trajan à Septime-Sévère*, Rome, 1972.

9 See J.B. Ward-Perkins *et al.*, *The Severan Buildings of Lepcis Magna: An Architectural Survey*, London, 1993.

10 For water-management, see B.D. Shaw, *Environment and Society in Roman North Africa*, Aldershot, 1995, part III, 'Water and power'; also the UNESCO Libyan valleys survey of 1979–80, the final report by G.W.W. Barker *et al.* (eds) *Farming the Desert: The UNESCO Libyan Valleys Archaeological Survey*, London, 1996–.

11 On Tripolitania, see D.J. Mattingly, *Tripolitania*, London, 1995.

12 For inscriptions referring to *saltus* and *conductores*, see D.P. Kehoe, *The Economics of Agriculture on Roman Imperial Estates in North Africa*, Göttingen, 1988.

13 This inscription can also be found in Reynolds and Ward-Perkins, *The Inscriptions of Roman Tripolitania*, no. 117; C. Flavius Pudens is honoured in nos 118–25 as well.

14 On Mauretania, see D. Fishwick, 'The annexation of Mauretania', *Historia* 20 (1971), pp. 467–87; N. Mackie, 'Augustan colonies in Mauretania', *Historia* 32 (1983), pp. 332–58.

15 For a guide to Apuleius' works, see *The Cambridge History of Classical Literature*, vol. II, *Latin Literature*, Cambridge, 1982, pp. 774–86; S.J. Harrison, *Apuleius: a Latin sophist*, Oxford, 2000.

16 See M. Bénabou, *La résistance africaine à la romanisation*, Paris, 1976.

17 The main collection of inscriptions are in *CIL* VIII; A. Merlin, *Inscriptions latines de la Tunisie*, Paris, 1944; S. Gsell and H.-G. Pflaum, *Inscriptiones latines de l'Algérie*, Paris, 1922–.

18 On the use of local languages in Africa, see Millar, 'Local cultures in the Roman empire'. On the Ghirza tombs, see D.J. Mattingly, 'Family values: art and power at Ghirza in the Libyan Pre-Desert', in S. Scott and J. Webster (eds) *Roman Imperialism and Provincial Art*, Cambridge, 2003. On the continuing practice of Punic religious customs, see G.C. Picard, *Les religions de l'Afrique antique*, Paris, 1954; Marcel Leglay, *Saturne africain: monuments*, 2 vols, Paris, 1961–6, and Marcel Leglay, *Saturne africain: histoire*, Paris, 1966.

29 RELIGION

1 For general accounts of religion in Rome and the empire, see M. Beard, J. North and S. Price (eds) *Religions of Rome 1: A History*, Cambridge, 1997; R. MacMullen, *Paganism in the Roman Empire*, New Haven, Conn. and London, 1981; J.H.W.G. Liebeschutz, *Continuity and Change in Roman Religion*, Oxford, 1979; J. Scheid, *An Introduction to Roman Religion*, transl. J. Lloyd, Bloomington, In., 2003; idem, *Quand faire c'est croire*, Auben, 2005; R. Turcan, *The Gods of Ancient Rome*, Edinburgh, 2001; J.B. Rives, *Religion in the Roman Empire*, 2006; J. Rüpke (ed.) *A Companion to Roman Religion*, Oxford, 2007; V.M. Warrior, *Roman Religion*, Cambridge, 2007.

2 J. Bremmer, 'Atheism in antiquity' in M. Martin (ed.) *The Cambridge Companion to Atheism*, Cambridge, 2006, Chapter 1.

3 See H.W. Attridge, 'The philosophical critique of religion under the early empire', *ANRW* II.16.1 (1978), pp. 45–78.

4 See J.G. Griffiths, *Apuleius of Madauros, The Isis-book (Metamorphoses XI)*, Leiden, 1975.

5 For collections of sources in English translation, see M. Beard, J. North and S. Price (eds) *Religions of Rome 2: A Sourcebook*, Cambridge, 1997, which includes painting, sculpture and coins as well as inscriptions and literary texts; F.C. Grant, *Hellenistic Religions*, New York, 1953; F.C. Grant, *Ancient Roman Religion*, New York, 1957.

6   See J. Bremmer and N. Horsfall, *Roman Myth and Mythography*, London, 1987; P. Veyne, *Did the Greeks believe in their myths? An essay in the constitutive imagination*, transl. P. Wessing, Chicago and London, 1988.

7   Aelius Aristides, *Orations* 42 (Asclepius), 43 (Zeus), 45 (Sarapis); S. Mitchell and P. van Nuffelen (eds) *One God: pagan monotheism in the Roman empire*, Cambridge, 2010, traces the relationship between polytheistic and monotheistic ideas.

8   On the importance of place for religious cult, see D. Frankfurter, 'Traditional Cult', in D.S. Potter (ed.) *A Companion to the Roman Empire*, Malden, Ma. and Oxford, 2006, pp. 547-52.

9   On temples and sacrifices, see J.E. Stambaugh, 'The functions of Roman temples', *ANRW* II.16.1 (1978), pp. 554–608.

10 R. Turcan, *The Cults of the Roman Empire*, transl. A. Nevill, Oxford and Cambridge, Ma., 1996, pp. 119, 256.

11 On priests, see M. Beard and J. North (eds) *Pagan Priests*, London, 1990; J. Scheid, 'Le prêtre et le magistrat', in C. Nicolet (ed.) *Des ordres à Rome*, Paris, 1984, pp. 243–80; J. Scheid, 'The priest', in A. Giardina (ed.) *The Romans*, Chicago and London, 1993, pp. 55–84.

12 On Alexander, see R. Lane Fox, *Pagans and Christians*, Harmondsworth, 1986, pp. 241–50.

13 The long inscribed records of the proceedings of the Arval Brethren, dating from 21 BC– AD 241, can be found in *CIL* VI, nos 2,023–119; a few are translated in LR 2, pp. 516–19.

14 For stability and change, see J. North, 'Conservatism and change in Roman religion', *PBSR* 44 (1976), pp. 1–12; J. North, 'Novelty and choice in Roman religion', *JRS* 70 (1980), pp. 186–91.

15 M. Beard, 'The sexual status of the Vestal Virgins', *JRS* 70 (1980), pp. 12–27; M. Beard, 'Re-reading (Vestal) virginity', in R. Hawley and B. Levick (eds) *Women in Antiquity: New Assessments*, London and New York, 1995, pp. 21–43; R.L. Wildfang, *Rome's Vestal Virgins*, London, 2006.

16 See R.M. Grant, *Greek Apologists of the Second Century*, Philadelphia, 1988; H. Chadwick, *Early Christian Thought and the Classical Tradition*, Oxford, 1966.

17 *Res Gestae* 20.4; Suet., *Aug.* 31.1–4.

18 On the worship of Sulis Minerva, see B. Cunliffe *et al.*, *The Temple of Sulis Minerva at Bath*, 2 vols, Oxford, 1985.

19 See I.M. Barton, 'Capitoline temples in Italy and the provinces (especially Africa)', *ANRW* II.12.1 (1982), pp. 259–342.

20 H. Engelmann, D. Knibbe and R. Merkelbach (eds) *Die Inschriften von Ephesos*, Bonn, 1980, nos 1,063–4; M.R. Lefkowitz and M. Fant (eds) *Women's Life in Greece and Rome: A Source Book in Translation*, 2nd edn, London, 1992, no. 430. More generally, see J. Scheid, 'The religious roles of Roman women', in P. Schmitt Pantel (ed.) *A History of Women in the West: From Ancient Goddesses to Christian Saints*, Cambridge, Mass., 1992, pp. 377–408.

21 See J. North, 'The development of religious pluralism', in J. Lieu, J. North and T. Rajak (eds) *The Jews among Pagans and Christians in the Roman Empire*, London and New York, 1992, pp. 174–93.

22 See in general, R. Turcan, *Les cultes orientaux dans le monde romain*, Paris, 1989.

23 On the worship of Jupiter Dolichenus, see M. Hörig, 'Iupiter Dolichenus', *ANRW* II.17.4 (1984), pp. 2136–79; P. Merlat, *Jupiter Dolichenus: essai d'interprétation et de synthèse*, Paris, 1960.

24 For some of the evidence, see BNP 12.5, 'The mysteries of Mithras'; R. Merkelbach, *Mithras*, Meisenheim, 1984; M.J. Vermaseren, *Mithras the Secret God*, London, 1963; M. Claus, *The Roman Cult of Mithras: the god and his mysteries*, transl. R. Gordon, Edinburgh, 2000; R. Beck, *The Religion of the Mithras Cult in the Roman Empire – Mysteries of the Unconquered Sun*, Oxford, 2006.

25 On the worship of Isis, see H.S. Versnel, *Ter Unus: Isis, Dionysos, Hermes: Three Studies in Henotheism*, Leiden, 1990; R.A. Wild, 'The known Isis-Sarapis sanctuaries of the Roman period', *ANRW* II.17.4 (1984), pp. 1739–851; R.E. Witt, *Isis in the Graeco-Roman World*, London, 1971.

26 See M. Goodman, *Mission and Conversion: proselytizing in the religious history of the Roman Empire*, Oxford, 1994, chaps.1–2.

27 On the imperial cult, see Chapter 12; S.R.F. Price, *Rituals and Power: The Roman Imperial Cult in Asia Minor*, Cambridge, 1984; D. Fishwick, 'The development of provincial ruler cult in the western Roman empire', *ANRW* II.16.2 (1978), pp. 1201–53; D. Fishwick, *The Imperial Cult in the Latin West*, 3 vols., Leiden, 1987–2004; I. Gradel, *Emperor Worship and Roman Religion*, Oxford, 2002, on the worship of emperors in Italy.

28 M. Beard, 'The Roman and the foreign: the cult of the "Great Mother" in imperial Rome', in N. Thomas and C. Humphrey (eds) *Shamanism, History and the State*, Ann Arbor, Michigan, 1994, pp. 164–90; R. Turcan, *Les religions de l'Asie dans la vallée du Rhône*, Leiden, 1972, pp. 83–8, 124–7; R. Duthoy, *The Taurobolium, its Evolution and Terminology*, Leiden, 1969.

30 JUDAISM

1 On the boundaries of the Jewish religious community, see S.J.D. Cohen, *The Beginnings of Jewishness: boundaries, varieties, uncertainties*, Berkeley, 1999; for the attitudes taken by Greek and Roman authors to the Jews, see the collections of evidence in M. Stern, *Greek and Latin Authors on Jews and Judaism*, 3 vols, Jerusalem, 1974–84; M. Whittaker, *Jews and Christians: Graeco-Roman Views*, Cambridge, 1984.

2 For an introduction to these sources, see G. Stemberger, *Introduction to the Talmud and Midrash*, 2nd edn, Edinburgh, 1996; M. Goodman and P. Alexander (eds), *Rabbinic Texts and the History of Late-Roman Palestine*, Oxford, 2010.

3 Translations of much of the material can be found in J.H. Charlesworth (ed.) *The Old Testament Pseudepigrapha*, 2 vols, New York, 1983.

4 On the Dead Sea Scrolls, see L.H. Schiffman (ed.) *Encyclopedia of the Dead Sea Scrolls*, Oxford, 2000; C. Hempel (ed.) *The Dead Sea Scrolls: Texts and Context*, Leiden, 2010.

5 On the Leontopolis temple, see R. Hayward, 'The Jewish temple at Leontopolis: a reconsideration', *Journal of Jewish Studies* 33 (1982), pp. 429–43.

6 See the discussions of pilgrimage in J. Jeremias, *Jerusalem in the Time of Jesus*, London, 1969, pp. 58–84; S. Safrai and M. Stern (eds) *The Jewish People in the First Century*, 2 vols, Assen/Amsterdam, 1974–6, vol. 2, Chap. 17; M. Goodman, *Judaism in the Roman World: collected essays*, Leiden, 2007, Chapter 5. On the religious ideology of the rebels in the two revolts, see M. Goodman, *Rome and Jerusalem: the clash of ancient civilizations*, London, 2007.

7 For a fine analysis of Judaism as 'covenantal nomism', see E.P. Sanders, *Judaism: Practice and Belief, 63 BCE–66 CE*, London and Philadelphia, 1992, Chap. 13.

8 Arguments for considering the canon as still fluid are given in J. Barton, *Oracles of God: Perceptions of Ancient Prophecy in Israel after the Exile*, London, 1986.

9   On synagogues in general, see L.I. Levine, *The Ancient Synagogue: the first thousand years*, New Haven, 2nd edn, 2005.

10 For the texts in translation, see G. Vermes, *The Complete Dead Sea Scrolls in English*, London, 1998.

11 Text in E. Qimron and J. Strugnell (eds) *Qumran cave 4 V, Miqsat ma'ase ha-Torah*, Oxford, 1994.

12 *Mishnah Avodah Zara* 2.6; on olive oil, see Joseph., *JW* 2.591–2; *AJ* 12.120; cf. M. Goodman, 'Kosher olive oil in antiquity', in P.R. Davies and R.T. White (eds) *A Tribute to Geza Vermes*, Sheffield, 1990, pp. 227–45.

13 On apocalyptic, see C.C. Rowland, *The Open Heaven: A Study of Apocalyptic in Judaism and Early Christianity*, London, 1982; J.J. Collins, *The Apocalyptic Imagination*, 2nd edn, Grand Rapids, Mi, 1998.

14 See the discussion of this problem in R. Gray, *Prophetic Figures in Late Second Temple Palestine*, New York, 1993, Chap. 1.

15 Discussions of messianism in J. Klausner, *The Messianic Idea in Israel*, London, 1956; E. Schürer, *The History of the Jewish People*, rev. edn, vol. 2, pp. 488–554; J. Neusner, W.S. Green and E.S. Frerichs (eds) *Judaisms and their Messiahs at the Turn of the Christian Era*, Cambridge, 1987; W. Horbury, *Jewish Messianism and the Cult of Christ*, London, 1998; M. Bockmuehl and J. Carleton Paget (eds.) *Redemption and Resistance: the Messianic hopes of Jews and Christians in antiquity*, London, 2008.

16 On the 'fourth philosophy' contrast M. Hengel, *The Zealots: Investigations into the Jewish Freedom Movement in the Period from Herod I until 70 AD*, Edinburgh, 1989, to R.A. Horsley, *Bandits, Prophets, and Messiahs: Popular Movements in the Time of Jesus*, Minneapolis, 1985.

17 On the Pharisees, see Joseph., *JW* 2.162–3; *AJ* 13.171–3, 288, 294, 297–8, 17.41, 18.12–17; *Life* 2.191. On the Rabbinic texts, see J. Neusner, *The Rabbinic Traditions about the Pharisees before 70*, 3 parts, Leiden, 1971. On the extent of the Pharisees' influence, see J. Neusner, *Politics to Piety*, Leiden, 1971, and the summary of arguments in D. Goodblatt, 'The place of the Pharisees in first-century Judaism: the state of the debate', *Journal for the Study of Judaism* 20 (1989), pp. 12–30; M. Goodman, *Judaism in the Roman World*, Chapter 9.

18 See J. Le Moyne, *Les Sadducéens*, Paris, 1972; Goodman, *Judaism in the Roman World*, Chapter 10.

19 See G. Vermes and M. Goodman, *The Essenes According to the Classical Sources*, Sheffield, 1989; T.S. Beall, *Josephus' Description of the Essenes Illustrated by the Dead Sea Scrolls*, Cambridge, 1988.

20 See arguments in M. Goodman, *Judaism in the Roman World*, Chapter 11.

21 On Philo, see S. Sandmel, *Philo of Alexandria: An Introduction*, New York and Oxford, 1979.

22 This is argued more fully in M. Goodman, 'Sadducees and Essenes after 70 CE', in S.E. Porter, P. Joyce and D.E. Orton (eds) *Crossing the Boundaries: Essays in Biblical Interpretation in Honour of Michael D. Goulder*, Leiden, 1994, pp. 347–56.

23 On such Rabbinic legislation, see G. Alon, *The Jews in their Land in the Talmudic Age*, vol. 1, Jerusalem, 1980, pp. 107–18.

24 A useful introduction to early Rabbinic Judaism is L.H. Schiffman, *From Text to Tradition: A History of Second Temple and Rabbinic Judaism*, Hoboken, New Jersey, 1991, Chaps 10, 12–13; a good collection of texts can be found in H. Maccoby, *Early Rabbinic Writings*, Cambridge, 1988.

25 M. Goodman, *State and Society in Roman Galilee AD 132–212*, 2nd edn, London and Portland, Or., 1983, Chap. 7; S.J.D. Cohen, in L.I. Levine (ed.) *The Galilee in Late Antiquity*, New York and Jerusalem, 1992, pp. 157–73.

26 Goodman, *State and Society*, pp. 111–18, argues against such recognition; D. Goodblatt, *The Monarchic Principle: Studies in Jewish Self-government in Antiquity*, Tübingen, 1994, Chap. 6, claims that the patriarch received wide authority within Jewish circles soon after AD 70; for references to more recent discussions, see S.T. Katz (ed.) *The Cambridge History of Judaism*, vol. 4, *The Late Roman-Rabbinic Period*, Cambridge, 2006.

31 CHRISTIANITY

1 For good general accounts, see H. Chadwick, *The Early Church*, 2nd edn, London 1993; R. Lane Fox, *Pagans and Christians in the Mediterranean World from the Second Century AD to the Conversion of Constantine*, Harmondsworth, 1986; W.H.C. Frend, *The Rise of Christianity*, London, 1984; T.D. Barnes, *Early Christianity and the Roman Empire*, London, 1984; R. MacMullen, *Christianizing the Roman Empire (AD 100–400)*, New Haven, Conn. and London, 1984; H. Chadwick, *The Church in Ancient Society from Galilee to Gregory the Great*, Oxford, 2001. New epigraphic and papyrological material pertinent to early Christianity is collected in a series of documents edited by G.H.R. Horsley, *New Documents Illustrating Early Christianity*, vols 1–6, North Ryde, N.S.W., 1981–92.

2 H. Chadwick (ed.) *Origen, Against Celsus*, Cambridge, 1953.

3 See T.D. Barnes, *Constantine and Eusebius*, Cambridge, Mass., 1981.

4 For apology, see R.M. Grant, *Greek Apologists of the Second Century*, Philadelphia, 1988; H. Chadwick, 'Justin Martyr's defence of Christianity', in his *History and Thought of the Early Church*, London, 1982.

5 On Jesus in his Jewish context, see J.D. Crossan, *The Historical Jesus: The Life of a Mediterranean Jewish Peasant*, Edinburgh, 1993; J.H. Charlesworth, *Jesus within Judaism*, New York, 1988; E.P. Sanders, *Jesus and Judaism*, 2nd edn, London, 1987; G. Vermes, *Jesus the Jew*, London, 1976; J. Bowker, *Jesus and the Pharisees*, Cambridge, 1973; G. Bornkamm, *Jesus of Nazareth*, London, 1960.

6 See C. Rowland, *Christian Origins: From Messianic Movement to Christian Religion*, London, 1985.

7 For Jewish Christianity, see J. Daniélou, *The Theology of Jewish Christianity*, London, 1964; A.F. Segal, 'Jewish Christianity', in H.W. Attridge and G. Hata (eds) *Eusebius, Christianity and Judaism*, Leiden, 1992, pp. 326–51.

8 On Paul, see F. Watson, *Paul, Judaism and the Gentiles*, Cambridge, 1986; W.D. Davies, *Paul and Rabbinic Judaism*, 4th edn, London, 1980; A.D. Nock, *Saint Paul*, London, 1938.

9 On the basis of morality in the Early Church, see W.A. Meeks, *The Origins of Christian Morality: The First Two Centuries*, New Haven, Conn. and London, 1993. On Christian asceticism in particular, see P. Brown, *The Body and Society: Men, Women and Sexual Renunciation in Early Christianity*, New York, 1988; J. McNamara, *A New Song: Celibate Women in the First Three Christian Centuries*, New York, 1985.

10 On the scarcity of archaeological evidence for Christianity before c. 180, see G.F. Snyder, *Ante Pacem: archaeological evidence of Church life before Constantine*, revised edn, Macon. Ga., 2003; on Paul's claims as representative, see E.P. Sanders, *Paul, the Law and the Jewish People*, Philadelphia, 1983, p. 189; for discussion of the structure of Christian communities

and the demography of expansion in the third century, see R. Stark, *The Rise of Christianity: a sociologist reconsiders history*, Princeton, 1996.

11 On the social background of Christians, see W.A. Meeks, *The First Urban Christians: The Social World of the Apostle Paul*, New Haven, Conn., 1983; J.G. Gager, *Kingdom and Community: The Social World of Early Christianity*, Englewood Cliffs, New Jersey, 1975; E.A. Judge, *The Social Pattern of Christian Groups in the First Century*, London, 1960.

12 See Averil Cameron, 'Neither male nor female', *Greece and Rome* 27 (1980), pp. 60–8; on Perpetua, see J. Salisbury, *Perpetua's passion: the death and memory of a young Roman woman*, London, 1997.

13 See in general D. Boyarin, *Border Lines: the partition of Judaeo-Christianity*, Philadelphia, 2004; J.M. Lieu, *Christian Identity in the Jewish and Graeco-Roman World*, Oxford, 2004; A.H. Becker and A.Y. Reed, eds, *The Ways that Never Parted: Jews and Christians in Late Antiquity and the Early Middle Ages*, Tübingen, 2003.

14 See W. Bauer, *Orthodoxy and Heresy in Earliest Christianity*, Philadelphia, 1971; H. Chadwick, *Heresy and Orthodoxy in the Early Church*, Aldershot, 1991.

15 On Gnosticism, see G. Filoramo, *A History of Gnosticism*, Oxford, 1990; E. Pagels, *The Gnostic Gospels*, New York, 1979; H. Jonas, *The Gnostic Religion*, 2nd edn, Boston, 1963; R.M. Grant, *Gnosticism and Early Christianity*, 2nd edn, New York, 1966.

16 On Marcion, see Jonas, *The Gnostic Religion*, Chap. 6.

17 See C.F. Evans, 'The New Testament in the making', *The Cambridge History of the Bible*, vol. 1, Cambridge, 1970, pp. 232–84.

18 On Montanism, see T.D. Barnes, 'The chronology of Montanism', *Journal of Theological Studies* 21 (1970), pp. 403–8.

19 For the persecution of Christians, see W.H.C. Frend, *Martyrdom and Persecution in the Early Church: A Study of Conflict from the Maccabees to Donatus*, Oxford, 1965.

20 For the Christian attitude to pagans, see R.P.C. Hanson, 'The Christian attitude to pagan religions up to the time of Constantine the Great', *ANRW* II.23.2 (1980), pp. 910–73.

21 For the Lyons martyrs, see Eusebius, *Church History* 5.1.

22 The shift is traced by A. Cameron, *Christianity and the Rhetoric of Empire: The Development of Christian Discourse*, Berkeley, Calif. and London, 1991.

32 SEVERANS TO CONSTANTINE

1 For a fuller account of this period, see A.K. Bowman, P. Garnsey and A. Cameron (eds) *The Cambridge Ancient History*, 2nd edn, vol. 12, Cambridge, 2005; D.S. Potter, *The Roman Empire at bay, AD 180–395*, London, 2004; O. Hekster, *Rome and its Empire, AD 193–284*, Edinburgh, 2008.

2 For a useful summary of scholarship on this subject, see J.N. Bremmer, 'The Vision of Constantine', in A.P.M.H. Lardinois, M.G.M. van der Poel and V.J.C. Hunink (eds) *Lands of Dreams*, Leiden, 2006, pp. 57–79.

BIBLIOGRAPHICAL NOTES

PART I: INTRODUCTION

General histories of the Early Roman Empire vary greatly in their emphasis and scale. The most useful brief introduction is C.M. Wells, *The Roman Empire*, 2nd edn, London, 1992. The clear, detailed political narrative in H.H. Scullard, *From the Gracchi to Nero: A History of Rome from 133 BC to AD 68*, 5th edn, London, 1982, reissued with a new introduction in 2011, is still well worth using, although the social and economic sections of the book are now very out of date. F.G.B. Millar, *The Roman Empire and its Neighbours*, 2nd edn, London, 1981, describes the empire from a wide perspective and over a long period. Volumes X (1996) and XI (2000) of the revised *Cambridge Ancient History* cover the period 44 BC–AD 180 in great detail, and often with magisterial authority. Students will find much helpful information in *The Oxford Classical Dictionary*, 4th edn, Oxford, 2010; G. Shipley *et al* (eds.) *The Cambridge Dictionary of Classical Civilization,* Cambridge, 2006; D.S. Potter (ed.) *A Companion to the Roman Empire*, Malden, Ma. and Oxford, 2006.

Many of the literary sources for Roman history in this period are published by the Loeb Classical Library in parallel texts of the original language and a translation. Many of these authors and writings have also been discussed in monographs by modern scholars; of these, the most important, because of its numerous allusions to a variety of historical problems, is R. Syme, *Tacitus*, 2 vols., Oxford, 1958. Collections of selected inscriptions in the original languages can be found in V. Ehrenberg and A.H.M. Jones (eds) *Documents Illustrating the Reigns of Augustus and Tiberius*, 2nd edn, Oxford, 1955; E.M. Smallwood (ed.) *Documents Illustrating the Principates of Gaius, Claudius and Nero*, Cambridge, 1967; E.M. Smallwood (ed.) *Documents Illustrating the Principates of Nerva, Trajan and Hadrian*, Cambridge, 1966. Much can also be learnt simply from reading the grand *corpora* of inscriptions: *Corpus Inscriptionum Latinarum* (especially *CIL* VI, inscriptions from Rome, which has a computer-generated index) and H. Dessau (ed.) *Inscriptiones Latinae Selectae*, 3 vols., Berlin, 1892–1916. The most useful collection of sources in translation is N. Lewis and M. Reinhold (eds) *Roman Civilization: Selected Readings*, 2 vols.,

3rd edn, New York, 1990. More selective are R.K. Sherk (ed.) *The Roman Empire: Augustus to Hadrian*, Cambridge, 1988, and D. Braund (ed.) *Augustus to Nero: A Sourcebook on Roman History 31 BC–AD 68*, London, 1985. For the most recent inscriptions, see the periodic epigraphic surveys in the *Journal of Roman Studies*, most recently A.E. Cooley, S. Mitchell and B. Salway, 'Roman Inscriptions 2001–2005' *JRS* 97 (2007), pp. 176–263. J. Bodel (ed.) *Epigraphic Evidence: ancient history from inscriptions*, London, 2001, provides an excellent introduction.

Useful collections of maps can be found in R.J.A. Talbert (ed.) *Atlas of Classical History*, London and New York, 1985; T.J. Cornell and J.F. Matthews, *Atlas of the Roman World*, Oxford, 1992; and especially in R.J.A. Talbert (ed.) *Barrington Atlas of the Greek and Roman World, Princeton*, N.J., 2000.

For a general picture of the Roman world in 50 BC, see M. Crawford, *The Roman Republic*, 2nd edn, London, 1992. On the Late Iron Age in northern Europe, see B.W. Cunliffe, *The Celtic World*, 2nd edn, London, 1992. On the eastern Mediterranean, there is a fine summary in F. W. Walbank, *The Hellenistic World*, 3rd impression with amendments, London, 1992.

For a general discussion of the 'Roman' characteristics of Roman society, see G. Alföldy, *The Social History of Rome*, London, 1985 (now rather out of date); M. Goodman, *Rome and Jerusalem: the clash of ancient civilizations*, London, 2007, chapters 4–10. For the specific topics discussed in Chapter 2, the reader is referred to works cited in the notes. Much evidence is cited in Lewis and Reinhold, *Roman Civilization*, and there are some good, more specialized sourcebooks, such as T. Wiedemann, *Greek and Roman Slavery*, London, 1981; J.F. Gardner, *Women in Roman Law and Society*, London, 1986; J.F. Gardner and T. Wiedemann, *The Roman Household: A Sourcebook*, London, 1991.

For an account of the history of the classical world as it appears to inhabitants of that world in the second century AD, see R.J. Lane Fox, *The Classical World: an epic history from Homer to Hadrian*, London, 2005.

PART II: ÉLITE POLITICS

There is an excellent discussion of the languages and political life of Republican Rome, which firmly scotches earlier, simplistic views about senatorial politics and shows the continuities between Republic and principate, in T.P. Wiseman (ed.) *Roman Political Life, 90 BC–AD 69*, Exeter, 1985. The relation between political rhetoric and practice is one theme of the collected studies of Peter Brunt, *The Fall of the Roman Republic: And Related Essays*, Oxford, 1988. The best introduction to the mechanics of political life is still L.R. Taylor, *Party Politics in the Age of Caesar*, Berkeley, Calif., 1949, and L.R. Taylor, *Roman Voting Assemblies from the Hannibalic War to the Dictatorship of Caesar*, Ann Arbor, Michigan, 1966.

The classic discussion of the transition from Republic to principate in R. Syme, *The Roman Revolution*, Oxford, 1939, uses prosopography to trace a history of political cabals operating behind the scenes. The allusive rhetorical style does not appeal to all readers, and some prosopographical links discovered by Syme may be less significant than he assumed, but the book is still exciting. Syme continued his prosopographical studies down to AD 14 in *The Augustan Aristocracy*, Oxford and New York, 1986, his last great work; his *Roman Papers* (edited by E. Badian and A.R. Birley in 7 vols., Oxford, 1979–91) are also full of insights. M. Hammond, *The Augustan Principate in Theory and Practice during the Julio–Claudian Period*, Cambridge, Mass., 1933, approaches the transition primarily as an issue of constitutional change; the contributors to F.G.B. Millar and E. Segal (eds) *Caesar Augustus: Seven Aspects*, Oxford, 1984, see the issue as the adaptation of Roman society to a monarchy.

Bibliography on the political issues which arose during the rule of emperors after Augustus has been given in the appropriate places in the notes. For a continuous narrative, now rather out of date, see A. Garzetti, *From Tiberius to the Antonines: A History of the Roman Empire, AD 14–192*, London, 1974.

PART III: THE STATE

The views of E.N. Luttwak, *The Grand Strategy of the Roman Empire from the First Century AD to the Third*, Baltimore, 1976, who analysed the function of the Roman army as 'defence-in-depth', were much influenced by the policies of the Cold War. Among the most influential responses to Luttwak is B. Isaac, *The Limits of Empire: The Roman Army in the East*, rev. edn, Oxford, 1992, which argues that the Roman military acted essentially as a police force. Both books cover periods much longer than the Early Empire, which may have affected their interpretations; in particular, Luttwak read back into earlier centuries the aggressive stance towards the empire of Sassanians and Germanic barbarians, first fully attested only in the third century.

For discussions of the way the state operated, see A.W. Lintott, *Imperium Romanum: Politics and Administration*, London, 1993, and P. Garnsey and R. Saller, *The Roman Empire: Economy, Society and Culture*, London, 1987, Chap. 2, 'Government without bureaucracy'; both books emphasize the lack of institutional structures. F.G.B. Millar, *The Emperor in the Roman World (31 BC–AD 337)*, 2nd edn, London, 1992, provides in effect a survey of the administration of the whole empire and its link to the emperor. His major argument, that government was shaped not by policy but by pressure from the governed, may lay undue stress on the significance of the epigraphic evidence on which he largely relies: such inscriptions naturally emphasize the role of successful petitions to the authorities. Both J.E. Lendon, *The Art of Government in the Roman World*, Oxford, 1997, and C. Ando, *Imperial Ideology and Provincial Loyalty in the Roman Empire*, Los Angeles, Ca., 2000, attempt to explain how and why the inhabitants of the empire accepted imperial rule, and the role they played in the maintenance of this system of government. For the institutions through which the state operated, many of the collected studies in A.H.M. Jones, *The Roman Economy: Studies in Ancient Economic and Administrative History*, ed. P.A. Brunt, Oxford, 1974, and P.A. Brunt, *Roman Imperial Themes*, Oxford, 1990, are fundamental. On the operation of the senate, R.J.A. Talbert, *The Senate of Imperial Rome*, Princeton, New Jersey, 1984, provides a superb description of the institution itself. R. Saller, *Personal Patronage under the Early Empire*, Cambridge, 1982, analyses the way that senators brokered power that ultimately derived from the emperor. K. Hopkins, *Death and Renewal*, Cambridge, 1983, includes a detailed discussion of the families which provided senators and suggests reasons for their rapid turnover. The best sourcebook on the government of the empire is B. Levick, *The Government of the Roman Empire: A Sourcebook*, London, 1985, which includes translations and discussions of much evidence not easily encountered elsewhere.

On the role of the army in society, many insights can be gleaned from R. MacMullen, *Soldier and Civilian in the Later Roman Empire*, Cambridge, Mass., 1963, even though it refers to a rather later period (from AD 200 to 400). G.R. Watson, *The Roman Soldier*, London, 1969, gives a good idea of what it was like to be a legionary. G. Webster, *The Roman Imperial Army of the First and Second Centuries AD*, 3rd edn, London, 1985, is a formal account of the organization and deployment of the military; for the beginning of the principate, L.J.F. Keppie, *The Making of the Roman Army: From Republic to Empire*, London, 1984, is now authoritative. J.B. Campbell, *The Emperor and the Roman Army, 31 BC–AD 235*, Oxford, 1984, explains how the military machine was controlled by the state. J.E. Lendon, *Soldiers and Ghosts: a history of battle in classical antiquity*, New Haven, Conn., 2005, analyses the use of military traditions by commanders to motivate their armies. Much evidence about Roman military life derived from archaeological evidence can be found in numerous studies published in the MAVORS series. For written records, see R.O. Fink, *Roman Military Records on Papyrus*, Cleveland, Ohio, 1971; A.K. Bowman and J.D. Thomas (eds) *The Vindolanda Writing-Tablets (tabulae Vindo-landenses II)*, London, 1994.

Much the most influential recent book on the image of the emperor has been P. Zanker, *The Power of Images in the Age of Augustus*, Ann Arbor, Michigan, 1988. Emperor worship has been much studied in recent years, with a new emphasis on its religious significance for worshippers; seminal in this reappraisal has been S.R.F. Price, *Rituals and Power: The Roman Imperial Cult in Asia Minor*, Cambridge, 1984.

On the political unity of the empire, A.N. Sherwin-White, *The Roman Citizenship*, 2nd edn, Oxford, 1973, is fundamental. On the way that local magistrates used civic evergetism to mediate between the desires of their compatriots and the Roman state, see G.M. Rogers, *The Sacred Identity of Ephesos: Foundation Myths of a Roman City*, London, 1991. On the extent of economic unity scholarly opinion remains divided; few historians would now attempt the magisterial overview provided by M.I. Rostovtzeff, *The Social and*

Economic History of the Roman Empire, 2nd edn, rev. P.M. Fraser, Oxford, 1957. An excellent survey of the debates among economic historians can be found in P. Garnsey and R. Saller, *The Roman Empire: Economy, Society and Culture*, London, 1987. Discussion of recent work on the nature of the Roman economy can be found in W. Scheidel, I. Morris and R. Saller (eds), *The Cambridge Economic History of the Greco-Roman World*, Cambridge, 2007. N. Morley, *Trade in Classical Antiquity*, Cambridge, 2007, provides a concise and engaging introduction to ancient trade, usefully summarizing theoretical debates. J.P. Oleson (ed.), *The Oxford Handbook of Engineering and Technology in the Classical World*, Oxford, 2008, is an indispensable resource for a variety of economic subjects, from aqueducts to weaving. N. Purcell and P. Horden, *The Corrupting Sea*, Oxford, 2000, is an important but dense work emphasising the significance of networks in the ancient Mediterranean. Only rarely does sufficient evidence survive for quantitative analysis, but such material as is available is brilliantly exploited by, among others, R. Duncan-Jones in *The Economy of the Roman Empire: Quantitative Studies*, 2nd edn, Cambridge, 1982; R. Duncan-Jones, *Structure and Scale in the Roman Economy*, Cambridge, 1990.

For the archaeological evidence of Roman culture across the empire, readers will find much in an excellent survey in J. Wacher (ed.) *The Roman World*, 2 vols., London, 1987.

PART IV: SOCIETY

On opposition to the imperial state, see M. Goodman, 'Opponents of Rome: Jews and others', in L. Alexander (ed.) *Images of Empire*, Sheffield, 1991, pp. 222–38. R. MacMullen, *Enemies of the Roman Order: Treason, Unrest, and Alienation in the Empire*, Cambridge, Mass., 1967, has a stimulating, rather impressionistic, account of particular sorts of deviants. Ch. Wirszubski, *Libertas as a Political Idea at Rome during the Late Republic and Early Principate*, Cambridge, 1950, traces the history of the political rhetoric adopted by the senatorial opponents of emperors.

A provocative account of cultural change in the late Republic and early empire can be found in A. Wallace-Hadrill, *Rome's Cultural Revolution*, Cambridge, 2008. P. Stewart, *The Social History of Roman Art*, Cambridge, 2008, provides a very readable overview of current scholarship. Especially useful on social history are S. Dixon, *The Roman Family*, Baltimore, 1992; K. Bradley, *Slavery and Society at Rome*, Cambridge, 1994; and T.G. Parkin and A.J. Pomeroy, *Roman Social History: A Sourcebook*, London and New York, 2007. Two marginalized groups, old people and children, have now received proper attention in two very good works: T.G. Parkin, *Old Age in the Roman World: A Cultural and Social History*, Baltimore, 2003, and B. Rawson, *Children and Childhood in Roman Italy*, Oxford, 2003.

On the transformation of the empire in general, much can be learned from the series of workshop volumes produced since 2000 by the international network on 'Impact of Empire' (see http://www.impactofempire.org). On particular regions, see J. Patterson, *Landscapes and Cities: rural settlement and civic transformation in early imperial Italy*, Oxford 2006 (with excellent summary of recent archaeological work); G. Woolf, *Becoming Roman: the origins of provincial civilization in Gaul*, Cambridge, 1998; D.J. Mattingly, *An Imperial Possession: Britain in the Roman Empire*, London, 2006; M. Goodman, *Rome and Jerusalem: the clash of ancient civilizations*, London, 2007.

PART V: HUMANS AND GODS

On traditional religions, R. Lane Fox, *Pagans and Christians in the Mediterranean World of the Second Century AD to the Conversion of Constantine*, Harmondsworth, 1986, may be singled out as a rare attempt to empathize with ancient polytheistic beliefs and practices. Many other studies reduce the study of ancient paganism to a set of puzzles about the popularity of particular cults. R. MacMullen, *Paganism in the Roman Empire*, New Haven, Conn. and London, 1981, tries to bring home to readers the complexities of paganism. H.S. Versnel, *Ter Unus: Isis, Dionysos, Hermes: Three Studies in Henotheism*, Leiden, 1990, and other studies tackle what may properly be described as pagan theology; since the evidence lies mainly in vague statements on inscriptions, the results are not always clear-cut. The past two decades have produced a great number of new studies on ancient religious history. M. Beard, J. North and S. Price, *Religions of Rome*, 2 vols., Cambridge, 1998, is an essential reference work with interpretation in volume 1 and evidence of all kinds laid out with admirable clarity in volume 2. R. Turcan, *The Gods of Ancient Rome*, London, 2001, has a good account of the variety of rites and rituals in Roman cults. J. Scheid, *An Introduction to Roman Religion*, Bloomington, In., 2003, provides distinctive interpretations of the calendar, rituals, priests, spaces, and basic theologies underlying the religious aspects of life in the city of Rome in the late Republic and early Empire.

Much scholarship on Judaism and Christianity in this period implicitly carries modern theological debates back into the study of the ancient world. Such anachronistic battles are probably inevitable, simply because historians interested enough to write about these religions are usually committed to a modern faith which in some way derives from Judaism or Christianity in the Roman period. One effect is the production of history far more polemical and intense than in most other areas of ancient history. Less justified is the assumption of some scholars that disputes in this area are in principle an expression of faith and therefore incapable of resolution. The study of Judaism and Christianity as part of the religious history of the period may help to encourage a more balanced approach.

Judaism in the Early Empire has mostly been studied as the background to early Christianity and rabbinic Judaism. For acerbic but mostly justified observations on the distortions thus engendered in the views of earlier scholars, see J. Neusner, *The Rabbinic Traditions about the Pharisees before 70*, 3 vols., Leiden, 1971, and E.P. Sanders, *Paul and Palestinian Judaism: A Comparison of Patterns of Religion*, London, 1977. Even with the best will, the effects of hindsight are hard to avoid; E.P. Sanders, *Judaism: Practice and Belief, 63 BCE–66 CE*, London and Philadelphia, 1992, makes a brave attempt to describe Judaean Judaism in its own terms, stressing (perhaps over-stressing) the significance of the Jerusalem Temple cult for all Jews. The standard reference work for Judaism in this period is E. Schürer, rev. G. Vermes, F.G.B. Millar *et al., The History of the Jewish People in the Age of Jesus Christ (175 BC–AD 135)*, 3 vols., Edinburgh, 1973–87, but the categories into which the material about Jewish religion is divided reflect Schürer's presuppositions as a nineteenth-century Protestant. Among other general introductions, S. J. D. Cohen, *From the Maccabees to the Mishnah*, 2nd edn, Philadelphia, 2006, is clear and balanced; L.H. Schiffman, *From Text to Tradition: A History of Second Temple and Rabbinic Judaism*, Hoboken, New Jersey, 1991, starts from the assumption that the rabbinic tradition was normative unless there is evidence to the contrary. For a greater sense of the extent of variety within Judaism, see M. Goodman, *Judaism in the Roman World: collected essays*, Leiden, 2007. On rabbinic Judaism, see Schiffman, *From Text to Tradition*, Chaps 10 and 13; L.I. Levine, *The Rabbinic Class of Roman Palestine in Late Antiquity*, Jerusalem and New York, 1989. Numerous studies by J. Neusner (e.g. *Judaism: The Evidence of the Mishnah*, 2nd edn, Atlanta, Georgia, 1988) have helped to clarify the structure of many rabbinic texts; his attempts to reconstruct the Judaisms of the authors of these texts by postulating their underlying philosophies are not always so successful (cf. the strictures of E. P. Sanders, *Jewish Law from Jesus to the Mishnah: Five Studies*, London and Philadelphia, 1990). For a fine collection of early rabbinic texts in translation, see H. Maccoby, *Early Rabbinic Writings*, Cambridge, 1988. Much useful information can be found in the relevant volumes of *The Cambridge History of Judaism*, vol.3, ed. W. Horbury, W.D. Davies and J. Sturdy, Cambridge, 1999; vol. 4, ed. S.T. Katz, Cambridge, 2006.

Modern scholarship on Christianity in the first centuries is even more affected by contemporary theology than studies of Judaism. Research on the life of Jesus, which was dormant during much of the twentieth century because of radical doubts about the historicity of the Gospels, has now revived with attempts to place Jesus within first-century Judaism. Among the more successful efforts are E.P. Sanders, *Jesus and Judaism*, 2nd edn, London, 1987, and J.D. Crossan, *The Historical Jesus: The Life of a Mediterranean Jewish Peasant*, Edinburgh, 1993; there is widespread agreement about the framework and thrust of Jesus' actions but little consensus about his probable teachings. Many histories of the Early Church after Jesus do little more than chart the appearance of theological notions in the extant literature. The clearest general introduction is H. Chadwick, *The Early Church*, 2nd edn, London, 1993. A clear institutional history of the Church can be found in W.H.C. Frend, *The*

Rise of Christianity, London, 1984. Attempts to take a more historical approach have mostly relied on sociological models derived from observation of the behaviour of religious groups in more recent times; among the most influential of these are J. Gager, *Kingdom and Community: The Social World of Early Christianity*, Englewood Cliffs, New Jersey, 1975; W.A. Meeks, *The First Urban Christians: The Social World of the Apostle Paul*, New Haven, Conn. and London, 1983; and R. Stark, *The Rise of Christianity: a sociologist reconsiders history*, Princeton, N.J., 1996.

Index

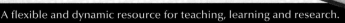